# STATISTICAL
# METHODS
## FOR THE SOCIAL &
## BEHAVIOURAL SCIENCES

Sara Miller McCune founded SAGE Publishing in 1965 to support the dissemination of usable knowledge and educate a global community. SAGE publishes more than 1000 journals and over 800 new books each year, spanning a wide range of subject areas. Our growing selection of library products includes archives, data, case studies and video. SAGE remains majority owned by our founder and after her lifetime will become owned by a charitable trust that secures the company's continued independence.

Los Angeles | London | New Delhi | Singapore | Washington DC | Melbourne

# STATISTICAL METHODS

## FOR THE SOCIAL &
## BEHAVIOURAL SCIENCES

### A MODEL-BASED APPROACH

## DAVID B. FLORA

Los Angeles | London | New Delhi
Singapore | Washington DC | Melbourne

Los Angeles | London | New Delhi
Singapore | Washington DC | Melbourne

SAGE Publications Ltd
1 Oliver's Yard
55 City Road
London EC1Y 1SP

SAGE Publications Inc.
2455 Teller Road
Thousand Oaks, California 91320

SAGE Publications India Pvt Ltd
B 1/I 1 Mohan Cooperative Industrial Area
Mathura Road
New Delhi 110 044

SAGE Publications Asia-Pacific Pte Ltd
3 Church Street
#10-04 Samsung Hub
Singapore 049483

Editor: Michael Ainsley
Editorial assistant: John Nightingale
Production editor: Tom Bedford
Copyeditor: Sheree Van Vreede
Proofreader: Thea Watson
Indexer: Cathy Heath
Marketing manager: Susheel Gokarakonda
Cover design: Wendy Scott
Typeset by: C&M Digitals (P) Ltd, Chennai, India
Printed in the UK

**Library of Congress Control Number: 2017955066**

**British Library Cataloguing in Publication data**

A catalogue record for this book is available from the British Library

ISBN 978-1-4462-6982-4
ISBN 978-1-4462-6983-1 (pbk)

At SAGE we take sustainability seriously. Most of our products are printed in the UK using FSC papers and boards. When we print overseas we ensure sustainable papers are used as measured by the PREPS grading system. We undertake an annual audit to monitor our sustainability.

für Julia

# CONTENTS

*Online Resources*    x

*About the Author*    xi

*Acknowledgements*    xii

*Preface*    xiii

**1   Foundations of Statistical Modeling Demonstrated with Simple Regression**    **1**

Chapter overview    1

What is a statistical model?    2

Significance testing and effect sizes    6

Simple regression models    9

Basic regression diagnostic concepts    27

Chapter summary    39

Recommended reading    40

**2   Multiple Regression with Continuous Predictors**    **42**

Chapter overview    42

What is multiple regression?    43

Multiple regression with two predictors    44

Multiple regression with $P$ = two or more predictors    62

Regression diagnostics revisited    72

Chapter summary    85

Recommended reading    86

**3   Regression with Categorical Predictors**    **87**

Chapter overview    87

What is the general linear model?    88

Using dummy-code variables    92

Using contrast-code variables    97

The analysis of covariance (ANCOVA) model and beyond    104

Regression diagnostics with categorical predictors    108

Chapter summary    111

Recommended reading    112

**4 Interactions in Multiple Regression: Models for Moderation**     **113**

    Chapter overview     113
    What is statistical moderation?     114
    Interactions with a categorical moderator     114
    Interactions with a continuous moderator     131
    Chapter summary     142
    Recommended reading     143

**5 Using Multiple Regression to Model Mediation and Other Indirect Effects**     **144**

    Chapter overview     144
    What are mediation and indirect effects?     145
    Specification of the simple indirect-effect model     147
    Estimation and inference for the indirect effect     151
    Chapter summary     161
    Recommended reading     161

**6 Introduction to Multilevel Modeling**     **163**

    Chapter overview     163
    What is multilevel modeling?     164
    Nonindependent observations     164
    The unconditional multilevel model     171
    Conditional multilevel models     179
    Distinguishing within-cluster effect from between-clusters effect     190
    Formal model comparisons     199
    Cross-level interactions     202
    Three-level models     205
    Assumption checking for MLM     205
    Chapter summary     208
    Recommended reading     212

**7 Basic Matrix Algebra for Statistical Modeling**     **213**

    Chapter overview     213
    Why matrix algebra?     213
    Kinds of matrices and simple matrix operations     214
    Elementary matrix algebra     218
    Matrix calculations for statistical applications     227
    Chapter summary     236
    Recommended reading     237

**8 Exploratory Factor Analysis**     **238**

    Chapter overview     238
    What is exploratory factor analysis?     239
    EFA with continuous observed variables     240

Research example for EFA with continuous observed variables    241
Estimation of the common factor model    247
Determining the optimal number of common factors    257
Using model fit statistics to determine the optimal number of factors    262
Factor rotation    265
Exploratory factor analysis with categorical observed variables    275
Assumptions and diagnostics for EFA    280
Chapter summary    283
Recommended reading    284

**9  Structural Equation Modeling I: Path Analysis**    **285**

Chapter overview    285
What is structural equation modeling?    286
Path analysis    288
Path analysis: Model specification    289
Path analysis: Model identification    302
Path analysis: Model estimation    306
Model fit evaluation    316
Assumptions and diagnostics for path analysis models    331
Chapter summary    333
Recommended reading    333

**10  Structural Equation Modeling II: Latent Variable Models**    **335**

Chapter overview    335
What are latent variable models?    336
Confirmatory factor analysis    337
Structural regression models    367
Chapter summary    386
Recommended reading    387

**11  Growth Curve Modeling**    **389**

Chapter overview    389
What is growth curve modeling?    390
Growth curve models for linear change    397
Growth curve models for nonlinear change    419
Chapter summary    434
Recommended reading    435

*References*    437
*Index*    447

# ONLINE RESOURCES

Visit https://study.sagepub.com/flora to find a range of additional resources for both students and lecturers, to aid study and support teaching.

The online resources are:

- Files containing annotated **input and output** for the most popular statistical analysis software packages (R, SAS®, IBM SPSS Statistics® and MPlus®), allowing you to implement statistical procedures no matter your software preference.
- A series of **datasets**, enabling you to apply statistical techniques to real data. When you see this icon in the margin, that means there's a dataset online that corresponds to the worked example in the text.

# ABOUT THE AUTHOR

David B. Flora, PhD, is an associate professor in the Department of Psychology at York University in Toronto, Canada. Dr Flora has also served as a coordinator of the Quantitative Methods Area in York's graduate program in psychology and as a coordinator of York's Statistical Consulting Service. As a quantitative psychologist, Dr Flora is a co-author on numerous articles focused on quantitative methodology itself as well as on a wide range of articles in which advanced quantitative methods are applied to substantive research topics in psychology. Dr Flora earned his PhD from the Quantitative Psychology program at the University of North Carolina at Chapel Hill. Although he now lives in Toronto, Dr Flora is a Tar Heel born and a Tar Heel bred, and when he dies he'll be a Tar Heel dead.

# ACKNOWLEDGEMENTS

If this book is at all successful at presenting and explaining its subject matter, it is because I have had the privilege of learning from many outstanding teachers and mentors. In fact, some of the writing in this text has evolved from their lecture notes. In alphabetical order, these teachers and mentors include Ken Bollen, Laurie Chassin, Patrick Curran (my graduate school advisor, whose enthusiasm about this book I have appreciated), Siek-Toon Khoo, Bud MacCallum, Abigail Panter, Dave Thissen, and Jack Vevea. My undergraduate statistics instructor Brad Hartlaub was the first to emphasize to me the importance of *writing* about data analyses. A few of my colleagues at York University – Rob Cribbie, John Fox, Michael Friendly, Georges Monette, and Jolynn Pek – have enhanced my understanding of this book's subject matter. I also thank Phil Chalmers for helping me create a few of the book's figures and other general computing assistance. Finally, I thank Michael Carmichael, Mila Steele, Michael Ainsley, and John Nightingale at SAGE Publications for steering me through this whole process.

Of course, none of the individuals named here is responsible for any inaccuracies which may appear in the following pages.

# PREFACE

This book is intended for graduate students as well as for more seasoned faculty and researchers alike in the behavioural and social sciences; the statistical methods and concepts covered herein are also widely used in education, the health sciences and business and organizational research. As an advanced text, this book was written for PhD-level students and researchers who are already comfortable with the topics typically covered in a first-year sequence of graduate-level applied statistics (see subsequent discussion) who wish to learn about more advanced procedures that are commonly used. As such, this text is suitable for a general second (or advanced) course in statistical methods for the behavioural and social sciences.

The book might be best understood as a survey of the advanced statistical methods most commonly used in modern research in psychology and related fields in the behavioural and social sciences. That is, each chapter gives an overview of a major topic which could be expanded into a full book on its own, and indeed, good book-length treatments are available for each topic (many of these resources are cited in the current text). I hope that the chapters in this text can provide a sufficient foundation for readers to begin using a given statistical modeling method for their data. But I also strongly encourage readers to delve deeper into any statistical topic that is especially pertinent for their research interests; the books and articles cited in the current text (particularly the Recommended Reading section concluding each chapter) should provide direction.

Because this text covers advanced statistical methods and is aimed at readers who have completed coursework in basic statistics and data analysis, it is necessary to assume comfort (more than just familiarity) with a wide range of fundamental topics and principles. If necessary, readers should review basic statistics before tackling this book. The following are the most critical topics readers are assumed to understand:

- Basic high school-level algebra; no experience with calculus is assumed (although concepts from calculus are mentioned in a few places, familiarity with them is not necessary for more general comprehension of the relevant material)
- Major concepts in research methods and design, including principles of sampling
- Describing and representing univariate distributions using frequency tables, descriptive statistics, and graphs
- Basic definitions and rules of probability (this text adheres to the frequentist conception of probability)
- Concepts of sampling distributions and standard error; the central limit theorem
- Logic of null hypothesis significance testing (and limitations of null hypothesis testing), including $Z$ and $t$ tests, $\chi^2$ tests, and definitions of Type I and Type II errors and statistical power

- Basic one-way analysis of variance (ANOVA)
- Definition and interpretation of confidence intervals (CIs); correspondence between confidence intervals and hypothesis tests
- Simple correlation and regression (although these topics are also detailed in Chapter 1)

Readers should also be familiar with American Psychological Association (APA) style (APA, 2010) for presenting statistical results (e.g., $t(272) = 2.91$, $p = .003$); this style guide is used widely in fields other than psychology.

The following topics are extremely important, and they are touched on in this text but not comprehensively detailed:

- The importance of quality measurement, collecting reliable and valid scores for variables of interest
- Multiple comparison control (i.e., accumulation of Type I error probability across a family of null hypothesis tests)
- Concerns regarding 'data dredging' or '$p$ hacking': These problems may be less severe when researchers (1) adhere to rigorous research design principles, (2) take reliable and valid measurements, and (3) choose statistical models that match theories as closely as possible and evaluate models with a wide lens, not abusing null hypothesis significance testing
- Principles for drawing causal inferences from statistical results

## PURPOSES AND PERSPECTIVE OF THIS BOOK

Probably the most common reason for setting out to write a textbook is that an instructor of a given course finds all currently available books unsatisfactory. That was my feeling as I planned and taught a course titled 'Multivariate Analysis', which is aimed at PhD-level graduate students in psychology. Although there is a wide range of textbooks already available on the general topic of multivariate data analysis, each one of them has certain limitations. Indeed, I have noticed that syllabi for similar courses taught at other universities often list several potential textbooks, implying that no one of them is entirely suitable.

The primary reason that I struggled to find an appropriate textbook for my course was that the particular topics typically emphasized in so-called 'multivariate' texts usually did not overlap well with the topics I felt should be emphasized to prepare graduate students for careers in which they are likely to need to understand the data analytic techniques that are most common in modern research in psychology and the social sciences. In particular, even recently published multivariate texts devote entire chapters to traditional multivariate statistical methods such as multivariate analysis of variance (MANOVA), discriminant function analysis, and canonical correlation analysis. Yet, these methods are hardly used in psychological research anymore, and in my roles as a research collaborator and statistical consultant, I almost never encounter studies for which these methods seem ideally suited. Even during my own graduate training in quantitative psychology, we were told that 'although we are learning about these methods, you will probably never use them!'

Instead, the statistical methods most commonly used in modern research in psychology and the social sciences generally entail developing, estimating, and testing *models* for data. In his landmark paper, Rodgers (2010) explained that a 'quiet methodological revolution' has occurred in which psychology has moved beyond rigid data analytic methods which empha-size statistical tests above all else in favour of more flexible methods for *modeling* data based on substantive theories and expertise regarding the underlying processes which give rise to empir-ical data. Perhaps most prominent among these modeling procedures is multiple regression, which of course is addressed in most, if not all, multivariate texts. But popular modern appli-cations of multiple regression for modeling hypotheses regarding *moderation* and *mediation* seem to receive little, if any, attention. Another important modeling method also commonly covered in most traditional multivariate texts is *exploratory factor analysis*, but it is usually preceded by a distracting treatment of principal components analysis, or even worse, princi-pal components analysis is falsely presented as if it is a *type* of factor analysis (see Chapter 8). Finally, few multivariate textbooks include chapters on both *multilevel modeling* (also known as hierarchical linear modeling) and *structural equation modeling*, although both have become extremely common in modern research.

Finally, a handful of texts present statistical methods in concert with their implementa-tion using a single particular software package (most commonly SPSS). In my experience, researchers (in graduate school and beyond) often become so wedded to one specific statisti-cal software package that they are later handcuffed by the limitations of that software when they encounter problems. For example, many newly developed statistical techniques become widely available before they are added to SPSS or SAS.

My hope is that if students have a solid understanding of the basic principles underlying a given statistical procedure, then that foundation will allow them to carry out the procedure using whichever software package implements the procedure most appropriately. Nonetheless, I recognize that students come to understand statistical procedures more completely when they can apply them using example data analyses, and for that reason, the website for this text includes annotated input and output files from several prominent software packages (i.e., R, SAS, SPSS, and Mplus) for each of the major statistical modeling procedures presented herein. For the most part, however, statistical software concerns are not addressed in the main body of this text because I do not want computing to become a distraction from the conceptual statisti-cal principles described in the book.

In closing, it is important to disclaim that I am a psychologist, and for that reason, the statistical methods and example data analyses presented in this text primarily draw on psy-chological research. But the methods and techniques I present (and any accompanying advice for data analysis) are broadly applicable across a wide range of disciplines.

## A NOTE ON EQUATIONS

As a text on advanced statistical modeling methods, it is necessary to present statistical models using equations. I strongly believe that having an understanding of the key equations underlying a statistical model is critical to understanding how the model represents empirical data or addresses a substantive research question. Yet, I have tried to keep the text nontechnical. Most equations in the text just involve simple addition and multiplication; occasionally exponentials or logarithms are used. Even the matrix algebra equations presented in Chapter 7 and subsequent chapters can be characterized as organized collections of simple algebraic operations based on addition and multiplication. Nonetheless, throughout the text, I have tried to explain the conceptual meaning of each potentially unfamiliar element within a given equation rather than assuming that these mathematical expressions are self-explanatory. **Equations are numbered if they are referred to in the text; un-numbered equations tend to be explained immediately without any need to refer to them again.**

Most equations presented in this text are variations of regression equations. As such, just as the conceptual content of later chapters builds on the content introduced in earlier chapters, the equations presented in later chapters usually build on equations first seen in earlier chapters. In many instances throughout the text, a newly introduced equation is compared with an equation presented earlier, either in the same chapter or in a previous chapter. Therefore, as one proceeds through the text, it is wise to keep track of the equations (particularly the numbered equations) as they appear so that one can compare a new equation with previous equations to identify which features are familiar from previous equations and which are new elaborations. Doing so should consequently help one understand the meaning of the particular statistical model that the equation pertains to.

Also, in digesting these equations, it is important not to get overwhelmed by notation. Whenever a symbol is introduced for the first time, its meaning is explained. I have attempted to keep the use of notation consistent throughout the text, but I have also tried to keep my use of notation consistent with the methodological literature on the topics covered in this text so that readers can more easily consult other resources, which does introduce some inconsistency from one chapter to another (especially when moving from multilevel modeling to structural equation modeling). To help prevent confusion about the Greek letters used for notation, at the beginning of each chapter there is a table giving the Greek letters used in that chapter, its English name, and a brief statement of what the Greek letter represents within that chapter.

# FOUNDATIONS OF STATISTICAL MODELING DEMONSTRATED WITH SIMPLE REGRESSION

## CHAPTER OVERVIEW

The major objective of this chapter is to develop an understanding of the principles of statistical modeling in general and the simple linear regression model in particular. These principles provide a conceptual foundation for the remainder of the text. The main topics of this chapter include:

- Definition and description of statistical modeling as a guiding theme for the text
- Perspective on effect-size meaning and significance testing used in this book
- Orientation toward the simple linear regression model
- The intercept-only model as a model against which to compare the simple linear regression model
- Foundational principles for simple linear regression
- Specification and estimation of the simple linear regression model
- Statistical inference with the simple linear regression model
- Dichotomous variables in simple linear regression
- Basic concepts for regression diagnostics as they pertain to simple linear regression
- Outliers and unusual cases from the perspective of simple linear regression

**Table 1.0**  Greek letter notation used in this chapter

| Greek letter | English name | Represents |
|---|---|---|
| $\beta$ | Lowercase 'beta' | Regression model parameter (intercept or slope, depending on subscript) |
| $\varepsilon$ | Lowercase 'epsilon' | Regression model error term |
| $\mu$ | Lowercase 'mu' | Population mean |
| $\sigma$ | Lowercase 'sigma' | Population standard deviation |
| $\rho$ | Lowercase 'rho' | Population correlation |
| $\alpha$ | Lowercase 'alpha' | Probability of Type I error |

## WHAT IS A STATISTICAL MODEL?

### A trivial example

Before formally defining *statistical model*, I will begin with a trivial example model that demonstrates some of the fundamental ideas about models. Growing up in the United States, I became accustomed to thinking about temperature on the Fahrenheit scale. I know how chilly 40°F is, and I know how warm 75°F is. In Canada, where I now live, temperature is usually reported on the Celsius scale. Unfortunately, I do not automatically have a good sense of what a temperature such as 13°C feels like (should I wear a jacket if I go outside?), so I find that I am constantly converting temperatures reported in Celsius into the approximate Fahrenheit temperature in my head. Of course, there is a known, precise relation between °F and °C, but the conversion isn't always easy for me to calculate in my head, so I use an approximation that I can calculate quickly. Specifically, I multiply the temperature in °C by two and add 30 to arrive at a value that I know is at least near the temperature in °F.

This approximation is my *model* for °F given the reported °C, and it can be expressed using the following mathematical equation:

$$°\hat{F} = 2(°C) + 30. \tag{1.1}$$

The hat symbol (^) over F on the left-hand side of the equation indicates that the formula produces a *predicted* value for °F given a particular value for °C. That is, the value for °C is known, or observed, whereas the value for $°\hat{F}$ is unobserved. (The predicted value is also known as the *model-implied* or *fitted* value.) So if I am told that it is 13°C outside and I am wondering whether I should wear a jacket, then I can quickly calculate

$$°\hat{F} = 2(13) + 30 = 56.$$

Thus, my predicted value for the temperature on the Fahrenheit scale is $°\hat{F} = 56$, which is not terribly cold but chilly enough that I will probably put on a jacket.

Now, I know that my model does not usually produce the actual, precise value for °F given some temperature in °C. That is, deriving the true °F using this approximation is error-prone, and so another way I can write the model is

$$°F = 2(°C) + 30 + \varepsilon, \tag{1.2}$$

where $\varepsilon$ is the error term representing the inaccuracy involved in reproducing the true °F using this formula. Next, with some simple algebra, we see that we can substitute Equation 1.1 into Equation 1.2 such that

$$°F = °\hat{F} + \varepsilon$$

or

$$\varepsilon = °F - °\hat{F}. \tag{1.3}$$

Thus, the error, $\varepsilon$, gives the difference between the true temperature on the Fahrenheit scale (°F) and the temperature on the Fahrenheit scale predicted by the model ($°\hat{F}$). Equations 1.1 and 1.2 are different ways of expressing the same model for the relation between °C and °F.

All statistical models are like my temperature model in Equation 1.1 in that they generate predicted values for some outcomes but do so with error. Of course there is an established, true relation between the Fahrenheit and Celsius scales, specifically

$$°F = 1.8(°C) + 32. \tag{1.4}$$

Note that Equation 1.4 is not really a *model* because there is no error term; given a value for °C, we can use Equation 1.4 to calculate the *exact*, true value for °F.

We can also use Equation 1.4 to evaluate the quality of the model expressed in Equations 1.1 and 1.2. That is, we can use Equation 1.4 to calculate values for the model's error term, $\varepsilon$, across different values of °C; in other words, we can use Equation 1.4 to find out how well our predicted values, $°\hat{F}$, reproduce the true values, °F. For example, if it is 0°C outside (i.e., the temperature at which water freezes), the true °F is 1.8(0) + 32 = 32°F, but the model's predicted value is 2(0) + 30 = 30° $\hat{F}$. Thus, the model is inaccurate by 2°F, or using Equation 1.3, we have $\varepsilon = 32 - 30 = 2$. So although it's not precise, the model does a reasonably good job of predicting °F when °C is 0, or freezing. But how well does the model do when, for example, it's 13°C? Will the model lead to me being too warm in a light jacket, or will I wish that I had put on something heavier? Again, using Equation 1.4, the true °F corresponding to 13°C is 55.4°F, and now $\varepsilon = -0.6$, which is reasonably accurate given the model's purpose; that is, I am unlikely to regret my decision to wear a jacket.

To get a more complete picture of how good the model is across a wider range of values for °C, we can plot Equations 1.1 and 1.4 in the same graph, as shown in Figure 1.1. I have chosen a range of –15°C to 45°C for the x-axis to represent the wide range of outside temperatures experienced in a given year in North America (having lived in Phoenix, Arizona, and Toronto, I am familiar with both extremes). Clearly, Equations 1.1 and 1.4 are both equations for straight lines but with different intercept and slope values. But in the figure, we see that the lines cross above 10°C, where both the predicted value $°\hat{F}$ and the true value °F equal 50. Thus, for 10°C, the model perfectly reproduces the true °F (i.e., $\varepsilon = 0$). To the left of 10°C, the line for the predicted values is below the line for the true values, indicating that when the temperature is below 10°C, the model underestimates the true °F and the corresponding values for the error term $\varepsilon$ are all positive. To the right of 10°C, the predicted line is above the true line, indicating that when the temperature is above 10°C, the model overestimates °F and the values for $\varepsilon$ are negative. Nonetheless, across the range of °C plotted, the predicted line never deviates far from the observed line, indicating that the model is good enough for the purpose of predicting degrees Fahrenheit across the range of temperatures most commonly experienced in North America. But if we were to extend the model in either direction, to extremely cold temperatures or extremely hot temperatures, the model's predictions would clearly deteriorate.

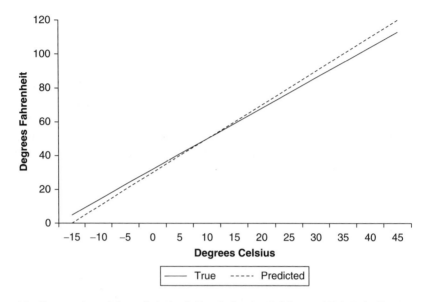

**Figure 1.1**   True and model-predicted relation between Celsius and Fahrenheit

In behavioural and social research, we can never know the *true* relation between any two variables. Equation 1.4 gives us the known, exact relation between Celsius and Fahrenheit, but there is no analogous version of Equation 1.4 for the types of variables studied in the social and behavioural sciences. Thus, there is no precise way to evaluate the quality of a statistical model in the manner illustrated in Figure 1.1. Instead, other methods for evaluating models must be used, and some of them are discussed throughout this book. Nevertheless, this temperature example demonstrates some key ideas about models:

1.  They are developed to give a useful simplification of some natural phenomenon (e.g., an easy way to calculate the relation between Celsius and Fahrenheit).
2.  They give predictions, but by virtue of the model being a simplification of nature, these predictions have error (e.g., the difference between model-implied, or predicted, Fahrenheit and true Fahrenheit).
3.  They are tailored to serve a particular use, for which the errors are hopefully small, that might not generalize to other uses (e.g., understanding the relation between Celsius and Fahrenheit across the range of temperatures commonly experienced in North America but not the extreme heat near the surface of the sun).

As statistician George Box famously stated, 'All models are wrong but some are useful' (Box, 1979: 208).

## Statistical model defined

With these ideas in mind, drawing from Pearl (2000: 202) and Rodgers (2010: 5), a **statistical model** is a set of one or more mathematical expressions (e.g., equations) that provides an idealized representation of reality; this representation represents reality in important ways but is necessarily a simplification that ignores certain features of reality. More formally, a statistical model specifies a univariate or multivariate population probability density function which is hypothesized to generate sample data (Myung, 2003).

The use of such statistical models to analyse quantitative data from behavioural and social empirical research studies is the unifying theme of this text. In particular, the text is focused on modeling procedures that are especially popular for analysing data in behavioural and social research, namely, multiple regression, factor analysis, multilevel modeling, and structural equation modeling (SEM). These modeling procedures are popular in modern research mostly because of their broad capacity to help answer a wide range of sophisticated research questions and, in so doing, to help with the development and evaluation of important substantive theories.

Rodgers (2010) also distinguished between two roles for models. The first is focused on evaluating models (and comparing competing models) for a given dataset using existing statistical modeling methods such as regression and SEM. This first role is the main topic of this text, although many of the principles addressed here also apply to the second role. The second role 'involves the development of mathematical models to match topics of explicit interest to researchers. Within this second framework, substantive scientists study behaviour and from that process develop mathematical models specific to their research domain' (Rodgers, 2010: 8). See Rodgers for examples of research based on this second approach. SEM, for example, is a prominent statistical method commonly used for the first role, and its flexibility makes SEM adaptable to many different applications, whereas models developed for the second role are often specific to a particular application.

First and foremost, statistical models are fundamentally **descriptive** in that they provide descriptions of the associations among one or more operational variables (i.e., the actual observed measurements in a research study rather than the more abstract concepts) in terms of a small set of patterns which are summarized with mathematical formulas. But moving beyond basic description, the two other major purposes of statistical models are **explanation** and **prediction**. Building a model for the purpose of explanation means that the model is meant to represent a theoretical account for the variation in some important dependent variable or outcome; typically this account (either explicitly or implicitly) represents the actual causal mechanisms, or a subset of potential causal mechanisms, that produce changes in the outcome. The adage that 'correlation does not imply causation' certainly extends to statistical models for observational data, but nonetheless, such models may still represent theoretical causal mechanisms. The models presented in this book are mainly presented with the goal of theoretical explanation in mind. But determining whether the associations among variables in a statistical model truly represent causal effects ultimately is the shared responsibility of researchers producing those results and the consumers of that research, all of whom must carefully consider the quality of the research design (e.g., were observations properly sampled and measured? What are potential confounding effects?) as well as the statistical analysis itself.

Models built for theoretical explanation usually are used only to describe outcomes that are observed within a given dataset (e.g., what is the association between personality and depression among university students?), whereas models built for the purpose of prediction are meant to provide accurate forecasts for critical outcomes that have not yet been observed (e.g., given a high school student's score on an academic achievement test, what is her likely university grade-point average?). Principles for developing statistical models for the different purposes of explanation and prediction tend to be complementary but not always. For further discussion of these issues, see Pedhazur (1997, especially pp. 195–8, and references therein).

Throughout this text, I frequently use the terms *predictor* and *predicted values* but doing so does not imply that I am referring to pure prediction in this sense of estimating unobserved values or future outcomes. Instead, I use these terms in a more descriptive mathematical sense. In any statistical model fitted to a dataset, the score on an independent or explanatory variable for a given research participant, or case, in that dataset can be used to obtain, or *predict,* values on the dependent or outcome variable for that same case; hence, this explanatory variable may be referred to as a *predictor*. If the predicted value on the outcome variable for a given case is close to the actual observed value for that case in the dataset, then the statistical model has performed well (for that case).

 Section recap

### Statistical models

A **statistical model** is a set of one or more mathematical expressions that provides an idealized representation of reality; this representation represents reality in important ways but is necessarily a simplification that ignores certain features of reality.

Fundamentally, models describe the variability of an important outcome or dependent variable as a function of one or more predictors or independent variables; these descriptions may reflect (causal) explanation or may simply be used for prediction.

## SIGNIFICANCE TESTING AND EFFECT SIZES

*Null hypothesis significance testing* (NHST) has been the dominant paradigm in data analysis for behavioural and social research since the middle of the 20th century, and criticism of NHST is just as old (e.g., Jones, 1952; Rozeboom, 1960). In psychology, debate over the usefulness (or lack thereof) of NHST bubbled over as a result of a now-famous article by Cohen (1994), leading the American Psychological Association (APA) to create a Task Force on Statistical Inference (TFSI) consisting of a team of eminent quantitative methodologists. The Task Force was charged with evaluating the possibility of banning NHST from psychology journals (or at least those published by APA). They ultimately concluded that although NHST has its flaws, it should remain available as a tool for data analysts but should also be supplemented with (if not subsumed by) other statistical information (see Wilkinson and the Task Force on Statistical Inference, 1999).

What has happened since then? In the APA's flagship journal, Rodgers (2010) argued that a 'quiet methodological revolution, a modeling revolution' has occurred which has made the NHST controversy mostly irrelevant. In particular:

A basic thesis of this article is that the heated (and interesting) NHST controversy during the 1990s was at least partially unnecessary. In certain important ways, a different methodological revolution precluded the need to discuss whether NHST should be abandoned or continued. This quiet revolution, a modeling revolution, is now virtually complete within methodology. But within the perspective of the diffusion of innovations, this revolutionary thinking is only beginning to spread to the applied research arena and graduate training in quantitative methods. Identifying the revolution is one mechanism that will promote its diffusion. The methodological revolution to which I refer has involved the transition from the NHST paradigms developed by Fisher and Neyman-Pearson to a paradigm based on building, comparing, and evaluating statistical/mathematical models. (Rodgers, 2010: 3-4).

This book adheres to the premise by Rodgers that a modeling revolution has occurred, and indeed, it's focused on 'building, comparing, and evaluating' models as the dominant paradigm in data analysis for modern behavioural and social research. But, as Rodgers implied, modeling is hardly a new enterprise in quantitative methodology (in fact, several prominent applied statistics texts already take this perspective, e.g., Maxwell and Delaney, 1990, 2004). Modeling is already a major data-analytic approach for most quantitative research in the behavioural and social sciences; the 'quiet revolution' is 'almost complete.' The task now is to give this epistemological system a more explicit focus in how researchers are trained, which this book aims to help accomplish.

It is important to understand that this focus on modeling does not imply that NHST is no longer used; instead, NHST still plays 'an important though not expansive role' (Rodgers, 2010: 1) in the context of comparing models and evaluating estimates of their parameters. Thus, my perspective for this book is that significance testing through the calculation and reporting of $p$ values is one tool that can be useful for evaluating and comparing models (or parts of models), but other tools [e.g., confidence intervals (CIs)] can be helpful as well. I readily acknowledge that students and researchers often misunderstand the exact meaning of a significance test and related concepts (definitions of $p$ value, Type I and II error, etc.) and that NHST has limitations, and we will keep these issues in mind as we use NHST to examine models. I won't review these definitions and limitations here because they have been thoroughly addressed elsewhere, and frankly I wish to move beyond them (but readers not familiar with these issues should at least consult Cohen, 1994, and Wilkinson and TFSI, 1999).

It is satisfying to recognize that the father of NHST, Sir Ronald Fisher, advocated a model-based approach for statistical inference in the context of nonrandom sampling. Statistics textbooks commonly present statistical inference (i.e., generalizing from sample statistics to population parameters) using NHST as being valid only when the data come from a simple random sample, but behavioural and social research is often conducted using nonrandom samples. Thus, a critical aspect of Fisher's model-based approach is the acknowledgement that there is no basis for statistical inference when observations are nonrandomly sampled from a finite population, but *inference is legitimate under nonrandom sampling from an infinite population* (Fisher, 1922). With this infinite-population inference approach, the researcher first specifies a statistical model that represents the process that generated the outcome variable(s) according to certain population parameters, which are the target of inference. Next, a parametric distributional assumption is imposed on the model to represent the link between the fixed, observed values of the outcome variable and the realizations of a random variable. Finally, it is critical to incorporate model parameters to account for any meaningful departure from simple random sampling and the sampling design that was used (i.e., sampling based on stratification or clustering or disproportionate sampling). For a detailed discussion of Fisher's model-based inferential framework, please read Sterba (2009). This framework (along with some adaptations discussed by Sterba) represents the perspective used in this text for model-based statistical inference assuming an infinite population. This is also the perspective widely adapted across almost all of behavioural research, even if it's not explicitly acknowledged (although certain areas of social research are more concerned with finite-population inference).

One result of the NHST controversy in psychology is that it has led to a greater emphasis on the importance of **effect-size** calculation and reporting. Put simply, effect size is the extent to which a predictor is associated with an outcome variable. In other words, effect size is the strength of the relation between two variables. As such, effect size is really a simple concept (but see Kelley and Preacher, 2012, for a thorough discussion of defining *effect size*), but it is my impression that the cries for more effect-size reporting have made the issue overly complicated and have needlessly confused students and researchers. These pleas seem to have created an impression among psychologists in particular that effect-size reporting must always consist of a sophisticated-sounding standardized effect-size statistic (e.g., Cohen's *d* or omega squared) when simpler, familiar descriptive statistics (e.g., unstandardized mean differences), graphs, and estimates of *model parameters* are often (if not always) more effective at conveying effect size in meaningful units (Wilkinson and TFSI, 1999; for further discussions of this issue, see Baguley, 2009, and Frick, 1999). To the extent that quality research reports (e.g., journal articles) in the behavioural and social sciences have *always* included descriptive statistics, graphs, and estimates of model parameters, they have therefore also always included effect-size information, even prior to the recent pleas for effect-size reporting (see Pek and Flora, in press, for further discussion).

The models presented in this text share the property that the associations among variables are represented with parameters (e.g., a regression slope coefficient) and, thus, that the size of a given parameter *is* a measure of effect size. This point was emphasized and demonstrated by Steinberg and Thissen (2006), who argued that when results of statistical models are reported, effect sizes 'are *most clearly* expressed in tabular or graphical presentation of parameter estimates' (p. 413; emphasis mine). The parameters need not be standardized; in fact, Wilkinson and TFSI (1999) exclaimed that, 'If the units of measurement are meaningful on a practical level (e.g., number of cigarettes smoked per day), then we usually prefer an unstandardized measure (regression coefficient or mean difference) to a standardized measure (*r* or *d*)' (p. 599). Thus, although there is a potentially overwhelming plethora of standardized effect-size statistics available to researchers, this text is focused on interpretation of the estimates of a model's parameters as the primary mode for effect-size conveyance.

 Section recap

### Effect size and significance testing

**Effect size** is simply the extent to which one or more predictor (or explanatory) variables is associated with an outcome (or response) variable. In other words, effect size is the strength of the relation between one or more independent variables and a dependent variable.

In the context of statistical modeling, parameter estimates *are* effect-size statistics and these effects are usually most clearly conveyed in unstandardized form.

Despite its logical flaws, null hypothesis significance testing (NHST) remains a useful tool for testing the effects in a model and for comparing models.

## SIMPLE REGRESSION MODELS

All statistical methods covered in this text involve using parametric models. A parametric model is a mathematical expression that uses parameters to represent hypothetical relations among variables in the population. In other words, the model represents a hypothetical process that generates the outcome variable(s) according to certain population parameters. The first model we will examine extensively is the **simple linear regression model**. I expect that any reader of this text is already familiar with simple regression as it is almost always covered in introductory statistics textbooks and courses. Here, the purpose of studying the simple regression model in some detail is to establish a solid foundation for presenting more complicated and advanced modeling procedures because the same statistical principles and methods continue to apply as the two-variable simple regression model is expanded into larger models for more than two variables. Indeed, a few ideas addressed here even for simple regression may be new for some readers. This chapter also provides a familiar context, simple regression, in which to introduce the reader to the terminology, notation, and style that will be used throughout this text.

To begin nailing down the terminology and notation used in this text, let's take a quick, initial look at the simple linear regression model. It is a model for the score of case, or individual $i$ on some outcome variable $Y$, given that individuals score on some predictor variable $X$. 'Individual $i$' is a potentially observed unit in the (infinite) population of interest; most often, these units of observation are individual people (i.e., research participants), but of course in certain research areas, the units of observation might instead be animals, cities, parent–child dyads, or business firms, among other possibilities. One way to write the simple regression model is with the linear equation

$$Y_i = \beta_0 + \beta_1 X_i + \varepsilon_i. \tag{1.5}$$

The parameters in the model are the **intercept**, denoted $\beta_0$, and the **slope**, denoted $\beta_1$. The slope term is also often called the **regression coefficient** because in the language of basic algebra, $\beta_1$ is the coefficient of $X_i$ in the equation. There are three variables in this simple regression model in that there are three terms with the subscript $i$, indicating that they vary across observations. The parameters do not have the $i$ subscript because they are constants; they do not vary across observations.

The outcome variable is $Y_i$; other terms that are more or less synonymous with *outcome variable* include *dependent variable, response,* and *criterion*. The predictor variable is $X_i$; other terms that are more or less synonymous with *predictor variable*, depending on context, include *independent variable, regressor, explanatory variable,* and *covariate*. Often, researchers prefer to use the terms *independent* and *dependent* variable in the context of experimental research, whereas the terms *predictor* and *outcome* variable are used in observational, naturalistic research, and finally the terms *explanatory* and *response* variables might be generalizable to any research context. Personally, I view these sets of terms as essentially interchangeable regardless of the research context because they are treated the same way mathematically when statistical models are fitted to data. For brevity, and perhaps just out of habit, I primarily use the terms *predictor* and *outcome* variable throughout this text (although, incidentally, most examples come from observational research contexts, but the principles presented in this text apply to models for experimental data as well).

The third variable in Equation 1.5 is the **disturbance** or **error** term, $\varepsilon_i$, which represents the inaccuracy of the model's ability to reproduce the value of the outcome variable perfectly for a given observation. Unlike $Y_i$ and $X_i$, which are directly measured by the researcher, the error is an unobserved variable that is not directly measured and instead arises as a property of the model. Although it is not explicitly indicated in Equation 1.5, the simple regression model also includes a parameter, $\sigma^2$, to capture the variance of the errors; that is, $\sigma^2 = \mathrm{VAR}(\varepsilon_i)$.

This text follows the standard notational practice in the statistics and methodology literature of using Greek letters to represent *population* parameters. There is an unfortunate tendency in some research areas (as well as the output format of the IBM SPSS Statistics® software package) to use the lowercase Greek letter beta ($\beta$) to denote the *sample* statistic estimating the standardized regression slope (often referring to it as the 'beta weight'),[1] whereas a capital Roman letter $B$ is used to denote the sample statistic estimating the unstandardized regression slope.[2] I feel that the latter notational practice is likely to become confusing as the ordinary linear regression model is expanded into more elaborate models, and it is much clearer if Greek letters such as $\beta$ are always used to represent population parameters. Estimates of model parameters calculated from sample data are statistics, but they will also be referred to as **parameter estimates** throughout this text. To distinguish parameter estimates from the actual parameter symbolically, we use the 'hat' symbol. For example, $\hat{\mu}$, or 'mu hat', is the estimate of the population mean parameter $\mu$ (also commonly denoted as $\bar{Y}$ to represent the sample mean of variable $Y$), whereas $\hat{\beta}$, or 'beta hat', is the sample estimate of a population regression slope parameter $\beta$.

 Section recap

### Simple linear regression model

The simple linear regression model for the relation between an outcome variable $Y$ and a predictor $X$ is

$$Y_i = \beta_0 + \beta_1 X_i + \varepsilon_i.$$

The intercept parameter, $\beta_0$, is the predicted value of $Y$ when $X$ equals 0.
The slope parameter, $\beta_1$, is the predicted amount that $Y$ changes when $X$ increases by 1.
The magnitude of $\beta_1$ is therefore a (population) effect size for the association between $X$ and $Y$.

---

[1]Standardized regression slopes are defined and discussed in Chapter 2.

[2]Contrary to popular impression, this notational practice is also not consistent with the APA style guide; see APA, 2010: 119 and 122.

## Research example for the simple regression model

To provide a context in which the simple regression model might be used, let's consider an actual research study: A graduate-student researcher is interested in whether and how certain personality characteristics relate to aggression. The researcher collects a sample of $N = 275$ undergraduate university students who each complete the Buss-Perry Aggression Questionnaire (BPAQ; Buss and Perry, 1992) and the Barratt Impulsiveness Scale (BIS; Barratt, 1994), among other questionnaires. At a basic level, the researcher wants to devise a *model* for aggression (operationalized with BPAQ scores) to represent (or describe or explain) how and why people vary on this important outcome.

This dataset is available on the text's webpage (https://study.sagepub.com/flora) along with annotated input and output from several popular statistical software packages showing how to reproduce the analyses presented in this chapter.

Before beginning to fit models to empirical data, it is always wise to examine the data descriptively and especially graphically. Thus, for this example, we begin by looking at the sample distribution of the outcome variable, BPAQ scores. Because the BPAQ score is an (approximately) continuous variable and there are $N = 275$ observations, it's best to examine its distribution graphically rather than with a frequency table, for instance, with the boxplot and histogram in Figure 1.2. These plots show that the sample distribution of BPAQ scores is unimodal and (approximately) symmetric, with the bulk of the scores falling between 2.0 and 3.0. The center of the distribution seems to be just above 2.5, and there are no outliers.

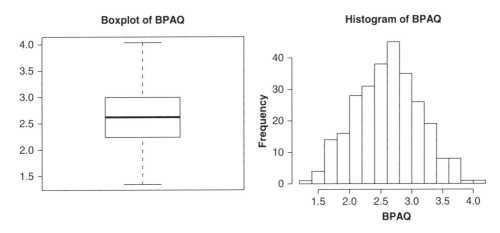

**Figure 1.2** Univariate distribution of BPAQ scores

Next, we might apply a density smoother (technically, a *kernel density estimate*) over the histogram of the sample data to approximate the (infinite) population probability distribution (see Wand and Jones, 1995). Likewise, we can superimpose the normal distribution curve that best fits the sample data; the histogram with the smoother and normal curve is shown in Figure 1.3. Now we can see that the sample distribution of BPAQ is remarkably close to a normal distribution; although the estimated density has a few small bumps, it is close to the superimposed normal curve.[3] Having an outcome variable with a distribution that's so close to a normal distribution is nice but unusual. But as we will see in later chapters, it is not always problematic for the outcome to be non-normal, and sometimes we don't need to do anything about it at all. Next, we might wish to have some numerical summaries, or descriptive statistics, to describe the sample distribution of BPAQ more specifically, as shown in Table 1.1. These summary statistics essentially support the observations made earlier from the graphs.

**Table 1.1**  Univariate descriptive statistics from aggression dataset

| Variable | Min | Q1 | Mdn | Q3 | Max | M | SD | Skewness | Kurtosis |
|---|---|---|---|---|---|---|---|---|---|
| BPAQ | 1.35 | 2.24 | 2.62 | 3.00 | 4.03 | 2.61 | 0.52 | 0.01 | −0.41 |
| BIS | 1.42 | 1.42 | 2.27 | 2.54 | 3.15 | 2.28 | 0.35 | 0.36 | −0.22 |
| Age | 17.00 | 18.00 | 18.00 | 20.00 | 50.00 | 20.21 | 4.96 | 3.70 | 15.43 |
| Alcohol | 0.00 | 3.00 | 12.00 | 24.00 | 96.00 | 16.00 | 15.87 | 1.50 | 3.09 |

*Note. N = 275. Min = minimum, Q1 = first quartile (or 25th percentile), Mdn = median (or 50th percentile), Q3 = third quartile (or 75th percentile), Max = maximum, M = mean, SD = standard deviation.*

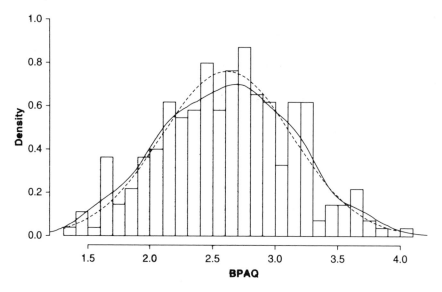

**Figure 1.3**  Histogram of BPAQ with fitted kernel density smoother (solid curve) and fitted normal distribution (dashed curve)

## Initial model for Y: Intercept-only model

Our first model for the BPAQ outcome variable isn't interesting or substantively informative, but it will give us a standard against which to compare the main regression model

---

[3]Note that the y-axis for Figure 1.3 is 'density,' or relative frequency on a probability scale, whereas the y-axis of the previous histogram in Figure 1.2 is just raw 'frequency,' on the scale of the number of cases at each observed value of BPAQ. Scaling frequency into relative frequency does not affect the shape of a distribution.

that incorporates the BIS predictor. In the absence of any predictor variable, the best model for BPAQ scores is simply an expression of the distribution's central tendency, such as the population mean, $\mu$. Of course we also know that there is variation around the mean, in that many (if not all) of the observations are not exactly equal to the mean. With this in mind, we can express this initial model like so:

$$Y_i = \mu + \varepsilon_i, \tag{1.6}$$

where $Y_i$ is the BPAQ score for case $i$ and the error term, $\varepsilon_i$, indicates that case $i$ is likely to have a value of $Y$ that deviates from the mean. This model is referred to as the **intercept-only model** because we can view it as a regression model without any predictors; that is, Equation 1.6 can be rewritten as

$$Y_i = \beta_0 + \varepsilon_i, \tag{1.7}$$

where $\beta_0 = \mu$. Note also that Equation 1.7 is equivalent to Equation 1.5 if $\beta_1 = 0$. This intercept-only model also includes the parameter $\sigma^2$ for the error variance; that is, $\sigma^2 = \text{VAR}(\varepsilon_i)$. In the intercept-only model, the error variance summarizes the extent to which observations differ from the mean, which is the value of $Y$ predicted by the model for every case in the population.

The parameter estimates for the intercept-only model are the familiar sample mean, $\bar{Y}$ (recall that $\bar{Y} = \hat{\mu}$, and therefore, for this model, $\bar{Y} = \hat{\beta}_0$), and sample variance, $s_Y^2 = \hat{\sigma}^2$. The square root of the sample variance, $\sqrt{s^2} = s$, is of course the sample standard deviation. Recall that the sample variance is calculated from the squared deviations of the mean from each observation:

$$\text{VAR}(Y) = s_Y^2 = \frac{\sum_{i=1}^{N}(Y_i - \bar{Y})^2}{N-1} = \frac{SS_Y}{N-1}, \tag{1.8}$$

where $SS$ stands for **sum of squares**.

Next, if we substitute the sample mean for the population mean (i.e., substitute the parameter estimate for the parameter) in the model, we have

$$Y_i = \hat{\mu} + e_i$$

or

$$Y_i = \bar{Y} + e_i.$$

Thus,

$$Y_i - \bar{Y} = e_i.$$

Note that because we have substituted parameter estimates for the actual population parameters, the deviation between the observed $Y_i$ and the value of $Y_i$ predicted by the model expressed in terms of parameter estimates is a **residual** term denoted $e_i$. In general, for both the intercept-only model and more complex regression models, the residual $e_i$ for a given case $i$ based on the estimated model will almost always differ from the error term $\varepsilon_i$ based on the true population model.

Next, following from the definition of $SS$, we have

$$\sum_{i=1}^{N} (Y_i - \bar{Y})^2 = \sum_{i=1}^{N} (Y_i - \hat{\mu})^2 = \sum_{i=1}^{N} e_i^2 = SS_e.$$

This is a simple but important result that generalizes to other, more elaborate models: The sum of squared residuals is the sum of squared deviations of the model's predicted $Y$ (here, the predicted $Y$ is just the mean) from the individual observed $Y$ values.

From Table 1.1, we see that the sample mean BPAQ score is 2.61 which, absent any predictor variables, gives the estimated predicted value of BPAQ for all cases in the population. Yet, the standard deviation of BPAQ is 0.52, indicating that there are substantial individual differences in the BPAQ outcome variable; soon we will incorporate predictor variables to explain this variability.

Furthermore, given the shape of the BPAQ distribution displayed in Figure 1.3, we should be comfortable that it is a reasonable approximation of a normal distribution such that $Y_i \sim N(\mu, \sigma^2)$; that is, the outcome $Y$ is distributed as a normal variable with population mean $\mu$ and variance $\sigma^2$. This statement then implies that the errors from the intercept-only model are also sampled from a normal distribution such that $\varepsilon_i \sim N(0, \sigma^2)$; that is, $\varepsilon$ is distributed as a normal variable with mean 0 and variance $\sigma^2$. Therefore, in this basic intercept-only model, the variance of the outcome variable equals the variance of the errors, but that won't be the case as soon as we add other variables to the model. Because the variance of the errors equals the variance of $Y$, the model has not explained *any* of the variation in the outcome. One way to evaluate the quality of subsequent models is to see how much of the variation in $Y$ is explained; that is, how much smaller is the error variance compared with the observed variance of $Y$? In other words, how much better is a model with one or more predictors of $Y$ than a model without any predictors?

 Section recap

## Intercept-only model

The **intercept-only model** is

$$Y_i = \beta_0 + \varepsilon_i.$$

Because this model has no predictor variables, its parameter estimates are the sample mean $\bar{Y} = \hat{\mu}$ and sample variance $s^2 = \hat{\sigma}^2$.

Because the model does not explain any of the outcome variable's variability, the residual variance is equal to the observed variance of $Y$.

Subsequent models which do include one or more predictors can be compared with this initial model to determine the amount of observed variance that is explained by the predictor(s).

## Focal model for Y: Simple regression with a single predictor

In the current research example, the main goal is to model aggression (measured with BPAQ) as a function of personality traits, such as impulsivity (measured with the BIS), not merely to describe the univariate distribution of BPAQ scores without any predictors. Thus, answering the actual substantive research question depends on devising a model that's more elaborate than the intercept-only model. Hopefully for this hypothetical personality researcher, the new model with BIS will be a statistical improvement over the basic intercept-only model. Again, before estimating the model, we should investigate the data graphically. Now that we are introducing a second variable, BIS scores, we can use a scatterplot to visualize the distribution of BPAQ scores conditioned on BIS scores, as depicted in Figure 1.4. The plot suggests that those with higher impulsivity scores tend to have higher aggression scores. That is, BPAQ scores covary with BIS scores, but the relation is far from perfect.

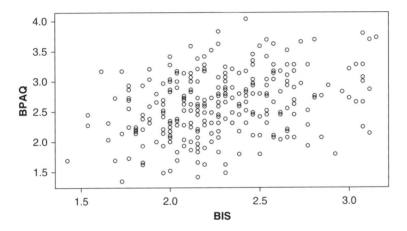

**Figure 1.4** Scatterplot of BPAQ scores against BIS scores

The sample **product-moment covariance** between two variables is the fundamental, basic ingredient that allows us to estimate the parameters of linear models (including advanced linear models, such as structural equation models). Consider the formula for the sample variance again:

$$\text{VAR}(Y) = s_Y^2 = \frac{\sum_{i=1}^{n}(Y_i - \bar{Y})^2}{N-1} = \frac{\sum_{i=1}^{n}(Y_i - \bar{Y})(Y_i - \bar{Y})}{N-1} = \frac{SS_Y}{N-1}.$$

This is an index of the amount that Y varies with itself. The formula for sample covariance is similar, but it incorporates both Y and X:

$$\text{COV}(Y,X) = s_{YX} = \frac{\sum_{i=1}^{n}(Y_i - \bar{Y})(X_i - \bar{X})}{N-1} = \frac{SCP}{N-1},$$

where SCP stands for **sum of cross-products** in that $(Y_i - \bar{Y})(X_i - \bar{X})$ is the *cross-product* between Y and X for a given case. Thus, $s_{YX}$ is an index of the amount that Y covaries with X in the sample. In our current research example, the covariance between BPAQ scores and BIS scores is $s_{YX} = 0.06$. But the value of a covariance depends on the scales of $Y$ and $X$; for this reason, covariance can be difficult to interpret as a basic descriptive statistic measuring the (linear) association between $X$ and $Y$.

Therefore, to aid interpretation of the association between two variables, the covariance can be standardized into the **Pearson product-moment correlation** (usually simply referred to as the 'correlation' or 'correlation coefficient'). The population correlation is represented with the Greek letter *rho*, $\rho$, whereas the sample correlation is represented with the Roman letter *r*. Thus, *r* estimates $\rho$. As readers are likely aware, a correlation is *always*[4] a value between $-1$ and $+1$, which is obtainable with the formula

$$r = \frac{\text{COV}(Y,X)}{\sqrt{\text{VAR}(Y) * \text{VAR}(X)}} = \frac{s_{YX}}{\sqrt{s_Y^2 s_X^2}}. \tag{1.9}$$

In our current example, the correlation between BPAQ and BIS is $r = .32$, which is consistent with the earlier observation that individuals with higher BIS scores tend to have higher BPAQ scores. More impulsivity is associated with more aggression. A 95% CI estimate of $\rho$ is $(.21, .42)$; that is, with 95% confidence, the interval from .21 to .42 captures the population correlation. In other words, a population correlation between BPAQ and BIS in the range of .21 to .42 is likely to have produced these data.

The correlation describes the extent to which two variables are *linearly* associated, implying that a straight line going through the middle of the points in the bivariate scatterplot (i.e., the simple regression line) does an adequate job of representing, or modeling, the pattern of covariation between $Y$ and $X$. It is easier to assess the quality of the straight-line model if we also add a nonparametric LOWESS ('LOcally WEighted Scatterplot Smoothing') regression curve to the plot, which is designed to capture more subtle, nonlinear regularities in the data that might not be well represented with the parametric regression line (see Fox, 2008: 21–4 and 496–507 for details on how LOWESS curves are calculated). Because it's nonparametric and is susceptible to chance variations in sample data, this LOWESS curve is difficult to use for population inference, but it can help evaluate the adequacy of the parametric linear regression model, given the observed data.[5] As shown in Figure 1.5 for the current example, the LOWESS curve is consistent with the straight line, so we should be comfortable using the line as a model for the data. Hence, although the relation between BPAQ and BIS is not particularly

---

[4] Here, the word 'always' is emphasized because when estimating certain advanced models, the obtained parameter estimates sometimes imply that a correlation between two variables is greater than $+1$ or less than $-1$. Such an estimated model solution must be discarded as *improper* because any correlation outside the $-1$ to $+1$ range is inherently nonsensical. This result commonly occurs in the context of advanced modeling procedures such as multilevel modeling (Chapter 6) and structural equation modeling (Chapters 9 and 10).

[5] The LOWESS curve is especially susceptible to chance variations in data when the sample size is small; in this case, only a few cases may cause the curve to display dramatic bends. In such a situation, the curve may *overfit* the data rather than smoothing over minor, sample-specific variation. One can control the extent to which a LOWESS curve captures such minor data characteristics by adjusting its *span* (see Fox and Weisberg, 2011: 117). In our current example, the sample size is rather large, and so the LOWESS curve is resistant to the influence of just a few unusual cases.

strong, it does appear as if the ordinary simple regression line is a reasonable model for the relation. That is, there doesn't seem to be any particular pattern in the data that would be grossly misrepresented by the straight line that best fits the data, namely, the **least-squares regression line**, which is defined later in this section.

As a quick aside, when a scatterplot shows a consistent nonlinear trend, the bivariate association may be effectively described using **Spearman's rank-order correlation coefficient**. Spearman's correlation is calculated by first transforming both variables into ranks, and then Spearman's correlation is the product-moment correlation between the two sets of ranks (see Chapter 8 for an example). The discrepancy between this rank-order correlation and the original, raw-score, product-moment correlation can be used as a diagnostic to determine whether a linear regression model is likely to be distorted by nonlinear patterns in the data.

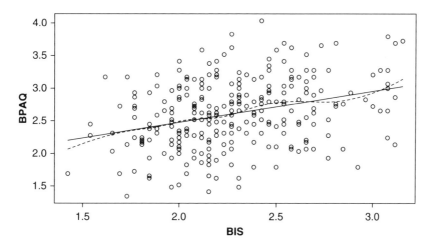

**Figure 1.5** Scatterplot of BPAQ scores against BIS scores with fitted linear regression line (solid line) and fitted LOWESS curve (dashed line)

But before considering the actual mathematical formulas for the linear model, it is important to distinguish between **predicted values** of Y, also known as *fitted* or *model-implied* values, and **observed values** of Y. The observed values of Y are the actual measured values for the outcome that are in the dataset. In the current example, there are $N = 275$ participants, or cases, with BPAQ aggression scores. Each of the 275 BPAQ scores is an observed value of Y. We can see in Figure 1.5 that most of the observed values do not fall on the regression line, and some are far from the line. The predicted values of Y, represented as $\hat{Y}$, are the Y values determined by the regression line across the X continuum. As we are using BIS impulsivity scores to predict or model BPAQ scores, then the $\hat{Y}$ values are the predicted, model-implied BPAQ scores at each possible BIS score (i.e., at each value of X). Because the prediction is not perfect (the correlation between BPAQ and BIS does not equal 1), most of the observed BPAQ scores do not equal the score that is predicted by the linear regression of BPAQ on BIS. Next, the **residual** for the individual, or case, i is the difference between that participant's observed Y value and the corresponding predicted $\hat{Y}$ value, given the *estimated* linear effect of the observed value for the predictor X:

$$e_i = Y_i - \hat{Y}_i.$$

So observed scores falling on an estimated regression line have residuals equal to zero, whereas observed scores that are far from the line have large residuals.

 Section recap

### Foundations for a simple linear regression model

A scatterplot of an outcome variable against a potential predictor helps determine whether it is appropriate to model the relation between the two variables using a straight-line function, i.e., a linear regression equation.

**Covariance** is a descriptive value measuring the strength of linear association between two variables; the **product-moment correlation** is a covariance which has been standardized to range between –1 and +1.

A **predicted value**, $\hat{Y}$, is the outcome variable score for individual $i$ that is predicted from the regression line given that individual's score on the predictor variable, $X_i$.

An **observed value**, $Y_i$, is the actual outcome variable score for individual $i$ regardless of that individual's score on the predictor variable, $X_i$.

Given a population regression equation, the regression error for individual $i$ is $\varepsilon_i = Y_i - \hat{Y}_i$.

Given an estimated regression equation, the **residual** for individual $i$ is $e_i = Y_i - \hat{Y}_i$.

## Simple linear regression: Model specification

**Model specification** simply refers to establishing the model's parameters with one or more equations giving the hypothetical mathematical relations among the variables. Often specification also involves statements about a model's assumptions regarding variance terms or probability distribution, although these assumptions sometimes arise because of estimation method (see later discussion in this section) and are not always a part of specification. Specification of the simple linear regression model was presented earlier, but here it is reiterated with slightly more detail.

The one-predictor linear regression model can be specified in two equivalent ways. The first expression is in terms of the predicted values of the outcome variable:

$$\hat{Y}_i = \beta_0 + \beta_1 X_i, \tag{1.10}$$

where $\hat{Y}_i$ is the predicted value on the outcome for case $i$ and $X_i$ is the observed value of the predictor for the same case $i$. As described previously, $\beta_0$ is the intercept parameter for the line, which is the value of $\hat{Y}$ when $X = 0$. $\beta_1$ is the slope parameter of the line, also called the regression coefficient, which is the amount that $\hat{Y}$ differs when $X$ increases by one unit. In other words, a one-unit increase in $X$ is associated with a change in $\hat{Y}$ equal to $\beta_1$. Of course sometimes $\beta_1$ is a negative number, indicating the amount that $\hat{Y}$ decreases per unit increase in $X$, just as a correlation can be positive or negative.

The second way of expressing the same model substitutes the observed $Y$ for the predicted $Y$ on the left-hand side of the equation:

$$Y_i = \beta_0 + \beta_1 X_i + \varepsilon_i, \tag{1.11}$$

where $Y_i$ is the observed score on the outcome for case $i$; $\beta_0$, $\beta_1$, and $X_i$ are the same as that presented earlier, and $\varepsilon_i$ is the error term. Because $\varepsilon_i = Y_i - \hat{Y}_i$, it is easy to see that the two expressions of the model (Equations 1.10 and 1.11) are algebraically equivalent. Finally, a third parameter of the model is the variance of the errors, $\sigma^2 = \text{VAR}(\varepsilon_i)$, which captures the extent to which observed values differ from predicted values.

Because $\beta_1$ measures the amount or extent to which the predictor variable is related to the outcome, it is an effect-size parameter. More specifically, because $\beta_1$ describes the linear effect of $X$ on $Y$ in terms of the scale of $Y$, it is an *unstandardized* effect-size measure. The correlation is a type of *standardized* effect-size measure because it indicates the strength of the linear relation between two variables on a standard scale from −1 to +1 rather than the observed scale of the outcome variable.

## Simple linear regression: Model estimation

In statistical modeling, **estimation** refers to the process of calculating estimates of model parameters from sample data. For any particular kind of model, there are many potential methods of estimation, but of course, some are better than others, where 'better' typically means that parameter estimates from an optimal estimation method are **unbiased, consistent**, and **efficient**, provided the method's assumptions are met. Briefly, a parameter estimate is unbiased if the mean of its sampling distribution equals the true value of the parameter at a given sample size; an estimate is consistent if its value approaches the parameter value as the sample size increases toward infinity; and an estimate is efficient if, compared with other estimation methods, its sampling distribution has the smallest variance.

In simple linear regression, the model parameters $\beta_0$ and $\beta_1$ are most commonly estimated from sample data using formulas derived using the **ordinary least-squares (OLS)** method of estimation. When its assumptions are met, parameter estimates calculated with OLS are unbiased, consistent, and efficient. These assumptions are addressed in both this chapter and subsequent chapters on linear regression.

The OLS formulas give values for $\hat{\beta}_0$ and $\hat{\beta}_1$ such that the set of squared residuals in the sample are as small as possible. More specifically, the line defined by the OLS estimates of $\hat{\beta}_0$ and $\hat{\beta}_1$ minimizes the **sum of squared residuals**, which is also known as the **error sum of squares**:[6]

$$SS_e = \sum_{i=1}^{N} e_i^2 = \sum_{i=1}^{n} (Y_i - \hat{Y}_i)^2.$$

Substituting the simple regression line as the model for $\hat{Y}$, we see that the residual sum of squares is

$$SS_e = \sum_{i=1}^{N} (Y_i - \hat{Y}_i)^2 = \sum_{i=1}^{N} (Y_i - [\hat{\beta}_0 + \hat{\beta}_1 X_i])^2.$$

---

[6]But the term 'error sum of squares' is misleading because of the distinction between *residuals*, which are deviations from $\hat{Y}$ based on sample estimates of the parameters, and *errors*, which are deviations from $\hat{Y}$ based on the true (but unknown) parameters. In practice, this sum-of-squares term can only be calculated using residuals.

The goal of OLS estimation is then to find parameter estimates, $\hat{\beta}_0$ and $\hat{\beta}_1$, that make the quantity $SS_e$ as small as possible. Calculus is required to show the derivation of the formulas for $\hat{\beta}_0$ and $\hat{\beta}_1$ that lead to the minimization of squared residuals (see Fox, 2008: 78–81). The result of this basic calculus problem gives the OLS estimate of $\beta_1$ as

$$\hat{\beta}_1 = \frac{\text{COV}(Y,X)}{\text{VAR}(X)} = r\left(\frac{s_Y}{s_X}\right). \tag{1.12}$$

With this expression, it is easy to see that if both $X$ and $Y$ are standardized (i.e., transformed so that their sample means equal 0 and variances equal 1), then the slope estimate is equal to the correlation.[7] Next, given the estimate of $\beta_1$, the OLS estimate of $\beta_0$ is

$$\hat{\beta}_0 = \bar{Y} - \hat{\beta}_1 \bar{X}.$$

Incidentally, when both $X$ and $Y$ are standardized, the intercept estimate equals zero.

For the current example modeling BPAQ aggression scores as a function of BIS impulsivity scores, the parameter estimates are $\hat{\beta}_0 = 1.52$ and $\hat{\beta}_1 = 0.48$, and thus, the estimated OLS regression line is

$$\hat{Y}_i = 1.52 + 0.48 X_i.$$

This is the equation of the line going through the middle of the points in the scatterplot in Figure 1.5. In fact, an OLS regression line is guaranteed to pass through the point $(\bar{X}, \bar{Y})$. The slope estimate $\hat{\beta}_1 = 0.48$ indicates that a one-unit increase in BIS scores predicts an increase of 0.48 in BPAQ scores. Again, this is the effect of BIS on BPAQ; it *is* an effect-size estimate for this data analysis. The intercept estimate $\hat{\beta}_0 = 1.52$ indicates that with a BIS score equal to zero, the predicted BPAQ score is 1.52. In this example, the intercept parameter is not substantively useful because a BIS score equal to 0 is outside of the range of the data, given the way that the questionnaire is scored. The intercept parameter often is of little interest in ordinary regression modeling, but in certain contexts, the interpretation of the intercept may be extremely important.

 Section recap

### Specification and estimation of the simple linear regression model

**Specification** establishes a model's parameters using one or more equations giving the hypothetical mathematical relations among the variables. Often specification also involves statements about a model's assumptions regarding variance terms or probability distributions.

Once a model is specified, **estimation** is the procedure by which the model's parameters are estimated from sample data.

**Ordinary least squares** (OLS) is the most common estimation method for linear regression. OLS produces the parameter estimates that minimize the sum of squared residuals.

---

[7]Standardized regression coefficients are discussed in Chapter 2.

## Simple linear regression: Statistical inference

The relation between BPAQ and BIS scores is clearly evident in the scatterplot, but the simple regression slope estimate $\hat{\beta}_1 = 0.48$ does not seem like a strong effect size given the observed scales of BPAQ and BIS. Thus, an important aspect of model interpretation does in fact involve significance testing and confidence interval estimation to determine whether this slope estimate is distinguishable from a population slope equaling zero (using a significance test) or, more comprehensively, to determine a plausible range for the value of the population slope (using a confidence interval or CI).

To make such inferences from the OLS parameter estimates to the unknown population parameters, it is necessary to make some assumptions about the error random variable, that is, the deviations from the estimated model. Primarily, we assume that $\varepsilon_i \sim N(0, \sigma^2)$, meaning that the errors come from a normal distribution with its mean equal to zero and variance equaling $\sigma^2$. Thus, in contrast to popular perception, in OLS regression, the normal distribution assumption is about the unmeasured errors and there is *no* explicit assumption that either measured variable $Y$ or $X$ is normal. Additionally, the fact that there is no $i$ subscript on $\sigma^2$ is important because it reflects the assumption that the error variance is the same (i.e., *constant variance*) for all observations, regardless of their value for $X$. This constant variance assumption is also known as **homogeneity of variance** or **homoscedasticity**: The variance of the errors is assumed homogeneous, or constant, across all values of $X$. Finally, there are a few other assumptions for OLS regression that we address in later chapters.

Usually, we are most interested in testing the null hypothesis that the regression slope equals zero:

$$H_0: \beta_1 = 0.$$

Note that if the null hypothesis is true, the regression model

$$Y_i = \beta_0 + \beta_1 X_i + \varepsilon_i$$

becomes

$$Y_i = \beta_0 + 0 \times X_i + \varepsilon_i$$

or

$$Y_i = \beta_0 + \varepsilon_i,$$

which is the intercept-only model presented earlier (Equation 1.7). Thus, the significance test for the slope $\hat{\beta}_1$ is also a *model comparison* test indicating whether the one-predictor, simple regression model is significantly different from the intercept-only model.

The ratio of the OLS estimate of a simple regression slope to its estimated *standard error* follows a $t$ distribution with $(N - 2)$ degrees of freedom. Thus, the null hypothesis for the slope is evaluated with a $t$ test:

$$t = \frac{\hat{\beta}_1}{s_{\hat{\beta}_1}}, \tag{1.13}$$

where $s_{\hat{\beta}_1}$ is the estimated standard error of $\hat{\beta}_1$. A formula for this standard error estimate is

$$s_{\hat{\beta}_1} = \sqrt{\frac{SS_e / (n-2)}{SS_x}}.$$

Recall that the **standard error** of a statistic is the standard deviation of its sampling distribution; hence, the standard error reflects the average amount that a statistic (such as a sample mean or a regression slope estimate) randomly drawn from its sampling distribution is expected to differ from the true parameter value.

Additionally, we can get a confidence interval estimate of $\beta_1$ using the usual symmetric confidence interval approach based on the $t$ distribution:

$$\hat{\beta}_1 \pm s_{\hat{\beta}_1} \times t_{\alpha},$$

where $t_{\alpha}$ is the appropriate *critical t* value for a $(1 - \alpha)\%$ confidence interval and $\alpha$ is the predetermined probability of a Type I error (usually $\alpha = .05$, leading to 95% confidence intervals). Of course, there is an exact correspondence between the $t$ test and the confidence interval in that the null hypothesis is not rejected at the given alpha level if the confidence interval overlaps 0 and is rejected if the confidence interval does not contain zero. Ultimately, though, the confidence interval is more informative than the null hypothesis significance test: Not only does the confidence interval indicate whether 0 (the value given by the null hypothesis) is a plausible value for the population slope parameter, but also the confidence interval gives a whole range of plausible values for the plausible parameter values.

This form of the $t$ test and confidence interval construction also applies to the intercept estimate, $\hat{\beta}_0$, but these results are often of little, if any, substantive interest (although standard statistical software does typically include the estimated standard error, $t$, and $p$ value of $\hat{\beta}_0$ within regression modeling output).

In the current example of the regression of BPAQ aggression scores on BIS impulsivity scores, $s_{\hat{\beta}_1} = 0.085$. Therefore, we have

$$t = \frac{\hat{\beta}_1}{s_{\hat{\beta}_1}} = \frac{0.4777}{0.0854} = 5.59.$$

The two-tailed $p$ value for this $t$ statistic is less than .0001, so using the conventional Type I error probability $\alpha = .05$, we reject the null hypothesis that the population slope equals zero. Thus, even though the effect-size estimate $\hat{\beta}_1$ is somewhat small, its true population value is likely to differ from zero. Furthermore, this $t$ test implies that the simple regression model with BIS as a predictor explains the data significantly better than the intercept-only model does.

Compared with the null hypothesis test, more specific information regarding the likely value of the population regression slope is given by a confidence interval around the slope estimate. Here, the 95% confidence interval estimate of $\beta_1$ is (0.31, 0.65), suggesting that a population slope of any value between 0.31 and 0.65 is likely to have produced these data. Hence, the data suggest that the population effect size could be as large as 0.65. This would seem like a large effect given that the BPAQ and BIS have similar scales; a one-point increase in BIS would predict a BPAQ score that is larger by 0.65 BPAQ units. But the lower end of the confidence interval suggests that the population effect could be 0.31, less than half as large as that suggested by the upper end.

Additionally, recall that in the intercept-only model, the variance of the residuals equals the variance of $Y$:

$$\text{VAR}(Y_i) = \text{VAR}(\beta_0 + \varepsilon_i) = \text{VAR}(\varepsilon_i).$$

Therefore, the intercept-only model does not explain any variance in $Y$. Let's call the intercept-only model for our current example 'Model 0'. The variance of BPAQ, and thus of the residuals from Model 0, equals 0.2746. Then, let Model 1 be the simple linear regression of BPAQ on BIS. The residual variance from Model 1 equals 0.2463. Thus, adding the predictor BIS has reduced the residual variance by $(0.2746 - 0.2463) = 0.0283$. The ratio $(0.0283) / (0.2746) = 0.1031$ then indicates the proportion of variance in BPAQ explained by Model 1. The (positive) square root of this proportion, $\sqrt{.1031}$, equals the correlation of .32 between BIS and BPAQ given earlier.

More generally, the **coefficient of determination**, $R^2$, is a descriptive statistic often reported as a measure of the overall standardized effect size given by a regression model. This statistic may be calculated as

$$R^2 = \frac{\text{VAR}(Y) - \text{VAR}(e)}{\text{VAR}(Y)}.$$

Because the sample-size terms in the numerator and denominator of this equation cancel out, it simplifies to an expression based on sum-of-squares terms:

$$R^2 = \frac{SS_Y - SS_e}{SS_Y}. \tag{1.14}$$

Consequently, in addition to the significance test for $\hat{\beta}_1$, we can also compare the intercept-only model to the one-predictor simple regression model using $R^2$, which indicates the proportion of variance in the $Y$ that's accounted for by including $X$ in the model. In simple linear regression, $R^2$ also equals the squared correlation, $r^2$, between $X$ and $Y$ and the $p$ value for the $t$ test for $\hat{\beta}_1$ is identical to the $p$ value for the significance test of the correlation. Hence, in our current example, we can also conclude that the proportion of the variance in $Y$ accounted for by BIS is significantly greater than zero.

 Section recap

### Statistical inference with the simple linear regression model

The null hypothesis that $\beta_1 = 0$ can be evaluated using a $t$ test in which

$$t = \frac{\hat{\beta}_1}{s_{\hat{\beta}_1}},$$

where $s_{\hat{\beta}_1}$ is the estimated standard error of $\hat{\beta}_1$.

*(Continued)*

(Continued)

Even more information about the true parameter value is provided by a confidence interval, which can be calculated with

$$\hat{\beta}_1 \pm s_{\hat{\beta}_1} \times t_{\alpha'}$$

where $t_\alpha$ is the *critical t* value for a $(1-\alpha)\%$ confidence interval with $\alpha$ as the predetermined Type I error probability.

The validity of these inferential methods depends on the assumption that the errors are normally distributed with constant (homogenous) variance across the range of $X$.

The **coefficient of determination**, $R^2$, gives the proportion of outcome variable variance explained by the predictor(s) in a regression model.

## Simple regression with a dichotomous predictor

Contrary to what is presented in some introductory statistics texts, the predictor variable in a simple correlation or regression analysis need not be continuous. The predictor can also be dichotomous (i.e., categorical with two values or categories, or binary) without violating any assumptions, although the outcome variable should still be continuous. For instance, continuing with our applied research example, we can use simple linear regression to model the relation between BPAQ aggression scores and gender. A scatterplot depicting the relation between BPAQ and gender is in Figure 1.6, with gender *dummy-coded* so that 0 = male and 1 = female. Because gender is a nominal variable, the choice of numerical values for its two categories is completely arbitrary, and the results presented here generalize to any numerical coding scheme for a binary variable. But dummy codes of 0 and 1 produce an especially convenient interpretation of the OLS regression parameters, as

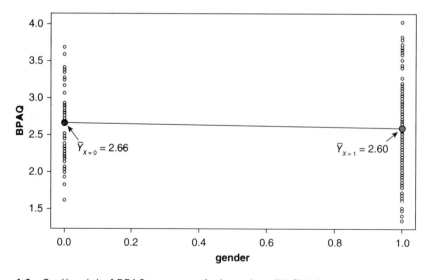

**Figure 1.6** Scatterplot of BPAQ scores against gender with fitted regression line

we will see later in the book (dummy coding is addressed further in Chapter 3). In addition to providing further insights about the simple regression model, the primary purpose of this section is to build a foundation for Chapter 3, which describes how categorical predictors with any number of categories (i.e., not just binary variables) can be incorporated in a linear regression model.

Because there are only two possible values of $X$, 0 and 1, a straight line is the mathematically simplest way to connect the middle of the points in the plot above $X = 0$ to the middle of the points above $X = 1$. Specifically, when $X$ is binary and coded 0 or 1, the OLS regression line is the line connecting the point $(0, \bar{Y}_{X=0})$ to the point $(1, \bar{Y}_{X=1})$. This line is superimposed in Figure 1.6, which provides the scatterplot of BPAQ scores against gender.

Once the binary predictor has been coded into two numerical values (such as the dummy codes used here), the formulas presented earlier for the OLS regression parameter estimates are directly applicable with the two dichotomous values used for $X_i$. In our current example with gender dummy coded, the estimated OLS regression line modeling BPAQ scores as a function of gender is

$$\hat{Y}_i = 2.66 - 0.06X_i.$$

Because $\hat{\beta}_0$, the estimated intercept, is the predicted value of $Y$ when $X = 0$, then 2.66 is the predicted BPAQ score among males. The intercept estimate is in fact the mean BPAQ score for males:

$$\hat{Y}_{male} = 2.66 - 0.06(0) = 2.66 = \bar{Y}_{male}.$$

Next, because $\hat{\beta}_1$, the estimated slope, is the predicted difference in $Y$ when $X_i$ changes by one unit, then –0.06 is the predicted difference in $Y$ between males and females. This parameter estimate thus gives the difference between the male mean and the female mean:

$$\hat{Y}_{female} = 2.66 - 0.06(1) = 2.60 = \bar{Y}_{female}.$$

Once again, the estimated regression slope represents the unstandardized effect size; the simple mean difference between males and females on the outcome is $\hat{\beta}_1 = 0.06$. Here, this is a small effect given that the range of observed BPAQ scores is approximately 1.0 to 4.0. Additionally, the plot in Figure 1.6 clearly illustrates the weakness of the effect. Thus, even though the scale of the BPAQ operational variable is essentially meaningless, we can easily tell that this simple mean difference is a small effect without converting it to some type of standardized effect size.

Moving on to inference, when the predictor in a simple regression model is binary, the $t$ test of whether the slope significantly differs from 0 (Equation 1.13) is equivalent to the well-known independent-groups $t$ test comparing the outcome variable means of the two groups formed by the dichotomous predictor variable:

$$t = \frac{\hat{\beta}_1}{s_{\hat{\beta}_1}} = \frac{\bar{Y}_2 - \bar{Y}_1}{s_{\bar{Y}_2 - \bar{Y}_1}},$$

where $s_{\bar{Y}_2 - \bar{Y}_1}$ is the standard error of the difference between means calculated using the familiar pooled-variance statistic formed under the homogeneity of variance assumption. Thus, the independent-groups $t$ test is a special case of significance testing in OLS regression. Likewise, the $p$ value for the correlation between a dichotomous $X$ and a continuous $Y$ will be equal to that for the $t$ test.[8] In the current example, this $t$ test is not significant, $t(273) = -0.797, p = .43$, implying that the gender difference on BPAQ scores may not differ from zero in the population. Finally, the confidence interval for the regression slope is identical to a confidence interval for the difference between two independent means; in the current example, the 95% confidence interval is $(-0.22, 0.09)$, conveying a range of plausible values for the population mean difference $(\mu_{female} - \mu_{male})$.

Because the number of male participants $(n = 57)$ is much smaller than the number of females $(n = 218)$ in this sample, we should pay extra attention to the viability of the homogeneity of variance assumption because it is well known that the consequences of heterogeneous variance for the $t$ test are more serious when the group sample sizes are markedly discrepant. The sample variances of BPAQ are similar across gender $(s^2_{male} = 0.26, s^2_{female} = 0.28)$, which should restore some comfort with the homogeneity of variance assumption despite the unbalanced sample size. But regardless of the homogeneity of variance assumption, as we observed earlier, the estimated effect size is tiny, and therefore, nonsignificance seems to be the appropriate result for this $t$ test.

## Dichotomous outcome?

In contrast to the previous section where a continuous outcome variable is regressed on a dichotomous predictor, it is critical to recognize that when the outcome itself is dichotomous, the simple linear regression model is not appropriate for the data. If $Y_i$ is coded as either 0 or 1 for each observation $i$, then the regression line will typically produce predicted values, $\hat{Y}$, that are outside the range from 0 to 1 and thus improper. Furthermore, the residuals cannot be normally distributed with homogeneity of variance, which leads to incorrect significance tests and confidence intervals for the parameters (Fox, 2008: 337). Instead, it is more reasonable to model dichotomous outcomes using a nonlinear modeling procedure such as logistic regression (or, similarly, probit regression). More generally, whenever the outcome variable is categorical, whether dichotomous or with multiple categories, the ordinary linear regression model is likely to produce misleading results and alternative nonlinear models for categorical outcomes, such as those within the class of generalized linear models, are more appropriate (see Fox, 2008, for a textbook-length treatment of these models). Fortunately, having a solid understanding of ordinary linear regression provides an excellent foundation for learning about logistic regression and other generalized linear models.

---

[8]The product-moment correlation between a dichotomous variable and a continuous variable calculated according to the formula presented earlier (Equation 1.9) is a special type of correlation known as the *point-biserial* correlation. Here, the point-biserial correlation between gender and BPAQ is $r = -.05$. In that the correlation is a type of standardized effect measure, the same value is obtained regardless of the numerical coding scheme used for the dichotomous variable (dummy-coded or otherwise).

## Section recap

### Dichotomous variables in the simple linear regression model

When a continuous outcome variable is regressed on a dummy-coded dichotomous (or binary) predictor, the intercept estimate will equal the mean of the group coded zero, $\hat{\beta}_0 = \bar{Y}_{X=0}$, and the slope estimate will equal the difference between the means of the two groups, $\hat{\beta}_1 = (\bar{Y}_{X=1} - \bar{Y}_{X=0})$.

Furthermore, the $t$ test for the slope estimate is equivalent to the independent-groups $t$ test and a $(1 - \alpha)\%$ confidence interval for the population slope is identical to a $(1 - \alpha)\%$ confidence interval for the difference between the two population means.

It is generally inappropriate to model a dichotomous outcome variable (or any categorical outcome) using a linear regression model.

# BASIC REGRESSION DIAGNOSTIC CONCEPTS

**Regression diagnostics** are graphical and numeric methods for evaluating the extent to which a regression model fitted to data is an adequate representation of that data and for evaluating the trustworthiness of inferential conclusions about the model's parameter estimates. In particular, regression diagnostics are used to check the extent to which the model's assumptions have been violated and to examine whether any unusual or outlying observations may be impacting the results. Although diagnostic methods primarily show their strength when applied to multiple regression models (i.e., models with two or more predictors), I introduce the basic concepts here because they can be more plainly and simply illustrated with the simple regression model.

## Linearity

First and foremost, as emphasized earlier, the simple regression model specifies a *linear* relation between the predictor and outcome variables. Linearity is most easily examined with a scatterplot of the observed variables (although this may not be sufficient when we move to multiple regression), which can be enhanced with a superimposed nonparametric regression curve as demonstrated previously in Figure 1.5. In this example, the straight-line regression model did seem to be a good representation of the positive (but weak) relation between BPAQ scores and BIS scores.

But let's also consider an example where things don't work out so well. The student researcher who collected the BPAQ aggression data was also interested in studying alcohol use among university students. Therefore, $N = 270$ participants in her study also answered questions about their quantity and frequency of alcohol use over the past year, which the researcher then combined to produce an overall alcohol-use index.[9] Next, although most of the undergraduate-student participants were 18 or 19 years old, there was a considerable

---

[9]Specifically, the study used the Quantity × Frequency index described in Chassin, Flora, and King (2004).

number of nontraditional students who were in their late-20s or 30s, and even a few as old as 50. The results reported in the literature suggest that heavy alcohol use is most common among young adults and declines thereafter. Thus, the researcher is interested in examining the association between age and alcohol use in her sample.

Although I recommend examining data descriptively before proceeding with model fitting, and we will look at the alcohol-use data momentarily, for didactic purposes, let's first consider the results from the OLS simple regression of alcohol use on age. The estimated regression slope is $\hat{\beta}_1 = -0.46$, indicating that for each one-year increase in age, the predicted amount of alcohol use declines by 0.46 of a point on the alcohol-use scale. This estimated effect seems somewhat weak given that the alcohol-use scale ranges from 0 to as high as 95 in the current sample, but it is significantly different from zero, $t(268) = 2.41$, $p = .02$. Further demonstrating the weakness of the effect, $R^2$ is only .02. Thus, the researcher might be tempted to conclude that there is a small, but significant, negative relation between age and alcohol use, and stop there. But as we see next, this conclusion, although correct in a broad sense, also may be an oversimplification of the data.

The scatterplot of alcohol use by age in Figure 1.7 (enhanced with the fitted regression line and a nonparametric LOWESS regression curve) supports the notion that high amounts of alcohol use are less common among older participants compared with those in early adult-hood. But this simple observation seems to neglect some other complexities in the data. One immediately noticeable issue is that there are far fewer participants at the older ages than at age 20 and younger, implying that these data give us scant information about the population level of alcohol use among older individuals. But more pertinent to our discussion of the adequacy of the linear regression analysis is that the LOWESS curve suggests that the typical amount of alcohol use increases from the youngest age until around age 23, but then decreases steadily until around age 35.[10] This nonlinear pattern is consistent with the results

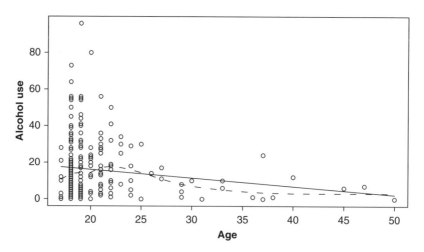

**Figure 1.7** Scatterplot of alcohol-use scores against age with fitted linear regression line (solid line) and fitted LOWESS curve (dashed line)

---

[10]As described in Footnote 5, with small samples, the LOWESS curve may overfit the data. Here, though, N is large, especially at the younger ages, implying that the LOWESS curve is likely capturing meaningful trends in the data.

in the published literature on alcohol use among young adults and is therefore important to recognize in these data, but the straight-line model only captures the broad observation that older participants tend to have lower amounts of alcohol use than younger participants. Nonetheless, this subtle nonlinear trend is not the only challenge that these data pose for the linear regression model, as we will see shortly.

## Distribution of residuals

Next, recall from earlier that correct inference for the regression parameters assumes that the errors are normally distributed with constant, or homogeneous, variance, $\varepsilon_i \sim N(0, \sigma^2)$. When this assumption is violated, the Type I error rate (if the null hypothesis is true) and power (if the null hypothesis is false) of the $t$ test for the slope parameter estimate is compromised, and the width of its confidence intervals are incorrect. Because of the central limit theorem, if the sample size is large (>100 or so for a simple regression model), then the normality assumption is less critical, and hypothesis tests and confidence intervals are still valid, as long as the other assumptions are met. Nevertheless, non-normality still impacts the efficiency of OLS estimates, meaning that alternative estimators of the regression parameters can produce smaller standard errors and therefore are associated with greater statistical power and more narrow confidence intervals for the estimates. Therefore, it is important to evaluate the tenability of the assumption that the errors are normally distributed with homogeneity of variance.

Recall that the *errors* from the population model (Equation 1.11) differ from the *residuals* from the regression equation formed with the sample-based OLS parameter estimates. Because the errors are unobservable, we must instead work with the residuals. With most statistical software packages, it is possible to extract the residuals from a fitted regression model and then the residuals can be examined like any other variable. Returning to the example regression of BPAQ aggression scores on BIS impulsivity scores, Figure 1.8 presents a histogram of the residuals from this model. Not surprisingly, given the approximate

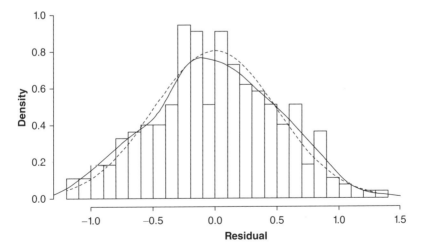

**Figure 1.8**  Histogram of residuals from OLS regression of BPAQ scores on BIS scores with fitted kernel density smoother (solid curve) and fitted normal distribution (dashed curve)

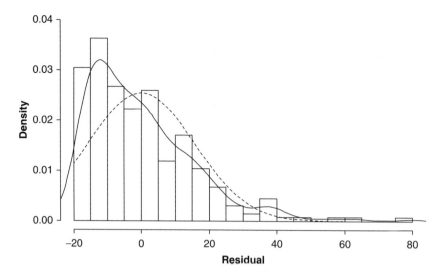

**Figure 1.9** Histogram of residuals from OLS regression of alcohol-use scores on age with fitted kernel density smoother (solid curve) and fitted normal distribution (dashed curve)

normal distribution of BPAQ and its reasonably linear (but weak) association with BIS, these residuals appear to provide a reasonable approximation of a normal distribution. In contrast, Figure 1.9 gives a histogram of residuals from the regression model of alcohol use on age, which is clearly non-normal.

## Homoscedastic versus heteroscedastic residuals

Perhaps more important than determining whether residuals are normally distributed is determining whether they are **homoscedastic**, meaning that their variance is consistent across the values of the predictor $X$; in other words, it's important to examine the residuals for homogeneity of variance. In our example regression of BPAQ scores on BIS scores, because the predictor (BIS) is approximately continuous, it's best to examine the residuals conditioned on BIS using a scatterplot, as in Figure 1.10. To aid interpretation, the scatterplot in this figure is enhanced with a nonparametric LOWESS curve along with smoother applied to the root-mean-square positive and negative residuals from the LOWESS curve (see Fox and Weisberg, 2011: 117–18), which give a graphical summary of the spread of the data in the plot. Because these dashed curves are approximately equidistant from each other as they move from low to high levels of BIS, the residuals in the plot are in fact evidencing homoscedasticity; that is, the spread of the data is constant across the values of the predictor, BIS. Therefore, we can be satisfied that the homogeneity of variance assumption is met for this linear model. Incidentally, the fact that the solid LOWESS curve in the plot is mostly straight and horizontal is further evidence that a linear model is a good representation of the relation between BPAQ and BIS scores.

Unlike the model regressing BPAQ on BIS, the estimated linear model predicting alcohol use from age appears to have **heteroscedastic** residuals, that is, residuals which are unevenly spread across the age predictor. In particular, Figure 1.11 displays a scatterplot of this model's

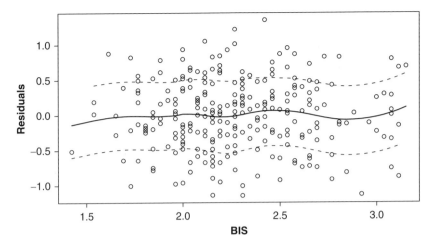

**Figure 1.10** Scatterplot of residuals against BIS scores with fitted LOWESS curve (solid line) and smoothed root-mean-square positive and negative residuals from the LOWESS curve (dashed lines)

residuals against age, again enhanced with the nonparametric LOWESS spread. In this figure, the residuals are more spread out at younger ages (especially around age 20) compared with higher values of age. Thus, the homogeneity of variance assumption is violated for this model, which then casts doubt on the inferential conclusion that the linear slope in the regression of alcohol on age significantly differs from zero. Note that Figure 1.11 also further illustrates the nonlinear pattern in the data.

Investigating the variability in a dataset can have value beyond just evaluating the homogeneity of variance assumption for regression. Here, for example, it may be of substantive importance to recognize there is much more variation in the amount of alcohol use among

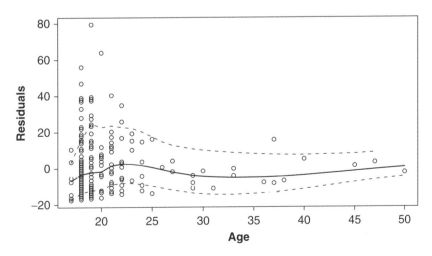

**Figure 1.11** Scatterplot of residuals against age with fitted LOWESS curve (solid line) and smoothed root-mean-square positive and negative residuals from the LOWESS curve (dashed lines)

younger undergraduates than among older undergraduates (see Figure 1.7). Just as there is a considerable number of younger students who report high amounts of alcohol use, there are many other younger students reporting zero or near-zero levels of use. Yet students older than 25 or so consistently report low amounts of alcohol use. For these data, this observation should only be considered descriptive because there are many fewer older students in the sample than there are younger students. Nonetheless, it is a strong pattern in the data that could be substantively informative for theory or applied practice.

 Section recap

### Basic concepts for regression diagnostics

**Regression diagnostics** are graphical and numeric procedures used to check the extent to which an estimated model's assumptions have been violated and to examine whether any unusual or outlying observations may be impacting the results.

The OLS linear regression assumptions of linear association, normally distributed errors, and homogeneity of error variance can be effectively assessed using univariate (e.g., histograms) and bivariate (e.g., scatterplots) plots of the residuals from an estimated regression model.

## Examining outliers and unusual cases

In regression, as with most statistical procedures, it is important to be concerned about influential observations, which can dramatically distort results. Data points that appear as outliers in simple scatterplots are often influential, but sometimes they are not, and sometimes such outlying observations may even be considered 'good' cases. Therefore, although I strongly endorse examining data with basic scatterplots, it can also be valuable to use more sophisticated methods for determining whether a sample has any unusual cases and whether such cases are a cause for concern about the results of a regression analysis. To this end, a variety of statistical measures has been developed to assess the extent to which each observation or case in a regression analysis may be considered influential. In general, a case or observation's *influence* is a function of its *leverage* and *discrepancy*.

**Leverage** is the extent to which an individual case is close to or far from the rest of the cases in terms of scores on the predictor variable(s) only. In the case of simple regression with a sole predictor $X$, the sample-based leverage of a given case $i$, which is also known as its **hat value**, is defined as

$$h_i = \frac{1}{N} + \frac{(X_i - \bar{X})^2}{\sum_{i=1}^{N}(X_i - \bar{X})^2} .$$

(1.15)

Equation 1.15 shows that leverage for case $i$ is a function of how much the case deviates from the mean of $X$ relative to the overall variation in $X$ for the whole sample. Leverage ranges from 0 to 1, with larger values indicative of stronger leverage.

**Discrepancy** is the extent to which case $i$ has an extreme value of $Y$ relative to its predicted value $\hat{Y}_i$. In other words, discrepancy is essentially the magnitude of the residual for case $i$; that is, $e_i = Y_i - \hat{Y}_i$. Discrepancy is most commonly assessed using a standardization of the residuals, which facilitates comparison of a given case with the rest of the sample. A common sample-based discrepancy measure is the **Studentized residual**, which helps determine whether a given residual is extreme relative to the other residuals.

There are two kinds of Studentized residuals, namely, the *internally* and *externally* Studentized residuals, and it is crucial to distinguish between them. The internally Studentized residual (also simply called the 'standardized residual') $e_i'$ for case $i$ is calculated based on the standard deviation of all residuals ($s_e$), including case $i$ in the calculation of that standard deviation:

$$e_i' = \frac{e_i}{s_e \sqrt{1 - h_i}}, \tag{1.16}$$

where $e_i$ is the residual ($Y_i - \hat{Y}_i$) for case $i$ and $h_i$ is the hat value, or leverage, for case $i$. Next, the externally Studentized residual $e_i^*$ (also known as the 'Studentized deleted residual' or the 'Jackknife residual') for case $i$ is based on the standard deviation of the residuals from a regression equation estimated using all observations *except* for case $i$:

$$e_i^* = \frac{e_i}{s_{e(-i)} \sqrt{1 - h_i}}, \tag{1.17}$$

where $s_{e(-i)}$ is the standard deviation of the residuals from the regression model estimated after removing case $i$ from the data.

The logic of removing case $i$ for getting the $s_{e(-i)}$ term in Equation 1.17 is that if this case is an outlier, it is based on a potentially incorrect regression model and will inflate the standard deviation of the residuals (i.e., the $s_e$ term in Equation 1.16 for the internally Studentized residuals) from the primary model. Thus, to measure whether a case's residual is extreme relative to the *other* residuals, that case should be removed before getting a measure of the standard deviation of the residuals of the other cases from the model estimated without including the potentially extreme case $i$.

More formally, the externally Studentized residual (but not the internally Studentized residual) follows a $t$ distribution with $N - 2 - P$ degrees of freedom (where $P$ is the number of predictors in the model, with $P = 1$ for simple regression). Yet, although the externally Studentized residual is distributed as a $t$ statistic, it should not be evaluated against the usual $t$ distribution critical values because of the multiple comparison problem (i.e., there are many potential significance tests because there are many cases whose Studentized residuals can be calculated). Nonetheless, the $t$ distribution allows a rough guideline whereby externally Studentized residuals greater than 2.5 or so can be considered extreme.

If a case has extreme leverage or discrepancy, it may not have an excessive impact on the actual estimates of the parameters obtained from the data. But **influence** combines leverage and discrepancy to measure the extent to which a case affects a model's parameter estimates. One common measure of influence is **Cook's distance**, defined as

$$D_i = \frac{e_i^*}{P + 1} \times \frac{h_i}{1 - h_i}, \tag{1.18}$$

where $P$ is again the number of predictors in the regression model. A large value of $D_i$ indicates that case $i$ has substantial influence on the parameter estimates. From Equation 1.18, it is easy to see that Cook's $D$ is a function of both leverage (i.e., $h_i$) and discrepancy (i.e., $e_i^*$), and that case $i$ will have a large value of $D_i$ when both $h_i$ and $e_i^*$ are large. But a small value of $h_i$ can compensate for a large $e_i^*$ (and vice versa) to produce a $D_i$ that is not particularly large. Another popular influence statistic is known as *DFFITS*, which is

$$DFFITS_i = e_i^* \sqrt{\frac{h_i}{1 - h_i}}$$

for case $i$. Clearly, Cook's $D$ and *DFFITS* provide essentially identical information about a given case (specifically, $D_i \approx DFFITS_i^2 / (P + 1)$), and so it is not necessary to calculate both influence measures within the same regression analysis. Another common influence measure, *DFBETAS*, directly measures the extent to which a given case influences a given regression parameter estimate.

 Section recap

### Outliers and unusual cases

After a linear regression model has been fitted to sample data, the **leverage, discrepancy,** and **influence** of each case in the sample can be assessed.

Leverage, measured with **hat values**, represents the degree to which a case is extreme relative to the distribution of the predictor variable(s) only.

Discrepancy, measured with **Studentized residuals**, represents the degree to which the observed outcome variable score for a case is extreme relative to its predicted outcome variable score.

Influence, measured with **Cook's distance** or **DFFITS**, represents the degree to which the leverage and discrepancy of a case combine to affect the model's parameter estimates.

If a case is an outlier with respect to leverage or discrepancy, it still might not have undue influence on the estimates of the regression parameters.

## A data-based illustration of leverage, discrepancy, and influence

To understand the concepts of leverage, discrepancy, and influence further, let's consider a made-up dataset of only $N = 11$ cases.[11] In this dataset, there is a clear positive relation between $X$ and $Y$ which is well represented by a simple linear regression model, as depicted in panel (a) of Figure 1.12. The OLS estimated regression equation from these data is

$$\hat{Y}_i = 3.00 + 0.50X_i,$$

[11]These 11 cases comprise 'dataset 1' from Anscombe's (1973) famous fictitious datasets.

with $R^2 = .67$. The data, along with the Studentized residuals, hat values, and Cook's $D$ resulting from this model are in Table 1.2. At this point, we simply note that none of the Studentized residuals or hat values seems particularly extreme, and consequently, neither are the Cook's $D$s, which is not surprising given the apparent lack of outlying observations in Figure 1.12(a).

Next, I added a 12th case (case $i = 12$) that has a large leverage but a small discrepancy, or residual, from the estimated regression model. This case appears as a clear outlier in panel (b) of Figure 1.12. With this new outlying case added to the data, the estimated regression equation becomes

$$\hat{Y}_i = 2.93 + 0.51X_i,$$

which is similar to the original equation but now $R^2 = .81$. The data with the new case along with the new Studentized residuals, hat values, and Cook's $D$s are in Table 1.3. Here, we see that case 12 has a much larger leverage ($h_{12} = 0.46$) than do the other cases. But because its residual is small ($e_{12}^* = 0.11$), it has minimal influence ($D_{12} = 0.01$). As a consequence, the estimated regression equation barely changes when this case is added to the data. Additionally, however, this case has also increased $R^2$ from .67 to .81 and has decreased the standard error of the regression slope from .12 to .08. For this reason, a high-leverage, low-discrepancy case is often referred to as a 'good leverage' case because it improves the precision of the parameter estimates (where precision refers to sampling variability of the estimates, as measured by their standard error). Thus, some outliers are indeed 'good'!

Panel (c) of Figure 1.12 shows the same data, except now case 12 has low leverage coupled with high discrepancy. With this outlying case, the estimated regression equation is

$$\hat{Y}_i = 3.50 + 0.50X_i.$$

Although the outlier has shifted the intercept, the slope estimate is identical to the initial model but $R^2 = .37$. The corresponding Studentized residuals, hat values, and Cook's $D$s are in Table 1.4. Now, we see that case 12 has an extreme Studentized residual ($e_{12}^* = 2.66$), but because it has no leverage ($h_{12} = 0.00$), it does not have much influence ($D_{12} = 0.32$). Although this Cook's $D$ is larger than those for the other 11 cases, it is still small in an absolute sense, as Cook's $D$ values are often not considered large until they are near 1.00 or greater. Yet, this case has substantially reduced $R^2$ from that obtained with the original 11 cases, and the standard error of the slope has increased from .12 to .21. Thus, cases with large discrepancy are harmful for the precision of the parameter estimates even when they have little influence.

Finally, panel (d) of Figure 1.12 shows the data with an outlying case that has both large leverage and large discrepancy and, consequently, large influence. Here, as shown in Table 1.5, case 12 clearly has an extreme Studentized residual ($e_{12}^* = -2.54$), moderately large leverage ($h_{12} = 0.62$), and hence substantial influence ($D_{12} = 7.77$). Thus, this outlier has radically affected the estimated regression equation, which is

$$\hat{Y}_i = 6.28 + 0.11X_i,$$

and has reduced $R^2$ to .10. No doubt, an outlier with large discrepancy and large leverage is a 'bad leverage' case!

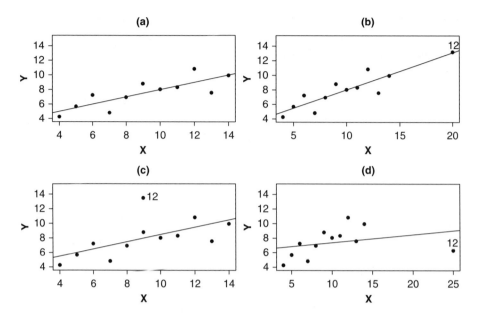

**Figure 1.12**   Scatterplots with fitted OLS regression lines. Panel (a): Plot of $N = 11$ original cases; Panel (b): Plot of $N = 11$ original cases plus high-leverage, low-discrepancy case indicated as case '12'; Panel (c): Plot of $N = 11$ original cases plus low-leverage, high-discrepancy case indicated as case '12'; Panel (d): Plot of $N = 11$ original cases plus high-influence case indicated as case '12'.

**Table 1.2**   Data for original $N = 11$ cases

| Case $i$ | X | Y | $\overset{\centerdot}{e}_i$ | $h_i$ | $D_i$ |
|---|---|---|---|---|---|
| 1 | 10 | 8.04 | 0.03324 | 0.00909 | 0.00006 |
| 2 | 8 | 6.95 | −0.04332 | 0.00909 | 0.0001 |
| 3 | 13 | 7.58 | −1.77793 | 0.14545 | 0.48921 |
| 4 | 9 | 8.81 | 1.11029 | 0.00000 | 0.06164 |
| 5 | 11 | 8.33 | −0.1481 | 0.03636 | 0.0016 |
| 6 | 14 | 9.96 | −0.04051 | 0.22727 | 0.00038 |
| 7 | 6 | 7.24 | 1.1019 | 0.08182 | 0.12676 |
| 8 | 4 | 4.26 | −0.72516 | 0.22727 | 0.1227 |
| 9 | 12 | 10.84 | 1.63487 | 0.08182 | 0.27903 |
| 10 | 7 | 4.82 | −1.45488 | 0.03636 | 0.15434 |
| 11 | 5 | 5.68 | 0.16607 | 0.14545 | 0.00427 |

*Note.* OLS estimates are $\hat{\beta}_0 = 3.00$, $\hat{\beta}_1 = 0.50$, $R^2 = .67$; $e^*$ is the Studentized residual; $h$ is the hat value; $D$ is Cook's distance.

**Table 1.3**   Data for original $N = 11$ cases plus high leverage, low discrepancy case ($i = 12$)

| Case $i$ | X | Y | $\overset{\centerdot}{e}_i$ | $h_i$ | $D_i$ |
|---|---|---|---|---|---|
| 1 | 10 | 8.04 | 0.01934 | 0.00003 | 0.00002 |
| 2 | 8 | 6.95 | −0.04489 | 0.01663 | 0.00011 |
| 3 | 13 | 7.58 | −1.79147 | 0.04303 | 0.23211 |
| 4 | 9 | 8.81 | 1.15984 | 0.00380 | 0.06420 |

| Case $i$ | X | Y | $e_i^*$ | $h_i$ | $D_i$ |
|---|---|---|---|---|---|
| 5 | 11 | 8.33 | −0.17614 | 0.00531 | 0.00151 |
| 6 | 14 | 9.96 | −0.08804 | 0.07547 | 0.00073 |
| 7 | 6 | 7.24 | 1.16450 | 0.06944 | 0.12226 |
| 8 | 4 | 4.26 | −0.68820 | 0.15846 | 0.07552 |
| 9 | 12 | 10.84 | 1.62209 | 0.01965 | 0.15103 |
| 10 | 7 | 4.82 | −1.51887 | 0.03851 | 0.16004 |
| 11 | 5 | 5.68 | 0.19664 | 0.10942 | 0.00462 |
| 12 | 20 | 13.20 | 0.11400 | 0.46024 | 0.00774 |

Note. OLS estimates are $\hat{\beta}_0 = 2.93$, $\hat{\beta}_i = 0.51$, $R^2 = .81$; $e^*$ is the Studentized residual; $h$ is the hat value; $D$ is Cook's distance.

**Table 1.4** Data for original $N = 11$ cases plus low-leverage, high-discrepancy case ($i = 12$)

| Case $i$ | X | Y | $e_i^*$ | $h_i$ | $D_i$ |
|---|---|---|---|---|---|
| 1 | 10 | 8.04 | −0.22376 | 0.00909 | 0.00255 |
| 2 | 8 | 6.95 | −0.26736 | 0.00909 | 0.00364 |
| 3 | 13 | 7.58 | −1.27509 | 0.14545 | 0.24116 |
| 4 | 9 | 8.81 | 0.39087 | 0.00000 | 0.00694 |
| 5 | 11 | 8.33 | −0.33076 | 0.03636 | 0.00744 |
| 6 | 14 | 9.96 | −0.30150 | 0.22727 | 0.02048 |
| 7 | 6 | 7.24 | 0.37428 | 0.08182 | 0.01386 |
| 8 | 4 | 4.26 | −0.69090 | 0.22727 | 0.10753 |
| 9 | 12 | 10.84 | 0.67770 | 0.08182 | 0.04543 |
| 10 | 7 | 4.82 | −1.07490 | 0.03636 | 0.07855 |
| 11 | 5 | 5.68 | −0.16877 | 0.14545 | 0.00422 |
| 12 | 9 | 13.50 | 2.65637 | 0.00000 | 0.32074 |

Note. OLS estimates are $\hat{\beta}_0 = 3.50$, $\hat{\beta}_1 = 0.50$, $R^2 = .37$; $e^*$ is the Studentized residual; $h$ is the hat value; $D$ is Cook's distance.

**Table 1.5** Data for original $N = 11$ cases plus high-influence case ($i = 12$)

| Case $i$ | X | Y | $e_i^*$ | $h_i$ | $D_i$ |
|---|---|---|---|---|---|
| 1 | 10 | 8.04 | 0.35938 | 0.00032 | 0.00590 |
| 2 | 8 | 6.95 | −0.10609 | 0.01580 | 0.00062 |
| 3 | 13 | 7.58 | −0.05929 | 0.02063 | 0.00020 |
| 4 | 9 | 8.81 | 0.82906 | 0.00516 | 0.03336 |
| 5 | 11 | 8.33 | 0.45620 | 0.00129 | 0.00962 |
| 6 | 14 | 9.96 | 1.17522 | 0.03901 | 0.09626 |
| 7 | 6 | 7.24 | 0.16970 | 0.05448 | 0.00230 |
| 8 | 4 | 4.26 | −1.39718 | 0.11638 | 0.24357 |
| 9 | 12 | 10.84 | 1.74128 | 0.00806 | 0.15249 |
| 10 | 7 | 4.82 | −1.20204 | 0.03224 | 0.09440 |
| 11 | 5 | 5.68 | −0.63704 | 0.08253 | 0.04035 |
| 12 | 25 | 6.30 | −2.53549 | 0.62411 | 7.77290 |

Note. OLS estimates are $\hat{\beta}_0 = 6.28$, $\hat{\beta}_1 = 0.11$, $R^2 = .10$; $e^*$ is the Studentized residual; $h$ is the hat value; $D$ is Cook's distance.

With larger datasets, it is tedious and impractical to examine lists of leverage, discrepancy, or influence as we have done here for a small, contrived dataset. Instead, one can plot these values with simple index plots. For example, our regression of BPAQ aggression scores on BIS impulsivity scores was based on a dataset with $N = 275$ cases. An index plot of the hat values for the $N = 275$ cases used to fit this model is in Figure 1.13. With these plots, it is important to pay attention to the scale of the vertical $y$-axis. Recall from earlier that hat values range from 0 to 1. Therefore, Figure 1.13 does not display any cases with extreme leverage as they are all around .025 or less. An index plot of the Studentized residuals from the same model regressing BPAQ on BIS is in Figure 1.14. Because an individual Studentized residual is $t$ distributed, any value above 2.0 or so (or less than –2.0) may be considered large. Although there are some cases in this sample that are strongly discrepant from their predicted values of $Y$ given the model, because of the large sample size, we should expect a few extreme cases to appear, and note that none of these Studentized residuals is radically greater than 2.0 (or below –2.0). But we should determine whether these cases are also influential, and thus, the index plot of Cook's $D$ from the same model of BPAQ on BIS is in Figure 1.15. Although a few cases have values of Cook's $D$ which are much larger than those for most of the sample, none of them is an extremely large $D$ in an absolute sense as only values near $D = 1.0$ or larger are considered strongly influential. Therefore, in this example, no unusual or outlying cases have an excessive impact on the results of our regression modeling analysis. Because we are only dealing with a simple, one-predictor regression at this point, this conclusion should not come as a surprise because the original scatterplot of BPAQ by BIS (Figure 1.4) did not have any apparent outliers. But when we consider models with multiple predictors, looking at the simple scatterplots of $Y$ by each $X$ may not be enough to determine whether there are any outlying or influential cases (so-called *multivariate outliers*). In that situation, it will be prudent to examine the leverage, discrepancy, and especially influence of cases to evaluate the quality and reliability of the complete regression model.

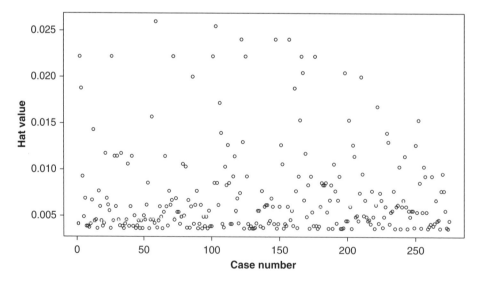

**Figure 1.13**  Hat values indicating leverage of $N = 275$ individual cases used to regress BPAQ scores on BIS scores

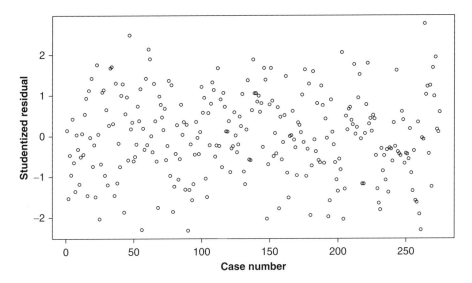

**Figure 1.14** Studentized residuals indicating discrepancy of $N = 275$ individual cases used to regress BPAQ scores on BIS scores

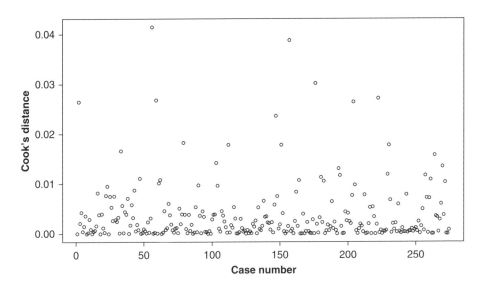

**Figure 1.15** Cook's distance indicating influence of $N = 275$ individual cases used to regress BPAQ scores on BIS scores

## CHAPTER SUMMARY

The major objective of this chapter was to develop an understanding of the principles of statistical modeling in general and the simple linear regression model in particular. These principles provide a conceptual foundation for the remainder of the text. A summary of these principles is as follows:

- A **statistical model** is a set of one or more mathematical expressions that provides an idealized representation of reality.
- **Effect size** is simply *the extent to which* one or more predictor (or explanatory) variables is associated with an outcome (or response) variable. In other words, effect size is the *strength of the relation* between a predictor variable and an outcome. In the context of statistical modeling, parameter estimates are effect-size statistics.
- The simple linear regression model for the relation between an outcome variable $Y$ and a predictor $X$ is $Y_i = \beta_0 + \beta_1 X_i + \varepsilon_i$.

  o The **intercept parameter**, $\beta_0$, is the predicted value of $Y$ when $X$ equals 0.
  o The **slope parameter**, $\beta_1$, is the predicted amount that $Y$ changes when $X$ increases by 1. The magnitude of $\beta_1$ is therefore a (population) effect size for the association between $X$ and $Y$.

- A **predicted value**, $\hat{Y}_i$, is the outcome variable score for individual $i$ that is *predicted* from the regression line given that individual's score on the predictor variable, $X_i$, whereas an **observed value**, $Y_i$, is the actual outcome variable score for individual $i$ regardless of that individual's score on the predictor variable, $X_i$.

  o In a population regression equation, the regression **error** for individual $i$ is $\varepsilon_i = Y_i - \hat{Y}_i$.
  o In an *estimated* regression equation, the **residual** for individual $i$ is $e_i = Y_i - \hat{Y}_i$.

- Model **estimation** is the procedure by which the model's parameters are estimated from sample data.

  o Ordinary least squares (OLS) is the most common estimation method for linear regression. OLS produces the parameter estimates that minimize the sum of squared residuals.

- The validity of inferential statistics associated with a regression model (i.e., $t$ tests and confidence intervals for regression slopes) depends on the assumption that $\varepsilon_i$ is normally distributed with constant (homogenous) variance across the range of $X$.
- **Regression diagnostics** are graphical and numeric procedures used to check the extent to which an estimated model's assumptions have been violated and to examine whether any unusual or outlying observations may be impacting the results.

## RECOMMENDED READING

Anscombe, F.J. (1973). Graphs in statistical analysis. *The American Statistician, 27,* 17–21.

- In this famous and easy-to-read paper, Anscombe primarily relies on the simple regression model to describe the importance of graphing data in concert with numerical statistical calculations.

Cohen, J. (1994). The earth is round ($p < .05$). *American Psychologist, 49,* 997–1003.

- This now-legendary and entertaining paper presents a thorough critique of null hypothesis significance testing.

Rodgers, J.L. (2010). The epistemology of mathematical and statistical modeling: A quiet methodological revolution. *American Psychologist, 65,* 1–12.

- This important, state-of-the-art overview discusses how statistical modeling has quietly become the dominant perspective for data analysis in psychology and related fields. Rodgers also argues that the debate over null hypothesis significance testing was irrelevant.

Sterba, S.K. (2009). Alternative model-based and design-based frameworks for inference from samples to populations: From polarization to integration. *Multivariate Behavioral Research, 44*, 711–40.

- This paper provides an interesting historical context to the model-based framework for statistical inference (based on the work of R.A. Fisher, the father of null hypothesis significance testing), justifying the use of inference from nonrandom samples, which are prevalent in much of the behavioural and social sciences. This tradition is contrasted with a design-based framework which relies on random sampling, and the paper ultimately describes an integration of the two perspectives.

Wilkinson, L., & The Task Force on Statistical Inference (1999). Statistical methods in psychology journals: Guidelines and explanations. *American Psychologist, 54*, 594–604.

- This paper is the APA task force's response to a call to ban null hypothesis significance testing. In addition to *not* recommending a ban, the paper presents a set of helpful guidelines regarding statistical information to be presented in a research article. In particular, the importance of incorporating quality graphs in a data analysis is emphasized.

# MULTIPLE REGRESSION WITH CONTINUOUS PREDICTORS

## CHAPTER OVERVIEW

The major objective of this chapter is to develop the main principles underlying multiple linear regression, beginning with an extensive treatment of the model with two continuous predictors and then building models with more than two predictors. The principles described in this chapter provide a foundation for the more advanced statistical models presented in the remainder of the text. The main topics of this chapter include:

- Specification and estimation of the two-predictor multiple regression model
- Distinction between the simple, bivariate (or marginal) effect of a predictor and the partial regression effect
- Multiple correlation
- Statistical inference for multiple regression
- Standardized regression coefficients
- Multiple regression with $P$ = two or more predictors
- Simultaneous and hierarchical regression
- Stepwise regression and other predictor selection methods
- Assumptions for OLS estimation of linear regression models and how to check them
- Consequences of assumption violation and remedies
- Outliers and unusual observations in multiple regression

**Table 2.0** Greek letter notation used in this chapter

| Greek letter | English name | Represents |
|---|---|---|
| $\beta$ | Lowercase 'beta' | Regression model parameter (intercept or slope, depending on subscript) |
| $\varepsilon$ | Lowercase 'epsilon' | Regression model error term |
| $\sigma$ | Lowercase 'sigma' | Population standard deviation ($\sigma^2$ is variance) |
| $\rho$ | Lowercase 'rho' | Population correlation |
| $\alpha$ | Lowercase 'alpha' | Probability of Type I error |

# WHAT IS MULTIPLE REGRESSION?

Substantive theories in the behavioural and social sciences are typically too complex to be represented by a simple one-predictor model such as the simple linear regression model. Instead, we are usually aware that individual differences in an outcome variable of interest can be described or explained by variation in several predictors. Investigating a series of simple regression models (or, equivalently, a series of correlations), with a separate model for each potential predictor of an outcome, yields an inefficient representation of substantive theory in terms of statistical models. Additionally, as we will see in considerable detail, the predictors themselves are often correlated with each other in important ways that should be accounted for to understand the relation between a given predictor and the outcome variable. Otherwise, misleading substantive conclusions could be reported. Therefore, as our goal is to develop a statistical model that matches substantive theory as closely as possible, we should be able to incorporate all potentially important variables simultaneously when modeling the variation in an important outcome variable.

One straightforward way to do so is to expand the simple linear regression model into the **multiple linear regression model**. Although multiple regression can theoretically incorporate any number of predictors, we will first examine the model with only two predictors. This two-predictor model itself may also be an oversimplification of the substantive phenomena under study, but it will allow us to explicate the major statistical concepts central to multiple regression more clearly. These basic concepts from the two-predictor model then generalize easily to models with more than two predictors, which are addressed later on in this chapter. Throughout the chapter, we examine regression models with continuous predictors; methods for incorporating categorical predictors are presented in Chapter 3.

## Research example for multiple regression

To motivate the two-predictor multiple regression model, we will continue with the study presented in Chapter 1 in which a graduate-student researcher is interested in how certain personality characteristics relate to self-reported aggression. In the simple regression analysis from Chapter 1, aggression scores (obtained with the Buss-Perry Aggression Questionnaire, BPAQ) were modeled as a linear function of impulsivity scores (obtained with the Barratt Impulsivity Scale, BIS) using a sample of $N = 275$ undergraduate research participants. But now suppose that the researcher has hypothesized that participant age is also an important predictor of aggression (specifically, aggression decreases with age), and therefore, her statistical model for BPAQ scores should incorporate *both* BIS scores and age.

As a reminder, this dataset is available on the text's webpage (https://study.sagepub.com/flora); the webpage also provides annotated input and output from several popular statistical software packages showing how to reproduce the analyses presented in the current chapter.

Before specifying and estimating a formal model for BPAQ scores as a function of both BIS scores and age, it is helpful to explore the bivariate relations between BPAQ and age and between BIS and age. Figure 2.1 gives scatterplots of BPAQ by age and BIS by age (measured in terms of years). Perhaps the most noticeable aspect of the data which can be gleaned from these scatterplots is that there are many more younger participants (around age 18 to 22) than there are older participants (age 25 and up). But it does appear that BPAQ scores are lower, on average, for older participants relative to younger participants, although we might be concerned about the assumptions for OLS regression if we include age as a linear predictor of BPAQ (more on that later). Additionally, there is a small but significant negative correlation between age and BPAQ, $r = -.21$, $p < .001$, with a 95% confidence interval (CI) of $(-.32, -.09)$. The relation between BIS and age is less pronounced, but the highest BIS scores occur mainly at the younger ages; the correlation between BIS and age is small but significant, $r = -.14$, $p = .02$, with a 95% CI of $(-.25, -.02)$. Therefore, these graphs and bivariate statistics do suggest that it is potentially important to incorporate age when modeling BPAQ scores from BIS scores.

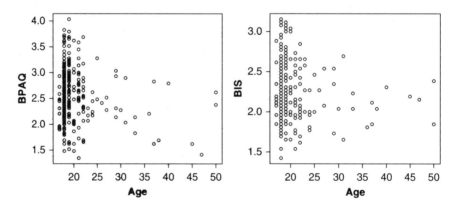

**Figure 2.1**  BPAQ scores by age (left panel) and BIS scores by age (right panel)

## MULTIPLE REGRESSION WITH TWO PREDICTORS

### Two-predictor multiple linear regression: Model specification

The two-predictor regression equation is a straightforward expansion of the simple regression equation given in Chapter 1 (see Equations 1.10 and 1.11). When we apply our current example, the outcome variable $Y$ is the BPAQ score and the two predictors are $X_1 = $ BIS score and $X_2 = $ age. Thus, we specify a regression model that predicts $Y$ as a linear function of both $X_1$ and $X_2$:

$$\hat{Y}_i = \beta_0 + \beta_1 X_{1i} + \beta_2 X_{2i}, \qquad (2.1)$$

which is equivalent to

$$Y_i = \beta_0 + \beta_1 X_{1i} + \beta_2 X_{2i} + \varepsilon_i, \qquad (2.2)$$

where, like with simple regression, $\varepsilon_i = Y_i - \hat{Y}_i$. Therefore, the model parameters are $\beta_0$, $\beta_1$, and $\beta_2$, as well as the error variance, $\sigma_\varepsilon^2 = \text{VAR}(\varepsilon_i)$.

The interpretations of these parameters are similar to those for the parameters of the simple regression model, but of course now the interpretations are based on the fact that there are two predictors in the model. The intercept $\beta_0$ is the predicted value of $Y$ when both $X_1$ and $X_2$ equal zero. Once again, the intercept parameter is often not of substantive interest, although exceptions occur when cases with values of zero on both predictors have a particular meaning. Next, $\beta_1$ is the **partial regression coefficient** (or **partial regression slope**) for $X_1$ and represents the predicted difference in $Y$ associated with a one-unit increase in $X_1$, *holding $X_2$ constant*, or *controlling $X_2$*. Similarly, $\beta_2$ is the partial regression coefficient (or slope) representing the predicted difference in $Y$ associated with a one-unit increase in $X_2$, holding $X_1$ constant. Finally, again expanding from simple regression, the error term $\varepsilon_i$ represents the difference between $Y_i$, which is the observed score on the outcome variable for individual $i$, and $\hat{Y}_i$, which is the score on the outcome variable that's predicted from individual $i$'s scores on *both $X_1$ and $X_2$*. The assumptions for the model, detailed later, pertain to $\varepsilon_i$ and its variance across individuals, $\sigma^2 = \text{VAR}(\varepsilon_i)$.

Thus, like simple regression, the slope coefficient represents the effect size relating a predictor to the outcome, but the critical difference from simple regression is that in multiple regression, this effect of one predictor controls, or holds constant, the effects of the other predictor (or predictors) in the model. In a later subsection, I give a detailed demonstration of the distinction between the **partial** effect of $X_1$ (obtained with multiple regression) in which a second predictor, $X_2$, is controlled, and the **marginal** effect of $X_1$ (obtained with simple regression) in which the second predictor is ignored. In short, although researchers usually expect a partial effect to be smaller than the marginal effect, in certain situations, it can be larger or even of an opposite sign. Similarly, it is possible for the estimated partial effect to be statistically significant when the corresponding marginal effect is not (or vice versa).

Geometrically, the two-predictor linear regression equation describes a flat plane rather than a line, as shown in the three-dimensional scatterplot in Figure 2.2 for a small sample of made-up data. In the figure, the shaded gray grid is the regression plane fitted to these data; the particular tilt of the plane is determined by the fact that the partial regression slope for $X_1$ is positive, whereas the partial slope for $X_1$ is negative. If the partial slopes of both $X_1$ and $X_2$ had been zero, then the plane would be perfectly parallel to the axes of both $X_1$ and $X_2$ (analogous to a flat line in a simple regression model). The plane's surface gives the $\hat{Y}$ values associated with any particular combination of $X_1$ and $X_2$. Unlike unobserved $\hat{Y}$ values, observed values of $Y$ do not fall exactly on the plane. Thus, the distance between any observed $Y$ and its predicted location on the plane is its residual. In Figure 2.2, the black spheres are the $N = 12$ individual observed data points, and the dotted lines connecting the data points to the plane represent the residuals. Points above the plane have positive residuals, and points below the line have negative residuals (some of which are hard to see because they are hidden by the surface of the plane). For a more detailed and enlightening presentation of the geometry of regression, see Monette (1990).

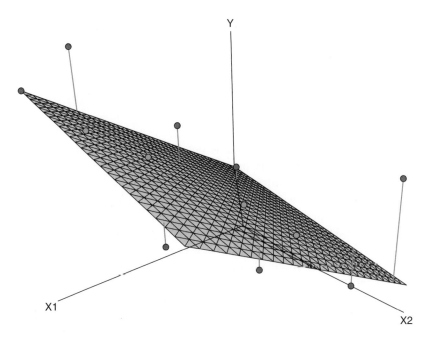

**Figure 2.2**   Three-dimensional regression plane fitted to contrived data ($N = 12$)

 Section recap

### Specification of the two-predictor multiple regression model

The multiple linear regression model with two predictors is

$$Y_i = \beta_0 + \beta_1 X_{1i} + \beta_2 X_{2i} + \varepsilon_i.$$

where

- The intercept, $\beta_0$, is the predicted value of $Y$ when both $X_1$ and $X_2$ equal zero
- $\beta_1$ is the **partial regression coefficient** (or slope) for $X_1$ and represents the predicted difference in $Y$ associated with a one-unit increase in $X_1$, *holding $X_2$ constant*, or *controlling $X_2$*
- $\beta_2$ is the partial regression coefficient (or slope) representing the predicted difference in $Y$ associated with a one-unit increase in $X_2$, holding $X_1$ constant
- The error term $\varepsilon_i = (Y_i - \hat{Y}_i)$ is the difference between $Y_i$, the observed score on the outcome variable for individual $i$, and $\hat{Y}_i$, the score on the outcome variable that's predicted from individual $i$'s scores on both $X_1$ and $X_2$

## Two-predictor multiple regression: Model estimation

Once again, **estimation** refers to the practice of using sample data to estimate the population parameters of a given statistical model. In the current two-predictor regression context, the goal is to find estimates of the intercept and partial slope coefficients which are denoted $\hat{\beta}_0$, $\hat{\beta}_1$, and $\hat{\beta}_2$. Whereas Equation 2.2 is an expression of the 'true' model in terms of population parameters, the estimated model is

$$Y_i = \hat{\beta}_0 + \hat{\beta}_1 X_{1i} + \hat{\beta}_2 X_{2i} + e_i.$$

Consequently, we again distinguish between the error term $\varepsilon_i$ from the population model and the residual term $e_i$ from the estimated model. Now, as with one-predictor simple regression, the parameters of the two-predictor multiple regression model are most commonly estimated using the ordinary least-squares (OLS) criterion, meaning that the collection of squared residuals from the sample are made as small as possible, or minimized. That is, the goal is to find the values of $\hat{\beta}_0$, $\hat{\beta}_1$, and $\hat{\beta}_2$ that make the sum of squared residuals as small as possible:

$$SS_e = \sum_{i=1}^{N} e_i^2 = \sum_{i=1}^{N} (Y_i - \hat{Y}_i)^2 = \sum_{i=1}^{N} (Y_i - [\hat{\beta}_0 + \hat{\beta}_1 X_1 + \hat{\beta}_2 X_2])^2. \tag{2.3}$$

A calculus problem to minimize $SS_e$ (see Fox, 2008: 78–81) shows that when there are only two predictors, the OLS estimate of the partial regression slope $\beta_1$ is

$$\hat{\beta}_1 = \frac{r_{YX_1} - r_{YX_2} r_{X_1 X_2}}{1 - r_{X_1 X_2}^2} \left( \frac{s_Y}{s_{X_1}} \right), \tag{2.4}$$

where $r_{YX_1}$ is the product-moment correlation between $Y$ and $X_1$, $r_{YX_2}$ is the correlation between $Y$ and $X_2$, $r_{X_1 X_2}$ is the correlation between $X_1$ and $X_2$, $s_Y$ is the standard deviation of $Y$, and $s_{X_1}$ is the standard deviation of $X_1$. Similarly, the OLS estimate of $\beta_2$ is

$$\hat{\beta}_2 = \frac{r_{YX_2} - r_{YX_1} r_{X_1 X_2}}{1 - r_{X_1 X_2}^2} \left( \frac{s_Y}{s_{X_2}} \right). \tag{2.5}$$

Finally, the OLS estimate of the intercept parameter is

$$\hat{\beta}_0 = \bar{Y} - \hat{\beta}_1 \bar{X}_1 - \hat{\beta}_2 \bar{X}_2. \tag{2.6}$$

From these formulas, it is clear that the OLS estimate of the partial regression slope $\beta_1$ depends on not only the correlation between $X_1$ and $Y$ but also on the correlation between $X_1$ and $X_2$ as well as on the correlation between $X_2$ and $Y$. Thus, we can see computationally how the partial regression slope $\beta_1$ gives the relation between $X_1$ and $Y$ *while controlling* $X_2$. (Likewise, $\hat{\beta}_2$ depends on the correlation between $X_2$ and $Y$ as well as on the correlation between $X_1$ and $X_2$ and on the correlation between $X_1$ and $Y$.) It is also instructive to notice that if the correlation between $X_1$ and $X_2$ equals zero, then the formula for the partial regression coefficient $\hat{\beta}_1$ reduces to the formula for a simple regression coefficient (cf. Equation 1.12). Given the availability of two predictors, $X_1$ and $X_2$, Equations 2.4 and 2.5 give the respective OLS estimates of the partial effects of $X_1$ and $X_2$ with $Y$, whereas Equation 1.12 gives the OLS estimate of the marginal effect of a given predictor, ignoring the other predictor. Thus, the partial regression slope for $X_1$ will equal its marginal relation with $Y$ only when the correlation between $X_1$ and $X_2$ equals zero (which is never precisely the case with real data).

Table 2.1 gives the means, standard deviations, and correlations for the example data from which we wish to model BPAQ scores ($Y$) as a function of both BIS scores ($X_1$) and age ($X_2$). The descriptive, summary statistics in this table give sufficient information to estimate the regression parameters for the two-predictor regression model. Applying the OLS formulas for the partial regression coefficients (Equations 2.4 and 2.5), we get

$$\hat{\beta}_1 = \frac{r_{YX_1} - r_{YX_2}r_{X_1X_2}}{1 - r^2_{X_1X_2}}\left(\frac{s_Y}{s_{X_1}}\right) = \frac{.32 - (-.21)(-.14)}{1 - (-.14)^2}\left(\frac{0.52}{0.35}\right) = 0.44$$

and

$$\hat{\beta}_2 = \frac{r_{YX_2} - r_{YX_1}r_{X_1X_2}}{1 - r^2_{X_1X_2}}\left(\frac{s_Y}{s_{X_2}}\right) = \frac{-.21 - (.32)(-.14)}{1 - (-.14)^2}\left(\frac{0.52}{4.96}\right) = -0.017.$$

Thus, controlling age (or holding age constant), a one-point increase in BIS is associated with a 0.44 increase in BPAQ score; this is the unstandardized effect-size estimate for BIS. Next, controlling for scores on the BIS, a one-year increase in age is associated with a 0.02 decrease in BPAQ score; this is the unstandardized effect-size estimate for age. Finally, applying Equation 2.6, the estimated intercept term is

$$\hat{\beta}_0 = \bar{Y} - \hat{\beta}_1\bar{X}_1 - \hat{\beta}_2\bar{X}_2 = 2.61 - (0.444 \times 2.28) - (0.017 \times 20.91) = 1.95,$$

indicating that the predicted BPAQ score is 1.95 for a person with BIS = 0 and age = 0. Putting these parameter estimates together, the estimated model is

$$\hat{Y}_i = 1.95 + 0.44X_1 - 0.02X_2.$$

The estimated coefficient of $X_1$, BIS scores, is larger than the coefficient for $X_2$, age (in absolute value). Nevertheless, because these two variables have different scales, at this point, we cannot say that BIS score predicts aggression more strongly than age does. We will return to this issue later.

**Table 2.1** Correlations, means, and standard deviations

|  | BPAQ | BIS | Age |
|---|---|---|---|
| BPAQ | 1 | – | – |
| BIS | .32 | 1 | – |
| Age | −0.21 | −0.14 | 1 |
| M | 2.61 | 2.28 | 20.21 |
| SD | 0.52 | 0.35 | 4.96 |

Note. N = 275. M = mean, SD = standard deviation.

## Section recap

### Estimation of the two-predictor multiple regression model

The parameters of the multiple linear regression model are most often estimated using ordinary least squares (OLS).

OLS estimation provides the intercept and slope estimates ($\hat{\beta}_0$, $\hat{\beta}_1$, and $\hat{\beta}_2$) that minimize the sum of squared residuals, $SS_e = \sum_{i=1}^{N} e_i^2 = \sum_{i=1}^{N} (Y_i - \hat{Y}_i)^2$.

In the two-predictor model, the slope estimate for $X_1$ depends on not only the correlation between $X_1$ and $Y$ but also the correlations between $X_1$ and $X_2$ and between $X_2$ and $Y$. In this way, $\hat{\beta}_1$ gives the effect of $X_1$ on $Y$ while controlling $X_2$.

---

## Illustration of the distinction between a partial effect and a marginal effect

From the OLS formulas for the regression parameters (Equations 2.4 and 2.5), we can see computationally how the partial regression slope $\beta_1$ gives the relation between $X_1$ and $Y$ while controlling $X_2$. As mentioned, researchers often expect that the effect of one predictor should be weaker when a second predictor is controlled. Indeed, that is the case for the example regression analyses of the BPAQ outcome variable presented in Chapter 1 and continued in this chapter. Specifically, in Chapter 1, we saw that the estimated simple regression coefficient for BIS was 0.48, yet in the estimated multiple regression model in this chapter, by controlling age, the partial regression coefficient for BIS is lower at 0.44. It is entirely possible, however, for the partial effect of a given predictor, obtained by controlling one or more additional predictors, to be stronger (or even of the opposite sign) than the corresponding marginal effect for that predictor. Many researchers (and journal reviewers) find the latter situation perplexing, often declaring that 'there must be something wrong' with the analyses or the data themselves, when in fact there is nothing wrong at all. One can determine that this scenario is possible by carefully considering different patterns of correlations among the predictors and outcome variables that would lead to a partial regression slope estimated with Equation 2.4 to be *larger* than the marginal slope for the same predictor estimated with Equation 1.12. Geometrically, this pattern of correlations determines the particular tilt of the three-dimensional regression plane representing the linear regression of $Y$ on $X_1$ and $X_2$. But perhaps the difference between a marginal and a partial regression slope is most clearly illustrated using two-dimensional graphs in which the variable to be controlled, $X_2$, is dichotomous, as shown in Figure 2.3.

The left-hand panel of Figure 2.3 shows a scatterplot of made-up data in which the marginal relation between $X_1$ and $Y$ is clearly strongly positive. For these data, the estimated marginal effect, that is, the slope of the simple regression of $Y$ on $X_1$, is $\hat{\beta} = 0.58$, which is significantly different from zero, $t(47) = 5.52$, $p < .0001$. But these results were obtained by ignoring a second predictor, $X_2$, which is dichotomous.[1] The right-hand panel of Figure 2.3 is

---

[1] Recall from Chapter 1 that the relation between a dichotomous predictor and a continuous outcome is necessarily linear. Here, $X_2$ is dichotomous to simplify the demonstration, but the principles described readily generalize to a continuous version of $X_2$.

a scatterplot of the same data, with different symbols used to distinguish the values of $X_2$. Now we can see that *within* a given value of $X_2$, the relation between $X_1$ and $Y$ is not particularly strong. This is what is meant by 'holding $X_2$ constant'; one focuses on the relation between $X_1$ and $Y$ within each value of $X_2$. When we estimate the two-predictor regression model for these data (Equation 2.1), the estimated partial relation between $Y$ and $X_1$ is $\hat{\beta}_1 = 0.18$, which is not significant, $t(46) = 1.30$, $p = .20$.[2] Thus, for these data, the partial relation between $X_1$ and $Y$ (i.e., the relation that *partials out* or *holds constant* $X_2$) is much weaker than the marginal relation between $X_1$ and $Y$.[3] In fact, the statistically significant marginal effect of $X_1$ becomes a nonsignificant partial effect when $X_2$ is controlled.

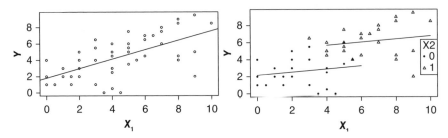

**Figure 2.3**   Scatterplots for contrived data with marginal regression slope for $X_1$ (left panel) and partial regression slope for $X_1$, holding $X_2$ constant (right panel)

As emphasized earlier, the partial relation between $Y$ and $X_1$ will not always be weaker than the marginal relation; sometimes it will be stronger. Figure 2.4 presents another made-up dataset. Like the data in Figure 2.3, the left-hand panel of Figure 2.4 shows a clear, positive marginal relation between $X_1$ and $Y$. Specifically, the slope of the simple regression of $Y$ on $X_1$ is $\hat{\beta} = 0.46$, which is significantly different from zero, $t(48) = 4.98$, $p < .0001$. But once again, these results were obtained by ignoring a second dichotomous predictor, $X_2$. The right-hand panel of Figure 2.4 is a scatterplot of the same data, again with different symbols used to distinguish the values of $X_2$. In contrast with the previous example, with these data, the relation between $X_1$ and $Y$ is even stronger within a given value of $X_2$. When we estimate the two-predictor regression model for these data, the estimated partial relation between $Y$ and $X_1$ is $\hat{\beta}_1 = 1.00$ with $t(47) = 9.62$, $p < .0001$. Thus, for these data, the partial relation between $X_1$ and $Y$ is much stronger than the marginal relation between $X_1$ and $Y$.[4] These data provide an example of a phenomenon known as **enhancement**, which occurs when the partial effect of a given predictor is greater than the corresponding marginal effect.[5] Although both the

---

[2]Inference for multiple regression is addressed later in this chapter.

[3]Note also that the data in Figure 2.3 do not depict an interaction between $X_1$ and $X_2$. If there were an interaction, the relation between $X_1$ and $Y$ would differ across the values of $X_2$, but the partial regression slopes in the right-hand panel of Figure 2.3 are parallel, reflecting the lack of an interaction in the model. Interactions are addressed in Chapter 4.

[4]Note once again that this difference also does not arise because of an interaction between $X_1$ and $X_2$.

[5]Specifically, enhancement occurs when the standardized partial effect exceeds the standardized marginal effect while the total proportion of variance explained by the model (i.e., multiple $R^2$) is greater than $r^2_{YX_1} + r^2_{YX_2}$. **Suppression** is the situation in which the standardized partial effect exceeds the standardized marginal effect but $R^2$ is less than $r^2_{YX_1} + r^2_{YX_2}$. For further details, see Friedman and Wall (2005).

marginal and partial effects of $X_1$ are statistically significant in this example, it's important also to recognize that it's possible for a marginal effect to be nonsignificant, whereas the corresponding partial effect controlling for one or more additional predictors is significant.

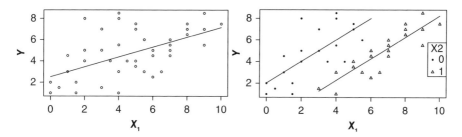

**Figure 2.4** Scatterplots for contrived data with marginal regression slope for $X_1$ (left panel) and partial regression slope for $X_1$, holding $X_2$ constant (right panel)

Finally, it is also possible for the partial relation between $Y$ and $X_1$ to be negative when the marginal relation is positive (or vice versa), as the new set of made-up data in Figure 2.5 illustrate. Here again, the left-hand panel of the figure shows that the marginal relation between $X_1$ and $Y$ is positive, specifically with $\hat{\beta}_1 = 0.34$, $t(48) = 2.67$, $p = .01$. But now, as depicted in the right-hand side of Figure 2.5, when we control for $X_2$, the partial relation between $Y$ and $X_1$ is negative, in particular, $\hat{\beta}_1 = -0.38$, which is also significant, $t(47) = -3.19$, $p = .003$.[6] These data provide an example of a phenomenon known as *Simpson's paradox*, which occurs when the sign of a partial effect of a given variable is the opposite sign of the corresponding marginal effect.

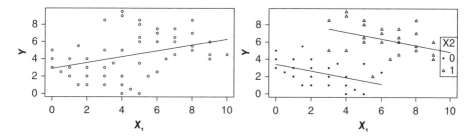

**Figure 2.5** Scatterplots for contrived data with marginal regression slope for $X_1$ (left panel) and partial regression slope for $X_1$, holding $X_2$ constant (right panel)

 Section recap

### Distinction between partial effect and marginal effect of a predictor

The coefficient of a predictor in a multiple regression model (i.e., its **partial effect**) is often smaller than its coefficient in a simple regression model (i.e., its **marginal effect**). In this case, the partial effect could be nonsignificant despite the marginal effect being significant.

*(Continued)*

---

[6]And, once again, there is no interaction between $X_1$ and $X_2$.

(Continued)

But it is also possible for the partial effect of a predictor to be larger than its corresponding marginal effect. In this case, the partial effect could be significant even though the marginal effect is nonsignificant.

Finally, it is even possible for the partial effect of a predictor to be negative even though the marginal effect is positive (or vice versa).

---

## Multiple correlation

The **coefficient of determination**, or $R^2$, was introduced in Chapter 1 in the context of the simple regression model. Recall that a squared correlation, $r^2$, between $X$ and $Y$ is the proportion of outcome variable variance explained by the model in simple regression. But in the present context of a two-predictor model, the squared correlation between a single predictor and $Y$ gives only the marginal proportion of variance explained by that predictor. Returning to our running empirical example, it might appear as if $r^2_{YX_1} = (.32)^2 = 10.24\%$ of the variance in BPAQ scores is explained by BIS scores and $r^2_{YX_2} = (-.21)^2 = 4.41\%$ of the variance in BPAQ scores is explained by age. Yet, because there is a nonzero correlation between these two predictors, they share some variation, and therefore, we cannot say that the total amount of variability in aggression explained by the two predictors is simply $14.65\% = (10.24\% + 4.41\%)$. Instead, the total amount of variability in aggression scores explained by the two predictors should be adjusted to account for the fact that the two predictors are correlated. In Chapter 1, $R^2$ was defined as the proportion of outcome variable variance explained by a regression model according to Equation 1.14; that logic also applies to multiple regression, as we will see later. But first, an equivalent approach to understanding and calculating $R^2$ is developed.

Once we have estimates of the parameters of the regression model (e.g., the OLS estimates), we can hypothetically compute a predicted outcome variable score for each research participant $i$ by plugging that person's observed values of $X_1$ and $X_2$ into the estimated regression equation. For each participant, or case, $i$ we will then have an observed outcome variable score $Y_i$ and a model-implied, or predicted value $\hat{Y}_i$. With these two values, we can then compute the residual, $e_i = Y_i - \hat{Y}_i$, for each case. Using the running example, the first participant in the data file (case $i = 1$) has BPAQ = 2.62, age = 18, and BIS = 2.15. To compute the predicted $Y$ for this person, we plug her observed $X$ values into the estimated regression equation:

$$\hat{Y}_i = 1.95 + 0.44X_1 - 0.02X_2$$

$$\hat{Y}_i = 1.95 + 0.44(2.15) - 0.02(18),$$

which gives us $\hat{Y}_1 = 2.54$. The residual for case $i = 1$ is therefore

$$e_1 = Y_1 - \hat{Y}_1 = 2.62 - 2.54 = 0.08.$$

We could follow this procedure to calculate $\hat{Y}$ for the remaining cases in the dataset, leading to a list of observed $Y$ values paired with predicted $\hat{y}$ values. Although our current multiple regression model only consists of two predictors, this procedure can be followed for a model with any number of predictors. The correlation between $Y$ and $\hat{Y}$ is $R$, the **multiple correlation**. $R$ is formally defined as the maximum correlation that can be achieved between the outcome $Y$ and the linear combination of the predictors, $X_1$ and $X_2$; this linear combination is represented by the variable $\hat{Y}$. For the two-predictor model, $R$ is also formulated as

$$r_{Y\hat{Y}} = R = \sqrt{\hat{\beta}_1 r_{Y1} + \hat{\beta}_2 r_{2Y}} .$$

The coefficient of determination referred to in Chapter 1 is more commonly called the **squared multiple correlation**, or $R^2$, and it gives the proportion of variance in the outcome $Y$ that is accounted for by the model as a whole. In the current two-predictor multiple regression, the 'model' is the optimal linear combination of $X_1$ and $X_2$, where 'optimal' refers to the linear combination using regression coefficients obtained by minimizing the squared residuals (i.e., OLS estimation). Thus, $R^2$ is a type of standardized effect size giving the overall effect of the predictors on the outcome in a standard metric ranging from 0 to 1. In the aggression example, multiple $R^2 = .1299$, indicating that 12.99% of the variability in BPAQ scores is explained by the optimal linear combination of the two predictors, age and BIS scores. This value for $R^2$ is slightly smaller than the sum of the two individual $r^2$ values giving the simple bivariate associations between each predictor and the outcome. That is, $(R^2 = .13) < (r_1^2 + r_2^2 = .1465)$. That's because multiple $R^2$ accounts for the correlation between the two predictors (or, generally, the correlations among all predictors in a model).

Often, a statistic known as **adjusted $R^2$**, or $\tilde{R}^2$, is reported alongside or instead of the squared multiple correlation, $R^2$. This statistic is calculated as

$$\tilde{R}^2 = 1 - (1 - R^2)\frac{N-1}{N-P-1},$$

where $P$ is the total number of predictors in the regression model. So far, we have only considered multiple regression models with $P = 2$, but we can see from this formula that as $P$ increases, the adjustment to the original $R^2$ will be larger. The original $R^2$ will only increase as additional predictors are added to a model, even if these new predictors are only trivially important. Thus, one rationale for $\tilde{R}^2$ is to provide a statistic that penalizes a model for being overly complex (i.e., too many unnecessary predictors). This penalty is larger with smaller values of the original $R^2$ and with smaller sample sizes. In my experience, although the original $R^2$ is a negatively biased estimate of the population proportion of variance explained (i.e., $\rho_{Y\hat{Y}}^2$), whereas $\tilde{R}^2$ is unbiased, the difference between $R^2$ and $\tilde{R}^2$ is usually not large enough to impact major substantive conclusions regarding an estimated model. Additionally, when $R^2$ is near zero, it is possible for $\tilde{R}^2$ to have a negative value, which is a nonsensical result. Finally, the distributional theory that allows significance tests for $R^2$ and model comparisons based on changes in $R^2$ (explained shortly) does not easily generalize to $\tilde{R}^2$. For these reasons, I do not find that reporting $\tilde{R}^2$ as a matter of routine is particularly important or informative.

 Section recap

### Multiple correlation

Given an estimated regression model, the correlation between $Y$ and $\hat{Y}$, where $\hat{Y}$ represents the optimal linear combination of the predictors in the model, is known as the **multiple correlation, $R$.**

Multiple $R^2$ represents the proportion of outcome variable variance explained by the linear combination of the predictors.

Because its calculation accounts for the correlations among the predictors, multiple $R^2$ is usually smaller than the simple sum of individual squared correlations between each predictor and the outcome.

## Two-predictor multiple regression: Inference

Often we would like to know whether $R^2$ is significantly greater than zero; in other words, we want to test whether the model is likely to explain a nonzero proportion of variability in the outcome variable in the population. The null hypothesis for this inferential question can be expressed as

$$H_0 : \rho^2_{Y\hat{Y}} = 0,$$

where $\rho^2_{Y\hat{Y}}$ is the population squared multiple correlation. The alternate hypothesis is

$$H_1 : \rho^2_{Y\hat{Y}} > 0.$$

Rejection of this **omnibus null hypothesis** in favour of the alternate hypothesis leads to a conclusion that the set of predictors, taken together, in the regression model explains a significant proportion of variance in the outcome variable. We can test this null hypothesis using the **analysis of regression variance**, which leads to an $F$ distributed test statistic.

Readers familiar with traditional one-way analysis of variance (ANOVA) for group mean comparisons will recognize that the analysis of regression variance follows the same logic. In fact, traditional ANOVA for group mean comparisons is mathematically a special case of the more general ANOVA for linear regression models (the formal expression of the traditional ANOVA model as a special type of linear multiple regression model is presented in Chapter 3).

From one-way, independent-groups ANOVA, recall that the total variability of the dependent variable is partitioned into between-groups variability (i.e., variation among group means) and within-groups variability (i.e., variation among individual cases within each group). If between-groups variability is substantially larger than the within-groups variability, then the independent variable (i.e., the group membership variable) accounts for a significant proportion of dependent variable variation.

In the regression ANOVA, the equivalent procedure is to partition the total variability of $Y$ into variability explained by the model and variability caused by random sampling error (i.e., individual differences) around the model. Specifically,

$$SS_{total} = SS_{model} + SS_{error},$$

where $SS_{total}$ is the total sum of squares for $Y$, $SS_{model}$ is the sum of squares explained by the model, and $SS_{error}$ is the error sum of squares.

The $SS_{total}$ term is the sum of the squared deviations of observed values of $Y$ from the mean of $Y$:

$$SS_{total} = \sum_{i=1}^{N}(Y_i - \bar{Y})^2.$$

This term should be familiar from introductory statistics as $SS_{total} = SS_Y$, a part of the definitional formula for calculating the variance and standard deviation of $Y$.

Next, $SS_{model}$ (also known as $SS_{regression}$) is the sum of the squared deviations of predicted values of $Y$, that is, $\hat{Y}$, from the mean of $Y$:

$$SS_{model} = \sum_{i=1}^{N}(\hat{Y}_i - \bar{Y})^2.$$

Because the predicted values are based on the influence of the predictors (see Equation 2.1), $SS_{model}$ represents how much the model that includes these predictors deviates from the overall mean of $Y$. Recall from Chapter 1 that the mean of $Y$ can be viewed as the predicted value of $Y$ in the intercept-only model; hence, $SS_{model}$ represents a comparison of predicted values from a focal model (i.e., a model including predictors of interest) with the predicted values from the intercept-only model. Consequently, we can view the regression ANOVA $F$ test as a test of whether the focal regression model significantly differs from the intercept-only model of Chapter 1.

Finally, the $SS_{error}$ term is also known as $SS_{residual}$ because it is simply the sum of the squared residuals across all observations, which was previously defined in Equation 2.3 as $SS_e$. Therefore, the sum-of-squares decomposition for regression can be more fully expressed as

$$\sum_{i=1}^{N}(Y_i - \bar{Y})^2 = \sum_{i=1}^{N}(\hat{Y}_i - \bar{Y})^2 + \sum_{i=1}^{N}(Y_i - \hat{Y}_i)^2.$$

This mathematical expression is an instance of a fundamental concept in all of parametric statistical modeling that observed variation in an outcome variable equals model-implied variation plus error variation. Given these definitions, an alternative formula for the squared multiple correlation is

$$R^2 = SS_{model}/SS_{total}.$$

This expression for $R^2$ is identical to that given as Equation 1.14 in Chapter 1 because $SS_{model} = SS_Y - SS_e$.

Next, just as $SS_{total} = SS_Y$ is divided by a degrees of freedom (df) term (i.e., $N - 1$) to arrive at an estimate of the variance of $Y$ (see Equation 1.8), so too are $SS_{model}$ and $SS_{error}$ divided by their respective $df$ terms to obtain variance, or **mean square** terms (so-called because each is the mean of a set of squared deviations). Specifically, we have

$$MS_{model} = SS_{model}/df_{model},$$

with $df_{model} = P$, where $P$ is the number of predictors in the regression model (up to this point, we have only considered simple regression models, which have $P = 1$, and two-predictor multiple regression models, which have $P = 2$). Additionally,

$$MS_{error} = SS_{error}/df_{error},$$

with $df_{error} = N - P - 1$. Note also that just as $SS_{model}$ plus $SS_{error}$ equals $SS_{total}$, it is also the case that

$$df_{total} = df_{model} + df_{error}.$$

Ultimately, if variance explained by the model, or $MS_{model}$, is substantially larger than variance as a result of random error, $MS_{error}$, then the data suggest that the model accounts for a substantial portion of variance in $Y$. More formally, the ratio $MS_{model}/MS_{error}$ gives a test statistic which, under the omnibus null hypothesis expressed earlier, is distributed as an $F$ statistic with $P$ and $N - P - 1$ degrees of freedom. If the $p$ value corresponding to the observed $F$ statistic is less than a nominal alpha level (typically $\alpha = .05$), the null hypothesis is rejected.

It is common for statistical software to summarize results from the regression ANOVA using an ANOVA table; a generic form of this table is in Table 2.2, whereas the ANOVA results for the BPAQ aggression example are in Table 2.3. Continuing with our example regression of BPAQ scores on BIS scores and age, the ANOVA indicates that $F(2, 272) = 20.31$, which is significant with $p < .0001$. Therefore, the $R^2$ value of .1299 is significantly greater than zero, indicating that the optimal linear combination of age and BIS (i.e., optimal by the OLS estimation criterion) accounts for a significant proportion of variability in aggression.

**Table 2.2**  Generic ANOVA table for regression

| Source | df | SS | MS | F |
|---|---|---|---|---|
| Model | $P$ | $SS_{model}$ | $SS_{model}/df_{model}$ | $MS_{model}/MS_{error}$ |
| Error | $N - P - 1$ | $SS_{error}$ | $SS_{error}/df_{error}$ | – |
| Total | $N - 1$ | $SS_Y$ | – | – |

**Table 2.3**  ANOVA table for the regression of BPAQ scores on BIS scores and age

| Source | df | SS | MS | F |
|---|---|---|---|---|
| Model | 2 | 9.77 | 4.89 | 20.31 |
| Error | 272 | 65.46 | 0.24 | – |
| Total | 274 | 75.23 | | |

The omnibus null hypothesis that the model does not explain any outcome variable variance can be equivalently expressed in terms of the individual regression coeffcients. In our current context of a two-predictor model, this form of the omnibus null hypothesis is

$$H_0: \beta_1 = \beta_2 = 0.$$

Thus, the $F$ test just presented can also be understood as a test of the *joint* significance of the estimated coefficients for a given model, taken as a set.

Usually, however, a researcher is more interested in separate significance tests for each partial regression coefficient. This interest implies null and alternate hypotheses for the population regression coefficient for predictor $X_1$:

$$H_0: \beta_1 = 0$$

and

$$H_1: \beta_1 \neq 0$$

and for the population regression coefficient of predictor $X_2$:

$$H_0: \beta_2 = 0$$

and

$$H_1: \beta_2 \neq 0.$$

We can evaluate these null hypotheses using a version of the $t$ statistic, which is essentially the same as presented in Chapter 1 for simple regression (Equation 1.13):

$$t = \frac{\hat{\beta}_p}{s_{\hat{\beta}_p}},$$

where $\hat{\beta}_p$ is the estimated partial regression coefficient for the $p$th predictor and $s_{\hat{\beta}_p}$ is the estimated standard error of $\hat{\beta}_p$. More generally, as with any use of a $t$ statistic, this $t$ statistic is a function of an observed effect-size statistic, or parameter estimate, divided by the estimated standard error of that parameter estimate. The degrees of freedom for this $t$ test is $df_{error}$ from the overall regression ANOVA.

Because the model now incorporates two predictors instead of just one, the formula for the standard error of a given parameter estimate is more complex than that given in Chapter 1 for simple regression. In the two-predictor linear regression, a formula for the estimated standard error of the OLS-estimated partial regression coefficient for a given predictor $X_p$ is

$$s_{\hat{\beta}_p} = \frac{s_Y}{s_{X_p}} \sqrt{\frac{1-R^2}{N-2-1}} \sqrt{\frac{1}{1-r_{X_1 X_2}^2}}, \tag{2.7}$$

where $r_{X_1 X_2}^2$ is the squared correlation between $X_1$ and $X_2$. Although this formula may seem complicated, three aspects should be intuitively logical. First, as with any standard error estimate, the larger the sample size, the smaller the standard error. Next, the larger $R^2$ is, the smaller the standard error is. And finally, the larger the correlation between the two predictors is, the larger the standard error is. At this point, it is important to recognize that it is possible, and even somewhat common, for the joint test of a set of predictors to be significant (i.e., the omnibus null hypothesis that $\beta_1$ and $\beta_2$ are simultaneously equal to 0, or that $R^2 = 0$, is rejected) when none of the separate $t$ tests for the individual regression coefficients is significant. This situation becomes more likely as $r^2_{X_1 X_2}$ increases.

We can also use the standard error term to construct confidence intervals for the partial regression coefficients:

$$\hat{\beta}_p \pm s_{\hat{\beta}_p} \times t_\alpha.$$

To reiterate from Chapter 1, although researchers typically focus on the significance of a given parameter estimate or effect, the confidence interval estimate for that parameter is ultimately more informative. The significance test merely indicates whether a population regression coefficient is likely to equal zero, whereas the confidence interval gives a whole range of plausible values for the population regression coefficient.

In our current example regression of BPAQ scores, the BIS partial regression slope $\hat{\beta}_1 = 0.44$ has a corresponding $t(272) = 5.22$, which is significant with $p < .0001$. Therefore, controlling age, the population regression coefficient for BIS scores is unlikely to be zero. The 95% CI around this parameter estimate is (0.276, 0.611), indicating that a population partial regression slope for BIS in the range of 0.276 to 0.611 is consistent with the sample data, such that participants with higher values of impulsivity (measured with BIS) tend to have higher values of aggression (measured with BPAQ). The partial regression slope for age, $\hat{\beta}_2 = -0.02$, is also significant with $t(272) = -2.91$, $p = .0039$, and the 95% CI around this parameter estimate is (−0.029, −0.006). Therefore, controlling BIS scores, a population partial regression slope for age in the range of −0.029 to −0.006 is consistent with these sample data, such that older participants tend to have lower BPAQ aggression scores.

 Section recap

### Statistical inference for multiple regression

The **analysis of regression variance** (regression ANOVA) is used to test the omninus null hypothesis that the population proportion of variance explained equals zero ($H_0 : \rho^2_{Y\hat{Y}} = 0$), in other words, to determine whether multiple $R^2$ is statistically significant.

With this regression ANOVA, the total variability of the outcome variable is partitioned into variability explained by the model ($MS_{model} = SS_{model}/df_{model}$) and error variability ($MS_{error} = SS_{error}/df_{error}$). The test statistic for the omnibus null hypothesis is then $F = MS_{model}/MS_{error}$.

In addition to this omnibus test that all partial regression coefficients equal zero, each regression coefficient can be tested for statistical significance using $t$ tests, with $t = \hat{\beta}_p/s_{\hat{\beta}_p}$.

More usefully, a $(1 - \alpha)$% confidence interval can be constructed for each partial regression coefficient with $\hat{\beta}_p \pm s_{\hat{\beta}_p} \times t_\alpha$.

## Standardized regression coefficients

In behavioural and social science research, important variables often have an arbitrary scale. For example, in our running example of the regression of BPAQ scores on BIS scores and age, only the age variable has a clear, well-understood scale, namely, the number of years since a person's birth. The other two variables, scores on the BPAQ and BIS questionnaires, are operationalizations of abstract psychological constructs, namely, aggression and impulsivity, respectively. The constructs themselves, although they are hypothetical variables, have an unknowable scale, and hence any operationalization of them has an arbitrary scale. Consequently, it can be challenging to interpret the magnitude of effects (e.g., regression coefficients) for such operational variables; does a 0.44 increase in BPAQ score per one-point increase in BIS constitute a small effect or a large effect? Furthermore, researchers often desire to compare the effects of different predictors on a given outcome variable. Doing so requires that the effects be based on the same scales of measurement. One purported solution to these issues is to transform the estimated 'raw' regression coefficients, which are based on the scales of the observed, operational variables, into **standardized regression coefficients**, which are based on a common, standard scale (almost always with mean = 0 and variance = 1). But this practice does little to aid interpretation, and might even produce misleading conclusions, as I briefly discuss next.

Recall our estimated regression model that

$$\hat{Y}_i = 1.95 + 0.44X_1 - 0.02X_2,$$

or, with the variable names,

$$\widehat{BPAQ}_i = 1.95 + 0.44(BIS_i) - 0.02(age_i) + e_i.$$

Because the age and BIS predictors have different scales, one cannot say that BIS has a stronger effect on BPAQ scores than age based solely on these unstandardized regression coefficients. But if each variable is standardized before estimating the regression model, then the variables are on the same scale. Standardization gives the variables the same mean and variance, but it does not change the correlations among them. If we then estimate the regression model using these standardized variables, the resulting partial regression coefficients are known as standardized regression coefficients.

More specifically, if $Y$, $X_1$, and $X_2$ are each standardized using their population means and standard deviations to produce

$$Z_{Y_i} = \frac{Y_i - \mu_Y}{\sigma_Y},$$

$$Z_{X_{1i}} = \frac{X_{1i} - \mu_{X_1}}{\sigma_{X_1}},$$

and

$$Z_{X_{2i}} = \frac{X_{2i} - \mu_{X_2}}{\sigma_{X_2}},$$

then the new variables $Z_Y$, $Z_{X_1}$, and $Z_{X_2}$ each have population mean $\mu_Z = 0$ and population standard deviation $\sigma_Z = 1$. The regression of $Z_Y$ on $Z_{X_1}$ and $Z_{X_2}$ is then

$$\hat{Z}_{Y_i} = \beta_1^* Z_{X_{1i}} + \beta_2^* Z_{X_{2i}}.$$

In this model, $\beta_1^*$ is the standardized population regression coefficient for standardized predictor $Z_{X_1}$, representing the predicted *standard deviation* difference in $Y$ from an increase in $X_1$ equal to 1 *standard deviation*, controlling $X_2$. Similarly, $\beta_2^*$, the standardized population regression coefficient for standardized predictor $Z_{X_2}$, represents the predicted standard deviation difference in $Y$ from a 1 standard deviation increase in $X_2$, controlling $X_1$.[7] (The intercept term in the standardized regression equation is always zero and, hence, not shown.)

Of course, in practice, the variables cannot be standardized based on their population means and standard deviations, in addition to the other realities of estimating regression parameters from sample data. The sample-estimated standardized regression coefficients can be obtained by standardizing $Y$, $X_1$, and $X_2$ using their sample means and standard deviations and then regressing this sample-standardized $Y$ on the sample-standardized $X_1$ and $X_2$. Alternatively, and much more commonly, $\hat{\beta}_p$, the unstandardized regression coefficient estimate for predictor $X_p$, is transformed into a standardized coefficient, $\hat{\beta}_p^*$, with:

$$\hat{\beta}_p^* = \hat{\beta}_p \frac{s_{X_p}}{s_Y}.$$

This formula produces a standardized regression coefficient based on sample estimates of the standard deviations of $Y$ (i.e., $s_Y$) and $X_p$ (i.e., $s_{X_p}$).

In the aggression running example, the standardized regression coefficient for BIS is $\hat{\beta}_1^* = 0.30$ and that for age is $\hat{\beta}_2^* = -0.17$. Thus, BIS does appear to have a stronger unique effect on aggression than age does. In general, though, comparing standardized regression coefficients is a flawed approach to ranking the importance of separate predictors in a regression model. Alternative procedures for assessing variable importance are reviewed by Chao, Zhao, Kupper, and Nylander-French (2008). A promising choice among these methods is to compare so-called *Pratt's Indices* (see Thomas, Hughes, and Zumbo, 1998) to determine the proportion that each predictor uniquely contributes to the overall multiple $R^2$.

Overall, I take a dim view toward standardized regression coefficients, and I feel that psychologists in particular overuse these statistics. Other statistical methodologists judge standardized coefficients even more harshly than I do; for a clear, thorough critique, see King (1986: 669–74; also see Berk, 2004: 117–19; Pedhazur, 1997: 320–22; Richards, 1982). My primary criticism of standardized coefficients is that their literal interpretation is cumbersome, increasing the level of abstraction from the substantive meaning of the actual data. Consider

---

[7]As explained in Chapter 1, there is a regrettable tendency to refer to standardized regression coefficients, including sample-estimated standardized coefficients, as 'beta weights' or just 'betas.' As a reminder, in this text, I adhere to the common statistical notation of using the lowercase Greek letter beta, i.e., $\beta$, to represent an unstandardized population regression coefficient, the sample estimate of which is $\hat{\beta}$. Herein, I denote a population standardized regression coefficient as $\beta*$, the sample estimate of which is $\hat{\beta}*$. The APA style guide (APA, 2010) uses the English characters $b$ and $b*$ to represent sample estimates of unstandardized and standardized (respectively) regression coefficient estimates (see p. 119), whereas the Greek letter $\beta$ represents the probability of Type II error in a null hypothesis test (see p. 122).

the effect of the age predictor in the current example: The interpretation of its standardized coefficient estimate, $\hat{\beta}_2^* = -0.17$, is that a 1-standard-deviation increase in age is associated with a 0.17-standard-deviation decrease in BPAQ scores. Yet, the interpretation of the original, unstandardized coefficient for age, $\hat{\beta}_2 = -0.02$, is simpler and based on the actual scales of the variables: A one-year increase in age is associated with a 0.02 decrease in BPAQ scores. Of course, as mentioned, BPAQ scores have an arbitrary scale as one particular operationalization of an abstract psychological construct, aggression. But standardizing this scale makes it no less arbitrary. And of course it is much easier to understand age in terms of years rather than in terms of standard-deviation units.

Standardized coefficients can also produce seemingly paradoxical results when researchers wish to compare the importance of predictors. Consider this hypothetical example (cf. Fox, 2008: 94–6): Suppose a regression of income ($Y$, in dollars) on years of education ($X_1$) and years of job experience ($X_2$) produces the estimated regression equation

$$\hat{Y}_i = 2000 + 200X_{1i} + 100X_{2i},$$

indicating that each additional year of education is associated with $200 higher income, whereas each additional year of experience is associated with $100 higher income. Thus, according to the unstandardized coefficients, education has double the effect on income than experience; an additional year of education has more benefit than an additional year of experience. Now, say we have $s_Y = 400$, $s_{X_1} = 2$, and $s_{X_2} = 5$. The standardized coefficient for education is therefore $200 \times (2 / 400) = 1.0$, and the standardized coefficient for experience is $100 \times (10 / 400) = 2.5$. Consequently, the standardized coefficient for experience is larger than that for education, implying the opposite conclusion than that suggested by the unstandardized coefficients, namely, that experience is more important than education. But because the unstandardized coefficients are based on well-understood, meaningful units (dollars per year), their interpretation is clear, whereas the standardized coefficients are based on the abstract, confusing units of standard deviations of dollars per standard deviations of years of education or per standard deviations of years of experience.

The example in the previous paragraph demonstrates that in the case where variables have a meaningful scale (such as number of cigarettes smoked per day, age in years, heart rate, and number of errors in a cognitive task), it is certainly best to interpret unstandardized regression coefficients. When variables operationalizing abstract constructs (such as the BPAQ aggression scale) are included, then it is more tempting to interpret standardized regression coefficients. But even these variables have scales that may become well understood as the research literature around them grows. For example, any clinical psychologist studying anxiety knows whether a five-point decrease on the popular Penn State Worry Questionnaire (PSWQ; Meyer, Miller, Metzger, and Borkovec, 1990) represents a meaningful or important change.

In addition to the interpretational limitations of standardized regression coefficients, a more technical limitation is that in practice, the standardization must be based on sample standard deviation, which varies across studies, rather than population standard deviation. For this reason, standardized coefficients even for the same predictors are not directly comparable across studies, even if one does deem them comparable across predictors within a given study. Furthermore, because the unstandardized coefficients are standardized using sample standard deviations, there is additional sampling variability associated with them. Consequently, their standard errors are different from those for unstandardized coefficients, and thus, the $p$ values for unstandardized coefficients should not be applied to the standardized coefficients.

The implication is that when an unstandardized coefficient estimate is significant, one cannot automatically assume that the corresponding standardized estimate is also significant. Constructing correct confidence intervals for standardized coefficients is also a difficult statistical problem.

These concerns about standardized coefficients notwithstanding, I do recognize that it is common practice to report them in many subdisciplines within the behavioural and social sciences. It can be daunting for a researcher to eschew the expectations of journal editors and reviewers, and so I expect that a recommendation never to report standardized coefficients would be ignored. In fact, in later chapters focusing on structural equation modeling, I will rely on standardized parameter estimates for interpreting models with latent variables. But at this point, I urge readers to be cognizant of the limitations of standardized regression coefficients , and if they must be reported in a research article or presentation, I strongly recommend that they be reported in addition to, and not instead of, the corresponding unstandardized regression coefficients.

 Section recap

### Standardized regression coefficients

The sample standardized regression coefficient for predictor $X_p$ can be calculated as

$$\hat{\beta}_p^* = \hat{\beta}_p \frac{s_{X_p}}{s_Y} .$$

This $\hat{\beta}_p^*$ gives the expected *standard deviation* change in Y per *1-standard-deviation* increase in $X_p$.

Exclusive reliance on standardized regression coefficients is statistically problematic and can elicit misleading substantive conclusions. If standardized regression slopes are reported, the original, unstandardized coefficients should always be reported as well.

## MULTIPLE REGRESSION WITH $P =$ TWO OR MORE PREDICTORS

As mentioned at the beginning of the chapter, a substantive theory about a given outcome variable often involves even more than just two predictor variables or background covariates.[8] Thus, the statistical model for that outcome should be flexible enough to incorporate multiple predictors. For instance, continuing with our running example, the researcher may wish to

---

[8]The term *covariate* often refers to a predictor variable that is of tangential theoretical importance, but it is believed to account potentially for a nontrivial portion of the outcome variable's variability. Mathematically, a covariate is not treated differently from any other predictor. In certain procedures in SPSS and other software packages, however, 'covariate' refers to any continuously distributed predictor, whereas a 'factor' is any categorical predictor.

examine the contribution of several personality variables, in addition to impulsivity, to the prediction of aggression, while continuing to account for the age covariate. It is straightforward to expand the multiple regression model to include more than two predictor variables. To illustrate, the model for BPAQ aggression scores will be expanded to include operationalizations of two personality variables, openness and conscientiousness, as well as the BIS impulsivity scores and age.

## P-predictor multiple regression: Model specification

Equation 2.1 gave the multiple regression model in which an outcome variable, $Y$, is expressed as an additive linear function of two predictors, $X_1$ and $X_2$. A third predictor, $X_3$, is easy to add to the model:

$$\hat{Y}_i = \beta_0 + \beta_1 X_{1i} + \beta_2 X_{2i} + \beta_3 X_{3i} . \tag{2.8}$$

Equation 2.8 is identical to Equation 2.1, except of course now $X_3$ is added along with its partial regression slope coefficient, $\beta_3$. And to generalize completely, the multiple regression model for $P$ predictors (where $P$, the total number of predictors, equals any finite positive integer greater than 1) can be written as

$$\hat{Y}_i = \beta_0 + \beta_1 X_{1i} + ... + \beta_P X_{Pi},$$

or, equivalently,

$$Y_i = \beta_0 + \beta_1 X_{1i} + ... + \beta_P X_{Pi} + \varepsilon_i,$$

again with $\varepsilon_i = Y_i - \hat{Y}_i$. An even more general expression of the model in which $P$ can equal any finite positive integer greater than or equal to 1 is

$$Y_i = \beta_0 + \left( \sum_{p=1}^{P} \beta_p X_{pi} \right) + \varepsilon_i . \tag{2.9}$$

It should be easy to see that if $P = 1$, Equation 2.9 reduces to Equation 1.5 and that if $P = 2$, Equation 2.9 reduces to Equation 2.2.

Similar to before, the intercept parameter, $\beta_0$, represents the predicted value of $Y$ when *all* predictors equal zero. And now for the $p$th predictor $X_p$, its partial regression coefficient (or slope) $\beta_p$ represents the predicted difference in $Y$ when $X_p$ increases by one unit, holding all other predictors in the model constant. That is, $\beta_p$ gives the unique effect of $X_p$ over and above all of the other predictors included in the model.

When the regression model included only one predictor (i.e., the simple regression model), we could easily visualize it as a straight line going through a two-dimensional scatterplot (e.g., Figure 1.5). When the model included two predictors, the geometric representation of the model is a three-dimensional regression plane (Figure 2.2). Now, if there are more than two predictors, the geometric surface implied by the regression equation has more than three dimensions and therefore is much more challenging to visualize with a single plot.[9]

## P-predictor multiple regression: Model estimation

Ordinary least-squares (OLS) continues to be the optimal method for estimating parameters from sample data for a regression model with more than two predictors (as long as the assumptions are met, as presented later in this chapter). Again, the goal of OLS is to find the parameter estimates that minimize the residual sum of squares, which, for the P-predictor equation, is

$$\sum_{i=1}^{N} e_i^2 = \sum_{i=1}^{N} (Y_i - \hat{Y}_i)^2 = \sum_{i=1}^{N} (Y_i - [\hat{\beta}_0 + \hat{\beta}_1 X_1 + \ldots + \hat{\beta}_p X_p])^2.$$

The scalar equations that give the OLS solutions for the parameter estimates become complex as more than $P = 2$ predictors are included. As we will see in Chapter 7, the OLS estimates instead can be expressed with a compact matrix equation. But for now, rest assured that the OLS estimates of the regression parameters again account for the pattern of correlations not only between each predictor and the outcome, but also the correlations among the predictors themselves. In this way, the partial regression slope for a given predictor continues to be distinct from the marginal slope that ignores the other predictors.

## P-predictor multiple regression: Inference and model comparisons

As with the one- and two-predictor regression models, when there are multiple predictors we again may be interested in testing hypotheses about multiple $R^2$ and a given individual partial regression slope, $\hat{\beta}_p$. Specifically for $R^2$, the null hypothesis is again $H_0 : \rho_{Y\hat{Y}}^2 = 0$. This null hypothesis is evaluated with the $F$ test presented before, with

$$F = \frac{MS_{model}}{MS_{error}} = \frac{SS_{model} \big/ df_{model}}{SS_{error} \big/ df_{error}},$$

where $SS_{model}$, $SS_{error}$, $df_{model}$, and $df_{error}$ are defined precisely as given earlier in the context of the two-predictor model. If the null hypothesis is rejected, $R^2$ is significantly greater than zero, again suggesting that the model explains more than zero variation in $Y$ in the population.

The significance of an estimated model's $R^2$ is often of limited substantive interest as researchers are typically more interested in the effects of individual predictors on their own.

---

[9]But one way to visualize the partial relation between a given predictor and the outcome, controlling for all other predictors, is to produce the two-dimensional *added-variable plot* for that predictor given the regression model. A complete definition and presentation of these plots is beyond the scope of this text given that they can be misleading when used for assessing model assumptions, although they are useful for examining influential cases. See Fox (2008: 268–72) and Fox and Weisberg (2011: 292–94) for details.

For a given individual partial regression coefficient $\hat{\beta}_p$ for predictor $X_p$, the null hypothesis is $H_0: \beta_p = 0$. If this null hypothesis is rejected, then the linear relation between $X_p$ and $Y$ is significant, holding all other predictors constant. As with the two-predictor model, this null hypothesis is evaluated with

$$t = \frac{\hat{\beta}_p}{s_{\hat{\beta}_p}}.$$

Here, the calculation of $s_{\hat{\beta}_p}$, the standard error of $\hat{\beta}_p$, is a generalization of the standard error for the two-predictor model:

$$s_{\hat{\beta}_p} = \frac{s_Y}{s_{X_p}} \sqrt{\frac{1-R_Y^2}{N-P-1}} \sqrt{\frac{1}{1-R_{X_p|X_{(-p)}}^2}}, \tag{2.10}$$

where $R_Y^2$ is the model's multiple $R^2$ and $R_{X_p|X_{(-p)}}^2$ is the multiple $R^2$ in a model regressing $X_p$ on all other predictors in the model. Equation 2.10 is almost identical to Equation 2.7, except the substitution of the $R_{X_p|X_{(-p)}}^2$ term here for the $r_{X_1X_2}^2$ term from Equation 2.7 indicates that in the current multiple predictor case, the standard error term for predictor $X_p$ is a function of the extent to which $X_p$ is correlated with all other predictors, whereas the $R_Y^2$ term also accounts for the extent to which the whole set of predictors relates to the dependent variable $Y$. When a model contains only two predictors, Equation 2.10 reduces to Equation 2.7 because in that situation, $R_{X_p|X_{(-p)}}^2 = r_{X_1X_2}^2$. Additionally, it is straightforward to use this standard error estimate to obtain a confidence interval for a given regression coefficient $\hat{\beta}_p$ with

$$\hat{\beta}_p \pm s_{\hat{\beta}_p} \times t_\alpha,$$

which is the same confidence interval formula for the one- or two-predictor models, except here it is more generally based on the estimated standard error for a $P$-predictor model. For both the $t$ test and the confidence interval, the degrees of freedom is the $df_{error}$ term from the regression ANOVA.

Equation 2.10 leads to the insight that the standard error for a given predictor $X_p$ becomes increasingly large as model size (i.e., the total number of predictors, $P$) increases, which in turn reduces the statistical power for the $t$ test of the individual coefficient, $\hat{\beta}_p$. Thus, although it is important to specify a realistic model that contains each potentially important predictor or covariate lest misleading conclusions be reached, there is also a practical advantage to estimating the most *parsimonious* model possible that does not include trivial effects which detract from the main theoretically important variables. It is often difficult to achieve a balance between parsimony and adequate comprehensiveness when faced with a large number of potential predictors and covariates, and a variety of model-building strategies have been proposed in the methodological literature to address this difficulty. Next, we address the most prominent of these strategies, keeping in mind that the most important goal is to specify the model that directly reflects the research questions under consideration, letting substantive theory be one's primary guide for model building.

 **Section recap**

### Multiple regression with $P$ = 2 or more predictors

The $P$-predictor multiple linear regression model can be expressed as

$$Y_i = \beta_0 + \left( \sum_{p=1}^{P} \beta_p X_{pi} \right) + \varepsilon_i ,$$

where $P$, the total number of predictors, is any finite integer greater than or equal to 1.

The partial regression slope coefficient $\beta_p$ gives the expected change in $Y$ per one-unit increase in $X_p$, while holding all other predictors in the model constant.

Once again, estimates of the regression slope coefficients are optimally obtained using OLS, which leads to an $F$ test for the model's multiple $R^2$ and $t$ tests, and $t$-based confidence intervals for each $\hat{\beta}_p$.

## Simultaneous regression

In **simultaneous regression**, all predictor variables of interest (and potentially important covariates of lesser substantive interest) are included *at once* in a single model to represent the relation between each predictor and the outcome while controlling all other predictors. The two-predictor regression models we have already discussed were examples of simultaneous regression. For instance, BPAQ aggression scores were regressed on age and BIS scores simultaneously such that $\hat{\beta}_1$ was the estimated regression slope for BIS, holding age constant, and $\hat{\beta}_2$ was the estimated regression slope for age, holding BIS constant.

To extend the example further, say the researcher also wants to examine how other personality traits, such as openness and conscientiousness, relate to aggression. In her study, the researcher also included measures of these traits from the NEO personality inventory (McCrae and Costa, 2004), namely, NEOo and NEOc, as respective operationalizations of the openness and conscientiousness constructs. Thus, using simultaneous regression, she might estimate a four-predictor model that incorporates all predictors of interest as well as the age covariate:

$$\hat{Y}_i = \beta_0 + \beta_1 X_{1i} + \beta_2 X_{2i} + \beta_3 X_{3i} + \beta_4 X_{4i},$$

where $\hat{Y}_i$ is the model-predicted BPAQ score for case $i$, $X_{1i}$ is that person's BIS score, $X_{2i}$ is her age, $X_{3i}$ is her score on the NEOo scale, and $X_{4i}$ is her score on the NEOc scale.

When this model is fitted to our ongoing dataset using the OLS estimation, we get $R^2 = .13$, $F(4, 270) = 10.46$, $p < .001$, indicating that the set of four predictors explains 13% of the observed variance in the BPAQ aggression scores. More specifically, as shown in Table 2.4, whereas the partial regression slopes for BIS and age are individually significant, neither NEOo nor NEOc is a significant unique predictor of BPAQ scores over and above the other three predictors in the model.

**Table 2.4** Simultaneous regression coefficients for BPAQ outcome variable

| Predictor variable | $\hat{\beta}$ | $SE(\hat{\beta})$ | t | p | 95% CI |
|---|---|---|---|---|---|
| BIS | 0.37 | 0.11 | 3.48 | <.001 | (.16, .58) |
| Age | −0.02 | 0.01 | 2.70 | .007 | (−.03, −.00) |
| NEOo | −0.02 | 0.06 | 0.28 | .782 | (−.13, −.10) |
| NEOc | −0.07 | 0.06 | 1.15 | .252 | (−.20, .05) |

Note. N = 275. SE = standard error.

In general, a predictor that has a strong, robust relation with an outcome variable will continue to have a strong partial effect even when there are several other variables in the regression model. But a potential difficulty with simultaneous regression is that when there is a large number of predictors, including them all reduces the statistical power to find that any one of them is a uniquely significant predictor (as is evident from Equation 2.10, in that a larger value of $P$ increases the standard error of any given $\hat{\beta}$). Thus, the inclusion of one or more trivial covariates might mask the contribution of a key substantive predictor.

To deal with this problem, researchers occasionally inspect the product-moment correlations between potential predictors and the outcome variable, and then they include in a simultaneous regression model only those predictors or covariates with a significant marginal correlation with the outcome. Although it is always prudent to examine descriptive statistics before proceeding with formal model fitting, as we saw previously in this chapter, this strategy has the potential to obscure important effects because the effect of a focal predictor may be made either stronger or weaker with the inclusion of a given covariate, which itself may or may not be strongly correlated with the outcome. Again, the main consideration when choosing variables for inclusion in a regression model is their theoretical role in the research questions under consideration. Or, if alternative theories imply the inclusion of other variables, then it may be important to include them as well, or to specify a different, competing model which can then be compared with the main model of interest (perhaps using the hierarchical strategy described next). Finally, if there is a conceptual reason or past empirical evidence that covariates of tangential substantive importance may also qualify the regression results, then it is also wise to estimate a model including these variables. If such variables turn out to have little influence on the model as a whole, then they might be removed to form a more parsimonious model including only the predictors directly related to the main substantive research questions.

 Section recap

### Simultaneous regression

In simultaneous regression, *all* predictor variables or covariates of potential theoretical or empirical importance are included at once in a single model.

## Hierarchical regression

**Hierarchical regression**,[10] also known as **sequential regression**, is essentially a model-comparison procedure. Here, an initial model with a smaller number of predictors (or 'block' of predictors) is compared with a subsequent model with the same predictors in the initial model plus one or more new predictors (which form a second block). If a formal null hypothesis test indicates that $R^2$ significantly increases from the initial model to the next, then one concludes that the set (or block[11]) of predictors that was added significantly explains variability of the outcome variable, over and above the controlling predictors and covariates that were in the initial model.

Reconsidering the example analysis presented earlier, suppose that the researcher considers the personality traits of openness and conscientiousness to be separate indicators of a more general trait, self-control. Consequently, the researcher would like to know whether the NEOo and NEOc, taken together as indicators of a general self-control construct, predict BPAQ aggression scores over and above the BIS scores and age. Hence, following a hierarchical procedure, the researcher specifies two models: Model 1 contains the set of controlling variables that have been shown to be important in a previous analysis, specifically BIS and age, whereas Model 2 is an expansion of Model 1 that also includes the set of self-control variables, NEOo and NEOc. That is, we have

$$\text{Model 1: } \hat{Y}_i = \beta_0 + \beta_1 X_{1i} + \beta_2 X_{2i},$$

where again $\hat{Y}_i$ is the model-predicted BPAQ score for case $i$, $X_{1i}$ is that person's BIS score, and $X_{2i}$ is her age. Next, we also have

$$\text{Model 2: } \hat{Y}_i = \beta_0 + \beta_1 X_{1i} + \beta_2 X_{2i} + \beta_3 X_{3i} + \beta_4 X_{4i},$$

where again $X_{3i}$ is her score on the NEOo scale and $X_{4i}$ is her score on the NEOc scale.

Formally speaking, Model 1 is *nested* within Model 2 because we can express Model 1 as a constrained version of Model 2 in which both $\beta_3$ and $\beta_4$ equal 0:

$$\text{Model 1: } \hat{Y}_i = \beta_0 + \beta_1 X_{1i} + \beta_2 X_{2i} + 0 \times X_{3i} + 0 \times X_{4i}.$$

This representation leads to the idea that we would like to perform a test of the joint significance of two regression coefficients, $\beta_3$ and $\beta_4$, taken together. The null hypothesis for this joint test is thus

$$\text{H}_0: \beta_3 = \beta_4 = 0;$$

---

[10]Not to be confused with *hierarchical linear modeling*, the main topic of Chapter 6.

[11]Sometimes the separate sets or 'blocks' of variables are instead called 'steps'. It is important to distinguish between this sense of the word 'step' in which the data analyst directly chooses which variables are included in a given step and the sense of the word 'step' in a 'stepwise' regression in which a computer algorithm chooses the sequence of variables. Stepwise regression is addressed later in this chapter.

that is, the population partial regression slopes for $X_{3i}$ and $X_{4i}$ both equal zero. Equivalently, we can express the null hypothesis in terms of the squared multiple correlations for Model 1 and Model 2:

$$H_0 : \rho_1^2 = \rho_2^2;$$

that is, the population proportion of variance explained is equal across the two models. Hence, if the sample $R^2$ is significantly greater for Model 2 than for Model 1, then we can conclude that the set of predictors that was added to Model 1 to form Model 2 significantly predicts the outcome variable, over and above the set of predictors in Model 1.

With our current dataset, $R^2 = .1299$ when only BIS and age are in the initial model (i.e., Model 1). When NEOo and NEOc are added to form Model 2, $R^2$ increases to .1342. The change in $R^2$ is thus $.1342 - .1299 = .0043$. Obviously this is a tiny difference, but for completeness, we can test its significance. The significance of a change in $R^2$ is tested using the $F$ statistic

$$F = \left( \frac{R_{M2}^2 - R_{M1}^2}{1 - R_{M2}^2} \right)\left( \frac{N - P_1 - P_2 - 1}{P_2} \right)$$

with $(P_2, N - P_1 - P_2 - 1)$ degrees of freedom. In this equation, $R_{M2}^2$ is $R^2$ for Model 2 (i.e., the complete model with all predictors included), $R_{M1}^2$ is $R^2$ for Model 1, $P_1$ is the number of variables in Model 1, and $P_2$ is the number of variables added to Model 1 to build Model 2. Keep in mind that this $F$ test, expressed in terms of $R^2$ values, is equivalent to a joint significance test of the individual regression coefficients for the set of predictors added to Model 1 to form Model 2. In the current example, we have

$$F = \left( \frac{R_{M2}^2 - R_{M1}^2}{1 - R_{M2}^2} \right)\left( \frac{N - P_1 - P_2 - 1}{P_2} \right) = \left( \frac{.1342 - .1299}{1 - .1342} \right)\left( \frac{275 - 2 - 2 - 1}{2} \right) = 0.67.$$

With 2 and 270 degrees of freedom, this $F$ statistic has a $p$ value $= .51$; therefore, adding the set of self-control variables, NEOo and NEOc, to the model does not account for a significant proportion of variance in BPAQ beyond that already accounted for by BIS and age.

The results from a hierarchical regression are usually given in a table like Table 2.5. Here, note that the results for Model 2 are the same results that were obtained just by following a simultaneous regression strategy from the beginning, entering the four predictors simultaneously; that is, the numerical results under Model 2 in Table 2.5 are identical to those for the simultaneous regression in Table 2.4. It is my impression that researchers often perform hierarchical regression unnecessarily when a basic simultaneous regression would be more concise and convey the same key results. Frequently, this practice occurs when researchers would like to confirm that a single, critically important predictor variable remains significantly related to the outcome variable over and above a potentially large set of controlling variables. They set up two 'blocks' of variables, the first containing all of the controlling variables, and the second containing only the final, critical variable, and they test whether $R^2$ significantly changes with the addition of the second block to the model. In other words, researchers are statistically comparing a model with $P$ predictors with a model with $P + 1$ predictors. The $F$ test corresponding to this change in $R^2$ is equivalent to the $t$ test for the single predictor added to form the second model (i.e., the single predictor in the second block) that would be obtained by estimating a single model including all $P + 1$ predictors simultaneously (specifically, $F = t^2$), rendering use of the hierarchical strategy redundant.

The main advantage of hierarchical regression, then, is that one can test whether a *group* of predictors significantly increases $R^2$ over and above a controlling set of predictors or covariates. It is possible for the increase in $R^2$ to be significant even when none of the individual regression coefficients of the added predictors is significant on its own. That is, the joint test for a set of two or more regression slope estimates will have more statistical power than any one-parameter significance test for a single predictor in the same set. Therefore, if one can justify grouping together predictors as a conceptual whole (as earlier where NEOo and NEOc are considered two indicators of a more general self-control construct), then hierarchical regression can be useful for answering research questions about that conceptual grouping.

**Table 2.5**  Hierarchical regression coefficients for BPAQ outcome variable

| Variable | $\hat{\beta}$ | $SE(\hat{\beta})$ | t | p | 95% CI |
|---|---|---|---|---|---|
| Model 1 | | | | | |
| BIS | 0.44 | 0.09 | 5.22 | <.001 | (.28, .61) |
| Age | −0.02 | 0.01 | 2.91 | .004 | (−.03, −.01) |
| Model 2 | | | | | |
| BIS | 0.37 | 0.11 | 3.48 | <.001 | (.16, .58) |
| Age | −0.02 | 0.01 | 2.70 | .007 | (−.03, −.00) |
| NEOo | −0.02 | 0.06 | 0.28 | .782 | (−.13, .10) |
| NEOc | −0.07 | 0.06 | 1.15 | .252 | (−.20, .05) |

*Note.* N = 275. $R^2$ for Model 1 = .13, F(2, 272) = 20.31, $p < .001$, $\Delta R^2$ for Model 2 = .004, F(2, 270) = 0.67, p = .51.

 Section recap

### Hierarchical regression

In **hierarchical regression**, an initial model (Model 1) with a smaller number of predictor variables is compared with a second model (Model 2) with the same predictors plus one or more additional predictors.

If $R^2$ is significantly greater (according to an $F$ test) for Model 2 than for Model 1, then the set of predictors that was added to Model 1 to form Model 2 accounts for a significant proportion of variance in the outcome variable over and above the predictors or covariates included in Model 1.

The individual regression slope estimates (and their standard errors and associated $t$ tests) in Model 2 are identical to what would have been obtained if Model 2 was estimated in just a single simultaneous regression model, without estimating Model 1. For this reason, hierarchical regression is most useful when more than one variable is added to Model 1 to form Model 2, to obtain a joint test for a set of predictors.

## Stepwise regression and other predictor selection methods

Sometimes a research study will have many predictors, and a researcher will want to construct a regression model containing the 'optimal' set of predictors with regard to maximizing multiple $R^2$ with as few predictors as possible. In this way, the researcher obtains a semblance of balance between parsimony and a thorough representation of the strongest predictors of an outcome variable. Predictor selection methods known as *forward, backward,* and *stepwise* regression undertake an atheoretical search for the optimal model from the available sample data. Because I am opposed to the use of such procedures in most situations, I only describe them briefly. Yet, it is important to address them because they do appear regularly in the behavioural and social science literature.

In **forward selection**, the predictor in the dataset (or in a set of potential predictors identified by the user) with the largest correlation with the outcome variable is entered into the model first by an automated computer algorithm. Next, the algorithm finds the predictor that leads to the largest increase in $R^2$ given that the first predictor is already in the model. The computer continues this procedure until the $R^2$ change from adding one of the remaining predictors is no longer significant (or the $R^2$ increase is no longer greater than some value prespecified by the user, such as .01). In **backward selection** (also known as backward elimination), the computer algorithm begins with all potential predictors in the model, and works 'backward' by removing the predictor which leads to a nonsignificant decrease in $R^2$ (or leads to the smallest decrease in $R^2$) and continues removing predictors one at a time, eventually obtaining a model with as few predictors as needed to maintain an overall $R^2$ value that is not substantially smaller than the $R^2$ with all possible predictors. **Stepwise regression** uses a combination of forward and backward selection: After selecting the first three predictors in a forward fashion, variables may be alternately removed (i.e., stepping backward) and added (stepping forward) until $R^2$ no longer changes substantially.

Each of these three types of predictor selection methods is *data driven* in that they completely ignore the theoretical importance or logical groupings of individual predictors. As such, these methods capitalize on chance relations in the sample which are unlikely to be replicated in another sample and, hence, are unlikely to exist in the population. Additionally, because the $F$ tests presented at each stage of the model selection procedure are 'one-at-a-time' tests that ignore the other stages, the $p$ values for these tests are incorrect because of the multiple comparison problem. Furthermore, as we will see in later chapters, certain types of predictors are meaningful only when grouped with other predictors (e.g., dummy-coded variables used to represent a multicategory variable or lower order terms grouped with higher order interaction terms), but predictor selection methods can easily lead to a model in which one of these terms is included without the others, which severely limits the interpretational meaningfulness of the model. In general, predictor selection is potentially useful when the main goal of the regression analysis is pure prediction of the values of an outcome variable with little or no interest in theoretical explanation for *why* individuals vary on the outcome variable. Even in that case, because of the tendency to capitalize on chance, models developed based on a predictor selection method should be considered tentative until they are cross-validated with a new sample. But most often in behavioural and social science, the purpose of a regression analysis is theoretical explanation, which demands that researchers carefully consider the variables to be included in a model based on theory instead of relying on one of these predictor selection methods (see Pedhazur, 1997: 211–40 for further discussion and critique).

An alternative approach to examining the relative importance among a large set of potential predictors is a class of methods known as **recursive partitioning** using *classification and regression trees*, which can overcome the pitfalls of forward, backward, and stepwise regression, to some extent. Recursive partitioning methods can also account for potential interactions and nonlinear associations among predictors and the outcome, which forward, backward, and stepwise regression cannot do. For a pedagogical description of recursive partitioning methods, see Strobl, Malley, and Tutz (2009).

 Section recap

### Predictor selection methods

Predictor selection methods, namely, **forward**, **backward**, and **stepwise regression**, rely on a computer algorithm to select a subset of predictors from a larger set of predictors, with the goal of maximizing $R^2$ using the smallest number of predictors necessary.

These predictor selection strategies *should be avoided at all costs* because

- They are completely atheoretical and can produce models with extremely limited or even nonsensical interpretations.
- They capitalize on chance relations in sample data and are based on incorrect *p* values, thereby producing results which are unlikely to replicate or adequately represent a true population model.

An alternative predictor selection method which can overcome these limitations is known as **recursive partitioning**.

## REGRESSION DIAGNOSTICS REVISITED

Regression diagnostics were introduced in Chapter 1; here I generalize those basic concepts to models with more than one predictor variable. As a reminder, regression diagnostics are methods for evaluating the extent to which an estimated regression model is a reasonable representation of the data and for evaluating the trustworthiness of inferential conclusions about the parameter estimates. Specifically, diagnostics are used to check the extent to which model assumptions have been violated and to examine whether any unusual or outlying observations may unduly affect the results.

Although I have alluded to the assumptions of the linear regression model already, here I present them more completely and formally. For the most part, the assumptions all can be stated in terms of the true model-based error term, $\varepsilon_i$, from the general multiple linear regression model given in Equation 2.9. In practice, these assumptions are assessed by examining the residuals $e_i$ based on the estimated regression model.

1. **Linearity.** This assumption is succinctly stated as $E(\varepsilon_i) = 0$; that is, the *expected value* of the error for individual *i* equals zero (i.e., the population mean of the errors equals zero) regardless of the value of $X_{pi}$, reflecting the idea that the partial relation between *Y* and

each $X$ is linear.[12] Although we can view the residual $e_i$ as an estimate of the true error $\varepsilon_i$, a consequence of OLS estimation is that the mean of the residuals always equal zero, whereas violation of the linearity assumption implies that the mean of the errors does not equal zero.

2. **Constant variance.** $VAR(\varepsilon_i) = \sigma^2$; that is, the variance of the errors is constant, or homogeneous, across all possible combinations of values for the predictors.

3. **Normality.** $\varepsilon_i \sim N(0, \sigma^2)$; that is, the errors are normally distributed with mean and constant variance as stated earlier. Recall from Chapter 1 that this assumption does not require that any of the individual observed variables, $Y$ or any $X_p$, are normally distributed.

4. **Independence.** $\varepsilon_i$, $\varepsilon_j$ are independent for $i \neq j$; that is, the errors for any two cases in the population are assumed to be independent. Although numerical diagnostics are available for assessing nonindependence (e.g., the Durbin-Watson test for time-series data), at this point, it is preferable to evaluate this assumption through careful consideration of research design rather than through any numerical or graphical diagnostic methods. For example, in psychotherapy research, the units of observation (clients) are typically clustered within different therapists delivering treatment, and thus, two clients sharing the same therapist are likely to have nonindependent errors in a regression model for treatment effects (unless the therapist effects are properly incorporated). Multilevel models, covered in Chapter 6, are often used to handle research designs such as this one which produce nonindependent cases.

5. **Each $X$ is fixed, or independent of** $\varepsilon$; that is, the predictors are measured without error. In behavioural and social science research, this assumption is often violated in the sense that many predictors are imperfect operationalizations of unobservable constructs. If this assumption is ignored (as often occurs), the estimated regression coefficients are biased (generally they are too small). If the scores for each observed $X$ have strong reliability, then this measurement error bias might be minimal. Structural equation models, the topic of Chapters 9 to 10, can be used to account for measurement error explicitly. Certain predictors such as experimental condition, gender, and age can usually be considered free of measurement error.

In sum, examination of the sample-based residuals, $e_i$, is used primarily to evaluate the linearity, constant variance, and normality assumptions, whereas the independence and fixed $X$ assumptions are more commonly addressed in terms of study design. Next, I present plots for assessing the linearity, constant variance, and normality assumptions for multiple regression, followed by brief discussions of a few procedures for addressing assumption violation, namely, *polynomial regression*, *transformations*, and *weighted least-squares* estimation. Then I address the concept of *multicollinearity*; although absence of multicollinearity is not a formal assumption of multiple regression, it is still an important concept to be aware of. This chapter ends by reviewing the concepts of leverage, discrepancy, and influence as they pertain to the examination of outlying or unusual cases in the context of multiple regression.

---

[12]Another way to state this assumption is to say that the model is 'linear in its parameters'. The important implication of this statement is that the model can contain nonlinear terms such as interaction terms (e.g., $X_3 = X_1 \times X_2$) or polynomial terms (e.g., $X_3 = X_1^2$) without producing a violation of the linearity assumption, despite the fact that the regression surface for a model with such terms is not flat. Technically, if we define the deterministic component of the model in Equation 2.9 as $\mu = \beta_0 + \beta_1 X_{1i} + \ldots + \beta_p X_{pi}$, then the model is linear in its parameters if the partial derivatives of $\mu$ with respect to its parameters are not themselves a function of the parameters.

## Linearity and constant variance

In Chapter 1, the adequacy of the simple linear regression model for the relation between a dependent variable $Y$ and a single predictor $X$ was examined with a scatterplot of $Y$ by $X$ (see Figure 1.5). In the multiple regression context, it is informative to construct separate scatterplots of $Y$ by each predictor as a matter of data exploration. But as explained earlier, such a plot only depicts the marginal relation between $Y$ and a given predictor $X_p$, whereas the multiple regression model is concerned with the partial relation between $Y$ and $X_p$, holding the other predictors constant. Consequently, scatterplots of the marginal relations between $Y$ and each $X$ are insufficient for assessing the linearity and constant variance assumptions for a multiple regression model. Instead, plotting the model's residuals against each predictor is a more direct way of assessing whether the partial relations are linear and whether the spread of residuals is constant across the values of a given $X_p$.

For example, consider again the regression of BPAQ scores ($Y$) on BIS scores ($X_1$) and age ($X_2$) presented earlier. With this model fitted to the data, a plot of the residuals ($e_i$) against BIS ($X_1$) appears in Figure 2.6. In general, if the linear model is correct, then the residuals are independent of the predictors and therefore a plot of residuals by a given predictor should be a *null plot* in the sense that there are no systematic features in the plot, such as nonlinear trends or trends related to the variation or spread of residuals. Figure 2.6 is reasonably interpreted as a null plot; the added LOWESS regression line does not pick up any strong nonlinear pattern in the residuals, and the variation of residuals (the vertical spread of residuals) is relatively consistent across the values of BIS (the horizontal axis; to aid this visualization, the plot is enhanced with dashed lines representing a smoothed nonparametric estimate of the positive and negative residual variance from the LOWESS curve following Fox and Weisberg, 2011: 117–18).

Using the same model, Figure 2.7 depicts a plot of residuals against age ($X_2$). Unlike Figure 2.6, there does appear to be a nonlinear trend in the residuals as a function of age, such that residuals tend to increase up to age 19 or so and then decrease to age 23 or 24

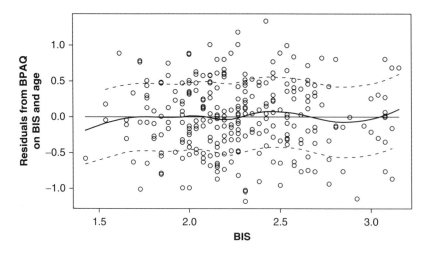

**Figure 2.6** Scatterplot of residuals against BIS scores with fitted LOWESS curve (solid line) and smoothed nonparametric positive and negative residual variance from the LOWESS curve (dashed lines)

before leveling out. Therefore, there seems to be a nonlinear relation between age and BPAQ scores that is not captured by the basic two-predictor linear regression of BPAQ on BIS and age, and it may be advisable to revise the model to account for this nonlinear pattern (using, for example, polynomial terms for age, which are introduced later). Despite this nonlinear pattern, the spread of the residuals is relatively homogenous as a function of age. Here, the nonparametric smoothed estimation of the variance function is especially helpful because there are many more observations at younger ages than at older ages. Without this plot enhancement, one might be tempted to conclude that the residuals are more spread out at younger ages than at older ages, but this interpretation neglects that there are many observations with small residuals clustered tightly together around ages 18 and 19. Yet, the dashed lines representing the spread of residuals are for the most part evenly spaced vertically across the values of age. Nonetheless, the fact that there are many fewer cases at the older ages still indicates that one should be careful about interpreting any age effects (or lack of effect) in these data, including the nonlinear trend.

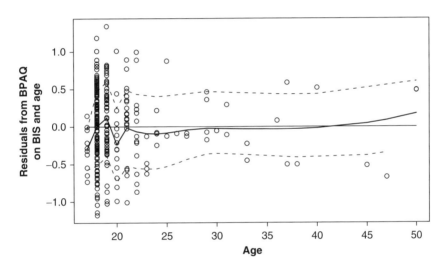

**Figure 2.7** Scatterplot of residuals against age with fitted LOWESS curve (solid line) and smoothed nonparametric positive and negative residual variance from the LOWESS curve (dashed lines)

It is also common to assess the linearity and homogeneity of variance assumptions by plotting the residuals against $\hat{Y}$, where $\hat{Y}$ of course represents the predicted value of $Y$ as a function of all $X$s in the model taken together. It is somewhat common for residual variance to increase as $\hat{Y}$ increases, indicating nonconstant variance. Figure 2.8 shows the plot of residuals by predicted values for the regression of BPAQ scores ($Y$) on BIS scores ($X_1$) and age ($X_2$). In this plot, it does appear as if the spread of the residuals is somewhat constant across the predicted values. There is a slight indication of nonlinearity in the LOWESS curve which results from the age effects noted earlier; because this curvature is slight, it is likely that the overall results from the model are not strongly distorted by any nonlinear influence of age. Plots of residuals against observed predictors (i.e., each $X_p$) or predicted values (i.e., $\hat{Y}$) can also reveal the presence of outliers or unusual cases. There are no clear outliers in Figures 2.6 to 2.8 (with the possible exception of a case with an extremely low predicted value in Figure 2.8). But should an outlier be detected, it may be a good or bad leverage case or may have little influence, as described in Chapter 1 and again later in this chapter.

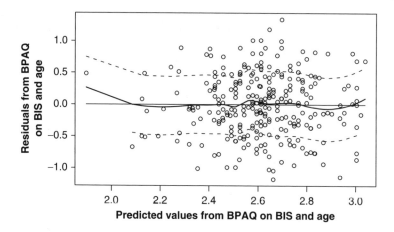

**Figure 2.8**  Scatterplot of residuals against predicted values with fitted LOWESS curve (solid line) and smoothed nonparametric positive and negative residual variance from the LOWESS curve (dashed lines)

## Normality

In Chapter 1, the assumption of normally distributed errors was evaluated simply by looking at a univariate histogram of a residuals; the same approach can be used in the multiple regression context. A histogram of the residuals from the regression of BPAQ on BIS and

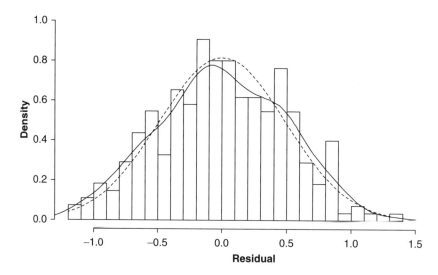

**Figure 2.9**  Histogram of residuals from regression of BPAQ on BIS and age with fitted kernel density smoother (solid curve) and fitted normal distribution (dashed curve)

age, enhanced with a fitted normal distribution and nonparametric density smoother, is in Figure 2.9. In this example, it is clear that the residuals are approximately normally distributed; there are no strong differences between the fitted normal curve and the smoothed density estimate.

## Consequences of assumption violation and remedies

When a model is estimated using a large sample size, as in our model of BPAQ scores ($N = 275$), multiple regression with OLS estimation can tolerate a considerable degree of assumption violation in that general substantive conclusions are unlikely to be grossly incorrect. But, if the *functional form* of the model (so far, a linear function is the only functional form we have addressed) is badly misspecified, such that a linear model is fitted to a strongly nonlinear data pattern among variables, then severe problems may occur, such as radically misleading slope coefficient estimates and significance tests. As discussed in Chapter 1, a common situation in which a linear regression model represents a misspecification occurs when the dependent variable is categorical. If the outcome has only two categories, then a linear model is a radical misspecification and a logistic regression model will likely be a superior alternative. If the outcome has more than two ordered categories, then ordinal logistic regression is often preferable to linear modeling, whereas an outcome with more than two nominal categories may be appropriately modeled with multinomial logistic regression. Logistic regression models are beyond the scope of this text; for detailed treatments, see Agresti (2002) or Fox (2008), among others. For better or worse, ordered, categorical outcome-variable data are frequently fitted to linear models in the behavioural and social sciences; when the number of categories is large (e.g., seven or more), then a linear model might give a reasonable representation of the data. But it is always wise to check plots of residuals to satisfy oneself of the adequacy of a linear model.

Of course, even continuous dependent variables can be nonlinearly related to a given predictor. As has been demonstrated, a nonparametric LOWESS curve can be used to help describe the nature of such nonlinear relations (although LOWESS curves tend to be useful only when $N > 100$ or so). But because these curves are nonparametric, they are not particularly useful for theoretical explanation or confirmation. Alternatively, curvilinear relations can be explicitly modeled using a polynomial regression model which, as described later, is really just a simple application of the multiple regression modeling approach already developed in this chapter.

Next, violation of the normality or constant variance assumptions for OLS regression still produces unbiased and consistent parameter estimates, but the efficiency of the estimates is compromised. Consequently, significance tests for $R^2$ and the individual regression coefficients have less power and confidence intervals are wider than when assumptions are met. Non-normal observed variables (particularly non-normal outcome variables) are commonly transformed to result in a new variable with a distribution more closely approximating a normal distribution, which is then included in a regression model in place of the original variable; the residuals from this model may then more closely approximate a normal distribution and may display less heteroscedasticity. Another potential remedy for nonhomogeneous variance is to use weighted least-squares (WLS) estimation in place of OLS. Transformations and WLS are briefly discussed later in this chapter.

 Section recap

**Assumptions for OLS estimation of linear regression models**

The assumptions for linear regression with OLS estimation can be formally expressed in terms of the errors from the population regression model:

1. If the partial association between each $X_p$ and $Y$ is linear, then $E(\varepsilon_i) = 0$; that is, the *expected value* of the error for individual $i$ equals zero regardless of the value of $X_{pi}$. This assumption can be checked with scatterplots of residuals against each $X_p$ or against $\hat{Y}$.

2. $VAR(\varepsilon_i) = \sigma^2$; that is, the variance of the errors is homogeneous across all possible combinations of values for the predictors. This assumption also can be checked with scatterplots of residuals against each $X_p$ or against $\hat{Y}$.

3. $\varepsilon_i \sim N(0, \sigma^2)$; that is, the errors are normally distributed with mean $= 0$ and constant variance. This assumption can be checked by graphing the univariate distribution of the residuals.

4. $\varepsilon_i, \varepsilon_j$ are independent for $i \neq j$; that is, the errors for any two cases in the population are assumed to be independent. This assumption is checked by careful consideration of a study's research design, particularly its sampling scheme.

5. Each $X$ is fixed, or independent of $\varepsilon$; that is, the predictors are measured without error. This assumption can be satisfied by ensuring that the scores on the predictors are highly reliable.

## Polynomial regression

If there is a curvilinear relation between a continuous outcome variable and a given predictor, $X_p$, then we can model the curvature using a **polynomial regression** model. This class of models includes terms for $X_p^k$ to represent the nonlinear relation between a dependent variable $Y$ and $X_p$, where the exponent $k$ gives the *order* of the model. For example, the polynomial regression of order $k = 2$, or the **quadratic regression** of $Y$ on a single $X$, includes both a linear term $X$ and a quadratic term $X^2$ so that the model is

$$Y_i = \beta_0 + \beta_1 X_i + \beta_2 X_i^2 + \varepsilon_i.$$

We can then proceed with OLS estimation to get estimates of the parameters $\beta_0$, $\beta_1$, and $\beta_2$. Specifically, the quadratic term $X^2$ is treated as just another variable in the model; that is, the previous model is equivalent to

$$Y_i = \beta_0 + \beta_1 X_{1i} + \beta_2 X_{2i} + \varepsilon_i$$

with $X_{2i} = X_{1i}^2$. If $\hat{\beta}_2$ is large, then there is substantial curvature in the relation between $X$ and $Y$, such that a scatterplot of $Y$ by $X$ should depict a single 'bend' in the data that is easily discerned visually.

The **cubic regression** of $Y$ on $X$ includes terms for $X$, $X^2$, and $X^3$:

$$Y_i = \beta_0 + \beta_1 X_i + \beta_2 X_i^2 + \beta_3 X_i^3 + \varepsilon_i.$$

Here, if $\hat{\beta}_3$ is large, then the curvature in the relation between $X$ and $Y$ is such that there is more than one visually apparent bend in the relation between $Y$ and $X$. More complex polynomial models are possible (i.e., models including $X^4$, $X^5$, and so on), but in practice, such effects are extremely difficult to interpret and usually represent an overfitting to data such that the model captures chance relations that are not replicable (regardless of their potential statistical significance in a given sample).

Note that in these polynomial models, terms for each power of $X$ up to the order $k$ are included as predictors of $Y$. That is, for the quadratic model, which is a polynomial model of order $k = 2$, terms are included for both $k = 1$ (i.e., $X^1 = X$) and for $k = 2$ (i.e., $X^2$).[13] The cubic model of order $k = 3$ therefore includes the terms $X^1$, $X^2$, and $X^3$. Additionally, it is important to recognize that it is possible to form a model in which there are nonlinear polynomial terms for one predictor whereas other predictors enter the model strictly linearly.

In Figure 2.7, we saw that the residuals from the regular linear regression of BPAQ scores on age and BIS scores seem to have a nonlinear relation with age, whereas in Figure 2.6, the residuals from this model are approximately linearly related to BIS scores. Therefore, it may be informative to expand this model to include nonlinear polynomial terms for the age predictor but retain only the linear term for BIS. Specifically, in Figure 2.7, it seems that the residuals from the regression of BPAQ scores on BIS and age increase as age increases from 17 to 19, go back down again from age 19 to 23, and then level out with older ages. Thus, there is more than one bend in the scatterplot, implying that a cubic (or even higher order) effect of age may be present. Nonetheless, a model with a cubic effect of age and a linear effect of BIS does not have a significantly greater $R^2$ than the original model with only linear terms for both age and BIS, $\delta R^2 = .005$, $F(2, 270) = 0.73$, $p = .48$. Therefore, the original linear model without the cubic effect of age seems to provide an adequate representation of the data; that is, the data only support the simpler conclusion that BPAQ scores tend to decrease with age. For a more complete treatment of the specification and interpretation of polynomial regression models, see Cohen, Cohen, West, and Aiken (2003: 196–215).

## Transformations

The residuals from a regression model are often (but not always) non-normal when the outcome variable is itself non-normal. As mentioned, **transformation** of a non-normal outcome variable often improves the distribution of residuals such that they more closely approximate a normal distribution, and transformation can also improve heteroscedasticity and nonlinearity and reduce the influence of extreme observations.

Specifically, a pronounced positive skewness can be reduced using a log-based transformation or a square root transformation (among other possibilities). For example, if $Y$ is positively

---

[13]Technically, there is also a term for $k = 0$ because $X^0 = 1$, and we can consider the intercept $\beta_0$ to be the regression coefficient for a constant $= 1$. See Chapter 7.

skewed, we might create a new variable $Y' = \ln(Y)$ or $Y' = \sqrt{Y}$. We then use $Y'$ as the out-come in a regression model and again proceed with OLS estimation. The residuals from the regression of $Y'$ should then be more normally distributed than those from a regression of the original, untransformed variable. Similarly, excess negative skewness can be reduced by squaring the variable (among other possibilities). More formally, routines such as the *Box-Cox* procedure (see Box and Cox, 1964) have been developed to determine the optimal transfor-mation for a given non-normally distributed variable (see Cohen, Cohen, West, and Aiken, 2003: 236–8). Regardless of the transformation chosen for a given variable, it is critical that the rank-ordering of cases not be affected. For example, if the original, $Y$ has both positive and negative observations, squaring $Y$ will make all observations positive, and consequently the lowest values of $Y$ (i.e., the most negative) may artificially become the largest, which in turn will lead to radically incorrect conclusions for any modeling of $Y' = Y^2$. A solution to this problem is to add a constant value to all observations of $Y$ so that they are all positive before squaring $Y$. Adding a constant as a part of a transformation can also help avoid illegal arith-metical operations, such as taking a logarithm of 0 or the square root of a negative number.

In general, researchers are often hesitant to analyse transformed variables because of the added interpretational complexity. For example, if $Y' = \ln(Y)$ is regressed on $X$, then the regres-sion coefficient $\beta$ for $X$ represents the predicted difference in the natural log of $Y$ that's associ-ated with a one-unit increase in $X$. But here, the effect of $X$ can easily be expressed in terms of the original scale of $Y$ by calculating the antilog, or exponentiation, of $\beta$; that is, $\exp(\beta) = e^\beta$. The exponentiated coefficient $\exp(\beta)$ then represents the predicted change in the original scale of $Y$ per one-unit increase of $X$. This idea of back-transforming regression coefficients can be used for any transformation of $Y$. Therefore, added interpretational difficulty seems like a small price to pay for obtaining more efficient regression estimates which have narrower confidence intervals and are more likely to be statistically significant. But, if a researcher finds that her major substantive conclusions are similar regardless of whether she models a trans-formed variable, as often occurs, then it is likely preferable to report results from the model of the original, untransformed variable.

## Weighted least squares

As an alternative to transformation, another method for handling heteroscedasticity (i.e., non-homogenous variance) is to estimate a regression model using WLS instead of OLS. In WLS, the goal is to find parameter estimates that minimize the weighted sum of squared residuals:

$$\sum_{i=1}^{N} w_i e_i^2 = \sum_{i=1}^{N} w_i (Y_i - \hat{Y}_i)^2,$$

where $w_i$, the weight for case $i$, depends on the variance of $e_i$ given the observed combina-tion of values of the predictors for case $i$. Under heteroscedasticity, WLS estimates are more efficient than OLS estimates, meaning that there is greater power for significance tests and confidence intervals are narrower compared with OLS. Nevertheless, there is considerable practical difficulty in conducting WLS, and so it is not particularly effective unless $N$ is large or homogeneity of variance is severely violated.

 Section recap

### Handling violated assumptions

Linear regression models estimated with OLS are robust to assumption violations, especially when $N$ is large.

Nonetheless, a nonlinear association between $Y$ and a given $X_p$ might be effectively modeled using **polynomial regression**, which is an adaptation of the linear regression model to include higher order powers of $X_p$ (such as $X_p^2$ for **quadratic regression** or $X_p^3$ for **cubic regression**).

If the residuals from a given model are highly non-normal or heteroscedastic, then instead fitting the model to a suitable **transformation** of $Y$ (such as $\ln(Y)$ or $\sqrt{Y}$) can produce residuals with a distribution better approximating normality and with less heteroscedasticity.

## Multicollinearity

As shown earlier in this chapter, in multiple regression, the partial relation between a predictor and the outcome variable is adjusted by the amount that the predictor is correlated with the other predictors in the model (e.g., Equation 2.4). When the correlations among predictors become close to 1 (or there is a more subtle, but regular, association among two or more predictors), there is substantial redundancy among predictors and, thus, an individual predictor contributes little *unique* information to the prediction of $Y$. This situation is known as **multicollinearity**. Multicollinearity can cause a host of problems for a regression analysis. In particular, individual regression coefficients can change dramatically in magnitude and even go from positive to negative (or vice versa) when a predictor is added that introduces multicollinearity. Also, the standard errors of slope estimates become inflated, leading to wide confidence intervals and low power. Fortunately, though, multicollinearity is a rare problem for the use of linear regression models in behavioural and social science (Fox, 2008) as long as researchers are careful and thoughtful about their selection of predictor variables for a model.

An easy and obvious way to check for potential multicollinearity is to inspect the simple, bivariate correlations among the candidate predictors for a regression model. In my experience, multicollinearity is usually not a concern until a correlation between two predictors becomes large, above .75 or so. There are situations, however, when problematic multicollinearity is not apparent just from the correlations among predictors. Thus, it is prudent to supplement regression diagnostic procedures with statistics that can help determine whether multicollinearity is likely to be a problem for an estimated model. A prominent example of such a statistic is the **variance inflation factor**, or *VIF*. This statistic describes the amount that the squared standard error of each estimated regression slope coefficient (i.e., the estimated variance of the sampling distribution of the parameter estimate) is increased relative to a hypothetical situation in which all of the predictor variables in the model are completely uncorrelated (refer to Equation 2.10 to see how the correlations among predictors influence the standard error of an estimated partial regression slope). A VIF statistic can be calculated for each predictor in a model; the VIF for generic predictor $X_p$ is

$$VIF_p = \frac{1}{1 - R^2_{X_p|X_{(-p)}}},$$

where $R^2_{X_p|X_{(-p)}}$ is the $R^2$ value obtained from a regression of $X_p$ on all other predictors. When $X_p$ is completely orthogonal (i.e., uncorrelated) to all other predictors, then it has $VIF = 1$; as predictors become more strongly correlated, VIF increases. Another commonly reported multicollinearity statistic is known as **tolerance**, or TOL, which is merely the inverse of VIF; that is,

$$TOL_p = \frac{1}{VIF_p}.$$

Thus, stronger correlations among predictors produce lower values of TOL.

If the VIF for a given predictor equals 4 (which is equivalent to $TOL = .25$), then its standard error is twice as large as it would be if the correlations among predictors all equaled zero. Therefore, variables with VIF of approximately 4 or larger may warrant further attention. Sophisticated methods are available for estimating models in which there is substantial multicollinearity among predictors (e.g., *ridge regression*). But in my experience, substantial multicollinearity is most likely to occur when researchers are careless about their choices of predictor variables for a given regression model. In these instances, close consideration of the substantive meaning of each predictor often reveals that one or more of them has substantial conceptual redundancy with another. Removing one of these problematic predictors then makes the multicollinearity issue disappear (see Fox, 2008: 342–43 for discussion). For example, multicollinearity is likely to be problematic when a set of predictors includes various subscales from a particular test or questionnaire as well as the total score of the test (the total score is linearly dependent on, and thus highly correlated with, any individual subscale score). A more subtle form of multicollinearity may occur when two variables that are near-polar opposites are included as predictors, such as two separate scales representing positive and negative mood.

As another example, suppose a researcher was interested in the effects of socioeconomic status (SES) on undergraduate grade-point average (GPA). To represent SES, the researcher might have several variables, including mother's income, father's income, and indexes of mother's and father's education. These predictor variables are likely to be highly correlated, potentially leading to high VIFs. But the researcher may view the model's representation of SES as incomplete if one or more of these predictors is removed from the model. Another solution, then, is to view these four variables as a *set* representing SES generally and to use hierarchical regression to determine whether this set of SES variables improves the prediction of GPA. In doing so, the researcher should focus exclusively on $R^2$ change for this set of predictors and its significance without paying attention to the individual coefficients or significance of any of the four SES variables separately because their individual coefficients and their standard errors are likely distorted by multicollinearity (but the $R^2$ change for the set of four predictors is not).

## Section recap

### Multicollinearity

**Multicollinearity**, which may be measured with the **variance inflation factor** (*VIF*), occurs when predictors are highly correlated with each other or there is otherwise a strong pattern of interdependence among them. Excess multicollinearity can have a drastic impact on multiple regression results.

Fortunately, problematic multicollinearity is uncommon in the behavioural and social sciences as long as researchers are thoughtful about choice of predictor variables for a given model.

## Examining outliers and influential observations

The concepts of **leverage**, **discrepancy**, and **influence** work essentially the same way for multiple regression as with simple regression. In simple regression, we could look at a simple two-dimensional scatterplot of $Y$ by $X$ to find outliers with large leverage or discrepancy. But with multiple regression, the regression surface has more than two dimensions and so it is difficult to discern from a plot of observed data whether a given case has large leverage, discrepancy, or influence on the regression parameters. Therefore, the numerical measures of leverage, discrepancy, and influence (which themselves may be plotted), which were defined and illustrated in Chapter 1, are much more valuable in the context of multiple regression.

The leverage, or hat value, of a given case is the extent to which a case differs from the rest of the cases in terms of scores on the set of predictors in the regression model only. The formula for the hat value of a given case from a simple, one-predictor model was given in Chapter 1 (Equation 1.15). With more than one predictor in a model, $h_i$, the hat value for case $i$, is expressed using a matrix formula because it must be a function of multiple predictors simultaneously. This matrix formula is presented in Chapter 7, but for now, recognize that $h_i$ measures the distance of case $i$ from the center of the multivariate distribution, or the 'centroid', of all predictor variables. Figure 2.10 gives an index plot of the hat values from

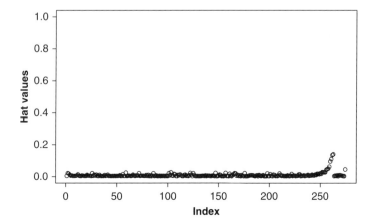

**Figure 2.10** Index plot of hat values from the regression of BPAQ on BIS and age

the multiple regression of BPAQ on BIS and age using the sample of $N = 275$ undergraduates presented earlier. The scale of this plot is set based on the fact that hat values can range from 0 to 1. Therefore, because none of the hat values approaches or exceeds 1, we can easily see that none of the cases in this dataset has extreme leverage (which might be mildly surprising because the age variable is strongly positively skewed).

Discrepancy is the extent to which case $i$ has an extreme value of $Y$ relative to its predicted value $\hat{Y}_i$; in other words, discrepancy is just the magnitude of the residual for case $i$ $(e_i = Y_i - \hat{Y}_i)$ for both the simple and multiple regression contexts. But as presented in Chapter 1, discrepancy is usually measured using externally Studentized residuals, which was defined in Equation 1.17, because the scale of the raw residuals is the same as the scale of the $Y$ variable itself. Figure 2.11 gives an index plot of the Studentized residuals from the regression of BPAQ on BIS and age. Because each $e_i^*$ is distributed as a $t$ statistic, we expect most values to fall between −2 and +2, with values well outside the range of −2.5 to +2.5 considered outliers. Therefore, none of the Studentized residuals in Figure 2.11 appears excessively outlying.

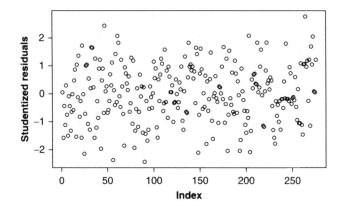

**Figure 2.11** Index plot of externally Studentized residuals from the regression of BPAQ on BIS and age

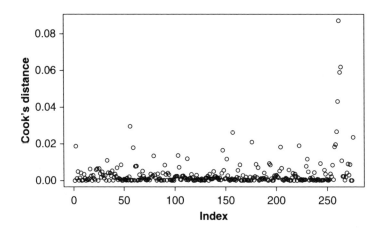

**Figure 2.12** Index plot of Cook's distance from the regression of BPAQ on BIS and age

Finally, influence combines both leverage and discrepancy to measure the extent to which a case influences a model's parameter estimates. Recall from Chapter 1 that Cook's distance, or $D_i$ (Equation 1.18), is a common measure of influence, with larger values of $D_i$ indicative of greater influence for case $i$ (another common influence statistic is *DFFITS*). Figure 2.12 shows an index plot of $D_i$ from the regression of BPAQ on BIS and age. A case with $D_i$ around 1 or greater may be considered influential. In Figure 2.12 none of the cases has a $D$ anywhere close to 1; therefore, none of them is excessively influential.

## Section recap

### Outliers and unusual observations in multiple regression

The concepts of leverage, discrepancy, and influence developed in Chapter 1 for simple regression easily generalize to multiple regression.

In multiple regression, leverage can again be measured with hat values, discrepancy can be measured with externally Studentized residuals, and influence can be measured with Cook's distance.

## CHAPTER SUMMARY

The principal objective of this chapter was to develop the major principles underlying multiple linear regression. The principles described in this chapter provide a foundation for the more advanced statistical models presented in the remainder of the text:

- The *P*-predictor multiple linear regression model can be expressed as

$$Y_i = \beta_0 + \left( \sum_{p=1}^{P} \beta_p X_{pi} \right) + \varepsilon_i,$$

  where $P$, the total number of predictors, is any finite integer greater than or equal to 1. The intercept, $\beta_0$, is the predicted value of $Y$ when all predictors equal zero.

  ○ The partial regression slope coefficient $\beta_p$ gives the expected change in $Y$ per one-unit increase in $X_p$, while holding all other predictors in the model constant.
  ○ The error term, $\varepsilon_i = (Y_i - \hat{Y}_i)$, is the difference between $Y_i$, the observed score on the outcome variable for individual $i$, and $\hat{Y}_i$, the score on the outcome that's predicted from individual $i$'s scores on all $P$ predictors.

- The parameters of the multiple linear regression model are most often estimated using ordinary least squares (OLS), which provides the intercept and slope estimates that minimize the sum of squared residuals, $SS_e = \sum_{i=1}^{N} e_i^2 = \sum_{i=1}^{N} (Y_i - \hat{Y}_i)^2$.
- The partial regression slope coefficient for a given $X_p$ obtained in a multiple regression model can be smaller or larger (or can have a different sign) than the marginal slope coefficient for the same $X_p$ obtained using a simple regression model that ignores the other predictors.
- Given an estimated regression model, the correlation between $Y$ and $\hat{Y}$, where $\hat{Y}$ represents the optimal linear combination of the predictors in the model, is known as **multiple R**. Multiple $R^2$ represents the proportion of outcome variable variance explained by the linear combination of the predictors.

- In **simultaneous regression**, all predictor variables or covariates of potential theoretical or empirical importance are included at once in a single model.
- In **hierarchical regression**, an initial model (Model 1) with a smaller number of predictor variables is compared with a second model (Model 2) with the same predictors plus one or more additional predictors.
- Predictor selection methods, namely, **forward**, **backward**, and **stepwise regression**, should be avoided.
- The assumptions for linear regression with OLS estimation can be formally expressed in terms of the errors from the population regression model:

  1. If the partial association between each $X_p$ and $Y$ is linear, then $E(\varepsilon_i) = 0$. This assumption can be checked with scatterplots of residuals against each $X_p$ or against $\hat{Y}$.
  2. $VAR(\varepsilon_i) = \sigma^2$; that is, the variance of the errors is homogeneous across all possible combinations of values for the predictors. This assumption also can be checked with scatterplots of residuals against each $X_p$ or against $\hat{Y}$.
  3. $\varepsilon_i \sim N(0, \sigma^2)$; that is, the errors are normally distributed with mean and variance of 0 and $\sigma^2$. This assumption can be checked by graphing the univariate distribution of the residuals.
  4. $\varepsilon_i, \varepsilon_j$ are independent for $i \neq j$. This assumption is checked by careful consideration of a study's research design, particularly its sampling scheme.
  5. Each $X$ is fixed, or independent of $\varepsilon$; that is, the predictors are measured without error. This assumption can be satisfied by ensuring that the scores on the predictors are highly reliable.

- **Multicollinearity**, which may be measured with the **variance inflation factor** (*VIF*), occurs when predictors are highly correlated with each other or there is otherwise a strong pattern of interdependence among them.

## RECOMMENDED READING

King, G. (1986). How not to lie with statistics: Avoiding common mistakes in quantitative political science. *American Journal of Political Science, 30,* 666–87.

- Despite coming from a political science perspective, the issues addressed in this nontechnical, didactic paper are equally prevalent in other behavioural and social sciences (now as in 1986). In particular, King discusses common misconceptions regarding standardized regression coefficients, multiple $R^2$, and the use of dichotomous variables in multiple regression.

Monette, G. (1990). Geometry of multiple regression and interactive 3-D graphics. In J. Fox & J.S. Long (Eds), *Modern methods of data analysis* (pp. 209–56). Newbury Park, CA: SAGE.

- Through the use of interesting examples and numerous graphs, Monette shows that substantial insight about multiple regression (and associated confidence intervals) can be gained by considering its underlying geometry.

Pek, J., & Flora, D.B. (In press). Reporting effect sizes in original psychological research: A discussion and tutorial. *Psychological Methods.* doi:dx.doi.org/10.1037/met0000126

- This paper offers a general discussion of effect-size reporting practices, emphasizing the value of unstandardized effect-size (e.g., unstandardized partial regression slopes) interpretation compared with standardized effect-size interpretation. Although most of the basic ideas are couched in terms of the multiple regression context or even simpler situations, the paper presents additional examples pertaining to statistical models discussed in later chapters of this text (e.g., ANOVA model, a regression model with an interaction, and a mediation model).

# REGRESSION WITH CATEGORICAL PREDICTORS

## CHAPTER OVERVIEW

Whereas Chapters 1 and 2 focused on simple and multiple regression models with continuous predictor variables, this chapter shows how categorical predictors can be incorporated into multiple regression models. In fact, following the concept of the general linear model, this chapter describes how any combination of continuous and categorical predictors can be included in a regression model. The main topics of this chapter include:

- Introduction to the concept of the general linear model
- Using dummy-code variables in regression models
- Expression of the analysis-of-variance (ANOVA) model as a multiple regression model
- Using contrast-code variables in regression models
- The analysis of covariance (ANCOVA) model and beyond
- Regression diagnostics with categorical predictors

**Table 3.0**  Greek letter notation used in this chapter

| Greek letter | English name | Represents |
| --- | --- | --- |
| $\beta$ | Lowercase 'beta' | Regression model parameter (intercept or slope, depending on subscript) |
| $\varepsilon$ | Lowercase 'epsilon' | Regression model error term |
| $\mu$ | Lowercase 'mu' | Population mean |
| $\eta$ | Lowercase 'eta' | $\eta^2$ is an effect size statistic equivalent to $R^2$ |
| $\psi$ | Lowercase 'psy' | A linear contrast |

## WHAT IS THE GENERAL LINEAR MODEL?

For several decades, data-analytic practice in behavioural research was falsely dichotomized into 'ANOVA methods' for data from controlled, randomized experiments and 'correlational methods' for data from observational studies without manipulated variables.[1] Through much of the 20th century, psychological research in particular was dominated by traditional, controlled experiments, and much modern research continues to involve experimental designs, the advantages of which are the isolation of the effects of a small number (e.g., one or two) of key independent variables and the ability to draw causal inferences unambiguously. Experimental designs typically involve one or two categorical independent variables (i.e., the variables manipulated to form discrete categories or groups) and a continuous dependent variable, which are precisely the types of variables for which Sir Ronald Fisher developed ANOVA around the year 1920. The statistical properties of the various forms of ANOVA are thoroughly understood and ANOVA continues to be well suited for the analysis of traditional, experimental data (therefore, its popularity continues); I have no criticism of the careful use of ANOVA for research designs (experimental or not) with only few categorical independent variables and a continuous dependent variable. Unfortunately, many researchers are comfortable analysing data *only* with ANOVA approaches, and many textbooks and statistics courses place excessive emphasis on ANOVA despite that many research designs produce data that cannot be adequately analysed using a traditional ANOVA method. A particularly egregious, yet common, data analytic practice involves categorizing a continuous predictor variable (often using a 'median split' to create 'high' and 'low' categories artificially) to render data into the ANOVA paradigm, which in turn can lead to grossly incorrect conclusions (see MacCallum, Zhang, Preacher, and Rucker, 2002). In other situations, a research design might include some combination of categorical and continuous independent variables or predictors. Here, the standard ANOVA can be expanded to include one or more continuous predictors, or covariates, to form what is known as **analysis of covariance**, or **ANCOVA**. Like ANOVA, the goal of ANCOVA is to analyse differences among the dependent variable means of the groups formed by the categorical independent variable(s), but in ANCOVA, these means are 'adjusted' based on one or more continuous covariates (ANCOVA is fully addressed later in this chapter).

It turns out, though, that multiple regression can incorporate a combination of any type and number of independent variables or predictors. Any predictor can be categorical or continuous and can arise from an experimental manipulation or naturalistic observation, and different types of predictors can be included within a single model. In fact, the statistical models representing group-mean differences in traditional ANOVA and ANCOVA (and even the between-groups *t* test for that matter) are specific types of multiple regression models, as we will see in this chapter. Reflecting its capacity to incorporate any combination of categorical and continuous predictors, the multiple regression model is often referred to as the **general linear model** (GLM), of which the ANOVA and ANCOVA models are special cases. Thus, the perspective that 'ANOVA is for experimental data; correlation and regression are for observational data' is patently false because ANOVA *is* a type of regression. Instead, we

---

[1]In this section of this chapter, the term 'ANOVA' pertains specifically to the partitioning of dependent variable variance into between-groups variance as a result of one or more discrete independent variables and within-groups variance, rather than the more general form of ANOVA, 'analysis of regression variance,' described in Chapter 2 in which dependent variable variance is partitioned into variance explained by any linear regression model and residual variance.

can view multiple regression, that is, the GLM, as a general data analytic system which can be applied to data from an extremely wide variety of research designs. This view was brought to the attention of the psychological research community by Cohen (1968), but regrettably, the false idea that separate statistical methods are needed for experimental and observational data has persisted to some extent. As modern research designs become more sophisticated, studies involving experimental manipulation often also involve nonmanipulated, observational predictors or covariates, which necessitates moving beyond the restrictive ANOVA model. But even for a simple one-way design with no continuous predictors, certain insights about the data which arise naturally from a regression modeling approach are not as easily obtained with a traditional ANOVA analysis, as we will see later. As discussed in Chapter 1, the major goal of statistical modeling is to find the model that optimally matches the research design and includes parameters pertaining to the main research questions. General linear modeling is an extremely flexible approach for attaining that goal across a wide variety of research studies.

To begin, recall that in Chapter 1, we saw that the relation between a continuous outcome variable and a dichotomous predictor (i.e., an independent variable with only two categories, such as biological sex) is guaranteed to be linear. Specifically, given any assignment of numerical values to the two categories of the binary variable to form predictor $X$, the simple regression model

$$\hat{Y}_i = \beta_0 + \beta_1 X_i$$

is the formula of the line connecting the two points formed by the mean of $Y$ at one value of $X$ and the mean of $Y$ at the other value of $X$ (see Figure 1.6). Furthermore, the $t$ test for the significance of the estimate $\hat{\beta}$ is equivalent to the independent-groups $t$ test comparing the means of $Y$ across the two groups. These insights pertain to any coding method used to assign numerical values to $X$. For example, if the dichotomous variable is sex, then males could be assigned $X = -1$ and females $X = +1$; or we could have $X = 1$ for males and $X = 2$ for females. Even a silly coding such as $X = 1.2$ for males and $X = 517.0$ for females would produce the statistical results just described; that is, the regression of $Y$ on $X$ would still be linear and the $t$ test for $\hat{\beta}$ would be identical to the between-groups $t$ test, but the actual values of the regression intercept and slope would change according to the coding of $X$. Thus, the assignment of numerical codes to the categories of a binary variable is arbitrary; as long as two different values are used to represent the two different categories of the predictor, then the simple linear regression described earlier is legitimate. But, as we saw in Chapter 1, if the coding system is chosen so that the values of $X$ for the two groups differ by exactly 1 (e.g., male = 0 and female = 1 or male = 1 and female = 2), then the estimated regression slope for $X$ equals the difference between the two sample means of $Y$ across the two levels of $X$. Finally, if the coding system is even more specifically chosen so that one level of $X$ equals 0 and the other equals 1, then the intercept of the regression equation represents the mean of $Y$ at the level coded 0. Of course, we can expand the simple linear regression model earlier to include a dichotomous $X$ along with any number of continuous predictors using the multiple regression approaches described in Chapter 2; in that case, the regression coefficient of the dichotomous $X$ is a partial regression slope reflecting the effect of the dichotomous predictor while holding the other predictors in the model constant.

Therefore, there are particular statistical interpretations to be drawn from the simple linear regression of a continuous outcome variable on a binary predictor. Given that a categorical predictor with only two values is easily incorporated into a regression model, how might we incorporate a categorical predictor variable with more than two categories? If such a multicategory predictor has an ordinal scale of measurement, then a single numerical predictor with values reflecting the ordering of the categories might be formed. For example, a three-category ordinal variable could be coded as $X = 0$, 1, or 2 for the three categories. A linear regression of a continuous outcome $Y$ on this $X$ will produce useful results only to the extent that a single straight line can connect the means of $Y$ across the three categories of $X$; otherwise, the results are potentially misleading. Often, though, a multicategory predictor has a nominal scale of measurement. In this situation, using a single numerical variable to represent the separate nominal categories in a regression model will produce mostly nonsensical results. The trick, then, is to represent the different levels of a multicategory predictor, regardless of whether it is nominal or ordinal, *using a set of separate dichotomous variables* to take advantage of the fact that the relation between a continuous $Y$ and a dichotomous $X$ is necessarily linear. There are numerous coding approaches to breaking down a multicategory predictor into several dichotomous variables. This chapter describes two of these approaches, *dummy coding* and *contrast coding*, because they seem to be the most useful and the most commonly applied.

 **Section recap**

### The general linear model

Any type of predictor variable, whether continuous or categorical (i.e., discrete), can be incorporated into a linear regression model. It does not matter whether the data arise from experimental research or from naturalistic, observational research.

Because it is capable of including any combination of categorical and continuous predictors, the multiple regression model is also known as the **general linear model** (GLM). The models underlying the independent-groups $t$ test, ANOVA, and ANCOVA are special cases of the general linear model.

The relation between a continuous $Y$ and a dichotomous $X$ is always linear. The trick to incorporating a predictor variable with more than two categories, whether nominal or ordinal, is to represent it using a set of separate dichotomous variables.

## Research example for regression with categorical predictors

In a study by Baumann, Seifert-Kessell, and Jones (1992), 66 students in Grade 4 were randomly assigned to receive one of three interventions designed to improve reading comprehension. The participants were evenly distributed ($n = 22$ per intervention group) among an 'instructional control' group, a 'Directed Reading-Thinking Activity' (DRTA) group, and a 'Think Aloud' (TA) group. After each group received its respective intervention, the participants completed an error-detection test designed to evaluate their reading comprehension. Note that this study, as presented so far, has a traditional experimental design with a three-level randomized, experimentally manipulated independent variable (i.e., intervention group) and an approximately continuous outcome variable (reading comprehension test scores).

The data from this design are well suited for the traditional, one-way ANOVA, but we will see how they can be explicitly analysed with an equivalent multiple regression approach.

This dataset is available on the text's webpage (https://study.sagepub.com/flora) along with annotated input and output from several popular statistical software packages showing how to reproduce the analyses presented in this chapter.

Consistent with Chapter 2, it is always prudent to consider descriptive statistics and graphs of a dataset before proceeding to any formal model-fitting procedure. Table 3.1 gives descriptive statistics of the error-detection reading comprehension test scores from the Baumann et al. (1992) study, broken down by the three intervention groups, whereas Figure 3.1 shows side-by-side boxplots of this outcome variable by treatment group (in general, side-by-side boxplots are more effective at conveying differences among treatment groups than bar charts are, despite their popularity; see Lane and Sandor, 2009). These results show that participants in the DRTA group had the highest test scores, on average, and that the TA group had a higher mean and median test score than the control group did. Yet, the boxplots show that there is considerable overlap of the test score distributions of the three groups, with the TA group having the largest spread in its participants' test scores. With these descriptive results in mind, we are ready to build a model for the population effect of the intervention group predictor variable on the reading comprehension test score outcome variable.

**Table 3.1** Descriptive statistics for reading comprehension scores conditioned on intervention group

| Group | M | SD | Mdn | Skewness | Kurtosis |
|---|---|---|---|---|---|
| Control | 6.68 | 2.77 | 6.50 | 0.32 | −0.92 |
| DRTA | 9.77 | 2.72 | 10.00 | −0.11 | −1.19 |
| TA | 7.77 | 3.93 | 7.00 | 0.23 | −1.20 |

Note. N = 66 (n = 22 per group). DRTA = Directed Reading-Thinking Activity, TA = Think Aloud, M = mean, Mdn = median, SD = standard deviation.

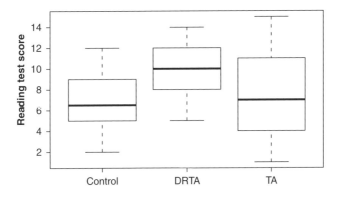

**Figure 3.1** Side-by-side box plots of reading comprehension scores by intervention group

## USING DUMMY-CODE VARIABLES

### Regression with dummy codes: Model specification

As mentioned, the general strategy to incorporating a discrete predictor with three or more categories in a linear multiple regression model is to represent the multicategory variable using a set of dichotomous variables to take advantage of the fact that the relation between any dichotomous predictor and a continuous dependent variable can only be linear. There are numerous approaches to this strategy; perhaps the most common and most easily understood approach is to use **dummy codes**, that is, *dummy-code variables* (also known as *indicator variables*).

We already saw the use of a dummy variable in Chapter 1 when we included gender as a predictor in a regression analysis by setting *male* = 0 and *female* = 1. Because gender was a nominal variable with two categories, we needed one dummy variable to distinguish male from female. But when a categorical predictor has more than two categories, more than one dummy-code variable is needed to distinguish the categories. In general, if a variable has $K$ categories, then $K - 1$ dummy codes are needed to distinguish among them. In our reading comprehension example, the intervention variable has three categories (control, DRTA, and TA), so we will need two dummy-code variables to represent it comprehensively.

In the creation of dummy codes, it is necessary to choose one category to represent a 'reference' or 'baseline' group, which becomes the category with a value of 0 on all dummy-code variables. With the gender predictor in the Chapter 1 example, *male* was the category dummy-coded 0 and, thus, served as the reference group. When a study has a clear control group, as in our current reading comprehension example, it is customary, but not necessary, to designate it as the reference group. Thus, for the three-group reading comprehension example, let's create two dummy variables as follows: Let dichotomous variable $D_1$ represent 'control vs. DRTA', and let dichotomous variable $D_2$ other represent 'control vs. TA'. Then participants in the control group are assigned the value 0 for both $D_1$ and $D_2$; participants in the DRTA group are assigned the value 1 for $D_1$ and 0 for $D_2$; finally, participants in the TA group are assigned the value 0 for $D_1$ and 1 for $D_2$ (see Table 3.2). It is critical to keep in mind that $D_1$ and $D_2$ are to be taken as a set: If we only knew that a participant has $D_1 = 0$, then it would be impossible to know whether that person is in the Control group or the TA group. But of course we also know that person's value of $D_2$, which, in combination with knowing that $D_1 = 0$, unambiguously indicates whether that person is in the Control group or the TA group.

Once these dummy variables are created, they become predictors in a multiple regression model:

$$\hat{Y}_i = \beta_0 + \beta_1 D_{1i} + \beta_2 D_{2i}. \tag{3.1}$$

In any multiple regression model, the intercept represents the predicted value of $Y$ for a hypothetical case with values of 0 on all predictors. Therefore, in the current reading comprehension example, $\beta_0$ represents the predicted $Y$ (i.e., the population mean) for a participant in the control group because control group participants are assigned the value of 0 for both $D_1$ and $D_2$. Next, the coefficient $\beta_1$ represents the predicted difference in $Y$ for a one-unit increase in $D_1$, holding $D_2$ constant. Therefore, $\beta_1$ is the predicted difference (i.e., the mean difference) in $Y$ for a participant in the DRTA group compared with a participant in the control group. It might be tempting to look at Table 3.2 and think that $D_1$ represents a comparison of the

**Table 3.2** Assignment of dummy-code values to intervention group categories

| | Dummy-code variable values | |
|---|---|---|
| Intervention group category | $D_1$ | $D_2$ |
| Control | 0 | 0 |
| DRTA | 1 | 0 |
| TA | 0 | 1 |

DRTA group with the other two groups combined, but a critical aspect of the dummy variable regression model in Equation 3.1 is that $D_1$ and $D_2$ are in the model simultaneously: The effect of $D_1$ holding $D_2$ constant means that $\beta_1$, the partial regression coefficient of $D_1$, is interpreted as a comparison of DRTA with the control group, over and above the effect of TA group membership. Likewise, then, coefficient $\beta_2$ for dummy variable $D_2$ is the predicted difference (i.e., the mean difference) in $Y$ for a participant in the TA group compared with a participant in the control group.

Generalizing beyond the reading comprehension example, $K - 1$ dummy variables are needed to represent a predictor with $K$ categories. The reference category is coded 0 on all dummy variables; that is, participants (or cases) who fall in the reference category have a value of 0 on all dummy variables. Each remaining category is coded 1 on its own dummy variable; that is, participants who fall in category $k$ are given a value of 1 on dummy variable $D_k$. These $K - 1$ dummy variables then comprehensively represent the original, categorical predictor in the regression model:

$$\hat{Y}_i = \beta_0 + \beta_1 D_{1i} + ... + \beta_{K-1} D_{(K-1)i}$$

or

$$Y_i = \beta_0 + \left( \sum_{k=1}^{K-1} \beta_k D_{ki} \right) + \varepsilon_i. \tag{3.2}$$

If there are no predictors in the model other than the $K - 1$ dummy variables, the intercept parameter $\beta_0$ is the predicted value of $Y$ (i.e., the population mean of $Y$) for cases in the reference category, and the partial slope parameter $\beta_k$ for dummy variable $D_k$ equals the difference between the population mean of $Y$ for category $k$ and the population mean of $Y$ for the reference category.

## Dummy codes: Regression ANOVA and interpretation of results

Continuing the reading comprehension example, we might first like to test the overall group effect; in other words, does intervention group membership significantly account for individual variation among reading comprehension test scores? Recall from Chapter 2 that multiple $R^2$ gives the proportion of variance in the outcome variable that is explained by the set of predictors in the model as a whole. Therefore, in the current context, multiple $R^2$ summarizes the effect of the two dummy variables taken together: Because the two dummy variables comprehensively represent the original three-category predictor, multiple $R^2$ summarizes the extent to which the reading comprehension outcome varies based on overall intervention group membership.

With the multiple regression model of Equation 3.1 fitted to the reading comprehension data using ordinary least-squares (OLS) estimation, we obtain $R^2 = .14$, which is significant with $F(2, 63) = 5.32$, $p = .007$. Therefore, intervention group membership does account for a significant proportion of variance in the reading comprehension test scores. It turns out that this $F$ test for $R^2$ is the same as we would have obtained using a traditional one-way ANOVA to test the omnibus null hypothesis that the population mean test scores of the three groups are equal. Furthermore, the analysis of regression variance table (Table 3.3) is the same as the traditional one-way ANOVA table, with $SS_{model} = SS_{between}$ and $SS_{error} = SS_{within}$. Additionally, $df_{model} = df_{between} = K - 1$ (i.e., the number of dummy variables representing the $K$-category predictor variable) and $df_{error} = df_{within} = N - K - 1$. Finally, the $R^2$ value of .14 equals the $\eta^2$ effect-size statistic often reported with ANOVA results, specifically:

$$\eta^2 = \frac{SS_{between}}{SS_{total}} = R^2.$$

In sum, the multiple regression of the outcome variable on the two dummy variables obtains results identical to those from a traditional one-way ANOVA procedure.

Of course, following a multiple regression procedure rather than a traditional ANOVA, we also obtain estimates of the regression coefficients for the dummy variables, whose general interpretation was given earlier. Continuing with the reading comprehension example, the intercept estimate is $\hat{\beta}_0 = 6.68$, which equals the mean test score of the control group, as can be seen in Table 3.1. This result should make a lot of sense: In any regression model, the intercept represents the predicted value for a hypothetical participant whose values for the predictors all equal 0, and here, a participant with a value of 0 for both predictors, $D_1$ and $D_2$, is a member of the control group. Thus, the predicted test score for the control group equals the mean of the control group. In Chapters 1 and 2, I stated that the intercept of a regression model is often not directly interpretable or informative, but in this dummy coding context, the intercept is meaningful.

Next, the estimated regression coefficient for dummy variable $D_1$ is $\hat{\beta}_1 = 3.09$ (95% CI: 1.17 to 5.01). Because of the way the dummy variables were created (Table 3.2), $\hat{\beta}_1$ represents a comparison of the DRTA group to the control group; specifically, from Table 3.1, one can determine that $\hat{\beta}_1 = 3.09$ equals the difference between the test score mean of the DRTA group and the mean of the control group. Additionally, because $\hat{\beta}_1$ is significant, $t(63) = 3.22$, $p = .002$, we can conclude that these two means are significantly different from each other. Finally, the estimated regression coefficient for dummy variable $D_2$ is $\hat{\beta}_2 = 1.09$ (95% CI: –0.83 to 3.01), which represents the difference between the TA group mean and the control group

**Table 3.3** ANOVA table for reading comprehension example

| Source | SS | df | MS | F |
|---|---|---|---|---|
| Model (between-groups) | 108.12 | 2 | 54.06 | 5.32 |
| Error (within-groups) | 640.50 | 63 | 10.17 | – |
| Total | 748.62 | 65 | – | – |

Note. $N = 66$.

mean. Because $\hat{\beta}_2$ is not significant, $t(63) = 1.14$, $p = .26$, these two means do not significantly differ. Complete results for the reading comprehension example are presented later in Table 3.6, where results from this dummy-code variable model can be compared with results obtained from equivalent models using alternative coding schemes (described later) for the multicategory intervention group predictor. As the table shows, one sense that the models are equivalent is that they each produce the same predicted values for participants in each category (i.e., the separate $\hat{y}$ values for participants in the control, DRTA, and TA groups); not coincidentally, these predicted values equal the sample means of each group and represent model-implied (or predicted) population means.

The inferential conclusions from the dummy variable model are nicely consistent with the graphical depiction of the distribution of test scores by intervention group in Figure 3.1 and descriptive statistics in Table 3.1. Note, however, that the regression results do not provide a direct comparison of the DRTA and TA group means. But this comparison is easily obtained simply by changing the dummy coding scheme so that either the DRTA or the TA group (instead of the control group) is the reference group and reestimating the model using these new dummy variables. The choice of reference group is arbitrary; although the interpretation of the specific regression coefficients will differ based on different dummy codings, the same overall ANOVA and $R^2$ values will result and the same predicted values for the outcome (i.e., model-implied population means) for the $K$ groups will be obtained. In general, separate models estimated using separate dummy coding systems to represent the same categorical predictor are **equivalent**. But, reestimating the model based on different dummy coding systems so that all possible pairwise group comparisons can be made lends an exploratory, post hoc flavour to the analyses, which has implications for the inferential conclusions, as described next.

Therefore, not only does a multiple regression approach produce the same ANOVA table as a traditional, one-way ANOVA, but also the estimated regression parameters and their significance tests provide specific mean comparisons which are not automatically produced with a standard ANOVA procedure. In practice, upon finding a significant $F$ test for the omnibus null hypothesis of a standard ANOVA, researchers will typically proceed to follow-up (i.e., post hoc) tests to examine more specific mean differences. But with a regression approach, these follow-up tests are automatically provided in the form of the $t$ tests for the estimated regression coefficients, which themselves are effect-size measures (unstandardized mean differences) for the comparison of categories. Nevertheless, the significance tests and confidence intervals (CIs) associated with the regression parameter estimates are *one-at-a-time* inferences in that the $p$ values (and CI widths) do not account for the presence of the other inferential tests drawn from the same model; as such, they are best viewed as **planned comparisons**. For the reading comprehension example, this planned comparison approach makes sense: The researchers likely expected before analysing their data that both interventions they developed (DRTA and TA) would lead to higher reading comprehension scores than the more traditional teaching approach given to the control group. But if a researcher cannot form specific hypotheses a priori about where specific population mean differences lie among three or more groups formed by a categorical predictor, then more conservative post hoc tests should be used for mean comparisons, such as the well-known Tukey multiple-comparison procedure.[2]

---

[2]Post hoc tests are beyond the scope of this text, but for a complete presentation, see Maxwell and Delaney (2004: 193–237).

## Formal expression of ANOVA model as a multiple regression model

As demonstrated earlier, a key result from the dummy-variable multiple regression model is that it can be used to reproduce the outcome variable means as a function of the groups formed by the categorical predictor variable. Likewise, the traditional ANOVA model is typically presented as a model for the population means of discrete groups or categories. A common expression of the ANOVA model is

$$Y_{ik} = \mu_k + \varepsilon_{ik}, \tag{3.3}$$

where $Y_{ik}$ is the outcome variable score for case $i$ in group $k$, $\mu_k$ is the population mean of $Y$ in group $k$, and $\varepsilon_{ik}$ is the difference between the group mean and the observed value of $Y$ for case $i$. In the dummy-variable multiple regression model (Equation 3.2), the predicted values determined by the values of the dummy variables are in fact the group means; thus,

$$\mu_k = \beta_0 + \beta_1 D_{1i} + \ldots + \beta_{K-1} D_{(K-1)i}. \tag{3.4}$$

Substituting the right-hand side of Equation 3.4 into Equation 3.3, we have

$$Y_{ik} = \beta_0 + \beta_1 D_{1i} + \ldots + \beta_{K-1} D_{(K-1)i} + \varepsilon_{ik}, \tag{3.5}$$

which is equivalent to Equation 3.2 (the subscript $k$ is included in the current context to emphasize that each case is a member of a particular group or category, indexed with $k$, but this subscript can be dropped without loss of generality).

 **Section recap**

### Using dummy-code variables

One way to represent a multicategory predictor in a multiple regression model is to use a set of **dummy-code variables**.

$K - 1$ dummy variables are needed to represent a predictor with $K$ categories. The reference or baseline category is coded 0 on all dummy variables. Each remaining category is coded 1 on its own dummy variable; i.e., dummy variable $D_k = 1$ for category $k$ and $D_k = 0$ for the reference category.

These $K - 1$ dummy variables then comprehensively represent the categorical predictor in the regression model:

$$Y_i = \beta_0 + \beta_1 D_{1i} + \ldots + \beta_{K-1} D_{(K-1)i} + \varepsilon_i.$$

If there are no other predictors in the model, the intercept estimate $\hat{\beta}_0$ equals the sample mean of $Y$ for the reference category. The slope estimate $\hat{\beta}_k$ for dummy variable $D_k$ equals the difference between the mean of $Y$ in category $k$ and the mean of $Y$ in the reference category.

This dummy variable regression model is statistically equivalent to the one-way ANOVA model. Therefore, the analysis of regression variance for testing the significance of multiple $R^2$ produces the same $F$ test as the traditional one-way ANOVA omnibus null hypothesis that the population mean of $Y$ is equal across all $k$ categories.

## USING CONTRAST-CODE VARIABLES

### Regression with contrast codes: Model specification

The dummy coding approach presented earlier is only one of many ways to represent a multi-category predictor variable in a multiple regression model. One potential drawback of dummy coding is that all regression coefficients are simple pairwise comparisons of a given category of the predictor to the reference category. Although these pairwise comparisons are easy to interpret, often researchers wish to make **complex comparisons** in which the aggregate of two or more groups is compared with either another group (e.g., two or more treatment conditions are compared with a single control condition) or compared with another aggregate of groups (e.g., two or more Western religious groups compared with two or more Eastern religious groups). In fact, in our current reading comprehension example, Baumann et al. (1992) explicitly planned a comparison of the two interventions, DRTA and TA, taken together as an aggregate, with the instructional control group. It is not possible to test this complex comparison using dummy-code variables; instead, it can be tested using **contrast codes**.

The complex comparison for the reading comprehension example implies the null hypothesis that the population mean test score of the control group ($\mu_1$) equals the average of the population mean test scores for the DRTA ($\mu_2$) and TA ($\mu_3$) groups:

$$H_0: \mu_1 = \frac{\mu_2 + \mu_3}{2},$$

which can be rearranged to

$$H_0: \mu_1 - \frac{\mu_2 + \mu_3}{2} = 0$$

or

$$H_0: 1\mu_1 - .5\mu_2 - .5\mu_3 = 0. \tag{3.6}$$

Equation 3.6 establishes the weights for a linear combination of population means, that is, a **linear contrast**:

$$\psi_1 = 1\mu_1 - .5\mu_2 - .5\mu_3.$$

In general, a linear contrast for a set of $K$ population means is any linear function of the form

$$\psi_k = c_1\mu_1 + c_2\mu_2 + \dots + c_K\mu_K = \sum_{k=1}^{K} c_k\mu_k$$

under the condition that the weights, or contrast codes, sum to zero; that is,

$$c_1 + c_2 + \dots + c_K = \sum_{k=1}^{K} c_k = 0.$$

Notice that the contrast from the reading comprehension example ($\psi_1$) meets the requirement that the contrast codes sum to zero ($1 - .5 - .5 = 0$). These contrast codes $c_k$ for each group then become the observed values of a variable $C$ used in a regression model for the outcome variable. But, similar to dummy coding, it is necessary to define $K - 1$ of these contrast-code variables so that the complete $K$-level predictor variable is represented in the multiple regression model. Most often, these contrasts are established so that they are *mutually orthogonal*, which is explained later.

In addition, Baumann et al. (1992) also planned a comparison of the two interventions to each other, ignoring the control group. This comparison implies the null hypothesis

$$H_0: \mu_2 = \mu_3$$

or

$$H_0: \mu_2 - \mu_3 = 0.$$

To see how this null hypothesis leads to a corresponding contrast, we can also incorporate the population mean of the control group explicitly:

$$H_0: 0\mu_1 + 1\mu_2 - 1\mu_3 = 0. \tag{3.7}$$

The control group has a weight of zero because the null hypothesis is a comparison of the two interventions, ignoring the control condition. The weights for the population means in the null hypothesis then give the contrast

$$\psi_2 = 0\mu_1 + 1\mu_2 - 1\mu_3.$$

In our current example, the contrasts $\psi_1$ and $\psi_2$ now provide observed values for the $K - 1$ contrast-code variables needed for a regression of reading comprehension test scores on the three-category predictor, intervention group.

Specifically, we create two variables, $C_1$ and $C_2$, whose values are determined by the two contrasts. As summarized in the **contrast matrix** in Table 3.4, participants in the control condition are given values of 1 for $C_1$ and 0 for $C_2$, participants in the DRTA condition are assigned values of $-.5$ for $C_1$ and 1 for $C_2$, and those in the TA condition are given values of $-.5$ for $C_1$ and $-1$ for $C_2$. Note how the values in the columns of the contrast matrix correspond to the weights of the contrasts $\psi_1$ and $\psi_2$; it may also be helpful to compare Table 3.4 with Table 3.2 to see how the contrast codes compare with dummy codes for this same research example. Finally, $C_1$ and $C_2$ become the predictors in a multiple regression model of the test score outcome variable:

$$\hat{Y}_i = \beta_0 + \beta_1 C_{1i} + \beta_2 C_{2i}, \tag{3.8}$$

which again is almost always estimated using OLS.

**Table 3.4** Contrast matrix showing assignment of contrast-code values to intervention group categories

| Intervention group category | Contrast-code variable values | |
| --- | --- | --- |
| | $C_1$ | $C_2$ |
| Control | 1 | 0 |
| DRTA | −0.5 | 1 |
| TA | −0.5 | −1 |

Generalizing beyond the reading comprehension example, a predictor with $K$ categories can be completely represented with a set of $K - 1$ contrast-code variables. The contrasts are constructed to allow the researcher to obtain planned comparisons among the means of the groups formed by the multicategory predictor, including complex comparisons in which the aggregate of two or more groups is compared with either another group or (in the case of $K \geq 4$) compared with another aggregate of groups. Each contrast $\psi_k$ of the $K - 1$ linear contrasts is constructed so that its numerical codes sum to 0; as demonstrated for the reading comprehension example, articulating the null hypothesis corresponding to a given contrast can guide its construction. After the contrast codes are used to form contrast variables (i.e., $C_1$, $C_2$ ,..., $C_{K-1}$), such that each participant is assigned the contrast-code values corresponding to her or his category, these $K - 1$ contrast variables then comprehensively represent the original, categorical predictor in the regression model:

$$\hat{Y}_i = \beta_0 + \beta_1 C_{1i} + ... + \beta_{K-1} C_{(K-1)i}$$

or

$$Y_i = \beta_0 + \left( \sum_{k=1}^{K-1} \beta_k C_{ki} \right) + \varepsilon_i.$$

Although estimates of the partial slope parameters $\beta_k$ lead to tests of the comparisons indicated by the contrasts, direct interpretation of their values is tricky, though, as demonstrated next.

## Contrast codes: Regression ANOVA and interpretation of results

When the model of Equation 3.8 is fitted to the reading comprehension data, the resulting $R^2$ and ANOVA table are identical to those obtained when the dummy coding approach was used to model the same data (i.e., $R^2 = .14$ and the ANOVA table matches Table 3.3). In general, the representation of a $K$-category predictor variable using $K - 1$ contrast codes is equivalent to using $K - 1$ dummy codes in that the two approaches produce the same decomposition of outcome variable variance into model and error sources and the same predicted values (i.e., model-implied population means) for the $K$ groups. Table 3.6 gives complete results for this new (but equivalent) model, showing that the predicted values obtained using dummy-code variables are the same as those obtained from the estimated regression equation using contrast codes. But the specific parameter estimates and the corresponding inferential conclusions are different from those obtained earlier with dummy variables.

Specifically, the estimated intercept of the regression of reading test scores on the contrast-code variables is $\hat{\beta}_0 = 8.08$. When an outcome variable is regressed on contrast-code variables, the intercept estimate equals the mean of the individual group means. Thus, here the estimated intercept of 8.08 equals the average of $\bar{Y}_{control} = 6.68$, $\bar{Y}_{DRTA} = 9.77$, and $\bar{Y}_{TA} = 7.77$ (see Table 3.1). Next, the estimated regression coefficient for contrast variable $C_1$ is $\hat{\beta}_1 = -1.39$, which represents the complex comparison of the DRTA and TA groups to the control group (i.e., $\psi_1$). Because this regression coefficient is significant, $t(63) = 2.51$, $p = .01$, the null hypothesis of Equation 3.6 is rejected; that is, contrast $\psi_1$ is significant. In other words, the average of the means of the two treatment groups (DRTA and TA) significantly differs from the mean of the control group. Regarding contrast $\psi_2$, the estimated regression coefficient for $C_2$ is $\hat{\beta}_2 = -1.00$, which represents the comparison of the DRTA and TA groups, ignoring the control group. This comparison is also significant, $t(63) = 2.08$, $p = .04$, indicating that the null hypothesis of Equation 3.7 is rejected. In other words, the means of the two treatment groups (i.e., DRTA and TA) significantly differ from each other.

Regarding the values of the regression coefficients themselves, the estimate $\hat{\beta}_1 = -1.39$ equals the product of a constant (specifically, $c = \frac{2}{3}$) and the difference between the sample mean test score of the control group and the average of the sample means of the treatment groups. That is, we have

$$\hat{\beta}_1 = c\left(\bar{Y}_{control} - \frac{\bar{Y}_{DRTA} + \bar{Y}_{TA}}{2}\right) = \frac{2}{3}\left(6.68 - \frac{9.77 + 7.77}{2}\right) = -1.39.$$

Likewise, the estimate $\hat{\beta}_2 = -1.00$ equals a constant (specifically, $c = 0.5$) times the difference between the sample mean test score of the TA group and the sample mean of the DRTA group:

$$\hat{\beta}_2 = c\left(\bar{Y}_{TA} - \bar{Y}_{DRTA}\right) = 0.5(7.77 - 9.77) = -1.00.$$

Thus, although tests of the slope estimates for the two contrast code variables provide inferential conclusions regarding the a priori null hypotheses, the regression coefficients themselves (and corresponding confidence intervals) are not directly interpretable when the contrasts are formed in the manner that led to the contrast matrix in Table 3.4.

## Improved contrasts

We can instead obtain more directly interpretable regression coefficients using the new contrast codes given in Table 3.5 (for further discussion of this issue, see Cohen et al., 2003: 333–34). In this revised contrast matrix, it is apparent that $C_1$ still represents a complex comparison of the control group with the two treatment groups and $C_2$ still represents a pairwise comparison of the DRTA group with the TA group; additionally, each contrast still meets the requirement that the sum of its codes equals zero (i.e., $\frac{2}{3} + (-\frac{1}{3}) + (-\frac{1}{3}) = 0$ and $0 + \frac{1}{2} + (-\frac{1}{2}) = 0$). But this revised contrast matrix was devised to satisfy another rule, namely, that the difference between the value of the set of positive contrast codes and the value of the set of negative contrast codes should equal 1 for each contrast. In Table 3.5, that is the case because for $C_1$ we have $\frac{2}{3} - (-\frac{1}{3}) = 1$ and for $C_2$ we have $\frac{1}{2} - (-\frac{1}{2}) = 1$.

**Table 3.5**  Revised contrast matrix showing assignment of contrast-code values to intervention group categories

| Intervention group category | Contrast-code variable values | |
|---|---|---|
| | $C_1$ | $C_2$ |
| Control | 2/3 | 0 |
| DRTA | –1/3 | 1/2 |
| TA | –1/3 | –1/2 |

When participants are assigned values for the $C_1$ and $C_2$ variables based on this revised contrast matrix and the regression model is estimated again, different parameter estimates are obtained, as shown in Table 3.6. Specifically, the intercept estimate is still $\hat{\beta}_0 = 8.08$, again equaling the average of the three group means. But the estimated slope coefficient for $C_1$ is now $\hat{\beta}_1 = -2.09$, which is equal to the difference between the sample mean of the control group and the average of the two treatment group means:

$$\hat{\beta}_1 = \left( \bar{Y}_{control} - \frac{\bar{Y}_{DRTA} + \bar{Y}_{TA}}{2} \right) = \left( 6.68 - \frac{9.77 + 7.77}{2} \right) = -2.09.$$

Additionally, the estimated slope coefficient for $C_2$ is now $\hat{\beta}_2 = -2.00$, which equals the difference between the sample mean of the TA group and the mean of the DRTA group:

$$\hat{\beta}_2 = \left( \bar{Y}_{TA} - \bar{Y}_{DRTA} \right) = (7.77 - 9.77) = -2.00.$$

Another advantage of using the current, revised contrast codes is that confidence intervals around $\hat{\beta}_1$ and $\hat{\beta}_2$ are also directly interpretable in terms of the mean comparisons specified by the null hypotheses indicated in Equations 3.6 and 3.7. That is, the 95% confidence interval for $\beta_1$, (–3.75, –0.43), indicates a range of plausible values for the difference between the population mean of the control group and the average of the population means of the treatment groups. Yet, the t tests for $\hat{\beta}_1$ and $\hat{\beta}_2$ are identical to those obtained with the first set of contrast codes, with $t(63) = -2.51$, $p = .01$ and $t(63) = -2.08$, $p = .04$, indicating that this alternative set of contrast-code variables leads to the same rejection of the null hypotheses behind contrasts $\psi_1$ and $\psi_2$.

Finally, the results obtained with the revised contrast-code variables are statistically equivalent to those obtained with both the dummy variables and the original contrast-code variables in that each method produces $R^2 = .14$ with $F(2, 63) = 5.32$, $p = .007$. Furthermore, as shown in Table 3.6, each method produces the same predicted values of Y for each category of the experimental intervention variable. As pointed out earlier, these predicted values equal the sample means of the control, DRTA, and TA groups.

As with the dummy coding approach, the contrast coding multiple regression approach to ANOVA provides the same omnibus ANOVA table and F test as a traditional, one-way ANOVA analysis, but the estimated regression coefficients and associated significance tests provide further detail regarding specific comparisons between groups. In particular, the strength of contrast coding is the ability to specify and test complex comparisons, with the regression slope estimates serving as effect-size measures (i.e., unstandardized mean differences) for the

**Table 3.6** Complete results for reading comprehension example across dummy coding and contrast coding of multicategory intervention group predictor

| Variable | $\hat{\beta}$ | $SE(\hat{\beta})$ | t | p | 95% CI |
|---|---|---|---|---|---|
| **Dummy variable model** | | | | | |
| (Intercept) | 6.68 | 0.68 | – | – | – |
| $D_1$ | 3.09 | 0.96 | 3.22 | .002 | (1.17, 5.01) |
| $D_2$ | 1.09 | 0.96 | 1.14 | .261 | (−0.83, 3.01) |

$\bar{Y}_{control} = 6.68 + 3.09(0) + 1.09(0) = 6.68,\ \bar{Y}_{DRTA} = 6.68 + 3.09(1) + 1.09(0) = 9.77,$
$\bar{Y}_{TA} = 6.68 + 3.09(0) + 1.09(1) = 7.77$

| | | | | | |
|---|---|---|---|---|---|
| **First contrast variable model** | | | | | |
| (Intercept) | 8.08 | 0.39 | – | – | – |
| $C_1$ | −1.39 | 0.56 | 2.51 | .015 | (−2.50, −0.28) |
| $C_2$ | −1.00 | 0.48 | 2.08 | .042 | (−1.96, 0.04) |

$\bar{Y}_{control} = 8.08 - 1.39(1) + 1.00(0) = 6.68,\ \bar{Y}_{DRTA} = 8.08 - 1.39(-.5) + 1.00(1) = 9.77,$
$\bar{Y}_{TA} = 8.08 - 1.39(-.5) + 1.00(-1) = 7.77$

| | | | | | |
|---|---|---|---|---|---|
| **Second contrast variable model** | | | | | |
| (Intercept) | 8.08 | 0.39 | – | – | – |
| $C_1$ | −2.09 | 0.83 | 2.51 | .015 | (−3.75, −0.43) |
| $C_2$ | 2.00 | 0.96 | 2.08 | .042 | (0.08, 3.92) |

$\bar{Y}_{control} = 8.08 - 2.09(\frac{2}{3}) + 2.00(0) = 6.68,\ \bar{Y}_{DRTA} = 8.08 - 2.09(-\frac{1}{3}) + 2.00(.5) = 9.77,$
$\bar{Y}_{TA} = 8.08 - 2.09(-\frac{1}{3}) + 2.00(-.5) = 7.77$

Note. $N = 66$. For all models, $R^2 = .14$, $F(2, 63) = 5.32$, $p = .007$. $SE$ = standard error.

contrasts representing the complex comparisons. For any given application, there are many potential approaches to specifying contrast codes (especially with $K = 4$ or more categories). The contrasts in both Table 3.4 and Table 3.5 are examples of *Helmert contrasts*, in which the first contrast is a comparison of the first group or category with an average of the other categories, the second contrast compares the second category with the average of the subsequent categories (or just the last category if there are only three) ignoring the first category, and so on if there are four or more categories of the predictor. Contrasts also may be specified in a more customized manner that does not adhere to the pattern implied by Helmert contrasts (see Cohen et al., 2003: 332–27).

It is desirable for a given set of contrasts representing a categorical predictor to be **mutually orthogonal**, meaning that each contrast accounts for a separate, unique proportion of variance from the overall proportion of outcome variable variance explained by the $K$-category predictor. Two contrasts are orthogonal if the products of the contrast codes within each category of the predictor sum to zero. In the reading comprehension example, the two contrasts in Table 3.4 are orthogonal to each other because the products of the values in each row of the contrast matrix sum to zero across the three categories of the predictor: $(1 \times 0) + (-0.5 \times 1) + (-0.5 \times -1) = 0$. Likewise, from Table 3.5 we have $(\frac{2}{3} \times 0) + (-\frac{1}{3} \times \frac{1}{2}) + (-\frac{1}{3} \times -\frac{1}{2}) = 0$. When a predictor has more than three categories, more than two contrasts are needed; if each possible pair in a given set of contrasts is orthogonal, then the set of contrasts is mutually orthogonal. When the sample sizes within each category of the predictor variable are equal (which is the case in the reading comprehension example, with $n = 22$ in each of the three intervention groups), the contrast-code variables $C_k$ are uncorrelated with each other; with unbalanced sample sizes, the $C_k$ will have nonzero correlations. An unbalanced sample size is usually presented as an important obstacle in traditional ANOVA analyses, but in the current multiple regression approach to ANOVA, unbalanced $n$ across the levels of a categorical predictor is handled automatically through the partialling of regression coefficients to account for correlations among the contrast-code variables (e.g., Equation 2.4).

 **Section recap**

### Using contrast-code variables

A multicategory predictor can also be represented in a multiple regression model using a set of **contrast-code variables**.

$K - 1$ contrast variables are needed to represent a predictor with $K$ categories. The contrasts $\psi_k$ are formed according to null hypotheses, including **complex null hypotheses**, which are typically based on planned comparisons.

For each contrast $\psi_k$, the contrast codes must sum to zero. These codes become the values assigned to $C_k$ contrast-code variables.

For the contrasts to be **mutually orthogonal**, the products of the codes for each pair of contrasts must also sum to zero.

For the regression coefficients of the contrast-code variables to be directly interpretable, for each contrast $\psi_k$, the difference between the value of the set of positive codes and the value of the set of negative contrast codes should equal 1.

The $K - 1$ contrast variables then comprehensively represent the categorical predictor in the regression model:

$$Y_i = \beta_0 + \beta_1 C_{1i} + \ldots + \beta_{K-1} C_{(K-1)i} + \varepsilon_i.$$

If there are no other predictors in the model, the intercept estimate $\hat{\beta}_0$ equals the average of the sample means of $Y$ across the groups formed by the multicategory predictor. The test of the slope estimate $\hat{\beta}_k$ for contrast variable $C_k$ is a test of the null hypothesis underlying contrast $\psi_k$.

This contrast variable regression model is statistically equivalent to the one-way ANOVA model as well as to the dummy variable model. Therefore, each model produces the same multiple $R^2$ (and corresponding $F$ test) and the same predicted values (i.e., model-implied population means) of the outcome $Y$ across the groups formed by the multicategory predictor.

# THE ANALYSIS OF COVARIANCE (ANCOVA) MODEL AND BEYOND

## ANCOVA: Model specification

The dummy coding and contrast coding approaches presented earlier illustrate how the relation between an outcome variable and any categorical predictor can be expressed with a linear regression model. Given that such multicategory predictors can be represented in a regression model, it is straightforward to expand the model further to include a combination of categorical and continuous predictors. The classic ANCOVA model is a prominent example. Originally, ANCOVA was developed for the context of an experimental (or quasi-experimental; see Reichardt, 2009) design in which there was a desire to test group differences on some outcome variable while accounting for potentially confounding, preexisting group differences on some other continuous variable, which was termed a *covariate*. Although the focus of the analysis was on the effect of the categorical predictor (e.g., an experimental manipulation), the continuous covariate was traditionally viewed as a nuisance to be controlled statistically. The general question ANCOVA attempts to answer is 'Would the groups differ on the outcome variable if they had been equivalent on the covariate?' In particular, expanding the logic of ANOVA, variability as a result of the covariate is removed from both between- and within-groups variability to adjust the omnibus ANOVA test for the influence of the covariate.

In modern research, the term *covariate* is more generally used to refer to any individual differences measure (which need not be continuous), and often there is explicit theoretical interest in the effects of individual covariates.[3] In the general linear model, that is, multiple regression, a 'covariate' is nothing more than another predictor variable on the right-hand side of the regression equation, regardless of its theoretical importance. This generality is easy to see when we consider the formal expression of the ANCOVA model:

$$Y_{ik} = \mu_k + \beta_X X_i + \varepsilon_{ik},$$  (3.9)

where, as in the ANOVA model of Equation 3.3, $Y_{ik}$ is the outcome variable score for case $i$ in group $k$, $\mu_k$ is the population mean of group $k$, and $\varepsilon_{ik}$ is the difference between the group mean and the observed value of $Y$ for case $i$. But the ANCOVA model also includes the continuous covariate $X$, whose relation with the outcome variable is a partial linear regression coefficient, $\beta_X$. As shown in Equation 3.4, $\mu_k$ can be expressed as a series of dummy-code predictors; consequently, the ANCOVA model can also be written as a function of dummy-code variables plus the effect of the continuous covariate. For example, if the predictor has $K = 3$ categories, the ANCOVA model with dummy-code variables is

$$Y_{ik} = \beta_0 + \beta_1 D_{1i} + \beta_2 D_{2i} + \beta_X X_i + \varepsilon_{ik},$$  (3.10)

where $D_1$ and $D_2$ are the two dummy-code variables. And then to generalize to more than three levels, the model is

---

[3]Unfortunately, with certain statistical software procedures, including the GLM procedure of SPSS, the term *covariate* still continues to refer explicitly to a continuous predictor, whereas categorical predictors are termed *factors*.

$$Y_{ik} = \beta_0 + \left(\sum_{k=1}^{K-1} \beta_k D_{ki}\right) + \beta_X X_i + \varepsilon_{ik}. \tag{3.11}$$

Of course, the predictor with $K$ categories or levels could be equivalently represented with contrast-code variables instead; in which case, a generic form of the ANCOVA model is

$$Y_{ik} = \beta_0 + \left(\sum_{k=1}^{K-1} \beta_k C_{ki}\right) + \beta_X X_i + \varepsilon_{ik}. \tag{3.12}$$

Hopefully it is becoming clear that the ANCOVA model is nothing more than a certain kind of multiple linear regression model in which an outcome variable $Y$ is regressed on a set of dichotomous predictors (representing a categorical predictor) and a single continuous predictor (the covariate). In fact, the ANCOVA model is a form of the general multiple regression model equation given in Chapter 2, Equation 2.9:

$$Y_i = \beta_0 + \left(\sum_{p=1}^{P} \beta_p X_{pi}\right) + \varepsilon_i,$$

in which some $X$ variables are dichotomous dummy- or contrast-code variables (e.g., $X_1 \equiv D_1$ or $C_1$, $X_2 \equiv D_2$ or $C_2$, etc.) and one or more of the $X$ variables is a continuous covariate. Therefore, all concepts introduced in Chapter 2 for multiple regression apply to the ANCOVA model (and the simpler ANOVA model, for that matter), and it is readily apparent that the model can be expanded to include any number of predictors, regardless of whether they are continuous or categorical.

Now let's return to the reading comprehension example. It turns out that Baumann et al. (1992) were interested in whether the groups differed in their postintervention reading test scores over and above any differences on a reading test score administered before the intervention. This is an example of a classic research question for which ANCOVA is often applied: 'Do groups differ on posttest scores, controlling pretest scores?' Or, 'Would the groups differ on the posttest if they had been equivalent on the pretest?' Put another way, the authors wanted to determine whether the groups had differential improvement, or change, in their reading scores from pretest to posttest. ANCOVA answers this question in the sense that if two participants are considered equal on the pretest, then they must have had different amounts of improvement if their posttest scores are different. Furthermore, as described earlier, Baumann et al. explicitly established a planned complex comparison of the two interventions (DRTA and TA) with the control group as well as a pairwise comparison of the two interventions with each other, ignoring the control group.

Therefore, to answer these research questions, we can specify a multiple regression model in which the reading posttest scores ($Y$) are regressed on the two contrast-code variables defined earlier in Table 3.5 to represent the three-category intervention variable ($C_1$ and $C_2$) as well as a covariate, the reading pretest scores ($X$):

$$\hat{Y}_i = \beta_0 + \beta_1 C_{1i} + \beta_2 C_{2i} + \beta_3 X_i. \tag{3.13}$$

Using this ANCOVA approach, the omnibus, overall effect of the intervention predictor is the joint effect of $C_1$ and $C_2$, taken together. To obtain this joint effect and its statistical significance, we can follow a hierarchical regression procedure as outlined in Chapter 2. Specifically, a model in which the posttest scores are regressed on the pretest scores only is compared with the complete model in Equation 3.13; the joint effect of $C_1$ and $C_2$ is then the change in $R^2$ across these two models.

## ANCOVA: Interpretation of results

When the reading comprehension posttest is regressed on the pretest alone, $R^2 = .32$.[4] When $C_1$ and $C_2$ (defined according to Table 3.5) are added to create the model in Equation 3.13, $R^2$ increases to .51. This $R^2$ change of .19 is statistically significant, $F(2, 62) = 12.17$, $p < .001$, indicating that the three-category intervention variable is significantly related to the posttest, holding the effect of the pretest constant. More loosely stated, the three groups significantly differ in terms of their improvement in reading comprehension from pretest to posttest. Next, the estimated regression coefficients for $C_1$ and $C_2$ and their statistical significance give results for the specific, planned comparisons among the three treatment groups. Pertaining to the effect of $C_1$, the DRTA and TA groups had significantly higher posttest scores than the control group did, $\hat{\beta}_1 = -2.83$, $t(62) = 4.40$, $p < .001$. Specifically, the coefficient estimate $-2.83$ is the difference between the control group posttest mean and the average of the DRTA and TA means, adjusted for the pretest. Pertaining to the effect of $C_2$, the DRTA group has significantly higher posttest scores than the TA group, $\hat{\beta}_2 = 1.59$, $t(62) = 2.17$, $p = .03$. Specifically, the difference between the DRTA group posttest mean and the TA mean equals 0.80, again adjusted for the pretest.

Whereas ANOVA is commonly presented as a method for comparing group means, ANCOVA is often presented as a method for comparing **adjusted means** across groups (also known as *conditional means*). Lengthy descriptions are given to convey the meaning of these adjusted means (e.g., Maxwell and Delaney, 2004: 415–20). But in the current multiple regression context, it is straightforward to see that these adjusted means are just the predicted values, $\hat{Y}_i$, for a hypothetical participant in each group whose value of the covariate equals the mean of that covariate. To demonstrate, consider the ANCOVA model of Equation 3.13 estimated with the reading comprehension data:

$$\hat{Y}_i = 1.291 - 2.831C_{1i} + 1.590C_{2i} + 0.693X_i,$$

where, once again, $Y$ is the reading comprehension posttest score, $C_1$ and $C_2$ are contrast variables formed according to Table 3.5, and $X$ is the reading comprehension pretest score. For participants in the control group, $C_1 = \frac{2}{3}$ and $C_2 = 0$, so the estimated model reduces to

$$\hat{Y}_i \mid control = -0.60 + 0.69X_i.$$

For DRTA participants, $C_1 = -\frac{1}{3}$ and $C_2 = \frac{1}{2}$; thus, the estimated model is

$$\hat{Y}_i \mid DRTA = 3.03 + 0.69X_i.$$

---

[4]It is not surprising to find a somewhat strong relation between the pretest and the posttest, given that it is essentially the same measure administered to the same participants across two occasions. In general, this tendency for an earlier measure to be related to a later measure of the same variable is known as *autocorrelation*.

Finally, for TA participants, $C_1 = -\frac{1}{3}$ and $C_2 = -\frac{1}{2}$, and the estimated model is

$$\hat{Y}_i \,|\, TA = 1.44 + 0.69 X_i.$$

Next, given a hypothetical value of the pretest equal to its mean, that is, letting $X_i = \bar{X} = 9.788$, we can use the previous three equations to calculate the adjusted means for each group, which are $\bar{Y}_{adjusted} \,|\, control = 6.19$, $\bar{Y}_{adjusted} \,|\, DRTA = 9.81$, and $\bar{Y}_{adjusted} \,|\, TA = 8.22$. Notice that these posttest means do not equal the original sample mean posttest scores of the three groups given in Table 3.1. Instead, these means are adjusted for the effect of the pretest on the posttest; this adjustment is nothing more than an application of the concept of a partial regression effect explained in Chapter 2.

As explained earlier, the ANCOVA model is applied to the reading comprehension example to provide an implicit test of whether the improvement, or change, in test scores differs across the three intervention groups; if the groups are considered equivalent on the pretest on average, that is, the pretest is a covariate held constant, than any posttest group differences are interpreted as differential average amounts of change. This is an example of a particularly common use of ANCOVA in which the covariate is a pretest of the same individual differences measure as the outcome variable, the posttest. An alternative and more intuitive approach to analysing group differences across two repeated measures is to examine group differences on the actual **change scores**, also known as *gain scores* or *difference scores*. The change score for case $i$ is simply $Y_{2i} - Y_{1i}$, where $Y_{2i}$ is the posttest score for case $i$ and $Y_{1i}$ is the pretest score for case $i$. There is a long and contentious debate among methodological researchers over which of these approaches to analysing group differences across two repeated measures (ANCOVA with pretest scores as covariate and posttest as outcome variable versus ANOVA with change scores as outcome variable) is most appropriate. The resolution of this debate is that the ANCOVA approach is preferable (because of a statistical power advantage) when group membership is formed by random assignment, whereas analysis of change scores is preferable when the group membership occurs naturally, without random assignment (because of the potential for misleading effects known as 'Lord's paradox'; see Maxwell and Delaney, 2004: 444–48 for a full discussion of these issues). Aside from these points, in the reading comprehension example, it turns out that a change score approach would not have been appropriate because Baumann et al. (1992) altered the reading comprehension test between administrations; thus, their pretest was not *commensurate* with the posttest, implying that it is not reasonable to calculate their difference. It is important to keep in mind, though, that the covariate in an ANCOVA can be any individual differences variable to be controlled, whether a pretest or not.

 Section recap

### Analysis of covariance model and beyond

The **analysis of covariance**, or ANCOVA, model is a multiple regression model (i.e., a special case of the general linear model) in which an outcome variable is regressed on a discrete

*(Continued)*

(Continued)

predictor (represented with dummy-code or contrast-code variables) as well as a covariate. ANCOVA was originally developed to determine whether group means differ over and above the effects of a potentially confounding covariate.

Traditionally, the covariate in an ANCOVA is a continuous variable, but in the multiple regression framework, the covariate is just another predictor in the regression equation which can be either continuous or discrete. Furthermore, the basic ANCOVA model can be easily expanded to include multiple predictors, which can be any combination of categorical and continuous variables.

Whereas the ANOVA model (Equation 3.3) can be used to reproduce the individual group means (i.e., $\hat{Y}$ values for each of the $K$ categories), the ANCOVA model can be used to produce **adjusted means**, which are $\hat{Y}$ values for each of the $K$ categories given a score on the covariate equal to the mean of the covariate.

The ANCOVA model is often used when the outcome variable is a posttest (or posttreatment) score and the covariate is a pretest (or pretreatment) score of the same measure. If participants are not randomly assigned to categories, though, results from this ANCOVA approach could be misleading, resulting from Lord's paradox. An alternative approach is to analyse simple change scores (posttest scores – pretest scores).

---

# REGRESSION DIAGNOSTICS WITH CATEGORICAL PREDICTORS

Multiple regression models incorporating categorical predictors are most commonly estimated using the OLS method described in Chapters 1 and 2. Therefore, the assumptions of OLS regression apply equivalently to models with categorical predictors and the same diagnostic procedures presented in Chapter 2 can be used.

To illustrate, Figure 3.2 gives a plot of the Studentized residuals by predicted values from the ANCOVA-type model in which the reading comprehension test scores were regressed on the pretest scores and the two contrast-code variables representing the three-level intervention predictor variable. The plot is enhanced with a LOWESS curve which has its span set to 1.0 to accommodate the small sample size (i.e., to avoid overfitting). This plot does suggest the presence of nonlinearity, but the sharp upward curve on the left side of the plot results from only two data points. To satisfy ourselves that nonlinearity is not a major concern for this estimated model, recall that the relation between a continuous outcome and a dichotomous predictor is necessarily linear; thus, the partial relations between the posttest scores and the two contrast-code variables in this example are both linear. Next, a scatterplot of the Studentized residuals by pretest scores (in Figure 3.3) shows only a slight curvature, which is not sufficient to warrant concern about nonlinearity. In sum, we can conclude that the original ANCOVA model with only linear terms for the regression of posttest scores on pretest scores and contrasts adequately captures the major regularities of these data.

The plot of Studentized residuals by predicted values also indicates that there are no major concerns regarding the homogeneity of variance assumption. To evaluate this assumption further, we could create scatterplots of the residuals by each contrast-code variable included in the actual regression model. But, in that these variables represent the original three-level

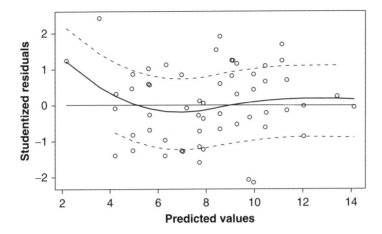

**Figure 3.2** Enhanced scatterplot of Studentized residuals against predicted values from regression of reading posttest scores on contrast variables and reading pretest scores (LOWESS span set to 1.0)

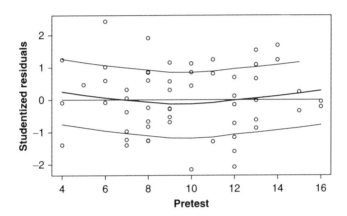

**Figure 3.3** Enhanced scatterplot of Studentized residuals against reading pretest scores (LOWESS span set to 1.0)

intervention variable, it is easier to discern the spread of the residuals across these three levels using a side-by-side box plot of the Studentized residuals by intervention group, as shown in Figure 3.4. At first, it may appear as if the residuals have a smaller spread in the DRTA group because the size of its box (i.e., the interquartile range) is noticeably smaller than that of the other two groups. But this difference is not drastic, and is somewhat compensated by the comparatively longer length of the whiskers (i.e., the range) of the DRTA box plot. Furthermore, the actual standard deviation of the residuals is similar across groups, although smallest for the DRTA group (standard deviation [SD] = 2.49 for Control, 2.00 for DRTA, and 2.69 for TA). Also notice from Figure 3.3 that the residuals are homogeneous across the levels of the pretest covariate. Finally, the histogram of Studentized residuals in Figure 3.5 indicates that the overall distribution of residuals from this model does not have any extreme departure from normality.

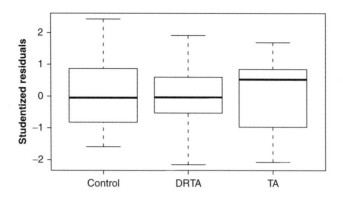

**Figure 3.4**  Side-by-side boxplots of Studentized residuals across intervention groups

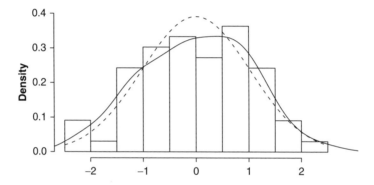

**Figure 3.5**  Histogram of Studentized residuals with fitted kernel density smoother (solid curve) and fitted normal distribution (dashed curve)

Given that this chapter presents a general multiple regression approach to ANCOVA, it is important to mention another model assumption which is typically presented in more traditional presentations of ANCOVA, namely, the assumption of **parallelism**, which is also known as **homogeneity of regression** (not to be confused with the homogeneity of variance assumption). In the multiple regression context, this assumption is simply understood as a statement that there is no interaction between the covariate and the categorical predictor; that is, the partial regression relation between the covariate and the outcome variable is consistent across the categories of the predictor. But this assumption is hardly unique to ANCOVA: Whenever there is a true interaction among predictors, any model that does not include a term to capture the interaction is **misspecified** (i.e., the model does not include parameters that exist in the population), and the parameter estimates and standard errors for that model are incorrect to some extent that might lead to misleading substantive conclusions. This situation occurs regardless of whether the predictors or covariates involved in the interaction are continuous or categorical. In traditional ANCOVA analyses, the lack of interaction is simply assumed, but when ANCOVA is explicitly implemented as a multiple regression model, the model is easily expanded to include any potentially important interactions. Multiple regression models with interaction effects are the major topic of Chapter 4.

## Section recap

### Regression diagnostics with categorical predictors

The same principles and procedures regarding regression diagnostics that were addressed in Chapters 1 and 2 readily generalize to models incorporating categorical predictors.

The traditional ANCOVA model carries an additional assumption known as **parallelism** or **homogeneity of regression**. Essentially, it is assumed that there is no interaction between the covariate and the discrete predictor variable. But explicitly implementing ANCOVA using multiple regression allows for an easy expansion of the model to include any important interactions.

## CHAPTER SUMMARY

This chapter explained how categorical predictors can be incorporated into multiple regression models. Following the concept of the **general linear model**, the chapter described how any combination of continuous and categorical predictors can be included in a regression model, regardless of whether the predictors arise from experimental research or naturalistic, observational research:

- The models underlying the independent-groups $t$ test, ANOVA, and ANCOVA are special cases of the general linear model.
- The relation between a continuous $Y$ and a dichotomous $X$ is always linear. The trick to incorporating a predictor variable with more than two categories, whether nominal or ordinal, is to represent it using a set of separate dichotomous variables, which may be **dummy-code variables** or **contrast-code variables**, among other possibilities.
- $K - 1$ dummy variables are needed to represent a predictor with $K$ categories. These $K - 1$ dummy variables comprehensively represent the categorical predictor in the regression model:

$$Y_i = \beta_0 + \beta_1 D_{1i} + \ldots + \beta_{K-1} D_{(K-1)i} + \varepsilon_i.$$

  - If there are no other predictors in the model, the intercept estimate $\hat{\beta}_0$ equals the sample mean of $Y$ for the reference category.
  - The slope estimate $\hat{\beta}_k$ for dummy variable $D_k$ equals the difference between the mean of $Y$ for category $k$ and the mean of $Y$ for the reference category.

- $K - 1$ contrast-code variables are needed to represent a predictor with $K$ categories. The contrasts $\psi_k$ are formed according to null hypotheses, including **complex null hypotheses**, which are typically based on planned comparisons. The $K - 1$ contrast variables comprehensively represent the categorical predictor in the regression model:

$$Y_i = \beta_0 + \beta_1 C_{1i} + \ldots + \beta_{K-1} C_{(K-1)i} + \varepsilon_i.$$

  - If there are no other predictors in the model, the intercept estimate $\hat{\beta}_0$ equals the average of the sample means of $Y$ across the groups formed by the multicategory predictor.
  - The test of the slope estimate $\hat{\beta}_k$ for contrast variable $C_k$ is a test of the null hypothesis underlying contrast $\psi_k$.

- The **analysis of covariance**, or **ANCOVA**, model is a multiple regression model in which an outcome variable is regressed on a categorical predictor as well as on a covariate.
- The traditional ANCOVA model carries an additional assumption known as **parallelism** or **homogeneity of regression**. Essentially, it is assumed that there is no interaction between the covariate and the categorical predictor. But explicitly implementing ANCOVA using multiple regression allows for an easy expansion of the model to include any important interactions.

## RECOMMENDED READING

Cohen, J. (1968). Multiple regression as a general data-analytic system. *Psychological Bulletin, 70*, 426–43.

- This clear, didactic paper debunked the traditional thinking that ANOVA is for experimental data, whereas regression is for observational data. Cohen outlines the strength of the general linear model to incorporate any combination of categorical and continuous predictors.

Lane, D.M., & Sandor, A. (2009). Designing better graphs by including distributional information and integrating words, numbers, and images. *Psychological Methods, 14*, 239–57.

- Among other good advice about graphs, this paper demonstrates why side-by-side box-plots are superior to bar charts (which are ubiquitous in experimental psychology) for illustrating group differences in the distribution of an outcome variable. Nonetheless, I don't agree with all of the guidelines in this paper; several of the touted graphs are cluttered with too much information.

MacCallum, R.C., Zhang, S., Preacher, K.J., & Rucker, D.D. (2002). On the practice of dichotomization of quantitative variables. *Psychological Methods, 7*, 19–40.

- For researchers who are inexperienced or uncomfortable with regression, this paper clearly and forcefully explains why it is rarely, if ever, a good idea to categorize a continuous predictor artificially (e.g., using a 'median split') so that traditional ANOVA procedures can be used instead of regression modeling.

# INTERACTIONS IN MULTIPLE REGRESSION: MODELS FOR MODERATION

## CHAPTER OVERVIEW

This chapter builds on the multiple regression models presented in earlier chapters by introducing interaction terms which are used to assess hypotheses about moderation in which the effect of one predictor varies according to another predictor. The main topics of this chapter include:

- Specifying a regression model for statistical moderation
- Probing an interaction with a dichotomous moderator
- Specifying a regression model for a multicategory moderator
- Probing an interaction with a multicategory moderator
- Probing an interaction with a continuous moderator
- Advice for interpreting interactions using multiple regression

**Table 4.0** Greek letter notation used in this chapter

| Greek letter | English name | Represents |
|---|---|---|
| $\beta$ | Lowercase 'beta' | Regression model parameter (intercept or slope, depending on subscript) |
| $\omega$ | Lowercase 'omega' | Simple intercept or simple slope parameter (depending on subscript) |
| $\alpha$ | Lowercase 'alpha' | Probability of Type I error |

## WHAT IS STATISTICAL MODERATION?

Thus far, we have focused on models in which the predictor variables have additive effects on an outcome variable. Often, however, two (or more) variables combine in a multiplicative fashion to predict an outcome variable. In this situation, there is an **interaction** between predictors, meaning that the effect of one predictor on the outcome depends on the value of another predictor. In other words, the relation between the first predictor and the outcome is different across different values of the second predictor. In the behavioural and social sciences, we often use the term **moderator** to refer to a variable that influences the relation between a **focal predictor** and an outcome; the focal predictor is then a predictor variable of central interest in a given model. In general, then, the term **moderation** is synonymous with interaction. As we will see later, determining which of two interacting variables is a moderator and which is a focal predictor is entirely a matter of how one wishes to interpret a given model; mathematically, the distinction is arbitrary.

## INTERACTIONS WITH A CATEGORICAL MODERATOR

### Research example for interaction with a categorical moderator

It may be easiest to begin understanding how to specify and interpret interactions in multiple regression when the moderator is a dichotomous variable. For example, Flora, Khoo, and Chassin (2007) were interested in determining whether parental alcoholism moderated the relation between an adolescent's level of externalizing behaviour and subsequent heavy alcohol use. Parental alcoholism was operationalized as a dichotomous variable which was dummy coded to equal 1 for *children of alcoholics* (COAs; adolescents who had at least one parent with a lifetime diagnosis of alcohol abuse or dependence) and 0 for *controls* (adolescents with neither parent reaching an alcohol disorder diagnosis). Later, we consider an operationalization of parental alcoholism that produces a three-category ordinally scaled variable reflecting a participant's number of alcoholic parents. Externalizing behaviour was operationalized using the Child-Behavior Checklist (Achenbach and Edelbrock, 1981), whereas the dependent outcome, heavy alcohol use, was measured using a composite of four self-report alcohol-use items (see Flora et al., 2007, for details). The regression analyses presented later use a subset of cases from a larger longitudinal dataset; these data come from $N = 165$ adolescents whose externalizing was observed at age 13 and alcohol use was observed at age 14.[1] Of these participants, 54.5% ($n = 90$) were COAs.

This dataset is available on the text's webpage (https://study.sagepub.com/flora) along with annotated input and output from several popular statistical software packages showing how to reproduce the analyses presented in this chapter.

---

[1]Flora et al. (2007) reported a more complex series of data analyses examining how parental alcoholism moderates the longitudinal relations between trajectories of externalizing and alcohol use. See Flora et al. for references regarding the recruitment of participants and procedure for the larger longitudinal study from which the current example data were drawn.

In this research example, we would like to know whether the relation between the focal predictor, externalizing behaviour, and the outcome, heavy alcohol use, is moderated by the binary parental alcoholism variable. That is, we hypothesize that the relation between externalizing behaviour and alcohol use varies according to parental alcoholism: Perhaps externalizing is more strongly related to alcohol use among adolescents who have an alcoholic parent than among those who are not children of alcoholics. But before estimating and interpreting a regression model for this hypothesis, it is prudent to examine the data descriptively.

Table 4.1 gives the correlations, means, and standard deviations for the three variables in this example. There is a small-to-moderate positive correlation between externalizing and heavy alcohol use, and the parental alcoholism variable is positively correlated with both externalizing and alcohol use. But these simple bivariate correlations do not convey any information whatsoever about our moderation hypothesis. It is more informative to plot the data and, specifically, to plot the relation between the focal predictor (externalizing) and the outcome (heavy alcohol use) separately for the two categories of the moderator (parental alcoholism), as shown in Figure 4.1. Now we can see that among the control participants, there does not appear to be any notable association between alcohol use and externalizing primarily because most of these participants have values at or near zero on the heavy alcohol-use outcome. Among COAs, though, there does seem to be a slight positive relation between externalizing and alcohol use. Thus, from a descriptive perspective, these sample data are consistent with the notion that the relation between externalizing and alcohol use differs according to parental alcoholism. But our ultimate goal, of course, is to build and test a population model that represents this moderation effect.

**Table 4.1**  Correlations, means, and standard deviations for adolescent alcohol-use example

| Variable | 1. | 2. | 3. |
|---|---|---|---|
| 1. Parental alcoholism (0 = control, 1 = COA) | 1.00 | – | – |
| 2. Externalizing behaviour | 0.21 | 1.00 | – |
| 3. Heavy alcohol use | 0.29 | 0.34 | 1.00 |
| M | 0.55 | 0.56 | 0.36 |
| SD | 0.50 | 0.44 | 0.67 |

Note. N = 165. M = mean, SD = standard deviation.

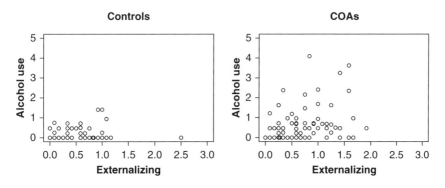

**Figure 4.1**  Scatterplots of heavy alcohol use across two levels of parental alcoholism

## Model specification and interpretation with a dichotomous moderator

A multiple regression model incorporating two predictors, $X_1$ and $X_2$, and an interaction between these predictors can be written as

$$\hat{Y}_i = \beta_0 + \beta_1 X_{1i} + \beta_2 X_{2i} + \beta_3 X_{3i},$$

where $X_3$ is a **cross-product** variable, or **product term**, that is formed by multiplying $X_1$ and $X_2$ together; that is, $X_3 = X_1 \times X_2$. Therefore, this model is equivalent to

$$\hat{Y}_i = \beta_0 + \beta_1 X_{1i} + \beta_2 X_{2i} + \beta_3 (X_{1i} \times X_{2i}). \tag{4.1}$$

Given this model, it is arbitrary as to whether one views $X_1$ as the focal predictor and $X_2$ as the moderator or vice versa; the conceptual difference between the focal predictor and the moderator mainly comes into play when one interprets the interaction, as we will see shortly. But for convenience at this point, let's say that $X_1$ is the focal predictor and $X_2$ is the moderator. The size of the partial regression coefficient $\beta_3$ represents the extent to which the interaction between $X_1$ and $X_2$ predicts the outcome $Y$, that is, the extent to which $X_1$ and $X_2$ have a multiplicative effect, or the extent to which $X_2$ moderates the relation between $X_1$ and $Y$. As with all multiple regression models considered so far, this model is most often estimated using the ordinary least-squares (OLS) method outlined in Chapter 2. Furthermore, it is straightforward to expand the model in Equation 4.1 to include additional predictors or covariates, following methods presented in Chapters 2 and 3, or even to add additional interactions. By no means is it necessary to estimate and interpret the interaction between two variables in isolation from other important predictors; Equation 4.1 and the examples given in this chapter involve models with only two predictors (and their interaction) merely for the sake of convenient simplicity. In practice, misleading results can be obtained if important predictors or covariates are omitted from a given model.

It is convenient to refer to the Equation 4.1 coefficients $\beta_1$ and $\beta_2$ as **first-order** (or *lower order*) effects and to the interaction effect $\beta_3$ as a **higher order** effect.[2] It is crucial to recognize that the relation between a given predictor and the outcome variable involves both its first-order effect and the higher order effect.[3] Recalling the original interpretations of partial regression coefficients from the earlier chapters, it is clear from Equation 4.1 that a one-unit increase in $X_1$ exerts an influence on $Y$ that is determined by both $\beta_1$ and $\beta_3$. Often, researchers are tempted to interpret first-order effects as 'main effects' in isolation from their interpretation of the interaction; doing so can be perilous. Instead, the first-order effect of a focal predictor, the coefficient $\beta_1$, represents the partial linear regression effect of that predictor *when the*

---

[2]Polynomial terms (see Chapter 2), such as a quadratic term $X^2 = X \times X$, are also higher order regression predictors.

[3]Occasionally researchers are tempted to estimate a model that includes a higher order product term but omits either one or both of the lower order predictors that comprise the product variable, such as

$$\hat{Y}_i = \beta_0 + \beta_1 X_{1i} + \beta_2 (X_{1i} \times X_{2i}).$$

Such a model violates the *principle of marginality* and is typically unrealistically restrictive (see Fox, 2008: 146–47). In general, models including interactions should almost always include both the higher order interaction effect and the first-order effects of the variables involved in the interaction.

*value of the moderator equals zero.* Next, the higher order effect, the interaction coefficient $\beta_3$, represents the amount that the slope for the focal predictor changes per one-unit increase in the moderator. Thus, in Equation 4.1, $\beta_1$ represents the partial regression relation between $X_1$ and $Y$ only among cases whose value of $X_2$ equals 0. This relation is easy to see algebraically: Setting $X_{2i} = 0$, Equation 4.1 reduces to

$$\hat{Y}_i = \beta_0 + \beta_1 X_{1i} + \beta_2 \times 0 + \beta_3 (X_{1i} \times 0)$$
$$= \beta_0 + \beta_1 X_{1i}.$$

(Likewise, $\beta_2$ represents the relation between $X_2$ and $Y$ among cases whose value of $X_1$ equals 0.) It may be that a value of zero for the moderator represents a nonsensical hypothetical participant for a particular research context; that is, there may not be any cases in the population with $X_2 = 0$. In this situation, a direct interpretation of $\beta_1$ that ignores $\beta_3$ is nonsense. A prominent approach to interpreting models with interactions, then, is to scale the moderator so that 0 is in fact a particularly meaningful and important value, as demonstrated later.

Returning to the adolescent heavy alcohol-use example, let's apply the model in Equation 4.1 with $X_1$ representing externalizing behaviour and $X_2$ as the dichotomous parental alcoholism variable. To estimate the model, the interaction term, $X_1 \times X_2$, is represented as a new variable, $X_3$, that is formed by multiplying $X_1$ and $X_2$ together.[4] When the alcohol-use variable is regressed on $X_1$, $X_2$, and $X_3$ using OLS estimation, the resulting parameter estimates are those given in Table 4.2. First and foremost, we should focus on the interaction effect, ignoring the other parameter estimates for the time being. Here, the estimated regression coefficient for the interaction term ($\hat{\beta}_3 = 0.57$) seems substantial given the standard deviation (*SD*) of the alcohol use outcome (*SD* = 0.67) and that the interaction is statistically significant. Therefore, at this point, we can conclude that the dichotomous parental alcoholism variable significantly moderates the relation between externalizing behaviour and alcohol use. But how, or in what way, does parental alcoholism affect the relation between externalizing and alcohol use? We can **probe** the interaction to answer this question, whereby we will arrive at a more specific interpretation of the effect of externalizing on alcohol use across the two categories of parental alcoholism.

**Table 4.2** Results for OLS regression of heavy alcohol use on externalizing behaviour, parental alcoholism, and their interaction

| Variable | $\hat{\beta}$ | $SE(\hat{\beta})$ | t | p | 95% CI |
|---|---|---|---|---|---|
| Intercept | 0.104 | 0.107 | – | – | – |
| $X_1$: Externalizing | 0.102 | 0.173 | 0.58 | .56 | (−0.240, 0.443) |
| $X_2$: COA | 0.002 | 0.155 | 0.01 | .99 | (−0.305, 0.308) |
| $X_3$: Externalizing × COA | 0.567 | 0.224 | 2.53 | .01 | (0.124, 1.010) |

*Note.* $N = 165$. $R^2 = .194$, $F(3,161) = 12.94$, $p < .001$. $SE$ = standard error.

[4]Some software regression procedures allow the user simply to enter 'var1*var2' as an independent variable (substituting the actual variable names in the data file for 'var1' and 'var2') instead of first creating a new variable equaling the product of 'var1' and 'var2'. See the software examples on the book's website for details.

Before moving on, though, I offer a word of advice. If an interaction effect is nonsignificant or otherwise deemed quantitatively trivial, it is helpful to drop the interaction from the model to obtain more easily interpreted slope estimates for the original, first-order predictors (e.g., instead of interpreting estimates of parameters from the model of Equation 4.1, interpret estimates from the model of Equation 2.1, which is equivalent to 4.1 if $\beta_3 = 0$). Although it is true that if the interaction effect is small and weak, the estimates of the first-order effects (e.g., $\hat{\beta}_1$ and $\hat{\beta}_2$ from estimating Equation 4.1) should be generally similar to the estimates obtained without the interaction included in the model ($\hat{\beta}_1$ and $\hat{\beta}_2$ from estimating Equation 2.1), in my experience, that is not always the case (especially if $\hat{\beta}_1$ or $\hat{\beta}_2$ is also small), and inferential conclusions regarding these first-order effects may change based on whether a trivial interaction effect is included. A more general principle is that when a larger model contains weak, trivially important effects, a smaller model without those effects included may be interpreted instead for the sake of parsimony.

 Section recap

### Specifying a regression model for statistical moderation

Statistical **moderation** occurs when the association between a focal predictor and an outcome variable differs across the levels of another predictor, the **moderator**.

Moderation can be assessed using multiple regression by testing the **interaction** between the focal predictor ($X_1$) and the moderator ($X_2$). Interactions are included in a multiple regression model by incorporating a **product term** ($X_1 \times X_2$) in the regression equation:

$$\hat{Y}_i = \beta_0 + \beta_1 X_{1i} + \beta_2 X_{2i} + \beta_3 (X_{1i} \times X_{2i}).$$

Here, $\beta_1$ and $\beta_2$ are the **first-order** (or lower order) effects of $X_1$ and $X_2$, respectively, whereas the interaction effect, $\beta_3$, is a **higher order** effect. The size of $\beta_3$ quantifies the extent of the interaction (or moderation) effect.

It is important not to interpret $\beta_1$ or $\beta_2$ as a so-called 'main effect'. Instead, $\beta_1$ represents the effect of $X_1$ only for a case which has $X_2 = 0$; likewise, $\beta_2$ represents the effect of $X_2$ only for a case which has $X_1 = 0$.

## Probing an interaction with simple-slope analysis

Occasionally, upon finding a significant interaction, researchers will 'split' their dataset according to the moderator, forming one dataset containing all participants with one value of the moderator (or with a particular range of values for the moderator) and a second dataset with all participants at the other value (or range of values) of the moderator. The next step is to estimate the relation between the focal predictor and the outcome variable separately using these two datasets, comparing results to determine the nature of the interaction. For instance, with the current data, we could create one dataset containing only the control participants and use this dataset to obtain the relation between alcohol use and externalizing among controls. Next, we could create a second dataset containing only COAs, use this second dataset to get the relation between alcohol use and externalizing among COAs, and then compare the results with the separate results obtained for controls. But this approach to probing an interaction by 'splitting' the data produces incorrect estimates of the standard error of the regression slopes relating the focal predictor to the outcome, which in turn leads to incorrect significance tests and confidence intervals for the relations between the focal predictor and the outcome across the values of the moderator. Instead, the nature of an interaction should be examined using the complete dataset, with careful interpretation of the estimated parameters of Equation 4.1. One approach to doing so is to probe an interaction using a **simple-slope analysis**.

With some basic algebra, one can see that Equation 4.1 is equivalent to

$$\hat{Y}_i = (\beta_0 + \beta_2 X_{2i}) + (\beta_1 + \beta_3 X_{2i})X_{1i}. \tag{4.2}$$

The first term in parentheses of Equation 4.2 gives what's called the **simple intercept** for $X_1$, and the second term in parentheses gives the **simple-slope** coefficient for $X_1$. That is, if we define the simple intercept for $X_1$ as

$$\omega_0 = (\beta_0 + \beta_2 X_{2i}) \tag{4.3}$$

and define the simple slope for $X_1$ as

$$\omega_1 = (\beta_1 + \beta_3 X_{2i}), \tag{4.4}$$

then Equation 4.2 can be written as

$$\hat{Y}_i = \omega_0 + \omega_1 X_{1i}. \tag{4.5}$$

Equation 4.5 is like a simple regression model of the form introduced in Chapter 1 (cf. Equation 1.10) in that $\omega_0$, the simple intercept for $X_1$, gives the predicted value of $Y$ when $X_1 = 0$ and $\omega_1$, the simple slope for $X_1$, gives the predicted change in $Y$ associated with a one-unit change in $X_1$. But it is clear from Equations 4.3 and 4.4 that $\omega_0$ and $\omega_1$ depend on $X_2$; thus, these terms reflect that the association between $X_1$ and $Y$ is moderated by $X_2$. (As mentioned, mathematically, it is arbitrary as to which variable, $X_1$ or $X_2$, is referred to as the moderator. Consequently, just as we can define the simple slope for $X_1$ that is a function of $X_2$, we can also define the simple slope for $X_2$ that is a function of $X_1$. Again, substantive context should determine which simple slopes are of primary importance.)

In the current example examining the interaction between the externalizing behaviour focal predictor ($X_1$) and the parental alcoholism moderator ($X_2$), the moderator is dichotomous (COA = 0 or COA = 1). Therefore, $\omega_0$ and $\omega_1$ each have only two possible values; that is, there are only two simple regression equations for the relation between externalizing and heavy alcohol use, one for each value of COA. For the control participants without an alcoholic parent, COA = 0 or $X_2 = 0$, and so using Equations 4.3 and 4.4, the simple intercept and simple slope for these participants are

$$\omega_{0|X_2=0} = \beta_0 + \beta_2 \times 0 = \beta_0$$

and

$$\omega_{1|X_2=0} = \beta_1 + \beta_3 \times 0 = \beta_1,$$

respectively. Thus, the simple intercept and simple slope for the effect of externalizing on alcohol use among control participants equal the intercept ($\beta_0$) and focal predictor slope ($\beta_1$) from the original regression model (i.e., Equation 4.1). This observation is consistent with the previous statement that in Equation 4.1, $\beta_1$ represents the partial regression relation between $X_1$ and $Y$ among cases whose value of $X_2$ equals 0. From Table 4.2, $\hat{\beta}_0 = 0.104$ and $\hat{\beta}_1 = 0.102$. Therefore, the estimated simple regression equation of alcohol use on externalizing for control participants is

$$\hat{Y}_i = 0.104 + 0.102(X_{1i}). \tag{4.6}$$

Next, for the children of alcoholics, COA = 1 or $X_2 = 1$, and so the simple intercept and simple slope for these participants are

$$\omega_{0|X_2=1} = \beta_0 + \beta_2 \times 1 = \beta_0 + \beta_2$$

and

$$\omega_{1|X_2=1} = \beta_1 + \beta_3 \times 1 = \beta_1 + \beta_3,$$

respectively. Again, using the estimates from Table 4.2,

$$\hat{\omega}_{0|X_2=1} = \hat{\beta}_0 + \hat{\beta}_2 = 0.104 + 0.002 = 0.106$$

and

$$\hat{\omega}_{1|X_2=1} = \hat{\beta}_1 + \hat{\beta}_3 = 0.102 + 0.567 = 0.669.$$

Therefore, the estimated simple regression equation of alcohol use on externalizing for children of alcoholics is

$$\hat{Y}_i = 0.106 + 0.669(X_{1i}). \tag{4.7}$$

Comparing Equation 4.6 with Equation 4.7 makes it clear that the effect of externalizing (i.e., the simple slope of externalizing) is much stronger among children of alcoholics than among controls; Figure 4.2 gives a plot of these estimated simple regression equations, more fully illustrating that the slope of externalizing strongly depends on the parental alcoholism moderator.

Because the coefficient for the interaction term ($\hat{\beta}_3 = 0.567$) is statistically significant, the simple-slope estimate of the COA group (i.e., the group with COA = 1) is significantly different from that of the control group (COA = 0). Additionally, a researcher might be interested in whether the simple slopes themselves are significant (i.e., significantly different from zero) or interested in confidence intervals for the individual simple slopes. In general, the $t$ test of the estimated first-order coefficient of the focal predictor ($\hat{\beta}_1$) is the $t$ test of the simple slope *among participants whose value of the moderator equals zero* ($\hat{\omega}_{1|X_2=0}$). This correspondence should be clear because, as shown earlier, $\omega_{1|X_2=0} = \beta_1$. Likewise, the confidence interval of the first-order slope estimate of the focal predictor corresponds to the

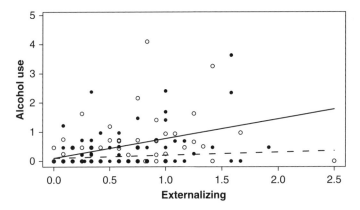

**Figure 4.2** Scatterplot of heavy alcohol use against externalizing with fitted regression moderated by parental alcoholism (solid line and solid data points for children of alcoholics [COAs], dashed line and open data points for control participants)

confidence interval of the simple slope among participants whose value of the moderator equals zero. Therefore, in the current example, the $t$ test of the slope estimate for externalizing from Table 4.2 indicates that the externalizing simple slope among control participants is not significant, $p = .56$, and that the one-at-a-time[5] 95% confidence interval (CI) for this simple slope is (–0.240, 0.443). Therefore, one needs only to look at the summary of the results from the original model with the interaction term included to find the estimate, significance (i.e., $t$ test), and confidence interval for the simple slope of the focal predictor among participants whose value of the moderator equals zero. Getting the significance and confidence interval of simple slopes at other values of the moderator is slightly more complex, as described next.

As shown earlier, the simple slope of the focal predictor among participants whose value of the moderator equals 1 is $\omega_{1|X_2=1} = \beta_1 + \beta_3$, which in the current example is the simple slope of the COA group. Because the sample estimate of this simple slope, $\hat{\omega}_{1|X_2=1}$, depends on two regression slope estimates, $\hat{\beta}_1$ and $\hat{\beta}_3$, its standard error is not readily discernible from the usual default statistical software output, which means that the $t$ test and confidence interval of this simple slope are also not immediately available. The standard error of this simple slope can be calculated using formulas provided by Bauer and Curran (2005), among other resources, but doing so requires calculation of the *asymptotic covariance matrix* of the regression coefficient estimates.[6] Although standard software can easily produce the values needed for this calculation, an alternative procedure is equally effective for testing simple slopes and constructing their confidence intervals and is perhaps more easily understood.

This alternative procedure takes advantage of the fact that the first-order regression coefficient for the focal predictor represents the simple slope among cases whose value of the

---

[5]The meaning of 'one at a time' is explained later in this chapter.

[6]Briefly, the asymptotic covariance matrix of the regression coefficient estimates contains the variances of the sampling distribution of the slope estimates (whose square roots are the standard errors of the individual slopes) as well as the covariances among the slope estimates from a hypothetically infinite number of samples.

moderator equals 0. The trick is to recode, or transform, the moderator to change which cases have a value of 0 on the moderator and then reestimate the model to obtain a different esti-mate of the first-order regression coefficient for the focal predictor; the $t$ test and confidence interval of this new estimate of the first-order regression coefficient then pertain to the simple slope at the new value of the moderator. To apply this procedure to the current example, we can simply recode the previous COA variable to create a new dummy variable, here called nCOA, such that nCOA = 0 for the children of alcoholics and nCOA = 1 for the control partici-pants. We then reestimate the model of Equation 4.1 with $X_1$ again representing externalizing behaviour, $X_2$ now representing the new nCOA variable, and the interaction term now being the product of the externalizing variable and nCOA.

The results from this model estimation are in Table 4.3. First, note that $R^2$ and its corresponding $F$ test are identical to those obtained earlier, indicating that the current model using the recoded COA variable is indeed equivalent to the previous model using the original COA variable. Next, the coefficients for the moderator (now nCOA instead of COA) and the interaction term match those obtained earlier (cf. Table 4.2), except they are now negative because nCOA is simply a reverse-coding of the original COA variable; likewise, the standard error of these coefficients remains unchanged.[7] Finally, the primary reason for reestimating the model using nCOA is to obtain a new first-order coefficient for the focal predictor, externalizing behaviour, along with its standard error, $t$ test, and confidence interval. This new first-order coefficient for externalizing ($\hat{\beta}_1 = 0.669$) equals the simple-slope estimate calculated earlier for the effect of externalizing among children of alcoholics. Thus, again we see that the first-order regression coefficient for the focal predictor represents the simple slope among cases whose value of the moderator equals 0 because here we have estimated the model using the nCOA variable as the moderator which is coded such that nCOA = 0 for the participants with an alcoholic parent. But now we also obtain the standard error of this simple-slope estimate which in turn produces a $t$ test and a confidence interval estimate of the population simple slope. The results in Table 4.3 therefore indicate that the externalizing simple slope among children of alcohol-ics is significant, $p < .001$, and the one-at-a-time 95% confidence interval for this simple slope is (0.387, 0.951).

**Table 4.3** Results for OLS regression of heavy alcohol use on externalizing behaviour, reverse-coded parental alcoholism, and their interaction

| Variable | $\hat{\beta}$ | $SE(\hat{\beta})$ | $t$ | $p$ | 95% CI |
|---|---|---|---|---|---|
| Intercept | 0.106 | 0.113 | – | – | – |
| $X_1$: Externalizing | 0.669 | 0.143 | 4.69 | <.001 | (0.387, 0.951) |
| $X_2$: nCOA | −0.002 | 0.155 | 0.01 | .560 | (−0.308, 0.305) |
| $X_3$: Externalizing × nCOA | −0.567 | 0.224 | 2.53 | .010 | (−1.010, −0.124) |

Note. $N = 165$. $R^2 = .194$, $F(3, 161) = 12.94$, $p < .001$.

[7]Additionally, the intercept has changed slightly because it now represents $\hat{Y}$ for participants who have a value of zero on externalizing and zero for nCOA, whereas the intercept for the original model estima-tion in Table 4.2 represents $\hat{Y}$ for participants who have a value of zero on externalizing and zero for the original COA variable.

In summary, this set of analyses has confirmed the hypothesis that parental alcoholism moderates the relation between externalizing behaviour and subsequent heavy alcohol use among adolescents via the significant interaction between the externalizing variable and the dichotomous parental alcoholism variable (either COA or nCOA). Next, the interaction was probed by finding simple slopes; specifically, the relation between externalizing and alcohol use was small ( $\hat{\omega} = 0.102$ ) and nonsignificant among control participants, but among children of alcoholics, externalizing was a stronger, significant predictor of heavy drinking ( $\hat{\omega} = 0.669$ ). This interaction effect is visualized in Figure 4.2, which shows the separate simple regression lines for the control and COA groups.

One point of concern for significance tests of simple slopes is that the comparison of their respective $p$ values with a nominal alpha level (typically .05) is valid for only a single test (Bauer and Curran, 2005). That is, testing more than simple slope for significance is an instance of the multiple comparisons problem: If the $p$ values for two simple slopes are both compared with a nominal alpha level of .05, then the probability of a Type I error across *both* tests (i.e., the family-wise Type I error probability) is greater than .05. This problem compounds as moderators have more than two levels and consequently significance tests are of interest for more than two simple-slope estimates. A well-known and easily implemented approach to handling this problem is to control the family-wise Type I error probability using a **Bonferroni-corrected** alpha level. Specifically, the Bonferroni-corrected alpha level is obtained by dividing the nominal alpha level for a given test (e.g., .05) by the number of significance tests to be carried out (e.g., the number of simple slopes). In the adolescent alcohol use example, there are two simple-slope estimates to be tested, and so the Bonferroni-corrected alpha level for each would be ($\alpha$ = .05) / 2 = .025. The simple slope for the COA participants is still significant using this corrected alpha level because the $p$ value for the first-order estimate of the externalizing predictor given in Table 4.3 is less than .025. This multiple comparison issue also applies to the calculation of confidence intervals for the simple slopes and is the reason that the confidence intervals reported earlier are referred to as 'one-at-a-time' confidence intervals; these confidence intervals provide valid coverage at 95% only if they are interpreted for a single simple-slope estimate. Yet again, though, we can easily apply the Bonferroni correction to obtain **simultaneous confidence intervals** for more than one simple-slope estimate. Specifically, if we take the confidence interval coverage to be (1 – $\alpha$)% (e.g., 1 – .05 = 95%), then to construct confidence intervals for two simple slopes with simultaneous 95% coverage, each one should be based on (1 – (.05 / .02)), or 97.5%. In the adolescent alcohol use example, the Bonferroni-corrected simultaneous 95% confidence interval is (–0.289, 0.493) for the externalizing simple slope among non-COAs; among COAs, the Bonferroni-corrected simultaneous 95% confidence interval is (0.346, 0.992). Notice that these simultaneous confidence intervals are wider than the corresponding one-at-a-time confidence intervals reported earlier.

The inferential conclusions given for this example should be considered tentative, however, because of violations of OLS regression assumptions. The principles and procedures of regression diagnostics presented in Chapter 2 apply directly to models incorporating interaction terms. In the current example, we can derive the residuals and predicted values from the estimated model regressing heavy alcohol use on externalizing behaviour, parental alcoholism, and their interaction just as with any multiple regression analysis. Here, the residuals clearly deviate from a normal distribution and there is a slight nonlinear and heteroscedastic pattern in the plot of residuals by predicted values (see Figure 4.3). These patterns occur primarily because the heavy alcohol-use outcome variable has a large frequency of observations equaling zero (many participants did not engage in any alcohol use). Yet, although the distribution of this variable is positively skewed, any transformation to reduce the skewness will not change the fact that many participants have the identical value on the outcome variable (after transformation, instead of many participants having a score equal to 0, these same participants will have a score equal to the transformation of 0).[8]

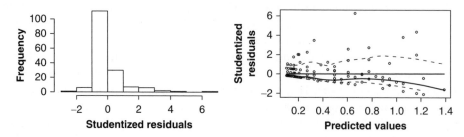

**Figure 4.3** Histogram of Studentized residuals (left panel) and scatterplot of Studentized residuals against predicted values (right panel) from regression of heavy alcohol use on externalizing, parental alcoholism, and their interaction

 Section recap

### Probing an interaction with simple-slope analysis

An important (e.g., statistically significant) interaction effect can be **probed** using a **simple-slope** analysis in which different (estimated) regression equations for the relation between the focal predictor and the outcome are obtained for different values of the moderator variable.

Formally, the simple-slope model can be expressed as

$$\hat{Y}_i = \omega_0 + \omega_1 X_{1i},$$

where $\omega_0 = (\beta_0 + \beta_2 X_{2i})$ is the simple intercept in the regression of $Y$ on $X_1$ and $\omega_1 = (\beta_1 + \beta_3 X_{2i})$ is the simple slope in the regression of $Y$ on $X_1$.

When $X_2 = 0$, the model reduces to

$$\hat{Y}_i = (\beta_0 + \beta_2 \times 0) + (\beta_1 + \beta_3 \times 0)X_{1i}$$
$$= \beta_0 + \beta_1 X_{1i}$$

and thus, the intercept and first-order effect from the original regression model (i.e., Equation 4.1) equals the simple intercept and simple slope for $X_1$ among cases with $X_2 = 0$.

---

[8]An alternative approach to analysing this alcohol-use variable is to treat it as two separate outcomes: A dichotomous variable representing whether each participant reported any alcohol use (which would need to be modeled using a categorical variable method such as logistic regression), and a continuous variable representing the amount of alcohol use reported by participants who have nonzero use (which would have nonrandom missing values for participants reporting zero use on the original variable).

Consequently, the confidence interval and $t$ test for $\hat{\beta}_1$ give the inferential results for the simple slope among cases with $X_2 = 0$.

If the moderator $X_2$ is a dichotomous dummy variable, these are inferential results for the focal predictor in the group coded 0.

The confidence interval and $t$ test for the simple slope among cases with $X_2 = 1$ can then be obtained by reverse-coding dummy variable $X_2$ so that the other group is coded 0 and by reestimating the model with the new, reverse-coded dummy variable (and the corresponding new interaction term).

# Model specification and interpretation with a multicategory moderator

The specification of a model for a dichotomous moderator presented earlier easily generalizes to models for categorical moderators with more than two levels by adapting the approaches outlined in Chapter 3. To demonstrate, we continue with the research example in which parental alcoholism is hypothesized to moderate the relation between externalizing behaviour and subsequent heavy alcohol use among adolescents. For the previous analysis, parental alcoholism was operationalized as a binary variable indicating whether each participant had at least one alcoholic parent or was a control participant. But it is also possible to operationalize parental alcoholism in terms of the number of alcoholic parents of each research participant. This operationalization produces a three-level categorical variable in which each participant has either no alcoholic parents, one alcoholic parent, or both parents are alcoholic. Then we can use a set of dummy-code variables to test whether this operationalization of parent alcoholism moderates the relation between externalizing and alcohol use, perhaps beginning by designating the control participants (i.e., those with zero alcoholic parents) as the reference group, as shown in Table 4.4. (Alternatively, of course, we could use contrast-code variables, among other possibilities, to represent this three-category moderator.)

**Table 4.4**  Assignment of dummy-code values to parental alcoholism moderator

| Number of alcoholic parents | Dummy-code variable values | |
| --- | --- | --- |
| | $D_1$ | $D_2$ |
| 0 | 0 | 0 |
| 1 | 1 | 0 |
| 2 | 0 | 1 |

To represent the interaction between any categorical moderator and a focal predictor comprehensively, it is necessary to create separate terms equaling the product of the focal predictor and each $K - 1$ dichotomous indicator variable (e.g., dummy-code variables or contrast-code variables) used to represent the $K$-category moderator. The interaction between the focal predictor and the $K$-category moderator is then represented by including these $K - 1$ product terms in a regression model simultaneously. In our current example, there are two dummy-code variables which, taken together, represent the three-category parental alcoholism moderator. Specifically, as defined in Table 4.4, $D_1$ represents a comparison of the control group with participants with one alcoholic parent and $D_2$ represents a comparison of the control group with participants with two alcoholic parents. Thus, to model the interaction between the three-category moderator and the externalizing behaviour focal predictor, it is necessary to create product terms for both of these dummy-code variables. Specifically, with $X_1$ again representing externalizing behaviour, we create two new variables, the first of which is equal to $(X_1 \times D_1)$ and the second is $(X_1 \times D_2)$ and include them in a regression model along with the first-order effects of the focal predictor and the moderator:

$$\hat{Y}_i = \beta_0 + \beta_1 X_{1i} + \beta_2 D_{1i} + \beta_3 D_{2i} + \beta_4 (X_{1i} \times D_{1i}) + \beta_5 (X_{1i} \times D_{2i}). \tag{4.8}$$

Generalizing beyond the $K = 3$ categories situation, a multiple regression model with $K - 1$ dummy-code variables and the interactions between these dummy variables and a focal predictor can be expressed as

$$\hat{Y}_i = \beta_0 + \beta_X X_i + \left( \sum_{k=1}^{K-1} \beta_k D_{ki} \right) + \left( \sum_{j=1}^{J-1} \beta_j (X_{1i} \times D_{ji}) \right),$$

where $j$ indexes the $J = K$ product terms formed by multiplying each dummy variable by the focal predictor.

To test the general hypothesis that parental alcoholism moderates the relation between externalizing and alcohol use, it might be advantageous to follow a hierarchical regression strategy in which the product terms $(X_1 \times D_1)$ and $(X_2 \times D_2)$ are considered together as a set (or 'block') to test the joint significance of the estimates of the two interaction coefficients, $\beta_4$ and $\beta_5$. In other words, if $R^2$ for the model in Equation 4.8 is significantly greater than $R^2$ for a more restricted model that does not include the two interaction terms (i.e., a model in which $\beta_4$ and $\beta_5$ both equal zero), that is,

$$\hat{Y}_i = \beta_0 + \beta_1 X_{1i} + \beta_2 D_{1i} + \beta_3 D_{2i}, \tag{4.9}$$

then we can conclude that the three-category parental alcoholism variable moderates the relation between externalizing ($X_1$) and the alcohol use outcome variable. The main reason for following this hierarchical strategy is that it is possible for the two interaction coefficients to be jointly significant as a set when neither of them is significant on its own. In other words, it is possible to obtain a significant $F$ test for the overall $R^2$ change across the models in Equations 4.8 and 4.9 even when neither of the separate $t$ tests for the $\hat{\beta}_4$ and $\hat{\beta}_5$ interaction coefficient estimates is significant. If this result occurs, one can still say that the categorical variable significantly moderates the relation between the focal predictor and the outcome. Additionally, if the individual test for either $\hat{\beta}_4$ or $\hat{\beta}_5$ is significant, one can conclude that there is significant moderation. In general, it is certainly not necessary for all regression coefficients for the product terms involving a $K$-category moderator to be significant for one to be able to conclude that there is significant moderation.

Returning to the alcohol use example, estimation of the model without interaction terms (Equation 4.9) obtains $R^2 = .18$, whereas estimation of the model with the two product terms for the interaction (Equation 4.8) obtains $R^2 = .22$. Although this increase in $R^2$ is somewhat small, it is significant, $\Delta R^2 = .04$, $F(2, 159) = 3.59$, $p = .03$, supporting the hypothesis that the three-category parental alcoholism variable moderates the association between externalizing and heavy alcohol use. Further results from the estimation of the moderation model are in Table 4.5. The estimated coefficient for the product term of the first dummy variable ($\hat{\beta}_4 = 0.574$) is significant. Because $D_1$ represents a comparison of the control group with participants with one alcoholic parent, this result indicates that the effect of externalizing is significantly greater among participants with one alcoholic parent than among those with no alcoholic parents (i.e., the simple slope of externalizing is significantly greater for those with one alcoholic parent compared with the simple slope of those with no alcoholic parents). Next, the estimated coefficient for the product term of the second dummy variable ($\hat{\beta}_4 = 0.812$) is not significant, which indicates that the effect of externalizing among participants with two alcoholic parents does not significantly differ from the externalizing effect among control participants. It may be surprising that the estimated coefficient for this second product term is not significant even though it has a greater magnitude than the estimated coefficient for the first product term, which is significant. This result occurs because there are only nine participants in the sample who have two alcoholic parents, which leads to high standard error terms for the first- and second-order estimated coefficients for the $D_2$ variable (see Table 4.5).

**Table 4.5** Results for OLS regression of heavy alcohol use on externalizing behaviour, parental alcoholism (number of alcoholic parents), and their interaction

| Variable | $\hat{\beta}$ | $SE(\hat{\beta})$ | t | p | 95% CI |
|---|---|---|---|---|---|
| Intercept | 0.104 | – | – | – | – |
| $X_1$: Externalizing | 0.102 | 0.171 | 0.59 | .554 | (−0.237, 0.440) |
| $D_1$: Controls vs. one alcoholic parent | −0.048 | 0.158 | 0.20 | .764 | (−0.360, 0.265) |
| $D_2$: Controls vs. two alcoholic parents | 0.273 | 0.380 | 0.72 | .474 | (−0.478, 1.024) |
| $X_1 \times D_1$ | 0.574 | 0.226 | 2.54 | .012 | (0.128, 1.019) |
| $X_2 \times D_2$ | 0.812 | 0.580 | 1.34 | .164 | (−0.334, 1.957) |

*Note. N = 165. R² = .217, F(5, 159) = 8.83, p < .001.*

 **Section recap**

### Specifying a regression model for a multicategory moderator

A categorical moderator with K categories should be incorporated in a regression model using a set of K - 1 dummy-code variables (or an equivalent representation such as contrast-code variables).

Next, to represent the interaction between the focal predictor and the categorical moderator comprehensively, J product terms should be formed by multiplying each K dummy-code variable by the focal predictor, X. Then, these J = K products are included

*(Continued)*

(Continued)

as predictors in the regression model along with first-order terms for the focal predictor and the dummy variables:

$$\hat{Y}_i = \beta_0 + \beta_X X_i + \left(\sum_{k=1}^{K-1} \beta_k D_{ki}\right) + \left(\sum_{j=1}^{J-1} \beta_j (X_{1i} \times D_{ji})\right).$$

Hierarchical regression can be used to determine whether the *set* of $J = K$ product terms significantly increases multiple $R^2$; if so, one concludes that the $K$-category variable significantly moderates the effect of the focal predictor.

## Probing an interaction with a multicategory moderator

Interactions involving a multicategory moderator can be probed in the same manner that was described earlier for a dichotomous moderator. With a $K$-category moderator, simple-slope analysis can be used to obtain $K$ simple-slope estimates for the effect of the focal predictor across each category of the moderator. In general, although models with categorical moderators can be equivalently specified using contrast-code variables (among other coding systems), simple-slope analysis is much easier if the moderator is represented using dummy-code variables.

Returning to the example analysis, given that the three-category parental alcoholism variable significantly moderates the relation between externalizing and alcohol use, we can proceed to probe the interaction using a simple-slope analysis. First, because the dummy-code variables were specified so that the control group (i.e., those with no alcoholic parents) has a value of zero on both $D_1$ and $D_2$, the first-order coefficient for the externalizing focal predictor is the simple slope for the participants with zero alcoholic parents; this interpretation is easy to see if one plugs in a value of 0 for both $D_1$ and $D_2$ in Equation 4.8. From Table 4.5, we can see that this simple-slope estimate ($\hat{\beta}_1 = 0.102$) is not significantly different from zero, $p = .55$. Appropriately, this result is consistent with the simple-slope results for the control group obtained earlier using the binary parental alcoholism moderator.

Next, the estimated coefficient for the $X_1 \times D_1$ term gives the amount that the externalizing slope increases for a one-unit increase in $D_{1i}$; therefore, the estimated simple slope for participants with one alcoholic parent is $(\hat{\beta}_1 + \hat{\beta}_4) = (0.102 + 0.574) = 0.676$. To obtain a confidence interval and determine whether this simple-slope estimate is significant, we can expand on the procedure outlined earlier for the dichotomous parental alcoholism variable. Specifically, we create new dummy-code variables with the one-alcoholic parent group as the reference group, that is, so that participants with one alcoholic parent (rather than those with no alcoholic parents) are given a value of zero on both of these two new dummy variables. When the model is reestimated using these new dummy variables and new product terms crossing the new dummy variables with the externalizing focal predictor, the new estimated first-order coefficient of the externalizing focal predictor is the simple-slope estimate for participants with one alcoholic parent, and the standard statistical software output provides the standard error and subsequent $t$ test and confidence interval for this simple slope (see Table 4.6 for complete results for this model). With the current data, the simple-slope estimate of the one-alcoholic parent group is significant,[9] $\hat{\beta} = 0.675$, $t(159) = 4.60$, $p < .001$.[10] Therefore, among participants with one alcoholic parent, externalizing behaviour significantly predicts alcohol use; a one-at-a-time 95% confidence interval for this effect is (0.385, 0.965). Finally, recall from Chapter 3 that different dummy coding systems for a multicategory predictor produce equivalent regression models; here, that is again the case as multiple $R^2$ and the corresponding $F$ test given with Table 4.6 are identical to those for the original model reported in Table 4.5. Furthermore, the estimated coefficient (and corresponding standard error) for $X_1 \times D_1$ in Table 4.6 is the same as that in Table 4.5 (with the sign reversed) because both represent the interaction between externalizing and the comparison of the control group with participants with one alcoholic parent.

**Table 4.6** Results for OLS regression of heavy alcohol use on externalizing behaviour, parental alcoholism (number of alcoholic parents), and their interaction, with one-alcoholic parent as reference category

| Variable | $\hat{\beta}$ | SE($\hat{\beta}$) | t | p | 95% CI |
|---|---|---|---|---|---|
| Intercept | 0.057 | – | – | – | – |
| $X_1$: Externalizing | 0.675 | 0.146 | 4.60 | <.001 | (0.385, 0.965) |
| $D_1$: One alcoholic parent vs. controls | 0.047 | 0.158 | 0.30 | .764 | (−0.265, 0.360) |
| $D_2$: One vs. two alcoholic parents | 0.321 | 0.384 | 0.84 | .405 | (−0.437, 1.079) |
| $X_1 \times D_1$ | −0.574 | 0.226 | 2.54 | .012 | (−1.019, −0.128) |
| $X_2 \times D_2$ | 0.238 | 0.573 | 0.42 | .679 | (−0.894, 1.370) |

Note. $N = 165$. $R^2 = .217$, $F(5, 159) = 8.83$, $p < .001$.

Similarly, referring back to the results in Table 4.5 from the original dummy coding system, the estimated coefficient for $X_1 \times D_2$ gives the amount that the externalizing slope increases for a one-unit increase in $D_2$; therefore, the estimated simple slope for participants with two alcoholic parents is $\left(\hat{\beta}_1 + \hat{\beta}_S\right) = (0.102 + 0.812) = 0.914$. Once again, we can obtain a confidence interval and significance test for this simple slope by reestimating the model using a new set of dummy-code variables, this time specified so that the reference group is the two-alcoholic parent group (see Table 4.7 for complete results). With the model estimated using this final set of dummy variables (and new product terms using these dummy variables), the first-order estimate for the externalizing focal predictor now gives the simple slope for the two-alcoholic parent group. Specifically, we obtain $\hat{\beta} = 0.913$, $t(159) = 1.65$, $p = .10$. Therefore, among participants with two alcoholic parents, externalizing behaviour does not significantly predict alcohol use, despite the fact that the estimated simple slope for the two-alcoholic parent group is larger than the significant simple-slope estimate of the one-alcoholic parent group. Again, this potentially confusing result is explained by the fact that there are only nine participants with two alcoholic parents in the current sample.

---

[9]Even using a Bonferroni-corrected $\alpha$ level of $(.05 / 3) = .017$.

[10]This new simple-slope estimate is slightly different from that given earlier because of a minor rounding error.

**Table 4.7** Results for OLS regression of heavy alcohol use on externalizing behaviour, parental alcoholism (number of alcoholic parents), and their interaction, with two-alcoholic parents as reference category

| Variable | $\hat{\beta}$ | $SE(\hat{\beta})$ | $t$ | $p$ | 95% CI |
|---|---|---|---|---|---|
| Intercept | 0.377 | – | – | – | – |
| $X_1$: Externalizing | 0.913 | 0.554 | 1.65 | .101 | (−0.181, 2.007) |
| $D_1$: Two alcoholic parents vs. controls | −0.273 | 0.380 | 0.72 | .474 | (−1.024, 0.478) |
| $D_2$: One vs. two alcoholic parents | −0.321 | 0.384 | 0.84 | .405 | (−1.079, 0.437) |
| $X_1 \times D_1$ | −0.812 | 0.580 | 1.40 | .164 | (−1.957, 0.334) |
| $X_2 \times D_2$ | −0.238 | 0.573 | 0.42 | .679 | (−1.370, 0.894) |

*Note.* $N = 165$. $R^2 = .217$, $F(5, 159) = 8.83$, $p < .001$.

In sum, the current analyses using the three-category parental alcoholism moderator based on the number of alcoholic parents offers little substantive improvement over the previous analyses using the simpler dichotomous parental alcoholism variable primarily because of the small number of participants with two alcoholic parents. But the main purpose of this analysis was to show that the basic concepts and strategies for specifying and interpreting models for moderation hypotheses that were introduced for a dichotomous moderator easily generalize to situations where a hypothesized moderator has more than two categories. In particular, the model incorporates interaction terms which are the product of the focal predictor and the set of variables (i.e., dummy-code variables) representing the moderator. Next, substantial (e.g., statistically significant) interactions can be probed using a simple-slope analysis. The critical point here is that the first-order regression coefficient for the focal predictor represents the simple slope for the level of the moderator equaling coded zero on all dummy variables. Consequently, if one recodes the set of dummy variables which together represent the moderator to change the reference group for the dummy coding system and reestimates the model (after also calculating new product terms with the new set of dummy variables), then one obtains the simple slope (and corresponding standard error, confidence interval, and $t$ test) for the new group of participants representing the reference category.

 Section recap

### Probing an interaction with a multicategory moderator

With a $K$-category moderator, simple-slope analysis can be used to obtain $K$ simple-slope estimates for the effect of the focal predictor across each category of the moderator.

Although models with multicategory moderators can be equivalently specified using contrast-code variables (among other coding systems), simple-slope analysis is much easier if the categorical moderator is represented using dummy-code variables.

The estimated first-order slope coefficient for the focal predictor represents the simple-slope estimate for the reference category in the dummy coding system. To obtain the simple-slope estimate (and associated standard error, confidence interval, and significance test) for another category, change the dummy coding system so that the other category becomes the reference category and reestimate the model using the new dummy-code variables (as well as the corresponding new product terms).

---

## INTERACTIONS WITH A CONTINUOUS MODERATOR

### Research example for interaction with a continuous moderator

To demonstrate the interpretation of an interaction effect from a continuous moderator, let's move to a new research example. In this example, we are interested in modeling the hypothesis that perceived social support buffers, or moderates, the relation between daily hassles (i.e., minor stressors) and subsequent psychological symptomatology. That is, we hypothesize that a positive association between hassles and symptoms should be weaker among individuals with higher levels of social support compared with those with lower social support. This empirical example is drawn directly from Howell (2007), who adapted research by Compas, Wagner, Slavin, and Vannatta (1986) and by Wagner, Compas, and Howell (1988). Specifically, a sample of $N = 56$ university students completed the Adolescent Perceived Events Scale (Compas, Davis, Forsythe, and Wagner, 1987) as an operationalization of daily hassles, the Social Support Questionnaire (Sarason, Levine, Basham, and Sarason, 1983) to provide social support scores, and the Hopkins Symptom Checklist (Derogatis, Lipman, Rickels, Uhlenhuth, and Covi, 1974) to provide outcome variable scores representing psychological symptomatology.

This dataset is also available on the text's webpage (https://study.sagepub.com/flora) along with annotated input and output from several popular statistical software packages showing how to reproduce the analyses presented herein.

Table 4.8 gives descriptive statistics for these data, whereas Figure 4.4 gives a scatterplot matrix of the three operational variables of hassles, social support, and symptoms. As one

**Table 4.8** Correlations, means, and standard deviations for hassles example

|  | 1. | 2. | 3. |
|---|---|---|---|
| 1. Hassles | 1.00 | – | – |
| 2. Social support | –.167 | 1.00 | – |
| 3. Symptoms | .577 | –.133 | 1.00 |
| $M$ | 170.20 | 28.96 | 90.43 |
| $SD$ | 124.34 | 8.16 | 21.01 |

*Note.* $N = 56$.

might expect, there is a substantial positive linear association between hassles and symptoms, $r = .58$. But social support is only weakly associated with hassles ($r = -.17$) and symptoms ($r = -.13$). Importantly, however, this pattern of correlations offers no hint about the possibility of an interaction between hassles and social support in the prediction of symptoms, and so we should still proceed with estimating a regression coefficient for this potential interaction. At this point, we also recognize that the sample distributions of hassles and symptoms are both positively skewed and seem to have some outlying cases. These issues may become relevant when we assess regression diagnostics for any model fitted to these data. Also, the standard deviation of the hassles predictor is large, which will be helpful to keep in mind when interpreting regression coefficients for this variable.

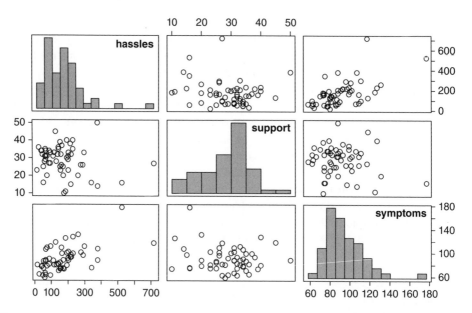

**Figure 4.4** Scatterplot matrix for hassles, social support, and psychological symptoms (diagonal gives univariate histogram of each variable)

## Model specification and interpretation with a continuous moderator

Once again, repeating Equation 4.1, a multiple regression model incorporating two predictors, $X_1$ and $X_2$, and an interaction between these predictors can be written as

$$\hat{Y}_i = \beta_0 + \beta_1 X_{1i} + \beta_2 X_{2i} + \beta_3 (X_{1i} \times X_{2i}) \, ,$$

where $X_1$ is the focal predictor and $X_2$ is the moderator. When the moderator is continuous rather than categorical, it is straightforward to estimate this model (again, OLS is the most common estimation method), but interpreting the interaction, in particular conducting a simple-slope analysis, is somewhat more challenging. In general, $\beta_1$, the first-order coefficient for the focal predictor, again represents the simple linear regression slope relating the focal predictor to the outcome when the value of the moderator equals zero.

Additionally, $\beta_3$, the coefficient of the interaction term, again represents the amount that the slope for the focal predictor changes per one-unit increase in the moderator. But with a continuous moderator, a 'one-unit increase' may not be as easy to contextualize as with a categorical moderator where a 'one-unit increase' simply means belonging to the next category or group; nonetheless, a simple-slope analysis can still effectively convey the influence of a continuous moderator.

Applying the research example, to test the hypothesis that the regression of symptoms on hassles is moderated by social support, we estimate the model in Equation 4.1 with hassles as $X_1$, the focal predictor, and social support as $X_2$, the moderator. Once again, the interaction between the focal predictor and the moderator is represented with a product term that is created by multiplying $X_1$ and $X_2$ together to create a new variable, $X_3 = (X_1 \times X_2)$, which is included in the regression model. The results of fitting this model to the data are summarized in Table 4.9. First and foremost, the interaction is significant, $\hat{\beta} = -0.005$, $t(52) = 2.14$, $p = .03$, which supports the hypothesis that social support moderates the relation between hassles and symptoms. Furthermore, because the estimated coefficient for the interaction is negative, we can conclude that higher levels of social support are associated with a weaker association between hassles and symptoms. But to understand the nature of this interaction more completely, we can probe it using a simple-slope analysis, which is presented next.

**Table 4.9** Results for OLS regression of psychological symptoms on daily hassles, social support, and their interaction

| Variable | $\hat{\beta}$ | SE($\hat{\beta}$) | $t$ | $p$ | 95% CI |
|---|---|---|---|---|---|
| Intercept | 45.751 | – | – | – | – |
| $X_1$: Hassles | 0.233 | 0.066 | 3.51 | <.001 | (0.100, 0.366) |
| $X_2$: Social support | 1.008 | 0.589 | 1.71 | .093 | (–0.173, 2.190) |
| $X_3$: Hassles × social support | –0.005 | 0.002 | 2.14 | .034 | (–0.010, –0.000) |

Note. $R^2 = .389$, $F(3, 52) = 11.01$, $p < .001$.

## Probing an interaction with a continuous moderator

As was the case for a dichotomous moderator, the first-order estimated coefficient for the focal predictor gives the simple slope of the focal predictor when the continuous moderator equals zero. In the current example, the results in Table 4.9 indicate that for a hypothetical participant whose social support score equals zero, the estimated simple linear regression slope of hassles is strong (given the scales of social support and hassles) and statistically significant, $\hat{\beta} = 0.23$, $t(52) = 3.51$, $p < .001$. But it is critical to recognize that the social support scores range from 10 to 50; therefore, this simple slope represents the effect of hassles on symptoms for a hypothetical participant whose social support score is outside the observed range of the social support scale. Indeed, this example demonstrates why it is important *not* to interpret first-order slope estimates as 'main effects'. Instead, it is much more informative to obtain simple-slope estimates at levels of the moderator which are representative of participants with prototypical scores, such as participants with a mean level of the moderator.

For example, it is likely of interest to estimate the relation between hassles and symptoms among participants with a mean level of social support.[11] Plugging the $\hat{\beta}$ estimates from Table 4.9 into Equations 4.3 and 4.4, the estimated simple intercept and simple slope for the relation between hassles and symptoms are

$$\hat{\omega}_0 = 45.751 + 1.008X_2$$

and

$$\hat{\omega}_1 = 0.233 - 0.005X_2,$$

respectively. Next, using the sample mean of social support (28.964) as the value of $X_2$, we obtain $\hat{\omega}_0 = 74.958$ and $\hat{\omega}_1 = 0.086$. Therefore, adapting Equation 4.5, the estimated simple linear regression of symptoms on hassles, among participants who have a mean level of social support, is

$$\hat{Y}_{i|X_2=28.964} = 74.958 + 0.086X_{1i}.$$

Thus, there is a positive association between hassles and symptoms for participants with an average level of social support.

Usually researchers wish to proceed further to determine whether a given simple-slope relation is statistically significant or to construct a confidence interval for the simple slope. To do so, we can adapt the procedure outlined earlier for a categorical $Y$ moderator to the current application with a continuous moderator. Specifically, we can first recode the original moderator so that a value of zero on the recoded moderator represents a particularly meaningful or prototypical level of that variable, such as the mean level. Next, we reestimate the model using the recoded moderator and its product with the focal predictor, and then the estimated first-order coefficient of the focal predictor will be the simple-slope estimate for individuals who have that particular prototypical value of the moderator.[12] Critically, when the model is reestimated using the recoded moderator, computer software output will automatically include the standard error and $t$ test for this first-order slope coefficient, thereby indicating the statistical significance of the simple slope; the corresponding confidence interval is also easily obtained. This approach is demonstrated next using the hassles by social support interaction example.

Typically, researchers obtain simple-slope estimates (and their significance or confidence intervals) for a low level of the moderator, a medium level of the moderator, and a high level

---

[11]Because social support is an (approximately) continuous variable, there might not be any participants in the sample whose social support score is exactly equal to the mean, or any other 'prototypical' score for that matter. Nevertheless, for the purposes of understanding and interpreting a model for the moderating effect of social support, it is informative to consider the hypothetical individual who has an average level of social support.

[12]Likewise, the intercept will shift. As always, the intercept represents the $\hat{Y}$ for participants who have a value of zero on all predictors; centering the moderator shifts its scale, changing the meaning of the value zero, which corresponds to a shift of the intercept. This shift corresponds to the calculation of a simple intercept as per Equation 4.3.

of the moderator. Often, and with little forethought, 'low' is taken as 1 standard deviation less than the mean of the moderator, 'medium' is the mean of the moderator, and 1 standard deviation above the mean is used as a 'high' level of the moderator. Yet, for many moderators, especially those with asymmetric distributions, 1 standard deviation above and below the mean may not be particularly meaningful or representative of values, and one might even fall outside the observed range of the data. For instance, if a positively skewed moderator does not have any observations falling below zero, subtracting 1 standard deviation from the mean could lead to a meaningless negative value. Estimating the simple slope at such a level of the moderator will not be substantively informative. Referring to our current example, we can see in Figure 4.4 that the distribution of social support is somewhat symmetric, suggesting that it would not be unreasonable to estimate simple slopes for the effect of hassles at 1 standard deviation above and below the mean of social support. But, 1 standard deviation above the mean of social support (i.e., $28.96 + 8.16 = 37.12$; see Table 4.8) is approximately the 89th percentile of the distribution; less than 11% of the sample has a value of social support above this level (1 standard deviation below the mean is approximately the 21st percentile of this distribution). Thus, it might be preferable to obtain simple-slope estimates at values of the moderator which are more representative of prototypical levels of social support, such as values corresponding to the 25th and 75th percentiles of the social support sample distribution. For consistency, the 'average' level of the moderator could also be defined as the 50th percentile, that is, the median, rather than the sample mean.

Therefore, to proceed with the current analysis, we recode, or **center**, the original social support variable three ways to obtain three versions of this moderator for which the value of zero represents either the 25th percentile of social support, the median of social support, or the 75th percentile of social support. We then reestimate the regression model for moderation using each of these three versions of the social support moderator to obtain three different first-order slope estimates for the hassles focal predictor, which are the simple-slope estimates for the regression of symptoms on hassles at low, medium, and high levels of social support. The computer output from each model estimation will also automatically provide the standard error and $t$ test for the corresponding simple-slope estimate, which is the principal advantage to using this method for probing a significant interaction or moderation effect.

To begin, the 25th percentile of the sample distribution of the social support variable equals 25.00. Thus, a new moderator variable, $X_{2L}$, is created by centering the original social support variable such that

$$X_{2L} = X_2 - 25.00,$$

where $X_2$ is the original social support variable. This transformation of $X_2$ does not change the shape or spread of the distribution of the original $X_2$; it merely shifts its center so that the 25th percentile of the distribution of $X_{2L}$ equals zero. Moreover, the correlation between $X_{2L}$ and $X_2$ equals +1.00. Next, adapting Equation 4.1, the regression model to be estimated is now

$$\hat{Y}_i = \beta_0 + \beta_1 X_{1i} + \beta_2 X_{2Li} + \beta_3 (X_{1i} \times X_{2Li}),$$

or, equivalently,

$$\hat{Y}_i = \beta_0 + \beta_1 X_{1i} + \beta_2 X_{2Li} + \beta_3 X_{3i},$$

noting that $X_1$ is again the hassles predictor and, importantly, the product term $X_3$ is now the product of $X_1$ and $X_{2L}$ (rather than the product of $X_1$ and the original $X_2$). The results from fitting this model to the data are in Table 4.10. Compare Table 4.9 with Table 4.10. First, notice that the model $R^2 = .39$ and its corresponding $F$ test are identical to that obtained when the model was estimated using the original, uncentered social support variable, reflecting that the current model is equivalent to the first model estimated for these data. Additionally, the estimated interaction coefficient, $\hat{\beta} = -0.005$, as well as its standard error, $t$ test, and confidence interval, are identical to what we obtained earlier using the original, uncentered social support variable.

**Table 4.10**  Results for OLS regression of psychological symptoms on daily hassles, social support (centered at 25th percentile), and their interaction

| Variable | $\hat{\beta}$ | $SE(\hat{\beta})$ | $t$ | $p$ | 95% CI |
|---|---|---|---|---|---|
| Intercept | 70.960 | – | – | – | – |
| $X_1$: Hassles | 0.106 | 0.019 | 5.55 | <.001 | (0.068, 0.144) |
| $X_2$: Centered social support | 1.008 | 0.589 | 1.71 | .093 | (−0.173, 2.190) |
| $X_3$: Hassles × centered social support | −0.005 | 0.002 | 2.14 | .034 | (−0.010, −0.000) |

Note. $R^2 = .389$, $F(3, 52) = 11.01$, $p < .001$.

Of primary interest from these results, however, is the estimated first-order coefficient for the focal predictor, hassles. As always, the first-order coefficient of the focal predictor is the simple slope for the focal predictor among participants whose value of the moderator equals zero. Therefore, here, because the social support moderator was centered at its 25th percentile, the estimated coefficient for hassles ($\hat{\beta} = 0.106$) gives the simple-slope relation between hassles and symptoms for participants at a low level of social support (i.e., the 25th percentile). Moreover, the $t$ test for the hassles first-order coefficient tells us that this simple-slope estimate is significantly greater than zero, $t(52) = 5.55$, $p < .001$. Yet again, we should compare the $p$ value for a simple slope to a Bonferroni-corrected $\alpha$ level. Here, we are testing three simple slopes (i.e., at high, average, and low social support), and so the corrected $\alpha$ level is $(.05 / 3) = .017$.

Next, to find the estimated simple-slope relation between hassles and symptoms for participants who have a medium level of social support, we can again center the original social support variable, this time by subtracting the median (31.00) from each observation to create the new variable

$$X_{2M} = X_2 - 31.00.$$

Now the model to be estimated is

$$\hat{Y}_i = \beta_0 + \beta_1 X_{1i} + \beta_2 X_{2Mi} + \beta_3 X_{3i},$$

where $X_3$ is now the product of $X_1$ and $X_{2M}$. The results from estimating this new version of the model are in Table 4.11. Once again, we obtain the same $R^2$ and the same interaction estimate. But the first-order coefficient of the hassles focal predictor has changed again, this time giving the simple-slope effect for participants who have a value of zero on the new $X_{2M}$ variable, which is the median value of social support. Specifically, the estimated coefficient for hassles ($\hat{\beta} = 0.076$) is now the simple-slope relation between hassles and symptoms for participants with a median level of social support. Although this simple-slope estimate is also significant using the Bonferroni-corrected $\alpha$ level, $t(52) = 3.61$, $p < .001$, it is smaller than the simple slope reported earlier for participants with a low level of social support (i.e., $\hat{\beta} = 0.076$ vs. $\hat{\beta} = 0.106$).

**Table 4.11** Results for OLS regression of psychological symptoms on daily hassles, social support (centered at median), and their interaction

| Variable | $\hat{\beta}$ | $SE(\hat{\beta})$ | t | p | 95% CI |
|---|---|---|---|---|---|
| Intercept | 77.011 | – | – | – | – |
| $X_1$: Hassles | 0.076 | 0.021 | 3.61 | <.001 | (0.034, 0.118) |
| $X_2$: Centered social support | 1.008 | 0.589 | 1.71 | .093 | (–0.173, 2.190) |
| $X_3$: Hassles × centered social support | –0.005 | 0.002 | –2.14 | .034 | (–0.010, –0.000) |

Note. $R^2 = .389$, $F(3, 52) = 11.01$, $p < .001$.

Finally, to get the estimated simple-slope relation between hassles and symptoms for participants who have a high level of social support, we can center the original social support variable by subtracting the 75th percentile (34.00) from each observation to create the new variable

$$X_{2H} = X_2 - 34.00.$$

The last model to be estimated is

$$\hat{Y}_i = \beta_0 + \beta_1 X_{1i} + \beta_2 X_{2Hi} + \beta_3 X_{3i},$$

where $X_3$ is the product of $X_1$ and $X_{2H}$. The results from this last version of the model estimation are in Table 4.12. Now the first-order coefficient of the hassles focal predictor ($\hat{\beta} = 0.060$) gives the simple-slope effect for participants who have a value of zero on $X_{2H}$, which is the 75th percentile of social support. Specifically, among participants with a high level of social support, although there is a positive linear association between hassles and symptoms, this effect is not significant using the Bonferroni-corrected $\alpha$ level, $t(52) = 2.41$, $p = .019$. Importantly, we again see that as social support increases, the association between hassles and symptoms decreases.

In summary, this simple-slope analysis is a numerically focused method to probing and interpreting the significant interaction between hassles and social support in the prediction of psychological symptoms. In other words, given that the interaction is statistically significant, we have sample-based evidence that social support moderates the relation between hassles and symptoms, but we need to carry out additional analyses to understand the nature of the interaction, which is the purpose of the simple-slope analysis. The simple-slope results presented earlier indicate that there is a significant, positive association between hassles and

**Table 4.12**  Results for OLS regression of psychological symptoms on daily hassles, social support (centered at 75th percentile), and their interaction

| Variable | $\hat{\beta}$ | $SE(\hat{\beta})$ | t | p | 95% CI |
|---|---|---|---|---|---|
| Intercept | 80.036 | – | – | – | – |
| $X_1$: Hassles | 0.060 | 0.025 | 2.41 | .019 | (0.010, 0.111) |
| $X_2$: Centered social support | 1.008 | 0.589 | 1.71 | .093 | (−0.173, 2.190) |
| $X_3$: Hassles × centered social support | −0.005 | 0.002 | −2.14 | .034 | (−0.010, −0.000) |

*Note.* $R^2 = .389$, $F(3, 52) = 11.01$, $p < .001$.

symptoms at low and medium levels of social support but the relation is not significant for those with high social support. Of course, we must remember to focus on effect size and not just on statistical significance; in the results earlier, it is clear that the relation between hassles and symptoms becomes notably weaker as social support increases; specifically, the estimated effect of hassles is $\hat{\beta} = 0.11$ at the 25th percentile of social support, $\hat{\beta} = 0.08$ at median social support, and $\hat{\beta} = 0.06$ at the 75th percentile of social support. Therefore, these data appear to support the hypothesis that social support is protective against the effect of hassles on psychological symptoms (but see the discussion on regression diagnostics later). We can understand a moderation effect more profoundly with a well-constructed graphical display of the interaction, such as that given in Figure 4.5 for the current example.

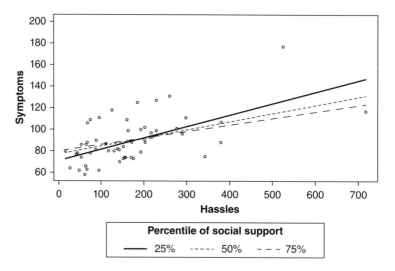

**Figure 4.5**  Scatterplot of psychological symptoms against hassles showing estimated regression lines for individuals with low (25th percentile), medium (median), and high (75th percentile) levels of social support

It is important to recognize that with a continuous moderator, technically there is an infinite number of simple-slope relations between the focal predictor and the outcome variable, one for each of the hypothetically infinite number of possible values of the moderator, although not all values of a truly continuous moderator will be represented in any given dataset.

In contrast, when a moderator is categorical, it is possible (and advisable) to estimate the simple slope for all observed values of the moderator (e.g., for both COAs and non-COAs in the example given earlier in this chapter). In the hassles example, however, we chose to estimate and interpret simple slopes at only three of many possible values of the social support variable; these three values were chosen because they represent prototypical levels of social support in the actual empirical data. Interactions may be easier to interpret when the simple-slope relation between the focal predictor and the outcome are significant at a given level of the moderator and nonsignificant at another level. But in some situations, it can happen that all estimated simple slopes are significantly greater than zero (or significantly less than zero). In other situations, it may be that none of the estimated simple slopes significantly differs from zero, but perhaps one of the estimated slopes is positive whereas another is negative, which is potentially of great interpretational importance. Once again, it is critical to pay attention to the effect size, that is, the actual direction and magnitude of the simple-slope estimate itself. Furthermore, a graphical display usually helps illuminate the size of an interaction effect.

 Section recap

### Probing an interaction with a continuous moderator

The interaction between a focal predictor and a continuous moderator can be probed using a simple-slope analysis.

In so doing, one must choose particular values of the moderator at which to obtain simple-slope estimates for the effect of the focal predictor. Preferably, these values of the moderator represent levels which are especially theoretically important or represent a prototypical individual within a given range of the moderator's distribution (e.g., low, medium, and high levels of the moderator).

One should not automatically assume that the 1 standard deviation below the mean, the mean, and 1 standard deviation above the mean are good choices for low, medium, and high levels of the moderator. The 25th, 50th (i.e., median), and 75th percentiles are often preferable.

The first-order coefficient of the focal predictor is the simple slope for a hypothetical case with a value of zero for the moderator. Therefore, one can obtain the simple slope for any given value of the original moderator by **centering** the moderator at that level and reestimating the regression model. The first-order coefficient of the focal predictor then corresponds to the simple slope effect for a hypothetical participant with that particular value of the moderator.

Once again, the principles of regression diagnostics addressed in Chapter 2 apply to regression models with interaction effects. For the current example examining the moderating effect of social support on the relation between hassles and symptoms, there was no evidence that any of the assumptions for OLS estimation of regression models was violated, despite that the sample distributions of the hassles and symptoms variables were both notably positively skewed. Nevertheless, there was one case in the dataset with a disproportionately large influence on the estimated model, with Cook's $D = 1.05$. The large influence of this case can be traced back to the fact that this participant also has an outlying value on the psychological symptoms outcome variable equal to 177; the maximum value of symptoms among the other cases is 131. When this case is completely removed from the dataset and the model is reestimated, the interaction between social support and hassles is no longer significant, $\hat{\beta} = -0.002$, $p = .52$. It is not good science for the primary result from a model to hinge on the inclusion of a single case, but also there is no reason to believe that this participant is not a legitimate representative of the population who should be included in the dataset. Thus, as an alternative to deleting the influential case from the dataset completely, one might set the outlying value of the outcome variable equal to the maximum value observed among the other cases; here, that means changing the symptom score for this case from 177 to 131. After doing so, the reestimated model again obtains a nonsignificant interaction between social support and hassles, $\hat{\beta} = -0.002$, $t(51) = 0.66$, $p = .30$. Therefore, we are forced to conclude that the current sample data do *not* adequately support the hypothesis that social support moderates the relation between hassles and symptoms in the population.

## Is centering continuous predictors *always* necessary for testing an interaction?

The answer to this question is a definite 'no' despite that many researchers are under the opposite impression. Centering predictors involved in an interaction is valuable for interpretation of that interaction, as demonstrated earlier, but otherwise its importance for estimating and reaching inferential conclusions from models including interactions has been greatly exaggerated in the methodological literature (see Edwards, 2009; Kromrey and Foster-Johnson, 1998). Often, researchers advocate centering to remove *nonessential multicollinearity* among the first-order predictors and their product term (e.g., Cohen et al., 2003), the idea being that the first-order predictors are necessarily highly correlated with the product term. Indeed, multicollinearity can be problematic, as discussed in Chapter 2, but this issue is of little, if any, concern for the product terms used to model interaction effects. A model with interactions based on centered predictors is fully equivalent to the same model with predictors in their original, noncentered form in that centering does not change the fit of the model to data (i.e., $R^2$ is not affected nor are the $\hat{Y}$ values). Furthermore, as we have seen, the estimated coefficient for the product term and its standard error are not affected by whether the predictors involved in the interaction are centered;[13] consequently, centering has no impact on conclusions about the magnitude or significance of the interaction effect itself. Finally, regardless of any multicollinearity concerns, it is not sensible to center dummy-code variables representing a categorical moderator because doing so destroys much of the interpretational advantage gained by using dummy codes in the first place, as described in Chapter 3 and in the earlier sections of this chapter.

---

[13]In the example analysis provided earlier, only the continuous moderator was centered (at representative low, medium, and high values) to probe the interaction, whereas the focal predictor was left uncentered. But regardless of whether one centers both the focal predictor and the moderator or only the moderator, doing so does not change the estimated interaction coefficient or its standard error.

What centering the moderator does affect is the estimate of the first-order coefficient of the focal predictor as well as its standard error.[14] But this change is merely a simple algebraic manipulation of the model undertaken to aid interpretation; it does not affect the fundamental statistical properties of the model. As thoroughly emphasized earlier, the first-order coefficient of the focal predictor represents the linear slope (i.e., the simple slope) of the relation between the focal predictor and the outcome among cases with a value of zero on the moderator. Centering the moderator simply shifts the center of its distribution (without otherwise affecting the distribution) so that the first-order coefficient for the focal predictor also shifts (along with the intercept) to obtain a simple slope with a particular interpretational usefulness based on the moderator (e.g., simple slope at the median of the moderator). As demonstrated earlier in the chapter, any given simple-slope estimate can also be obtained algebraically (see Equations 4.2 to 4.5) using results obtained from a model estimated without centering any of its predictors. The chief value of centering, therefore, is to obtain the automatic output from statistical software that indicates whether the first-order estimate of the focal predictor (i.e., the simple slope) is statistically significant, although the significance of a given simple slope can also be obtained algebraically without centering (see Bauer and Curran, 2005).

In summary, when a multiple regression model contains an interaction, the relations of the predictors involved in the interaction with the outcome variable must be interpreted within the context of the interaction; it is dangerous, if not outright incorrect, to attempt to describe the 'main effect' of a predictor over and above the effect of the interaction. Centering predictors does not lead to 'main effect' estimates; instead, centering leads to simple-slope estimates that are interpreted as pertaining to participants who have a value of zero on the centered moderator. In practice, researchers with hypotheses about moderation should focus first and foremost on the magnitude and statistical significance of the interaction effect (i.e., the estimated coefficient for the product term in the regression model); centering is not at all necessary for this purpose. After determining that there is an important moderation effect, a simple-slope analysis involving centering of the moderator is one useful approach to interpreting the nature of the interaction, although there are other approaches to probing an interaction which may not explicitly entail centering (such as graphical methods, e.g., Fox, 2003).

The principles of model specification and model building that are covered in Chapter 2 also apply to models including interaction terms. In particular, if one of a researcher's hypotheses involves moderation, then the regression model to be estimated should include the interaction term that is relevant to that hypothesis. If the estimated interaction effect is too small to support the moderation hypothesis (i.e., it is not practically or statistically significant), the model that contains the interaction is still most closely matched to the theory that inspired the data analysis; just as a model should include all theoretically important predictors, it should also include all theoretically important interaction terms, regardless of their actual estimated magnitude from a given sample of data. In this situation, a researcher should still probe the interaction to confirm that there is no substantively meaningful change in simple-slope estimates for the focal predictor across the levels of the moderator. But, because of the nonessential multicollinearity of the product term with the first-order predictors, to interpret the overall effects (i.e., 'main effects') of these predictors without the influence of the

---

[14]Centering the focal predictor will also change the first-order coefficient of the moderator. But centering the focal predictor is unnecessary for interpreting (i.e., probing) the interaction, and so in the example earlier, the hassles focal predictor was not centered.

interaction (even though it is weak), then the researcher should respecify the model by dropping the interaction term (especially if the theory motivating the moderation hypothesis was weak in the first place), as recommended earlier in this chapter.

## Section recap

**Advice for interpreting interactions using multiple regression**

The purpose of centering a continuous predictor is to facilitate probing an interaction using simple-slope analysis, not to remove multicollinearity.

The estimated coefficient and standard error of the interaction term is the same regardless of whether predictors are centered.

If a model includes an interaction, even if it is weak, then the effects of its constituent predictors should be interpreted in the context of the interaction (i.e., by probing the interaction), not as 'main effects'.

If one wants to interpret the overall, 'main effect' of a first-order predictor, ignoring any interaction, then the interaction term(s) should be omitted from the model.

## CHAPTER SUMMARY

This chapter built on the multiple regression models presented in earlier chapters by introducing interaction terms which are used to assess hypotheses about moderation in which the effect of one predictor varies according to another predictor. Statistical **moderation** occurs when the association between a focal predictor and an outcome variable differs across the levels of another predictor, the **moderator**:

- Interactions are included in a multiple regression model by incorporating a **product term** $(X_1 \times X_2)$ in the regression equation:

$$\hat{Y}_i = \beta_0 + \beta_1 X_{1i} + \beta_2 X_{2i} + \beta_3 (X_{1i} \times X_{2i}),$$

  where $\beta_1$ and $\beta_2$ are the **first-order** (or lower order) effects of $X_1$ and $X_2$, respectively, whereas the interaction effect, $\beta_3$, is a **higher order** effect. The size of $\beta_3$ quantifies the extent of the interaction (or moderation) effect.
- It is important not to interpret $\beta_1$ or $\beta_2$ as a so-called 'main effect'. Instead, $\beta_1$ represents the effect of $X_1$ *only* for a case which has $X_2 = 0$; likewise, $\beta_2$ represents the effect of $X_2$ *only* for a case which has $X_1 = 0$.
- An important (e.g., statistically significant) interaction effect can be **probed** using a **simple-slope** analysis in which different (estimated) regression equations for the relation between the focal predictor and the outcome are obtained for different values of the moderator variable.
- When $X_2 = 0$, the model $\hat{Y}_i = \beta_0 + \beta_1 X_{1i} + \beta_2 X_{2i} + \beta_3 (X_{1i} \times X_{2i})$ reduces to

$$\hat{Y}_i = \beta_0 + \beta_1 X_{1i},$$

and thus the intercept and first-order effect for $X_1$ equals the *simple intercept* and *simple slope* for the focal predictor among cases with $X_2 = 0$.

- If the moderator $X_2$ is a dichotomous dummy variable, $\hat{\beta}_1$ is the simple-slope estimate for the category coded zero.
- To represent the interaction between the focal predictor and a multicategory moderator comprehensively, $J$ product terms should be formed by multiplying *each K* dummy-code variable by the focal predictor, $X$. Then, these $J = K$ products are included as predictors in the regression model along with first-order terms for the focal predictor and the dummy variables:

$$\hat{Y}_i = \beta_0 + \beta_X X_i + \left( \sum_{k=1}^{K-1} \beta_k D_{ki} \right) + \left( \sum_{j=1}^{J-1} \beta_j (X_{1i} \times D_{ji}) \right).$$

- Hierarchical regression can be used to determine whether the set of $J = K$ product terms significantly increases multiple $R^2$; if so, one concludes that the $K$-category variable significantly moderates the effect of the focal predictor.
- In a simple-slope analysis for probing the interaction between a focal predictor and a continuous moderator, one must choose particular values of the moderator at which to obtain simple-slope estimates for the effect of the focal predictor. Preferably, these values of the moderator represent levels which are especially theoretically important or represent a prototypical individual within a given range of the moderator's distribution (e.g., low, medium, and high levels of the moderator).

## RECOMMENDED READING

Bauer, D.J., & Curran, P.J. (2005). Probing interactions in fixed and multilevel regression: Inferential and graphical techniques. *Multivariate Behavioral Research, 40,* 373–400.

- This paper clearly explains the statistical properties of probing interactions using simple-slope analysis and demonstrates the method with an applied example. As its title indicates, the paper also explains how interactions from multilevel models can be probed; multilevel modeling is the topic of Chapter 6.

Kromrey, J.D., & Foster-Johnson, L. (1998). Mean centering in moderated multiple regression: Much ado about nothing. *Educational and Psychological Measurement, 58,* 42–67.

- This paper provides an empirical demonstration to debunk the common belief that it is always necessary to center predictors to obtain valid estimates of moderation effects. Consequently, the potential value of centering is clarified.

# USING MULTIPLE REGRESSION TO MODEL MEDIATION AND OTHER INDIRECT EFFECTS

## CHAPTER OVERVIEW

This chapter describes how multiple regression models may be used to assess hypotheses regarding indirect effects and statistical mediation, which occurs when a variable predicts or influences an outcome indirectly through another variable, an intervening variable. The main topics of this chapter include:

- Conceptualization of indirect effects and mediation
- Specification of the simple indirect-effect model
- Estimation and inference for the indirect effect
- Moderated indirect effects

**Table 5.0**  Greek letter notation used in this chapter

| Greek letter | English name | Represents |
|---|---|---|
| $\alpha$ | Lowercase 'alpha' | Parameter in regression of mediator (or intervening variable) on independent variable (intercept or slope, depending on subscript) |
| $\beta$ | Lowercase 'beta' | Parameter in regression of dependent variable on mediator (or intervening variable) (intercept or slope, depending on subscript) |
| $\varepsilon$ | Lowercase 'epsilon' | Regression model error term |

*Note.* The probability of a Type I error is also symbolized using $\alpha$ (but not italicized).

# WHAT ARE MEDIATION AND INDIRECT EFFECTS?

Up to this point, I have mostly avoided discussing causality and the extent to which statistical analyses may be used to test causal hypotheses. The main reason for not addressing causality explicitly is that I view it as primarily an issue of substantive theory development and subsequent research design much more so than an issue of actual data analysis (for a concise and cogent discussion of causality in the context of statistical modeling, see Chapter 3 of Bollen, 1989; also Murnane and Willett, 2011). Although I stress the importance of finding the optimal match of a given statistical model to a substantive theory to evaluate that theory using empirical data, the focus of this text is the actual data analysis via model fitting, regardless of whether the substantive theory under consideration explicitly involves a causal process. A given statistical model simply represents how two or more variables are associated with each other with no consideration of whether the associations arise from causal processes. For example, the simple linear regression of $Y$ on $X$ can be a useful model for the relation between these two variables if their association is such that differences in $X$ cause differences in $Y$ or if the association between $X$ and $Y$ simply serves a descriptive or a predictive purpose. As stated in Chapter 1, models are fundamentally descriptive, but they can be used for causal inference.

That being said, one particular class of causal hypotheses, namely, hypotheses of **mediation**, has become so popular and pervasive in the behavioural and social sciences that statistical approaches to modeling and testing mediation demand special attention. In its most simple form, mediation is a causal process whereby an independent variable has a causal influence on a second variable, typically known as the **mediator** or **intervening variable**, which in turn has a causal influence on a dependent or outcome variable. Put another way, a mediation hypothesis stipulates that an independent variable has an **indirect effect** (also known as a **mediated effect**) on a dependent variable through the putative mediator. The model implied by a mediation hypothesis is depicted in Figure 5.1, in which the independent variable is denoted $X$, the mediator or intervening variable is $M$, and the dependent variable is $Y$.

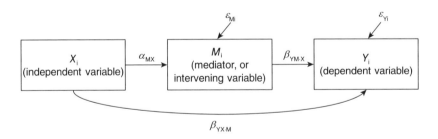

**Figure 5.1** Simple indirect-effect model

Given my earlier comments, it is valuable to recognize that this model can be fitted to data and evaluated regardless of whether the substantive theory leading to the model explicitly specifies causal relations among $X$, $M$, and $Y$. If the substantive theory implying the model in Figure 5.1 is not a theory of causality, one can still use it to estimate and interpret the indirect effect, but one cannot claim that a significant or otherwise substantial indirect effect is evidence of causal mediation per se. Nonetheless, causal effects can and do manifest themselves in observational data, and there is no sin in discussing causality in the context of observational research as long as we recognize that we cannot absolutely confirm a causal relation without true experimental evidence. Of course, randomized experimentation is the gold-standard approach for confirming causal relations. If a study involving hypotheses about mediation does incorporate a randomized experimental manipulation, most often only the independent variable $X$ is randomized, and so the relation between $M$ and $Y$ still cannot be considered causal through the traditional experimental approach.[1] Another concern with the simple indirect-effect model is that it is statistically equivalent to a handful of other models which are not consistent with an indirect effect or causal mediation explanation; research design is particularly important for helping choose among these models (see Pek and Hoyle, 2016).

To make these points concrete, reconsider the research example from Chapter 4 in which parental alcoholism predicted subsequent adolescent heavy alcohol use. These data are used again in this chapter to model an indirect effect of parental alcoholism on heavy alcohol use through the potential intervening variable of externalizing behaviour. In this analysis, parental alcoholism is associated with subsequent externalizing, which in turn is associated with subsequent alcohol use, confirming the hypothesis of an indirect effect. But it may be difficult to conceive of these relations as being causal in any strict sense; hence, although we will confirm that there is an indirect effect, we may not be justified referring to this effect as causal mediation. In another example, we examine the effect of an experimental manipulation on rated self-presentation, which in turn leads to a higher positive affect during a social interaction. Here, the effect of the manipulation on self-presentation is considered causal, as is the effect of self-presentation on positive affect. Thus, finding a significant indirect effect of the manipulation on positive affect through self-presentation can be considered evidence of causal mediation. In sum, finding a substantial indirect effect using the model in Figure 5.1 may or may not be indicative of causal mediation, depending on whether the underlying substantive theory stipulates causal effects.

Indirect effects, whether causal mediational effects or not, are commonly estimated using ordinary least-squares (OLS) multiple regression models, which is the topic of this chapter. In particular, this chapter focuses on the simple three-variable model depicted in Figure 5.1, which I refer to as the *simple indirect-effect model*. Of course it is possible to expand this model to incorporate additional predictors or covariates, additional mediators or intervening variables, or even additional outcome variables. Larger models with indirect effects, particularly those with multiple intervening variables or multiple outcome variables, are more commonly estimated using structural equation modeling, which is addressed in Chapters 9 and 10 of this text, where we will revisit the estimation and interpretation of indirect effects.

 Section recap

### Conceptualization of indirect effects and mediation

**Mediation** refers to a causal chain in which a primary independent variable or predictor causes differences in an **intervening variable**, or **mediator**, which then causally affects a primary outcome or dependent variable.

---

[1] It is hypothetically possible to establish a causal link between a nonrandomized mediator $M$ and an outcome $Y$ using Rubin's (1974) causal model, also known as the 'potential outcomes' or 'counterfactual' framework. Giving an adequate description of this approach is beyond the scope of this text, but for a presentation in the context of modeling mediation hypotheses, see Coffman and Zhong (2012) or Imai, Keele, and Tingley (2010).

In other words, the predictor variable has an **indirect effect** (or **mediated effect**) on the outcome variable through the intervening variable.

The simple indirect-effect model can be used to estimate and test a hypothesized indirect effect regardless of whether the effects in the model can legitimately be considered causal mediation effects; a given indirect effect could be considered merely descriptive.

---

## SPECIFICATION OF THE SIMPLE INDIRECT-EFFECT MODEL

Unlike the regression models we have examined so far, the **simple indirect-effect model** depicted in Figure 5.1 has not one, but two, dependent or outcome variables. First, the hypothesized mediator or intervening variable ($M$ in Figure 5.1) is a dependent variable predicted by the main predictor ($X$ in Figure 5.1). Next, the main outcome variable ($Y$ in Figure 5.1) is predicted by both the intervening variable and the main predictor. Put another way, the intervening variable $M$ serves as both a predictor (of $Y$) and an outcome (of $X$). Because the overall model has two outcome variables, there are two regression equations. The first equation is the regression of the intervening variable on the main predictor:

$$M_i = \alpha_0 + \alpha_{MX}X_i + \varepsilon_{Mi}. \tag{5.1}$$

This equation is nothing more than a simple regression equation of the type described in Chapter 1 (e.g., Equation 1.5), just with slightly different notation: The value of $M$ for individual $i$ is a linear function of an intercept parameter $\alpha_0$ plus the product of a slope parameter $\alpha_{MX}$ and the value of $X$ for case $i$, plus an error $\varepsilon$ specific to case $i$. In the literature on mediation analysis, it is common to symbolize the regression relation between the main predictor and the intervening variable with the letter $a$, which is the reason that here we represent this slope with the Greek letter $\alpha$ but maintain our preference for using Greek letters to represent population parameters. Furthermore, the subscript $MX$ for this parameter is used to indicate that the slope pertains to the regression of the intervening variable $M$ on the predictor $X$. Finally, the error term $\varepsilon_{Mi}$ includes an $M$ subscript to distinguish it from the error term in the regression equation for the outcome variable $Y$, given next. Despite this change in notation, it is important to keep in mind that the interpretation of the parameters in this regression equation is no different from that described in Chapter 1 for simple linear regression.

Next, in the simple indirect-effect model, the dependent variable $Y$ is usually regressed on both the intervening variable $M$ and the main predictor variable $X$:

$$Y_i = \beta_0 + \beta_{YM.X}M_i + \beta_{YX.M}X_i + \varepsilon_{Yi}. \tag{5.2}$$

This equation should be familiar as an instance of the two-predictor regression model described in Chapter 2 (e.g., Equation 2.2), where now the two predictors are $M$ and $X$. The partial regression slope parameter for $M$ is $\beta_{YM.X}$, with the $YM.X$ subscript indicating that this parameter pertains to the regression of $Y$ on $M$, controlling $X$. Likewise, the partial regression slope for $X$ is $\beta_{YX.M}$, with the $YX.M$ subscript indicating that it refers to the regression of $Y$ on $X$, controlling $M$. Finally, the error term $\varepsilon_{Yi}$ includes a $Y$ subscript to distinguish it from the error term for the intervening variable in Equation 5.1. Although the notation has changed slightly, the interpretation of the parameters in Equation 5.2 is the same as the parameter interpretation for the two-predictor linear regression model presented in Chapter 2.

In the current context, the main purpose of specifying and estimating Equations 5.1 and 5.2 is to provide the information needed to calculate the indirect effect. Taken together, these two equations form the simple indirect-effect model; it may be helpful to see how these equations map onto their depiction in Figure 5.1. The indirect effect or mediation hypothesis specifies that $X$ predicts $Y$ indirectly through the intervening variable $M$; in other words, $X$ leads to $M$ and then $M$ leads to $Y$. Therefore, the indirect effect consists of the effect of $X$ on $M$, which is represented with the $\alpha_{MX}$ parameter, *and* the effect of $M$ on $Y$, which is represented with the $\beta_{YM.X}$ parameter. Specifically, the indirect effect, represented as a population parameter, is the product of these two slope parameters, $\alpha_{MX} \times \beta_{YM.X}$, which, for brevity, is symbolized as $\alpha\beta$, without the subscripts, for the remainder of this chapter. This indirect-effect parameter is often referred to as the **product of coefficients** in the methodological literature. The size of $\alpha\beta$ represents the extent to which the main predictor affects the outcome variable indirectly through the intervening variable or the extent to which mediation is present; $\alpha\beta$ is thus an unstandardized effect-size statistic.

The indirect effect $\alpha\beta$ is of central importance in this chapter, but it may also be informative to provide terminology for the other effects in the overall simple indirect-effect model as they are typically referred to in the literature. In particular, the **direct effect** of the main predictor $X$ on the outcome variable $Y$ is the partial regression slope $\beta_{YX.M}$ for the regression of $Y$ on $X$ controlling $M$. The **total effect**, representing the total, overall effect of $X$ on $Y$, is then the sum of the direct effect and the indirect effect, that is, $(\alpha_{MX} \times \beta_{YM.X}) + \beta_{YX.M}$.[2] It is important to recognize, though, that it is possible for the indirect effect to be greater (i.e., of a stronger magnitude in absolute value) than the total effect, which occurs when the indirect effect and the direct effect have opposite signs (a scenario known as *inconsistent mediation*; MacKinnon, Krull, and Lockwood, 2000). Although such a result may seem counterintuitive, it is nonetheless entirely sensible both theoretically and empirically, and it is basically an extension of the principle described in Chapter 2 whereby a partial regression coefficient for a given predictor obtained by controlling some third variable can potentially be larger or of an opposite sign than the marginal effect that ignores the third variable (e.g., a suppression effect). MacKinnon et al. (2000) offered a clear presentation of the equivalence of inconsistent mediation and suppression, providing empirical research examples of the phenomenon.

Regardless of their respective signs, the total effect of $X$ on $Y$ can be decomposed into the direct effect and the indirect effect. This decomposition implies that we can interpret the direct effect parameter $\beta_{YX.M}$ as an unstandardized effect size, indicating the predicted difference in $Y$ per one-unit increase in $X$, holding $M$ constant, just as any partial regression coefficient is an unstandardized effect size, as described in Chapter 2. Similarly, the indirect-effect parameter $\alpha\beta$ is also an unstandardized effect size, indicating the predicted difference in $Y$ per one-unit increase in $X$ that occurs through the intervening variable $M$.

For simplicity, this chapter focuses on the simple indirect-effect model with only three observed variables, a single main predictor $X$, a single intervening variable $M$, and a single outcome variable $Y$. In practice, however, such simplicity is typically not realistic in that there are usually other important predictors or covariates to control. Following the logic

---

[2]It also happens that, if all OLS assumptions are met for linear regression, the total effect $(\alpha_{MX} \times \beta_{YM.X}) + \beta_{YX.M}$ equals the marginal regression slope obtained from the simple regression of $Y$ on $X$, ignoring $M$.

of Chapter 2 (see Equation 2.9), Equation 5.1 is easily expanded to include any number of additional predictors:

$$M_i = \alpha_0 + \alpha_{MX_1} X_{1i} + \left( \sum_{p=2}^{P} \alpha_{MX_p} X_{pi} \right) + \varepsilon_{Mi}, \tag{5.3}$$

where $X_1$ is the main predictor (e.g., an experimental treatment indicator) for examining a given indirect effect and $P$ is the total number of predictors. Similarly, Equation 5.2 can also be expanded to include additional predictors or covariates:

$$Y_i = \beta_0 + \beta_{YM \cdot X_1} M_i + \beta_{YX_1 \cdot M} X_{1i} + \left( \sum_{p=2}^{P} \beta_{MX_p} X_{pi} \right) + \varepsilon_{Yi}. \tag{5.4}$$

The set of predictors in Equation 5.4 for $Y$ need not be identical to the set of predictors in Equation 5.3 for $M$. Additionally, some of the additional predictors in Equation 5.4 might themselves be intervening variables; this possibility of multiple intervening variables, also known as multiple mediation, is touched on in Chapter 9. In conclusion, although we estimate and interpret indirect effects using only the three-variable simple intervening model in this chapter, it is important to keep in mind that in practice, such indirect effects may be biased to a misleading extent if other important predictors and covariates are not included in the regression models used to estimate a given indirect effect $\alpha\beta$.

 Section recap

### Specification of the simple indirect-effect model

In the simple indirect-effect model, both the intervening variable ($M$) and the main outcome variable ($Y$) are outcome variables predicted by the main predictor ($X$). Therefore, the model consists of two linear regression equations:

$$M_i = \alpha_0 + \alpha_{MX} X_i + \varepsilon_{Mi},$$

$$Y_i = \beta_0 + \beta_{YM \cdot X} M_i + \beta_{YX \cdot M} X_i + \varepsilon_{Yi}.$$

Of course, each of these equations can be expanded to include additional predictors or covariates.

From these two equations, the indirect effect of $X$ on $Y$ through $M$ is the **product of coefficients**, $\alpha_{MX} \times \beta_{YM \cdot X}$.

The **direct effect** of $X$ on $Y$ through $M$ is $\beta_{YX \cdot M}$, and the **total effect** of $X$ on $Y$ is $(\alpha_{MX} \times \beta_{YM \cdot X}) + \beta_{YX \cdot M}$.

It is possible for the indirect effect to be greater than the total effect.

## Research example for modeling a mediational indirect effect

To demonstrate the application of the simple indirect-effect model to estimate and interpret an indirect effect representing a hypothetical causal chain indicative of mediation, we borrow data from Study 2B of Dunn, Biesanz, Human, and Finn (2007; also reported in Biesanz, Falk, and Savalei, 2010). In this social-psychological experiment, 40 participants were randomly assigned either to 'put their best face forward' ($n = 18$) or not ($n = 22$) during a social interaction with their romantic partner. Researchers rated the participants' level of self-presentation (the extent to which they tried to put their best face forward) during the social interaction using a seven-point rating scale. At the end of the study, participants reported their level of positive affect, also using a seven-point rating scale. The researchers hypothesized that self-presentation would mediate the association between the experimental manipulation and subsequent levels of positive affect; specifically, they hypothesized that being instructed to self-present would cause higher self-presentation which in turn would lead to higher levels of positive affect.

This dataset is available on the text's webpage (https://study.sagepub.com/flora) along with annotated input and output from several popular statistical software packages showing how to reproduce the analyses presented in this chapter.

As with any statistical modeling exercise, it is important to begin by examining pertinent descriptive statistics and graphs. Figure 5.2 includes univariate histograms of self-presentation rating (the purported mediator, M) and positive affect (the outcome variable, Y), whereas Figure 5.3 includes plots of the bivariate associations of interest, which are the relations between the experimental condition (the predictor, or independent variable, X) and self-presentation rating and between self-presentation rating and positive affect. The plot of positive affect by self-presentation in Figure 5.3 has a useful feature that we have not seen in any of the previous plots in this text. This plot is a type of enhanced scatterplot referred to as a *bubble plot*. Because the self-presentation and positive affect variables both have ordered, categorical scales, there is considerable overlap of cases at certain points in the plot. The bubble plot depicts the number of cases at each data point by setting the size of the data points, or 'bubbles', to be proportional to the number of observed cases at each point: The larger the bubble, the greater the number of participants at that data point. In Figure 5.3, the bubble sizes help illuminate the pattern that participants with high self-presentation ratings tend to report a high positive affect. From these plots, it does appear that the data are in line with

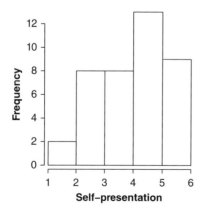
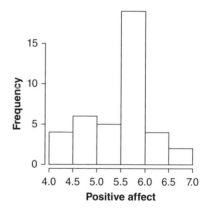

**Figure 5.2** Histograms of self-presentation (mediating variable) and positive affect (outcome variable)

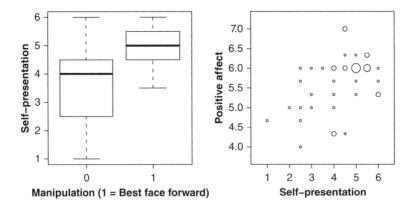

**Figure 5.3** Left panel: Boxplot showing distribution of self-presentation (mediator) against the best-face forward manipulation (independent variable) and right panel: Bubble plot showing positive affect (outcome variable) against self-presentation

the hypothesized relations described earlier. The next steps are to fit the simple indirect-effect model to the data and then to test the mediation hypothesis formally.

## ESTIMATION AND INFERENCE FOR THE INDIRECT EFFECT

As mentioned, the two equations that combine to form the simple indirect-effect model, Equations 5.1 and 5.2, are just linear regression equations, and so their parameters can be estimated using the same OLS estimation procedure applied in the preceding chapters. Therefore, the assumptions underlying OLS estimation also apply equivalently to the current context. Using this OLS regression approach to modeling indirect effects, the two equations are estimated separately. Specifically, Equation 5.1 is first estimated to obtain $\hat{\alpha}$, the sample estimate of the $\alpha_{MX}$ parameter, and then Equation 5.2 is estimated to obtain $\hat{\beta}$, the sample estimate of the $\beta_{YM\Delta X}$ parameter. These two parameter estimates are then multiplied together to obtain $\widehat{\alpha\beta}$, the sample estimate of the indirect effect.

Returning to the self-presentation example, complete results for the estimation of Equations 5.1 and 5.2 to form the simple indirect-effect model are given in Table 5.1. The first regression equation to be estimated is a regression of the self-presentation rating (the hypothesized mediator, $M$) on the dichotomous experimental condition variable (the main predictor, $X$). The estimated linear relation between condition and self-presentation is $\hat{\alpha}_{MX} = 1.13$, which is significant, $t(38) = 3.17$, $p = .003$, indicating that the mean self-presentation rating is 1.13 higher for participants assigned to 'put their best face forward'. We can see from Figure 5.3 that there is evidence of nonhomogenous variance of self-presentation across the two conditions, but a robust $t$ test (Welch's test) corroborates the finding that self-presentation significantly differs across the two groups.

Next is the regression of positive affect (the dependent variable, $Y$) on self-presentation rating ($M$), controlling experimental condition ($X$). The estimated linear relation between self-presentation rating and positive affect is $\hat{\beta}_{YM\cdot X} = 0.19$, which is also significant, $t(37) = 2.15$, $p = .038$, indicating that each one-point increase in self-presentation rating predicts a 0.19 increase in positive affect, holding the experimental condition variable constant. Importantly, the regression diagnostic procedures outlined in Chapter 2 do not indicate any substantial problems for this model with regard to OLS assumptions or influential cases.

**Table 5.1** Results for OLS regression models to estimate simple indirect-effect model for self-presentation example

| Predictor variable | Estimated coefficient | SE | t | p | 95% CI |
|---|---|---|---|---|---|
| Self-presentation outcome (mediator) | | | | | |
| X: Experimental manipulation | 1.13 | 0.36 | 3.17 | .003 | (0.41, 1.86) |
| Positive affect outcome (main dependent variable) | | | | | |
| X: Experimental manipulation | 0.32 | 0.22 | 1.45 | .155 | (−0.13, 0.78) |
| M: Self-presentation rating | 0.19 | 0.09 | 2.15 | .038 | (0.01, 0.38) |

Note. N = 40. SE = standard error.

Given the results from these two regression models, the estimated indirect effect is therefore $\widehat{\alpha\beta} = 1.13 \times 0.19 = 0.22$, indicating that being in the 'best face forward' experimental condition causes a 0.22 increase in positive affect through the self-presentation mediating variable compared with the control condition.[3] The direct effect, which is the partial regression relation between experimental condition and positive affect holding self-presentation rating constant, is $\hat{\beta}_{YX\cdot M} = 0.33$. Therefore, the total effect of the experimental manipulation on positive affect is $0.22 + 0.33 = 0.55$. In sum, the predicted positive affect score is 0.55 higher for participants instructed to put their best face forward relative to control participants; of this total difference, 0.22 is explained by higher levels of self-presentation occurring in the experimental condition.

At this point, researchers typically want to know whether a given indirect effect or mediated effect is itself statistically significant. The methodological literature has produced an overwhelming proliferation of approaches to testing the significance of an indirect effect, and there are several published simulation studies in which these methods are compared with each other. Rather than cataloguing each of these methods, we will instead focus on just two approaches: (1) the *test of the joint significance* of $\hat{\alpha}$ and $\hat{\beta}$ and (2) the *percentile bootstrap confidence interval* for the product, $\alpha\beta$. These approaches share the advantages of being simple compared with other methods and of having performed well in simulation studies (in terms of balancing Type I error control and power; in particular, see Biesanz et al., 2010, and MacKinnon, Lockwood, Hoffman, West, and Sheets, 2002). In passing, it is important also to mention two of the most commonly used approaches to assessing mediation and other indirect effects: (1) a method explicated by Baron and Kenny (1986) which has come to be known as the *causal steps* approach and (2) a significance test for $\widehat{\alpha\beta}$ based on a standard error approximation from Sobel (1982), which is commonly known as the *Sobel test*. Despite their popularity, the causal steps approach and the Sobel test consistently perform poorly in simulation studies compared with other methods, and so we will not consider them further.

## Joint significance of $\hat{\alpha}$ and $\hat{\beta}$

One way to think about the 'overall' null hypothesis for an indirect effect is to form separate null hypotheses for the two constituent paths in Figure 5.1 forming the indirect effect of X on Y

---

[3]Under the linearity assumption for these regression models, this indirect-effect estimate is a correct estimate of the causal mediation effect despite that the self-presentation mediator is not randomized (Imai et al., 2010).

through $M$. The logic is that for there to be an indirect effect, first the independent variable, or main predictor, must have a nonzero relation with the intervening variable (or mediator) and second the intervening variable must have a nonzero relation with the outcome variable (holding the main predictor constant). This logic implies rejection of two separate null hypotheses:

$$H_0: \alpha_{MX} = 0$$

and

$$H_0: \beta_{YM.X} = 0.$$

The **test of the joint significance** of $\hat{\alpha}$ and $\hat{\beta}$ simply states that if both of these null hypotheses are rejected, that is, if both $\hat{\alpha}$ and $\hat{\beta}$ are significantly different from zero, then one concludes that there is a significant indirect relation between the main predictor and outcome variables via the intervening variable.[4] In the current mediation example, the relation between experimental condition and self-presentation ratings was significant. Additionally, the relation between self-presentation and positive affect was significant, controlling the experimental condition. Therefore, the two constituent paths of the indirect effect are both significant, confirming the hypothesis that self-presentation ratings mediate the relation between the experimental manipulation and the reported positive effect.

## Percentile bootstrap confidence interval for $\widehat{\alpha\beta}$

Because the estimated indirect effect, $\widehat{\alpha\beta}$, is a single parameter estimate with its own sampling distribution, in principle, it is preferable to evaluate an obtained empirical value of $\widehat{\alpha\beta}$ with direct reference to the sampling distribution of $\widehat{\alpha\beta}$, rather than basing inference on separate sampling distributions of $\hat{\alpha}$ and $\hat{\beta}$, as with the joint test. In other words, testing the significance of an indirect effect should be based on a single null hypothesis for the single parameter $\alpha\beta$,

$$H_0: \alpha\beta = 0,$$

instead of the two separate null hypotheses for $\alpha_{MX}$ and $\beta_{YM.X}$ given in the previous paragraph. Currently, the most prominent approaches to evaluating this null hypothesis involve constructing confidence interval (CI) estimates of $\alpha\beta$: If a CI calculated from sample data does not overlap the value of $\alpha\beta$ specified by the null hypothesis (i.e., zero), then the null hypothesis is rejected with a given nominal alpha level.[5] Of course, the nominal alpha level is most

---

[4]This procedure is similar to the Baron and Kenny (1986) causal steps method but with one critical difference: The causal steps method requires statistical significance for the initial marginal relation between the independent and dependent variables (i.e., ignoring the mediator), which is commonly known as the $\tau$ or $c$ parameter, whereas the current joint significance approach does not include that step.

[5]Because the true sampling distribution of $\widehat{\alpha\beta}$ depends on the population values of $\alpha$ and $\beta$, there may not be an exact correspondence between the overlap of a CI estimate of $\alpha\beta$ with zero and the correct $p$ value for the null hypothesis, in contrast to the exact correspondence between hypothesis tests and CIs for parameters such as means and regression coefficients (Biesanz et al., 2010).

commonly .05, implying that the null hypothesis for $\alpha\beta$ is rejected if a 95% CI around $\widehat{\alpha\beta}$ does not contain zero. Rejection of the null hypothesis leads to the conceptual conclusion that the obtained indirect effect $\widehat{\alpha\beta}$ is significantly different from zero. But we should also keep in mind that the CI is much more informative than that: It gives a complete range of plausible values for the population indirect effect, $\alpha\beta$.

**Bootstrapping** is a method which, in general, can be used to derive an *empirical* sampling distribution of a particular statistic (such as $\widehat{\alpha\beta}$), referred to as a *plug-in statistic*, to obtain information about the variability of that statistic across different samples (the authoritative text on bootstrapping in general is Efron and Tibshirani, 1993). As such, bootstrapping approaches provide alternatives to inferential procedures (i.e., hypothesis tests and CIs) that are based on analytically derived, theoretical sampling distributions (such as a normal distribution for the sampling distribution of a regression coefficient as per the central limit theorem). Therefore, bootstrapping is particularly useful for situations in which a given theoretical sampling distribution is likely to be incorrect as a result of small sample size or assumption violation, when the sampling distribution has a known but complex form, or when there simply is no statistical theory about the sampling distribution of a given statistic.

Regarding the indirect effect, statistical theory tells us that the sampling distributions of $\hat{\alpha}$ and $\hat{\beta}$ are normal (and to account for uncertainty in the estimation of their standard error, these estimates are evaluated against a $t$ distribution rather than against a normal distribution), but it turns out that the theoretical sampling distribution of their product, $\widehat{\alpha\beta}$, is much more complex, with its shape depending on the population values of $\alpha$ and $\beta$ (MacKinnon, Lockwood, and Williams, 2004). Consequently, bootstrapping represents an attractive option for obtaining information about the sampling distribution of $\widehat{\alpha\beta}$ which then can be used to reach inferential conclusions about the population value of $\alpha\beta$. In particular, the **percentile bootstrap CI**, which is described next, is a straightforward approach to obtaining a CI estimate of $\alpha\beta$ that has performed well in simulation studies of inferential methods for the indirect effect.

Bootstrapping is a resampling procedure in which many random samples are drawn from the same overall dataset. Importantly, these samples are drawn *with replacement*, meaning that a particular case can be included in a random sample more than once.[6] Then, the plug-in statistic of interest (e.g., $\widehat{\alpha\beta}$) is calculated for each sample, and these values are collected to form an empirical sampling distribution of the plug-in statistic. More specifically, the steps involved in constructing a 95% percentile bootstrap CI for the indirect effect $\alpha\beta$ are given next. Take heart that these steps are automated by readily available functions in statistical software, but it is still valuable to understand the mechanics of the procedure:

1. Consider the original dataset of size N, a 'population reservoir' from which to draw samples.
2. Randomly sample cases with replacement from the population reservoir to get a **bootstrap sample**, also of size N. Note that this means sampling the entire record for each case, that is, the observed values of each variable for a randomly selected person (or other unit of observation), rather than sampling values from individual variables.

---

[6]Here's a simple example to illustrate sampling with replacement: Imagine randomly choosing a ball from a bag containing three balls: a red ball, a blue ball, and a green ball. For the first observation, one randomly grabs a single ball and observes its colour, such that the probability of obtaining any one colour is 1/3. Next, sampling with replacement implies that an observed ball is returned to the bag before any subsequent observations occur. Therefore, there are always three balls in the bag when one randomly selects the next ball to observe its colour, and the probability of observing any one colour remains 1/3 across all random draws.

3.  Using the current bootstrap sample, estimate the indirect-effect model to obtain a value of $\widehat{\alpha\beta}$ . The model estimated with the bootstrap sample should be specified to be the same as the original, complete indirect-effect model; that is, if there are covariates in the original model in addition to the main predictor and intervening variable (see Equations 5.3 and 5.4), then these covariates should also be included when $\widehat{\alpha\beta}$ is estimated with the bootstrap sample.

4.  Repeat steps 2 and 3 J times, where J is a large number (e.g., 1,000), leading to J bootstrap estimates of $\widehat{\alpha\beta}$ .

5.  Sort the J bootstrapped values of $\widehat{\alpha\beta}$ from low to high to construct the empirical sampling distribution of $\widehat{\alpha\beta}$ .

6.  To obtain a 95% percentile bootstrap CI estimate of $\alpha\beta$, find the bootstrapped values of $\widehat{\alpha\beta}$ at the 2.5th percentile and at the 97.5th percentile of the empirical sampling distribution. The lower limit of the CI is the $\widehat{\alpha\beta}$ value at the 2.5th percentile, and the upper limit is the value at the 97.5th percentile.

Applying this procedure to the self-presentation example, the first bootstrap sample produced $\widehat{\alpha\beta}$ = 0.18, the second bootstrap sample led to $\widehat{\alpha\beta}$ = 0.05, the third produced $\widehat{\alpha\beta}$ = 0.15, and so on, to a collection of J = 1,000 bootstrap estimates of $\widehat{\alpha\beta}$ . The distribution of these bootstrap estimates, depicted in Figure 5.4, represents an empirical sampling distribution of the $\widehat{\alpha\beta}$ statistic. The mean (0.22) and median (0.21) of this distribution are both close to the original point estimate of $\widehat{\alpha\beta}$ = 0.22, but its shape is notably positively skewed and kurtotic (skewness = 0.73, kurtosis = 1.30), which helps illustrate why it is not generally appropriate to test the significance of $\widehat{\alpha\beta}$ using a Z or t statistic. But because 95% of the $\widehat{\alpha\beta}$ estimates fall between the 2.5th percentile and the 97.5th percentile of this distribution, we can use the values of these percentiles as the lower and upper limits of a 95% CI for $\alpha\beta$ (alternatively, we could instead use the 0.05 and 99.50 percentiles to construct a 99% CI, for example).

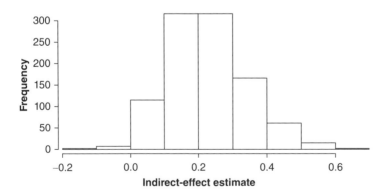

**Figure 5.4**  Histogram of empirical sampling distribution of $\widehat{\alpha\beta}$ across 1,000 bootstrap samples

Here, the 2.5 percentile value of this distribution is 0.03 and the 97.5 percentile is at 0.51; thus, the 95% percentile bootstrap CI estimate is (0.03, 0.51). Notice that this CI is not symmetric; the difference between the median of the bootstrap sampling distribution and the lower limit (0.21 – 0.03 = 0.18) is less than the difference between the upper limit and the median (0.51 – 0.21 = 0.30). This asymmetry is a consequence of the positive skewness of the bootstrap empirical sampling distribution, whereas CIs based on normal-theory estimates (e.g., CIs for a mean or for a single linear regression coefficient) are always symmetric. Nonetheless, because this percentile bootstrap CI does not overlap zero, we can conclude that the population indirect effect of the 'best face forward' experimental manipulation on positive affect that goes through the self-presentation mediator is unlikely to equal zero. Thus, self-presentation significantly mediates the relation between the experimental manipulation independent variable and the positive affect outcome variable. Finally, it is important to keep in mind that because boot-strapping is based on a random-sampling procedure, repeating this analysis with the same dataset may lead to a slightly different bootstrap percentile CI (even with rounding), although the result should be extremely close as long as the number of bootstrap samples is large.

### Section recap

**Estimation and inference for the indirect effect**

The two linear regression equations (Equations 5.1 and 5.2) forming the simple indirect-effect model can both be estimated using OLS.

The test of the **joint significance** of $\hat{\alpha}$ and $\hat{\beta}$ and the **percentile bootstrap confidence interval** for $\alpha\beta$ both provide tests of the indirect effect which adequately control Type I error and have high power compared with other popular tests of indirect effects.

In the test of joint significance, if both $\hat{\alpha}$ and $\hat{\beta}$ are significant according to their separate $t$ tests, then one concludes that the indirect effect of $X$ on $Y$ through $M$ is significant.

**Bootstrapping** the indirect effect estimate $\widehat{\alpha\beta}$ involves forming an empirical sampling distribution of $\widehat{\alpha\beta}$: Draw $J$ samples, each of size $N$, with replacement from the original dataset of $N$ cases. Calculate $\widehat{\alpha\beta}$ for each sample, and sort the $\widehat{\alpha\beta}$ estimates from low to high.

The 95% percentile bootstrap confidence interval for $\alpha\beta$ is formed from the values at the 2.5th and 97.5th percentiles of the bootstrap empirical sampling distribution of $\widehat{\alpha\beta}$.

If the 95% percentile bootstrap CI does not overlap 0, conclude that the indirect-effect estimate $\widehat{\alpha\beta}$ is significant with $\alpha = .05$.

## Research example for modeling a nonexperimental indirect effect

To demonstrate the application of the simple indirect-effect model to estimate and inter-pret an indirect effect arising from an observational, nonexperimental context, we again use the parental alcoholism example data described in Chapter 4, where we found that parental alcoholism moderates the prospective relation between externalizing behaviour and heavy alcohol use in a sample of adolescents. Here, we will instead estimate a model to examine the hypothesis that there is an indirect effect of parental alcoholism (operationalized as a dichoto-mous variable) on heavy alcohol use among adolescents through the intervening variable of externalizing behaviour.

Again, this dataset is available on the text's webpage (https://study.sagepub.com/flora) along with annotated input and output from several popular statistical software packages showing how to reproduce the analyses presented next.

At first, we will ignore the results from Chapter 4 about the interaction between parental alcoholism and externalizing and focus on estimating and interpreting the indirect effect while pretending that there is no moderation effect, but then we will reintroduce the interaction to investigate an instance of *moderated mediation*, or to avoid the implication of causality, a *moderated indirect effect*.

Referring back to Table 4.1, we see that there is a small correlation between parental alcoholism and externalizing behaviour ($r$ = .21; control group mean = 0.46, median = 0.33; children of alcoholics (COAs) group mean = 0.65, median = 0.58) and a slightly bigger correlation between externalizing behaviour and subsequent heavy alcohol use ($r$ = .34). Figure 5.5 illustrates these bivariate relations (also notice that there are two cases with outlying externalizing scores).

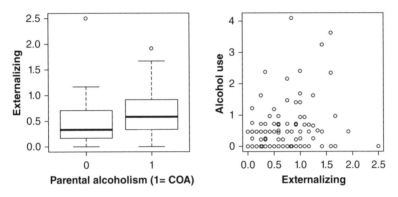

**Figure 5.5** Bivariate associations pertaining to indirect effect hypothesis for adolescent alcohol use example. Left panel: Side-by-side boxplot of externalizing behaviour (intervening variable) against parental alcoholism (main predictor). Right panel: Scatterplot of heavy alcohol use (main outcome variable) against externalizing behaviour (intervening variable)

Complete results from applying the simple indirect-effect model (Figure 5.1) to this example are in Table 5.2. The first regression model to be estimated is a regression of externalizing behaviour (the hypothesized intervening variable, $M$) on the dichotomous parental alcoholism variable (the main predictor, $X$). The estimated relation between parental alcoholism and externalizing is $\hat{a}_{MX}$ = 0.186, which is significant, $t(163)$ = 2.74, $p$ = .007, indicating that the predicted externalizing score is 0.186 higher for COAs compared with control participants. The next model is a regression of heavy alcohol use (the dependent variable, $Y$) on externalizing ($M$), controlling parental alcoholism ($X$). The estimated partial relation between externalizing and heavy alcohol use is $\hat{\beta}_{YM \cdot X}$ = 0.439, which is also significant, $t(163)$ = 3.92, $p$ < .001, indicating that each one-point increase in externalizing predicts a 0.439 increase in alcohol use, controlling parental alcoholism.

Given the results from these two regression models, the estimated indirect effect is $\widehat{\alpha\beta}$ = 0.186 × 0.439 = 0.082, indicating that parental alcoholism is associated with a 0.082 increase in the heavy alcohol-use variable via increased externalizing behaviour. This indirect effect is statistically significant according to the joint significance of $\hat{\alpha}$ and $\hat{\beta}$ and because a 95% percentile bootstrap CI of (0.02, 0.20) does not overlap zero. The direct

**Table 5.2** Results for OLS regression models to estimate simple indirect-effect model for adolescent alcohol use example

| Predictor variable | Estimated coefficient | SE | t | p | 95% CI |
|---|---|---|---|---|---|
| Externalizing outcome (mediator) | | | | | |
| X: Parental alcoholism | 0.19 | 0.07 | 2.74 | .007 | (0.05, 0.32) |
| Heavy alcohol use (main dependent variable) | | | | | |
| X: Parental alcoholism | 0.31 | 0.10 | 3.08 | .002 | (0.11, 0.50) |
| M: Externalizing behaviour | 0.44 | 0.11 | 3.92 | <.001 | (0.22, 0.65) |

*Note. N = 165.*

effect, which is the partial regression relation between parental alcoholism and alcohol use obtained by holding externalizing constant, is $\hat{\beta}_{YX \cdot M} = 0.307$. Therefore, the total effect of parental alcoholism on heavy alcohol use is $0.082 + 0.307 = 0.389$. In sum, the predicted heavy alcohol-use score is 0.389 for COAs relative to control participants; of this total difference, 0.082 is explained by higher levels of externalizing among COAs.

## A moderated indirect effect?

Recall from Chapter 4 that externalizing behaviour was also a significant moderator of the relation between parental alcoholism and adolescent heavy alcohol use. Therefore, the application of the simple indirect-effect model to these variables described in the previous two paragraphs provides an incomplete picture of the associations among these three variables. Consequently, to represent the pattern of relations among these variables more completely, the simple indirect-effect model of Figure 5.1 is expanded to include an interaction between $X$ and $M$, as depicted in Figure 5.6. This pattern of effects represents a particular type of **moderated indirect effect**, which also may be termed **moderated mediation** (in the context of explicit causal hypotheses) or **conditional indirect effect**, in which the indirect effect of $X$ on $Y$ through $M$ is qualified by an interaction between $X$ and $M$.

In my experience, when the main predictor in an indirect-effect model is a naturalistic, observational variable (e.g., a risk factor such as parental alcoholism) and not an experimental manipulation formed by random assignment to groups, it is common for this predictor to interact with the putative intervening variable in the prediction of the main outcome variable. Therefore, in the context of nonexperimental research, the model depicted in Figure 5.6 may often be more realistic than the simple indirect-effect model of Figure 5.1. Of course, it is also entirely possible that some other covariate could moderate either the relation between $X$ and $M$ or the relation between $M$ and $Y$ to provide other instances of moderated indirect effects (see Preacher, Rucker, and Hayes, 2007, for a comprehensive presentation of various forms of moderated mediation). But for now, we will continue to consider the situation in which the only variables in the analysis are a single $X$, a single $M$, and a single $Y$.

The model in Figure 5.6 again represents a set of two linear regression equations. The first, the regression of $M$ on $X$, is identical to Equation 5.1. But the equation for $Y$ needs to be expanded to include the interaction between $X$ and $M$:

$$Y_i = \beta_0 + \beta_{YX}X_i + \beta_{YM}M_i + \beta_{Y(XM)}(X_iM_i) + \varepsilon_{Yi}. \tag{5.5}$$

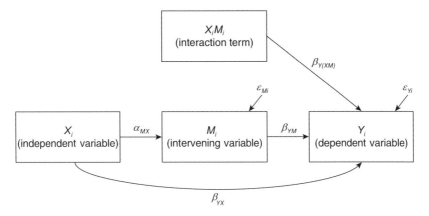

**Figure 5.6** Moderated indirect-effect model

Notice that this equation is just an application of Equation 4.1, the linear regression model for the interaction between two predictors, with $X = X_1$ and $M = X_2$. Next, the indirect effect of $X$ on $Y$ through $M$ is no longer simply the product of $\alpha_{MX}$ and $\beta_{YM}$ because the relation between $M$ and $Y$ is a function of both $\beta_{YM}$ and $\beta_{Y(XM)}$. Instead, as given by Preacher et al. (2007), the conditional indirect effect for a given level of $X$ is $\alpha_{MX} \times (\beta_{YM} + \beta_{Y(XM)}X)$, reflecting that the indirect effect is itself moderated by, or is conditioned on, the predictor $X$; that is, the value of the indirect effect changes across the different values of $X$. It is useful to recognize that the term in parentheses, $\beta_{YM} + \beta_{Y(XM)}X$, is equivalent to the *simple-slope* coefficient $\omega_1$ from Chapter 4 (Equation 4.4) for the effect of $M$ on $Y$ as a function of the moderator $X$.

Applying the adolescent heavy alcohol-use example, we still have $\hat{\alpha}_{MX} = 0.19$ as the estimated relation between parental alcoholism and externalizing behaviour. Next, returning to the results from Chapter 4 (see Table 4.2), there was a substantial interaction between the dichotomous parental alcoholism variable and externalizing in the prediction of heavy alcohol use, giving $\hat{\beta}_{Y(XM)} = 0.57$. In the current context, this interaction effect represents the extent to which the association between the intervening variable (externalizing) and the outcome variable (alcohol use) differs across the two levels of the dichotomous predictor (parental alcoholism). More specifically, the simple-slope analysis in Chapter 4 indicated that the relation between externalizing and alcohol use equalled 0.10 among control participants and equalled 0.67 among COAs. These values then provide the necessary ingredients for the estimated conditional indirect effect. Specifically, among control participants, we have $\hat{\alpha}_{MX} \times (\hat{\beta}_{YM} + \hat{\beta}_{Y(XM)}X) = 0.19 \times (0.10) = 0.02$, which is not significantly different from a population effect of zero based on a 95% percentile bootstrap confidence interval of (–0.01, 0.09). Among COAs, $\hat{\alpha}_{MX} \times (\hat{\beta}_{YM} + \hat{\beta}_{Y(XM)}X) = 0.19 \times (0.67) = 0.13$, which is distinguishable from a population effect of zero based on a 95% percentile bootstrap confidence interval of (0.03, 0.27).

Unfortunately, giving a conceptual interpretation to these conditional indirect-effect values is awkward because the implication is that the focal predictor $X$ predicts $Y$ indirectly through $M$, yet $X$ also moderates the relation between $Y$ and $M$. Or, we could equivalently say that $M$ is both an intervening variable and a moderator in the relation between $X$ and $Y$. Consequently, the usual phrasing for interpreting a regression effect as the predicted difference in $Y$ for a one-unit change in $X$ is difficult, if not impossible, to apply for this particular overall model (Figure 5.6) because the moderation effect is such that the predicted difference in $Y$ for a one-unit change in $X$ is different based on the level of $X$ (Coffman and Zhong, 2012, also suggested that the $\hat{\alpha}_{MX} \times (\hat{\beta}_{YM} + \hat{\beta}_{Y(XM)} X)$ parameter defined here is not interpretable as an indirect effect).

For the current example, we can reach a general conclusion that externalizing behaviour intervenes in the association between parental alcoholism and adolescent heavy alcohol use, but simultaneously, parental alcoholism moderates the relation between externalizing and heavy alcohol use. Yet giving exact, conceptual interpretations to the 0.02 (for the control group) and 0.13 (for the COA group) conditional indirect-effect estimates is difficult. Because conceptual interpretation of the actual values of the conditional indirect effects from this type of moderated-indirect-effect model is so difficult, my general advice for reporting this type of analysis is instead to focus on interpreting each constituent path in Figure 5.6. Despite the interpretational awkwardness that arises from this model, it nonetheless provides a comprehensive picture of how the $X$ and $M$ variables come together to describe and predict variation in the $Y$ outcome.

As mentioned, because these analyses are just an application of OLS regression techniques, the same assumptions and diagnostic procedures outlined in Chapter 2 are applicable here. For this adolescent heavy alcohol-use example, Figure 5.5 indicates that there are some outlying observations, and we know from Chapter 4 that the distribution of the alcohol-use variable is potentially problematic. After fitting Equation 5.5 to these data, there was no evidence of influential outliers (using Cook's $D$), but the relation between the residuals and predicted values was notably nonlinear and the residuals were non-normally distributed, which is consistent with the diagnostic results presented for these data in Chapter 4 (see Figure 4.3). Nonetheless, when the alcohol-use outcome variable is transformed using a square-root transformation, essentially the same conceptual conclusions can be drawn as those outlined earlier based on the nontransformed alcohol-use variable.[7]

## Section recap

### Moderated indirect effects

A **moderated indirect effect** (or **moderated mediation**, in the context of causal effects) occurs when the association between the main predictor variable and the intervening variable is moderated by another variable, the association between the intervening variable and the outcome is moderated by another variable, or both.

In nonexperimental research, it is likely that the main predictor variable will interact with the intervening variable in the prediction of the main outcome. Unfortunately, this type of moderated indirect effect is difficult to interpret.

---

[7]Similar results were also obtained with a natural log transformation.

# CHAPTER SUMMARY

This chapter described how multiple regression models may be used to assess hypotheses regarding **indirect effects** and statistical **mediation**, which refers to a causal chain in which a primary independent variable or predictor causes differences in an **intervening variable**, or **mediator**, which then causally affects a primary outcome or dependent variable:

- The simple **indirect-effect model** can be used to estimate and test a hypothesized indirect effect regardless of whether the effects in the model can legitimately be considered causal mediation effects; a given indirect effect could be considered merely descriptive.
- The simple indirect-effect model consists of two linear regression equations which can be estimated with OLS:

$$M_i = \alpha_0 + \alpha_{MX}X_i + \varepsilon_{Mi},$$

$$Y_i = \beta_0 + \beta_{YM.X}M_i + \beta_{YX.M}X_i + \varepsilon_{Yi},$$

  where $X$ is the main independent or predictor variable, $M$ is the intervening variable (or mediator), and $Y$ is the main outcome variable.
- From these two equations, the indirect effect of $X$ on $Y$ through $M$ is the **product of coefficients**, $\alpha_{MX} \times \beta_{YM.X}$.
- The test of the **joint significance** of $\hat{\alpha}$ and $\hat{\beta}$ and the **percentile bootstrap confidence interval** for $\alpha\beta$ both provide tests of the indirect effect which adequately control Type I error and have high power compared with other popular tests of indirect effects.
- A **moderated indirect effect** (or **moderated mediation**, in the context of causal effects) occurs when the association between the main predictor variable and the intervening variable is moderated by another variable, the association between the intervening variable and the outcome is moderated by another variable, or both.
- In nonexperimental research, it is likely that the main predictor variable will interact with the intervening variable in the prediction of the main outcome. Unfortunately, this type of moderated indirect effect is difficult to interpret.

# RECOMMENDED READING

Bollen, K.A. (1989). Causality and causal models. In K.A. Bollen, *Structural equations with latent variables* (pp. 40–79). New York: Wiley.

- Bollen gives a clear, complete discussion of causality and the conditions that must be met to draw valid causal inference from statistical models.

MacKinnon, D.P., Krull, J.L., & Lockwood, C.M. (2000). Equivalence of the mediation, confounding and suppression effect. *Prevention Science, 4,* 173–81.

- Through the use of several interesting examples, the authors describe how patterns of effects among three (or more variables) can be equivalently cast as representing mediation, confounding, or suppression.

Pek, J., & Hoyle, R.H. (2016). On the (in)validity of tests of simple mediation: Threats and solutions. *Social and Personality Psychology Compass, 10,* 150–63.

- This paper offers a didactic critique of the routine use of the simple mediation model. In particular, the authors point out that the simple indirect-effect model presented in this chapter is statistically equivalent to a handful of alternative models which are not consistent with a causal mediation process. The authors highlight the importance of research design for helping choose among these models.

Preacher, K.J., Rucker, D.D., & Hayes, A.F. (2007). Addressing moderated mediation hypotheses: Theory, methods, and prescriptions. *Multivariate Behavioral Research, 42,* 185–227.

- The authors clearly present several different types of models reflecting so-called moderated mediation and describe methods for testing indirect effects for each type.

# INTRODUCTION TO MULTILEVEL MODELING

## CHAPTER OVERVIEW

Each regression model presented in the previous chapters has relied on a strong assumption that the cases are statistically independent. After beginning with a discussion of the prevalence of nonindependent observations in behavioural and social science research, the current chapter focuses on a prominent modeling procedure for representing nonindependent observations, namely, multilevel modeling (MLM). The main topics of this chapter include:

- Discussion of nonindependent observations
- Specification of the unconditional multilevel model
- Estimation and inference for multilevel models
- Specification and interpretation of the random-intercepts multilevel model
- Specification and interpretation of the random-slopes multilevel model
- Specification and interpretation of multilevel models with Level 2 predictors
- Distinguishing within-cluster effects from between-clusters effects
- Formal model comparisons
- Specifying and interpreting cross-level interactions
- Assumption checking in MLM

**Table 6.0** Greek letter notation used in this chapter

| Greek letter | English name | Represents |
|---|---|---|
| $\beta$ | Lowercase 'beta' | Level 1 regression parameter (intercept or slope, depending on subscript) |
| $\varepsilon$ | Lowercase 'epsilon' | Level 1 error term |

*(Continued)*

**Table 6.0**   (Continued)

| Greek letter | English name | Represents |
|---|---|---|
| $\gamma$ | Lowercase 'gamma' | Level 2 regression parameter (intercept or slope, depending on subscript) |
| $\delta$ | Lowercase 'delta' | Level 2 error term |
| $\sigma$ | Lowercase 'sigma' | $\sigma^2$ is Level 1 error variance |
| $\tau$ | Lowercase 'tau' | $\tau^2$ is Level 2 error variance; $\tau$ is covariance between different Level 2 error terms |
| $\chi$ | Lowercase 'chi' | $\chi^2$ distribution |

## WHAT IS MULTILEVEL MODELING?

As outlined in Chapter 2, a key assumption of estimating regression models using ordinary least-squares (OLS) is that the cases (more precisely, the model-implied error terms) are independent. When this assumption is violated, results based on OLS estimation are incorrect to some extent and can therefore lead to misleading substantive conclusions. Various methods are available for dealing with this issue, but the most prominent and most generally applicable is to model the nonindependence directly using a *multilevel model* instead of a standard OLS regression approach. Fortunately, many of the ideas and principles of multiple regression that have been covered so far in this text generalize to multilevel modeling, and it is even possible to represent the standard multiple regression model (i.e., Equation 2.9) as a special type of multilevel model.

**Multilevel modeling** (**MLM**) is also commonly known as *hierarchical linear modeling (HLM;* not to be confused with the hierarchical regression technique described in Chapter 2), *mixed-effects modeling* or simply *mixed modeling*, and sometimes *random-effects modeling* or *random-coefficients modeling*. Although there are subtle reasons for preferring one of these terms over another depending on context and mainly according to custom within particular research fields, all of these names refer to essentially the same approach toward modeling data containing nonindependent observations. From this point forward, this text will use the term *multilevel modeling* or *MLM* to refer to this general modeling approach.

## NONINDEPENDENT OBSERVATIONS

Repeating Equation 2.9, recall that the standard linear regression model for $P$ predictors can be written as

$$Y_i = \beta_0 + \left( \sum_{p=1}^{P} \beta_p X_{pi} \right) + \varepsilon_i,$$

where $\varepsilon_i$ is the error term for participant $i$, such that

$$\varepsilon_i = Y_i - \hat{Y}_i.$$

The independence assumption invoked when one estimates the model using OLS is formally stated as

$$E(\varepsilon_i, \varepsilon_j) = 0, \quad i \neq j.$$

That is, information about the error for a generic case $i$ provides no information about the error of a different case $j$.

It is occasionally stated that if this independence assumption does not hold, the OLS slope estimates remain unbiased; but in certain situations, ignoring the causes of noninde-pendence can still lead to misleading estimates, as described later. But also under violation of the independence assumption, $R^2$ will be overestimated; that is, sample-based $R^2$ values will tend to be larger than their population analog $\rho^2$. Additionally, the mean-squared-error term from the analysis of regression variance may be substantially underestimated (i.e., smaller than it should be), leading to inflated Type I error rates for the significance test for $R^2$. Finally, and perhaps most importantly, the standard errors of the individual regression coefficient estimates will also tend to be underestimated, consequently leading to inflated Type I error rates for the $t$ tests of the regression slopes and confidence intervals for the slopes which are too narrow.

These consequences of ignored nonindependence are predictable given the perspective that nonindependence serves to reduce the *effective sample size* of a research study: Because observations that are nonindependent provide correlated, overlapping data, it is as if a study of $N$ nonindependent cases was conducted using fewer than $N$ completely independ-ent cases. Because sample size plays a critical role in the calculation of standard errors, standard error estimates are biased by ignored nonindependence among observations.

## Potential sources of nonindependence

Although the independence assumption for OLS regression technically pertains to the error term, usually it is evaluated with respect to observations of the outcome variable, $Y$. As men-tioned in Chapter 2, evaluation of independence is typically best achieved through careful consideration of research design and procedures, particularly sampling procedures. It turns out that it is much easier to describe research scenarios in which nonindependent outcome variable observations are likely than it is to define general conditions that guarantee complete independence of observations.[1]

Probably the most common and intuitive examples of nonindependent observations come from education research, where many research questions involve outcomes for individual stu-dents, but the students are sampled from classes, schools, and school districts. This situation is likely to produce nonindependent observations of individual students in that two students from the same class are likely to be more similar to one another (because they share the same teacher or other resources) compared with a pair of students who come from two different classes. Likewise, two classes might be more similar to one another when they are in the same school compared with two classes in different schools. In MLM terminology, we would say

---

[1] Even simple random sampling may not guarantee complete independence among observations.

that the data are **hierarchical**, such that students are **nested** or **clustered** within classes and classrooms are nested within schools.[2] More generally, hierarchical data arise when individual cases are nested within groupings of cases; because these individual cases are clustered into groups,[3] observations at the individual level are nonindependent.

In the educational context just described, the research procedure is often explicitly designed to produce hierarchical data to allow an examination of the relations among student-level characteristics, classroom characteristics, and perhaps even school-level or school-district characteristics. But in other contexts, aspects of the research procedure might unintentionally produce hierarchically nested data with nonindependent observations. For example, imagine a study in which a few different research assistants interview adult participants about alcohol use. Perhaps some of these interviewers are adept at building rapport with the participants, such that participants are more willing to discuss this sensitive topic; conversely, the other interviewers are less skilled, and the participants they interview are not as willing to disclose information. In this situation, although the participants may have been sampled completely randomly from the population, the responses provided by two participants interviewed by the same research assistant are likely to be more similar in certain respects[4] than are those provided by two participants with different interviewers. Consequently, having many participants nested within few interviewers is a likely cause of nonindependence resulting from shared interviewer characteristics. Therefore, even if the main purpose of a research study does not involve examination of relations among variables across different levels of a data hierarchy, certain aspects of the research procedure can still create a data structure characterized by nonindependence among individual observations. It is prudent, then, always to consider the possibility of nonindependence carefully because of the potential deleterious effects of ignored nonindependence on data analytic results and interpretation.

Hierarchically nested data appear regularly in behavioural and social research. To paraphrase a colleague, once one is aware of the possibility of hierarchical data structures, they begin to appear everywhere. For example:

- Psychotherapy clients are nested within therapists.
- Siblings are nested within families.
- Animal subjects are nested within litters.
- Homeless individuals are nested within service areas.
- Households are nested within neighbourhoods, which are then nested within cities.

---

[2]Sometimes, however, data structures with nonindependent cases are not strictly hierarchically nested, but such data can still be modeled by adapting the basic MLM approach presented in this chapter (see Snijders and Bosker, 2012: 205–15).

[3]These groups do not necessarily correspond to the different categories of a categorical independent variable. As explained in further detail later, if the grouping variable is considered 'fixed', then the traditional general linear modeling approaches outlined in Chapters 2 and 3 are appropriate; if the grouping is instead 'random', then MLM is appropriate.

[4]Not necessarily with respect to the participants' actual *amount* of alcohol use, but perhaps responses regarding attitudes would be similar, or the tendency to provide nonresponses (i.e., missing data) would be similar within those interviewed by a given interviewer.

- With longitudinal data, repeated observations are nested within a single person.
- In experimental designs, repeated trials of a task are nested within a condition, and then repeated conditions may be nested within participants.

Whenever there is a possibility that some feature of the research design might serve to introduce a hierarchical structure into the data, whether intentionally or not, MLM strategies are applicable.

When the hierarchical structure of nonindependent observations is directly modeled using MLM, correct standard errors of parameter estimates are obtained, such that Type I error rates for significance tests are maintained at their nominal level (provided other assumptions are met, as discussed later in this chapter), which does not occur when nonindependence is ignored. Additionally, although there are other corrective procedures to account for nonindependence, by explicitly representing whether variables are measured at an individual level or at a group level (i.e., different levels of the data hierarchy), MLM avoids potentially misleading results caused by the *ecological fallacy*, which pertains to making interpretations about individuals based on aggregated, group-level information, as well as from the *atomistic fallacy*, which pertains to making interpretations about groups based on individual-level relations (see Diez Roux, 2002). In MLM, individual-level outcomes can be modeled using individual-level predictors, group-level predictors, or both simultaneously, potentially including interactions between variables measured at different levels. For example, one can efficiently examine a student-level outcome (e.g., academic achievement) as a function of student-level variables (e.g., student socioeconomic status [SES]), class-level variables (e.g., teacher experience), and school-level variables (e.g., average SES of the school) using a single model. This approach is clearly more desirable than a disjointed series of separate OLS regression analyses (e.g., a separate regression model for each class using only student-level variables, in which class-level variables must be ignored, or a regression model in which the cases are classes, in which student-level characteristics must be averaged to produce class-level predictors).

 **Section recap**

### Nonindependent observations and multilevel modeling

Nonindependence of observations can occur purposefully with certain research designs, whereas other research designs and sampling procedures can unintentionally produce nonindependent observations.

If the independent observations assumption for OLS regression is violated, misleading parameter estimates can be obtained and standard errors are incorrect, leading to inflated Type I error rates and confidence intervals which are too narrow.

**Multilevel modeling (MLM)** is a procedure in which nonindependence among observations can be modeled directly.

In MLM, variables observed at any level of a data hierarchy can be included directly without averaging over groups of observations.

## Research example for MLM

Throughout this chapter, artificial data inspired by a research study by Hamermesh and Parker (2005) are used to illustrate the main concepts of MLM.[5] In the example analyses, these data are used to model course evaluation ratings given by individual university students as a function of student overall grade-point average (GPA) and a rating of each course instructor's physical attractiveness. It will be useful to keep in mind that a single attractiveness rating was given for each instructor by a team of research assistants rather than by each student in the instructor's course. The data are hierarchically structured such that students are clustered within instructors. That is, individual students are nested within courses, with each course taught by a different instructor, and so we might say that the instructor is the clustering or grouping variable (each instructor taught only one course in the current dataset). Therefore, course evaluation ratings given by two students in the same course are not independent observations because we would expect a higher level of consistency among evaluations of the same course than across different courses. Additionally, whereas the course evaluation rating and student GPA are individual, student-level variables, the instructor's physical attractiveness is an instructor-level variable. Therefore, whereas two students in the same course are likely to have different values for course evaluation and for their GPA, the instructor attractiveness rating is consistent across students in the same course.

This dataset is available on the text's webpage (https://study.sagepub.com/flora) along with annotated input and output from several popular statistical software packages showing how to reproduce the analyses presented in this chapter.

To understand the data organization more concretely, Table 6.1 displays the data for six of the $N = 463$ students in the dataset. Notice that the first two students (Student ID = 1 and 2) were in a course taught by the same instructor (Instructor ID = 1); whereas these two students gave the course different evaluation ratings and have different overall GPAs, the instructor's attractiveness rating is common to both students, reflecting that instructor attractiveness is a characteristic of the instructor, not of the individual students. Overall, the data were collected

**Table 6.1** Data for subset of $n = 6$ cases taken from larger sample of $N = 463$ for course-evaluation example

| Student ID | Instructor ID | Course evaluation | Student GPA | Instructor attractiveness |
|:---:|:---:|:---:|:---:|:---:|
| 1 | 1 | 4.3 | 2.10 | 0.20 |
| 2 | 1 | 3.6 | 3.79 | 0.20 |
| 98 | 2 | 4.0 | 2.26 | −0.83 |
| 99 | 2 | 2.1 | 1.83 | −0.83 |
| 462 | 94 | 3.2 | 3.39 | 0.33 |
| 463 | 94 | 4.1 | 1.69 | 0.33 |

---

[5]Despite that the data used for the analyses in this chapter were created to be similar to the original data from Hamermesh and Parker (2005), because the current data are artificial, the results and substantive conclusions reached herein do not validly represent Hamermesh and Parker's actual findings.

such that the 463 students are nested within 94 different instructors. A varying number of students provided ratings of each course; the dataset contains a mean number of 4.93 students for each instructor (not all students enrolled in a given course section provided data for this study).

As always, we should examine descriptive statistics and graphs of the data before proceeding to fit models. Doing so is somewhat challenging with hierarchically structured data because it is logical to examine some summaries of the individual level (e.g., across all of our $N = 463$ student respondents), whereas it may be more informative to consider other descriptives based on the cluster-level units (e.g., within each of the $J = 94$ different instructors; see Gelman and Hill, 2007, for a more thorough presentation of descriptive, exploratory analyses for multilevel data.)

To begin, the outcome variable, course evaluation rating, ranges from 2.10 to 5.00, with an overall (i.e., across all $N = 463$ individual cases) mean of 4.00 (median also $= 4.00$) and standard deviation of 0.55. But of course these course evaluation ratings are each targeted toward 1 of the 94 different instructors, and so it is probably more useful to look at the course evaluation ratings on an instructor-by-instructor basis. That is, one might prefer to examine descriptive statistics of the ratings for each instructor separately, such as $\bar{Y}_j$, the mean of the evaluation ratings of the course taught by the $j$th instructor, or $s_j$, the standard deviation of the ratings for this instructor. For example, the instructor with the highest average course evaluation is instructor 85, whose mean rating is $\bar{Y}_{85} = 4.79$, based on ratings provided by $n = 8$ students. The standard deviation of these eight ratings is $s_{85} = 0.18$. Next, although instructor 30 has the lowest average course evaluation rating, $\bar{Y}_{30} = 2.30$, only one student provided a rating for this particular instructor. The next lowest average course evaluation belongs to instructor 68, with $\bar{Y}_{68} = 2.57$, which comes from $n = 3$ students; the standard deviation of these three ratings is $s_{68} = 0.35$.

Similarly, we could examine the per-instructor descriptive statistics for the student GPA predictor variable, although it might also make sense to summarize student GPA across all $N = 463$ individual cases, ignoring the instructor clustering variable. Thus, the overall mean GPA, measured on a standard four-point scale,[6] is 2.38 with standard deviation 1.09. Instructor 5 had the privilege of teaching the study participants who had the highest average GPA,[7] $\bar{X}_5 = 3.87$ with standard deviation $s_5 = 0.35$. In contrast, the $n = 3$ student respondents enrolled in the course taught by instructor 11 have an average GPA of only $\bar{X}_{11} = 0.68$.

Finally, instructor physical attractiveness ratings are observed only at the level of each instructor. This variable ranges from a minimum of $-1.54$ to a maximum of 1.88. Hamermesh and Parker (2005) normed the attractiveness ratings so that their mean across the $J = 94$ instructors is $\bar{X} = 0.00$ (median $= -0.13$) with a standard deviation of 0.83. The correlation between instructor attractiveness and the individual course evaluation ratings is $r = .19$; the scatterplot in Figure 6.1 indicates that this low correlation seems to be an adequate summary of the weak bivariate association between these two variables (i.e., there is no strong nonlinear trend apparent in the plot).

Because a key aspect of the study is the association between student GPA and course evaluation rating, it is important also to explore the relation between these two variables descriptively. Similar to the univariate descriptives, these bivariate descriptives can either ignore the clustering of students within instructors or not. A simple scatterplot that ignores the nesting of students within instructors is in Figure 6.2, which suggests a moderate,

---

[6]This is the standard GPA scale used in the United States; an A average equals 4.0, a B average equals 3.0, and so on.

[7]Except instructor 61, where the $n = 1$ participating student has a 4.0 GPA.

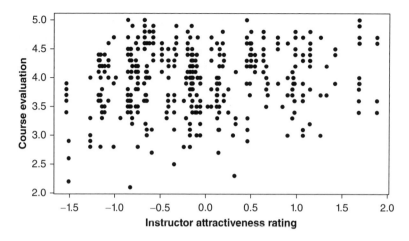

**Figure 6.1** Scatterplot of course evaluation ratings against ratings of instructor physical attractiveness

positive association between these variables. But in this plot, the nesting of students within instructors is not discernible, and the relation between GPA and course evaluation may not be consistent across the $J = 94$ instructors in the study: We might imagine that the most popular instructors receive high evaluations from both low-GPA students and high-GPA students (suggesting a weak within-instructor correlation), or that particularly ineffective instructors receive low evaluations from both weak and strong students (again suggesting a weak within-instructor correlation), whereas most instructors receive favourable feedback from students who earn good grades and less favourable feedback from students earning lower grades.

Figure 6.3 gives a set of scatterplots, each of which shows the relation between GPA and course evaluation for a single instructor; we can see that this relation varies from one instructor to the next. For instance, for instructor 20, the correlation between student GPA and course evaluation is $r = -.24$, which is in the opposite direction from the pattern shown in the overall plot (Figure 6.2) which does not distinguish the data from different instructors. But this correlation is based on data from only $n = 10$ student participants. The data for instructor 34 show a pattern more consistent with the overall pattern in Figure 6.2; for instructor $j = 34$, the correlation between course evaluation rating and student GPA is $r = .58$, but this correlation is based on only $n = 13$ students. In the current dataset, these individual per-instructor correlations between student GPA and course evaluation are difficult to take seriously because of the small number of students rating each course. As we will see, a key use of multilevel modeling is to obtain the average within-cluster (e.g., within-instructor) relation between a predictor and an outcome variable, while taking into account the number of cases $n$ within each cluster (e.g., $n =$ the number of students within a course section) providing data for that relation; parameters describing the variability of these within-cluster relations are also estimated. If we were to ignore the clustering of students within instructors and fit a regression line to the data in Figure 6.2, its slope would probably not equal the average of separate slopes of lines representing the separate within-cluster relations. The reason why will become apparent shortly.

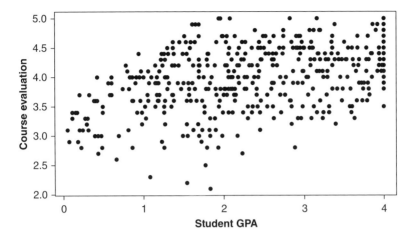

**Figure 6.2** Scatterplot of course evaluation rating against student GPA, ignoring clustering of students within instructors

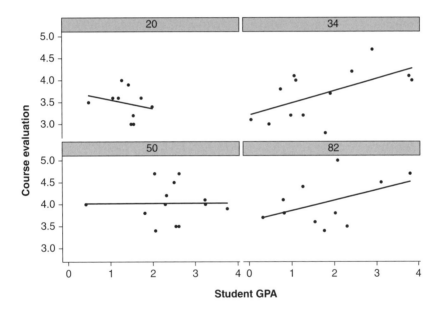

**Figure 6.3** Scatterplot of course evaluation rating against student GPA for each of four separate instructors (with regression lines separately fitted by OLS) selected from among the $J = 94$ instructors in the dataset. (Upper left panel, instructor $j = 20$; Upper right panel, instructor $j = 34$; Lower left panel, instructor $j = 50$; Lower right panel, instructor $j = 82$)

## THE UNCONDITIONAL MULTILEVEL MODEL

### The unconditional multilevel model: Model specification

Before building more complex models to represent associations between an outcome variable and predictor variables from hierarchical data structures, we will begin with the simplest multilevel model, the **unconditional model**, which is also known as an *intercept-only model*, the *random-effects analysis-of-variance (ANOVA) model*, or the *variance-components model*. This model is the multilevel generalization of the intercept-only regression model presented in Chapter 1, and thus, it serves an important pedagogic purpose in that it provides a simple, foundational model against which more complex (and more realistic) models can be compared. But in the MLM context, the unconditional model also serves the practical purpose of providing the parameters necessary for calculating an important numerical index known as the *intraclass correlation*.

The unconditional multilevel model or random-effects ANOVA model is a generalization of the traditional, fixed-effects one-way ANOVA model, a form of which was given in Equation 3.3. An equivalent expression of the ANOVA equation is given here as the **Level 1 equation** of the unconditional model, where *Level 1* refers to cases at the level of the individual participants in the data hierarchy (e.g., in the course-evaluation example, individual students are the Level 1 units):

$$Y_{ij} = \beta_j + \varepsilon_{ij} \text{ (Level 1).} \tag{6.1}$$

Here, $Y_{ij}$ is the observed value of the outcome $Y$ for individual $i$ in cluster $j$, $\beta_j$ is the mean of $Y$ within cluster $j$, and $\varepsilon_{ij}$ is the deviation of $Y_{ij}$ from the mean of cluster $j$. Additionally, $\varepsilon_{ij}$ is one of the model's error terms, in that the cluster mean $\beta_j$ is the predicted value of $Y$ for a person in cluster $j$. Applying the current example, $Y_{ij}$ is the observed course evaluation rating given by student $i$ for instructor $j$ and $\beta_j$ is the mean of the evaluations for instructor $j$. Here, and throughout this chapter, cluster membership is indexed with $j = 1, 2, ..., J$, and individual cases within a cluster $j$ are indexed with $i = 1, 2, ..., n_j$. Thus, $J$ is the total number of clusters in a sample of hierarchical data (e.g., $J = 94$ is the total number of course instructors in our example data), and $n_j$ is the total number of individual participants within a specific cluster $j$ (e.g., the number of students participating in the study who provide course evaluations for the $j$th instructor). The sum of all $n_j$ is the total number of cases (i.e., Level 1 units) in the dataset, $N$ (e.g., $N = 463$ students participating in the study).

At this point, it may be helpful to clarify that in MLM, *cluster* is a generic term representing the groups formed by the nesting, or grouping, of the individual cases in the dataset (e.g., in our example, the clustering variable is *instructor*, in that individual students are nested, or grouped, into courses taught by separate instructors). It is this grouping of individual cases in different clusters that leads to nonindependence of the individual-level data. In traditional ANOVA analyses (described in Chapter 3), there is usually only a small number of groups (e.g., levels of an independent variable formed by an experimental manipulation), but in MLM, there may be many groups or clusters of cases (e.g., $J = 94$ different course instructors in our current example) in a given dataset, and the intention is to generalize results to a hypothetical population of clusters.

The traditional ANOVA model is most appropriately applied when the independent variable is considered *fixed*, such that all relevant groups are directly represented in the data, and there is no intention of generalizing results beyond those levels of the grouping independent variable. For example, all treatment levels in an experimental manipulation are included in an analysis, or all levels of a naturally occurring categorical variable (e.g., gender or ethnicity) are included in a fixed-effects ANOVA analysis. On the other hand, *random-effects* ANOVA is more appropriate when only a sample of the possible levels of the grouping, or clustering, variable is included in the data, or when a purpose of the analysis is to make generalizations beyond the particular observed groups of the clustering variable.

One way to think about this distinction is to imagine a replication of a given study: If the study were repeated using the same procedures, would the identical set of groups be observed again (e.g., as a result of an identical experimental manipulation or an identical set of ethnic categories), or would a different set of groups end up being observed? If the latter, then a random-effects approach is more appropriate. Referring to our example data, it is likely that the study collected course evaluations and other data for only a selection of instructors at the particular university where the data were collected, whereas the research questions are more generally about course evaluation across all courses, not just those taught by the instructors included in the study. Thus, the random-effects ANOVA model, which is another name for the unconditional multilevel model, is a more appropriate model for representing the variability in student evaluations as a function of the instructor grouping variable. In the current unconditional model, $\beta_j$ is treated as a *random variable*, such that these means vary randomly across clusters, with a continuous population distribution.

As mentioned, Equation 6.1 gives the Level 1 equation of the unconditional model, where Level 1 refers to the lowest level of the data hierarchy, or the individual research participant level. *Level 2*, then, refers to the separate groups, or clusters, in the data hierarchy. In the current example, the Level 1 observations are specific to individual student participants, whereas the Level 2 units are the 94 different instructors (in that the students are clustered within courses taught by different instructors). In other examples, there may be a Level 3 of the data (e.g., different universities within which instructors are clustered) and potentially even more levels. The complete unconditional multilevel model can be specified using a separate equation for each level.

The Level 1 equation (Equation 6.1) can be thought of as a regression equation in which there are no predictors (i.e., no $X$s), but the intercept $\beta_j$ is allowed to vary across clusters (hence, the unconditional model is also known as the *intercept-only model*). With $\beta_j$ considered a random variable, we can write an equation with these Level 1 intercepts, or cluster means, as the outcome variable, which is the **Level 2 equation** of the unconditional model:

$$\beta_j = \gamma + \delta_j \text{ (Level 2).} \tag{6.2}$$

Here, $\gamma$ is the **grand mean** of $Y$ across all individuals regardless of their cluster and $\delta_j$ is the deviation of the mean of cluster $j$ from the grand mean; that is, $\delta_j = \beta_j - \gamma$. Returning to our example, $\gamma$ represents the population mean course evaluation averaged across all individual students, whereas $\delta_j$ is the difference between this grand mean and the mean evaluation for the particular course taught by the $j$th instructor.

The right-hand side of Equation 6.2, the Level 2 equation of the unconditional model, can be substituted for $\beta_j$ in Equation 6.1, the Level 1 equation, to get the so-called **reduced-form equation**, which is also known as the **combined equation**:

$$Y_{ij} = \beta_j + \varepsilon_{ij} = (\gamma + \delta_j) + \varepsilon_{ij}$$

or

$$Y_{ij} = \gamma + \delta_j + \varepsilon_{ij} \text{ (Combined).} \tag{6.3}$$

This reduced-form equation indicates that the observed value of $Y$ for individual $i$ within cluster $j$ is an additive combination of the grand mean ($\gamma$), the deviation of the mean of cluster $j$ from the grand mean ($\delta_j$), and the deviation of the individual's value of $Y$ from the cluster mean ($\varepsilon_{ij}$).

Using our example, Equation 6.3 states that the course evaluation rating from student $i$ for instructor $j$ is the sum of the grand mean evaluation (i.e., $\gamma$), the difference between instructor $j$'s mean course evaluation and the grand mean (i.e., $\delta_j$), and the deviation of the student $i$'s evaluation from instructor $j$'s course evaluation (i.e., $\varepsilon_{ij}$). Because $\gamma$ does not vary across individuals or clusters, it is often referred to as a **fixed effect**. Next, $\delta_j$ and $\varepsilon_{ij}$ do vary across clusters and individuals, respectively, and are therefore referred to as **random effects**. Because the models contain a mixture of fixed and random effects, MLM is often called *mixed-effects modeling* or simply *mixed modeling*.

Formally, $\beta_j$ and $\varepsilon_{ij}$ are random variables with assumed normal distributions, such that the Level 1 errors, $\varepsilon_{ij}$, are normally distributed with mean = 0 and variance = $\sigma^2$ and the Level 2 cluster means, $\beta_j$, are normally distributed with mean = $\gamma$ and variance = $\tau^2$. These statements are symbolized as $\varepsilon_{ij} \sim N(0, \sigma^2)$ and $\beta_j \sim N(\gamma, \tau^2)$, respectively. Thus, in the unconditional model, the outcome variable $Y$ has two components of variation: The variance of $\varepsilon_{ij}$ and the variability among the cluster means, $\tau^2$. As a result, the total variance of $Y$ can be partitioned into these two **variance components**:

$$\text{VAR}(Y_{ij}) = \text{VAR}\left(\gamma + \delta_j + \varepsilon_{ij}\right) = \text{VAR}(\delta_j) + \text{VAR}(\varepsilon_{ij}) = \tau^2 + \sigma^2.$$

Estimates of these variance components can be used to summarize the extent of the variation in $Y$ that results from nonindependence, that is, the grouping of observations into clusters.

In particular, the **intraclass correlation**, abbreviated **ICC**, is a descriptive statistic commonly used to summarize the extent to which the values of a given variable are characterized by the grouping of individual observations into clusters. Working from the variance components of the unconditional model, the *ICC* represents the ratio of variance resulting from clustering relative to total variance as

$$ICC = \frac{\tau^2}{\tau^2 + \sigma^2}.$$

If the *ICC* is equal to or near zero, there are minimal between-clusters differences in $Y$; as *ICC* increases, then a larger proportion of the observed variability results from the differences among the clusters. In other words, the *ICC* represents the extent to which members of the same cluster are more similar to one another than to members of other clusters. The sample estimate of this *ICC* index is routinely reported in studies using MLM to quantify the extent to which observations of a given variable $Y$ are nonindependent.

 Section recap

### Specification of the unconditional multilevel model

The **unconditional**, or *intercept-only*, multilevel model is also known as the *random-effects ANOVA model* and the *variance-components* model.

In traditional, fixed-effects ANOVA, the groups are taken as fixed entities and it is assumed that a given study includes data from all groups of interest.

In contrast, the groups (or clusters) in random-effects ANOVA are presumed to be randomly sampled from a population of groups; the goal of the model is to generalize beyond the particular sample of groups that was observed in a given study.

The **Level 1 equation** of the unconditional model is

$$Y_{ij} = \beta_j + \varepsilon_{ij},$$

where $Y_{ij}$ is the observed value of $Y$ for individual $i$ in cluster $j$, $\beta_j$ is the mean of $Y$ within cluster $j$, and $\varepsilon_{ij}$ is the deviation of $Y_{ij}$ from the mean of cluster $j$.

The **Level 2 equation** of the unconditional model is

$$\beta_j = \gamma + \delta_j,$$

where $\gamma$ is the **grand mean** of $Y$ across all individual cases and $\delta_j$ is the deviation of the mean of cluster $j$ from the grand mean; that is, $\delta_j = \beta_j - \gamma$.

The Level 2 equation can be substituted into the Level 1 equation to obtain the **reduced-form**, or **combined**, equation:

$$Y_{ij} = \gamma + \delta_j + \varepsilon_{ij}.$$

Because $\gamma$ does not vary across individuals or clusters, it is a **fixed effect**. Because $\delta_j$ and $\varepsilon_{ij}$ do vary across clusters and individuals, respectively, they are **random effects**.

Applying the reduced-form equation, the total variance of $Y$ can be partitioned into two **variance components**:

$$\mathrm{VAR}(Y_{ij}) = \mathrm{VAR}\left(\gamma + \delta_j + \varepsilon_{ij}\right) = \mathrm{VAR}(\delta_j) + \mathrm{VAR}(\varepsilon_{ij}) = \tau^2 + \sigma^2.$$

The variance components are used to calculate the **intraclass correlation**,

$$ICC = \frac{\tau^2}{\tau^2 + \sigma^2},$$

which quantifies the extent to which members of the same cluster are more similar to one another than to members of other clusters (i.e., the extent of nonindependence of observed values of $Y$).

## Estimation and inference for multilevel models

As described in Chapters 1 and 2, traditional linear regression models are usually estimated with OLS to minimize squared residuals. This OLS technique produces known, closed-form equations for obtaining parameter estimates from data (i.e., Equations 1.12 and 2.4 to 2.6). Unfortunately, such closed-form equations cannot be derived for most multilevel models, and instead, iterative algorithms must be used to obtain parameter estimates. This difficulty primarily arises because of the somewhat abstract nature of the distinct variance components of multilevel models; OLS regression has a single variance component, the variance of the errors, VAR($\varepsilon_j$), whereas multilevel models partition variance into Level 1 and Level 2 terms, as explained earlier.

In general, multilevel models are usually estimated using the **maximum likelihood** (or **ML**) technique because ML parameter estimates have desirable statistical properties in the context of MLM. In particular, ML estimates are *consistent* (meaning that estimates converge to their true population value as $N$ increases) and *efficient* (meaning that standard errors are minimal compared with other estimation methods). Furthermore, parameter estimates obtained with ML are asymptotically normally distributed, and thus, normal theory inference (significance testing and confidence interval estimation) is applicable using the usual $t$ and $Z$ distributions.

Maximum likelihood is commonly used as an estimation method for a wide variety of modeling procedures, including MLM and structural equation modeling (i.e., the topic of Chapters 9 and 10). The overall goal of ML, regardless of the type of model being estimated, is to determine the parameter estimates that are the most likely to have produced the current data. To do so, it is necessary to impose distributional assumptions for the random effects in the model. For the unconditional model, these assumptions are that both the Level 1 error term, $\varepsilon_{ij}$, and the Level 2 error term, $\delta_j$, are normally distributed, as mentioned earlier. Given these distributional assumptions, ML estimation often proceeds using an algorithm known as the *EM algorithm*; the details of this algorithm for MLM are beyond our scope here, but see Raudenbush and Bryk (2002: Chapters 3 and 14) for a complete description. For a more general tutorial on ML, see Myung (2003).

In the context of MLM, there are two general flavours of ML estimation, namely, **full-information maximum likelihood** (or **FIML**) and **restricted maximum likelihood** (or **REML**). In short, the FIML approach obtains estimates of the random-effect parameters (i.e., $\tau^2$ and $\sigma^2$ in the unconditional model) while assuming that the fixed-effect parameters are known (i.e., $\gamma$ in the unconditional model), whereas REML recognizes that there is uncertainty in the estimation of the fixed-effect parameters (which is akin to the need to divide a sum of squares by $N - 1$ instead of just $N$ when estimating a sample variance resulting from the population mean being unknown). In practice, fixed-effects parameter estimates are identical across FIML and REML, but the Level 2 random-effects estimates tend to be smaller with FIML, especially when there is a small number of Level 2 units (i.e., clusters) in the data. Consequently, REML is recommended when the number of Level 2 units is small (e.g., $J < 50$; Snijders and Bosker, 2012). Prominent software for MLM tends to use REML by default, with FIML available as an option. A particularly important feature of ML estimation, whether by REML or FIML, is that the parameter estimates account for the number of Level 1 observations ($n_j$) per Level 2 unit, so that clusters with more cases contribute more weight to the estimation of parameters.

Because estimation of multilevel models almost always uses an iterative algorithm, it is important to be aware of the possibility of obtaining **nonconvergence** or an **improper solution**. Nonconvergence occurs when the estimation algorithm has reached some maximum number of iterations without finding an optimal set of parameter estimates given the model and the data. An improper solution occurs when the algorithm does converge to an optimal set of parameter estimates but one or more of the estimates is out-of-bounds, such as a variance term estimated to be negative or an implied correlation greater than 1.[8] When either of these situations occurs (which is not rare), the data analyst usually must simplify the model being estimated.

---

[8] Often, software output will indicate an improper solution by warning that a particular estimated covariance or correlation matrix is *singular* or *nonpositive definite*. These terms are defined in Chapter 7.

A by-product of ML estimation is the **asymptotic covariance matrix** of the parameter estimates. The values in this covariance matrix summarize the multivariate sampling distribution of the parameter estimates, including the variance of each parameter estimate. For example, when the unconditional model is estimated using FIML or REML, the asymptotic covariance matrix includes the variance of the estimated grand mean parameter, $VAR(\hat{\gamma})$. The square root of this term ($\sqrt{VAR(\hat{\gamma})} = s_{\hat{\gamma}}$) is an estimate of the standard error of $\hat{\gamma}$, which then can be used to construct a confidence interval around $\hat{\gamma}$ and to test a null hypothesis for $\hat{\gamma}$. Specifically, because ML estimation produces approximately normally distributed parameter estimates (provided that $N$ is large), the ratio of the parameter estimate to its estimated standard error,

$$Z = \frac{\hat{\gamma}}{s_{\hat{\gamma}}},$$

can be used as a large-sample $Z$ test of the null hypothesis that $\hat{\gamma} = 0$. With the standard error taken from the asymptotic covariance matrix obtained by ML, this $Z$ test is more formally known as a **Wald test**.

A variation of the Wald test that is more appropriate for small samples refers the ratio of the parameter estimate to its estimated standard error to a $t$ distribution instead of the standard normal distribution:

$$t = \frac{\hat{\gamma}}{s_{\hat{\gamma}}}.$$

The degrees of freedom for this $t$ test equal $N - J - P - 1$, where $P$ is the total number of Level 1 predictors (to test the significance of the fixed effect of a Level 1 predictor), or $N - J - Q - 1$, where $Q$ is the total number of Level 2 predictors (to test the significance of the fixed effect for a Level 2 predictor). At this point, for the unconditional model, both $P = 0$ and $Q = 0$; models with Level 1 and Level 2 predictors are presented later. Finally, by default most MLM software produces Wald tests as $t$ tests rather than as $Z$ tests, but of course, a $t$ distribution converges to the standard normal distribution as $N$ increases.

Wald tests are most appropriately applied to estimates of fixed-effect parameters (e.g., $\hat{\gamma}$ in the unconditional model), but they are problematic for random-effect estimates (e.g., $VAR(\delta_j)$) because these parameters tend to have non-normal sampling distributions (e.g., the sampling distributions of a variance parameter with a true value near zero tends to be positively skewed because variance estimates cannot be negative). Instead, random-effect parameters may be tested using *likelihood-ratio tests*, which are described later in this chapter.

The results from fitting the unconditional model to the course evaluation data using REML are presented in Table 6.2, which indicates that the estimated grand mean course evaluation score is $\hat{\gamma} = 3.94$. Next, although it is possible to estimate each of the separate $\beta_j$ terms, that is, the course evaluation means for each instructor ($J = 94$ of them in this example!),[9] in the MLM context, we are generally more interested in describing the variation among these cluster means rather than in inspecting each mean. Describing this variation is consistent

---

[9] From Equation 6.2, each cluster mean $\beta_j$ depends on the grand mean, $\gamma$, as well as on an unobserved group-level error term, $\delta_j$. In MLM, the $\beta_j$ are often calculated as so-called *posterior means* using *empirical Bayes estimation*, which combines the actual data from a given cluster $j$ with information from an assumed normal population distribution for $\delta_j$. For further explanation, see Raudenbush and Bryk (2002: 45–48).

with the notion that the cluster means are randomly sampled from a population of cluster means, rather than all possible groups being represented in the sample data. Therefore, in the current example, the estimated variance of the mean course evaluations across instructors is $\text{VAR}(\delta_j) = \hat{\tau}^2 = 0.147$ and the standard deviation is thus $s = 0.38$, indicating that approximately 2/3 of instructors (in the population of instructors) have mean evaluation ratings falling in a seemingly narrow range between ~3.5 and 4.3 (i.e., $3.94 \pm 0.38$).

Finally, the estimated Level 1 variance term, that is, the variance of individual student course evaluation ratings around the mean instructor-level ratings, is $\hat{\sigma}^2 = 0.17$. Given this variance estimate and the Level 2 variance estimate $\hat{\tau}^2 = 0.147$, the estimated $ICC$ is

$$ICC = \frac{0.147}{0.147 + 0.170} = .46.$$

This is a large $ICC$, indicating that the variance in course evaluations is strongly explained by the clustering of students in classes. The implication of this result should be fairly obvious: A major reason that individual students give different course evaluation scores is that they are taught by different instructors. Consequently, if we wish to use variables such as student GPA to predict course evaluation ratings, we should take this source of nonindependence into account.

**Table 6.2**  Results for unconditional MLM fitted to course-evaluation data

| Fixed effect | Estimate | SE |
|---|---|---|
| $\gamma$ (grand mean) | 3.94 | 0.05 |
| **Random effects** | **Estimate** | **SD = $\sqrt{\text{variance estimate}}$** |
| $\tau^2$ (Level 2 variance) | 0.147 | 0.38 |
| $\sigma^2$ (Level 1 variance) | 0.170 | 0.41 |

Note. $N = 463$, $J = 94$. SD = standard deviation, SE = standard error.

 Section recap

### Estimation and inference for multilevel models

Multilevel models are most often estimated using the **maximum-likelihood** (**ML**) method. Either full-information ML (FIML) or restricted ML (REML) may be used, with REML recommended when there is a small number of clusters.

Because MLM parameter estimates often do not have closed-form solutions, ML estimation proceeds according to a computerized iterative algorithm. Occasionally, results cannot be interpreted because the algorithm does not converge (i.e., **nonconvergence**) or because illegitimate parameter estimates cannot be obtained (i.e., an **improper solution**).

Parameter estimates obtained with ML are consistent, efficient, and asymptotically normally distributed. As such, normal theory confidence intervals and significance tests (i.e., **Wald tests**) can be computed for estimates using standard errors extracted from the **asymptotic covariance matrix** of the estimates.

# CONDITIONAL MULTILEVEL MODELS

## Conditional multilevel models: Incorporating a Level 1 predictor

The multilevel model described thus far (Equations 6.1 to 6.3) is considered an unconditional model because it does not incorporate any predictors at either Level 1 or Level 2. That is, the distributions of $Y_{ij}$ and $\beta_j$ are not conditioned upon one or more predictor variables. Instead, the individual observations are simply a function of their cluster means plus an error term (Level 1) and the cluster means are a function of the grand mean plus another error term (Level 2). In practice, the primary purpose of the unconditional model is to provide the variance estimates needed to calculate the *ICC*. Substantive theory, however, stipulates that certain predictor variables are important for representing or explaining the variation in the outcome variable. Consequently, the model extends to incorporate predictors at either Level 1 (i.e., individual predictors such as student gender or GPA), Level 2 (cluster-level predictors such as instructor attractiveness or age), or both Level 1 and 2 (simultaneously considering individual and cluster-level predictors).

## The random-intercepts model

Returning to our running example, because GPA is an individual student-level predictor (each student *i* has her or his own GPA), this predictor is included in the Level 1 (i.e., the individual level) equation of a multilevel model. So, extending Equation 6.1 to include a single predictor, a conditional Level 1 equation is

$$Y_{ij} = \beta_{0j} + \beta_{1j}X_{ij} + \varepsilon_{ij} \text{ (Level 1)}, \tag{6.4}$$

where $X_{ij}$ represents an individual-level predictor such as the GPA for student *i* in the class taught by instructor *j*. This Level 1 equation is similar to the basic simple regression model presented in Chapter 1 (cf. Equation 1.11), but the critical difference is that now the intercept, $\beta_{0j}$, and the slope, $\beta_{1j}$, are both indexed with *j*, indicating that these regression parameters can vary across clusters. Applying the running example, having regression parameters vary across clusters implies that there may be a separate regression line representing the relation between student GPA and course evaluation for each instructor. Of course, like multiple regression, the Level 1 equation (Equation 6.4) can be expanded to include any number of predictors (i.e., $X_{1ij}, X_{2ij}, X_{3ij}$, etc.):

$$Y_{ij} = \beta_{0j} + \left( \sum_{p=1}^{P} \beta_{pj}X_{pij} \right) + \varepsilon_{ij} \text{ (Level 1)},$$

where *P* is the total number of Level 1 predictors.

Let's first consider a model in which only the intercepts vary across clusters, such that the intercept in the regression of $Y_{ij}$ on $X_{ij}$ can vary across the *J* clusters whereas the slope is constant. That is, there is a random term for the intercept but the slope is fixed across clusters, resulting in what is commonly referred to as the **random-intercepts** multilevel model. Thus, in the regression of course evaluation on student GPA, the intercepts will vary across instructors but we assume that the slope of these regression lines is the same for each instructor. Hence, the Level 2 model is expressed in terms of two separate equations, one for the random intercepts and one for the fixed slope:

$$\beta_{0j} = \gamma_{00} + \delta_{0j} \quad \text{(Level 2a),} \tag{6.5}$$

$$\beta_{1j} = \gamma_{10} \quad \text{(Level 2b).} \tag{6.6}$$

Equation 6.5, the Level 2a equation, indicates that the intercepts $\beta_{0j}$ from the Level 1 equation (i.e., Equation 6.4) are characterized by a fixed effect, $\gamma_{00}$, representing the mean intercept across all $J$ clusters, and a random effect, $\delta_{0j}$, representing the deviation of $\beta_{0j}$, the intercept specific to cluster $j$, from the mean intercept $\gamma_{00}$. Next, Equation 6.6, the Level 2b equation, indicates that the slopes $\beta_{1j}$ from the Level 1 equation are characterized only by a fixed effect, $\gamma_{10}$, representing the linear regression slope that is considered constant across all $J$ clusters. Of course, if a model includes more than one predictor, the partial regression slope coefficient $\beta_{pj}$ of each predictor $X_p$ then has its own version of Equation 6.6 (e.g., the coefficient $\beta_{2j}$ for predictor $X_2$ equals a parameter $\gamma_{20}$ which is constant across all $J$ clusters for a random-intercepts model. Thus, the Level 2c equation would be $\beta_{2j} = \gamma_{20}$).

Therefore, conceptually there is a separate regression line for each cluster (i.e., each class or instructor in our example), such that the lines have different intercepts but the same slope; this model is represented in Figure 6.4. The mean of these separate regression lines is determined by the fixed effects, which are the $\gamma_{00}$ intercept term and the $\gamma_{10}$ slope term. Next, instead of estimating a separate regression line for each cluster (although that is possible to do[10]), we summarize the random variation of these hypothetical regression lines using the parameter $\text{VAR}(\delta_{0j}) = \tau_{00}^2$, which represents the variance among the intercepts of the separate Level 1 regression lines across Level 2 units. More formally, we presume that the intercepts are randomly sampled from a normal distribution of intercepts with population mean equal to $\gamma_{00}$ and population variance of $\tau_{00}^2$; that is, $\beta_{0j} \sim N(\gamma_{00}, \tau_{00}^2)$. The random-intercepts model does

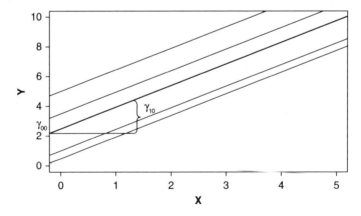

**Figure 6.4** Idealized depiction of a random-intercepts model (thin lines represent regression lines specific to individual clusters; heavy bold line represents mean regression line across all clusters. The intercept of the mean regression line is $\gamma_{00}$, and the slope of all lines is $\gamma_{10}$)

---

[10]Once again using the empirical Bayes approach mentioned in the previous footnote in this chapter.

not include an analogous random variance for the slope $\beta_{1j}$, so at this point the model indicates that the strength of the linear association between $X$ and $Y$ is constant across all clusters. Thus, in our running example, the Level 1 and Level 2 equations, taken together, suggest that there is a single regression line relating GPA to course evaluation for each instructor, and these regression lines have different intercepts but equal slopes.

The reduced-form equation for this random-intercepts model, obtained by substituting the Level 2 equations (Equations 6.5 and 6.6) into the Level 1 equation (Equation 6.4), is

$$Y_{ij} = \gamma_{00} + \gamma_{10}X_{ij} + \delta_{0j} + \varepsilon_{ij} \text{ (Combined).} \tag{6.7}$$

This reduced-form equation explicates that the observed value of the outcome variable for person $i$ in cluster $j$ is determined by two fixed effects, which are $\gamma_{00}$ (the mean intercept) and $\gamma_{10}X_{ij}$ (the fixed slope multiplied by that person's score on $X$), and two random effects, which are $\delta_{0j}$ (the deviation of the mean intercept from the random intercept specific to cluster $j$) and $\varepsilon_{ij}$ (the error term for person $i$ from that person's cluster-specific regression line). Thus, the model has four parameters to be estimated: two fixed-effect regression coefficients ($\gamma_{00}$ and $\gamma_{10}$) and two random-effect variance terms ($\tau_{00}^2$ and $\sigma^2$). In the example, the fixed effect parameters, $\gamma_{00}$ and $\gamma_{10}$, describe the mean regression of course evaluation on student GPA across all instructors, whereas the Level 2 variance term, $\tau_{00}^2$, quantifies how much the intercept of this regression relation varies across instructors.

The results from fitting the random-intercepts model to the course evaluation data (again using REML) are in Table 6.3. Here, the estimated fixed-effect slope $\hat{\gamma}_{10} = 0.17$ indicates that for each one-point increase in a student's GPA (which corresponds to improving by one letter grade, e.g., from a C average to a B average), the course evaluation rating provided by that student is predicted to increase by 0.17 (a Wald-based 95% CI for this effect is 0.13, 0.21). But remember that because the model does not include a random-slope variance component, this association between student GPA and course evaluation is considered equal across all instructors. Yet, as will be explained later in this chapter, this slope represents an ambiguous combination of the *within-cluster* effect of GPA and the *between-clusters* effect.

Next, the estimated mean intercept is $\hat{\gamma}_{00} = 3.55$, which represents the predicted mean course evaluation score for a given instructor received from students whose GPA = 0. Because the model includes a random-intercept variance component, the intercept in the regression of course evaluation ratings on GPA is presumed to vary across instructors. In particular, the estimated variance of the within-instructor intercepts is $\hat{\tau}_{00}^2 = 0.10$, which corresponds to a standard deviation of 0.32. By incorporating random intercepts, this model corrects for the nonindependence in the data in that the standard error (and hence confidence interval and significance test) of the regression relation between GPA and course evaluation accounts for the nesting of students within instructors. But a more interesting and perhaps more realistic model also allows the slopes of this regression relation to vary across instructors, which is a possibility we examine in the next section.

Finally, statistics analogous to $R^2$ from OLS multiple regression can be calculated for multilevel models. Recall that the Level 1 variance estimate from the unconditional model was $\hat{\sigma}^2 = 0.17$. With the inclusion of the Level 1 predictor GPA in the current random-intercepts model, the Level 1 residual variance estimate decreased to $\hat{\sigma}^2 = 0.15$. Thus, one might conclude that the unexplained variability in course evaluations was reduced by $(0.170 - 0.152) / (0.170) = 0.1059$, or 10.59%, resulting from the inclusion of the Level 1 explanatory variable,

GPA, implying that this predictor accounts for 10.59% of Level 1 variance. Yet, although we are focusing on the effect of a Level 1 predictor (i.e., individual student GPA), it turns out that calculating the proportion of Level 1 variance explained in this manner can produce improper negative values in certain situations.

Instead, Snijders and Bosker (2012) advocated a statistic which they referred to as $R_1^2$, which represents 'the proportional reduction of error for predicting an individual outcome' (p. 111). This statistic can be calculated as

$$R_1^2 = 1 - \frac{\hat{\sigma}_1^2 + \hat{\tau}_1^2}{\hat{\sigma}_0^2 + \hat{\tau}_0^2},$$

where $\hat{\sigma}_0^2$ is the Level 1 variance estimate from the unconditional model, $\hat{\tau}_0^2$ is the Level 2 variance estimate from the unconditional model, $\hat{\sigma}_1^2$ is the Level 1 residual variance from a random-intercepts model, and $\hat{\tau}_1^2$ is the Level 2 residual variance from the same random-intercepts model (note that for the purposes of this formula only, the subscripts for these variance terms are not consistent with the subscripting convention used earlier and throughout the remainder of the chapter). For the current example, we have

$$R_1^2 = 1 - \frac{0.152 + 0.103}{0.170 + 0.147} = .1956,$$

indicating that student GPA explains 19.56% of the *total* variability across individual course-evaluation ratings.

**Table 6.3**  Results for random-intercepts MLM fitted to course-evaluation data

| Fixed effects | Estimate | SE | t | p |
|---|---|---|---|---|
| $\gamma_{00}$ (mean intercept) | 3.55 | 0.06 | 59.67 | <.001 |
| $\gamma_{10}$ (GPA effect) | 0.17 | 0.02 | 8.69 | <.001 |
| **Random effects** | **Estimate** | **SD = $\sqrt{\text{variance estimate}}$** | | |
| $\tau^2$ (Level 2 variance) | 0.103 | 0.32 | – | – |
| $\sigma^2$ (Level 1 error variance) | 0.152 | 0.39 | – | – |

*Note.* N = 463, J = 94.

## Section recap

### Specification and interpretation of the random-intercepts multilevel model

The **random-intercepts** multilevel model can be used to regress an outcome variable on one or more individual-level (i.e., Level 1) predictors.

Conceptually, each cluster has its own linear regression equation for $Y_{ij}$. The intercepts of these equations ($\beta_{0j}$) randomly vary across clusters, but the slopes ($\beta_j$) for predictor $X_{ij}$ are considered the same for each cluster:

$$Y_{ij} = \beta_{0j} + \beta_{1j}X_{ij} + \varepsilon_{ij} \qquad \text{(Level 1)},$$

$$\beta_{0j} = \gamma_{00} + \delta_{0j} \qquad \text{(Level 2a)},$$

$$\beta_{1j} = \gamma_{10} \qquad \text{(Level 2b)},$$

$$Y_{ij} = \gamma_{00} + \gamma_{10}X_{ij} + \delta_{0j} + \varepsilon_{ij} \qquad \text{(Combined)}.$$

Consequently, the model accounts for the fact that observations nested within clusters are nonindependent.

Instead of estimating each of $J$ regression equations, the hypothetical set of regression equations for the $J$ clusters is summarized by two fixed-effect parameters:

- $\gamma_{00}$, which represents the mean of the $\beta_{0j}$ intercepts
- $\gamma_{10}$, which represents the constant slope coefficient for predictor $X_{ij}$

And one random-effects parameter:

- $\tau_{00}^2$, which represents the variance of the random intercepts (i.e., VAR($\delta_{0j}$), where $\delta_{0j}$ is the difference between $\gamma_{00}$ and $\beta_{0j}$ for cluster $j$)

---

## The random-slopes model

As alluded to earlier, we can also allow slopes to vary across clusters to examine how much the magnitude of the relation between $X_{ij}$ and $Y_{ij}$ varies across clusters. In our running example, this flexibility of MLM allows the linear relation between GPA and course evaluation to vary across instructors. Conceptually, incorporating this possibility makes sense because some instructors may be well liked (or disliked!) by all students, regardless of those students' GPAs, whereas other instructors may receive high ratings only from students who have high GPAs. Furthermore, the OLS regression lines for the four instructors in Figure 6.3 suggest that the linear association between GPA and course evaluation does indeed vary across instructors. A question is whether the sample data can fully support a comprehensive model for all instructors with this added complexity.

To specify this **random-slopes** multilevel model, the Level 1 equation remains the same as Equation 6.4 from the random-intercepts model:

$$Y_{ij} = \beta_{0j} + \beta_{1j}X_{ij} + \varepsilon_{ij} \text{ (Level 1)}.$$

Likewise, the Level 2a equation for the random-intercept term of the Level 1 equation, $\beta_{0j}$, remains the same as Equation 6.5 from the previous model; that is, we continue to allow intercepts to vary across clusters:

$$\beta_{0j} = \gamma_{00} + \delta_{0j} \text{ (Level 2a)}.$$

But now, the Level 2b equation for the slope term of the Level 1 equation, $\beta_{1j}$, also includes a random-effect term:

$$\beta_{1j} = \gamma_{10} + \delta_{1j} \text{ (Level 2b)}.$$

Here, in contrast to Equation 6.6, the $\gamma_{10}$ parameter now represents the mean slope for the linear relation between $X$ and $Y$, averaged across the $J$ clusters, rather than a single slope assumed to be the same for all clusters. The term $\delta_{1j}$ then represents the deviation between this mean slope and the slope that is particular to cluster $j$. Therefore, the Level 1 and Level 2 equations, taken together, suggest that there is a separate regression line relating $X$ to $Y$ for each cluster, and these regression lines have both different intercepts and different slopes, as illustrated in Figure 6.5.[11]

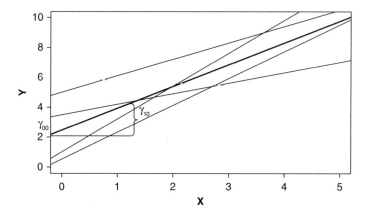

**Figure 6.5** Idealized depiction of a random-slopes model (thin lines represent regression lines specific to individual clusters; heavy bold line represents mean regression line across all clusters. The intercept of the mean regression line is $\gamma_{00}$, and the slope of the mean line is $\gamma_{10}$)

As with the previous models, we can substitute the Level 2 equations into the Level 1 equation to arrive at a single reduced-form expression for the random-slopes model:

$$Y_{ij} = \gamma_{00} + \gamma_{10}X_{ij} + \delta_{0j} + \delta_{1j}X_{ij} + \varepsilon_{ij} \text{ (Combined)}. \tag{6.8}$$

The parameter representing the variance of the intercepts is again $\text{VAR}(\delta_{0j}) = \tau_{00}^2$. But now the model also has varying slopes, and so the parameter capturing this variation is $\text{VAR}(\delta_{1j}) = \tau_{11}^2$. Overall, this random-slopes model has six parameters to be estimated: two fixed effects ($\gamma_{00}$ and $\gamma_{10}$, the mean intercept and slope, respectively), three random variance terms ($\tau_{00}^2$, the intercept variance; $\tau_{11}^2$, the slope variance; and $\sigma^2$, the Level 1, individual error variance), and a covariance between the random intercepts and the random slopes, which is denoted $\tau_{01}$. This covariance parameter quantifies the extent to which the random intercepts covary with the random slopes. In other words, the model includes a parameter to represent the possibility that clusters with higher intercepts may tend to have higher slopes for the relation between $X$ and $Y$ (or higher intercepts could be associated with lower slopes, which would produce a

[11]It is possible to specify and estimate a model which has randomly varying slopes but with a single intercept that is constant across groups; nevertheless, such models are extremely unusual and unrealistic for most applications. Consequently, as a general rule, when a MLM is referred to as a random-slopes model, keep in mind that the intercepts are also presumed to vary randomly.

negative covariance). Formally, we now presume that both the random intercepts and the random slopes are randomly sampled from normal distributions such that $\beta_{0j} \sim N(\gamma_{00}, \tau_{00}^2)$ and $\beta_{1j} \sim N(\gamma_{10}, \tau_{11}^2)$.[12]

Unfortunately, when this random-slopes model is fitted to the course evaluation data, neither the REML nor the FIML algorithm converges to a final set of parameter estimates. This result occurs partly because there is a large number of instructors in the dataset ($J = 94$), but there are data for only a few students in each course who participated in the study (i.e., the $n_j$ is small for most clusters). Consequently, to examine the possibility that the relation between student GPA and course evaluation ratings varies across instructors, it is necessary to alter the model in some way. An alternative model specification which does allow random slopes is presented later in this chapter.

 ## Section recap

### Specification and interpretation of the random-slopes multilevel model

With the **random-slopes** multilevel model, each cluster has its own linear regression equation for $Y_{ij}$. Like the random-intercepts model, the intercepts of these equations ($\beta_{0j}$) randomly vary across clusters, but unlike the random-intercepts model, the slopes ($\beta_{1j}$) for predictor $X_{ij}$ also randomly vary across clusters:

$$Y_{ij} = \beta_{0j} + \beta_{1j}X_{ij} + \varepsilon_{ij} \qquad \text{(Level 1),}$$

$$\beta_{0j} = \gamma_{00} + \delta_{0j} \qquad \text{(Level 2a),}$$

$$\beta_{1j} = \gamma_{10} + \delta_{1j} \qquad \text{(Level 2b),}$$

$$Y_{ij} = \gamma_{00} + \gamma_{10}X_{ij} + \delta_{0j} + \delta_{1j}X_{ij} + \varepsilon_{ij} \qquad \text{(Combined).}$$

Instead of estimating each of $J$ regression equations, the hypothetical set of regression equations for the $J$ clusters is summarized by two fixed-effect parameters:

- $\gamma_{00}$, which represents the mean of the $\beta_{0j}$ intercepts
- $\gamma_{10}$, which represents the mean of the $\beta_{1j}$ slope coefficients for predictor $X_{ij}$

Also, there are now three random-effects parameters:

- $\tau_{00}^2$, which again represents the variance of the random intercepts (i.e., VAR($\delta_{0j}$), where $\delta_{0j}$ is the difference between $\gamma_{00}$ and $\beta_{0j}$ for cluster $j$)
- $\tau_{11}^2$, which represents the variance of the random slopes (i.e., VAR($\delta_{1j}$), where $\delta_{1j}$ is the difference between $\gamma_{10}$ and $\beta_{1j}$ for cluster $j$)
- $\tau_{01}$, which represents the covariance between $\delta_{0j}$ and $\delta_{1j}$

[12]In fact, we further presume that the intercepts and slopes are randomly sampled from a *bivariate* normal distribution with covariance parameter $\tau_{01}$.

## Conditional multilevel models: Incorporating a Level 2 predictor

Earlier, we considered models in which there was a single Level 1 predictor; specifically, we were interested in the relation between student GPA and course evaluation while accounting for the nesting of students within classes. But there may be situations in which one is primarily interested in the influence of a Level 2 predictor when there is no Level 1 predictor (or while controlling a Level 1 predictor, as shown later in this chapter). Continuing with our running example, suppose we want to examine how the course evaluation ratings vary as a function of the instructor's physical attractiveness. That is, do students who are enrolled in courses with more attractive instructors tend to give higher course evaluations? As explained earlier, instructor physical attractiveness is an instructor-level characteristic; hence, this predictor enters the model in the Level 2 equation.

At this point, we wish to specify a model in which a Level 2 variable (e.g., instructor attractiveness) is included as a predictor, but no Level 1 predictors are included as covariates. Therefore, the Level 1 equation of the current model is identical to Equation 6.1 of the completely unconditional model:

$$Y_{ij} = \beta_j + \varepsilon_{ij} \ \text{(Level 1)},$$

where again, $\beta_j$ represents the mean of $Y$ for cluster $j$. But now, the Level 2 equation is expanded to include a predictor, $W$, of these cluster means:

$$\beta_j = \gamma_0 + \gamma_1 W_j + \delta_j \ \text{(Level 2)}, \tag{6.9}$$

where $W_j$ is the value of the Level 2 predictor variable for cluster $j$. Thus, the Level 2 equation is essentially a type of simple regression equation in which the cluster means are the outcome variable being regressed on the Level 2 predictor, $W$. For this reason, this model is sometimes called a *means-as-outcomes model*. Here, the fixed-effect parameter $\gamma_0$ is an intercept representing the predicted mean of $Y$ for a hypothetical cluster with a value of 0 for $W$, whereas the fixed-effect parameter $\gamma_1$ is the slope parameter indicating the predicted change in $\beta$ for a one-unit increase in $W$. Finally, $\delta_j$ is now a random-effect error term capturing the difference between the value of $\beta_j$ (the mean of $Y$ in cluster $j$) and the value of $\beta_j$ predicted by its regression on $W_j$. Consequently, the Level 2 variance term, $VAR(j) = \tau^2$, is now an error variance representing the variance of the cluster means that remains after accounting for the Level 2 predictor $W$.

Again, the Level 2 equation can be combined with the Level 1 equation, leading to

$$Y_{ij} = \gamma_0 + \gamma_1 W_j + \delta_j + \varepsilon_{ij} \ \text{(Combined)}.$$

Thus, we can see that although the Level 2 equation (Equation 6.9) presents $W$ as a predictor of the cluster means $\beta_j$, the reduced-form, or combined, equation indicates that this Level 2 predictor also can be thought of as a predictor of the main outcome variable, $Y$. Applying this model to our example, $Y_{ij}$ is again the observed course evaluation given by student $i$ for instructor $j$, $\beta_j$ is the mean course evaluation for instructor $j$, and $W_j$ is the physical attractiveness rating of instructor $j$, whereas $\delta_j$ is the instructor-level random effect (i.e., error term) and $\varepsilon_{ij}$ is the individual student-level random effect.

The results from fitting this model to the course evaluation data (again using REML) are in Table 6.4. The fixed-effect intercept estimate $\hat{\gamma}_0 = 3.94$ is the predicted mean course evaluation rating for an instructor whose physical attractiveness level is scored as 0. In the current analysis, because of the way the attractiveness variable was created, an instructor scored as 0 is a hypothetical professor with *mean* physical attractiveness,[13] and therefore, this estimated mean intercept represents the predicted mean course evaluation for an instructor with average attractiveness. The estimate of the fixed Level 2 slope is $\hat{\gamma}_1 = 0.12$, indicating that for each one-point increase in attractiveness rating, an instructor's mean evaluation is predicted to increase by 0.12 (95% CI: 0.01, 0.22). The estimated Level 2 error variance is $\hat{\tau}^2 = 0.139$. Comparing this variance estimate with the Level 2 variance estimate from the completely unconditional model (for which $\hat{\tau}^2 = 0.147$), we can determine that including the instructor-level attractiveness predictor reduced the variance of the Level 2, between-instructor means by $(0.147 - 0.139) / (0.147) = 5.44\%$. Finally, the estimated Level 1, or individual student-level error variance is $\hat{\sigma}^2 = 0.17$, which is identical to that obtained for the completely unconditional model because the current model also does not include any Level 1 predictor. Thus, the proportion of total variance reduced by the instructor attractiveness predictor is $(0.147 - 0.139) / (0.147 + 0.170) = 2.52\%$.

**Table 6.4** Results for regression of course-evaluation data on instructor attractiveness rating

| Fixed effects | Estimate | SE | t | P |
|---|---|---|---|---|
| $\gamma_0$ (intercept) | 3.94 | 0.04 | 89.12 | <.001 |
| $\gamma_1$ (attractiveness effect) | 0.12 | 0.05 | 2.15 | .034 |
| **Random effects** | **Estimate** | **SD = $\sqrt{\text{variance estimate}}$** | | |
| $\tau^2$ (Level 2 error variance) | 0.139 | 0.37 | – | – |
| $\sigma^2$ (Level 1 variance) | 0.170 | 0.41 | – | – |

*Note. N = 463, J = 94.*

## Conditional multilevel models: Including both Level 1 and Level 2 predictors

The previous models considered only Level 1 and Level 2 predictors in isolation from each other. That is, first a random-intercepts model was specified to examine the simple relation between a Level 1 predictor, student GPA, and the course evaluation outcome without including any Level 2 predictor; next, a model was specified to examine the simple effect of a Level 2 predictor, instructor attractiveness, without including any Level 1 predictor. But because any given research context is likely to give theoretical importance to both Level 1 and Level 2 predictors, we should build a model that can include one or more predictors at both levels simultaneously. In the current example, the main substantive research question is whether instructor attractiveness predicts course evaluations. But we have also determined that student GPA is an important predictor of course evaluations. Therefore, we would like to determine whether there is a relation between instructor attractiveness (a Level 2 variable, $W$) and course evaluation over and above the effect of student GPA (a Level 1 variable, $X$).

---

[13]The mean attractiveness rating across all 94 instructors is $\bar{W} = 0$ with standard deviation $s_w = 0.38$.

To do so, we might first expand the random-intercepts model to include a Level 2 predictor. The idea here is that the regression of $Y$ on $X$ varies across clusters, and now we wish to incorporate a cluster-level variable to explain or predict that variation. Consequently, the Level 1 equation remains identical to Equation 6.4, which regresses the outcome variable on the Level 1 predictor $X$:

$$Y_{ij} = \beta_{0j} + \beta_{1j}X_{ij} + \varepsilon_{ij} \text{ (Level 1)}.$$

Next, the Level 2 equation for the random-intercepts is expanded to include the Level 2 predictor $W$:

$$\beta_{0j} = \gamma_{00} + \gamma_{01}W_j + \delta_{0j} \text{ (Level 2a)}.$$

Consequently, this equation for the intercepts is similar to Equation 6.9. But here, the Level 2 outcome, $\beta_{0j}$, is the random intercept for cluster $j$ from the regression of $Y$ on $X$ in the Level 1 equation, whereas in Equation 6.9, the Level 2 outcome, $\beta_j$, is simply the mean of $Y$ for cluster $j$. Therefore, we are now using a Level 2 variable, $W$, to predict the different cluster-level intercepts in the regression of $Y$ on $X$ in the Level 1 equation.

Next, although we are not yet allowing the Level 1 slope term, $\beta_{1j}$, to vary across clusters, we still need to specify a Level 2 equation to provide a framework for that possibility later on:

$$\beta_{1j} = \gamma_{10} \text{ (Level 2b)}.$$

And so this Level 2b equation is the same as the Level 2b equation (Equation 6.6) from the original random-intercepts model, indicating that $\gamma_{10}$ is the linear slope in the regression of $Y$ on $X$ that is assumed constant across all clusters. Putting the Level 1 and 2 equations together, the reduced form equation is

$$Y_{ij} = \gamma_{00} + \gamma_{01}W_j + \gamma_{10}X_{ij} + \delta_{0j} + \varepsilon_{ij} \text{ (Combined)}. \tag{6.10}$$

Now we can see that the outcome variable $Y$ is in fact simultaneously regressed on both a Level 1 predictor, $X_{ij}$, for which the fixed-effect coefficient is $\gamma_{10}$, and a Level 2 predictor, $W_j$, for which the fixed-effect coefficient is $\gamma_{01}$. The variance of the Level 2 random effect is $\text{VAR}(\delta_{0j}) = \tau_{00}^2$, representing the variability among the random intercepts that remains after accounting for the Level 2 predictor, whereas the variance of the Level 1 random effect is $\text{VAR}(\varepsilon_{ij}) = \sigma^2$, representing the variability of the dependent variable $Y$ that remains after accounting for the Level 1 predictor $X$.

The results from fitting this model to the course evaluation data (using REML) are in Table 6.5. Here, the estimated fixed intercept $\hat{\gamma}_{00} = 3.55$ represents the predicted mean course evaluation for an instructor with mean attractiveness (i.e., attractiveness rated = 0) from a hypothetical student with GPA = 0. Once again, because there are no students with such a low GPA, this estimate has limited interpretational value. More importantly, $\hat{\gamma}_{01} = 0.12$ (95% CI: 0.03, 0.21) is the predicted increase in the mean course evaluation per one-point increase in instructor attractiveness, holding student GPA constant. This effect is significant, $t(92) = 2.62$, $p = .01$; therefore, more attractive instructors tend to receive higher course evaluations, even when controlling student GPA. Next, $\hat{\gamma}_{10} = 0.17$ (95% CI: 0.13, 0.21) is approximately the predicted increase in mean course evaluation per one-point increase in student GPA, holding instructor attractiveness constant. Yet, as with the earlier random-intercepts model, the precise interpretation of this GPA effect represents an ambiguous blend of within- and between-instructor effects of GPA on course evaluation; we return to this issue shortly. Finally, the estimated Level 1 residual variance was $\hat{\sigma}^2 = 0.15$ and the estimated Level 2 residual variance was $\hat{\tau}_{00}^2 = 0.09$.

**Table 6.5** Results for regression of course-evaluation data on instructor attractiveness rating

| Fixed effects | Estimate | SE | t | p |
|---|---|---|---|---|
| $\gamma_{00}$ (mean intercept) | 3.55 | 0.06 | 60.66 | <.001 |
| $\gamma_{10}$ (GPA effect) | 0.17 | 0.02 | 8.84 | <.001 |
| $\gamma_{01}$ (attractiveness effect) | 0.12 | 0.05 | 2.62 | .010 |

| Random effects | Estimate | SD = $\sqrt{\text{variance estimate}}$ | | |
|---|---|---|---|---|
| $\tau_{00}^2$ (Level 2 error variance) | 0.093 | 0.31 | – | – |
| $\sigma^2$ (Level 1 error variance) | 0.153 | 0.39 | – | – |

Note. N = 463, J = 94.

 **Section recap**

### Specification and interpretation of multilevel models with Level 2 predictors

The unconditional model is easily expanded to include one more cluster-level variable, that is, Level 2 predictors.

In particular, the Level 2 equation is expanded into a linear regression equation in which the group means, $\beta_j$, are an outcome variable regressed on a cluster-level predictor $W_j$:

$$Y_{ij} = \beta_j + \varepsilon_{ij} \qquad \text{(Level 1)},$$

$$\beta_j = \gamma_0 + \gamma_1 W_j + \delta_j \qquad \text{(Level 2)},$$

$$Y_{ij} = \gamma_0 + \gamma_1 W_j + \delta_j + \varepsilon_{ij} \qquad \text{(Combined)}.$$

Here, the fixed-effect parameter $\gamma_0$ represents the predicted mean of Y (i.e., predicted value of $\beta$) for a cluster with W = 0 and the fixed-effect parameter $\gamma_1$ represents the predicted increase in the mean of Y for a one-unit increase in W.

The random-intercepts model is also easily expanded to include a Level 2 predictor, allowing the outcome variable Y to be regressed on both Level 1 and Level 2 predictors simultaneously:

$$Y_{ij} = \beta_{0j} + \beta_{1j} X_{ij} + \varepsilon_{ij} \quad \text{(Level 1)},$$

$$\beta_{0j} = \gamma_{00} + \gamma_{01} W_j + \delta_{0j} \quad \text{(Level 2a)},$$

(Continued)

(Continued)

$$\beta_{1j} = \gamma_{10} \qquad \text{(Level 2b)},$$

$$Y_{ij} = \gamma_{00} + \gamma_{01}W_j + \gamma_{10}X_{ij} + \delta_{0j} + \varepsilon_{ij} \quad \text{(Combined)}.$$

Now, rather than being a predictor of the cluster means, the Level 2 variable W is a linear predictor of the random intercepts of the clusters:

- $\gamma_{00}$ represents the predicted intercept of the Level 1 equation (i.e., predicted value of $\beta_0$) for a cluster with $W = 0$.
- $\gamma_{01}$ represents the predicted increase in the Level 1 intercept for a one-unit increase in W.

Because this model does not have randomly varying slopes, $\gamma_{10}$ again represents the constant slope coefficient for predictor $X_{ij}$; i.e., the value of $\beta_{1j}$ is presumed the same for all clusters.

---

## DISTINGUISHING WITHIN-CLUSTER EFFECT FROM BETWEEN-CLUSTERS EFFECT

Earlier, when describing the random-intercepts model, I mentioned that the fixed-effect slope parameter $\gamma_{10}$ for the effect of a Level 1 predictor (e.g., the effect of student GPA on course evaluation ratings) represented an ambiguous combination of a within-cluster effect of the predictor and the between-clusters effect. In other words, the linear relation between

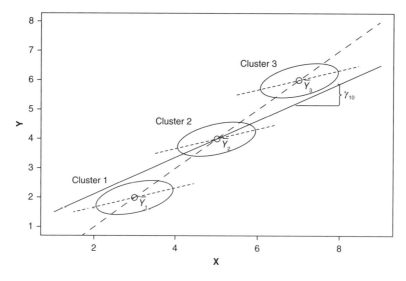

**Figure 6.6** Idealized graph showing that the $\gamma_{10}$ parameter is the slope of a line (the solid line) that lies between a within-cluster slope (the dotted regression lines) and a between-clusters slope (the dashed line connecting the cluster means) (the ovals are data ellipses representing where 95% of the individual, Level 1 data points might lie for each of three different hypothetical Level 2 clusters)

the original, raw-scale Level 1 predictor and the outcome variable represents a blend of an individual-level effect on the outcome and a cluster-level effect. Figure 6.6 gives an idealized graphical representation illustrating that the $\gamma_{10}$ parameter is the slope of a line (the solid line) that lies between a within-cluster slope (the dotted regression lines) and a between-clusters slope (the dashed line connecting the cluster means); in the plot, the ovals are 'data ellipses' representing where most of (e.g., 95%) the individual, Level 1 data points might lie for each of three different hypothetical Level 2 clusters. (Also notice that this plot depicts a random-intercepts model; the within-cluster regression lines have varying intercepts but not varying slopes.) Whether this blend of two separate regression effects is problematic from a conceptual perspective is a matter of some disagreement among methodologists, and the importance of the issue depends on the particular research context.

## Centering a Level 1 predictor

It turns out that we can disentangle the within-cluster effect of a Level 1 predictor $X$ from its between-clusters effect by centering $X$ before including it in the model.[14] In the current two-level MLM context, there are two basic approaches to centering a Level 1 predictor: **grand mean centering** and **cluster mean centering** (also known as *centering within-cluster* or *group mean centering*). A grand-mean-centered Level 1 predictor, $X_{ij\bullet\bullet}$, is created by simply subtracting the grand mean of $X$ from each observed $X_{ij}$:

$$X_{ij\bullet\bullet} = X_{ij} - \bar{X}_{\bullet\bullet},$$

where $\bar{X}_{\bullet\bullet}$ is the grand mean of $X$, that is, the mean of all individual values of $X$, ignoring cluster membership. If we just include $X_{ij\bullet\bullet}$ as the Level 1 predictor instead of the original $X_{ij}$, we still do not obtain an unambiguous estimate of the within-cluster effect of $X$. Instead, we can obtain an unambiguous estimate of the within-cluster effect of $X$ by estimating a model using the cluster-mean-centered version, $X_{ij\bullet}$. Specifically, the cluster-mean-centered Level 1 predictor can be expressed as

$$X_{ij\bullet} = X_{ij} - \bar{X}_{\bullet j},$$

where $\bar{X}_{\bullet j}$ is the mean of $X$ within cluster $j$.

Applying our running example, the GPA of individual student $i$ in cluster $j$ is cluster mean centered by subtracting the mean of the GPAs for the students *with the same instructor j*. Table 6.6 shows how these different versions of the Level 1 predictor are created for four students in the example data; two students are in the class taught by instructor $j = 1$, whereas the other two students are in the class taught by instructor $j = 2$. Reestimating a random-intercepts model (e.g., Equations 6.4 to 6.7) using a cluster-mean-centered Level 1 predictor, $X_{ij\bullet}$, in place of the original, uncentered $X_{ij}$, leads to a fixed-effect slope parameter, $\gamma_{10}$, which represents the specific within-cluster effect of the Level 1 predictor, that is, the slope of the dotted lines in Figure 6.5. We further examine models with such a cluster-mean-centered predictor shortly.

---

[14]A complete explanation of why centering accomplishes this result is beyond the scope here, but see Enders and Tofighi (2007) for details.

**Table 6.6** Original, uncentered and centered GPA data for four students from overall course-evaluation dataset

| *i* | *j* | $X_{ij}$ | $\bar{X}_{..}$ | $X_{j..} = X_{ij} - \bar{X}_{..}$ | $\bar{X}_{.j}$ | $X_{ij.} = X_{ij} - \bar{X}_{.j}$ |
|---|---|---|---|---|---|---|
| Student | Instructor | GPA | GPA grand mean | Grand-mean-centered GPA | GPA cluster means | Cluster-mean-centered GPA |
| 1 | 1 | 2.10 | 2.38 | −0.28 | 2.73 | −0.63 |
| 95 | 1 | 1.20 | 2.38 | −1.18 | 2.73 | −1.53 |
| 2 | 2 | 4.00 | 2.38 | 1.62 | 2.70 | 1.30 |
| 98 | 2 | 2.26 | 2.38 | −0.12 | 2.70 | −0.44 |

Cluster mean centering is often recommended when there is a strong theoretical reason to focus on an individual's relative position within the cluster (e.g., Snijders and Bosker, 2012). For instance, one might use cluster mean centering if one believed that the key predictive effect of student GPA on course evaluation was whether a student had higher or lower GPA relative to the other students rating the same instructor (known as a 'frog pond effect'), whereas one is less interested in the effect of a student's GPA relative to all other students, regardless of the instructor being rated. Enders and Tofighi (2007) more broadly recommended cluster mean centering 'in situations in which the primary substantive interest involves a Level 1 predictor' (p. 128). In the current example, it seems to make sense to consider GPA relative to other students rating the same instructor, which is the within-cluster effect. Yet, one might also be interested in whether the overall, average GPA for a given class predicts the average course evaluation for the instructor of that class, which is the between-clusters effect. That is, does the mean GPA of students rating instructor *j* predict the mean course evaluation of instructor *j*? Therefore, the following models are specified so that we can obtain separate slope coefficients for the within-cluster effect and the between-clusters effect.

### Reincorporating the Level 1 means

As mentioned, using a cluster-mean-centered Level 1 predictor produces an unambiguous within-cluster effect of that Level 1 variable. The between-clusters effect can be obtained by creating a Level 2 predictor which, for a given cluster *j*, equals the mean of the corresponding Level 1 predictor within that cluster. Specifically, this Level 2 variable, $W_j$, is defined as $W_j = \bar{X}_{.j}$. In the current example, to obtain the between-clusters effect of GPA on the average course evaluation for a given instructor, the value of $W_j$ for instructor *j* equals the mean GPA of the students rating the course taught by that instructor *j*.

Now we are ready to specify a model which will unambiguously represent both the within-cluster and between-clusters effects of the original Level 1 predictor, $X_{ij}$. Specifically, this model incorporates the cluster-mean-centered Level 1 variable, $X_{ij.}$, to produce the within-cluster effect and the Level 2 variable, $W_j = \bar{X}_{.j}$, to produce the between-clusters effect. Consequently, the equations for the random-intercepts version of this model are

$$Y_{ij} = \beta_{0j} + \beta_{1j}X_{ij.} + \varepsilon_{ij} \qquad \text{(Level 1),}$$

$$\beta_{0j} = \gamma_{00} + \gamma_{01}\overline{X}_{\bullet j} + \delta_{0j} \qquad \text{(Level 2a),} \qquad (6.11)$$

and

$$\beta_{1j} = \gamma_{10} \qquad \text{(Level 2b).} \qquad (6.12)$$

The reduced-form equation is therefore

$$Y_{ij} = \gamma_{00} + \gamma_{01}\overline{X}_{\bullet j} + \gamma_{10}X_{ij\bullet} + \delta_{0j} + \varepsilon_{ij} \qquad \text{(Combined).} \qquad (6.13)$$

This current model is a specific form of the more general expression given in Equation 6.10, with the current model explicitly indicating that the Level 1 predictor has been cluster mean centered $(X_{ij\bullet})$ and the Level 2 predictor is defined as $W_j = \overline{X}_{\bullet j}$, the cluster means of the Level 1 variable. An idealized version of this model is depicted in Figure 6.7; once again the graph includes hypothetical data ellipses for each of three clusters. Here, the within-cluster effect $(\gamma_{10})$ is the common slope of the dotted lines within the separate ellipses of the three clusters and the between-clusters effect $(\gamma_{01})$ is the slope of the dashed line connecting the cluster-specific means of $Y$ across the three clusters.

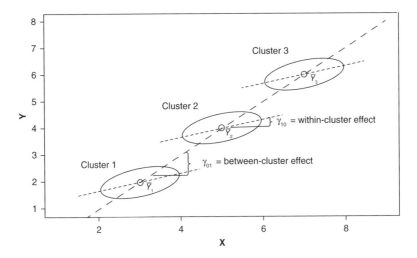

**Figure 6.7**   Idealized graph for model with the $\gamma_{10}$ parameter representing the slope of the within-cluster regression lines (the dotted lines) and the $\gamma_{01}$ parameter is the slope of the between-clusters regression line (the dashed line connecting the cluster means) (the ovals are data ellipses representing where 95% of the individual, Level 1 data points might lie for each of three different hypothetical Level 2 clusters)

Returning to the course evaluation example, the Level 1 predictor $X_{ij\bullet}$ is the deviation of the GPA of student $i$ in the course taught by instructor $j$ from the mean GPA of students in the same course $j$, whereas the Level 2 predictor $\overline{X}_{\bullet j}$ is the mean GPA of the students in the course taught by instructor $j$. Consequently, the Level 1 slope coefficient $\beta_{1j}$ represents the linear association between student GPA and course evaluation within the course taught by instructor $j$. Because the Level 1 predictor is cluster mean centered, $\beta_{1j}$ represents the effect of a student's GPA relative to other students in the same course, not relative to all students across all instructors. Next, because the Level 2 equation for these within-cluster effects (Equation 6.12) contains only a fixed effect, $\gamma_{10}$, and no random error term, then the Level 1 within-course effect $\beta_{1j}$ is considered equal across all instructors; $\gamma_{10}$ therefore represents a constant within-course effect. Moving to the effect of the Level 2 predictor $\bar{X}_{\cdot j}$, its coefficient $\gamma_{01}$ is the between-clusters effect of GPA, representing the predicted increase in the mean course evaluation for instructor $j$ associated with a one-point increase in the mean GPA for students in course $j$.

Table 6.7 gives the results for fitting this model (again using REML). The estimated within-course effect of student GPA on course evaluation is $\hat{\gamma}_{10} = 0.14$ (95% CI: 0.10, 0.18). Recall that earlier when we estimated the random-intercepts model using the original, uncentered version of GPA as the Level 1 predictor, we obtained $\hat{\gamma}_{10} = 0.17$. But this previous estimate was a blend of the within-cluster effect of GPA and the between-clusters effect, whereas the current estimate of $\hat{\gamma}_{10} = 0.14$ is the effect of GPA that is only a result of within-course differences in GPA. Next, the estimate of the Level 2 slope is $\hat{\gamma}_{01} = 0.35$ (95% CI: 0.25, 0.45), giving the between-courses effect of mean GPA on mean course evaluation across instructors. That is, a one-point increase in mean GPA in course $j$ predicts a 0.35 increase in the mean course evaluation for the $j$th instructor. Therefore, the between-instructors GPA effect ($\hat{\gamma}_{01} = 0.35$) is stronger than the within-instructor GPA effect ($\hat{\gamma}_{10} = 0.14$), suggesting that teaching a course with high-GPA students on average has a stronger influence on instructors' course evaluation ratings than does the GPA of individual students relative to other students within the same course.

The sole Level 2 random-effect estimate for this model is $\widehat{\text{VAR}}(\delta_{0j}) = \hat{\tau}_{00}^2 = 0.08$, which is the variance of the error term from the Level 2a equation (Equation 6.11), giving the variance among the intercepts in the Level 1 regression of course evaluation on student GPA that remains after accounting for the Level 2 predictor, the per-instructor mean GPA. One way to think about this error variance is to recognize that the random-intercepts model is specified such that the intercepts in the regression of course evaluation on (cluster-mean centered) student GPA can vary from instructor to instructor; including the Level 2 predictor, the instructor-level GPA means, explains some of this variation in the intercepts. The $\tau_{00}^2$ parameter quantifies the remaining intercept variability. Because the current model does not include random slopes, that is, the

**Table 6.7** Results for regression of course-evaluation data on cluster-mean-centered GPA and GPA cluster means

| Fixed effects | Estimate | SE | $t$ | $p$ |
|---|---|---|---|---|
| $\gamma_{00}$ (mean intercept) | 3.12 | 0.12 | 25.65 | <.001 |
| $\gamma_{10}$ (Level 1 GPA effect) | 0.14 | 0.02 | 6.80 | <.001 |
| $\gamma_{01}$ (Level 2 GPA effect) | 0.35 | 0.05 | 7.04 | <.001 |

| Random effects | Estimate | SD = $\sqrt{\text{variance estimate}}$ | | |
|---|---|---|---|---|
| $\tau_{00}^2$ (Level 2 error variance) | 0.083 | 0.29 | – | – |
| $\sigma^2$ (Level 1 error variance) | 0.153 | 0.39 | – | – |

Note. $N = 463$. Level 1 GPA effect refers to cluster-mean-centered GPA; Level 2 GPA effect refers to $J = 94$ GPA means per cluster.

Level 1 within-course effect of student GPA is considered constant across all courses, there is no error term in the Level 2b equation (Equation 6.12) and thus no analogous variance term for the Level 1 slopes. Finally, the Level 1 random effect variance estimate is $\widehat{VAR}(\varepsilon_{ij}) = \hat{\sigma}^2 = 0.15$, which represents the variance among individual students' course evaluations that remains after accounting for GPA and the nesting of students within instructors.

## Alternative approach

It turns out that regressing the outcome variable on both the cluster-mean-centered Level 1 predictor $X_{ij\bullet}$ and the Level 2 cluster means $\bar{X}_{\bullet j}$ is not the only way to disentangle the within-cluster effect of $X$ from the between-clusters effect. Alternatively, one can simply regress the outcome on the original, uncentered Level 1 predictor $X_{ij}$ as well as on the Level 2 cluster means $\bar{X}_{\bullet j}$ so that the reduced-form equation of the model is

$$Y_{ij} = \gamma_{00} + \gamma_{01}\bar{X}_{\bullet j} + \gamma_{10}X_{ij} + \delta_{0j} + \varepsilon_{ij} \text{ (Combined).} \tag{6.14}$$

This model is identical to that represented in Equation 6.13, but now the Level 1 predictor is the original, uncentered $X_{ij}$ rather than the cluster-mean-centered version $\bar{X}_{\bullet j}$.

At this point, based on regression principles, it should be no surprise that the partial slope $\gamma_{10}$ for $X_{ij}$ obtained in the current model by controlling the Level 2 means will be different from the original $\gamma_{10}$ from Equation 6.7 which did not control the Level 2 means. But more precisely, by controlling the Level 2 means, the current fixed-effect slope for the Level 1 predictor $\gamma_{10}$ is equal to the $\gamma_{10}$ obtained using the cluster-mean-centered predictor according to Equation 6.13, even though the Level 1 predictor in the current model (Equation 6.14) is not cluster mean centered. Yet, the slope coefficient $\gamma_{01}$ for the Level 2 cluster means $\bar{X}_{\bullet j}$ in the current model is not the same as the between-clusters effect $\gamma_{01}$ of Equation 6.13. Instead, the between-clusters effect can be obtained from the current Equation 6.14 as $(\gamma_{10} + \gamma_{01})$. For a detailed explanation of this issue, see Raudenbush and Bryk (2002: 135–41).

To illustrate, Table 6.8 gives results obtained when the model in Equation 6.14 is fitted to the course evaluation data (with REML) using the uncentered student GPA and the instructor-level GPA means as predictors. Once again, we get $\hat{\gamma}_{10} = 0.14$, representing the within-course effect of an individual student's GPA relative to other students in the same course (furthermore, the fixed-effect intercept estimate and random-effects parameter estimates are the same as those presented in Table 6.7). But the estimated coefficient of the instructor-level GPA means is now $\hat{\gamma}_{01} = 0.21$ and no longer represents the between-courses effect of mean GPA. But, the between-clusters effect obtained earlier does in fact equal the sum of the current fixed-effect slope estimates, $(\hat{\gamma}_{10} + \hat{\gamma}_{01}) = (0.14 + 0.21) = 0.35$.

In conclusion, this issue of separating the within-cluster effect of a Level 1 predictor from its between-clusters effect is admittedly confusing. Table 6.9 outlines the different approaches just presented and may be a helpful guide for distinguishing among the different models for the effects of a Level 1 predictor. At this point, it may seem that estimating the model of Equation 6.13 (regressing $Y$ on the cluster-mean-centered Level 1 variable $X_{ij\bullet}$ and the Level 2 cluster means $\bar{X}_{\bullet j}$) is the most straightforward approach to easily obtaining clearly interpretable effects. But applying the model of Equation 6.14 (regressing $Y$ on the uncentered Level 1 variable $X_{ij}$ and the Level 2 cluster means $\bar{X}_{\bullet j}$) may be advantageous when one expands the model to include an interaction term involving the Level 1 predictor $X$, as is discussed later.

**Table 6.8** Results for regression of course-evaluation data on uncentered GPA and GPA cluster means

| Fixed effects | Estimate | SE | t | p |
|---|---|---|---|---|
| $\gamma_{00}$ (mean intercept) | 3.12 | 0.12 | 25.65 | <.001 |
| $\gamma_{10}$ (Level 1 GPA effect) | 0.14 | 0.02 | 6.80 | <.001 |
| $\gamma_{01}$ (Level 2 GPA effect) | 0.21 | 0.05 | 3.90 | <.001 |

| Random effects | Estimate | SD = $\sqrt{\text{variance estimate}}$ | | |
|---|---|---|---|---|
| $\tau_{00}^2$ (Level 2 error variance) | 0.083 | 0.29 | – | – |
| $\sigma^2$ (Level 1 error variance) | 0.153 | 0.39 | – | – |

*Note. N = 463. Level 1 GPA effect refers to cluster-mean-centered GPA; Level 2 GPA effect refers to J = 94 GPA means per cluster.*

**Table 6.9** Comparison of random-intercepts models for effects of a Level 1 predictor with estimates from regressions of course-evaluation outcome on student GPA

| | Fixed-effect parameter | | | |
|---|---|---|---|---|
| | $\gamma_{10}$ | | $\gamma_{01}$ | |
| Model (Equation) | Interpretation | Estimate | Interpretation | Estimate |
| $Y_{ij} = \gamma_{00} + \gamma_{10}X_{ij} + \delta_{0j} + \varepsilon_{ij}$ (6.7) <br><br> Level 1 predictor un-centered | Blend of within-cluster and between-clusters effect | 0.17 | (none) | (none) |
| $Y_{ij} = \gamma_{00} + \gamma_{01}\bar{X}_{\bullet j} + \gamma_{10}X_{ij\bullet} + \delta_{0j} + \varepsilon_{ij}$ <br><br> (6.13) <br><br> Level 1 predictor cluster-mean-centered, cluster means as Level 2 predictor | Within-cluster effect | 0.14 | Between-clusters effect | 0.35 |
| $Y_{ij} = \gamma_{00} + \gamma_{01}\bar{X}_{\bullet j} + \gamma_{10}X_{ij} + \delta_{0j} + \varepsilon_{ij}$ <br><br> (6.14) <br><br> Level 1 predictor uncentered, cluster means as Level 2 predictor | Within-cluster effect | 0.14 | Difference between within-cluster and between-clusters effect | 0.21 |

 Section recap

## Distinguishing within-cluster effect from between-clusters effect

The effect of any Level 1 predictor, $X_{ij}$, can be disaggregated into a within-cluster effect and a between-clusters effect.

The within-cluster effect can be obtained by regressing $Y_{ij}$ on the Level 1 **cluster-mean-centered** predictor $X_{ij\bullet} = X_{ij} - \bar{X}_{\bullet j}$, where $\bar{X}_{\bullet j}$ is the mean of X within cluster j.

The between-clusters effect is obtained by regressing $Y_{ij}$ on the cluster means $\bar{X}_{\bullet j}$, which itself is a type of Level 2 predictor.

Therefore, a random-intercepts model to obtain both the within- and between-clusters effects of a single variable $X_{ij}$ is

$$Y_{ij} = \beta_{0j} + \beta_{1j}X_{ij\bullet} + \varepsilon_{ij} \qquad \text{(Level 1),}$$

$$\beta_{0j} = \gamma_{00} + \gamma_{01}\bar{X}_{\bullet j} + \delta_{0j} \qquad \text{(Level 2a),}$$

$$\beta_{1j} = \gamma_{10} \qquad \text{(Level 2b),}$$

$$Y_{ij} = \gamma_{00} + \gamma_{01}\bar{X}_{\bullet j} + \gamma_{10}X_{ij\bullet} + \delta_{0j} + \varepsilon_{ij} \qquad \text{(Combined),}$$

with the fixed-effect parameter $\gamma_{10}$ representing the within-cluster effect and the fixed-effect parameter $\gamma_{01}$ giving the between-clusters effect.

An alternative random-intercepts model for obtaining separate within- and between-clusters effects of $X$ uses the original uncentered Level 1 predictor along with the cluster means as a Level 2 predictor:

$$Y_{ij} = \beta_{0j} + \beta_{1j}X_{ij} + \varepsilon_{ij} \qquad \text{(Level 1),}$$

$$\beta_{0j} = \gamma_{00} + \gamma_{01}\bar{X}_{\bullet j} + \delta_{0j} \qquad \text{(Level 2a),}$$

$$\beta_{1j} = \gamma_{10} \qquad \text{(Level 2b),}$$

$$Y_{ij} = \gamma_{00} + \gamma_{01}\bar{X}_{\bullet j} + \gamma_{10}X_{ij} + \delta_{0j} + \varepsilon_{ij} \qquad \text{(Combined),}$$

with the fixed-effect parameter $\gamma_{10}$ representing the within-cluster effect and the between-clusters effect equaling the sum of the two fixed-effect parameters, $(\gamma_{10} + \gamma_{01})$.

## Revisiting the random-slopes model

Another advantage of cluster mean centering is that it can help stabilize the estimation of more complex models because cluster mean centering reduces high correlations between within-cluster intercepts and slopes; such high correlations can cause difficulties for ML estimators. Recall from earlier that when we tried to estimate a model (i.e., Equation 6.8) with slopes for the effect of student GPA on course evaluation that randomly varied across instructors, we were not able to obtain a converged solution. That initial random-slopes model was estimated using an uncentered Level 1 variable, however. Alternatively, then, we can specify a random-slopes model using the cluster-mean-centered Level 1 variable $X_{ij\bullet}$. At this point, however, we will not yet incorporate the cluster means $\bar{X}_{\bullet j}$ as a Level 2 predictor. The equations for this alternative model are thus

$$Y_{ij} = \beta_{0j} + \beta_{1j}X_{ij\bullet} + \varepsilon_{ij} \qquad \text{(Level 1),}$$

$$\beta_{0j} = \gamma_{00} + \delta_{0j} \qquad \text{(Level 2a),}$$

$$\beta_{1j} = \gamma_{10} + \delta_{1j} \qquad \text{(Level 2b)},$$

$$Y_{ij} = \gamma_{00} + \gamma_{10}X_{ij\bullet} + \delta_{0j} + \delta_{1j}X_{ij\bullet} + \varepsilon_{ij} \quad \text{(Combined)}. \qquad (6.15)$$

These equations are identical to those presented previously for the random-slopes model with the critical difference being that here the cluster-mean-centered Level 1 predictor $X_{ij\bullet}$ is used in place of the uncentered predictor $X_{ij}$. Therefore, the Level 2 variance parameters for the current model are the same as for the previous random-slopes model, with the variance of the intercepts being $\text{VAR}(\delta_{0j}) = \tau_{00}^2$, the variance of the slopes being $\text{VAR}(\delta_{1j}) = \tau_{11}^2$, and the covariance between the random intercepts and the random slopes being $\tau_{01}$. Recall that this covariance parameter quantifies the extent to which clusters with higher intercepts tend to have higher slopes (or higher intercepts could be associated with lower slopes, which would produce a negative value for $\tau_{01}$).

When this revised version of the random-slopes model is fitted to the course evaluation data (using REML) with cluster-mean-centered student GPA as the Level 1 predictor, we do obtain a properly converged solution, the results of which are in Table 6.10. Because the model now specifies that the effect of student GPA on course evaluations varies across instructors, the fixed-effect estimate $\hat{\gamma}_{10} = 0.14$ represents the mean within-cluster slope of the different within-instructor regressions of course evaluation on student GPA, that is, the predicted change in course evaluation associated with a one-point increase in GPA, averaged across all instructors. The estimated random-slope variance is $\hat{\tau}_{11}^2 = 0.002$, which corresponds to a standard deviation of 0.05. Thus, there may be substantial variation in these slopes across the within-instructor regressions of course evaluation on GPA given that the estimate of the mean slope is 0.14. The fixed-intercept estimate $\hat{\gamma}_{00} = 3.93$ is the estimated mean intercept, which, because GPA was cluster mean centered, represents the predicted mean course evaluation for a given instructor (i.e., it is still the mean of the cluster means, as was obtained earlier with the simpler random-intercepts model). The estimate of the intercept variance is $\hat{\tau}_{00}^2 = 0.15$ (corresponding to a standard deviation = 0.39), indicating the amount of variability in the different intercepts across the within-class regressions of course evaluation on GPA. Because GPA was cluster mean centered, this intercept variance represents the variance of the mean course evaluations across different instructors.

Next, for ease of interpretation, it is helpful to convert the estimated covariance between random intercepts and slopes, $\hat{\tau}_{01}$, into a correlation. Thus, with the current example, the correlation between the random intercepts and slopes is $r_{01} = -.26$. This negative correlation indicates that larger within-course intercepts in the regression of course evaluation on GPA are associated with smaller slopes for that regression. This effect might seem complicated, but it makes sense for the following reason: when even students with low GPAs give an instructor high course evaluations, it is likely that students with high GPAs also give good course evaluations. Thus, for these instructors, there would be a weak association (small slope) between student GPA and course evaluation. But often high-quality instructors teach particularly difficult courses; students with lower GPAs might not appreciate the quality of the difficult course, whereas students with higher GPAs may give better evaluations of such a course, leading to a strong relation (large slope) between student GPA and course evaluation.

**Table 6.10** Results for random-slopes model for course-evaluation data using cluster-mean-centered GPA

| Fixed effects | Estimate | SE | t | p |
|---|---|---|---|---|
| $\gamma_{00}$ (mean intercept) | 3.93 | 0.05 | 86.76 | <.001 |
| $\gamma_{10}$ (Level 1 GPA effect) | 0.14 | 0.02 | 6.58 | <.001 |

| Random effects | Estimate | SD = $\sqrt{\text{variance estimate}}$ | | |
|---|---|---|---|---|
| $\tau_{00}^2$ (intercept variance) | 0.153 | 0.39 | – | – |
| $\tau_{11}^2$ (slope variance) | 0.002 | 0.05 | – | – |
| $\sigma^2$ (Level 1 error variance) | 0.149 | 0.39 | – | – |
| $r_{01}$ (intercept-slope correlation) | −0.258 | | – | – |

*Note. N = 463.*

## FORMAL MODEL COMPARISONS

In the results given in Table 6.10, the estimated slope variance of $\hat{\tau}_{11}^2 = 0.002$ may seem somewhat small, which might lead one to question whether this model with randomly varying slopes is too complex for these data. If $\tau_{11}^2$ is exactly zero, then the model with random intercepts and random slopes (i.e., Equation 6.15) reduces to a model with only random intercepts and a single fixed slope (the covariance between intercept and slope, $\tau_{01}$, also necessarily disappears), which returns us to the random-intercepts model (i.e., Equation 6.7). In other words, the random-intercepts model is *formally nested* within a model with both random intercepts and random slopes, which means that one can use a **likelihood-ratio test** (also known as the *deviance test*) to determine whether the random-intercepts model fits the data significantly worse than the current random-slopes model. If the models do not significantly differ, then we can conclude that the slope-variance estimate $\hat{\tau}_{11}^2$ does not significantly differ from zero.

In particular, the ML estimation procedure (whether REML or FIML) uses an algorithm to maximize the log of the likelihood of the current model's parameter estimates given the data. The *log-likelihood* value of a given estimated model multiplied by –2 is known as the model's *deviance statistic*, D:

$$D = -2\ln(likelihood).$$

The difference between the deviance statistics of two nested models then produces a likelihood-ratio test statistic which follows $\chi^2$ distribution in large samples:

$$(D_2 - D_1) \sim \chi^2(df = q_1 - q_2);$$

where for two nested models, $D_1$ is the deviance of the more general model with $q_1$ parameters to be estimated and $D_2$ is the deviance of the *restricted* model with $q_2$ parameters to be estimated. Thus, degrees of freedom for this $\chi^2$ statistic equals the difference between the number of parameters to be estimated for the two models, $q_1 - q_2$. If the $\chi^2$ statistic is significant, then one rejects the null hypothesis that the simpler model with fewer parameters (i.e., the restricted model) fits the data equally as well as the more complex model.

In our current context, the random-slopes model is more general than the random-intercepts model because the random-slopes model contains all of the same parameters of the random-intercepts model, plus additional parameters to represent the variance of the slopes ($\tau_{11}^2$) and the covariance between intercepts and slopes ($\tau_{01}$). Put another way, the random-intercepts model is a simplified, or restricted, version of the random-slopes model in which the slope variance and intercept-slope covariance have both been constrained to equal zero ($\tau_{11}^2 = \tau_{01} = 0$).

It is important to keep in mind that with REML estimation, the likelihood-ratio test should be used only to compare models which differ with respect to random effects (i.e., restricted vs. freely estimated $\tau$ parameters), as in the current context of comparing a random-intercepts model with a random-slopes model. Nested models which differ according to their fixed effects (i.e., restricted vs. freely estimated $\gamma$ parameters) can be formed by dropping one or more predictor variables from the combined equation, which is analogous to the hierarchical regression method described in Chapter 2. In this situation, a likelihood-ratio test might be used to evaluate a complex null hypothesis that the fixed effects (i.e., the $\gamma$ slope coefficients) of two or more predictors equal zero, but such a test is only appropriate if the nested models are both estimated using FIML (models estimated with FIML also can be used to compare models with differing random effects).

Applying this likelihood-ratio test to compare the random-intercept and random-slopes models of the course evaluation data, the log-likelihood of the random-intercepts model estimated earlier (i.e., the model of Equation 6.7) was –302.90. This model's deviance is therefore $-2 \times (-302.90) = 605.80$. The log-likelihood of the estimated random-slopes model (Equation 6.15) is –302.65, leading to a deviance of $-2 \times (-302.65) = 605.30$. Finally, the difference between these two deviance statistics, $(605.80 - 605.30) = 0.50$, is treated as a $\chi^2$ statistic with two degrees of freedom. The statistic has two degrees of freedom because the random-slopes model has two more parameters ($\tau_{11}^2$ and $\tau_{01}$) than the random-intercepts model. Because $\chi^2$ (2) = 0.50 gives $p = .78$, the random-intercepts model does not fit the data significantly differently than the random-slopes model,[15] and consequently, we may conclude that the more parsimonious random-intercepts model is preferable for these data.

As alternatives to the likelihood-ratio test, statistics known as *information criteria* are also commonly used to choose between competing models. Specifically, **Akaike's Information Criterion**, or **AIC**, for a given model is calculated as

$$AIC = D + 2q,$$

where, again, $D$ is the model's deviance and $q$ is its number of parameters to be estimated. Next, the **Bayesian Information Criterion**, or **BIC**, is

$$BIC = D + q \ln N.$$

The individual values of *AIC* and *BIC* for a given model are not meaningful in isolation from other models. Instead, *AIC* and *BIC* are only used to compare models with each other. In particular, for two or more competing models estimated from the same data, the model with the

---

[15]Equivalently, we could say that we fail to reject the null hypothesis that $\tau_{11}^2 = \tau_{01} = 0$.

lowest value of *AIC* or the lowest value of *BIC* is said to have the best fit to the data. Importantly, *AIC* and *BIC* both penalize models for complexity. In an absolute sense, adding more and more parameters (i.e., additional random or fixed effects for additional predictors) will always improve model fit (by decreasing the deviance, *D*), although that improvement will eventually become trivial (analogous to the idea from OLS multiple regression that additional predictors will always increase $R^2$, although that increase eventually becomes miniscule). But with *AIC* and *BIC*, this decrease in *D* that occurs by increasing a model's complexity will eventually become offset by the increase in the number of parameters, *q*, as is hopefully apparent from their formulas. Consequently, *AIC* and *BIC* will favour a more parsimonious model with fewer parameters relative to a more complex model containing parameters which do little to explain the data.

Although statistical software commonly reports both *AIC* and *BIC*, in practice, researchers tend to pay closer attention to the comparison of *BIC* across competing models. Additionally, it is important to keep in mind that like all statistics, *AIC* and *BIC* are subject to sampling error, and therefore, small differences in *AIC* or *BIC* from one model to the next may not be statistically reliable. Additionally, the sampling error of *AIC* and *BIC* may even increase with greater sample size (Preacher and Merkle, 2012).

Returning to the course evaluation example, we can use *AIC* and *BIC* to help choose between the random-intercepts model for the effect of student GPA and the random-slopes model. For the random-intercepts model, *AIC* = 613.80 and *BIC* = 630.33. For the random-slopes model, *AIC* = 617.30 and *BIC* = 642.10. Thus, both *AIC* and *BIC* are lower for the random-intercepts model, and hence, both favour retaining the random-intercepts model as the more optimal model for the data relative to the random-slopes model. In the current analyses, *AIC* and *BIC* are consistent with each other and with the likelihood-ratio test in terms of choosing the random-intercepts model. But in practice, it is possible for these statistics to give seemingly conflicting results; in this case, one should select the model that most directly addresses the research questions of interest.

 Section recap

### Formal model comparisons

One model is formally nested within another if it can be formed by setting restrictions (or constraints) on the parameters of the more general model.

For example, a random-intercepts model is nested within a random-slopes model because the random-intercepts model can be formed by restricting the Level 2 slope variance parameter (as well as the intercept-slope covariance parameter) to equal zero.

A **likelihood-ratio test** can be used to determine whether a nested model (i.e., a more restricted model) fits the data significantly worse than a more general model with additional parameters.

The likelihood-ratio test statistic is $(D_2 - D_1)$, where $D_2 = -2\ln likelihood_2$ is the **deviance** of the restricted model and $D_1 = -2\ln likelihood_1$ is the deviance of the general model.

This statistic is referred to a $\chi^2$ distribution with degrees of freedom equal to $q_1 - q_2$, where $q_1$ is the number of parameters in the general model and $q_2$ is the number of parameters in the restricted model.

*(Continued)*

(Continued)

With REML estimation, likelihood-ratio tests can be used only to compare models with differing random-effects parameters. If nested models have differing fixed-effects parameters, likelihood-ratio tests are only valid if the models are estimated with FIML.

Competing models can also be compared using the **AIC** or **BIC** statistic, with BIC being more commonly relied upon. The model with the lowest value of AIC or BIC is preferred as the best-fitting model.

Although both AIC and BIC are a function of a model's log-likelihood, they also account for model complexity (i.e., the number of parameters to be estimated). Thus, all else being equal, simpler models produce lower values of AIC and BIC.

## CROSS-LEVEL INTERACTIONS

Earlier, we developed a model to examine the association between the course evaluation ratings and a Level 2 predictor, instructor physical attractiveness, controlling the Level 1 variable, student GPA. In particular, the model incorporated this Level 2 variable as a predictor $W_j$ of the random intercepts in the regression of $Y$ on the Level 1 variable $X$ as follows:

$$Y_{ij} = \beta_{0j} + \beta_{1j}X_{ij} + \varepsilon_{ij} \qquad \text{(Level 1)},$$

$$\beta_{0j} = \gamma_{00} + \gamma_{01}W_j + \delta_{0j} \qquad \text{(Level 2a)},$$

but without any random error for the slopes:

$$\beta_{1j} = \gamma_{10} \qquad \text{(Level 2b)},$$

which led to the reduced-form equation given earlier as Equation 6.10 and repeated here:

$$Y_{ij} = \gamma_{00} + \gamma_{01}W_j + \gamma_{10}X_{ij} + \delta_{0j} + \varepsilon_{ij} \quad \text{(Combined)}.$$

(At this point, for the sake of simplifying the presentation, we are not yet 'adding back the means' of the Level 1 predictor, $\bar{X}_{\bullet j}$, to separate the within- and between-clusters effect of $X$.)

If a Level 2 variable can be used to explain variation in intercepts in the regression of $Y$ on the Level 1 predictor $X$, we might also wonder whether a Level 2 variable can predict the slopes in the regression of $Y$ on the Level 1 variable $X$. Applying the course evaluation example, we would like to determine whether the relation between student GPA ($X$) and course evaluation ($Y$) for a given instructor can be predicted from the instructor's physical attractiveness ($W$). Put another way, if the relation between GPA and course evaluation randomly varies across instructors, we can model this slope variation as a function of an instructor-level characteristic, such as attractiveness. Thus, we can expand the Level 2b equation to incorporate $W$ as well as an error term, $\delta_{1j}$ (because we can't expect $W$ to explain potential slope variation perfectly). Therefore, just as the randomly varying intercepts can be regressed on $W$ in the Level 2a equation, so too can the random slopes be regressed on $W$:

$$\beta_{1j} = \gamma_{10} + \gamma_{11}W_j + \delta_{1j} \quad \text{(Level 2b)}.$$

Now, if we substitute this expanded version of the Level 2b equation and the previous Level 2a equation into the Level 1 equation, the reduced-form equation becomes

$$Y_{ij} = \gamma_{00} + \gamma_{01}W_j + \gamma_{10}X_{ij} + \gamma_{11}W_jX_{ij} + \delta_{0j} + \delta_{1j}X_{ij} + \varepsilon_{ij} \text{ (Combined)}. \tag{6.16}$$

Consequently, regressing the slopes on a predictor $W$ ends up incorporating an interaction between the Level 1 predictor, $X$, and the Level 2 predictor, $W$; this term, $\gamma_{11}W_jX_{ij}$, is called a **cross-level interaction**. Hence, the combined equation (Equation 6.16) indicates that the model as a whole has four fixed-effect parameters: the overall, mean intercept ($\gamma_{00}$), the first-order effect of Level 1 predictor $X$ ($\gamma_{10}$), the first-order effect of Level 2 predictor $W$ ($\gamma_{01}$), and the cross-level interaction between $X$ and $W$ ($\gamma_{11}$). The model's random-effect variance parameters are the Level 1 error variance (VAR($\varepsilon_{ij}$) = $\sigma^2$), two Level 2 error variances (VAR($\delta_{0j}$) = $\tau_{00}^2$ and VAR($\delta_{1j}$) = $\tau_{11}^2$), as well as a residual covariance between the Level 2 error terms (COV($\delta_{0j},\delta_{1j}$) = $\tau_{10}$).

Now that the basic framework for specifying a cross-level interaction is established, we must return to the concept of centering. Recall from earlier that the effect of a Level 1 predictor ($\gamma_{10}$) is a blend of within- and between-cluster effects, unless the cluster means of the predictor are included as a Level 2 covariate. For this reason, estimating the model presented in Equation 6.16 can produce a spurious cross-level interaction (i.e., a Type I error for the Wald test of $\hat{\gamma}_{11}$; Enders and Tofighi, 2007). But if we expand the Level 2a equation for the random intercepts to include the cluster means, $\bar{X}_{\bullet j}$, as well as the potential interaction between $\bar{X}_{\bullet j}$ and the other Level 2 variable $W_j$, then the overall model will include effects which disentangle the within- and between-cluster effects of $X_{ij}$, each of which is moderated by the Level 2 predictor, $W_j$. Specifically, the model represented in reduced-form Equation 6.16 is altered slightly to obtain

$$Y_{ij} = \beta_{0j} + \beta_{1j}X_{ij} + \varepsilon_{ij} \qquad \text{(Level 1)},$$

$$\beta_{0j} = \gamma_{00} + \gamma_{01}W_j + \gamma_{02}\bar{X}_{\bullet j} + \gamma_{03}(\bar{X}_{\bullet j} \times W_j) + \delta_{0j} \qquad \text{(Level 2a)},$$

$$\beta_{1j} = \gamma_{10} + \gamma_{11}W_j + \delta_{1j} \qquad \text{(Level 2b)},$$

$$Y_{ij} = \gamma_{00} + \gamma_{01}W_j + \gamma_{02}\bar{X}_{\bullet j} + \gamma_{03}\bar{X}_{\bullet j}W_j + \gamma_{10}X_{ij} + \gamma_{11}W_jX_{ij} + \delta_{0j} + \delta_{1j}X_{ij} + \varepsilon_{ij} \qquad \text{(Combined)}. \tag{6.17}$$

Here, the Level 1 predictor is presented in its original, uncentered form, but the cluster-mean-centered $X_{ij}$ could be used instead, and the model would still be separating the within-cluster effect of $X$ from the between-clusters effect. But the advantage of using the uncentered $X_{ij}$ (while also including the cluster means as a Level 2 predictor) at this point is that, should the cross-level interaction $\gamma_{11}$ turn out to be important (e.g., statistically significant), then it will be much easier to probe the interaction across the whole sample, ignoring the nesting of the data, rather than by recentering $X$ using different values for each cluster.

Applying the combined Equation 6.17 to the course evaluation example indicates that there are two coefficients representing the interaction between student GPA and instructor attractiveness: $\gamma_{03}$ is the coefficient for the Level 2 interaction based on the between-clusters effect of mean GPA per instructor, whereas $\gamma_{11}$ pertains to the cross-level interaction based on the within-cluster effect of individual student GPA. The purpose of the model is to determine whether instructor attractiveness predicts the slopes in the regression of course evaluation on student GPA; thus, the main conceptual focus is on the $\gamma_{11}$ coefficient for the cross-level interaction. The results from fitting this model fitted to the data using REML are in Table 6.11. The cross-level interaction between student GPA and professor attractiveness is not significant, $t(367) = 0.12$, $p = .90$. Thus, instructor attractiveness does not predict the varying slopes in the different regressions of course evaluation rating on student GPA across instructors. Additionally, the Level 2 interaction between mean GPA per-instructor and instructor attractiveness is also nonsignificant, $t(90) = 1.19$, $p = .24$.

If either of these interactions had been significant, we could probe it by calculating simple-slope effects in much the same way that interactions are probed in single-level OLS regression. Specifically, the strategy for probing interactions explained in Chapter 4 can be used with MLM; see Bauer and Curran (2005) for further detail and a worked example. But this strategy of finding simple-slope effects across the levels of moderator (e.g., student GPA) by centering the moderator at high, medium, and low values is much simpler if the Level 1 moderator is not centered using a different centering value for each cluster (i.e., the way $X_{ij}$ is cluster mean centered using the mean of each cluster). The simple-slope effects will still represent pure within-cluster effects if the Level 2 means $\bar{X}_j$ are included in the model, as just explained in the context of Equation 6.14.

**Table 6.11**  Results for model with course-evaluation regressed on cross-level interaction between student GPA and instructor attractiveness

| Fixed effects | Estimate | SE | t | p |
|---|---|---|---|---|
| $\gamma_{00}$ (overall intercept) | 3.09 | 0.12 | 26.19 | <.001 |
| $\gamma_{10}$ (student GPA first-order effect) | 0.14 | 0.02 | 6.43 | <.001 |
| $\gamma_{01}$ (attractiveness first-order effect) | 0.28 | 0.12 | 2.31 | .023 |
| $\gamma_{02}$ (GPA cluster means first-order effect) | 0.23 | 0.05 | 4.34 | <.001 |
| $\gamma_{03}$ (attractiveness × GPA means) | −0.07 | 0.06 | 1.19 | .237 |
| $\gamma_{11}$ (attractiveness × student GPA) | 0.00 | 0.03 | 0.12 | .902 |

| Random effects | Estimate | SD = √variance estimate | | |
|---|---|---|---|---|
| $\tau^2_{00}$ (intercept error variance) | 0.071 | 0.27 | – | – |
| $\tau^2_{11}$ (slope error variance) | 0.001 | 0.03 | – | – |
| $\sigma^2$ (Level 1 error variance) | 0.152 | 0.39 | – | – |
| $r_{01}$ (intercept-slope error correlation) | −0.107 | | – | – |

Note. N = 463. Student GPA effect refers to uncentered GPA; Level 2 GPA effect refers to J = 94 GPA means per cluster.

## Section recap

### Specifying and interpreting cross-level interactions

Just as the random-intercepts model can be expanded to include one (or more) Level 2 predictors of the cluster-specific intercepts, the random-slopes model can be expanded to include Level 2 predictors of both the cluster-specific intercepts and the cluster-specific slopes:

$$Y_{ij} = \beta_{0j} + \beta_{1j}X_{ij} + \varepsilon_{ij} \qquad \text{(Level 1)},$$

$$\beta_{0j} = \gamma_{00} + \gamma_{01}W_j + \gamma_{02}\bar{X}_{\bullet j} + \gamma_{03}(\bar{X}_{\bullet j} \times W_j) + \delta_{0j} \qquad \text{(Level 2a)},$$

$$\beta_{1j} = \gamma_{10} + \gamma_{11}W_j + \delta_{1j} \qquad \text{(Level 2b)}.$$

(Here, the Level 2 cluster means $\bar{X}_{\bullet j}$ are included in the Level 2a equation so that the model separates the within- and between-clusters effects of $X$.)

Including $W_j$ as a predictor of the random slopes $\beta_{1j}$ creates a **cross-level interaction** between $X_{ij}$ and $W_j$ in the combined equation:

$$Y_{ij} = \gamma_{00} + \gamma_{01}W_j + \gamma_{02}\bar{X}_{\bullet j} + \gamma_{03}\bar{X}_{\bullet j}W_j + \gamma_{10}X_{ij} + \gamma_{11}W_j X_{ij} + \delta_{0j} + \delta_{1j}X_{ij} + \varepsilon_{ij} \quad \text{(Combined)},$$

where $\gamma_{11}$ is the fixed-effect coefficient for this cross-level interaction.

Cross-level interactions can be probed using simple-slopes analyses.

---

## THREE-LEVEL MODELS

So far, this chapter has only considered two-level models for data characterized by only two levels of hierarchical nesting, for example, individual students nested within different courses or instructors. Although the Level 1 units (e.g., students) are nonindependent, these models still assume independence for the Level 2 units (e.g., instructors). It is possible, however, for there to be nonindependence among the Level 2 units. For instance, a study may be conducted such that Level 2 instructor units are sampled from different universities, and the data for instructors from the same university may be correlated as a result of certain university characteristics. In this situation, a three-level model may be most appropriate for the data.[16] In this situation, any of the two-level models presented earlier can be expanded to include a third level. Specifically, the $\gamma$ parameters, which are fixed effects in the two-level model, can instead be considered random effects which randomly vary across Level 3 units (for a complete presentation, see Chapter 8 of Raudenbush and Bryk, 2002). Unfortunately, because of their complexity, three-level models are often difficult to estimate, requiring particularly large datasets, and are cumbersome to interpret.

## ASSUMPTION CHECKING FOR MLM

Essentially, the same assumptions and diagnostic principles for multiple regression that were described in Chapters 1 and 2 can be generalized to MLM. The added complexity is that these standard regression assumptions now apply to each level of the model. Here, I summarize these assumptions only briefly; more detailed treatments are in Raudenbush and Bryk (2002: Chapter 9) and in Snijders and Bosker (2012: Chapter 10).

---

[16]In the current running example on course evaluation data, all $J = 94$ instructors were sampled from the same university and can be considered independent.

To provide a particular MLM context, consider the equations for a random-intercepts model with a single predictor at both Level 1 and Level 2:

$$Y_{ij} = \beta_{0j} + \beta_{1j}X_{ij} + \varepsilon_{ij} \quad \text{(Level 1)},$$

$$\beta_{0j} = \gamma_{00} + \gamma_{01}W_j + \delta_{0j} \quad \text{(Level 2a)},$$

$$\beta_{1j} = \gamma_{10} + \delta_{1j} \quad \text{(Level 2b)}.$$

The Level 1 equation specifies a linear relation between $X$ and $Y$, and so the foremost assumption is that the linear functional form is indeed an adequate representation of the association between $X$ and $Y$. Because the model stipulates that this linear association varies from cluster to cluster, it is preferable to evaluate linearity by plotting $Y$ by $X$ separately for each cluster, which is similar to that shown earlier in Figure 6.3, although doing so is challenging when the number of clusters $J$ is large or the within-cluster sample sizes $n_j$ are small. Next, the Level 2b equation also specifies a linear functional form, this time for the regression of the random intercepts, $\beta_{0j}$, on the Level 2 predictor $W_j$. Here, linearity can be evaluated by extracting the predicted intercept for each cluster and plotting them against the Level 2 predictor. For an example from the course evaluation data, Figure 6.8 gives a scatterplot of the random intercepts from the regression of course evaluation ratings on student GPA (i.e., intercepts extracted from the model summarized in Table 6.8) against the Level 2 predictor instructor attractiveness; although the association is not strong, the linear functional form seems like an appropriate representation of this relation.

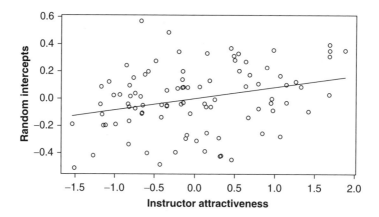

**Figure 6.8** Scatterplot of random intercepts from the regression of course evaluation ratings on student GPA against instructor attractiveness

The formal assumptions for MLM focus on the random effects at each level. First, the Level 1 errors $\varepsilon_{ij}$ are assumed to be independent and normally distributed. Additionally, the variance of the Level 1 errors, $\sigma^2$, is assumed to be constant within and across each Level 2 unit (i.e., each cluster). These Level 1 assumptions can be evaluated by adopting the graphical methods presented in Chapter 2, whereas the homogeneity of variance assumption can also be tested using statistics presented by Raudenbush and Bryk (2002). For models fitted to the course evaluation example data, however, this homogeneity of variance assumption is difficult to assess because the sample size $n_j$ is small within each cluster (here, $n_j < 14$ for all clusters). But Figure 6.9 shows that the Level 1 residuals (i.e., $\hat{\varepsilon}_{ij}$) from the random-intercepts model presented in Table 6.8 are approximately normally distributed (despite some outlying observations on the left of the distribution).

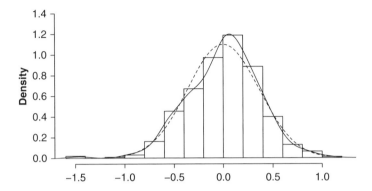

**Figure 6.9** Histogram of Level 1 residuals from the regression of course evaluation ratings on student GPA with fitted kernel density smoother (solid curve) and fitted normal distribution (dashed curve)

Regarding Level 2, analogous assumptions are made for both the Level 2a error term $\delta_{0j}$ and the Level 2b error term $\delta_{1j}$. Specifically, these error terms are also assumed independent and normally distributed. Next, whenever a Level 2 variable $W_j$ is included as a predictor of either random intercepts (in the Level 2a equation) or random slopes (in the Level 2b equation), then the Level 2 error terms should have homogeneous variance across the values of this $W_j$. Finally, it is assumed that the Level 2 error terms are independent from the Level 1 errors.

Procedures similar to those used for checking the Level 1 error term assumptions can be adapted to check assumptions for the Level 2 error terms. A complication is that the Level 2 outcomes (i.e., $\beta_{0j}$ and $\beta_{1j}$) are not directly observed, which introduces additional uncertainty in the estimation of the true Level 2 error terms; once again, for further details, see Raudenbush and Bryk (2002). Returning to the estimated random-intercepts model in which course evaluation ratings are regressed on GPA and instructor attractiveness, Figure 6.10 gives a scatterplot of the Level 2a residuals ($\hat{\delta}_{0j}$) against the attractiveness Level 2 predictor; the homogeneity of variance assumption appears tenable. But because this particular model has no predictor for the random slopes, this homogenous variance assumption is not applicable for the Level 2b error term $\delta_{1j}$.

A benefit of estimating multilevel model using maximum likelihood (either REML or FIML) is that the parameter estimates themselves remain accurate even under modest assumption violations, as long as N is large. But the standard errors, and consequently the confidence intervals and significance tests, may be distorted by assumption violations. Yet, remedies are available. First, as described in Chapter 2, non-normal variables can be transformed prior to model fitting, which may lead to less severe violations of the normality and homogeneity of variance assumptions compared with models fitted to data for nontransformed variables. Instead of, or in addition to, transforming problematic variables, robust standard errors can be obtained for the fixed-effect estimates (specifically, so-called 'sandwich' or 'Huber-corrected' standard errors; see Raudenbush and Bryk, 2002: 276–80).

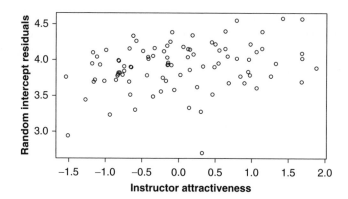

**Figure 6.10** Scatterplot of random intercept residuals (from the regression of course evaluation ratings on student GPA and instructor attractiveness) against instructor attractiveness

 Section recap

### Assumption checking in MLM

In general, the assumptions and accompanying diagnostic procedures that pertain to OLS multiple regression generalize to multilevel models estimated with maximum likelihood. With MLM, the added complication is that these assumptions apply to each level of the model.
In particular:

- The linear functional form of both the Level 1 and Level 2 equations should correctly represent the data.
- The Level 1 errors, $\varepsilon_{ij}$, are assumed normally distributed with homogenous variance within and across each Level 2 unit (i.e., each cluster).
- The Level 2 errors, $\delta_{0j}$ for random intercepts and $\delta_{ij}$ for random slopes, are assumed normally distributed with homogeneous variance across the levels of any Level 2 predictors.
- The Level 1 errors are assumed independent of the Level 2 errors.

When one or more assumptions may be violated, fixed-effects estimates nonetheless may not be severely affected, and robust standard errors can be used to obtain improved inferential statistics.

## CHAPTER SUMMARY

The current chapter focused on a prominent modeling procedure for incorporating nonindependent observations, namely, multilevel modeling (MLM):

- Multilevel models are most often estimated using the **maximum-likelihood (ML)** method. Either full-information ML (FIML) or restricted ML (REML) may be used.
- The **unconditional**, or *intercept-only*, multilevel model is also known as the *random-effects analysis-of-variance (ANOVA)* model and the *variance-components* model.

- In contrast to traditional fixed ANOVA, the groups (or clusters) in random-effects ANOVA are presumed to be randomly sampled from a population of groups; the goal of the model is to generalize beyond the particular sample of groups that was observed in a given study.
- The **Level 1 equation** of the unconditional multilevel model is

$$Y_{ij} = \beta_j + \varepsilon_{ij},$$

where $Y_{ij}$ is the observed value of $Y$ for individual $i$ in cluster $j$, $\beta_j$ is the mean of $Y$ within cluster $j$, and $\varepsilon_{ij}$ is the deviation of $Y_{ij}$ from the mean of cluster $j$.
- The **Level 2 equation** of the unconditional multilevel model is

$$\beta_j = \gamma + \delta_j,$$

where $\gamma$ is the **grand mean** of $Y$ across all individual cases and $\delta_j$ is the deviation of the mean of cluster $j$ from the grand mean; that is, $\delta_j = \beta_j - \gamma$.
- The Level 2 equation can be substituted into the Level 1 equation to obtain the **reduced-form**, or **combined**, equation:

$$Y_{ij} = \gamma + \delta_j + \varepsilon_{ij}.$$

- The variance components from the unconditional multilevel model are used to calculate the **intraclass correlation**, which quantifies the extent to which members of the same cluster are more similar to one another than to members of other clusters (i.e., the extent of nonindependence of observed values of $Y$).
- In the **random-intercepts** multilevel model, conceptually, each cluster has its own linear regression equation for $Y_{ij}$. The intercepts of these equations ($\beta_{0j}$) randomly vary across clusters, but the slopes ($\beta_j$) for predictor $X_{ij}$ are considered the same for each cluster:

$$Y_{ij} = \beta_{0j} + \beta_{1j}X_{ij} + \varepsilon_{ij} \qquad \text{(Level 1)},$$

$$\beta_{0j} = \gamma_{00} + \delta_{0j} \qquad \text{(Level 2a)},$$

$$\beta_{1j} = \gamma_{10} \qquad \text{(Level 2b)},$$

$$Y_{ij} = \gamma_{00} + \gamma_{10}X_{ij} + \delta_{0j} + \varepsilon_{ij} \qquad \text{(Combined)}.$$

- Instead of estimating each of $J$ regression equations, the hypothetical set of regression equations for the $J$ clusters is summarized by two fixed-effect parameters:

  ○ $\gamma_{00}$, which represents the mean of the $\beta_{0j}$ intercepts
  ○ $\gamma_{10}$, which represents the constant slope coefficient for predictor $X_{ij}$

- And one random-effects parameter:

  ○ $\tau_{00}^2$, which represents the variance of the random intercepts (i.e., $\text{VAR}(\delta_{0j})$)

- With the **random-slopes** multilevel model, each cluster has its own linear regression equation for $Y_{ij}$. Both the intercepts of these equations ($\beta_{0j}$) and the slopes ($\beta_{1j}$) randomly vary across clusters:

$$Y_{ij} = \beta_{0j} + \beta_{1j}X_{ij} + \varepsilon_{ij} \qquad \text{(Level 1)},$$

$$\beta_{0j} = \gamma_{00} + \delta_{0j} \qquad \text{(Level 2a)},$$

$$\beta_{1j} = \gamma_{10} + \delta_{1j} \qquad \text{(Level 2b)},$$

$$Y_{ij} = \gamma_{00} + \gamma_{10}X_{ij} + \delta_{0j} + \delta_{1j}X_{ij} + \varepsilon_{ij} \qquad \text{(Combined)}.$$

- In the random-slopes model, there are two fixed-effect parameters:

    - $\gamma_{00}$, which represents the mean of the $\beta_{0j}$ intercepts
    - $\gamma_{10}$, which represents the mean of the $\beta_{1j}$ slope coefficients for predictor $X_{ij}$

- And three random-effects parameters:

    - $\tau_{00}^2$, which represents the variance of the random intercepts (i.e., VAR($\delta_{0j}$))
    - $\tau_{11}^2$, which represents the variance of the random slopes (i.e., VAR($\delta_{1j}$))
    - $\tau_{01}$, which represents the covariance between $\delta_{0j}$ and $\delta_{1j}$

- The unconditional model is easily expanded to include one or more cluster-level variables, that is, Level 2 predictors. In particular, the Level 2 equation is expanded into a linear regression equation in which the group means, $\beta_j$, are an outcome variable regressed on a cluster-level predictor, $W_j$:

$$Y_{ij} = \beta_j + \varepsilon_{ij} \qquad \text{(Level 1)},$$

$$\beta_j = \gamma_0 + \gamma_1 W_j + \delta_j \qquad \text{(Level 2)},$$

$$Y_{ij} = \gamma_0 + \gamma_1 W_j + \delta_j + \varepsilon_{ij} \qquad \text{(Combined)}.$$

- The random-intercepts model is also easily expanded to include one or more Level 2 predictor, allowing the outcome variable $Y$ to be regressed on both Level 1 and Level 2 predictors simultaneously:

$$Y_{ij} = \beta_{0j} + \beta_{1j}X_{ij} + \varepsilon_{ij} \qquad \text{(Level 1)},$$

$$\beta_{0j} = \gamma_{00} + \gamma_{01}W_j + \delta_{0j} \qquad \text{(Level 2a)},$$

$$\beta_{1j} = \gamma_{10} \qquad \text{(Level 2b)},$$

$$Y_{ij} = \gamma_{00} + \gamma_{01}W_j + \gamma_{10}X_{ij} + \delta_{0j} + \varepsilon_{ij} \qquad \text{(Combined)}.$$

- The effect of any Level 1 predictor, $X_{ij}$, can be disaggregated into a **within-cluster effect** and a **between-clusters effect**. A random-intercepts model to obtain both the within- and between-clusters effects of a single variable $X_{ij}$ is

$$Y_{ij} = \beta_{0j} + \beta_{1j}X_{ij\bullet} + \varepsilon_{ij} \qquad \text{(Level 1)},$$

$$\beta_{0j} = \gamma_{00} + \gamma_{01}\overline{X}_{\bullet j} + \delta_{0j} \qquad \text{(Level 2a)},$$

$$\beta_{1j} = \gamma_{10} \qquad \text{(Level 2b),}$$

$$Y_{ij} = \gamma_{00} + \gamma_{01}\bar{X}_{\bullet j} + \gamma_{10}X_{ij\bullet} + \delta_{0j} + \varepsilon_{ij} \qquad \text{(Combined),}$$

with $\gamma_{10}$ representing the within-cluster effect and $\gamma_{01}$ giving the between-clusters effect.

- An alternative random-intercepts model for obtaining separate within- and between-clusters effects of $X$ uses the original, uncentered Level 1 predictor along with the cluster means as a Level 2 predictor:

$$Y_{ij} = \beta_{0j} + \beta_{1j}X_{ij} + \varepsilon_{ij} \qquad \text{(Level 1),}$$

$$\beta_{0j} = \gamma_{00} + \gamma_{01}\bar{X}_{\bullet j} + \delta_{0j} \qquad \text{(Level 2a),}$$

$$\beta_{1j} = \gamma_{10} \qquad \text{(Level 2b),}$$

$$Y_{ij} = \gamma_{00} + \gamma_{01}\bar{X}_{\bullet j} + \gamma_{10}X_{ij} + \delta_{0j} + \varepsilon_{ij} \qquad \text{(Combined),}$$

with $\gamma_{10}$ representing the within-cluster effect and the between-clusters effect equaling $(\gamma_{10} + \gamma_{01})$.

- The random-slopes model can be expanded to include Level 2 predictors of both the cluster-specific intercepts and the cluster-specific slopes:

$$Y_{ij} = \beta_{0j} + \beta_{1j}X_{ij} + \varepsilon_{ij} \qquad \text{(Level 1),}$$

$$\beta_{0j} = \gamma_{00} + \gamma_{01}W_j + \gamma_{02}\bar{X}_{\bullet j} + \gamma_{03}(\bar{X}_{\bullet j} \times W_j) + \delta_{0j} \qquad \text{(Level 2a),}$$

$$\beta_{1j} = \gamma_{10} + \gamma_{11}W_j + \delta_{1j} \qquad \text{(Level 2b).}$$

- Including $W_j$ as a predictor of the random slopes $\beta_{1j}$ creates a **cross-level interaction** between $X_{ij}$ and $W_j$ in the combined equation:

$$Y_{ij} = \gamma_{00} + \gamma_{01}W_j + \gamma_{02}\bar{X}_{\bullet j} + \gamma_{03}\bar{X}_{\bullet j}W_j + \gamma_{10}X_{ij} + \gamma_{11}W_jX_{ij} + \delta_{0j} + \delta_{1j}X_{ij} + \varepsilon_{ij} \qquad \text{(Combined),}$$

where $\gamma_{11}$ is the fixed-effect coefficient of the cross-level interaction.

- A **likelihood-ratio test** can be used to determine whether a nested model (i.e., a more restricted model) fits the data significantly worse than a more general model with additional parameters.
- With REML estimation, likelihood-ratio tests can be used only to compare models with differing random-effects parameters. If nested models have differing fixed-effects parameters, likelihood-ratio tests are only valid if the models are estimated with FIML.
- Competing models can also be compared using the **AIC** or **BIC** statistic, with BIC being more commonly relied upon. Although both AIC and BIC are a function of a model's log-likelihood, they also account for model complexity (i.e., the number of parameters to be estimated).
- In general, the assumptions and accompanying diagnostic procedures that pertain to OLS multiple regression generalize to multilevel models estimated with maximum likelihood. With MLM, the added complication is that these assumptions apply to each level of the model.

## RECOMMENDED READING

Bauer, D.J., & Curran, P.J. (2005). Probing interactions in fixed and multilevel regression: Inferential and graphical techniques. *Multivariate Behavioral Research, 40,* 373–400.

- Although this paper was also recommended in Chapter 4, it is well worth revisiting here. In particular, this article describes methods (i.e., using simple slopes) for probing interactions in multilevel models, including cross-level interactions. Empirical research examples are provided to illustrate the methods.

Enders, C.K., & Tofighi, D. (2007). Centering predictor variables in cross-sectional multilevel models: A new look at an old issue. *Psychological Methods, 12,* 121–38.

- This paper provides a clear, comprehensive discussion of how and why centering predictors in multilevel models affects parameter interpretations, specifically the disambiguation of within- and between-cluster effects. But I do not entirely agree with the authors' recommendation to center categorical predictors.

# BASIC MATRIX ALGEBRA FOR STATISTICAL MODELING

## CHAPTER OVERVIEW

This chapter is unique in that no new statistical procedures are introduced. Rather, the current chapter aims to introduce matrix algebra in the gentlest way possible. After a discussion on why it is useful to know a little about matrix algebra, the main topics of the chapter include:

- Kinds of matrices and simple matrix operations
- Matrix addition and subtraction
- Multiplication with matrices
- Determinants and matrix inversion
- Matrix calculations for statistical applications
- Matrix equations for linear regression
- Eigenvalues and eigenvectors

## WHY MATRIX ALGEBRA?

The previous chapters of this text have focused on models for a single outcome variable, $Y$. Consequently, each model could be specified using only a single equation with the exception of the simple indirect-effect model, or mediation model, of Chapter 5. But recall that the overall indirect-effect model was examined using two separate models which were estimated separately from each other, one model for the intervening variable or mediator and a second model for the main outcome variable. Additionally, each multilevel model in Chapter 6 was expressed using several equations (i.e., a Level 1 equation along with a set of Level 2 equations), but in each instance, it was possible to combine the separate equations into a single reduced-form equation (e.g., Equations 6.3 and 6.7) because there was always a single outcome variable, $Y$. But as we move forward, the models will be truly **multivariate** in nature in that there will usually be more than one dependent or outcome variable; that is, we will have $Y_1$, $Y_2$,..., $Y_Q$ outcomes instead of a single $Y$. As a result, there will be a separate equation for each of the $Q$ outcomes, but the parameters in the equations will all be estimated simultaneously rather than through one-at-a-time, separate analyses of each $Y$.

When the number of outcome variables $Q$ for a given multivariate model becomes large, it can be onerous to write out the entire model using a separate equation for each $Y$. Instead, being able to express mathematical relations using *matrices* will greatly facilitate our ability to describe multivariate statistical methods; a set of $Q$ separate equations can often be expressed using a single, compact matrix equation. Additionally, univariate models for only a single outcome variable can be understood as a special case of a multivariate model, and therefore, they also are represented within a more general matrix framework. Matrix operations form the foundation for all statistical computing. The statistical procedures implemented in software such as R, SAS®, and SPSS, even the simple ones, are all programmed in terms of matrix operations. To demonstrate, this chapter will present the matrix formulas for simple descriptive statistics and OLS regression.

This chapter provides only a light introduction to the standard notational conventions and algebraic operations for matrices as they pertain to statistical modeling. Having these conventions under our belt will allow me to present the modeling procedures of the remaining chapters in a concise fashion which is consistent with how these methods are represented in the behavioural and social science methodological literature as well as within certain computer software implementations. My hope is that this material will also give readers a certain level of comfort with matrix formulas that will enhance their comprehension of methodological research papers, including those I cite throughout this text. At its core, the mathematical background needed for this chapter is minimal and really involves nothing more complex than the simple algebra of the previous chapters; there is still no calculus involved. The main foci of this chapter are definitions, notation, and mathematical rules for matrices. Some details and examples of matrix computations are presented in this chapter, but given their complexity and tedium, the work of matrix calculation is best left for computers. Readers who desire more comprehensive treatments of matrix algebra and its application to statistics are referred to Fox (2009) and to Carroll, Green, and Chaturvedi (1997).

> The text's webpage (https://study.sagepub.com/flora) provides annotated input and output from several popular statistical software packages showing how to reproduce the matrix calculations presented in this chapter.

## KINDS OF MATRICES AND SIMPLE MATRIX OPERATIONS

A **matrix** is an organized, rectangular array of quantities known as **elements**. Most often, an element is a single **scalar** term, such as a numerical value or an algebraic symbol representing a numerical value.[1] For an initial example matrix, consider matrix **A**:

---

[1] It is possible, though, to have a matrix of matrices, which is known as a *block matrix*. An element of a block matrix is another smaller matrix.

$$A = \begin{bmatrix} a_{11} & a_{12} \\ a_{21} & a_{22} \\ a_{31} & a_{32} \end{bmatrix} = \begin{bmatrix} 1.0 & 3.0 \\ 0.2 & 4.6 \\ 8.5 & -2.3 \end{bmatrix}.$$

It is a standard notational convention to symbolize a matrix with a letter in bold-faced font (e.g., **A**), whereas an individual scalar term is symbolized in lowercase, italic font (e.g., $a_{11}$). Element $a_{ij}$ of **A** is the entry in the $i$th row and $j$th column. Thus, $a_{11} = 1.0$ is the entry in the first row, first column of **A**; $a_{12} = 3.0$ is the entry in the first row, second column; $a_{21} = 0.2$ is in the second row, first column; and so on. A matrix is characterized by the number of rows, $I$, and the number of columns, $J$, which define the matrix's **order** or **dimension**. Matrix **A** has dimension ($3 \times 2$) because there are $I = 3$ rows and $J = 2$ columns.[2]

If a research study has $N$ cases (e.g., $N$ research participants) and $P$ variables, then the data for the study are typically saved in a **data matrix** of dimension $N \times P$. That is, when you open a data file in a program such as SPSS or Microsoft Excel, you are looking at an $N \times P$ data matrix, although you may not explicitly think of it as a matrix. Other examples of matrices with which you are likely already familiar are correlation matrices and covariance matrices, which are described in detail later in this chapter.

The **transpose** of a given matrix **X**, denoted **X**′ (or $\mathbf{X}^{\mathsf{T}}$), is formed by writing the rows of **X** as the columns of **X**′. Thus, the transpose of matrix **A** given earlier is

$$\mathbf{A}' = \begin{bmatrix} 1.0 & 0.2 & 8.5 \\ 3.0 & 4.6 & -2.3 \end{bmatrix}.$$

For any matrix, $(\mathbf{X}')' = \mathbf{X}$. The ability to transpose a matrix is particularly useful for making matrices *conformable* for multiplication, which is described later.

A matrix consisting of only one column is called a **column vector**. Vectors are often symbolized with a bold letter in lowercase. For example,

$$\mathbf{a} = \begin{bmatrix} a_1 \\ a_2 \\ \vdots \\ a_I \end{bmatrix}$$

is a generic ($I \times 1$) column vector. Similarly, a matrix consisting of only one row is called a **row vector**, such as the ($1 \times J$) vector **b**′ :

$$\mathbf{b}' = \begin{bmatrix} b_1 & b_2 & \cdots & b_J \end{bmatrix}.$$

When a vector is a row vector, it is common to attach the 'prime' symbol to the vector name (which is why this row vector is called **b**′ instead of just **b**), which indicates that the row vector is the transpose of some column vector. By convention, a vector is generally assumed to be a column vector (such as **a** ) unless it is explicitly written as a transpose (such as **b**′).

A **square matrix** of dimension $J$ has $J$ rows and $J$ columns. The entries $c_{jj}$ (that is, $c_{11}$, $c_{22}, \ldots, c_{JJ}$) of a square matrix **C** comprise the main **diagonal** of the matrix.

---

[2]A single scalar value can be considered a ($1 \times 1$) matrix.

Thus, by definition, the diagonal goes from the top-left of a square matrix to the bottom-right. For example,

$$C = \begin{bmatrix} -5 & 1 & 3 \\ 2 & 2 & 6 \\ 7 & 3 & -4 \end{bmatrix}$$

is a square matrix of dimension $J = 3$ because the number of rows (3) equals the number of columns (3). The elements of the diagonal are $c_{11} = -5$, $c_{22} = 2$, and $c_{33} = -4$. The elements above the diagonal of a square matrix (here, $c_{12} = 1$, $c_{13} = 3$, and $c_{23} = 6$) form the **upper triangle**, whereas the elements below the diagonal (here, $c_{21} = 2$, $c_{31} = 7$, and $c_{32} = 3$) form the **lower triangle**. The **trace** of a square matrix $C$, denoted tr($C$), equals the sum of its diagonal elements. Given the current $C$, we have

$$\text{tr}(C) = \sum_{j=1}^{J} c_{jj} = -5 + 2 + -4 = -7.$$

Next, a square matrix $A$ is **symmetric** if $A = A'$, that is, if $a_{ij} = a_{ji}$ for all $i$ and $j$. Consequently, the matrix $C$ is not symmetric (e.g., because $c_{12} \neq c_{21}$, $c_{13} \neq c_{31}$, etc.). But the matrix $D$,

$$D = \begin{bmatrix} -5 & 1 & 3 \\ 1 & 2 & 6 \\ 3 & 6 & -4 \end{bmatrix},$$

is symmetric because $D = D'$ (the elements in the upper triangle are a mirror image of the elements in the lower triangle; $d_{12} = d_{21}$, $d_{13} = d_{31}$, and $d_{23} = d_{32}$).

All **correlation matrices**, which are typically denoted $R$, are square, symmetric matrices with each diagonal element equal to 1. For example, the correlations given in Chapter 2 in Table 2.1 can be organized in a matrix as

$$R = \begin{bmatrix} 1.00 & 0.32 & -0.21 \\ 0.32 & 1.00 & -0.14 \\ -0.21 & -0.14 & 1.00 \end{bmatrix}.$$

But because a correlation matrix is symmetric, usually only the lower triangle is displayed when the correlation matrix is presented as a table in a research report, as in the original Table 2.1, reproduced as Table 7.1. Or, equivalently, one might present only the upper triangle of a symmetric matrix, as in Table 7.2. Additionally, because each diagonal element of a correlation matrix equals 1, the trace of a correlation matrix equals the total number of variables in the correlation matrix; in the current example, tr($R$) = 3.

**Table 7.1** Correlation matrix as a lower triangle

|      | BPAQ | BIS | Age |
|------|------|-----|-----|
| BPAQ | 1    | –   | –   |
| BIS  | .32  | 1   | –   |
| Age  | −.21 | −.14 | 1  |

**Table 7.2**  Correlation matrix as an upper triangle

|  | BPAQ | BIS | Age |
|---|---|---|---|
| BPAQ | 1 | .32 | −.21 |
| BIS | − | 1 | −.14 |
| Age | − | − | 1 |

Recall from Equation 1.9 that a correlation is simply a covariance that has been standardized according to the standard deviations of the two variables being correlated:

$$r_{XY} = \frac{\text{COV}(X,Y)}{\sqrt{\text{VAR}(X)}\sqrt{\text{VAR}(Y)}} = \frac{s_{XY}}{s_X s_Y}.$$

Therefore, the covariances among a set of two or more variables can also be contained within a square, symmetric matrix, a **covariance matrix**, which is often denoted **S**. For example, with three variables $Y$, $X_1$, and $X_2$, the (population) covariance matrix is

$$\mathbf{S} = \begin{bmatrix} \text{VAR}(Y) & & \\ \text{COV}(Y,X_1) & \text{VAR}(X_1) & \\ \text{COV}(Y,X_2) & \text{COV}(X_1,X_2) & \text{VAR}(X_2) \end{bmatrix} = \begin{bmatrix} \sigma_Y^2 & & \\ \sigma_{YX_1} & \sigma_{X_1}^2 & \\ \sigma_{YX_2} & \sigma_{X_1 X_2} & \sigma_{X_2}^2 \end{bmatrix}.$$

Whereas the diagonal elements of a correlation matrix all equal 1, the diagonal elements of a covariance matrix are the variances of the variables.

Moving on, a square matrix is called a **diagonal matrix** if all elements equal 0 except those on the main diagonal:

$$\mathbf{D} = \begin{bmatrix} d_1 & 0 & \cdots & 0 \\ 0 & d_2 & \cdots & 0 \\ \vdots & \vdots & \ddots & \vdots \\ 0 & 0 & \cdots & d_J \end{bmatrix}.$$

An especially important type of diagonal matrix is an **identity** matrix **I**, in which each diagonal element equals 1:

$$\mathbf{I} = \begin{bmatrix} 1 & 0 & \cdots & 0 \\ 0 & 1 & \cdots & 0 \\ \vdots & \vdots & \ddots & \vdots \\ 0 & 0 & \cdots & 1 \end{bmatrix}.$$

Another important type of matrix (which need not be square) is a **zero matrix**, **0**, in which all elements equal zero:

$$\mathbf{0} = \begin{bmatrix} 0 & 0 & \cdots & 0 \\ 0 & 0 & \cdots & 0 \\ \vdots & \vdots & \ddots & \vdots \\ 0 & 0 & 0 & 0 \end{bmatrix}.$$

 Section recap

## Kinds of matrices and simple matrix operations

A **matrix** is an organized, rectangular array of quantities known as **elements**. Most often, an element is a single **scalar** term, such as a numerical value or an algebraic symbol representing some numerical value.

Element $a_{ij}$ of matrix **A** is the entry in the $i$th row and $j$th column.

A matrix is characterized by the number of rows, $I$, and the number of columns, $J$, which define the matrix's **order** or **dimension**.

The **transpose** of a given matrix **X**, denoted **X′** (or **X**$^{T}$), is formed by writing the rows of **X** as the columns of **X′**. For any matrix, $(X')' - X$.

A matrix consisting of only one column (i.e., with dimension $I \times 1$) is called a **column vector**. Similarly, a matrix consisting of only one row (i.e., with dimension $1 \times J$) is called a **row vector**.

A **square matrix** of dimension $J$ has $J$ rows and $J$ columns. The entries $c_{ii}$ (that is, $c_{11}$, $c_{22}$,..., $c_{JJ}$) of a square matrix **C** comprise the main **diagonal** of the matrix.

The **trace** of a square matrix **C**, denoted tr(**C**), equals the sum of its diagonal elements.

A square matrix **A** is **symmetric** if $A = A'$, that is, if $a_{ij} = a_{ji}$ for all $i$ and $j$.

All **correlation matrices**, which are often denoted **R**, are square, symmetric matrices with each diagonal element equal to 1.

A **covariance matrix**, which is often denoted **S**, is a square, symmetric matrix with off-diagonal elements that are the covariances between variables; the diagonal elements of a covariance matrix are the variances of the variables.

A square matrix is called a **diagonal matrix** if all elements equal 0 except those on the main diagonal.

An important type of diagonal matrix is an **identity** matrix **I**, in which each diagonal element equals 1.

Another important type of matrix (which need not be square) is a **zero matrix**, **O**, in which all elements equal zero.

---

# ELEMENTARY MATRIX ALGEBRA

## Matrix addition and subtraction

The major strength, indeed the purpose, of matrix algebra is that it provides a framework for algebraically manipulating large amounts of numerical entities using small, concise matrix expressions. As we will see, a set of many equations expressed using scalar terms can often be reexpressed using only a few (or even only one) matrix equation. The cost of this efficiency is that matrix algebra adheres to a strict set of rules, some of which are immediately intuitive and some of which are not.

Two matrices can be added only if they have the same dimension; then their sum is formed by adding the corresponding elements. Thus, if **A** and **B** are both of dimension $(I \times J)$, then their sum, $C = A + B$, is also of dimension $(I \times J)$, with $c_{ij} = a_{ij} + b_{ij}$. For example, matrices

$$A = \begin{bmatrix} 1 & 2 & 3 \\ 4 & 5 & 6 \end{bmatrix}$$

and

$$B = \begin{bmatrix} -5 & 1 & 2 \\ 3 & 0 & -4 \end{bmatrix}$$

both have dimension (2 × 3), and so their sum is another (2 × 3) matrix

$$C = A + B = \begin{bmatrix} 1+(-5) & 2+1 & 3+2 \\ 4+3 & 5+0 & 6+(-4) \end{bmatrix} = \begin{bmatrix} -4 & 3 & 5 \\ 7 & 5 & 2 \end{bmatrix}.$$

Likewise, if $D = A - B$, then $D$ is also of dimension ($I \times J$), with $d_{ij} = a_{ij} - b_{ij}$:

$$D = A - B = \begin{bmatrix} 1-(-5) & 2-1 & 3-2 \\ 4-3 & 5-0 & 6-(-4) \end{bmatrix} = \begin{bmatrix} 6 & 1 & 1 \\ 1 & 5 & 10 \end{bmatrix}.$$

Furthermore, the negative of a matrix $B$, such as $E = -B$, is of the same dimension as $B$, with elements $e_{ij} = -b_{ij}$:

$$E = -B = \begin{bmatrix} 5 & -1 & -2 \\ -3 & 0 & 4 \end{bmatrix}.$$

Because matrix addition, subtraction, and negation are performed in an *element-wise* way (e.g., for addition, element *i,j* from one matrix is added to element *i,j* from the other matrix, and so on, across all $I \times J$ elements), essentially the same intuitive laws are obeyed as for the corresponding scalar operations. Specifically, matrix addition is *commutative* in that

$$A + B = B + A$$

and matrix addition is *associative* in that

$$(A + B) + C = A + (B + C).$$

Additionally, negation of a matrix distributes through parentheses in the same way as with scalar algebra, and so

$$-(-A) = A$$

and

$$(A - B) = A + (-B) = -(B - A).$$

It is also intuitively clear that subtracting a matrix from itself produces a zero matrix of the same dimension,

$$A - A = 0,$$

and that

$$A + 0 = A.$$

Finally, it is also the case that

$$(\mathbf{A} + \mathbf{B})' = \mathbf{A}' + \mathbf{B}' ;$$

that is, the transpose of a sum of two matrices equals the sum of the two matrices individually transposed.

 **Section recap**

### Matrix addition and subtraction

Two matrices can be added only if they have the same dimension; then their sum is formed by adding corresponding elements.

Thus, if **A** and **B** are both of dimension ($I \times J$), then their sum, **C** = **A** + **B**, is also of dimension ($I \times J$), with $c_{ij} = a_{ij} + b_{ij}$.

Likewise, if **D** = **A** − **B**, then **D** is also of dimension ($I \times J$), with $d_{ij} = a_{ij} - b_{ij}$.

The negative of a matrix **B**, such as **E** = −**B**, is of the same dimension as **B**, with elements $e_{ij} = -b_{ij}$.

Matrix addition is *commutative* in that **A** + **B** = **B** + **A**.

Matrix addition is *associative* in that (**A** + **B**) + **C** = **A** + (**B** + **C**).

## Multiplication with matrices

The operation and rules for multiplying a scalar term by a matrix are also straightforward. The product of a scalar $c$ and a ($I \times J$) matrix **A** is an ($I \times J$) matrix **B** = $c$**A** in which $b_{ij} = c \times a_{ij}$. For example, if $c = 3$ and

$$\mathbf{A} = \begin{bmatrix} 1 & 3 \\ 2 & 5 \\ 8 & -2 \end{bmatrix},$$

then their product is

$$\mathbf{B} = 3 \times \begin{bmatrix} 1 & 3 \\ 2 & 5 \\ 8 & -2 \end{bmatrix} = \begin{bmatrix} 3 \times 1 & 3 \times 3 \\ 3 \times 2 & 3 \times 5 \\ 3 \times 8 & 3 \times -2 \end{bmatrix} = \begin{bmatrix} 3 & 9 \\ 6 & 15 \\ 24 & -6 \end{bmatrix}.$$

The product of a scalar and a matrix is also commutative such that

$$c\mathbf{A} = \mathbf{A}c$$

and *distributive* such that

$$\mathbf{A}(b + c) = \mathbf{A}b + \mathbf{A}c$$

and

$$c(\mathbf{A} + \mathbf{B}) = c\mathbf{A} + c\mathbf{B}.$$

Finally, it is also true that

$$0\mathbf{A} = \mathbf{0},$$

$$1\mathbf{A} = \mathbf{A},$$

and

$$(-1)\mathbf{A} = -\mathbf{A}.$$

Whereas these rules for multiplying a matrix by a scalar are straightforward, the operation and rules for multiplying two matrices together are considerably more complex. First, it might not even be possible to multiply two given matrices together; two matrices must be **conformable** for multiplication to be possible. Two matrices $\mathbf{A}$ and $\mathbf{B}$ are conformable for multiplication in the order given (i.e., $\mathbf{AB}$ rather than $\mathbf{BA}$) if the number of columns of the left-hand matrix ($\mathbf{A}$) is equal to the number of rows of the right-hand matrix ($\mathbf{B}$). Thus, $\mathbf{A}$ and $\mathbf{B}$ are conformable for multiplication if $\mathbf{A}$ has dimension ($I \times J$) and $\mathbf{B}$ is of dimension ($I \times K$). For example, the following two matrices are conformable:

$$\mathbf{A} = \begin{bmatrix} 2 & 1 \\ 4 & 2 \\ 6 & 3 \end{bmatrix}, \mathbf{B} = \begin{bmatrix} 1 & 3 \\ 3 & 1 \end{bmatrix},$$

meaning that it is possible to calculate the product $\mathbf{AB}$ because the number of columns of $\mathbf{A}$ equals the number of rows of $\mathbf{B}$. But it is not possible to calculate the product of these two matrices in the opposite order as $\mathbf{BA}$ because the number of columns of $\mathbf{B}$ does not equal the number of rows of $\mathbf{A}$. It is possible, though, to calculate $\mathbf{BA}'$, which shows the usefulness of transposing a matrix.

Unlike addition and subtraction of matrices and the multiplication of a matrix by a scalar, the operation of multiplying two matrices together is not simply element-wise. Let $\mathbf{C} = \mathbf{AB}$ be the matrix product of ($I \times J$) matrix $\mathbf{A}$ and ($J \times K$) matrix $\mathbf{B}$; also, let $\mathbf{a}'_i$ represent the $i$th row of $\mathbf{A}$ and $\mathbf{b}_j$ represent the $j$th column of $\mathbf{B}$. Then $\mathbf{C}$ is a matrix of dimension ($J \times K$) with elements calculated as

$$c_{ij} = \mathbf{a}'_i \bullet \mathbf{b}_j = \sum_{n=1}^{J} a_{in} b_{nj}.$$

Element $c_{ij}$ is known as the **dot product** of row $i$ from matrix $\mathbf{A}$ and column $j$ from matrix $\mathbf{B}$. For example, using matrices $\mathbf{A}$ and $\mathbf{B}$ in the previous paragraph, because $\mathbf{A}$ has dimension ($3 \times 2$) and $\mathbf{B}$ has dimension ($2 \times 2$), then their product $\mathbf{C}$ will be ($3 \times 2$). Thus, the six elements of $\mathbf{C}$ are $c_{11}$, $c_{12}$, $c_{21}$, $c_{22}$, $c_{31}$, and $c_{32}$, each of which is a dot product of the corresponding row of $\mathbf{A}$ and column of $\mathbf{B}$. The dot product of the first row of $\mathbf{A}$ and the first column of $\mathbf{B}$ is

$$c_{11} = \mathbf{a}'_1 \bullet \mathbf{b}_1 = (2 \quad 1) \bullet (1 \quad 3) = (2 \times 1) + (1 \times 3) = 5.$$

Next, the dot product of the first row of **A** and the second column of **B** is

$$c_{12} = a_1' \bullet b_2 = (2 \quad 1) \bullet (3 \quad 1) = (2 \times 3) + (1 \times 1) = 7.$$

The remaining dot products are

$$c_{21} = a_2' \bullet b_1 = (4 \quad 2) \bullet (1 \quad 3) = (4 \times 1) + (2 \times 3) = 10,$$

$$c_{22} = a_2' \bullet b_2 = (4 \quad 2) \bullet (3 \quad 1) = (4 \times 3) + (2 \times 1) = 14,$$

$$c_{31} = a_3' \bullet b_1 = (6 \quad 3) \bullet (1 \quad 3) = (6 \times 1) + (3 \times 3) = 15,$$

and

$$c_{32} - a_3' \bullet b_2 = (6 \quad 3) \bullet (3 \quad 1) = (6 \times 3) + (3 \times 1) = 21.$$

Therefore, the resulting matrix product is

$$\mathbf{C} = \mathbf{AB} = \begin{bmatrix} c_{11} & c_{12} \\ c_{21} & c_{22} \\ c_{31} & c_{32} \end{bmatrix} = \begin{bmatrix} 5 & 7 \\ 10 & 14 \\ 15 & 21 \end{bmatrix}.$$

For another example, if instead we have

$$\mathbf{D} = \begin{bmatrix} 1 & 2 \\ 3 & 4 \end{bmatrix} \text{ and } \mathbf{E} = \begin{bmatrix} 0 & 3 \\ 2 & 1 \end{bmatrix},$$

because **D** has dimension (2 × 2) and **E** has dimension (2 × 2), then their product **F** will also be (2 × 2). The dot product of the first row of **D** and the first column of **E** is

$$f_{11} = d_1' \bullet e_1 = (1 \quad 2) \bullet (0 \quad 2) = (1 \times 0) + (2 \times 2) = 4.$$

Next, we have

$$f_{12} = d_1' \bullet e_2 = (1 \quad 2) \bullet (3 \quad 1) = (1 \times 3) + (2 \times 1) = 5,$$

$$f_{21} = d_2' \bullet e_1 = (3 \quad 4) \bullet (0 \quad 2) = (3 \times 0) + (4 \times 2) = 8,$$

and finally

$$f_{22} = d_2' \bullet e_2 = (3 \quad 4) \bullet (3 \quad 1) = (3 \times 3) + (4 \times 1) = 13.$$

Therefore,

$$\mathbf{F} = \begin{bmatrix} 4 & 5 \\ 8 & 13 \end{bmatrix}.$$

Matrix multiplication is generally not commutative. That is, it is often (but not always) the case that **AB** ≠ **BA**. For example, using matrices **D** and **E**, when we **postmultiplied D** by **E**, we obtained

$$\mathbf{F} = \mathbf{DE} = \begin{bmatrix} 4 & 5 \\ 8 & 13 \end{bmatrix}.$$

But if we instead **premultiply D** by **E**, the result is

$$\mathbf{ED} = \begin{bmatrix} 9 & 12 \\ 5 & 8 \end{bmatrix} \neq \mathbf{F}.$$

Other rules for matrix multiplication follow more intuitively. Matrix multiplication is associative, meaning that $\mathbf{A}(\mathbf{BC}) = (\mathbf{AB})\mathbf{C}$. Furthermore, matrix multiplication is also distributive with respect to addition in that

$$(\mathbf{A} + \mathbf{B})\mathbf{C} = \mathbf{AC} + \mathbf{BC}$$

and

$$\mathbf{A}(\mathbf{B} + \mathbf{C}) = \mathbf{AB} + \mathbf{AC}.$$

Next, the identity and zero matrices play roles with respect to matrix multiplication analogous to those of the numbers 0 and 1 in scalar algebra. In particular,

$$\underset{(I \times J)}{\mathbf{A}} \underset{(J \times J)}{\mathbf{I}} = \underset{(I \times I)}{\mathbf{I}} \underset{(I \times J)}{\mathbf{A}} = \mathbf{A},$$

meaning that the post- or premultiplying any matrix **A** by the conformable identity matrix results in the same original matrix **A**. Furthermore,

$$\underset{(I \times J)}{\mathbf{A}} \underset{(J \times K)}{\mathbf{0}} = \underset{(I \times K)}{\mathbf{0}}$$

and

$$\underset{(M \times I)}{\mathbf{0}} \underset{(I \times J)}{\mathbf{A}} = \underset{(M \times J)}{\mathbf{0}},$$

meaning that the post- or premultiplying any matrix **A** by the conformable zero matrix results in another zero matrix. A further property of matrix multiplication is that $(\mathbf{AB})' = \mathbf{B'A'}$; that is, the transpose of a product is the product of the transposes taken in the opposite order. Finally, the powers of a square matrix are the products of the matrix with itself. That is,

$$\mathbf{A}^2 = \mathbf{AA},$$

$$\mathbf{A}^3 = \mathbf{AAA} = \mathbf{AA}^2 = \mathbf{A}^2\mathbf{A},$$

and so on.

## Section recap

### Multiplication with matrices

The product of a scalar $c$ and a $(I \times J)$ matrix **A** is an $(I \times J)$ matrix $\mathbf{B} = c\mathbf{A}$ in which $b_{ij} = c \times a_{ij}$.

*(Continued)*

(Continued)

The product of a scalar and a matrix is commutative such that $c\mathbf{A} = \mathbf{A}c$, and *distributive* such that $\mathbf{A}(b + c) = \mathbf{A}b + \mathbf{A}c$

and

$c(\mathbf{A} + \mathbf{B}) = c\mathbf{A} + c\mathbf{B}$.

Two matrices $\mathbf{A}$ and $\mathbf{B}$ are **conformable** for multiplication in the order given (i.e., $\mathbf{AB}$ rather than $\mathbf{BA}$) if the number of columns of the left-hand matrix ($\mathbf{A}$) is equal to the number of rows of the right-hand matrix ($\mathbf{B}$).

Let $\mathbf{C} = \mathbf{AB}$ be the matrix product of $(I \times J)$ matrix $\mathbf{A}$ and $(J \times K)$ matrix $\mathbf{B}$; also, let $\mathbf{a}'_i$ represent the $i$th row of $\mathbf{A}$ and $\mathbf{b}_j$ represent the $j$th column of $\mathbf{B}$. Then $\mathbf{C}$ is a matrix of dimension $(I \times K)$ with elements calculated as

$$c_{ij} = \mathbf{a}'_i \bullet \mathbf{b}_j = \sum_{n=1}^{J} a_{in} b_{nj}.$$

Element $c_{ij}$ is known as the **dot product** of row $i$ from matrix $\mathbf{A}$ and column $j$ from matrix $\mathbf{B}$.

Matrix multiplication is generally not commutative. That is, it is often (but not always) the case that $\mathbf{AB} \neq \mathbf{BA}$.

Matrix multiplication is associative, meaning that $\mathbf{A}(\mathbf{BC}) = (\mathbf{AB})\mathbf{C}$.

Matrix multiplication is also distributive with respect to addition in that $(\mathbf{A} + \mathbf{B})\mathbf{C} = \mathbf{AC} + \mathbf{BC}$ and $\mathbf{A}(\mathbf{B} + \mathbf{C}) = \mathbf{AB} + \mathbf{AC}$.

---

## What about division? Determinants and matrix inversion

For any square matrix $\mathbf{A}$, a scalar, numeric value known as the **determinant** can be calculated, which is symbolized as $|\mathbf{A}|$ or $\det(\mathbf{A})$. Determinants are used in many complex matrix operations, including certain statistical applications. For instance, the determinant of a covariance matrix for a set of variables represents the multivariate *generalized variance* of those variables. Additionally, if $|\mathbf{A}| = 0$, then one or more columns of $\mathbf{A}$ can be expressed as a linear combination of other columns; that is, the columns are linearly dependent. As a simple example, with

$$\mathbf{A} = \begin{bmatrix} 3 & 1 & 4 \\ 4 & 1 & 5 \\ 2 & 3 & 5 \end{bmatrix},$$

it is easy to see that the third column equals the sum of the first two, and indeed, the determinant of this matrix is 0. Other examples are less obvious, of course. In general, a matrix with a determinant equal to 0 is called a **singular** matrix, implying that there is a linear dependency among its columns, which is problematic for certain statistical applications. Later, in Chapters 8 and 9, determinants of covariance matrices will appear in the maximum likelihood fitting function for factor analysis and structural equation modeling.

For a $(2 \times 2)$ matrix

$$\mathbf{A} = \begin{bmatrix} a_{11} & a_{12} \\ a_{21} & a_{22} \end{bmatrix},$$

the determinant is calculated as $|\mathbf{A}| = (a_{11}a_{22}) - (a_{12}a_{21})$. Next, for a $(3 \times 3)$ matrix

$$\mathbf{A} = \begin{bmatrix} a_{11} & a_{12} & a_{13} \\ a_{21} & a_{22} & a_{23} \\ a_{31} & a_{32} & a_{33} \end{bmatrix},$$

the formula is

$$|\mathbf{A}| = (a_{11}a_{22}a_{33}) - (a_{11}a_{23}a_{32}) + (a_{12}a_{23}a_{31}) - (a_{12}a_{21}a_{33}) + (a_{13}a_{21}a_{32}) - (a_{13}a_{22}a_{31}).$$

For the $(3 \times 3)$ matrix in the previous paragraph, applying this formula obtains

$$|\mathbf{A}| = (15) - (45) + (10) - (20) + (48) - (8) = 0,$$

confirming that the matrix is singular. For larger matrices, the formula is progressively more complex, such that hand calculation is extremely tedious.

Determinants are involved in the calculation of a matrix **inverse**. In matrix algebra, there is no direct analog of division, but many square matrices have an inverse, which then can be used to solve equations, as shown later. In scalar arithmetic, division can also be expressed using inverses. For example, the expression

$$(35 \div 7) = (35 \times \frac{1}{7}) = 5$$

is equivalent to the expression

$$35(7^{-1}) = 5$$

where $7^{-1}$ is the inverse of the scalar value 7. Note that, of course, the inverse of any scalar value $n$ has the property that $n^{-1}n = 1$; for example, $7 \times 7^{-1} = 1$. Analogously, the inverse of a square matrix $\mathbf{A}$ is itself a square matrix of the same dimension, written $\mathbf{A}^{-1}$, with the property that $\mathbf{AA}^{-1} = \mathbf{A}^{-1}\mathbf{A} = \mathbf{I}$.

Finding the inverse of a square matrix is not simply a matter of taking the inverse of each scalar element within the matrix. The correct process is too mathematically complex to present here (see Carroll et al., 1997: 136–43), but we can use matrix multiplication to establish whether one matrix is an inverse of another. For example, the matrix

$$\mathbf{A} = \begin{bmatrix} 2 & 9 \\ 1 & 4 \end{bmatrix}$$

has an inverse of

$$\mathbf{A}^{-1} = \begin{bmatrix} -4 & 9 \\ 1 & -2 \end{bmatrix}$$

because

$$\mathbf{AA}^{-1} = \begin{bmatrix} 2 & 9 \\ 1 & 4 \end{bmatrix} \begin{bmatrix} -4 & 9 \\ 1 & -2 \end{bmatrix} = \begin{bmatrix} 1 & 0 \\ 0 & 1 \end{bmatrix} = \mathbf{I}$$

and

$$\mathbf{A}^{-1}\mathbf{A} = \begin{bmatrix} -4 & 9 \\ 1 & -2 \end{bmatrix}\begin{bmatrix} 2 & 9 \\ 1 & 4 \end{bmatrix} = \begin{bmatrix} 1 & 0 \\ 0 & 1 \end{bmatrix} = \mathbf{I}.$$

But it is important to recognize that not all square matrices have inverses. If a square matrix does have a unique inverse, then the matrix is termed **nonsingular**; a square matrix without an inverse (corresponding to having a determinant equal to zero) is called singular. Singular matrices can cause problems in certain statistical applications; in these cases, software applications typically produce a warning message that a particular matrix related to the model being estimated is singular.

The ability to multiply matrices together and to take inverses of square matrices makes it straightforward to formulate systems of scalar equations, such as a set of several regression equations, as a single matrix equation, and then to solve for the unknown quantities in the system. For a brief example, consider the following system of two scalar linear equations with two unknowns, $x_1$ and $x_2$:

$$-5 = 2x_1 + 9x_2,$$

$$7 = x_1 + 4x_2.$$

Next, these two scalar equations are expressed as a single matrix equation:

$$\begin{bmatrix} -5 \\ 7 \end{bmatrix} = \begin{bmatrix} 2 & 9 \\ 1 & 4 \end{bmatrix}\begin{bmatrix} x_1 \\ x_2 \end{bmatrix}$$

or, more compactly,

$$\mathbf{y} = \mathbf{A}\mathbf{x}.$$

To solve for $\mathbf{x}$, we can premultiply both sides of the matrix equation by $\mathbf{A}^{-1}$:

$$\mathbf{A}^{-1}\mathbf{y} = \mathbf{A}^{-1}\mathbf{A}\mathbf{x},$$

which implies

$$\mathbf{A}^{-1}\mathbf{y} = \mathbf{I}\mathbf{x}$$

or simply

$$\mathbf{A}^{-1}\mathbf{y} = \mathbf{x}.$$

Thus, the solution for $\mathbf{x}$ is

$$\begin{bmatrix} -4 & 9 \\ 1 & -2 \end{bmatrix}\begin{bmatrix} -5 \\ 7 \end{bmatrix} = \begin{bmatrix} 83 \\ -19 \end{bmatrix} = \mathbf{x}.$$

## Section recap

### Determinants and matrix inversion

For any square matrix **A**, a scalar, numeric value known as the **determinant** can be calculated, which is symbolized as $|\mathbf{A}|$ or det(**A**).

If $|\mathbf{A}| = 0$, then **A** is referred to as a **singular** matrix, indicating that one or more columns of **A** can be expressed as a linear combination of other columns.

Determinants are involved in the calculation of a matrix **inverse**:

The inverse of a square matrix **A** is itself a square matrix of the same dimension, written $\mathbf{A}^{-1}$, with the property that $\mathbf{AA}^{-1} = \mathbf{A}^{-1}\mathbf{A} = \mathbf{I}$.

Not all square matrices have inverses. If a square matrix does have a unique inverse, then the matrix is termed **nonsingular**; a square matrix without an inverse (corresponding to having a determinant equal to 0) is singular.

Matrix inverses are useful for solving matrix equations in a manner analogous to the use of division in algebraic equations with only scalar terms.

# MATRIX CALCULATIONS FOR STATISTICAL APPLICATIONS

## Means

Recall that the formula for calculating a sample mean using scalar terms is

$$\bar{X} = \frac{1}{N}\sum_{i=1}^{N} X_i.$$

For instance, take a small sample of $N = 5$ with $X_i$ scores of [3, 4, 6, 2, 5]. The mean of these scores is thus

$$\bar{X} = \frac{1}{N}\sum_{i=1}^{N} X_i = \frac{1}{5}(3+4+6+2+5) = \frac{1}{5}(20) = 4.$$

To get the sample mean of a single variable $X_i$ using matrix algebra, first express the data (i.e., the sample values of $X_i$) as a column vector:

$$\mathbf{x} = \begin{bmatrix} 3 \\ 4 \\ 6 \\ 2 \\ 5 \end{bmatrix}.$$

To add up all the elements in a column vector **x**, we need to premultiply **x** by the conformable **unit vector**, **1**′. A unit vector is simply a vector of ones, which in the current example must have a length of 5 to be conformable with our data vector **x**:

$$\mathbf{1}' = \begin{bmatrix} 1 & 1 & 1 & 1 & 1 \end{bmatrix}.$$

Then the matrix expression for the summation of the data is

$$\sum_{i=1}^{N} X_i = \underset{(1\times N)}{\mathbf{1'}} \underset{(N\times 1)}{\mathbf{x}} .$$

Thus, the matrix formula for the sample mean of a single variable, $X$, is

$$\bar{X} = \frac{1}{N}\mathbf{1'x}.$$

With the example data, the matrix calculation of the mean is

$$\bar{X} = \frac{1}{5}[1 \ \ 1 \ \ 1 \ \ 1 \ \ 1]\begin{bmatrix} 3 \\ 4 \\ 6 \\ 2 \\ 5 \end{bmatrix} = \frac{1}{5}[20] = 4.$$

Next, rather than a single variable, consider a $(N \times P)$ data matrix $\mathbf{X}$, containing data for $P$ variables. For example, $\mathbf{X}$ could contain scores for $N = 5$ participants on $P = 3$ variables, $X_1$, $X_2$, and $X_3$:

$$\mathbf{X} = \begin{bmatrix} 3 & 7.8 & 0 \\ 4 & 8.0 & 0 \\ 6 & 8.2 & 1 \\ 2 & 7.9 & 1 \\ 5 & 8.1 & 1 \end{bmatrix}.$$

We would like to calculate the mean of each column (i.e., each variable) of $\mathbf{X}$. These three means will be collected in the vector $\bar{\mathbf{X}}' = \begin{bmatrix} \bar{X}_1 & \bar{X}_2 & \bar{X}_3 \end{bmatrix}$. The matrix formula for calculating a vector of means from a $(N \times P)$ data matrix is

$$\underset{(1\times P)}{\bar{\mathbf{X}}'} = \frac{1}{N} \underset{(1\times N)}{\mathbf{1'}} \underset{(N\times P)}{\mathbf{X}} .$$

Notice that this formula is a simple generalization of the matrix formula for calculating the mean of a single variable, in that the dimension of the data matrix has expanded from $(N \times 1)$ to $(N \times P)$. With the example data matrix, the means are calculated as

$$\bar{\mathbf{X}}' = \frac{1}{5}[1 \ \ 1 \ \ 1 \ \ 1 \ \ 1]\begin{bmatrix} 3 & 7.8 & 0 \\ 4 & 8.0 & 0 \\ 6 & 8.2 & 1 \\ 2 & 7.9 & 1 \\ 5 & 8.1 & 1 \end{bmatrix} = [4 \ \ 8.0 \ \ 0.6] = \begin{bmatrix} \bar{X}_1 & \bar{X}_2 & \bar{X}_3 \end{bmatrix}.$$

## Variance and covariance

Using scalar terms, the formula for the unbiased sample variance of a single variable $X_i$ is

$$s^2 = \frac{1}{N-1}\sum_{i=1}^{N}(X_i - \bar{X})^2.$$

An analogous matrix algebra approach to calculating the variance of $X$ involves first calculating a vector of deviation scores, $\mathbf{x}_D$:

$$\mathbf{x}_D = \mathbf{x} - \mathbf{1}\bar{X}.$$

For example, using the same data vector given earlier,

$$\mathbf{x} = \begin{bmatrix} 3 \\ 4 \\ 6 \\ 2 \\ 5 \end{bmatrix}, \text{ which has } \bar{X} = 4,$$

the deviation scores are

$$\mathbf{x}_D = \begin{bmatrix} 3 \\ 4 \\ 6 \\ 2 \\ 5 \end{bmatrix} - \begin{bmatrix} 1 \\ 1 \\ 1 \\ 1 \\ 1 \end{bmatrix} 4 = \begin{bmatrix} 3 \\ 4 \\ 6 \\ 2 \\ 5 \end{bmatrix} - \begin{bmatrix} 4 \\ 4 \\ 4 \\ 4 \\ 4 \end{bmatrix} = \begin{bmatrix} -1 \\ 0 \\ 2 \\ -2 \\ 1 \end{bmatrix}.$$

Given the deviation score vector, the matrix formula for the unbiased sample variance of $X$ is

$$s^2 = \frac{1}{N-1}\mathbf{x}_D'\mathbf{x}_D.$$

So with the example data, we have

$$s^2 = \frac{1}{4}\begin{bmatrix} -1 & 0 & 2 & -2 & 1 \end{bmatrix}\begin{bmatrix} -1 \\ 0 \\ 2 \\ -2 \\ 1 \end{bmatrix} = \frac{1}{4}10 = 2.5.$$

Next, again consider a complete $(N \times P)$ data matrix $\mathbf{X}$. To get the deviation scores for each column (i.e., each variable) in $\mathbf{X}$, generalize the deviation score formula from the previous paragraph to apply to a data matrix of dimension $(N \times P)$ rather than just $(N \times 1)$:

$$\underset{(N\times P)}{\mathbf{X}_D} = \underset{(N\times P)}{\mathbf{X}} - \underset{(N\times 1)}{\mathbf{1}}\underset{(1\times P)}{\bar{\mathbf{X}}'}.$$

Using the same data matrix given earlier,

$$\mathbf{X} = \begin{bmatrix} 3 & 7.8 & 0 \\ 4 & 8.0 & 0 \\ 6 & 8.2 & 1 \\ 2 & 7.9 & 1 \\ 5 & 8.1 & 1 \end{bmatrix}, \text{ which has } \bar{\mathbf{X}}' = \begin{bmatrix} 4 & 8.0 & 0.6 \end{bmatrix},$$

the matrix of deviation scores is calculated as

$$\mathbf{X_D} = \begin{bmatrix} 3 & 7.8 & 0 \\ 4 & 8.0 & 0 \\ 6 & 8.2 & 1 \\ 2 & 7.9 & 1 \\ 5 & 8.1 & 1 \end{bmatrix} - \begin{bmatrix} 1 \\ 1 \\ 1 \\ 1 \\ 1 \end{bmatrix} \begin{bmatrix} 4 & 8.0 & 0.6 \end{bmatrix},$$

leading to

$$\mathbf{X_D} = \begin{bmatrix} 3 & 7.8 & 0 \\ 4 & 8.0 & 0 \\ 6 & 8.2 & 1 \\ 2 & 7.9 & 1 \\ 5 & 8.1 & 1 \end{bmatrix} - \begin{bmatrix} 4 & 8 & .6 \\ 4 & 8 & .6 \\ 4 & 8 & .6 \\ 4 & 8 & .6 \\ 4 & 8 & .6 \end{bmatrix} = \begin{bmatrix} -1 & -0.2 & -0.6 \\ 0 & 0.0 & -0.6 \\ 2 & 0.2 & 0.4 \\ -2 & -0.1 & 0.4 \\ 1 & 0.1 & 0.4 \end{bmatrix}.$$

Now, given the matrix of deviation scores, the matrix formula

$$\mathbf{S} = \frac{1}{(N-1)} \mathbf{X_D'} \mathbf{X_D}$$

produces the complete **variance–covariance matrix** for data matrix $\mathbf{X}$. Because matrix $\mathbf{X_D}$ has dimension $(N \times P)$, it follows that the product $\mathbf{X_D'}\mathbf{X_D}$ will have dimension $(P \times P)$, and thus, the variance–covariance matrix $\mathbf{S}$ will also have dimension $(P \times P)$. Applying the example $\mathbf{X_D}$ from the previous paragraph,

$$\mathbf{S} = \frac{1}{N-1} \mathbf{X_D'} \mathbf{X_D} = \frac{1}{4} \begin{bmatrix} -1.0 & 0.0 & 2.0 & -2.0 & 1.0 \\ -0.2 & 0.0 & 0.2 & -0.1 & 0.1 \\ -0.6 & -0.6 & 0.4 & 0.4 & 0.4 \end{bmatrix} \begin{bmatrix} -1 & -0.2 & -0.6 \\ 0 & 0.0 & -0.6 \\ 2 & 0.2 & 0.4 \\ -2 & -0.1 & 0.4 \\ 1 & 0.1 & 0.4 \end{bmatrix},$$

which produces

$$\mathbf{S} = \frac{1}{4} \begin{bmatrix} 10.0 & 0.9 & 1.0 \\ 0.9 & 0.1 & 0.2 \\ 1.0 & 0.2 & 1.2 \end{bmatrix} = \begin{bmatrix} 2.5 & 0.225 & 0.25 \\ 0.225 & 0.025 & 0.05 \\ 0.25 & 0.05 & 0.3 \end{bmatrix}.$$

In a variance–covariance matrix $\mathbf{S}$, the diagonal elements are the variances of each column (i.e., each variable) in the original data matrix $\mathbf{X}$. For example, element $s_{11}$ is the variance of $X_1$, where $X_1$ is the variable represented in the first column of $\mathbf{X}$. The off-diagonal elements are product-moment covariances, each of which summarizes the linear relation between two variables, as described in Chapter 1. For example, element $s_{21}$ is the covariance between $X_2$ and $X_1$. A variance–covariance matrix is usually simply called a *covariance matrix*. Thus, it is important to keep in mind that a covariance matrix still has variances as its diagonal elements. In this sense, a variance can be thought of as 'the covariance of a variable with itself'.

## Standard deviation

Expressed using scalar terms, standard deviation $s$ is simply the square root of variance:

$$s = \sqrt{s^2} = (s^2)^{1/2}.$$

To get the standard deviations of each column (i.e., each variable) in a data matrix $\mathbf{X}$, we first need to define a diagonal matrix $\mathbf{D}$ which contains only the diagonal elements of the corresponding covariance matrix $\mathbf{S}$ calculated from $\mathbf{X}$:

$$\mathbf{D} = diag(\mathbf{S}).$$

Following from the example covariance matrix earlier,

$$\mathbf{D} = diag(\mathbf{S}) = diag \begin{bmatrix} 2.5 & 0.225 & 0.25 \\ 0.225 & 0.025 & 0.05 \\ 0.25 & 0.05 & 0.3 \end{bmatrix} = \begin{bmatrix} 2.5 & 0 & 0 \\ 0 & 0.025 & 0 \\ 0 & 0 & 0.3 \end{bmatrix}.$$

The standard deviations of the variables in $\mathbf{X}$ are then the diagonal elements of the matrix $\mathbf{D}^{1/2}$:

$$\mathbf{D}^{1/2} = \begin{bmatrix} 2.5^{1/2} & 0 & 0 \\ 0 & 0.025^{1/2} & 0 \\ 0 & 0 & 0.3^{1/2} \end{bmatrix} = \begin{bmatrix} 1.58 & 0 & 0 \\ 0 & 0.16 & 0 \\ 0 & 0 & 0.55 \end{bmatrix}.$$

(with rounding to two decimal places).

## Correlations

As presented in Chapter 1 (Equation 1.9), the sample product-moment correlation between two variables, $X$ and $Y$, can be calculated using scalar terms with

$$r_{XY} = \frac{s_{XY}}{\sqrt{s_X^2}\sqrt{s_Y^2}} = \frac{s_{XY}}{s_X s_Y},$$

where $s_X^2$ and $s_Y^2$ are the sample variances of $X$ and $Y$, $s_X$ and $s_Y$ are the standard deviations, and $s_{XY}$ is the product-moment covariance between $X$ and $Y$. To see how this scalar formula generalizes to a matrix formula, it is helpful to rearrange its terms as follows:

$$r_{XY} = \frac{s_{XY}}{\sqrt{s_X^2}\sqrt{s_Y^2}} = s_{XY} \left(s_X^2\right)^{-1/2} \left(s_Y^2\right)^{-1/2},$$

which then can be written as

$$r_{XY} = \left(s_X^2\right)^{-1/2} s_{XY} \left(s_Y^2\right)^{-1/2}.$$

The formula for converting a $P \times P$ sample covariance matrix, $\mathbf{S}$, for $P$ variables into the correlation matrix, $\mathbf{R}$, for these variables has an analogous form:

$$\mathbf{R} = \mathbf{D}^{-1/2}(\mathbf{S})\,\mathbf{D}^{-1/2},$$

where $\mathbf{D}$ is the $P \times P$ diagonal matrix of variances as defined earlier. By this process, the diagonal elements of $\mathbf{R}$ will always equal 1 and the off-diagonal elements will always fall between $-1$ and $+1$.

Following from the same three-variable running example used in the previous sections, we have

$$\mathbf{D}^{-1/2} = \begin{bmatrix} \dfrac{1}{2.5^{1/2}} & 0 & 0 \\ 0 & \dfrac{1}{0.025^{1/2}} & 0 \\ 0 & 0 & \dfrac{1}{0.3^{1/2}} \end{bmatrix} = \begin{bmatrix} \dfrac{1}{1.58} & 0 & 0 \\ 0 & \dfrac{1}{0.16} & 0 \\ 0 & 0 & \dfrac{1}{0.55} \end{bmatrix},$$

which leads to

$$\mathbf{R} = \mathbf{D}^{-1/2}\mathbf{S}\mathbf{D}^{-1/2} = \begin{bmatrix} \dfrac{1}{1.58} & 0 & 0 \\ 0 & \dfrac{1}{0.16} & 0 \\ 0 & 0 & \dfrac{1}{0.55} \end{bmatrix} \begin{bmatrix} 2.5 & 0.225 & 0.25 \\ 0.225 & 0.025 & 0.05 \\ 0.25 & 0.05 & 0.3 \end{bmatrix} \begin{bmatrix} \dfrac{1}{1.58} & 0 & 0 \\ 0 & \dfrac{1}{0.16} & 0 \\ 0 & 0 & \dfrac{1}{0.55} \end{bmatrix}.$$

Thus,

$$\mathbf{R} = \mathbf{D}^{-1/2}\mathbf{S}\mathbf{D}^{-1/2} = \begin{bmatrix} 1.00 & .90 & .29 \\ .90 & 1.00 & .58 \\ .29 & .58 & 1.00 \end{bmatrix},$$

which is indeed a symmetric matrix with diagonal elements equal to 1 and off-diagonal elements being product-moment correlations between $-1$ and $+1$.

 Section recap

### Matrix calculations for statistical applications

The vector of means of the columns (i.e., the variables) of a $(N \times P)$ data matrix $\mathbf{X}$ is

$$\underset{(1 \times P)}{\overline{\mathbf{X}}'} = \frac{1}{N}\underset{(1 \times N)}{\mathbf{1}'}\underset{(N \times P)}{\mathbf{X}}$$

where $\mathbf{1}'$ is a *unit vector* in which all elements equal 1.

The symmetric $(P \times P)$ **variance-covariance matrix** of a $(N \times P)$ data matrix $\mathbf{X}$ is

$$\mathbf{S} = \frac{1}{(N-1)}\mathbf{X}_D'\mathbf{X}_D$$

where $\mathbf{X}_D$ is a matrix of deviation scores calculated as $\underset{(N \times P)}{\mathbf{X}_D} = \underset{(N \times P)}{\mathbf{X}} - \underset{(N \times 1)}{\mathbf{1}} \underset{(1 \times P)}{\overline{\mathbf{X}}'}$ .

The diagonal elements of the covariance matrix $\mathbf{S}$ are the variances of the columns of $\mathbf{X}$, and the off-diagonal elements are the covariances among the columns of $\mathbf{X}$.

The standard deviations of the data matrix $\mathbf{X}$ are the diagonal elements of $\mathbf{D}^{1/2}$, where $\mathbf{D} = diag(\mathbf{S})$ is a diagonal matrix which contains only the diagonal elements (i.e., the variances) of the corresponding covariance matrix $\mathbf{S}$.

The symmetric $(P \times P)$ **correlation matrix** of a $(N \times P)$ data matrix $\mathbf{X}$ is

$$\mathbf{R} = \mathbf{D}^{-1/2}(\mathbf{S}) \, \mathbf{D}^{-1/2},$$

where $\mathbf{D}$ is again the diagonal matrix containing only the diagonal elements of the corresponding covariance matrix $\mathbf{S}$.

## Matrix equations for linear regression

The multiple linear regression model with one outcome variable and $P$ predictors can be expressed in matrix form as

$$\mathbf{Y} = \mathbf{X}\boldsymbol{\beta} + \boldsymbol{\varepsilon},$$

where $\mathbf{Y}$ is a vector of outcome scores for $N$ cases or individuals, $\mathbf{X}$ is a $(N \times (P + 1))$ matrix of scores on the $P$ predictor variables (as well as a column containing a constant equal to 1), $\boldsymbol{\beta}$ is a vector of $(P + 1)$ population linear slope coefficients (including an intercept parameter), and $\boldsymbol{\varepsilon}$ is a vector of error terms for the $N$ cases. Written another way, this matrix equation (for $P > 2$) is

$$\begin{bmatrix} y_1 \\ y_2 \\ \vdots \\ y_N \end{bmatrix} = \begin{bmatrix} 1 & x_{11} & x_{12} & \cdots & x_{1P} \\ 1 & x_{21} & x_{22} & \cdots & x_{2P} \\ \vdots & \vdots & \vdots & & \vdots \\ 1 & x_{N1} & x_{N2} & \cdots & x_{NP} \end{bmatrix} \begin{bmatrix} \beta_0 \\ \beta_1 \\ \vdots \\ \beta_P \end{bmatrix} + \begin{bmatrix} \varepsilon_1 \\ \varepsilon_2 \\ \vdots \\ \varepsilon_N \end{bmatrix}.$$

It is critical to realize that the matrix of predictor variables values, $\mathbf{X}$ (which is often referred to as the *design matrix*), has as its first column a constant value equal to 1 for all rows (i.e., all $N$ cases). This constant is included so that the intercept parameter, $\beta_0$, is used to model $Y$ for each case. One way to think about the intercept is that it is the regression coefficient for a 'variable' which is a constant value (=1) for each case. To illustrate, recall that a matrix equation is essentially a collection of separate scalar equations. Here, the regression matrix equation is a collection of $N$ individual linear equations, one for each of $i = 1, 2,..., N$ individuals. For a generic individual case $i$, the regression equation is

$$y_i = \beta_0 1 + \beta_1 x_{i1} + \beta_2 x_{i2} + \dots + \beta_P x_{iP} + \varepsilon_i,$$

which, of course, is mathematically the same as the more familiar expression

$$y_i = \beta_0 + \beta_1 x_{i1} + \beta_2 x_{i2} + \dots + \beta_P x_{iP} + \varepsilon_i.$$

The only difference between these two scalar equations is that the first explicitly indicates that the regression intercept parameter is the coefficient for a 'variable' which is set to equal 1 for all $N$ cases. Therefore this 'variable' is a constant, not a variable, which is why output from statistical software often reports the intercept estimate on a row labeled 'Constant' rather than 'Intercept'.

Recall from Chapter 2 that the regression parameters, that is, the intercept and slope coefficients in $\beta$, are usually estimated from sample data using the ordinary least-squares (OLS) method, which minimizes the sum of the squared residuals, $SS_e$. In matrix terms, the OLS solution for $\beta$ is obtained by minimizing the result of the (estimated) error vector $\hat{\varepsilon}$ premultiplied by its transpose; it turns out that $\hat{\varepsilon}'\hat{\varepsilon} = SS_e$. Because the estimated regression model

$$\mathbf{Y} = \mathbf{X}\hat{\beta} + \hat{\varepsilon}$$

implies

$$\hat{\varepsilon} = \mathbf{Y} - \mathbf{X}\hat{\beta},$$

minimizing $\hat{\varepsilon}'\hat{\varepsilon}$ is equivalent to finding a vector of parameter estimates, $\hat{\beta}$, which minimizes the value of $f$ in the matrix function

$$f = (\mathbf{Y} - \mathbf{X}\hat{\beta})'(\mathbf{Y} - \mathbf{X}\hat{\beta}).$$

Solving this minimization problem (which requires calculus) leads to the OLS solution

$$\hat{\beta} = (\mathbf{X}'\mathbf{X})^{-1}\mathbf{X}'\mathbf{Y}.$$

The $(N \times 1)$ vector of outcome variable predicted values, $\hat{\mathbf{Y}}$, from the estimated regression model is thus

$$\hat{\mathbf{Y}} = \mathbf{X}\hat{\beta} = \mathbf{X}(\mathbf{X}'\mathbf{X})^{-1}\mathbf{X}'\mathbf{Y},$$

or simply $\hat{\mathbf{Y}} = \mathbf{H}\mathbf{Y}$ where $\mathbf{H} = \mathbf{X}(\mathbf{X}'\mathbf{X})^{-1}\mathbf{X}'$. This matrix $\mathbf{H}$ is commonly called the **hat matrix**. Recall from Chapter 1 that another name for the leverage of a given case is *hat value*; the reason for this term is that the leverage values are the diagonal elements of the hat matrix.

 Section recap

### Matrix equations for linear regression

Expressed in matrix form, the multiple linear regression model is

$$\mathbf{Y} = \mathbf{X}\beta + \varepsilon,$$

where
  **Y** is a vector of outcome variable scores for $N$ cases or individuals

**X** is a $(N \times (P + 1))$ matrix of scores on the $P$ predictor variables (as well as a column containing a constant equal to 1)

$\boldsymbol{\beta}$ is a vector of $(P + 1)$ population linear slope coefficients (including an intercept parameter)

$\boldsymbol{\varepsilon}$ is a vector of error terms for the $N$ cases

The OLS solution for $\boldsymbol{\beta}$ is obtained by minimizing $\hat{\boldsymbol{\varepsilon}}'\hat{\boldsymbol{\varepsilon}}$, which is equivalent to finding the parameter estimates $\hat{\boldsymbol{\beta}}$ which minimize the function $f = (\mathbf{Y} - \mathbf{X}\hat{\boldsymbol{\beta}})'(\mathbf{Y} - \mathbf{X}\hat{\boldsymbol{\beta}})$.

The resulting OLS solution is $\hat{\boldsymbol{\beta}} = (\mathbf{X}'\mathbf{X})^{-1}\mathbf{X}'\mathbf{Y}$.

---

## Eigenvalues and eigenvectors

Many multivariate statistical procedures rely on calculation of the **eigenstructure** of certain symmetric matrices, such as covariance and correlation matrices. The eigenstructure of a symmetric matrix **S** can be expressed as

$$\mathbf{S} = \mathbf{U}\mathbf{D}\mathbf{U}', \tag{7.1}$$

where the columns of **U** are **eigenvectors** and **D** is a diagonal matrix with **eigenvalues** as diagonal elements (this **D** is not the same as the **D** matrix used earlier to calculate a covariance matrix). Eigenvalues and eigenvectors are also sometimes called *characteristic roots and vectors*.

Taking a few steps back, if **S** is a $(P \times P)$ symmetric matrix, **u** is a vector of length $P$, and $\lambda$ is a scalar such that

$$\mathbf{S}\mathbf{u} = \lambda\mathbf{u}, \tag{7.2}$$

then $\lambda$ is an eigenvalue of **S** and **u** is the corresponding eigenvector. The potential value of this relation may seem readily apparent: On the left-hand side of the equation, **u** is premultiplied by a full $(P \times P)$ matrix (i.e., **S**), but on the right-hand side, this matrix has been replaced by a single scalar term (i.e., $\lambda$). It is as if all of the numerical information in **S** has been collapsed into a single value, $\lambda$.

But for any given symmetric matrix, there will generally be more than one nonzero eigenvalue–eigenvector combination which satisfies Equation 7.2. Specifically, a $(P \times P)$ symmetric matrix has $P$ eigenvalues that are typically ordered from largest to smallest,

$$\lambda_1 \geq \lambda_2 \geq ... \geq \lambda_P,$$

and are respectively associated with eigenvectors

$$\mathbf{u}_1, \mathbf{u}_2, ..., \mathbf{u}_P.$$

The eigenvalues are arranged in descending order as the diagonal elements of a diagonal matrix

$$\mathbf{D} = \begin{bmatrix} \lambda_1 & 0 & \cdots & 0 \\ 0 & \lambda_2 & \cdots & 0 \\ \vdots & \vdots & \ddots & \vdots \\ 0 & 0 & \cdots & \lambda_P \end{bmatrix}$$

and the corresponding eigenvectors can be collected as columns in a matrix $\mathbf{U}$ (such that the first column of $\mathbf{U}$ is $\mathbf{u}_1$, the second column is $\mathbf{u}_2$, and so on). Next, Equation 7.2 can be expanded to

$$\mathbf{SU} = \mathbf{UD},$$

now showing that the original symmetric matrix multiplied by the set of eigenvectors can be expressed as the product of the eigenvectors and a simple diagonal matrix containing the eigenvalues. The matrix of eigenvectors $\mathbf{U}$ is *orthogonal*, meaning that $\mathbf{UU}' = \mathbf{I}$. Consequently, the latter equation can be rearranged to produce Equation 7.1, the eigenstructure equation for symmetric matrix $\mathbf{S}$.

If all eigenvalues of a symmetric matrix are positive, then the matrix is considered **positive definite**. Certain statistical estimation algorithms require positive-definite covariance (or correlation) matrices because nonpositive definite matrices are singular and cannot be inverted. Similarly, an estimated model implying a nonpositive definite covariance matrix of parameter estimates (i.e., in the multivariate sampling distribution of the estimates) is said to represent an *improper solution* which should not be interpreted. Ocassionally a statistical software procedure produces error messages indicating that results could not be obtained (or that the results that were obtained may be improper) because a particular matrix is nonpositive definite or singular.

 Section recap

### Eigenvalues and eigenvectors

Any square, symmetric matrix can be decomposed into its eigenstructure, which is a useful operation for certain advanced statistical applications.

The eigenstructure of a symmetric matrix $\mathbf{S}$ can be expressed as

$$\mathbf{S} = \mathbf{UDU}',$$

where the columns of $\mathbf{U}$ are **eigenvectors** and $\mathbf{D}$ is a diagonal matrix with **eigenvalues** as diagonal elements.

If all eigenvalues of a symmetric matrix are positive, then the matrix is **positive definite**. Certain statistical procedures require that a covariance (or correlation) matrix be positive definite.

## CHAPTER SUMMARY

This chapter was unique in that no new statistical procedures were introduced. Rather, the chapter gave a gentle introduction to matrix algebra:

- Expressing mathematical relations using matrices greatly facilitates the ability to describe multivariate statistical methods; a set of $Q$ separate equations can often be expressed using a single, compact matrix equation.

- Matrix operations form the foundation for all statistical computing.
- A matrix is an organized, rectangular array of quantities known as elements. Most often, an element is a single scalar term, such as a numerical value or an algebraic symbol representing some numerical value.

## RECOMMENDED READING

Carroll, J.D., Green, P.E., & Chaturvedi, A. (1997). *Mathematical tools for applied multivariate analysis: Revised edition.* San Diego, CA: Academic Press.

Fox, J. (2009). *A mathematical primer for social statistics.* Thousand Oaks, CA: SAGE.

These two texts are recommended for mathematically inclined readers who are interested in much more detail about matrix operations than given in the current chapter. As their titles indicate, both texts focus on the key matrix operations for statistical applications rather than other uses of matrix algebra (of which there are many). The Fox (2009) primer is less technical than the Carroll et al. (1997) text, although the latter is also elementary with respect to the field of matrix algebra.

# EXPLORATORY FACTOR ANALYSIS

## CHAPTER OVERVIEW

Exploratory factor analysis (EFA) is a well-known (and occasionally controversial) multivariate statistical technique which originated in the field of psychometrics but has been diversified to other areas in the behavioural and social sciences. After detailing EFA for the context of continuous observed variables, this chapter moves on to discuss the use of EFA of categorical observed variables (such as the individual items in a questionnaire). The main topics of this chapter include:

- Purpose of exploratory factor analysis
- Specification of the common factor model
- Communality and uniqueness
- Estimation of the common factor model

    o   Principal axis estimation
    o   Unweighted least-squares estimation
    o   Maximum likelihood estimation

- Determining the optimal number of common factors
- Factor rotation

    o   Orthogonal and oblique rotations
    o   Factor pattern versus factor structure

- Exploratory factor analysis with categorical observed variables
- Assumptions and diagnostics for EFA

**Table 8.0**  Greek letter notation used in this chapter

| Greek letter | English name | Represents |
|---|---|---|
| λ | Lowercase 'lambda' | Factor loading parameter |
| ε | Lowercase 'epsilon' | Regression error term (unique factor) |
| Λ | Uppercase 'lambda' | Factor loading matrix |
| P | Uppercase 'rho' | Population observed variable correlation matrix |
| Ψ | Uppercase 'psy' | Interfactor correlation matrix |
| Θ | Uppercase 'theta' | Error covariance matrix |
| χ | Lowercase 'chi' | $\chi^2$ distribution |
| τ | Lowercase 'tau' | Threshold parameter |

*Note.* This use of τ differs from that in Chapter 6 on multilevel modeling.

## WHAT IS EXPLORATORY FACTOR ANALYSIS?

Factor analysis, particularly **exploratory factor analysis** (or **EFA**), holds a prominent place in the history of empirical research in psychology, especially psychometric research on intelligence and cognitive abilities. From that beginning, the use of factor analysis spread to research on personality and psychopathology, among other areas of psychology, and has since spread to other social sciences. The general purpose of factor analysis is to develop a model which represents the pattern of associations among a potentially large number of empirically observed variables in terms of a small number of unobserved, or **latent**, variables. A latent variable is also referred to as a **factor** in the factor analysis literature.[1] In behavioural and social research, these factors typically represent constructs which cannot be directly measured, such as intelligence, attitudes, cognitive abilities, personality traits, preferences, and so on. Thus, factor analysis is commonly used in psychometric research to establish whether and to what extent certain observed, operational variables can be used to represent hypothetical latent variables or constructs.

Factor analysis originally developed as a method for representing the pattern of correlations obtained by administering many different tests to a sample of research participants. Scores from these tests typically elicited continuously distributed observed variables, and thus, it was natural for factor analysis to develop as a method for analysing Pearson product-moment correlation matrices according to Thurstone's (1947) *common factor model*. Eventually, researchers recognized that this common factor model was a linear model with continuous observed variables as outcome variables and the factors as explanatory predictors (Bartholomew, 2007, traces this history). In modern research, however, factor analysis is most commonly used to model the responses to individual items from one test or questionnaire, rather than to model total scores from many different tests or scales. Yet, because the most common kinds of

---

[1] In the general field of statistics, the term *factor* is commonly used to refer to any categorical (or discrete) variable. For instance, the phrase *factorial ANOVA* refers to the fact that ANOVA is used to test differences resulting from one or more categorical independent variables. Conversely, in factor analysis (and psychometrics in general), the word *factor* most often refers to any unobserved, or latent, variable. Usually these factors are assumed to be continuous, but there are methods for categorical latent variables.

test and questionnaire items, including Likert-type items, produce categorical variables (with dichotomous or ordered item-response categories) rather than continuous variables, this traditional linear factor analysis model for product-moment $\mathbf{R}$ is often problematic. Instead, alternative methods for factor analysing categorical, item-level variables are preferable for many applications.

Thus, the first part of this chapter presents EFA using the traditional, linear factor analysis model for analysing a Pearson product-moment correlation matrix $\mathbf{R}$, working through an example in which the observed variables are the total scores from a battery of nine different psychological tests. The second part of the chapter describes one prominent alternative method for EFA with item-level variables, namely, the factor analysis of *polychoric correlations*, working through an example in which the observed variables are 20 items from a single test. Because of the modern prevalence of EFA as an item-analysis procedure, this polychoric correlation method is more likely to be appropriate for readers wishing to perform EFA for their own research than is the traditional analysis of product-moment $\mathbf{R}$. But because this alternative method is a generalization of the traditional, linear factor analysis modeling approach, the first part of the chapter provides many of the basic, foundational principles needed to understand the alternative method presented later.

 Section recap

### Purpose of exploratory factor analysis

The general purpose of **exploratory factor analysis** (or **EFA**) is to develop a model which represents the pattern of associations among a potentially large number of empirically observed variables in terms of a small number of **factors**, which are **latent variables**.

The **common factor model** developed as a linear model with continuous test scores as outcome variables and the factors as explanatory predictors.

But in modern research, factor analysis is most commonly used to model the responses to individual items from one test or questionnaire, rather than to model total scores from many different tests.

The traditional linear factor analysis model does not work as well for individual item-level variables because they are typically categorical rather than continuous. Therefore, alternative methods for factor analysing categorical, item-level variables are preferable for many applications.

## EFA WITH CONTINUOUS OBSERVED VARIABLES

If there are many observed variables in a study, the pattern of correlations among them may be difficult to describe and understand. Some correlations may be large and others may be small or even near zero, and some may be positive and others may be negative. Inevitably, even if all correlations among the variables are large, a certain amount of variation will occur among them. Typically, a researcher will have some idea, based on substantive theory, that there is a conceptual theme underlying at least a few variables that helps explain why they are correlated. Often, the researcher will even have predictions that one or more particular theoretical constructs are causally related to certain observed variables. But if the theory is not strong enough to produce explicit, a priori hypotheses about which observed variables are directly measured by which constructs or there is little previous relevant research, then *exploratory* factor analysis is an appropriate method for modeling the pattern of correlations among the observed variables (as opposed to *confirmatory factor analysis*, which is covered in Chapter 10). When these observed variables are continuously distributed, product-moment correlations are often reasonable representations of their bivariate associations (see Chapter 1), which leads to the expression of EFA as a type of linear model, as we will see shortly.

## RESEARCH EXAMPLE FOR EFA WITH CONTINUOUS OBSERVED VARIABLES

In the process of developing a new self-report questionnaire called the Social Appearance Anxiety Scale (SAAS), Hart et al. (2008) administered this test to a sample of research participants as a part of a larger battery of other psychological tests purported to measure different aspects of social anxiety and body image. Specifically, $N = 109$ university students completed the SAAS in addition to the Brief Fear of Negative Evaluation Scale (BFNE), the Social Interaction Anxiety Scale (SIAS), the Social Phobia Scale (SPS), the Social Physique Anxiety Scale (SPAS), the Body-Image Ideals Questionnaire (BIQ), the Appearance Schemas Inventory (ASI), and finally the Appearance Evaluation (APEVAL) and Overweight-Preoccupation (OWPRE) subscales from the Multidimensional Body-Self Relations Questionnaire (see Hart et al. for references and descriptions of each of these tests). The researchers were interested in examining the latent structure of these nine tests; that is, they wanted to determine whether and how certain unobserved factors accounted for the pattern of correlations among the participants' scores on the tests.

This dataset is available on the text's webpage (https://study.sagepub.com/flora) along with annotated input and output from several popular statistical software packages showing how to reproduce the analyses presented in this chapter.

The product-moment correlation matrix **R** for the nine tests is given in Table 8.1. Although all of the correlations are statistically significant (all *ps* < .05), some are much stronger than others, and although most are positive, a few are negative. Given such a set of varying correlations among a set of observed variables, EFA may be used to uncover and understand the structure that produces the particular pattern of correlations. The main idea of EFA is that there exists a small number of factors, which are latent variables, within a given topic domain. These factors influence the observed variables to varying extents, thereby producing the correlations among them.

### Specification of the common factor model

As mentioned, although various other factoring methods were developed over the 20th century, Thurstone's (1947) **common factor model** represents the dominant approach to EFA that is in continuous use today. In the common factor model, observed variables (which are also sometimes referred to as *manifest variables* or *measured variables*) depend on

**Table 8.1** Product-moment correlations among nine social anxiety and body image variables

|  | BFNE | SIAS | SPS | SPAS | BIQ | ASI | APEVAL | OWPRE | SAAS |
|---|---|---|---|---|---|---|---|---|---|
| BFNE | 1.00 | – | – | – | – | – | – | – | – |
| SIAS | .71 | 1.00 | – | – | – | – | – | – | – |
| SPS | .67 | .80 | 1.00 | – | – | – | – | – | – |
| SPAS | .61 | .46 | .46 | 1.00 | – | – | – | – | – |
| BIQ | .64 | .48 | .41 | .63 | 1.00 | – | – | – | – |
| ASI | .53 | .33 | .45 | .49 | .59 | 1.00 | – | – | – |
| APEVAL | –.51 | –.45 | –.40 | –.78 | –.53 | –.34 | 1.00 | – | – |
| OWPRE | .39 | .31 | .37 | .59 | .47 | .43 | –.43 | 1.00 | – |
| SAAS | .81 | .76 | .77 | .59 | .57 | .48 | –.55 | .37 | 1.00 |

*Note. N = 109.*

two different types of latent variables, or factors. First, **common factors** directly influence more than one observed variable and account for the correlations among all observed variables (a given model might have only one common factor). Additionally, the common factors explain some portion of the variance of each observed variable. Second, a **unique factor** influences only one observed variable and explains the portion of the observed variable's variance that is not explained by common factors. Unique factors do not explain correlations among observed variables. Theoretically, each unique factor has two parts, a *specific* part representing systematic factors affecting only a single given observed variable, and an *error* part representing random variation. It is important to keep in mind, though, that the specific and error parts of a unique factor are theoretical and cannot be separated statistically within a given model.

A major aspect of EFA is determining the smallest number of factors, $M$, needed to explain adequately the relations among $P$ observed variables (i.e., the *battery* of observed variables) using both statistical and interpretational criteria. Although the number of common factors $M$ for a given battery can be any number from $M = 1$ to $M = P$, $M$ is usually presumed to be much smaller than $P$.

Given these ideas, the common factor model is a linear function which relates a given observed variable to the set of common factors and a unique factor. A general form of this linear equation is

$$Y_{pi} = \left( \sum_{m=1}^{M} \lambda_{pm} f_{mi} \right) + \varepsilon_{pi}, \tag{8.1}$$

where $Y_{pi}$ is the observed score on the $p$th observed variable for individual $i$, $f_{mi}$ is the score on the $m$th common factor for individual $i$, $\lambda_{pm}$ is the **factor loading** of the $p$th observed variable on the $m$th factor, and $\varepsilon_{pi}$ is the value on the $j$th unique factor for individual $i$. If there is only one common factor (i.e., $M = 1$), then Equation 8.1 simplifies to

$$Y_{pi} = \lambda_{p1} f_{1i} + \varepsilon_{pi}.$$

If there are two common factors ($M = 2$), the model is

$$Y_{pi} = \lambda_{p1}f_{1i} + \lambda_{p2}f_{2i} + \varepsilon_{pi},$$

and so on to the general form of Equation 8.1.

Thus, it should be evident that the common factor model is essentially a linear multiple regression model in which a given observed variable ($Y$) is the outcome and the common factors ($f_1...f_M$) are the predictor variables.[2] A factor loading is therefore a partial regression slope coefficient giving the strength of the linear relation between the $m$th common factor and the $p$th observed variable (holding the other common factors constant), and the unique factor is analogous to the error term in a multiple regression model. Yet, because a common factor is a latent variable, scores on this variable, which are termed **factor scores**, are unknown and indeterminate; one is never able to determine their values exactly.[3] Thus, the major statistical problem in EFA is to estimate the regression coefficients (i.e., the factor loadings) despite that values for the predictor variables are not available; the ordinary least-squares (OLS) estimation method for multiple regression described in earlier chapters cannot be used.

Equation 8.1 is a scalar equation giving the model for the $p$th of $P$ observed variables; in other words, the model specifies a separate regression equation for each observed variable. Because there are multiple observed variables, which are outcome variables, this is a type of multivariate multiple regression problem. Thus, the EFA of $P$ observed variables implies a set of $P$ scalar regression equations. These separate scalar equations can be compactly represented using a single matrix equation:

$$\mathbf{Y} = \mathbf{\Lambda}\mathbf{f} + \boldsymbol{\varepsilon}, \qquad (8.2)$$

where $\mathbf{Y}$ is the $P \times 1$ vector of observed variables, $\mathbf{\Lambda}$ is a $P \times M$ **factor loading matrix** (also known as the *factor pattern matrix*), $\mathbf{f}$ is the $M \times 1$ vector of common factors, and $\boldsymbol{\varepsilon}$ is the $P \times 1$ vector of unique factors. Just as the slope coefficients are the major parameters to be interpreted in regular multiple regression, the factor loading matrix includes the major parameters that are the focus in an EFA. Although they are not apparent in Equation 8.2, the other parameters of the model include the correlations among the common factors and the variances of the unique factors.

We will see how to estimate the EFA parameters from data shortly, but first we consider an estimated factor loading matrix for the example data from nine social anxiety tests, given

---

[2]But notice that there is no intercept parameter in Equation 8.1. Because EFA is (usually) an analysis of a correlation matrix, information about the measurement scales of the observed variables is not included, which implies that the intercept parameter equals 0. It is possible (if unusual), though, to specify and estimate EFA models with nonzero intercepts.

[3]But once a given factor model is estimated, there are methods for obtaining factor score estimates. MacCallum (2009: 134–35) presented factor scoring methods and discussed this historically contentious issue, ultimately recommending that research questions involving individual factor scores be examined using full structural equation models (see Chapter 10) rather than calculating factor score estimates to be used in subsequent analyses.

in Table 8.2. Because there are $P = 9$ observed variables and $M = 2$ factors, this factor loading matrix has dimension $9 \times 2$. Drawing from Equation 8.2, the elements of this matrix are the (estimated) regression coefficients relating each observed variable to each factor. For example, for the BFNE observed variable, the estimated regression equation is

$$Y_{1i} = 0.69f_{1i} + 0.24f_{2i} + e_{1i},$$

whereas for the SPAS observed variable, the estimated regression equation is

$$Y_{1i} = -0.03f_{1i} + 0.96f_{2i} + e_{1i}.$$

Because the EFA model is established such that the common factors all have variance equal to 1 (i.e., the predictor variables in the regression equation all have the same scale), we can conclude from the factor loadings that BFNE is more strongly related to the first factor than the second, whereas SPAS has a strong relation, or *salient* loading, on the second factor but not the first. More specifically, because a factor loading is a partial regression coefficient, a 1-standard-deviation increase in $f_1$ predicts a 0.69 increase in the observed BFNE score (holding $f_2$ constant), whereas a 1-standard-deviation increase in $f_2$ predicts only a 0.24 increase in the observed BFNE score (holding $f_1$ constant). Based on interpretation of the factor loading pattern, researchers usually ascribe a conceptual label to each factor. For example, here $f_1$ might be labeled 'social interaction anxiety' because of the shared conceptual content of the BFNE, SIAS, SPS, and SAAS tests, each of which has a salient loading on $f_1$. Next, $f_2$ might be labeled 'body image concern' because of the shared conceptual content of the SPAS, BIQ, APEVAL, and OWPRE tests. A situation where it is difficult to ascertain a shared conceptual content among observed variables with salient loadings on a given factor might indicate that the number of factors $M$ of the estimated model is either too small or too large.[4]

**Table 8.2** Estimated factor loading matrix for two-factor model of social anxiety data

| Variable | $f_1$ | $f_2$ |
|---|---|---|
| BFNE | 0.69 | 0.24 |
| SIAS | 0.92 | −0.07 |
| SPS | 0.92 | −0.08 |
| SPAS | −0.03 | 0.96 |
| BIQ | 0.24 | 0.55 |
| ASI | 0.26 | 0.39 |
| APEVAL | −0.02 | −0.79 |
| OWPRE | 0.01 | 0.61 |
| SAAS | 0.81 | 0.14 |

[4]Assuming that the estimated factor pattern has been *rotated*; the topic of factor rotation is addressed later in this chapter.

## Section recap

**Specification of the common factor model**

A major goal of EFA is to determine the number of common factors, $M$, that adequately explain the pattern of correlations among a set of $P$ observed variables.

Given a choice of the value of $M$, the common factor model relates these $M$ latent variables, or factors, to the observed variables with a linear regression function:

$$Y_{pi} = \left( \sum_{m=1}^{M} \lambda_{pm} f_{mi} \right) + \varepsilon_{pi}$$

where

$Y_{pi}$ is the score on the $p$th observed variable for individual $i$

$f_{mi}$ is the score on the $m$th **common factor** for individual $i$

$\lambda_{pm}$ is the **factor loading** (a type of partial regression slope coefficient) relating the $m$th common factor to the $p$th observed variable

$\varepsilon_{pi}$ is the score on the $p$th **unique factor** (a type of linear regression error term) for individual $i$.

Because there is a separate version of the scalar regression equation for each of the $P$ observed variables, these equations can be collected into a single matrix equation to represent the common factor model:

$$\mathbf{Y} = \mathbf{\Lambda f} + \mathbf{\varepsilon},$$

where

$\mathbf{Y}$ is the $P \times 1$ vector of observed variables

$\mathbf{\Lambda}$ is a $P \times M$ **factor loading matrix** (also known as the *factor pattern matrix*)

$\mathbf{f}$ is the $M \times 1$ vector of common factors

$\mathbf{\varepsilon}$ is the $P \times 1$ vector of unique factors

Therefore, the common factor model is a linear regression model in which the actual values of the predictor variables, the **factor scores**, are unknown. Consequently, the OLS formulas for multiple regression presented in Chapters 1 and 2 cannot be used to obtain estimates of the regression slope parameters, or factor loadings, in $\mathbf{\Lambda}$.

# Communality and uniqueness

As detailed in Chapter 2, the squared multiple correlation (also known as the coefficient of determination), denoted $\rho^2$ as a population parameter and $R^2$ as a sample estimate of the parameter, is a prominent quantity for describing a given multiple regression model. Specifically, the squared multiple correlation represents the proportion of variance in an outcome variable that is explained by the model's linear combination of predictor variables. Because the common factor model is a type of regression model, an analogous quantity, known as the **communality**, can be obtained for each observed variable in the context of EFA. In particular, the communality of a given observed variable represents the proportion of that variable's variance that is explained by the EFA model's linear combination of factors. Although the concept of communality is especially important for the development of *principal axis estimation* (described later in this chapter), communality estimates are also useful descriptive statistics for evaluating the quality of any estimated factor model. Unfortunately, in practice, researchers often overlook interpretation of communality estimates.

Repeating Equation 8.1, the scalar regression equation for a particular observed variable in an EFA is

$$Y_{pi} = \left( \sum_{m=1}^{M} \lambda_{pm} f_{mi} \right) + \varepsilon_{pi}.$$

Given this equation, the variance of $Y$ can be expressed as

$$VAR(Y_{pi}) = VAR\left( \left( \sum_{m=1}^{M} \lambda_{pm} f_{mi} \right) + \varepsilon_{pi} \right),$$

which can then be written as

$$VAR(Y_{pi}) = VAR\left( \sum_{m=1}^{M} \lambda_{pm} f_{mi} \right) + VAR\left( \varepsilon_{pi} \right).$$

This expression indicates that the variance of an observed variable can be partitioned into two terms: variance resulting from the common factors, or *common variance*, and variance resulting from the unique factor, or *unique variance*. The communality for observed variable $p$, or $h_p^2$, is the ratio of common variance to total variance; in other words, it is the proportion of observed variance that is explained by the common factors. The communality of the $p$th observed variable can be expressed formally as

$$h_p^2 = \frac{VAR\left( \sum_{m=1}^{M} \lambda_{pm} f_{mi} \right)}{VAR(Y_p)} = \frac{1 - VAR(\varepsilon_p)}{VAR(Y_p)}.$$

Next, the **uniqueness** of observed variable $p$, or $u_p^2$, is the proportion of observed variance of $Y_p$ that is not explained by the common factors:

$$u_p^2 = \frac{VAR(\varepsilon_p)}{VAR(Y_p)}$$

or

$$u_p^2 = 1 - h_p^2.$$

As these expressions suggest, it is always the case that the sum of the communality and uniqueness of a given observed variable equals 1; in other words, taken together, the common factors and the unique factor account for 100% of the observed variance of a given $Y_p$.

To illustrate briefly, the estimated two-factor model for the social anxiety example produces $\hat{h}^2 = 0.74$ for the BFNE observed variable but only $\hat{h}^2 = 0.38$ for the OWPRE variable. This small communality for OWPRE implies that either this observed variable has a large proportion of pure random error or there are additional systematic factors beyond $f_1$ ('social anxiety') and $f_2$ ('negative body image') which account for the observed variance of OWPRE.[5]

 Section recap

### Communality and uniqueness

In a given EFA model, the **communality** of the $p$th observed variable, $h_p^2$, is the proportion of variance explained by the set of common factors.

The communality is therefore the EFA version of the squared multiple correlation (the estimate of which is symbolized as $R^2$ in OLS multiple regression).

The **uniqueness** of the $p$th observed variable, $u_p^2$, is simply $1 - h_p^2$, giving the proportion of variance not explained by the common factors.

Interpretation of communality estimates (or, equivalently, uniqueness estimates) can help evaluate the quality of an estimated EFA model.

## ESTIMATION OF THE COMMON FACTOR MODEL

Earlier, we saw that the common factor model can be understood as a (multivariate) multiple linear regression model where the outcome variables are observed but the predictor variables (i.e., the factors) are unobserved. Because the participants' values for these predictors are not available, the usual OLS regression formulas for estimating the slope coefficients cannot be used. Thus, the fundamental estimation problem for EFA is to obtain regression coefficients (i.e., the factor loadings) for predictors (i.e., the factors) without having data for those predictors. It turns out that we can capitalize on the correlations among the observed variables themselves, which are the outcome variables in the common factor model, to estimate these regression coefficients that link the observed variables to the unobserved factors. Consequently, EFA is an analysis of correlations.

Given the matrix form of the common factor model,

$$\mathbf{Y} = \mathbf{\Lambda f} + \boldsymbol{\varepsilon},$$  (8.2 repeated)

---

[5]This finding for OWPRE does not necessarily imply that the two-factor model is incorrect or inadequate for the current dataset of only nine observed variables. It may not be defensible to estimate an alternative model with an additional common factor in an effort to increase the communality of OWPRE because the other observed variables may have weak, near-zero relations with that factor. Instead, at this point, we simply take the low communality of OWPRE as a descriptive statistic indicating that this particular observed variable shares little variance with the common factors that account for the correlations among the other variables.

it can be shown by algebraic manipulation that the **correlation structure** for the $P$ observed variables implied by the factor model is

$$\hat{\mathbf{P}} = \Lambda\Psi\Lambda' + \Theta. \tag{8.3}$$

Here, $\hat{\mathbf{P}}$ is the $P \times P$ **model-implied correlation matrix** for the population, which is also known as the *predicted correlation matrix* or as the *fitted correlation matrix*. If the common factor model is correct in the population (given the correct number $M$ of common factors and correct population parameter values), this $\hat{\mathbf{P}}$ equals the true population correlation matrix, **P**. On the right-hand side of Equation 8.3, $\Lambda$ is the same $P \times M$ matrix of factor loadings as in Equation 8.2 and $\Psi$ is the $M \times M$ matrix of correlations among the common factors (i.e., the interfactor correlation matrix). Finally, $\Theta$ is a diagonal matrix with diagonal values equal to the uniquenesses of the individual observed variables.

Notice that the factor scores themselves, given in Equation 8.2 as **f**, do not appear in the correlation structure expression in Equation 8.3. Yet the correlation structure does include all of the model's parameters, including the factor loadings (i.e., $\Lambda$), interfactor correlations (i.e., $\Psi$), and uniquenesses (i.e., the diagonal of $\Theta$; and therefore communalities are also easily obtained as $\mathbf{I} - \Theta$). Because these parameters are all present in the correlation structure equation, in practice, the observed sample correlations, contained in the sample correlation matrix **R**, provide sufficient data to estimate the entire model. Briefly stated, the estimation goal of EFA is to find the set of parameter values in $\Lambda$, $\Psi$, and $\Theta$ that produces (via the correlation structure equation) a model-implied correlation matrix, $\hat{\mathbf{P}}$, that matches the sample correlation matrix **R** as closely as possible, given that **R** is itself an estimate of the population correlation matrix P.

In other words, EFA is a model-fitting analysis of the correlations among observed variables, and one does not need the actual $N \times P$ dataset (i.e., the observed data for the $N$ cases on the $P$ observed variables) as long as the observed correlations are available. That is, as a first step to conducting an EFA, a computer software package automatically calculates the correlation matrix **R** (although it may not show it to the user as output), and then proceeds to fit one or more EFA models to **R** using one of the estimation procedures described next. Alternatively, if the user does not have access to the original $N \times P$ data matrix but does have a sample correlation matrix (e.g., the correlations in Table 8.1), with any software capable of EFA, it is possible to provide only these correlations as input data. For instance, many published studies include a table of correlations among the variables used in the study; any researcher can then borrow these correlations for a secondary data analysis using EFA.

Thus, the estimation task in EFA is to find the set of parameter values that reproduces the sample correlation matrix as closely as possible. Over the years, many estimation methods, which have often been referred to as 'factor extraction' methods, have been suggested; some of these methods are now obsolete. One old-fashioned method still commonly used today is *principal axis estimation*, which is sometimes simply referred to as the *principal factor method*. Modern estimation methods relying on computerized, iterative algorithms are more accurate with respect to reproducing a population correlation matrix and are therefore recommended (MacCallum, 2009). Among these are *unweighted least-squares* (ULS) estimation (not to be confused with OLS for the regular multiple regression model) and *maximum likelihood* (ML) estimation. Nevertheless, because there are many published studies using principal axis estimation and because many of the ideas behind this method are pedagogically important, the next section summarizes the logic of principal axis factoring before the ULS and ML estimation procedures are presented.

Regardless of which estimation method a researcher chooses, an initial, educated guess must be made about $M$, the number of common factors for the model because all EFA estimation procedures require that $M$ be specified beforehand. In that a major purpose of EFA is to uncover $M$, specifying a value of $M$ beforehand may seem like a bit of a 'chicken-and-egg' problem. But one can always estimate a model with $M$ equal to some particular value, and then if the fit or interpretation of the estimated model is unsatisfactory, one can then estimate a new model with more or fewer factors than were in the first model. Procedures for determining the optimal number of common factors are presented in detail later in this chapter.

Before proceeding with the details of EFA estimation methods, it is important to discuss **principal components analysis** (PCA), which is often incorrectly presented as a factor extraction method and, regrettably, is even the default estimator within the EFA procedures of certain statistical software packages (e.g., SPSS and SAS). Put simply, PCA is not a form of factor analysis. Although EFA and PCA are similar mathematically, they have fundamentally different purposes with respect to research application. PCA is a data-reduction method, in which many variables are collapsed into *components*, and nothing more. Factor analysis, on the other hand, is a more sophisticated modeling procedure which seeks to explain the pattern of correlations among observed variables using latent variables, or factors. A component from a PCA analysis is not a type of common factor; components contain a mixture of both common and unique variability, whereas EFA explicitly disentangles common variance from unique variance. Consequently, common factors are more realistic representations of unobservable, hypothetical constructs (via the model's explicit representation of measurement error), and thus, factor analysis is more appropriate than PCA for most research applications in the behavioural and social sciences (especially psychometric studies involving scale development and validation). For more detailed discussions of this issue, see Fabrigar, Wegener, MacCallum, and Strahan (1999); Preacher and MacCallum (2003); and Widaman (2007).

 **Section recap**

### Estimation of the common factor model

Although data for the common factors themselves (i.e., the factor scores) are not observable, an EFA model can be estimated according to the **model-implied correlation matrix**, which is a function of the model parameters but not the actual factor scores.

The model-implied correlation matrix is

$$\hat{\mathbf{P}} = \Lambda\Psi\Lambda' + \Theta,$$

where

$\hat{\mathbf{P}}$ is the $P \times P$ model-implied correlation matrix
$\Lambda$ is the $P \times M$ factor-loading matrix
$\Psi$ is the $M \times M$ interfactor correlation matrix
$\Theta$ is a diagonal matrix with diagonal values equal to the observed variable uniquenesses.

If the common factor model is correct in the population, $\hat{\mathbf{P}}$ equals the true population correlation matrix $\mathbf{P}$ among the observed variables.

*(Continued)*

(Continued)

In practice, the EFA model is estimated by finding the set of parameter estimates that produces a model-implied correlation matrix $\hat{\mathbf{P}}$ which matches the observed, sample correlation matrix $\mathbf{R}$ as closely as possible.

Although **principal components analysis** (PCA) is often presented as a method of factor extraction, PCA is not in fact a type of EFA. In most research applications in the behavioural and social sciences, EFA is more appropriate than PCA because common factors offer a more realistic representation of hypothetical constructs.

## Principal axis estimation

As mentioned earlier, **principal axis estimation** continues to be common, and there are numerous publications using this EFA method. The description of the principal axis method provided here is admittedly abstract and could benefit from a numerical presentation of a worked example. But I have decided not to present such a numerical example because I feel that iterative, algorithmic estimators should be preferred given modern computing capabilities, and a detailed example of principal axis might distract readers from this point.

For simplicity, begin by assuming that the interfactor correlations all equal zero; nonzero interfactor correlations can be reincorporated with factor rotation, which is described later in this chapter. Consequently, the $M \times M$ interfactor correlation matrix $\Psi$ is set to equal an $M \times M$ identity matrix I, and thus, the equation for the correlation structure

$$\hat{\mathbf{P}} = \Lambda\Psi\Lambda' + \Theta \qquad \text{(8.3 repeated)}$$

becomes

$$\hat{\mathbf{P}} = \Lambda I\Lambda' + \Theta,$$

which simplifies to

$$\hat{\mathbf{P}} = \Lambda\Lambda' + \Theta. \qquad (8.4)$$

Subtracting $\Theta$ from both sides of the equation yields

$$(\hat{\mathbf{P}} - \Theta) = \Lambda\Lambda'. \qquad (8.5)$$

The term on the left-hand side of Equation 8.5, $(\hat{\mathbf{P}} - \Theta)$, is the model-implied, population **reduced correlation matrix**. To estimate the factor loading matrix, the principal axis method uses a sample estimate of the reduced correlation matrix $(\mathbf{R} - \hat{\Theta})$, where $\hat{\Theta}$ is a sample estimate of the true $\Theta$. Thus, the population-based expression in Equation 8.4 is analogous to the sample-based expression

$$(\mathbf{R} - \hat{\Theta}) = \hat{\Lambda}\hat{\Lambda}'), \qquad (8.6)$$

where $\hat{\Lambda}$ is the sample estimate of the population factor-loading matrix.

To calculate an initial, sample reduced correlation matrix $(\mathbf{R} - \hat{\Theta})$, principal axis estimation begins by estimating the communalities of each observed variable in the factor model. Because $u_p^2 = 1 - h_p^2$, these initial communality estimates provide estimates of the diagonal values of $\Theta$, which are the $u_p^2$ uniqueness terms (recall that $\Theta$ is a diagonal matrix by definition, so all of its off-diagonal values equal zero).

There are many possible choices for **initial communality estimates** (also known as *prior communalities*), and EFA software packages typically include several of these options. A particularly common choice is to use an observed squared multiple correlation (SMC) for a given observed variable as its initial communality estimate. Specifically, in the context of EFA, the SMC for a given observed variable is calculated by regressing that variable on all other observed variables, and the $R^2$ estimate, or SMC, from this regression serves as the initial communality estimate for that variable. For instance, using our running example of social anxiety and body image variables, when the BFNE observed variable serves as an outcome variable regressed on the remaining eight observed variables, the resulting $R^2 = .74$ would be the initial communality estimate for BFNE.

The logic of using these SMCs as initial communality estimates is that they give the proportion of variability in an observed variable that is shared with the set of all other variables. Recall that in the common factor model, the communality of an observed variable is itself an SMC value giving the proportion of variability in an observed variable that is shared with the common factors. But at the beginning of the estimation procedure, information about the common factors is not available, and so the set of observed variables instead serves as the initial predictor set for obtaining the SMC, or communality value, of a given observed variable. Once the entire model is estimated, these initial communality estimates are updated based on the obtained factor pattern to provide **final communality estimates**. It is these final communality estimates that should be reported as the communality values of the observed variables in an application of EFA.

Once initial communality estimates are obtained, for each observed variable, the initial uniqueness is one minus its initial communality estimate. These uniqueness estimates then provide the diagonal elements of a $\hat{\Theta}$ matrix, which in turn is used to form the sample reduced correlation matrix $(\mathbf{R} - \hat{\Theta})$. It turns out that this reduced correlation matrix is the same as the original sample correlation matrix but with the initial communality estimates on its diagonal instead of 1s. This pattern occurs because each diagonal value of $\mathbf{R}$ equals 1, and the corresponding diagonal value of $\hat{\Theta}$ is a uniqueness term, and as defined earlier, $1 - u_p^2 = h_p^2$. Because $\hat{\Theta}$ is a diagonal matrix, the off-diagonal values of the reduced correlation matrix $(\mathbf{R} - \hat{\Theta})$ are all unchanged from the original $\mathbf{R}$.

Recall from Chapter 7 that the eigenstructure of a symmetric matrix has the form $\mathbf{UDU'}$ (i.e., Equation 7.1, where columns of $\mathbf{U}$ are eigenvectors and diagonal values of $\mathbf{D}$ are eigenvalues. Because the sample reduced correlation matrix is symmetric, its eigenstructure can be calculated, and the resulting eigenvectors and eigenvalues are used in principal axis estimation to calculate the estimated factor loading matrix, $\hat{\Lambda}$. In particular, extending Equation 8.6, we have

$$(\mathbf{R} - \hat{\Theta}) = \hat{\Lambda}\hat{\Lambda}' = \mathbf{UDU'}.$$

It turns out that each column of $\hat{\Lambda}$ is equal to an eigenvector multiplied by the square root of the corresponding eigenvalue. But some eigenvectors will correspond to extremely small eigenvalues, which implies that they reproduce a trivial amount of the numerical information in the reduced correlation matrix. Consequently, the estimated factor loading matrix $\hat{\Lambda}$ is formed by selecting only the eigenvectors whose eigenvalues indicate that a substantial amount of information from the correlation matrix will be retained. This selection is a result of the data analyst's decision about the number of common factors, $M$, in the model, where $M$ determines the number of columns for $\hat{\Lambda}$, which thereby determines the number of eigenvector–eigenvalue combinations needed for the principal axis solution.

Again, principal axis estimation is a somewhat outdated method of estimating an EFA model because more computationally intensive procedures (made feasible with modern computing capabilities) tend to produce more accurate results with respect to recovering the population model. Yet, it is still important to recognize the central role of eigenstructure in principal axis factoring because eigenvalue-based methods for determining the number of common factors, $M$, are still applicable with other estimation procedures. Estimation methods relying on iterative algorithms, particularly ULS and ML estimation, have better statistical properties than the more old-fashioned principal axis approach, and so we turn to these estimators next.[6]

 Section recap

### Principal axis estimation

**Principal axis estimation** is an outdated method of EFA model estimation, but it is still commonly used.

The population **reduced correlation matrix** is defined as $(\mathbf{P} - \Theta)$, where $\mathbf{P}$ is the population correlation matrix among the observed variables for an EFA and $\Theta$ is the diagonal matrix containing the uniqueness terms of the observed variables.

The principal axis method obtains an estimated factor loading matrix $(\hat{\Lambda})$ from the eigenstructure of a sample estimate of the reduced correlation matrix, $(\mathbf{R} - \hat{\Theta})$, according to the formula

$$(\mathbf{R} - \hat{\Theta}) = \hat{\Lambda}\hat{\Lambda}'.$$

Specifically, the sample reduced correlation matrix $(\mathbf{R} - \hat{\Theta})$ is simply the sample correlation matrix with diagonal values equal to communality estimates for the observed variables (rather than diagonal values equal to 1).

The factor loading matrix is estimated using **initial communality estimates** (also known as *prior communalities*). The prior communality of observed variable $p$ is often calculated as the squared multiple correlation (SMC), that is, $R^2$, obtained when $Y_p$ is regressed on the remaining $(P - 1)$ observed variables.

After the estimated factor loading matrix $\hat{\Lambda}$ is obtained, **final communalities** (i.e., final estimates of the population communalities) are calculated. In practice, final communality estimates should be reported and interpreted.

---

[6]The principal axis method can be expanded to an *iterative principal axis* method, in which an estimated $\hat{\Lambda}$ matrix leads to improved communality estimates, which then lead to a new, improved $\hat{\Lambda}$, and so on until the changes in $\hat{\Lambda}$ become negligible. This procedure is asymptotically equivalent to ULS estimation for EFA (MacCallum, 2009).

## Unweighted least-squares estimation

As detailed in Chapter 2, the most common estimation method in simple and multiple regression analysis is OLS. In OLS regression, parameter estimates are obtained that minimize the sum of squared residuals; the residuals represent the difference between the observed outcome variable values and the predicted (or model-implied) $\hat{Y}$ values. Thus, in standard regression analyses, the focus is on finding parameter estimates (i.e., regression slope coefficients) that fit the model to individual cases. But in EFA, the focus is on finding parameter estimates that fit the model to observed correlations, rather than to individual cases. Thus, the goal of **unweighted least squares** (**ULS**) estimation in EFA is to find the parameter estimates (i.e., factor loadings and uniquenesses) that minimize the squared **residual correlations**, which represent the difference between the actual, observed correlations in **R** and the model-implied correlations.

Unweighted least squares estimation in EFA, which is also known as **ordinary least squares** (**OLS**) or *minimum residual* (*MinRes*) estimation, is based on the minimization of a **fitting function** (which is also known as a *discrepancy function*). The ULS fitting function for EFA can be written as

$$F_{ULS} = \frac{1}{2} tr(\mathbf{R} - \hat{\mathbf{P}})^2. \tag{8.7}$$

Earlier, $\hat{\mathbf{P}}$ was presented in Equations 8.3 and 8.4 as the model-implied correlation matrix formed from the unknown, hypothetical parameters in $\Lambda$ and $\Theta$. But now, the $\hat{\mathbf{P}}$ in Equation 8.7 is calculated based on a set of sample-based estimates of the factor loadings, collected in the $\hat{\Lambda}$ matrix, and the uniquenesses, collected in the $\hat{\Theta}$ matrix, such that

$$\hat{\mathbf{P}} = \hat{\Lambda}\hat{\Lambda}' + \hat{\Theta} \tag{8.8}$$

under an initial simplifying assumption of uncorrelated common factors. Using a computerized iterative algorithm, ULS proceeds by trying numerous different $\hat{\Lambda}$ and $\hat{\Theta}$ matrices until the set of parameter estimates is found that produces the smallest possible value for $F_{ULS}$, with the obtained value from a given sample denoted $\hat{F}_{ULS}$. The fitting function in Equation 8.7 is a manipulation of the squared difference between the observed sample correlation matrix, **R**, and the model-implied correlation matrix, $\hat{\mathbf{P}}$, where the difference $(\mathbf{R} - \hat{\mathbf{P}})$ is known as the **residual correlation matrix**. Thus, by minimizing $F_{ULS}$, the squared residual correlations are minimized. Furthermore, it is clear that if the model perfectly reproduces the sample correlations such that $\hat{\mathbf{P}} = \mathbf{R}$, all residual correlations equal zero and $\hat{F}_{ULS} = 0$. In practice, though, one should not expect the model to fit the data perfectly, and thus, it is typical to obtain a value of $\hat{F}_{ULS}$ which is near 0 but still greater than 0. In sum, a good-fitting model is one for which the predicted, or model-implied, correlations match the observed correlations as closely as possible. For such a model, the residual correlations are very small and therefore the obtained value of $\hat{F}_{ULS}$ is near zero (although typically this value itself is not reported).

## Example of model-implied and residual correlation matrices

When the two-factor EFA model is fitted to the social anxiety example dataset using ULS, an estimated factor loading matrix is

$$\hat{\Lambda} = \begin{bmatrix} 0.85 & 0.17 \\ 0.78 & 0.40 \\ 0.77 & 0.41 \\ 0.82 & -0.46 \\ 0.71 & -0.15 \\ 0.58 & -0.08 \\ -0.72 & 0.35 \\ 0.55 & 0.27 \\ 0.87 & 0.26 \end{bmatrix}.$$

It is important to keep in mind that this factor loading matrix is *unrotated*, implying that it is probably not interpretable. In contrast, the factor loading matrix given earlier in Table 8.2 was rotated to improve interpretation; the concept of factor rotation is described later in this chapter. At this point, working with the unrotated factor loading matrix is sufficient for the purpose of presenting the predicted and residual correlation matrices because these correlation matrices are the same regardless of rotation.

Thus, applying Equation 8.8, the product of $\hat{\Lambda}$ with its transpose produces the estimated model-implied reduced correlation matrix. That is,

$$\hat{P} - \hat{\Theta} = \hat{\Lambda}\hat{\Lambda}'.$$

Using the current $\hat{\Lambda}$, we obtain the correlation matrix in Table 8.3 from calculating the product $\hat{\Lambda}\hat{\Lambda}'$. Because $\hat{\Lambda}\hat{\Lambda}' = \hat{P} - \hat{\Theta}$, the diagonal elements of this correlation matrix, rather than being equal to 1, correspond to the final communality estimates for each variable. The sample model-implied correlation matrix, $\hat{P}$, is obtained simply by making each diagonal value in Table 8.3 equal to 1 (which is equivalent to adding the uniqueness estimates to the communality estimates on the diagonal).

Next, the residual correlation matrix is the difference between the observed correlation matrix (see Table 8.1) and this model-implied correlation matrix, $R - \hat{P}$. The resulting residual correlation matrix for the current example is given in Table 8.4. One way to evaluate the adequacy of the factor model (i.e., whether there are enough common factors) is to inspect the off-diagonal elements of the residual correlation matrix. A substantial residual correlation

**Table 8.3** Model-implied correlation matrix (with final communalities on the diagonal) for two-factor model of social anxiety data

|  | BFNE | SIAS | SPS | SPAS | BIQ | ASI | APEVAL | OWPRE | SAAS |
|---|---|---|---|---|---|---|---|---|---|
| BFNE | .74 | .72 | .72 | .62 | .57 | .48 | −.55 | .42 | .78 |
| SIAS | .72 | .76 | .76 | .45 | .49 | .42 | −.42 | .32 | .78 |
| SPS | .72 | .76 | .76 | .45 | .48 | .42 | −.41 | .31 | .77 |
| SPAS | .62 | .45 | .45 | .88 | .65 | .51 | −.75 | .58 | .59 |
| BIQ | .57 | .49 | .48 | .65 | .52 | .43 | −.56 | .43 | .57 |
| ASI | .48 | .42 | .42 | .51 | .43 | .35 | −.45 | .34 | .49 |
| APEVAL | −.55 | −.42 | −.41 | −.75 | −.56 | −.45 | .64 | −.49 | −.53 |
| OWPRE | .42 | .32 | .31 | .58 | .43 | .34 | −.49 | .38 | .41 |
| SAAS | .78 | .78 | .77 | .59 | .57 | .49 | −.53 | .41 | .82 |

**Table 8.4** Residual correlation matrix (with uniquenesses on the diagonal) for two-factor model of social anxiety data

|  | BFNE | SIAS | SPS | SPAS | BIQ | ASI | APEVAL | OWPRE | SAAS |
|---|---|---|---|---|---|---|---|---|---|
| BFNE | .26 | −.01 | −.05 | −.01 | .07 | .05 | .04 | −.03 | .04 |
| SIAS | −.01 | .24 | .04 | .01 | .00 | −.09 | −.03 | −.01 | −.02 |
| SPS | −.05 | .04 | .24 | .01 | −.07 | .04 | .01 | .06 | .00 |
| SPAS | −.01 | .01 | .01 | .12 | −.02 | −.02 | −.03 | .01 | −.01 |
| BIQ | .07 | .00 | −.07 | −.02 | .48 | .17 | .03 | .03 | .00 |
| ASI | .05 | −.09 | .04 | −.02 | .17 | .65 | .10 | .09 | −.01 |
| APEVAL | .04 | −.03 | .01 | −.03 | .03 | .10 | .36 | .06 | −.02 |
| OWPRE | −.03 | −.01 | .06 | .01 | .03 | .09 | .06 | .62 | −.03 |
| SAAS | .04 | −.02 | .00 | −.01 | .00 | −.01 | −.02 | −.03 | .18 |

between any two variables suggests that the relation between those variables is not well explained by the factor model (although there is no concrete guideline or cut-off for how small residual correlations should be, I suggest that any residual correlation >.10 is worthy of further consideration with respect to potential model misfit).

 **Section recap**

### Unweighted least-squares estimation

**Unweighted least-squares** (ULS), also known as *ordinary least-squares* (OLS) or *minimum residual* (MinRes), estimation of an EFA model obtains the set of parameter estimates that minimizes the squared **residual correlation matrix**.

The residual correlation matrix is $(\mathbf{R} - \hat{\mathbf{P}})$, where $\hat{\mathbf{P}}$ is a model-implied correlation matrix calculated from a set of parameter estimates in $\hat{\Lambda}$ (an estimated factor loading matrix) and $\hat{\Theta}$ (a diagonal matrix with uniqueness estimates on the diagonal) according to the equation

$$\hat{\mathbf{P}} = \hat{\Lambda}\hat{\Lambda}' + \hat{\Theta}.$$

Specifically, ULS estimation uses an iterative algorithm to find the set of parameter estimates that minimizes the following **fitting function** (also known as a **discrepancy function**):

$$F_{ULS} = \frac{1}{2} tr(\mathbf{R} - \hat{\mathbf{P}})^2.$$

A good-fitting model is one for which the model-implied correlations match the observed correlations as closely as possible. For such a model, the residual correlations are near 0 and therefore the obtained value $\hat{F}_{ULS}$ is near zero.

## Maximum likelihood estimation

**Maximum likelihood** (ML), previously introduced in Chapter 6 for multilevel modeling, is a prominent estimation method for many statistical modeling procedures because it has well-understood, large-sample statistical properties. When all of its assumptions are met, these properties of ML are *asymptotically* optimal, meaning that ML outperforms other estimation procedures as the sample size grows to infinity. Briefly, 'the ML solution provides estimates of values of population parameters that most likely would have yielded the observed sample' (MacCallum, 2009: 128). Like ULS estimation for EFA, ML estimation of an EFA model also works using a fitting function. The ML fitting function, expressed in terms of correlation structure,[7] is

$$F_{ML} = \log|\widehat{\mathbf{P}}| + \text{tr}(\mathbf{R}\widehat{\mathbf{P}}^{-1}) - \log|\mathbf{R}| - P,$$

where $P$ is the number of observed variables in the analysis and $\widehat{\mathbf{P}}$ is as defined in Equation 8.8. As with the ULS method, ML uses an iterative algorithm to find the $\hat{\Lambda}$ and $\hat{\Theta}$ matrices that make the obtained value of $F_{ML}$, denoted $\hat{F}_{ML}$ for a given sample, as small as possible. Although the ML fitting function is slightly more complex than the ULS fitting function, one can see that $F_{ML}$ is essentially a comparison of the observed correlation matrix, $\mathbf{R}$, with the model-implied correlation matrix, $\widehat{\mathbf{P}}$, and that when $\widehat{\mathbf{P}} = \mathbf{R}$, the value of $F_{ML}$ equals 0.

A difference between ULS and ML is that the mathematical derivation of the ML fitting function begins with an assumption that the observed variables follow a multivariate normal distribution, whereas the ULS method makes no distributional assumptions for the observed variables. The assumptions for EFA are addressed further later in this chapter. Invoking this normality assumption, however, allows the ML method to produce a formal significance test for the fit of the model to the data, which in essence is a test of $M$, the number of factors. This test is also presented later. Although ML estimation has ideal statistical properties when its assumptions are met, there are situations in which ULS estimation performs better; Briggs and MacCallum (2003) offered a detailed comparison of these estimators, and ultimately they recommended that applied researchers fit EFA models using both ML and ULS and compare the solutions.

Regardless of the estimation method used in EFA, an important concern is the possibility of obtaining an *improper solution*. Specifically, it is possible for the final, estimated uniqueness of a given observed variable to be negative, which in turn corresponds to an estimated communality greater than 1. Given that communality represents a proportion of explained variance, any value above 1 is nonsensical; similarly, in that a uniqueness is also a variance term, any negative value is necessarily incorrect. An estimated communality greater than 1 is known as a *Heywood case*. Whenever an estimated EFA model contains one or more Heywood cases, the entire model solution is rendered improper and must be discarded, usually in favour of a simpler model. A similar problem that occasionally arises with iterative estimators such as ULS and ML is known as *nonconvergence*. Computerized algorithms are programmed to stop after some maximum number of estimation iterations (often set to 25 in software procedures for EFA). If the algorithm has not arrived at an optimal estimated model given the data by that point, then nonconvergence has occurred. In this situation, the researcher may increase

---

[7]The ML fitting function can also be expressed in terms of covariance structure, as presented in Chapter 9.

the maximum number of iterations (e.g., from 25 to 100). If, after increasing the number of iterations, a proper solution is given for the estimated model, then the researcher may proceed as usual. But it is possible to not reach convergence even after increasing the maximum number of iterations. Although the software will typically print the results for a nonconverged solution, like an improper solution, these results should be discarded. Improper solutions and nonconvergence are more likely to occur when there is a linear dependence among the observed variables (see the discussion of multicollinearity in Chapter 2), when the model includes too many common factors, or when the sample size is too small, among other possible causes. Often, problems involving improper and nonconverged solutions can be remedied by removing one or more problematic observed variable or by reducing $M$, the number of common factors in the model.

 **Section recap**

### Maximum likelihood estimation

**Maximum likelihood** (ML) estimation of an EFA model finds the set of parameter estimates (i.e., factor loadings and uniquenesses) that would be most likely to produce the observed correlations under the assumption that the observed variables follow a multivariate normal distribution.

Specifically, with ML estimation, a computerized, iterative algorithm is used to find the set of parameter estimates that produces the smallest value of the ML fitting function:

$$F_{ML} = \log|\hat{\mathbf{P}}| + \text{tr}(\mathbf{R}\,\hat{\mathbf{P}}^{-1}) - \log|\mathbf{R}| - P,$$

where $P$ is the number of observed variables and $\hat{\mathbf{P}}$ is the model-implied correlation matrix.

With any estimation method for EFA, it is possible to obtain an **improper solution**. For example, a set of parameter estimates could include one or more communalities greater than 1 (or, equivalently, a uniqueness estimate less than 0). A communality greater than 1 is known as a *Heywood case*.

Estimation methods which rely on an iterative algorithm, such as ULS and ML, can also lead to *nonconvergence*, which occurs when a maximum number of iterations has been reached but the algorithm has not settled on a set of parameter estimates which adequately minimizes the fitting function.

Any results obtained from a nonconverged or improper solution should be discarded and not interpreted.

## DETERMINING THE OPTIMAL NUMBER OF COMMON FACTORS

As stated previously, the overall purpose of EFA is to find and interpret a small number of common factors which adequately explain the pattern of the correlations among a larger number of observed variables. Thus, a major decision in an EFA is the number of common factors to have for the model, which corresponds to $M$, the number of columns of the factor loading matrix, $\Lambda$. To emphasize, determining the optimal value of $M$ is a decision that the researcher must make, and one should not blindly accept the default number of factors output by a computer software program. (With some software, the user must always explicitly indicate the number of factors for a given model estimation, whereas software such as SPSS and SAS produces a default number of factors that is based on the faulty *Kaiser criterion*, which is discussed next.) Instead, one should consult a variety of criteria to help reach a decision, allowing theoretical expectations and model interpretability to influence the decision. Doing so usually involves comparing several factor solutions, that is, comparing estimated models with differing numbers of factors. The objective is to obtain the simplest model possible (i.e., the fewest number of factors), the most parsimonious model, that still reasonably accounts for the pattern of correlations among the observed variables.

Following from that objective, many criteria for determining the optimal number of factors involve the eigenvalues of the correlation matrix being analysed because (roughly speaking) an eigenvalue characterizes the amount of information contained in a factor relative to the overall covariation among the observed variables. But estimating the factor model using ML also facilitates the calculation of more sophisticated model fit statistics, which are being increasingly advocated for evaluating EFA models (e.g., Preacher, Zhang, Kim, and Mels, 2013). This model-fit perspective is addressed after presentation of the more traditional eigenvalue-based methods.

Finally, interpretational quality is a critical aspect of determining the optimal number of factors. Even if statistical criteria strongly suggest a certain number of factors, each factor should have a meaningful, defensible interpretation after rotation (rotation is explained later). If a given rotated factor is not substantively interpretable, then the number of factors should probably be decreased. It is also important to be aware of the so-called *naming fallacy*, which occurs when researchers falsely ascribe a conceptual meaning to a factor that is weakly defined based on only one or two observed variables or by variables which bear little conceptual relation to each other.

## Kaiser criterion

The simplest method for determining the number of common factors is known variously as the **Kaiser criterion**, the *Kaiser-Guttman rule*, and the *eigenvalue-one rule*. With this method, the number of factors $M$ is set equal to the number of eigenvalues of the original, unreduced sample correlation matrix **R** that are greater than 1. Unfortunately, although this approach is probably the most widely used rule for determining the number of factors (largely because it is the default method in SPSS and SAS), it is well-known to be highly fallible for a variety of reasons (see Preacher and MacCallum, 2003, for a summary). Therefore, although it is important to be aware of this method, it is *not recommended*.

## Scree plot

A better method to determine the optimal number of common factors is to evaluate a graph known as a **scree plot** (evaluation of this graph is also sometimes called a *scree test*, although it does not represent a formal statistical hypothesis test; Cattell, 1966). A scree plot is simply a scatterplot of the eigenvalues of a correlation matrix against their ranks in terms of magnitude (with adjacent points usually connected with line segments). The eigenvalues either of the unreduced sample correlation matrix $\mathbf{R}$ or of the reduced sample correlation matrix, $(\mathbf{R} - \hat{\Theta})$, may be plotted, although most EFA software plots the eigenvalues of $\mathbf{R}$ by default. But given that the purpose of EFA is to explain covariation among variables using common factor variance, it makes more sense to plot the eigenvalues of a reduced correlation matrix, with diagonal values based on initial communality estimates such as SMCs, as explained earlier under the principal axis method, or with diagonal values based on final communality estimates for a one-factor model. The number of factors to retain as the value of $M$ is represented in a scree plot by the number of larger eigenvalues seen to the left before the remaining, smaller eigenvalues appear to level off.

Figure 8.1 displays the scree plot for the social anxiety example with the eigenvalues of the sample reduced correlation matrix $(\mathbf{R} - \hat{\Theta})$. Because eigenvalues represent the approximate amount of covariance explained by a factor (before rotation), it is clear from Figure 8.1 that the first unrotated factor would explain much more covariance in the observed variables than do the subsequent potential factors (because the first eigenvalue is much greater than the remaining eigenvalues). But there is also a noticeably larger gap between the second and third eigenvalue than there is between the third and fourth or between the fourth and fifth, suggesting that a potentially meaningful amount of covariation would be captured by a second factor. Overall, the eigenvalues appear to level off starting at the third factor, indicating that a two-factor model (i.e., $M = 2$) might be optimal for these data.

## Parallel analysis

The number of common factors suggested by a scree plot can be ambiguous, and thus, several methods have been developed to supplement the plot with more objective numerical criteria. One such method that has gained popularity in recent years is known as **parallel analysis** (Horn, 1965). With this procedure, the eigenvalues of the observed correlation matrix are

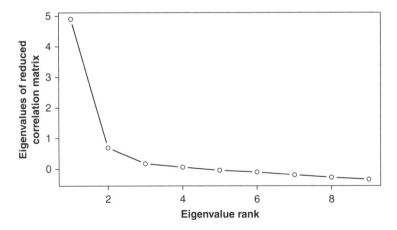

**Figure 8.1** Scree plot of eigenvalues of the reduced correlation matrix from the social anxiety data

compared with the eigenvalues of correlation matrices from data simulated to be completely random. Because the simulated data are based on variables which are uncorrelated in the population, there are no common factors underlying the variables, and so any nonzero sample correlations among the simulated data only result from sampling error. Thus, any eigenvalue from the observed $\mathbf{R}$ that exceeds the eigenvalues from the random data correlations likely represents a common factor rather than covariation caused by sampling error alone. The optimal number of factors is then taken to be equal to the number of eigenvalues from the observed correlations that are greater than the corresponding eigenvalues of the random data correlations. As with the scree plot, parallel analysis may be based on either the unreduced correlation matrix $\mathbf{R}$ or the reduced matrix $(\mathbf{R} - \hat{\Theta})$, but analysis of the reduced $\mathbf{R}$ is more consistent with the logic of the common factor model, and thus, the eigenvalues of the observed reduced correlation matrix should be compared with the eigenvalues from simulated reduced correlation matrices.

Specifically, parallel analysis begins by simulating a series of random datasets (often 100 datasets are generated), each with $N$ observations on a set of $P$ standard normal variables which are uncorrelated in the population, where $N$ is the sample size for the actual observed data and $P$ is the number of observed variables in the actual factor analysis. The (reduced) correlation matrix and its eigenvalues are then calculated for each random dataset. A distribution of these random eigenvalue sets is formed, and the eigenvalues from the (reduced) correlation matrix of the actual, observed data are typically compared with either the 95th percentile of the random eigenvalue distribution or the mean of the random eigenvalue distribution. That is, the first eigenvalue of the actual correlation matrix is compared with the 95th percentile (or the mean) of the distribution of the first eigenvalues of the simulated correlation matrices, the second eigenvalue of the actual data is compared with the 95th percentile (or the mean) of the distribution of the second eigenvalues of the simulated correlation matrices, and so on, until the observed eigenvalues no longer exceed the random eigenvalues.

Thus, parallel analysis is clearly computationally intensive. But it has become more popular largely because of the availability of automated routines which are available as macros or functions in popular statistical software.

To illustrate parallel analysis with the social anxiety example, 100 datasets, each with $N = 109$ and $P = 9$, were simulated from a standard normal multivariate distribution with all population correlations equal to zero. Next, the reduced correlation matrices were calculated for each random dataset (with their diagonal elements set equal to communality estimates for a one-factor model fitted to the random data), and then the eigenvalues of these matrices were computed. Table 8.5 presents the eigenvalues of the observed reduced correlation matrix along with the 95th percentile values and means of the eigenvalues from the simulated reduced correlation matrices. The second eigenvalue of the observed reduced $\mathbf{R}$ is greater than both the 95th percentile and the mean of the eigenvalue distributions of the second eigenvalue of the random reduced correlation matrices, whereas the third observed eigenvalue does not exceed either the 95th percentile or the mean of the third eigenvalues from the random data. Therefore, this parallel analysis indicates that $M = 2$ common factors may be appropriate for the social anxiety data regardless of whether the 95th percentile or the mean of the random eigenvalues is used. (Incidentally, a parallel analysis of unreduced correlation matrices suggested $M = 1$ factor). The results from a parallel analysis can be displayed graphically as an enhanced version of a scree plot, as shown in Figure 8.2. This figure illustrates that the first two observed eigenvalues exceed the corresponding random eigenvalues, but the third and subsequent observed eigenvalues are smaller than the corresponding random eigenvalues.

**Table 8.5** Parallel analysis results for social anxiety data

| Eigenvalue rank | Eigenvalues of observed reduced R | Mean eigenvalue, random reduced R | 95th percentile of eigenvalues, random reduced R |
|---|---|---|---|
| 1 | 4.903 | 0.794 | 1.126 |
| 2 | 0.693 | 0.340 | 0.424 |
| 3 | 0.175 | 0.224 | 0.309 |
| 4 | 0.061 | 0.121 | 0.182 |
| 5 | −0.042 | 0.039 | 0.084 |
| 6 | −0.098 | −0.053 | 0.010 |
| 7 | −0.194 | −0.130 | −0.080 |
| 8 | −0.276 | −0.218 | −0.149 |
| 9 | −0.344 | −0.323 | −0.229 |

*Note.* Random reduced correlation matrices were formed by simulating 100 datasets from a multivariate normal distribution, each with $P = 9$ variables with population correlations all equal to 0.

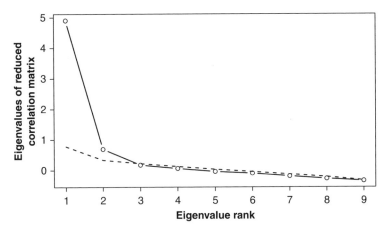

**Figure 8.2** Scree plot of social anxiety variables enhanced with parallel analysis results (solid line connects eigenvalues of observed reduced correlation matrix; dashed line connects mean of eigenvalues from simulated reduced correlation matrices)

 Section recap

### Determining the optimal number of common factors

Several methods for determining $M$, the optimal number of common factors for an EFA model, are based on the eigenvalues of either the original, unreduced correlation matrix **R** among the observed variables or, preferably, the reduced correlation matrix, $(\mathbf{R} - \hat{\Theta})$.

With the **Kaiser criterion** (i.e., the *eigenvalue-one rule*), the number of factors $M$ is taken as the number of eigenvalues of the unreduced correlation matrix that exceed 1.

*(Continued)*

(Continued)

Although it has been commonly used, the Kaiser criterion is known to be faulty, both conceptually and in practice. Therefore, more sophisticated methods for determining the optimal number of factors are to be preferred.

A **scree plot** is a graph of the eigenvalues of the (reduced) correlation matrix, with eigenvalues ordered from largest (left) to smallest (right). The optimal number of factors $M$ is determined by observing the point in the scree plot at which a given eigenvalue and all subsequent eigenvalues are approximately equal; $M$ is the number of eigenvalues which occur before the remaining eigenvalues seem to level off.

In essence, a **parallel analysis** is an attempt to apply an objective criterion to evaluating in a scree plot.

---

# USING MODEL FIT STATISTICS TO DETERMINE THE OPTIMAL NUMBER OF FACTORS

## Root-mean-square residual

In addition to the eigenvalue-based methods for determining the optimal number of factors of an EFA model for a given set of observed variables, statistics have been developed that evaluate the fit of a given factor model to the observed correlation matrix without using the eigenvalues. One of these statistics is the **root-mean-square residual** (**RMSR** or **RMR**),[8] which can be obtained regardless of the method used to estimate the factor model (whereas the other fit statistics described next derive from the statistical theory of ML estimation).

As its name implies, the RMR is a summary statistic based on the residual correlation matrix, $(\mathbf{R} - \hat{\mathbf{P}})$ (e.g., Table 8.4 for the social anxiety example). If a model has done a good job of explaining the observed correlations, then the individual elements of $(\mathbf{R} - \hat{\mathbf{P}})$ should be small. For a given set of estimates for an EFA model, one could calculate the mean of the squared residual correlations to get a sense of how well the residuals have been minimized overall. Taking the square root of this mean puts the statistic back into the original correlation metric, and thus, the RMR expresses the average residual correlation such that smaller values of RMR are indicative of better model fit. Of course, the more factors that are included in the model, the smaller the residual correlations, and so RMR is guaranteed to become smaller as $M$, the number of factors, increases. So the goal is to find the value of $M$ such that RMR is substantially smaller for a model fitted with $M$ factors compared with a model with $(M - 1)$ factors, but also RMR does not decrease appreciably when there are $(M + 1)$ factors.

For the social anxiety example, RMR = .106 for the one-factor model (i.e., $M = 1$), RMR = .050 for the two-factor model, and RMR = .025 for the three-factor model. The two-factor model explains the observed correlations substantially better than the one-factor model, but there is comparatively little improvement in RMR for the three-factor model. Therefore, the RMR statistics suggest that $M = 2$ is the optimal number of factors for the social anxiety data. This low RMR value for the two-factor model reflects the fact that most of the residual

---

[8]Often this statistic is reported as SRMR, which stands for *standardized root-mean-square residual*. In the current context of EFA with correlation matrices, SRMR and RMR are equivalent. When covariance matrices are analyzed (e.g., Chapters 9 and 10), SRMR and RMR differ.

correlations in Table 8.4, which was formed from the ULS-estimated two-factor model, are small; the largest residual correlation, between the BIQ and ASI observed variables, equals .17.

## Minimum fit-function $\chi^2$ exact-fit test

When a factor model is estimated using ML, the obtained minimized value of the fitting function, $\hat{F}_{ML}$, can be multiplied by $(N - 1)$ to obtain a statistic which follows a $\chi^2$ distribution under the assumption that the EFA model with $M$ factors is perfectly correct in the population.[9] Thus, ML estimation leads to a $\chi^2$ exact-fit test[10] for the null hypothesis that a model with $M$ factors perfectly fits the data. In practice, researchers then interpret a nonsignificant $\chi^2$ test as an indication that the optimal number of factors has been specified.

But because the $\chi^2$ exact-fit test is based on an unrealistic null hypothesis of perfect fit, it is overly sensitive to sample size (i.e., good models are rejected with large $N$) and tends to favour overly complex models (i.e., models with too many factors, such that all observed variables, except perhaps one or two, have weak loadings on the extra factors). Consequently, this test is not recommended. With the social anxiety example, the $\chi^2$ test was significant for each of the one-, two-, and three-factor models. For the four-factor model, $\chi^2$ (6) = 6.84, $p$ = .34, suggesting that a four-factor model is the correct population model for these variables. Yet, with only $P = 9$ observed variables, a four-factor model is likely to be overly complex and difficult to interpret.

## Root-mean-square error of approximation (RMSEA)

The **root-mean-square error of approximation** (or **RMSEA**) has become a prominent model fit statistic in structural equation modeling (SEM; the topic of Chapters 9 and 10), although it was originally developed from an EFA perspective (Steiger and Lind, 1980; also see Browne and Cudeck, 1992); further detail on RMSEA is presented in Chapter 9. This statistic overcomes a limitation of the $\chi^2$ exact-fit test by including a correction for model complexity. The sample estimate of RMSEA is[11]

$$\text{RMSEA} = \sqrt{\frac{\hat{F}_{ML}(N-1) - df}{df(N-1)}}. \tag{8.9}$$

All else being equal, RMSEA will favour a more parsimonious model (i.e., the model with greater $df$) over a less parsimonious model, with smaller values of RSMEA indicating better model fit. Browne and Cudeck (1993) suggested that RMSEA values of .05 or less indicate close fit, values below .08 indicate reasonable fit, and values above .10 indicate unacceptable fit. It is important to recognize these are only rough guidelines that do not hold in all situations,

---

[9]The degrees of freedom for this $\chi^2$ statistic equal $\dfrac{(P-M)^2 - (P+M)}{2}$, which is a function of the number of nonredundant elements of the observed covariance matrix minus the number of parameters to be estimated.

[10]This test is also formally a type of *likelihood-ratio test.*

[11]In situations where $df$ is greater than $\hat{F}_{ML}(N-1)$, RMSEA is set equal to 0.

and by no means should they be treated as strict cut-offs. For example, the results of simulation studies have indicated that RMSEA tends to be too big with sample sizes less than 200 (Curran, Bollen, Chen, Paxton, and Kirby, 2003).

A valuable quality of RMSEA is that confidence intervals can be constructed for it. Rather than depending on their somewhat arbitrary guidelines for specific RMSEA values, Browne and Cudeck (1992) recommended a model comparison procedure, whereby RMSEA is used to rank alternative models (e.g., models with differing numbers of common factors) in terms of their fit to data, in essentially the same way that was described earlier for RMR. Preacher et al. (2013) showed that confidence intervals (CIs) for RMSEA are especially useful for this purpose, recommending that the lower bound of the RMSEA 90% confidence intervals be used to select the optimal model (i.e., the optimal number of factors, $M$) in an EFA setting.

Returning to the social anxiety example, RMSEA = .143 with 90% CI of (.098, .178) for the two-factor model, which is indicative of poor fit. Moving to the three-factor model, we obtain RMSEA = .123 with 90% CI of (.064, .170); although the point-estimate of RMSEA is still in the poor-fit range, the lower bound of the CI suggests that the three-factor model may be adequate. Next, RMSEA does suggest that a four-factor model fits these data closely, with RMSEA = .044 and 90% CI of (.000, .133). Yet, as mentioned earlier, a four-factor model is likely to be difficult to interpret in this example because there are only $P = 9$ observed variables. Additionally, RMSEA seems to perform best with sample sizes of at least 200; here we only have $N = 109$.

There are many other model fit statistics; some of them are presented in the following chapters on SEM. It turns out that these SEM fit statistics are applicable to EFA because the EFA model is in fact a special case of SEM.

In summary, there is often no clear answer to the question of the optimal number of factors, which is certainly the case for the current social anxiety example. In this example, the scree plot, parallel analysis, and RMR statistic indicated that a two-factor model is well supported by the data, whereas the RMSEA fit statistic favoured a four-factor model or, perhaps, a three-factor model. At this point, it is clear that several estimated models should be examined for their interpretational quality. Thus, for the social anxiety example, we should obtain and attempt to interpret estimated, rotated factor loading matrices for each of the two-, three-, and four-factor models. In general, researchers should always examine several models by varying the number of factors, carefully considering the interpretational clarity of rotated factor loadings obtained from each. It is *exploratory* factor analysis after all!

 Section recap

### Using model fit statistics to determine the optimal number of factors

The optimal number of common factors $M$ for a given set of observed variables can be assessed using various model fit statistics in a model comparison procedure. For instance, the fit statistics of a model with $M$ factors might be compared with the fit statistics of a model with $(M-1)$ factors and a model with $(M+1)$ factors.

A popular model fit statistic for EFA is the **root-mean-square residual (RMR)**, which is calculated from an estimated model with $M$ factors by obtaining the mean of the residual correlations (i.e., the off-diagonal elements of $(\mathbf{R} - \hat{\mathbf{P}})$) squared, and then taking the square root of that mean. The lower its RMR is, the better a given model fits the data.

ML estimation of a given EFA model produces a $\chi^2$ **exact-fit test**, the null hypothesis of which is that a given model with $M$ factors fits the data perfectly. But because the perfect-fit null hypothesis is problematic, the $\chi^2$ fit test is not recommended.

The **root-mean-square error of approximation (RMSEA)** is a model fit statistic which overcomes a limitation of the $\chi^2$ fit test by including a correction for model complexity.

Like RMSR, lower values of RMSEA are indicative of better model fit. In particular, comparing the lower limit of 90% confidence intervals of RMSEA is a good strategy for model selection (i.e., choosing the model with the optimal number of factors $M$) as long as the sample size is large (i.e., $N > 200$).

Regardless of what a given statistic or method suggests as the optimal number of common factors $M$, a researcher should always estimate and interpret results from several competing EFA models (i.e., models with differing numbers of common factors).

## FACTOR ROTATION

When an EFA model with $M \geq 2$ factors is estimated, it turns out that there is an infinite number of factor loading matrices which explain the relations among the observed variables equally well, which is a statistical phenomenon known as *rotational indeterminacy*. Because of this issue, the initial factor loading matrix $\hat{\Lambda}$ obtained from a given estimation method (whether ULS, ML, principal axis, or another EFA estimation method) is almost always difficult to interpret with respect to assigning a conceptual meaning to the factors (i.e., the columns of $\hat{\Lambda}$). Therefore, for any model with $M \geq 2$ factors, researchers should always apply at least one method of **factor rotation** to obtain an alternative $\hat{\Lambda}$ matrix that is more interpretable than the initial, unrotated $\hat{\Lambda}$.

Consider again the unrotated $\hat{\Lambda}$ from the two-factor model fitted to the social anxiety data using ULS estimation, which is presented in Table 8.6. There, we see that all nine observed variables have moderate (e.g., 0.55) to strong (e.g., 0.85) loadings on the first factor, $f_1$, along with only small (e.g., 0.17) to moderate (e.g., 0.40) loadings on the second factor, $f_2$. Additionally, each variable is more strongly associated with $f_1$ than with $f_2$. Although this first unrotated factor might be taken to represent some general construct common to all observed variables (overall social anxiety?), any substantive meaning of $f_2$ is harder to decipher because most of the observed variables also have a moderate association with $f_2$, although some are in the opposite direction as their loadings on $f_1$ (e.g., the SPAS variable). In general, this factor pattern would be much easier to understand conceptually if some loadings were strong and others were near zero; achieving such a pattern is the goal of factor rotation.

To illustrate the concept of rotation, Figure 8.3 displays the geometric relations between the observed variables of the social anxiety example and the unrotated factors for the estimated two-factor model. In this figure, the factors are the axes; $f_1$ is the horizontal axis, and $f_2$ is the vertical axis. Each observed variable is represented as a single point in this space, with its coordinates relative to the axes given by its factor loadings. For example, taking values from Table 8.6, the coordinates of SPAS are (0.82, −0.46), meaning that it is far to the right on the positive end of the $f_1$ axis and moderately low relative to the negative end of the $f_2$ axis.

**Table 8.6** Unrotated factor loadings from two-factor model of social anxiety data

| Variable | $\hat{\Lambda}$ (loadings) | | Communality |
| | $f_1$ | $f_2$ | $\widehat{h^2}$ |
|---|---|---|---|
| BFNE | 0.85 | 0.17 | .74 |
| SIAS | 0.78 | 0.40 | .76 |
| SPS | 0.77 | 0.41 | .76 |
| SPAS | 0.82 | −0.46 | .88 |
| BIQ | 0.71 | −0.15 | .52 |
| ASI | 0.58 | −0.08 | .35 |
| APEVAL | −0.72 | 0.35 | .64 |
| OWPRE | 0.55 | −0.27 | .38 |
| SAAS | 0.87 | 0.26 | .82 |

This figure provides some visual confirmation of the verbal description given in the previous paragraph: Because most of the observed variables have moderate-to-strong positive loadings on $f_1$, they are clustered together toward the positive end of the $f_1$ axis. Furthermore, the $f_2$ loadings are all weak to moderate, and none of them is paired with a weak $f_1$ loading; consequently, the observed variables show a moderate vertical spread with respect to $f_2$, but none of them falls close to the $f_2$ axis itself.

Geometrically speaking, the goal of factor rotation is to rotate the axes (i.e., the factors) so that each observed variable is close to a large value on one axis and close to zero on all other axes. The absolute distance between any two observed variables themselves stays the same; what changes is the location of the axes. That is, the factors are rotated, whereas the relations of the observed variables to each other are unaltered. For this reason, rotation affects neither

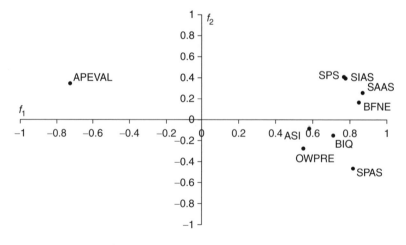

**Figure 8.3** Graphical representation of unrotated factor pattern for two-factor model of social anxiety data

the communality estimates of the observed variables nor the predicted and residual correlation matrices. For further description of the geometry of rotation, see Nunnally and Bernstein (1994: 493–506).

Table 8.7 displays a rotated estimated factor loading matrix, $\hat{\Lambda}_r$, for the social anxiety two-factor model, whereas Figure 8.4 depicts the geometric relations between the observed variables and these rotated factors. Unlike Figure 8.3, which showed the unrotated factors, in Figure 8.4, several variables (e.g., BFNE and SIAS) are close to the rotated $f_1$ (the horizontal axis) and near zero with respect to the rotated $f_2$, and several variables are close to the rotated $f_2$ axis and near zero on the rotated $f_1$ axis (although BIQ and ASI are more in-between the two axes). Accordingly, the rotated factor loading estimates in Table 8.7 show that most variables have a salient relation with one rotated factor along with a weak to near-zero relation with the other (except BIQ and ASI, which are moderately associated with both rotated factors). Notice, though, that the communality estimates in Table 8.7 are identical to those in Table 8.6.

Given this configuration, assigning a conceptual interpretation to the rotated factors is straightforward: $f_1$ is strongly determined by observed variables pertaining to anxiety involving social interaction (or 'social interaction anxiety'), whereas $f_2$ is more strongly characterized by the concept of negative body image (or 'body image concern'). Of course, this interpretation is straightforward for a researcher with substantive expertise regarding these observed variables; it is essential for substantive expertise to inform the interpretation of the common factors in an EFA model.

The goal of most rotation methods is to achieve **simple structure** (Thurstone, 1947) for the rotated factor loading matrix. Thurstone's precise definition of simple structure is more elaborate than most researchers realize (see McDonald, 1999: 179–80), but the general idea is that each rotated factor should be characterized by large loadings for a distinct set of observed variables and by small loadings for the other observed variables (i.e., **column parsimony**), whereas each observed variable should be influenced only by a subset (often one, preferably) of common factors (i.e., **row parsimony**). Many researchers confuse simple structure with a stricter criterion known as an **independent clusters solution**, in which each observed

**Table 8.7**  Rotated factor loadings from two-factor model of social anxiety data

| Variable | $\hat{\Lambda}$ (loadings) | | Communality |
|---|---|---|---|
| | $f_1$ | $f_2$ | $\hat{h}^2$ |
| BFNE | 0.69 | 0.24 | .74 |
| SIAS | 0.92 | −0.07 | .76 |
| SPS | 0.92 | −0.08 | .76 |
| SPAS | −0.03 | 0.96 | .88 |
| BIQ | 0.24 | 0.55 | .52 |
| ASI | 0.26 | 0.39 | .35 |
| APEVAL | −0.02 | −0.79 | .64 |
| OWPRE | 0.01 | 0.61 | .38 |
| SAAS | 0.81 | 0.14 | .82 |

*Note.* Factor loadings obtained with oblimin rotation (oblimin weight = 0.0).

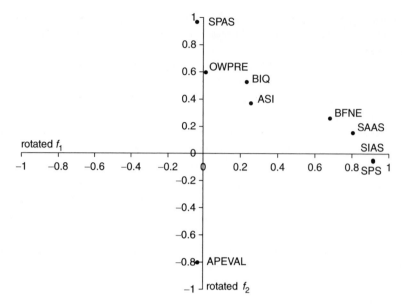

**Figure 8.4** Graphical representation of rotated factor pattern for two-factor model of social anxiety data

variable has a strong loading on one and only one common factor and near-zero loadings on all other factors (McDonald, 1999).

Specifically, *analytic rotation* (Browne, 2001) works by multiplying the initial factor loading matrix by a **transformation matrix** which is selected to provide an interpretable, rotated factor loading matrix, $\hat{\Lambda}_r$, that approximates simple structure:

$$\hat{\Lambda}_r = \hat{\Lambda}\mathbf{T}. \tag{8.10}$$

Complex methods, such as the *oblimin* procedure, are used to find the specific values in $\mathbf{T}$; in short, they are determined from the sine and cosine of the angles by which the factor axes are rotated (for details, see Browne, 2001, and Jennrich, 2007).

 Section recap

### Factor rotation

The purpose of **factor rotation** is to transform an initial, unrotated factor loading matrix, $\hat{\Lambda}$, into a more interpretable, rotated factor loading matrix, $\hat{\Lambda}_r$.

In general, analytic rotation methods seek to find a transformation of $\hat{\Lambda}$ which strikes a balance between **row parsimony**, by which each observed variable is strongly influenced by few (preferably one) rotated factors and has near-zero loadings with all other rotated factors, and **column parsimony**, by which each rotated factor has strong influences on a set of observed variables and near-zero factor loadings with all other variables.

## Orthogonal and oblique rotations

**Orthogonal rotation** occurs when the transformation matrix $\mathbf{T}$ in Equation 8.10 is a square, orthogonal matrix, meaning that $\mathbf{TT}' = \mathbf{I}$. Over the years, many orthogonal rotation methods have been developed. In particular, an orthogonal procedure known as *varimax* is probably the most commonly used of all rotation methods, orthogonal or otherwise. The popularity of varimax is likely because it was one of the earliest numerical methods, it is simple computationally, and it is the default rotation in popular software with EFA procedures (e.g., SPSS and SAS). But using an orthogonal rotation such as varimax ensures that the resulting rotated factors will themselves be orthogonal, such that the (estimated) interfactor correlation matrix, $\hat{\Psi}$, will continue to be restricted to equal an identity matrix, $\mathbf{I}$, as is the case when the initial, unrotated factor loading matrix is estimated (see Equations 8.3 to 8.6). In other words, the correlations among orthogonally rotated factors are all *exactly* equal to zero.

In practice, however, it is unrealistic to expect that common factors should be completely uncorrelated, and methodologists now almost unanimously agree that such overly simplistic orthogonal rotations should be avoided. In contrast, rotation methods that produce correlated factors are called **oblique rotations**. It is more realistic to allow factors to be correlated; thus, oblique rotation methods should be preferred in most situations.[12] If the optimal model solution has near-zero interfactor correlations, an oblique rotation will itself return weakly correlated factors, which is similar to an orthogonal rotation anyway.

Specifically, oblique rotation finds a transformation matrix for Equation 8.10 such that the diagonal elements of the matrix formed by $(\mathbf{T}^{-1}\mathbf{T}'^{-1})$ all equal 1. As a result, the estimated interfactor correlation matrix will be

$$\hat{\Psi} = \mathbf{T}^{-1}\mathbf{T}'^{-1}.$$

Recall from earlier in this chapter that estimation of the EFA model, whether by principal axis, ULS, or ML, begins by restricting $\Psi = \mathbf{I}$. Consequently, when the model is estimated, an unrotated, estimated factor loading matrix $\hat{\Lambda}$ is obtained with the property that the factors are still uncorrelated such that $\hat{\Psi} = \mathbf{I}$. Using an oblique rotation serves to reintroduce the interfactor correlations so that $\hat{\Psi}$ is no longer restricted to being an identity matrix.

Many oblique rotation methods have been developed, and of these, *promax* has been the most commonly used. Like varimax, the popularity of promax is likely a result of its relative simplicity and easy implementation with popular software (in fact, promax was explicitly developed as an oblique version of varimax). Nevertheless, promax does not regularly achieve simple structure as well as other oblique rotations, particularly the so-called 'direct rotations', such as the Crawford and Ferguson (1970) family of rotations which can be varied to influence

---

[12]An important exception occurs when a researcher hypothesizes that all observed variables are determined by a dominant *general factor*, but overall this general factor is not sufficient to explain remaining associations among clusters of observed variables, which may be accounted for with more minor common factors known as *specific factors*. When such a pattern is expected, an orthogonal *bifactor* rotation may be appropriate (see Reise, 2012); nonetheless, an oblique version of bifactor rotation can still achieve better results (Jennrich and Bentler, 2012).

the degree to which the factors are correlated (up to orthogonality) and to achieve a balance between row parsimony and column parsimony (see Jennrich, 2007). A prominent oblique rotation within this family is known as **oblimin** rotation. EFA software with oblimin rotation typically allows the user to alter a weighting parameter, often denoted as $\gamma$, which controls the balance between column and row parsimony, which in turn also affects the interfactor correlations. This oblimin weight is usually set to zero by default; in this situation, oblimin rotation is equivalent to a well-known rotation called *direct quartimin*. In practice, one might compare the results from a few different rotations and choose the one achieving the most interpretable factor loading matrix.

Returning to the social anxiety example, the rotated factor loadings in Table 8.7 were obtained using oblimin rotation with the oblimin weight set to 0.0 (i.e., direct quartimin rotation). Because this is a model with only two factors, there is a single correlation in the $\hat{\Psi}$ interfactor correlation matrix, which in this case is $r_{f_1f_2} = 0.63$, indicating that the correlation between $f_1$, 'social interaction anxiety', and $f_2$, 'body image concern', is moderate to strong.

For comparison, the factor loadings in Table 8.8 were obtained by increasing the oblimin weight to 0.5, which corresponds to a rotation method known as *biquartimin*. With this new rotation, the pattern of loadings is similar to that given earlier, such that $f_1$ could still be labeled 'social interaction anxiety' and $f_2$ 'body image concern'. Overall, large factor loadings have become larger and small loadings smaller. As a consequence, the BIQ and ASI variables are now even more strongly related to $f_2$ than to $f_1$, whereas under the first rotation, their placement among the factors was a little more ambiguous. But an undesirable result of this new rotation is that several factor loadings which had been close to zero with the oblimin weight set to 0.0 are now further from zero in the negative direction; for example, the $f_2$ loading for SIAS has gone from −0.07 to −0.22. Furthermore, increasing the oblimin weight has also increased the interfactor correlation from $r_{f_1f_2} = 0.63$ to $r_{f_1f_2} = 0.78$ (which is not necessarily problematic, however).

**Table 8.8** Rotated factor loadings from two-factor model of social anxiety data

| Variable | $\hat{\Lambda}$ (loadings) | | Communality |
| | $f_1$ | $f_2$ | $\widehat{h^2}$ |
|---|---|---|---|
| BFNE | 0.72 | 0.17 | .74 |
| SIAS | 1.04 | −0.22 | .76 |
| SPS | 1.04 | −0.24 | .76 |
| SPAS | −0.23 | 1.11 | .88 |
| BIQ | 0.16 | 0.59 | .52 |
| ASI | 0.21 | 0.41 | .35 |
| APEVAL | 0.13 | −0.90 | .64 |
| OWPRE | −0.11 | 0.70 | .38 |
| SAAS | 0.88 | 0.04 | .82 |

*Note.* Factor loadings obtained with oblimin rotation (oblimin weight = 0.5).

## Section recap

### Orthogonal and oblique rotations

Factor rotation methods can be classified according to whether they are **orthogonal** or **oblique**.

Orthogonal rotations, the most popular of which is *varimax*, force the interfactor correlations to equal 0 (i.e., the interfactor correlation matrix, Ψ, is forced to be an identity matrix). Because it is unrealistic to expect common factors to be uncorrelated, orthogonal rotations are generally not recommended.

Oblique rotations lead to common factors which are allowed to correlate with each other (i.e., the interfactor correlation matrix, Ψ, is no longer forced to be an identity matrix).

A popular type of oblique rotation is known as *promax*; nevertheless, promax generally does not approximate simple structure as well as other oblique rotations, such as **oblimin**.

Different forms of oblimin rotation can be obtained by adjusting the oblimin weight. Doing so affects the balance between row parsimony and column parsimony and changes the interfactor correlations.

In practice, it can be beneficial to compare factor loading matrices obtained with several rotations and ultimately choose the rotation producing the most interpretable set of factor loadings.

## Factor pattern versus factor structure

Recall that the factor loading matrix, Λ, contains regression coefficients relating the common factors (predictor variables) to the observed variables (outcome variables). That is, to repeat Equation 8.1, the population regression equation for a given observed variable is

$$Y_{pi} = \left( \sum_{m=1}^{M} \lambda_{pm} f_{mi} \right) + \varepsilon_{pi} \, ,$$

and repeating Equation 8.2, the matrix equation for all observed variables is

$$\mathbf{Y} = \mathbf{\Lambda f} + \varepsilon.$$

As mentioned previously, another name for Λ is *factor pattern matrix*. A different matrix, called the **factor structure matrix**, contains the correlations between observed variables and the factors. The EFA procedure of some software packages (e.g., SPSS) prints both matrices by default, and so it is important to understand the difference between them.

If the factors are uncorrelated (as with orthogonal rotation), the factor structure and factor pattern matrices are the same. In other words, if the factors are not correlated, their partial relations with the observed variables are the same as their simple, marginal relations, paralleling the result from ordinary multiple regression that the partial multiple regression slope for a given predictor variable equals its marginal, simple regression slope only when that predictor has zero correlation with the other predictors in the model (see Chapter 2). But if the factors are instead correlated (as occurs with oblique rotation), then the factor structure and factor pattern matrices are not the same. Specifically, the factor pattern matrix contains the unique relation between an observed variable and a given factor while controlling for the influence of all other factors, whereas the factor structure matrix contains the marginal correlations between the observed variables and the underlying factors, combining across the indirect influences of all other factors. For this reason, interpretation should focus on the factor pattern matrix instead of on the structure matrix, paralleling the importance of interpreting partial regression slopes from a multiple regression with correlated predictors rather than just the simple correlations between each predictors and the outcome variable.

Researchers often mistakenly believe that factor loadings cannot be greater than 1 (or less than –1). But loadings in the factor pattern matrix are regression slopes, not correlations, and as such may be greater than 1 (or less than –1), as occurs in Table 8.8. But elements of the factor structure matrix are correlations and thus must fall between –1 and +1. As mentioned earlier, sometimes a communality estimate will be greater than 1 (implying a uniqueness less than 1), which also signals an improper solution. But to reiterate, an estimated factor pattern *loading* exceeding 1 (or less than –1) is not problematic in and of itself.

 Section recap

### Factor pattern versus factor structure

An element of the factor pattern matrix (i.e., a factor loading) represents a partial regression slope coefficient giving the unique linear association between factor $m$ and observed variable $p$, holding the effect of the other factors on observed variable $p$ constant.

An element of a **factor structure matrix** represents the simple, marginal correlation between factor $m$ and observed variable $p$, ignoring the effect of all other factors on observed variable $p$.

When on oblique rotation is used, the rotated factors are correlated and the factor pattern matrix is different from the factor structure matrix. Interpretation should be primarily based on the factor pattern matrix because factor pattern values represent the effect of one factor while holding the other factors constant.

---

To conclude from the presentation of EFA so far, it is difficult to provide step-by-step instructions for EFA because there are so many aspects to the analysis which influence each other simultaneously and thus should be considered simultaneously. But in general, the major stages of an EFA can be enumerated as follows:

1. Estimate an initial model with $M$ factors based on a first educated guess about an appropriate number of factors. If there is absolutely no prior theory about a reasonable value for $M$, perhaps begin with a simple one-factor model. This stage also requires choosing an estimation method; if $N$ is small (e.g., <200) or weak common factors (i.e., factors defined by small-to-moderate loadings) are expected, then ULS may be preferable. Otherwise, use ML. Later, these analyses may be repeated with the other estimator.

2. Based on results from step 1, determine a potentially optimal number of factors $M$ by consulting a variety of criteria including a scree plot, parallel analysis, and model fit statistics such as RMR and RMSEA. Inspecting the final communality estimates and individual residual correlations should also be helpful. If there are one or more variables with weak communalities or there are substantial residual correlations (e.g., .10 or greater), then the current value of $M$ from step 1 may need to be increased. The conceptual interpretability of the rotated factor pattern (i.e., $\hat{\Lambda}_r$) is also critical; if there are uninterpretable factors, then the current value of $M$ may be too large. Keep in mind that the interpretational quality of $\hat{\Lambda}_r$ may depend on the rotation chosen, and so it might be prudent to examine different rotations (e.g., by increasing the oblimin weight from 0 to .5).

3. Based on results from step 2, estimate the model with the potentially optimal number of factors $M$ (unless it was already estimated in step 1) as well as the model with $(M - 1)$ factors and the model with $(M + 1)$ factors. Compare the models in terms of their fit to the data (i.e., using statistics such as RMR and RMSEA) and in terms of their parameter estimates, including the communality estimates, the rotated factor pattern $\hat{\Lambda}_r$, and the estimated interfactor correlation matrix $\hat{\Psi}$. Once again, try different rotations to enhance the interpretation of $\hat{\Lambda}_r$ for a given model. The final estimated model to report as best for the data is the one that optimizes the overall combination of each of these aspects of the analysis.

## Research example for EFA with continuous observed variables

Therefore, to complete the social anxiety EFA example, it is important also to examine one- and three-factor models. Up to this point, the chapter has focused on the estimated two-factor model for this example, which seems to provide a reasonable representation of the pattern of correlations among these nine observed variables, and the scree plot, parallel analysis, and RMR statistics all suggested that $M = 2$ factors may be appropriate for these data. RMSEA, on the other hand, was best for the three- and four-factor models, but given the current sample size ($N = 109$), this fit statistic may not be reliable. Nonetheless, it is important to examine the estimated models with $(M - 1) = 1$ factor and with $(M + 1) = 3$ factors: If the simpler model with $(M - 1)$ factors captures the major regularities in the data without producing substantially large residual correlations, than it may be preferred; conversely, if interpretable, conceptually important factors emerge in the model with $(M + 1)$ factors, then that model may be best for the current set of observed variables.

Table 8.9 gives the estimated factor loadings and communalities (obtained using ULS estimation) for the one-factor model. Note that with only one factor, the concept of rotation is not applicable. Each observed variable has a salient loading on the single factor, but the final communality estimate for OWPRE, in particular, is low. Additionally, in the residual correlation matrix from this one-factor model, there are notable residual correlations between SPAS and APEVAL ($r_{residual} = -.31$), SPAS and OWPRE ($r_{residual} = .22$), BIQ and ASI ($r_{residual} = .18$), and SIAS and SPS ($r_{residual} = .17$). As we saw in Table 8.4, however, the residual correlations from the estimated two-factor model were all near zero; additionally, the communalties for OWPRE and APEVAL are improved with the two-factor model. For these reasons, as well as because of the results from the scree plot and parallel analysis, the two-factor model is preferable to the one-factor model.

Next, Table 8.10 gives the estimated factor loadings and communalities (obtained using ULS estimation) for the three-factor model following oblimin rotation with oblimin weight $= 0$.

**Table 8.9**  Factor loadings from one-factor model of social anxiety data

| Variable | $\hat{\Lambda}$ (loadings) $f_1$ | Communality $\widehat{h^2}$ |
|---|---|---|
| BFNE | 0.88 | .77 |
| SIAS | 0.80 | .64 |
| SPS | 0.79 | .63 |
| SPAS | 0.72 | .52 |
| BIQ | 0.70 | .49 |
| ASI | 0.59 | .35 |
| APEVAL | −0.65 | .42 |
| OWPRE | 0.51 | .26 |
| SAAS | 0.90 | .80 |

Here, $f_1$ and $f_2$ would again likely be interpreted as 'social interaction anxiety' and 'body image concern' as they were with the two-factor model. In this new three-factor model, $f_3$ is primarily defined by a strong loading for ASI (along with a moderate loading for BIQ). So $f_3$ also seems to relate to content pertaining to body image. In fact, the major differences between the two-factor model and the three-factor model revolve around ASI in particular: Its loading on $f_2$ in the two-factor model is 0.39, whereas its loading on $f_2$ in the three-factor model is 0.00; the relations between the other variables and $f_2$ do not change nearly as much with the three-factor model. Additionally, the communality estimate for ASI has jumped from .35 with the two-factor model to .75 with the three-factor model, whereas the communalities of the other variables are mostly unchanged. Therefore, it seems as if the main purpose of the three-factor model relative to the two-factor model is to create an additional factor which primarily

**Table 8.10**  Rotated factor loadings from three-factor model of social anxiety data

| Variable | $\hat{\Lambda}$ (loadings) $f_1$ | $f_2$ | $f_3$ | Communality $\widehat{h^2}$ |
|---|---|---|---|---|
| BFNE | 0.64 | 0.15 | 0.21 | .75 |
| SIAS | 0.96 | −0.01 | −0.12 | .81 |
| SPS | 0.88 | −0.08 | 0.07 | .76 |
| SPAS | −0.03 | 0.95 | 0.06 | .92 |
| BIQ | 0.17 | 0.33 | 0.40 | .58 |
| ASI | 0.05 | 0.00 | 0.84 | .75 |
| APEVAL | −0.09 | −0.83 | 0.12 | .68 |
| OWPRE | −0.02 | 0.48 | 0.24 | .39 |
| SAAS | 0.78 | 0.12 | 0.08 | .81 |

*Note.* Factor loadings obtained with oblimin rotation (oblimin weight = 0.0).

accounts for content specific to ASI. In general, models with factors defined by salient load-ings for only one or two observed variables are to be avoided. In sum, then, we conclude that the two-factor model provides the optimal combination of fit to the data and interpretability for the social anxiety example. To deal with variables such as ASI and OWPRE which have small communality estimates in the two-factor model, we simply conclude that these vari-ables are not as strongly related to the constructs represented by the two common factors as the other observed variables are.

## EXPLORATORY FACTOR ANALYSIS WITH CATEGORICAL OBSERVED VARIABLES

At the beginning of this chapter, I explained that in modern applications of factor analysis, the observed variables are most commonly the responses to individual items from a single test or questionnaire, rather than total scores from many different tests. Because the most common kinds of test items, including Likert-type items, produce categorical variables (with dichotomous or ordered item-response categories) rather than continuous variables, the traditional linear factor analysis model for product-moment $R$ presented earlier is often prob-lematic. Specifically, treating item-response variables as continuous variables often leads to incorrect decisions about the number of common factors underlying the items and biased estimates of factor loadings, communalities, and interfactor correlations (see Flora, LaBrish, and Chalmers, 2012). These problems are most likely to occur when the item-level variables have five or fewer response categories because in these situations the associations among the items are not well approximated by the linear function implied by a Pearson product-moment correlation. If items have more than five ordered categories, then it is usually safe to fit EFA models to the product-moment correlations among them (i.e., to treat them as continuous variables), following the methods described earlier.

One procedure for factor analysing ordered-categorical item-level variables involves fitting the EFA model (i.e., Equation 8.3) to *polychoric correlations*, which are explicitly designed to measure the nonlinear bivariate associations among categorical, ordinally scaled variables, rather than the usual product-moment correlations.[13] Other procedures have been explicitly developed for the factor analysis of item-level variables, such as so-called 'full-information' methods based on item response theory (see Wirth and Edwards, 2007). Here, I have chosen to present the polychoric correlation approach because it can be under-stood as an extension of the correlation-based, linear factor analysis methods presented earlier and because this approach tends to perform as well as full-information procedures in many common situations (Forero and Maydeu-Olivares, 2009). The results of recent work (Barendse, Oort, and Timmerman, 2015) have supported the effectiveness of the limited-information approach using polychoric correlations specifically for the EFA context (most methodological work with polychoric correlations has instead been focused on confirma-tory factor analysis; see Chapter 10).

---

[13]Karl Pearson is responsible for the major developments behind both the polychoric correlation and the more well-known product-moment correlation, and so it is vague to refer to the latter simply as the 'Pearson correlation'.

## Polychoric correlations

The logic behind the **polychoric correlation** begins with the notion that an unobserved, continuous variable, known as a *latent response variable*, determines the observed values of the ordinal item response. **Threshold** parameters are used to relate this continuous latent response variable to an observed, ordinal variable. If a test or questionnaire item produces a dichotomously scored observed variable (e.g., an item scored 0 = *incorrect* or 1 = *correct*), then a single threshold parameter, $\tau$, is needed to relate that observed item-response variable to the corresponding latent response variable, such that

$$Y_i = \begin{cases} 0 \text{ if } Y_i^* \leq \tau \\ 1 \text{ if } Y_i^* > \tau \end{cases},$$

where $Y_i$ is an observed dichotomous variable (scored as 0 or 1 for each case $i$) and $Y_i^*$ is a normally distributed latent response variable. Similarly, if a Likert-type questionnaire item has three ordered response categories (e.g., 0 = *disagree*, 1 = *neutral*, and 2 = *agree*), then two threshold parameters, $\tau_1$ and $\tau_2$, are needed to link the item to its latent response variable:

$$Y_i = \begin{cases} 0 \text{ if } Y_i^* \leq \tau_1 \\ 1 \text{ if } \tau_1 < Y_i^* \leq \tau_2, \\ 2 \text{ if } Y_i^* > \tau_2 \end{cases}$$

where $Y_i$ is now an observed variable with three ordered categories (scored 0, 1, or 2 for each case $i$) and $Y_i^*$ is again a normally distributed latent response variable.[14] This association between a three-category item $Y$ and its normally distributed latent response variable is illustrated in Figure 8.5. In general, an observed item $Y$ with $C$ ordered categories is related to a latent, continuous variable $Y^*$ such that

$$Y_i = c \text{ if } \tau_c < Y_i^* \leq \tau_{c+1}, \tag{8.11}$$

with $\tau_0 = -\infty$ and $\tau_C = +\infty$. Thus, the number of finite threshold parameters for an item with $C$ categories equals $C - 1$.

Because the latent response variables are specified to be normally distributed, the threshold parameters are the $Z$ scores from a standard normal distribution which produce probabilities equal to the observed proportions of cases within each category of the observed, categorical variable. For instance, if an observed $Y$ has only $C = 2$ categories and 50% of participants fall into each category, then $Z = 0$ is the value that separates the lower .5 of the standard normal distribution from the upper .5 of the distribution; therefore, $\tau_1 = 0$ is the single threshold parameter for this observed $Y$ variable.

---

[14]Scoring the observed categories as 0, 1, or 2 is arbitrary from a statistical perspective. The threshold parameters and ultimate polychoric correlation for a pair of variables will be the same regardless of the numerical values assigned to the ordered categories (as long as those values are in ascending order themselves). For instance, items scored as 0 = *disagree*, 1 = *neutral*, and 2 = *agree* could instead be scored as −1 = *disagree*, 0 = *neutral*, and +1 = *agree* without affecting the thresholds or correlations.

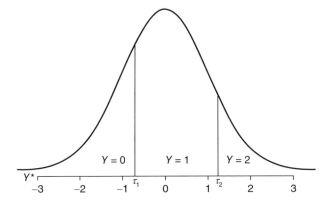

**Figure 8.5** Illustration of normally distributed latent response variable Y* categorized by thresholds $\tau_1$ and $\tau_2$ to produce three-category variable Y

Given the observed information from two ordered item-level variables, a polychoric correlation is then an estimate of the linear correlation between the continuous latent response variables giving rise to the observed item-level variables.[15] Specifically, although the formula for the polychoric correlation is too complex to present here, the univariate threshold parameters as well as the bivariate cross-tabulation of the observed items enter into a maximum likelihood procedure to arrive at the polychoric correlation estimate (see Olsson, 1979). This maximum likelihood function is derived by specifying that any pair of latent response variables follows a *bivariate* normal distribution; a key parameter of the bivariate normal distribution is the correlation between the two normally distributed continuous variables.

Once the polychoric correlations among all item-level variables are calculated, the common factor model is fitted to the polychoric correlation matrix, $\mathbf{R}_{polychoric}$, rather than to the usual product-moment correlation matrix. Specifically, a factor analysis of polychoric correlations implies that the common factor model is

$$\mathbf{Y^*} = \Lambda \mathbf{f} + \varepsilon,$$

which is nearly identical to the model in Equation 8.2 for observed continuous variables, except here the common factors in **f** are predictors of the continuous latent response variables in **Y***, with each variable in **Y*** linked to its corresponding observed variable via Equation 8.11. But like EFA of continuous variables, the model parameters are estimated from the correlation structure, where the correlations are now polychoric correlations. Thus, adopting Equation 8.3 leads to

$$\widehat{\mathbf{P}} = \Lambda \Psi \Lambda' + \Theta,$$

where $\widehat{\mathbf{P}}$ contains the model-implied correlations among the latent response variables in **Y***. Next, ULS estimation (rather than ML) of the EFA model is recommended (Lee, Zhang, and Edwards, 2012), the purpose of which is to minimize squared residual polychoric correlations according to the manner described earlier in this chapter for ULS estimation of EFA models.

---

[15]The *tetrachoric correlation* is a specific type of polychoric correlation that is obtained when both observed variables are dichotomous.

## Research example for EFA with item-level categorical variables

An article by Nissim et al. (2010) noted that although the Beck Hopelessness Scale (BHS; Beck, Weissman, Lester, and Trexler, 1974, cited in Nissim et al.) is often administered to seriously ill patients to measure a general hopelessness construct (which in turn predicts suicidal ideation), the conceptual content of the individual items suggests that the scale may take on a different interpretation among individuals with advanced cancer than the pessimistic cognitive style defining psychological hopelessness. To help examine this possibility, Nissim et al. used EFA to determine whether there are multiple common factors underlying responses to the items of the BHS given by patients with advanced cancer.

> This dataset is also available on the text's webpage (https://study.sagepub.com/flora) along with annotated input and output from several popular statistical software packages showing how to reproduce the analyses presented here.

The 20 BHS items are dichotomously scored (each item is given a *true* or *false* response), implying that an EFA of product-moment correlations is likely to produce misleading results, as discussed earlier. Therefore, Nissim et al. (2010) fitted various EFA models to the matrix of polychoric correlations[16] among the $P = 20$ items calculated with a sample of $N = 170$ patients with advanced cancer. In fact, Table 8.11 shows that the polychoric correlations among the first three items of the BHS are drastically different from the product-moment correlations among these items (positively worded items were reverse-scored prior to all data analyses).[17]

Both a scree plot and parallel analysis of the reduced polychoric correlation matrix suggest that a model with $M = 2$ common factors is optimal for the BHS items. Importantly, this parallel analysis compared the eigenvalues of the observed polychoric correlation matrix with eigenvalues of randomly generated polychoric correlation matrices rather than with randomly generated product-moment correlation matrices (see Garrido, Abad, and Ponsoda, 2013). Next, with one-, two-, and three-factor models each estimated using ULS, the RMR statistics are .112, .074, and .062, respectively. Ultimately, Nissim et al. (2010) decided that a two-factor model was optimal for their data. The results for the two-factor model are presented in Table 8.12; these factor loadings were obtained using oblimin rotation with the oblimin

**Table 8.11** Polychoric and product-moment correlations among the first three items of the Beck Hopelessness Scale

| Item | 1. | 2. | 3. |
|---|---|---|---|
| 1. I look forward to the future with hope and enthusiasm. | 1.00 | .19 | .39 |
| 2. I might as well give up because there is nothing I can do about making things better for myself. | .55 | 1.00 | .05 |
| 3. When things are going badly, I am helped by knowing they cannot stay that way forever. | .65 | .19 | 1.00 |

*Note.* $N = 170$. Polychoric correlations are below the diagonal, and product-moment correlations are above the diagonal.

---

[16]Because the items are dichotomous, one may also refer to the correlations as tetrachoric correlations.

[17]Correlations among only the first three items are presented to conserve space.

weight set to 0.5.[18] In this table, the items are reordered for ease of interpretation. Factor 1 is defined by salient loadings from items 1, 3, 5, 6, 7, 13, 15, and 19; this factor somewhat corresponds to the 'negative expectations' factor identified by Nissim et al. Factor 2 is defined by salient loadings from items 8, 9, 12, 14, 16, 17, and 20, which somewhat corresponds to the 'loss of motivation' factor identified by Nissim et al. The estimated interfactor correlation is $r = .62$. Finally, the communality estimates for this two-factor model are all strong, with the exception of $\widehat{h^2} = .35$ for item 4 and $\widehat{h^2} = .39$ for item 10.

The main take-away from this example EFA with the BHS items is that once one recognizes that the categorical nature of the observed item-level variables indicates that the analysis

**Table 8.12** Parameter estimates from two-factor model of items from the Beck Hopelessness Scale

| Item | | $\hat{\Lambda}$ (loadings) | | Communality |
|---|---|---|---|---|
| | | $f_1$ | $f_2$ | $\widehat{h^2}$ |
| 1. | I look forward to the future with hope and enthusiasm | 0.88 | 0.05 | .82 |
| 7. | My future seems dark to me | 0.73 | 0.19 | .74 |
| 3. | When things are going badly, I am helped by knowing they cannot stay that way forever | 0.93 | −0.41 | .56 |
| 5. | I have enough time to accomplish the things I want to do | 0.76 | −0.06 | .52 |
| 6. | In the future, I expect to succeed in what concerns me most | 0.91 | −0.01 | .82 |
| 13. | When I look ahead to the future, I expect that I will be happier than I am now | 0.85 | −0.21 | .55 |
| 15. | I have great faith in the future | 0.80 | 0.13 | .78 |
| 19. | I can look forward to more good times than bad times | 0.72 | 0.20 | .73 |
| 4. | I cannot imagine what my life would be like in 10 years | −0.14 | 0.67 | .35 |
| 9. | I just can't get the breaks, and there is no reason I will in the future | 0.12 | 0.84 | .85 |
| 11. | All I can see ahead of me is unpleasantness rather than pleasantness | 0.51 | 0.51 | .85 |
| 12. | I don't expect to get what I really want | 0.37 | 0.60 | .76 |
| 14. | Things just won't work out the way I want them to | 0.28 | 0.65 | .73 |
| 16. | I never get what I want so it's foolish to want anything | −0.28 | 0.98 | .70 |
| 17. | It is very unlikely that I will get any real satisfaction in the future | 0.26 | 0.76 | .88 |
| 20. | There is no use in really trying to get anything I want because I probably won't get it | −0.22 | 1.04 | .85 |
| 8. | I happen to be particularly lucky, and I expect to get more of the good things in life than the average person | 0.24 | 0.54 | .51 |
| 2. | I might as well give up because there is nothing I can do about making things better for myself | 0.45 | 0.34 | .51 |
| 18. | The future seems vague and uncertain to me | 0.39 | 0.45 | .57 |
| 10. | My past experiences prepared me well for the future | 0.20 | 0.48 | .39 |

*Note.* Factor loadings obtained with oblimin rotation (oblimin weight = 0.5).

---

[18]These results are somewhat different from those reported by Nissim et al. (2010) who used a different estimator (a type of *weighted* least squares) and different rotation (promax).

should be based on polychoric correlations rather than on product-moment correlations, the EFA proceeds in the same way as with continuous observed variables: Essentially the same criteria are available for determining the optimal number of common factors (noting that the randomly generated correlation matrices for parallel analysis should also be polychoric correlation matrices; see Garrido, Abad, and Ponsoda, 2016, for further recommendations regarding the use of model fit statistics for EFA with categorical variables), the same rotation methods are applicable, and finally the major parameter estimates (factor loadings, communalities, and interfactor correlations) are interpreted in the same manner.

 Section recap

### EFA with categorical observed variables

Treating item-level variables, which are categorical, as if they are continuous can lead to grossly inaccurate EFA results.

Fitting EFA models to **polychoric correlations** (rather than to the usual product-moment correlations) using ULS estimation properly accounts for the ordered categorical nature of item-level variables.

A polychoric correlation is an estimate of the correlation between two continuous, normally distributed, but unobserved variables known as *latent response variables*. A latent response variable $Y*$ is categorized according to **threshold** parameters, $\tau_c$, which then produce the observed, ordinally scaled categorical variable Y.

A factor analysis of the polychoric correlation matrix, $\mathbf{R}_{polychoric}$, implies that the common factor model is

$$\mathbf{Y^*} = \mathbf{\Lambda f} + \varepsilon,$$

such that the common factors in $\mathbf{f}$ are predictors of the vector of continuous latent response variables $\mathbf{Y^*}$, with each variable in $\mathbf{Y^*}$ linked to its corresponding observed, item-level variable according to the threshold parameters.

An EFA of item-level variables using polychoric correlations proceeds in the same way as with continuous observed variables:

- The same criteria are available for determining the optimal number of common factors
- The same rotation methods are applicable
- The major parameter estimates (factor loadings, communalities, and interfactor correlations) are interpreted in the same manner

## ASSUMPTIONS AND DIAGNOSTICS FOR EFA

As seldom as researchers examine potential assumption violations and influential cases in the context of ordinary regression modeling, doing so seems even rarer for EFA. For a comprehensive, nontechnical overview of this topic, see Flora et al. (2012).

First and foremost, because EFA is essentially an analysis of the correlations among observed variables, it is prudent to determine whether those correlations represent an adequate summary of the associations among the variables. As already detailed, if the observed variables are categorical (which is almost always the case with item-level variables), then they are not linearly related, and thus, standard product-moment correlations may be inadequate for factor analysis. Instead, EFA models may be fitted to the polychoric correlations among the observed variables. This polychoric correlation procedure tends to outperform analyses using product-moment correlations when items have five or fewer categories; with more than five ordered categories per observed variable, the bivariate associations among them more closely approximate linear relations and it may be preferable to fit EFA models using product-moment correlations (or to try both types of correlations and compare the results).

But if the observed variables are (approximately) continuous, then it is still important to evaluate whether their bivariate associations can be reasonably well summarized with a measure of linear association, that is, with product-moment correlations. Returning to the social anxiety example, Figure 8.6 presents a scatterplot matrix of the nine observed variables, which is just a collection of all possible bivariate scatterplots among the nine observed variables (with a depiction of each variable's univariate distribution on the diagonal). Within each of these individual scatterplots, it does appear as if a straight line would be a reasonable model for most bivariate associations, although a few relations also seem to have a curvilinear component (e.g., between SPS and SPAS). The polynomial regression approach described in Chapter 2 would be awkward and confusing to incorporate into an EFA, but it may be that a transformation of one or more observed variables would serve to 'linearize' the bivariate associations.

Alternatively, when the scores on the original, raw score variables show curvilinear relations, it may be that their *ranks* are linearly associated (converting a variable to ranks is also a form of transformation). This appears to be the case for the association between SPS and SPAS, as shown in Figure 8.7, where the original observations in the left panel of the figure have a noticeable nonlinear trend but the ranks of the observations in the right panel of the figure are more directly linearly associated. In this situation, Spearman's rank correlations may be

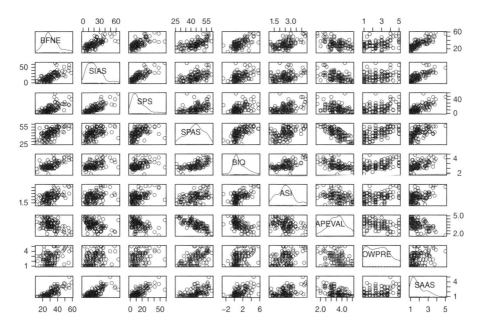

**Figure 8.6**  Scatterplot matrix for nine social anxiety and body image variables

used for EFA in place of the usual product-moment correlations. When two raw scale variables, $Y_1$ and $Y_2$, are converted into ranks, $Y_{1r}$ and $Y_{2r}$, then Spearman's rank correlation between $Y_1$ and $Y_2$ is simply the Pearson product-moment correlation between the ranks, $Y_{1r}$ and $Y_{2r}$. Continuing with the social anxiety example, when EFA is performed using Spearman's rank correlations rather than the original, raw score correlations, the optimal EFA model is again a two-factor model with a rotated factor pattern similar to that presented earlier. Therefore, in this particular example, the slight nonlinear trends among the observed variables do not seem to have any radically distorting effect on the original EFA. But in other situations, nonlinear associations among continuous variables could potentially lead to misleading conclusions from an EFA if they are ignored.

Beyond the importance of assessing linearity among variables, distributional assumptions for EFA depend on the estimation method. The ULS estimator (and by extension principal axis estimation) makes no assumption about the univariate or multivariate distributions of the observed variables. But the ML estimator is based on an assumption that the observed variables follow a multivariate normal distribution, although the parameter estimates maintain consistency when this assumption is violated. Methods for assessing multivariate normality are addressed in Chapters 9 and 10 in the SEM context; these are also applicable to ML estimation of EFA models. Finally, as detailed earlier, calculation of polychoric correlations for the EFA of item-level variables is based on an assumption that each pair of latent response variables has a bivariate normal distribution. Nevertheless, although this assumption is difficult to assess in practice, it is mild and violations do not seem to have severe effects on the polychoric correlations themselves nor on subsequent factor analysis results (Flora and Curran, 2004).

Next, just as influential observations can have dramatic effects on ordinary multiple regression analyses, as described in Chapter 2, the same is true for EFA. In fact, because the common factor model is a form of a regression model, many of the case diagnostic concepts and methods that are used for ordinary regression are also applicable to EFA, as described by Flora et al. (2012). Applying these methods, there are no excessively outlying or influential cases in the social anxiety example. Similar case diagnostic methods have not yet been examined for the EFA of categorical variables using polychoric correlations. But a particular problematic data feature for this procedure is known as **sparseness**, which occurs when the bivariate cross-tabulation of two observed variables produces cells with frequencies equal to zero (see Savalei, 2011). In this situation, it may be advantageous to collapse categories so that the univariate distributions of the observed ordinal variables are less skewed.

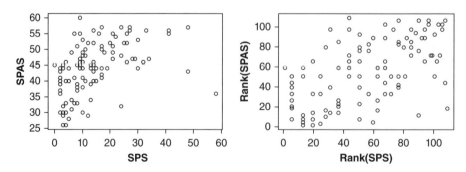

**Figure 8.7** Scatterplot of SPAS variable by SPS variable raw scores (left panel) and ranks (right panel)

## Section recap

### Assumptions and diagnostics for EFA

The most important assumption of EFA using product-moment correlations is that the observed variables are linearly related:

- If the observed variables (e.g., items) have five or fewer categories, this linearity assumption is grossly violated and a method which accounts for the categorical nature of the variables, such as factor analysing polychoric correlations, should be used instead.
- If the observed variables have more than five ordered categories or are continuous, then the linearity assumption may be checked using scatterplots.
- If models are fitted to product-moment correlations using ULS estimation (or principal axis), there is no distributional assumption for the observed variables.
- If models are fitted to product-moment correlations using ML, then the observed variables are assumed to follow a multivariate normal distribution.
- If models are fitted to polychoric correlations, each pair of latent response variables is assumed to follow a bivariate normal distribution. Nevertheless, this assumption is nearly impossible to assess, and mild violations do not have strong effects on EFA results.

Like any statistical modeling procedure, EFA results are potentially influenced by outlying observations. Case diagnostic principles from ordinary multiple regression analysis can be generalized to EFA.

## CHAPTER SUMMARY

Exploratory factor analysis (EFA) is a well-known (and occasionally controversial) multivariate statistical technique which originated in the field of psychometrics but has seen its use diversify to other areas in the behavioural and social sciences. After detailing EFA for the context of continuous observed variables, this chapter also discussed the use of EFA of categorical observed variables (such as the individual items from a questionnaire):

- The general purpose of **exploratory factor analysis** (or **EFA**) is to develop a model which represents the pattern of associations among a potentially large number of empirically observed variables in terms of a small number of **factors**, which are **latent variables**.
- A major goal of EFA is to determine the number of common factors, $M$, that adequately explain the pattern of correlations among a set of $P$ observed variables.
- Given a choice of the value of $M$, the **common factor model** relates these $M$ latent variables, or factors, to the observed variables with a linear regression function.
- Therefore, the common factor model is a linear regression model in which the actual values of the predictor variables, the **factor scores**, are unknown.
- The purpose of **factor rotation** is to transform an initial, unrotated factor loading matrix, $\hat{\Lambda}$, into a more interpretable, rotated factor loading matrix, $\hat{\Lambda}_r$.
- In modern research, factor analysis is most commonly used to model the responses to individual items from one test or questionnaire.

- The traditional linear factor analysis model does not work well for item-level variables because they are typically categorical with ordinal scales of measurement rather than continuous; the linear association implied by a product-moment correlation is a poor model for categorical, item-level variables.
- Fitting EFA models to **polychoric correlations** (rather than to the usual product-moment correlations) properly accounts for the ordered categorical nature of item-level variables.

## RECOMMENDED READING

Fabrigar, L.R., Wegener, D.T., MacCallum, R.C., & Strahan, E.J. (1999). Evaluating the use of exploratory factor analysis in psychological research. *Psychological Methods, 4,* 272–99.

- This article reviews the major decisions that must be made in an EFA and how these decisions can impact subsequent results and conclusions.

Flora, D.B., LaBrish, C., & Chalmers, R.P. (2012). Old and new ideas for data screening and assumption testing for exploratory and confirmatory factor analysis. *Frontiers in Quantitative Psychology and Measurement, 3* (55). doi:10.3389/fpsyg.2012.00055

- The first part of this paper demonstrates how principles of regression diagnostics can be applied to fitted EFA models, and the second part of the paper shows why categorical, item-level variables should not be treated as continuous variables.

MacCallum, R.C. (2009). Factor analysis. In R.E. Millsap, & A. Maydeu-Olivares (Eds), *The SAGE handbook of quantitative methods in psychology* (pp. 123–47). Thousand Oaks, CA: SAGE.

- Although a handful of factor analysis texts have been published over the decades, in my opinion, most of them have substantial flaws. This book chapter provides a brief, but comprehensive, treatment of EFA that is as good as any text. Much of the material in this chapter is inspired by MacCallum's chapter.

Preacher, K.J., & MacCallum, R.C. (2003). Repairing Tom Swift's electric factor analysis machine. *Understanding Statistics, 2,* 13–43.

- This paper gives a clear, nontechnical demonstration of the differences between EFA and principal components analysis; the advantages of using an oblique rather than an orthogonal rotation are also addressed.

# STRUCTURAL EQUATION MODELING I: PATH ANALYSIS

## CHAPTER OVERVIEW

Beginning with the current chapter, the remaining chapters of the text address various structural equation models. Over the past several decades, structural equation modeling (SEM) has become an extremely common procedure for multivariate data analysis in the behavioural and social sciences. To introduce the major principles of SEM, the current chapter focuses on path analysis models, which include only observed variables; ensuing chapters present models which include both observed and latent variables. The main topics of this chapter are:

- What is structural equation modeling?
- Specification of path analysis models
- Identification of path analysis models
- Estimation of path analysis models
- Standard errors, inference, and $R^2$ statistics
- Model fit evaluation
- Model evaluation and revision
- Estimated model interpretation
- Assumptions and diagnostics for path analysis models

**Table 9.0**  Greek letter notation used in this chapter

| Greek letter | English name | Represents |
| --- | --- | --- |
| $\gamma$ | Lowercase 'gamma' | Slope parameter in regression of $Y$ on $X$ |
| $\Gamma$ | Uppercase 'gamma' | Matrix of $\gamma$ parameters |
| $\beta$ | Lowercase 'beta' | Slope parameter in regression of one $Y$ on a different $Y$ |
| $B$ | Uppercase 'beta' | Matrix of $\beta$ parameters |

*(Continued)*

**Table 9.0** (Continued)

| Greek letter | English name | Represents |
|---|---|---|
| $\zeta$ | Lowercase 'zeta' | Regression error term |
| $\Phi$ | Uppercase 'phi' | Covariance matrix of exogenous variables |
| $\phi$ | Lowercase 'phi' | Variance or covariance element in $\Phi$ |
| $\Psi$ | Uppercase 'psy' | Covariance matrix of errors in $\zeta$ |
| $\psi$ | Lowercase 'psy' | Variance or covariance element in $\Psi$ |
| $\Sigma$ | Uppercase 'sigma' | Population covariance matrix among observed variables |
| $\theta$ | Lowercase 'theta' | Vector of all model parameters |
| $\chi$ | Lowercase 'chi' | $\chi^2$ distribution |

*Note.* Some of these Greek letters may have been used for different purposes in previous chapters.

## WHAT IS STRUCTURAL EQUATION MODELING?

**Structural equation modeling**, or **SEM**, is a general framework for specifying and estimating a wide variety of parametric, multivariate statistical models. Usually these models are designed to capture a set of linear relations among variables, but methods for various types of nonlinear SEM are now well established. Although they are not synonymous in all situations, several other names for SEM which readers might encounter include:

- *Covariance structure modeling* or *covariance structure analysis* stems from the fact that many common types of structural equation models are estimated directly from an observed covariance matrix rather than from the original raw data for all cases.
- Similarly, *correlation structure modeling* occurs when models are fitted to observed correlation matrices, which removes information about observed variable scales.
- *Simultaneous equation modeling* stems from the fact that a structural equation model usually consists of two or more separate regression equations which are estimated simultaneously.
- *Moment structure modeling* or *moment structure analysis* is a generalization of the covariance structure modeling idea to represent the idea that the data for certain models consist of both observed means (i.e., the first *moment* of a distribution) and observed variances and covariances (i.e., the second central moment).

In certain contexts (especially in literature from the 1970s and 1980s), SEM has also been referred to as *causal modeling*. Although SEM can certainly be used to help evaluate theories of causality, not all structural equation models need to address causal hypotheses, and methods other than SEM can test causal hypotheses (see Murnane and Willett, 2011, for an overview of causal inference, and see Pedhazur, 1997: 765–70, for an entertaining account of causality in the context of SEM). To repeat from earlier, statistical models are fundamentally descriptive but can be used for causal inference. That being said, much of the research comprising path analysis has been focused on evaluating causal hypotheses, but reaching valid conclusions regarding causality depends on assumptions regarding research design and variable selection beyond the standard statistical assumptions (again, see Bollen, 1989, and Pedhazur, 1997). Just because one uses path analysis (or another type of SEM) successfully does not imply that one has confirmed the presence of a particular causal process; the statistical procedure itself is not sufficient to establish causality.

Finally, SEM has also been called *LISREL modeling* (once again, particularly in literature from the 1970s and 1980s), which conflates the statistical methodology of SEM with a prominent software package known as LISREL, which has been (and still is) developed by Karl Jöreskog, who is one of the pioneering statistical researchers of SEM (e.g., Jöreskog and Sörbom, 1974, 2015).

Given its generality, SEM encompasses several other modeling methods as special cases. Among others, these specific types of SEM include:

- Univariate general linear models, including all of its submodels, such as the regression model underlying the independent-groups *t* test and analysis of variance (ANOVA), and all of the other simple and multiple regression models covered in Chapters 1 through 5
- Multivariate general linear models, which include the model underlying many of the traditional methods covered in multivariate statistical texts, such as multivariate analysis of variance and covariance (i.e., MANOVA and MANCOVA), canonical correlation analysis, and discriminant function analysis (in fact, approaching these methods as structural equation models has certain advantages; see Graham, 2008, and Green and Thompson, 2006, 2012)
- Path analysis, which is the main topic of this chapter
- Both exploratory factor analysis (see Chapter 8) and confirmatory factor analysis (covered in Chapter 10)
- Latent growth curve or trajectory modeling for repeated measures or longitudinal data (covered in Chapter 11)

This wide array of statistical models fits under the umbrella of SEM because a given SEM can (a) include any number of independent variables, predictors, or covariates and any number of dependent or outcome variables (and a variable can serve as both a predictor and an outcome in the same model); (b) include latent variables, which is critical for representing hypothetical constructs and accounting for measurement error; and (c) represent a mean structure, which is critical for repeated measures or longitudinal data as well as for other applications.

Although there were other influential developers around the same time, the birth of SEM as a comprehensive modeling framework is mainly attributed to a series of papers by Jöreskog in the late 1960s and 1970s (e.g., Jöreskog, 1969, 1970, 1973; see Matsueda, 2012, for a review of the history of SEM). Jöreskog referred to his general approach as the analysis of 'LInear Structural RELations' which he abbreviated LISREL. This approach involved specifying models using a particular set of parameter matrices with Greek letter symbols for notation as well as a set of conventions for representing models using *path diagrams*. This LISREL notation has evolved into the modern standard for the most part and serves as the notational system for SEM in this text (alternatives include the Bentler and Weeks, 1980, notation and the reticular action model, or RAM, notation of McArdle and McDonald, 1984).

 **Section recap**

### What is structural equation modeling?

**Structural equation modeling** (**SEM**) is a general framework encompassing a wide variety of statistical models as special cases.

*(Continued)*

(Continued)

Structural equation models can incorporate any number of independent or predictor variables and any number of dependent or outcome variables, as well as both observed variables and latent variables.

Jöreskog's LISREL approach continues to be a dominant system for representing structural equation models using a specific set of Greek letter notation and depictions of models using **path diagrams**.

## PATH ANALYSIS

As mentioned, a crucial strength of SEM is the ability to include latent variables. But many applications of SEM have no latent variables (except error terms, which are technically latent variables although they do not represent hypothetical constructs; Bollen, 2002). A structural equation model with only observed variables (also called manifest variables) and no latent variables (except error terms) is commonly called a **path analysis** model.

Because it is simpler to set aside latent variables for now, the current chapter uses path analysis to provide a framework for introducing most of the fundamental concepts of SEM. Specifically, path analysis gives us a simple context to step through the major concepts of the *specification*, *identification*, and *estimation* of structural equation models.

As with the models covered in earlier chapters, model **specification** is a set of mathematical statements about the relations among the variables of interest which establishes the set of parameters for the model. In SEM, specification is the formal expression of the hypothesized model in terms of mathematical equations or a **path diagram** (path diagrams are described and presented throughout this chapter as well as throughout Chapters 10 and 11).

Next, **identification** is the property of a model that determines whether the specified equations in the model are solvable based on the balance of 'knowns' and 'unknowns'. The 'knowns' are essentially the descriptive summary statistics (usually just variances and covariances) obtainable from the data, whereas the 'unknowns' are the population parameters. Unique estimates of the model parameters cannot be obtained unless the model is identified. Often, researchers specify models which are too complex and thus are not identified; in this situation, there is more than one set of parameter estimates which explain the observed data equally well.

Given that a specified model is identified, model **estimation** is the process of obtaining estimates of the hypothetical population parameters (i.e., parameter estimates) using empirical, sample data. The concept of estimation has already been addressed in earlier chapters (e.g., ordinary least-squares estimation of multiple regression models and maximum likelihood estimation of multilevel models or exploratory factor analysis models).

The topics of identification and estimation are abstract and technical, but having at least a rudimentary understanding is valuable because problems often arise in applied research, and a familiarity with the principles and terminology pertaining to identification and estimation can be helpful for troubleshooting when SEM software produces ominous warning messages in its output.

## Section recap

### What is path analysis?

**Path analysis** models are structural equation models which consist of only observed variables and no latent variables.

Because path analysis models do not include latent variables, they provide a simple context for presenting the fundamental concepts of model **specification**, **identification**, and **estimation** for SEM.

---

## Research example for path analysis: Social support and depression

Scott-Lennox and Lennox (1995) used path analysis to examine the relations between social support and depression among older adults with low income. Specifically, they examined the prediction of scores on the Center for Epidemiological Studies Depression Scale (CESD), an operational variable representing a person's level of depression, from scores on a Perceived Adequacy of Social Support Scale (PASS), an operational variable representing a person's level of perceived social support. The researchers also hypothesized that PASS scores would be determined by aspects of each participant's social support network, particularly support network *size* (essentially the number of close confidants named by each participant), support network *density* (how close the participant believes network members are to each other), and gender *homophily* (the proportion of the participant's total network that were the same gender as the participant). To examine these predictions, we have a sample of $N = 214$ cases simulated to be consistent with the summary statistics for the white female group reported by Scott-Lennox and Lennox (1995).[1]

This dataset is available on the text's webpage (https://study.sagepub.com/flora) along with annotated input and output from several popular statistical software packages showing how to reproduce the analyses presented in this chapter.

## PATH ANALYSIS: MODEL SPECIFICATION

The specification of a given structural equation model is a formal statement of the hypothesized associations among variables using either a set of one or more equations or, equivalently, a path diagram. Although model specification tends to be emphasized more explicitly in SEM, the concept is present in other statistical modeling procedures; for example,

---

[1]Specifically, Scott-Lennox and Lennox (1995) provided a sample correlation matrix, means, and standard deviations of these five observed variables for each of several groups. Unfortunately, although they reported the total sample size across all groups, they did not give the within-group sample sizes. Because the data for the current chapter are simulated, the results reported herein are not a valid reproduction of the results reported by Scott-Lennox and Lennox.

earlier chapters presented model specification for multiple regression (Equation 2.9), the simple indirect-effect model (Equations 5.1 and 5.2), the random-intercepts multilevel model (Equations 6.4 to 6.7), and the common factor model underlying exploratory factor analysis (Equations 8.1 and 8.2). In this chapter, model specification for path analysis is presented first for familiar regression models of increasing complexity (e.g., the simple regression model, the two-predictor multiple regression model, and so on) which can be understood as certain types of path analysis models; then, specification of the complete social support and depression example model is given along with a completely general matrix formulation that can be applied to any path analysis model. Once again, specifying a regression model as a path analysis model often implies a hypothesized causal process among the variables, but the use of path analysis (or SEM generally) itself is not sufficient to establish causality.

## Specification of a simple regression model

As mentioned, the linear regression model is a certain type of structural equation model. Indeed, the simple regression model (see Chapter 1) where a single observed, operational dependent variable or outcome, $Y$, is regressed on a single observed, operational independent variable or predictor, $X$, is the simplest model possible (aside from a trivial univariate, or intercept-only, model). Applying the social support and depression example, the simple linear regression of CESD scores on PASS scores can be specified as a structural equation model or, more specifically, as a path analysis model; the path diagram for this model is depicted in Figure 9.1. In path diagrams, observed variables are represented with rectangles, whereas arrows pointing from one observed variable to another are hypothesized, directional linear regression relations. Here, the path diagram makes it clear that the PASS observed variable is a direct predictor of the CESD observed variable; the regression slope for this relation is represented with the Greek letter $\gamma$, and the error term in this regression relation is represented with the letter $\zeta$.

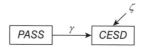

**Figure 9.1** Path diagram representing a simple linear regression model as a path analysis model

All path diagrams imply one or more regression equations. Here, letting $Y_i$ represent the observed score on the CESD variable for person $i$ and $X_i$ represent that person's score on PASS, the single regression equation corresponding to the path diagram in Figure 9.1 can be written as

$$Y_i = \gamma X_i + \zeta_i,$$ 

(9.1)

where $\gamma$ is the regression slope coefficient (also known as a *path coefficient*) and $\zeta_i$ is the error term for person $i$. Equation 9.1 is just a form of the simple regression model presented in Chapter 1, except there is no intercept parameter. It is common for path analysis models to exclude intercepts. This tendency is simply a by-product of the fact that these models are often estimated directly from the observed covariances among the variables (see the Estimation section later in this chapter) without consideration of the observed means; it turns out that omitting the intercept has no implications for the obtained estimates of the other parameters in the model. Finally, the path diagram also includes a short arrow connecting the $\zeta$ error term to $Y$; this arrow does not represent a parameter to be estimated from data and is instead assumed to be a constant equal to 1, which reflects the fact that Equation 9.1 can also be written as

$$Y_i = \gamma X_i + (1)\zeta_i.$$

In fact, sometimes this constant of 1 is explicitly written on the arrow connecting $\zeta$ to $Y$ to indicate that this particular arrow does not represent a free parameter to be estimated, in contrast to the arrow representing $\gamma$ which is a parameter to be estimated.

It is important to keep in mind that the parameters of this model consist of not only the regression slope coefficient, $\gamma$, but also of the variance of $X$ (i.e., $\sigma_X^2$) and the variance of $\zeta$ (i.e., $\sigma_\zeta^2$). The variance of the outcome variable $Y$ is not itself a model parameter; instead, the model represents the variance of $Y$ as a function of $\sigma_X^2$ and $\sigma_\zeta^2$. Specifically, if we take the variance of both sides of Equation 9.1, we obtain

$$\mathrm{VAR}(Y_i) = \mathrm{VAR}(\gamma X_i + \zeta_i) = \gamma^2 \sigma_X^2 + \sigma_\zeta^2.$$

This expression demonstrates the concept that the model explains the variance of the outcome variable according to a function of the set of parameters, which are $\gamma$, $\sigma_X^2$, and $\sigma_\zeta^2$. As we will see later, this concept generalizes to larger models and provides a basis for model estimation.

 Section recap

### Specification of simple regression as a path analysis model

The **specification** of a given structural equation model provides a formal statement of the associations among variables using either a set of one or more equations or, equivalently, a path diagram.

Using LISREL notation, a simple linear regression model is specified as

$$Y_i = \gamma X_i + \zeta_i,$$

where $\gamma$ is the slope coefficient parameter, $\zeta_i$ is the error term, and no intercept parameter is needed.

This model's parameter set includes the slope $\gamma$ as well as the variance of the predictor $(\sigma_X^2)$ and the error variance $(\sigma_\zeta^2)$.

## Specification of a multiple regression model

Just as a simple regression model can be specified as a structural equation model, a multiple regression model, in which a single observed outcome variable is regressed on two or more observed predictors, can also be represented as a structural equation model. Returning to the social support and depression example, the researchers hypothesized that the PASS variable would be determined by support network *size*, support network *density*, and support network gender *homophily*. A path analysis model consistent with this hypothesis is depicted in Figure 9.2.

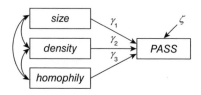

**Figure 9.2**   Path diagram representing a multiple regression model as a path analysis model

In path diagrams, curved double-headed arrows connecting separate variables represent non-directional relations; that is, they represent assumed covariances among variables, but no directional effect is hypothesized. Recall from Chapter 2 that a key idea in multiple regression modeling is to account for the correlations among predictor variables; equivalent, the path analysis model in Figure 9.2 is specified to include the covariances among the predictors size, density, and homophily.

Similar to the model presented in Figure 9.1, the model in Figure 9.2 contains only one outcome variable, which is now PASS, and thus, there is a single regression equation for the model. But now there are three predictors, and so this equation is a multiple regression equation:

$$Y_i = \gamma_1 X_{1i} + \gamma_2 X_{2i} + \gamma_3 X_{3i} + \zeta_i, \tag{9.2}$$

where $Y_i$ is the PASS variable score for person $i$, $X_{1i}$ is that person's *size* score, $X_{2i}$ is the *density* score, and $X_{3i}$ is the *homophily* score. Once again, the error term for person $i$ is represented as $\zeta_i$ and the model does not need to include an intercept parameter. Yet, this path analysis model is an example of the multiple regression models covered in Chapter 2, and thus, each slope coefficient ($\gamma_1$, $\gamma_2$, and $\gamma_3$) is the partial regression coefficient for its observed variable, representing the linear effect of that predictor while holding the other predictors constant. This interpretation is a result of the model including the covariances among the observed predictors, as depicted by the curved, double-headed arrows in Figure 9.2. Thus, the parameters of the current model include the three regression coefficients ($\gamma_1$, $\gamma_2$, and $\gamma_3$) as well as the variances of the predictors ($\sigma_{X_1}^2$, $\sigma_{X_2}^2$, and $\sigma_{X_3}^2$), the covariances among the predictors ($\sigma_{X_2 X_1}$, $\sigma_{X_3 X_1}$, and $\sigma_{X_3 X_2}$), and finally the error variance, $\sigma_{\zeta}^2$.

Of course, in multiple regression generally, and thus path analysis by extension, there can be any number of predictors, some of which might be things like dummy code variables to represent categorical predictors (as in Chapter 3) or product terms to represent interactions (as in Chapter 4), and the model specification (i.e., the path diagram and the regression equation) expands accordingly. That is, a general form of Equation 9.2 including any number $Q$ of observed variables is

$$Y_i = \left( \sum_{q=1}^{Q} \gamma_q X_{qi} \right) + \zeta_i.$$

This equation is essentially equivalent to Equation 2.9, which expressed the multiple regression of an outcome variable $Y$ on any number of predictors, except here the intercept parameter is dropped without any loss of generality.

## Section recap

### Specification of multiple regression as a path analysis model

Using LISREL notation, a multiple regression model with $Q$ predictors is specified as

$$Y_i = \left( \sum_{q=1}^{Q} \gamma_q X_{qi} \right) + \zeta_i,$$

where $\gamma_q$ is the slope parameter for predictor $X_q$, $\zeta_i$ is again the error term, and again no intercept parameter is needed.

This model's parameter set includes the slopes, the error variance, the variances of the predictors, and the covariances among predictors.

Analogous to ordinary least-squares (OLS) multiple regression, including the covariances among predictors as model parameters leads to the $\gamma$ slope coefficients being interpreted as partial regression slopes.

## Specification of a multivariate multiple regression model

With the exception of exploratory factor analysis (Chapter 8), the statistical models considered so far in this text have all been *univariate* in the sense that they each had a single dependent or outcome variable. In the context of path analysis, it is straightforward to extend a model into a *multivariate* scenario in which there are two or more outcome variables. Figure 9.3 depicts a generic example of a path analysis model in which two predictor variables, $X_1$ and $X_2$, simultaneously predict two outcomes, $Y_1$ and $Y_2$.

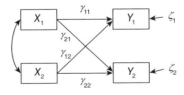

**Figure 9.3** Path diagram representing a multivariate regression model as a path analysis model

Because the model in Figure 9.3 has two outcome variables, the model specification consists of not one but two regression equations, one for each outcome:

$$Y_{1i} = \gamma_{11} X_{1i} + \gamma_{12} X_{2i} + \zeta_{1i},$$

$$Y_{2i} = \gamma_{21} X_{1i} + \gamma_{22} X_{2i} + \zeta_{1i}.$$

In these equations, it is important to follow the subscripts on the slope coefficients: The first subscript on the coefficient indicates the equation's outcome variable, and the second refers to the predictor variable. Thus, for example, $\gamma_{12}$ is the coefficient of $X_2$ in the prediction of $Y_1$ (i.e., $Y_1$ regressed on $X_2$), but $\gamma_{21}$ is the coefficient for the regression of $Y_2$ on $X_1$. These two scalar equations can be combined into a single matrix equation:

$$\begin{bmatrix} Y_1 \\ Y_2 \end{bmatrix} = \begin{bmatrix} \gamma_{11} & \gamma_{12} \\ \gamma_{21} & \gamma_{22} \end{bmatrix} \begin{bmatrix} X_1 \\ X_2 \end{bmatrix} + \begin{bmatrix} \zeta_1 \\ \zeta_2 \end{bmatrix}$$

or

$$\mathbf{y} = \mathbf{\Gamma x} + \mathbf{\zeta}.$$

A more complete general matrix formula for path analysis models is presented later in this chapter.

As referred to earlier, the LISREL approach to specifying structural equation models involves a particular use of matrices to collect the model parameters. According to this approach, the parameters of the current model in Figure 9.3 include the four regression coefficients (which are collected in the matrix $\mathbf{\Gamma}$), the covariance matrix of the predictors, and the covariance matrix of the error terms. Specifically, the variances and covariances among $\mathbf{x}$ are collected in the $\mathbf{\Phi}$ covariance matrix:

$$\mathbf{\Phi} = \begin{bmatrix} \sigma_{X_1}^2 & \\ \sigma_{X_1 X_2} & \sigma_{X_2}^2 \end{bmatrix},$$

and the error variances are contained in a covariance matrix named $\mathbf{\Psi}$:

$$\mathbf{\Psi} = \begin{bmatrix} \sigma_{\zeta_1}^2 & \\ 0 & \sigma_{\zeta_2}^2 \end{bmatrix}.$$

Here, $\mathbf{\Psi}$ is a diagonal matrix because the model does not include a covariance between $\zeta_1$ and $\zeta_2$; the model therefore indicates that any observed correlation between $Y_1$ and $Y_2$ should be completely explained by their shared associations with $X_1$ and $X_2$. Thus, there is a total of nine free parameters in this model: four regression coefficients in $\mathbf{\Gamma}$, three variance–covariance terms in $\mathbf{\Phi}$, and two error variances in $\mathbf{\Psi}$.

In the previous model, the error covariance is *fixed* or *constrained* to zero. But in path analysis (and SEM generally), it is possible to include error covariances as freely estimated model parameters. For example, the model in Figure 9.3 can be expanded to free the covariance between $\zeta_1$ and $\zeta_2$, the conceptual interpretation of which is that there is some remaining relation between $Y_1$ and $Y_2$ that is not explained by the effects of $X_1$ and $X_2$ on both $Y_1$ and $Y_2$. This expanded model is depicted in Figure 9.4; the curved, double-headed arrow connecting $\zeta_1$ and $\zeta_2$ represents this free error covariance parameter. The parameter matrices for this model are identical to those for the model in Figure 9.3, except the off-diagonal element of $\mathbf{\Psi}$, $\sigma_{\zeta_1 \zeta_2}$, is now *free* rather than fixed to 0:

$$\mathbf{\Psi} = \begin{bmatrix} \sigma_{\zeta_1}^2 & \\ \sigma_{\zeta_1 \zeta_2} & \sigma_{\zeta_2}^2 \end{bmatrix}.$$

Although researchers are often tempted to include them in models, it is important to be careful with error covariance parameters for several reasons:

1.  They can cause a model to be underidentified, which means it is not estimable.
2.  They are often difficult to interpret, if not completely illogical, within the substantive conceptualization of the model.
3.  Sometimes software will automatically include one or more error covariances by default, even if one does not intend such parameters to be a part of the model.

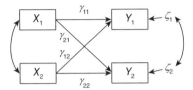

**Figure 9.4** Path diagram representing a multivariate regression model with a free error covariance parameter

## Specification of multivariate multiple regression as a path analysis model

A multivariate multiple regression model with two or more outcomes is specified with a separate scalar equation for each outcome variable.

For instance, if a path analysis model has two outcomes, $Y_1$ and $Y_2$, and two predictors, it is specified with two scalar equations:

$$Y_{1i} = \gamma_{11}X_{1i} + \gamma_{12}X_{2i} + \zeta_{1i},$$

$$Y_{2i} = \gamma_{21}X_{1i} + \gamma_{22}X_{2i} + \zeta_{1i}.$$

These two scalar equations can be expressed with a single matrix equation:

$$\begin{bmatrix} Y_1 \\ Y_2 \end{bmatrix} = \begin{bmatrix} \gamma_{11} & \gamma_{12} \\ \gamma_{21} & \gamma_{22} \end{bmatrix} \begin{bmatrix} X_1 \\ X_2 \end{bmatrix} + \begin{bmatrix} \zeta_1 \\ \zeta_2 \end{bmatrix}.$$

In addition to the $\gamma$ slope parameters, this model's parameter set includes $\Phi$ (the covariance matrix for the predictors $X_1$ and $X_2$) and $\Psi$ (the covariance matrix for the error terms $\zeta_1$ and $\zeta_2$).

Often, $\Psi$ is *fixed* (or *constrained*) to be a diagonal matrix, meaning that the covariance between any two error terms is set to equal 0. But in SEM it is possible to allow error covariance terms to be freely estimated, nonzero parameters.

## Specification of models for mediation and other indirect effects

Chapter 5 focused on the simple indirect-effect model (also called the simple mediation model) and briefly mentioned that such a model can be specified and estimated using a single structural equation model rather than two separate regression models (i.e., one OLS regression model with the purported mediator or intervening variable regressed on the main independent variable and another model with the main dependent variable regressed on both the mediator and the independent variable). In one of the applied examples in Chapter 5, a mediation model was presented in which the relation between a dichotomous best-face-forward experimental manipulation and participants' self-reported positive affect rating was mediated by a rating of the participants' level of self-presentation.

As explained in Chapter 5, an important aspect of the simple indirect-effect model is that the mediator or intervening variable is both an outcome variable being regressed on the main independent variable as well as a predictor of the main dependent variable. Thus, because there are two outcome variables (the main dependent variable and the mediator), two scalar regression equations are needed to represent the model. Continuing with the self-presentation example from Chapter 5, if we let $Y_1$ represent self-presentation, let $Y_2$ represent positive affect, and let $X$ represent the best-face-forward manipulation, then the regression equation for the self-presentation mediator can be written as

$$Y_{1i} = \gamma_{11}X_i + \zeta_{1i},$$ \hfill (9.3)

whereas the regression equation for the positive-affect dependent variable is

$$Y_{2i} = \gamma_{21}X_i + \beta_{21}Y_{1i} + \zeta_{2i}.$$ \hfill (9.4)

These equations are essentially the same as Equations 5.1 and 5.2, respectively, except here Equations 9.3 and 9.4 are expressed using the LISREL notation for SEM, which is explained in further detail later (additionally, Equations 9.3 and 9.4 do not have intercept parameters, unlike Equations 5.1 and 5.2). Furthermore, the path diagram of this model (in Figure 9.5) is essentially the same as that given in Figure 5.1, except now Figure 9.5 uses LISREL notation.

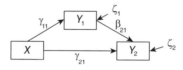

**Figure 9.5** Path diagram representing a simple indirect effect model (or simple mediation model)

A valuable feature of path analysis is that the same variable can serve as an outcome variable in one regression equation and as a predictor in another equation. For example, in Equation 9.3, $Y_1$ is the outcome variable, but in Equation 9.4 the same $Y_1$ is a predictor variable. More specifically, in SEM (and other statistical methods), variables can be classified according to whether they are *endogenous* or *exogenous*. An **exogenous** variable serves only as an independent variable (or predictor, explanatory variable, or covariate) in the complete set of regression equations in a given model. In a path diagram, exogenous variables directly 'point at' other variables but do not have any straight arrows pointing at them from other variables. In the simple mediation model, $X$ is the only exogenous variable. An **endogenous** variable serves as a dependent variable (or outcome or response variable) in at least one of the regression equations for the model. In a path diagram, if a variable has any straight arrow pointing at it from at least one other variable, then it is endogenous. In the simple mediation model, both $Y_1$ and $Y_2$ are endogenous.

In LISREL notation, an exogenous observed variable is represented as an $X$, whereas any endogenous observed variable is a $Y$. Consequently, Figure 9.5 and Equations 9.3 and 9.4 represent a purported mediating or intervening variable using a $Y$ rather than $M$. Additionally, the letter $\gamma$ denotes the partial regression slope parameter relating an exogenous variable to an endogenous variable, whereas $\beta$ is used to represent the partial regression slope relating one endogenous variable to another endogenous variable. This difference between $\gamma$ and $\beta$ is demonstrated in Equation 9.4, where the relation between $Y_2$ and $X$ is symbolized with a $\gamma$ coefficient but the relation between $Y_2$ and $Y_1$ is symbolized using a $\beta$. Within a given regression equation, this distinction between $\gamma$ and $\beta$ has no real statistical or interpretational impact; both are just partial regression coefficients representing linear effects in the same manner as has been the case for all multiple regression slope parameters throughout this text. The only reason for using different Greek letters to represent regression coefficients for exogenous versus endogenous variables is to foster a fuller understanding of the roles that different variables serve in the model, which in turn can be advantageous for understanding how models are represented across various SEM software procedures.

Once again, as described in Chapter 5, the *total effect* of an exogenous variable on the main dependent variable (i.e., $Y_2$ in the model in Figure 9.5) in a path model can be partitioned into the *direct* (i.e., $\gamma_{21}$) and *indirect effects* (i.e., the product of coefficients $\gamma_{11} \times \beta_{21}$). In fact, most SEM software procedures have routines for presenting these separate effects in their output along with bootstrapped confidence intervals (CIs) for the estimated indirect effect, consistent with their description in Chapter 5. This capability is especially advantageous for models with multiple intervening variables. For example, Figure 9.6 presents a model with two endogenous variables, labeled as $Y_1$ and $Y_2$, which mediate or intervene in the relation between the exogenous variable $X$ and the main dependent variable $Y_3$. Because this model has three endogenous variables, it is characterized by three separate regression equations:

$$Y_{1i} = \gamma_{11}X_i + \zeta_{1i},$$

$$Y_{2i} = \gamma_{21}X_i + \zeta_{2i},$$

and

$$Y_{3i} = \gamma_{31}X_i + \beta_{31}Y_{1i} + \beta_{32}Y_{2i} + \zeta_{3i}.$$

Now, $X$ predicts $Y_3$ indirectly through both $Y_1$ and $Y_2$, so there are two indirect effects, which may be quantified as $(\gamma_{11} \times \beta_{31})$ and $(\gamma_{21} \times \beta_{32})$. Most SEM software can provide bootstrapped confidence intervals for separate indirect effects within the same model. Therefore, the total effect of $X$ on $Y_3$ is the sum of $\gamma_{31}$ (the direct effect) and $(\gamma_{11} \times \beta_{31})$ and $(\gamma_{21} \times \beta_{32})$, the two indirect effects. For further detail on assessing multiple indirect effects within the same model, see Preacher and Hayes (2008).

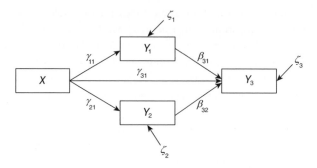

**Figure 9.6**  Path diagram representing a model with two mediators

Finally, an important distinction between the SEM approach to modeling mediation and the multiple regression approach of Chapter 5 is that using SEM, the regression parameters of both Equations 9.3 and 9.4 are estimated simultaneously, in a single shot, rather than using separate regression modeling analyses for each endogenous variable. This capability may become especially advantageous as models are expanded to include multiple intervening variables or other endogenous variables. Another potential advantage of using SEM to model indirect effects is the possibility of explicitly including error covariance parameters among endogenous intervening variables. For example, the model in Figure 9.6 implies that any relation between $Y_1$ and $Y_2$ is completely explained by their shared relation with $X$. But instead there could be a strong correlation between the errors $\zeta_1$ and $\zeta_2$, which may need to be included as a free parameter in the $\Psi$ matrix to achieve adequate model fit (model fit is covered later in this chapter).

 **Section recap**

### Specification of indirect-effect models as path analysis models

A key advantage of path analysis models is that a variable can appear as a predictor in one equation and as an outcome in another equation, which allows any number of mediation or indirect effects to be included in a single model.

Any variable appearing on the left-hand side of an equation in a model (i.e., any variable appearing as an outcome or dependent variable in at least one equation) is known as an **endogenous** variable.

A variable that appears only on the right-hand side of all equations in a model (i.e., any variable that serves only as a predictor or covariate) is known as an **exogenous** variable.

The simple mediation model can be specified using LISREL notation with

$$Y_{1i} = \gamma_{11}X_i + \zeta_{1i}$$

and

$$Y_{2i} = \gamma_{21}X_i + \beta_{21}Y_{1i} + \zeta_{2i}.$$

where $X$ is the main independent variable, $Y_1$ is the intervening variable (or mediator), and $Y_2$ is the main dependent variable.

## General model specification form for path analysis

The models in Figures 9.1 and 9.2 are incomplete versions of the full path analysis model hypothesized by Scott-Lennox and Lennox (1995). Their complete model posited that perceived social support (measured as PASS scores) would mediate the relations among the size, density, and homophily social support network characteristics and depression (measured by CESD scores). The path diagram for this hypothesized model is in Figure 9.7. The individual scalar regression equations comprising this model can be inferred from the path diagram; because there are two endogenous variables (PASS and CESD), there are two scalar regression equations. Letting PASS = $Y_1$ and CESD = $Y_2$, as well as size = $X_1$, density = $X_2$, and homophily = $X_3$, the regression equations are

$$Y_{1i} = \gamma_{11}X_{1i} + \gamma_{12}X_{2i} + \gamma_{13}X_{3i} + \zeta_1, \tag{9.5}$$

which reflects that size, density, and homophily are direct predictors of PASS, and

$$Y_{2i} = \beta_{21}Y_{1i} + \zeta_2, \tag{9.6}$$

which reflects that PASS is a direct predictor of CESD. Once again, these scalar equations can be collected into a single matrix equation, which, for the current example, is

$$\begin{bmatrix} Y_1 \\ Y_2 \end{bmatrix} = \begin{bmatrix} 0 & 0 \\ \beta_{21} & 0 \end{bmatrix}\begin{bmatrix} Y_1 \\ Y_2 \end{bmatrix} + \begin{bmatrix} \gamma_{11} & \gamma_{12} & \gamma_{13} \\ 0 & 0 & 0 \end{bmatrix}\begin{bmatrix} X_1 \\ X_2 \\ X_3 \end{bmatrix} + \begin{bmatrix} \zeta_1 \\ \zeta_2 \end{bmatrix}. \tag{9.7}$$

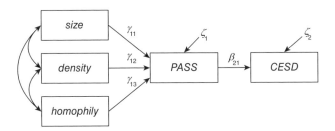

**Figure 9.7** Path diagram of hypothesized social support and depression model

The general matrix equation of any path analysis model is

$$\mathbf{Y} = \mathbf{BY} + \mathbf{\Gamma X} + \zeta, \tag{9.8}$$

where $\mathbf{Y}$ is a $P \times 1$ vector of endogenous variables, $\mathbf{X}$ is a $Q \times 1$ vector of exogenous variables, $\mathbf{B}$ is a $P \times P$ matrix of coefficients for the regression of endogenous variables on other endogenous variables, $\mathbf{\Gamma}$ is a $P \times Q$ matrix of coefficients for the regression of endogenous variables on exogenous variables, and $\zeta$ is a $P \times 1$ vector of errors in the equations (i.e., regression prediction errors), which are also commonly referred to as *disturbances* in the SEM context.

Notice that the example model in Figure 9.7 does not include every possible direct effect. An important concept in specifying models is the distinction between **free** parameters and

**fixed** (also known as *constrained* or *restricted*) parameters. For example, the current example model does not hypothesize a direct effect between size $(X_1)$ and CESD $(Y_2)$. Thus, this path does not appear as an arrow in the path diagram and the corresponding element of $\Gamma$ is *fixed* to zero, that is, $\gamma_{21} = 0$. But the model does hypothesize a direct effect between size $(X_1)$ and PASS $(Y_1)$; thus, this path appears as an arrow in the path diagram and the corresponding element of $\Gamma$, $\gamma_{11}$, is *free*, meaning that this parameter is to be estimated from the data, that is, it is 'freely estimated'. As one can see in the matrix equation for the current example model (Equation 9.7), there are several elements in $B$ and $\Gamma$ that are fixed to equal zero as a part of specifying the hypothesized model.

Regarding the $B$ matrix, which has elements representing the coefficients for the regression of individual endogenous variables on other endogenous variables, its diagonal elements are always fixed to zero because it does not make sense to regress a variable on itself. But as we have seen, one purpose of SEM is to allow the regression of one endogenous variable on another endogenous variable, which here is represented by the freed $\beta_{21}$ parameter representing the slope coefficient of the regression of CESD $(Y_2)$ on PASS $(Y_1)$. Sometimes, there are free $\beta$ parameters both above and below the diagonal of $B$; this situation produces a *nonrecursive* model with a feedback loop in the path diagram and can create an identification problem (the concept of identification is discussed later).

The regression coefficients in $B$ and $\Gamma$ are not the only parameters in a path analysis model. As we have already seen, the model also contains free parameters in $\Phi$, the $Q \times Q$ covariance matrix for the exogenous variables. Recall again that an important concept in multiple regression is that partial regression coefficients account for the correlations among the predictor variables; along these lines, it is standard for all elements of $\Phi$ to be freely estimated. In the current example, we have size $= X_1$, density $= X_2$, and homophily $= X_3$, so $\Phi$ is the $3 \times 3$ covariance matrix for these variables:

$$\Phi = \begin{bmatrix} \sigma^2_{X_1} & & \\ \sigma_{X_2 X_1} & \sigma^2_{X_2} & \\ \sigma_{X_3 X_1} & \sigma_{X_3 X_2} & \sigma^2_{X_3} \end{bmatrix}.$$

Next, $\Psi$ is the $P \times P$ covariance matrix for the error terms (i.e., $\zeta_p$) for the separate regression equations (there is one scalar equation and, thus, one error term for each endogenous variable). Hence, the diagonal elements of $\Psi$ are the variances of the $\zeta$ terms in the model; that is, they are error variances, not the variances of the endogenous $Y$ variables themselves. The error variance of an endogenous variable is the variance of that variable that remains after variance accounted for by its predictors has been removed. Additionally, as explained earlier, the error covariance between any two endogenous variables is the (linear) relation between those variables that remains after the model's regression effects have been removed (i.e., the correlation between two variables that is not explained by the model). The current example model has two endogenous variables, PASS and CESD; thus, there are two scalar regression equations, leading to two error terms, $\zeta_1$ and $\zeta_2$. The model must include free parameters to represent the variance of these error terms. There are no free error covariance parameters in the hypothesized model, so its $\Psi$ is a diagonal matrix:

$$\Psi = \begin{bmatrix} \sigma^2_{\zeta_1} & \\ 0 & \sigma^2_{\zeta_2} \end{bmatrix}.$$

## Section recap

### General model specification form for path analysis

The general matrix equation for any path analysis model is

$$\mathbf{Y} = \mathbf{BY} + \mathbf{\Gamma X} + \zeta,$$

where

$\mathbf{Y}$ is a $P \times 1$ vector of endogenous variables

$\mathbf{X}$ is a $Q \times 1$ vector of exogenous variables

$\mathbf{B}$ is a $P \times P$ matrix of coefficients in the regression of endogenous variables on other endogenous variables

$\mathbf{\Gamma}$ is a $P \times Q$ matrix of coefficients for the regression of endogenous variables on exogenous variables

$\zeta$ is a $P \times 1$ vector of errors in the equations (i.e., regression prediction errors), which are also commonly referred to as *disturbances* in the SEM context

In a structural equation model, parameters are either **free** or **fixed**. Any free parameter is a parameter to be estimated from the observed data, whereas a fixed parameter (also known as a **restricted** or **constrained** parameter) is set equal to a particular value (often 0 in path analysis models) a priori based on the hypothesized model.

The parameter set in a path analysis model also includes $\mathbf{\Phi}$, the $Q \times Q$ covariance matrix of $\mathbf{X}$, and $\mathbf{\Psi}$, the $P \times P$ covariance matrix among $\zeta$.

Most often, all elements of $\mathbf{\Phi}$ are free parameters, whereas $\mathbf{\Psi}$ is usually restricted to be a diagonal matrix (i.e., the error covariance parameters are fixed to 0).

## Alternative path diagram for the complete social support and depression example model

The path diagrams presented in Figures 9.1 to 9.7 adhere to conventions popularized by Jöreskog's LISREL approach (see Byrne, 1998: 13–17) as well as by Bollen's (1989) authoritative SEM text. A more elaborate set of conventions for drawing path diagrams has gained popularity

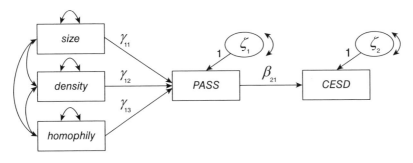

**Figure 9.8**  Alternative path diagram of hypothesized social support and depression model

and is now common in the methodological literature (see Ho, Stark, and Chernyshenko, 2012, for a full description). Figure 9.8 presents the social support and depression model according to this latter set of diagramming conventions. It is important to keep in mind that Figures 9.7 and 9.8 are merely alternative representations of the same model.

In Figure 9.8, each $\zeta$ error term is enclosed in an oval which makes explicit the idea that the error term in a regression model is in fact a certain type of latent variable: The error term is a variable in the sense that different individuals have different values for this variable, but these values are not observable because the true model parameters, which determine the values of $\zeta$, are unknown, thus making $\zeta$ a latent variable. Additionally, the single-headed arrows connecting each $\zeta$ to its endogenous variable are labeled with the value '1'. This label makes explicit that the relation between a given $\zeta$ and its endogenous variable is fixed to equal 1 rather than being a free parameter. More explicitly, Equations 9.5 and 9.6 can be written as

$$Y_{1i} = \gamma_{11}X_{1i} + \gamma_{12}X_{2i} + \gamma_{13}X_{3i} + 1 \times (\zeta_1)$$

and

$$Y_{2i} = \beta_{21}Y_{1i} + 1 \times (\zeta_2),$$

respectively, to emphasize the idea that the coefficient of each error term is a constant (rather than a free parameter) fixed to 1. Next, the remaining distinction between the path diagram in Figure 9.7 and the one in Figure 9.8 is that only the latter includes small, curved bidirectional arrows, one for each exogenous variable and one for each latent error. These small curved arrows represent the free variance parameters in the model, that is, the diagonal elements of $\Phi$ (the covariance matrix of $\mathbf{X}$) and the diagonal elements of $\Psi$ (the covariance matrix of $\zeta$).

The main advantage of the diagramming approach depicted in Figure 9.8 is that it explicitly represents all of the model's parameters, whereas the path diagram in Figure 9.7 does not explicitly represent the model's variance parameters (although covariance parameters are represented). Another small advantage of the diagram in Figure 9.8 is the indication that the relation between an error term and an endogenous variable is a fixed constant rather than a free parameter. Nonetheless, I prefer the simpler version of the path diagram depicted in Figure 9.7 for a couple of reasons:

1. Including the small double-headed arrows for the variance parameters makes the picture cluttered, especially for larger models with more variables.
2. It should be taken as understood that the variance parameters exist without explicitly depicting them; if the variables didn't have variance, then they would not be variables.

The LISREL-style path diagram in Figure 9.7 directly maps the regression equations themselves onto the diagram; that is, it shows how the variables (including error terms) combine additively on the right-hand side of Equation 9.8 to produce the set of outcome variables, $\mathbf{Y}$, on the left-hand side of the equation.

## PATH ANALYSIS: MODEL IDENTIFICATION

So far, this chapter has focused almost exclusively on model specification for path analysis; in other words, the focus has been on the path diagramming conventions and on defining the corresponding population parameters for a series of prototypical path analysis models, ending with the example model for the hypothetical relations among social support variables and a depression measure. Of course, upon specifying a path analysis model representing a hypothesized pattern of relations among observed variables, a researcher will next want to fit that model to data, that is, to estimate the model, to determine whether there is empirical support for the hypothesized pattern of variable relations and to interpret estimates of the model's parameters. But if the model is not identified, then any obtained results are not trust-worthy, if results are even obtained at all. In general, but not always, SEM software will alert the user if the model being estimated is potentially not identified, and so to some extent, it is not always necessary for a researcher to consider model identification before attempting to estimate a model. But problems with identification do occur regularly across a variety of SEM applications, and so when they are encountered, it is important to have a basic understanding of the concept of identification.

Simply put, a model is identified if it is theoretically possible to obtain a unique estimate of each parameter; conversely, if more than one set of parameter values fit the observed data equivalently, then the model is not identified. In short, the main question involved in model identification is whether the 'known' information from the data (which, in path analysis, is generally the number of variances and covariances among the observed variables) is adequate to arrive at a unique estimate of the 'unknown' terms, which are the model's free parameters. Thus, if a model specification is too complex (e.g., the path diagram contains too many direc-tional or nondirectional arrows representing free parameters connecting the variables), then it is not possible to arrive at unique parameter estimates from the observed data.

The identification concept applies not just to path analysis models but to all parametric statis-tical models. For instance, the basic simple and multiple regression models covered in Chapters 1 to 6 are all identified. From Chapter 8, though, exploratory factor analysis (EFA) models with two or more factors are not fully identified because of rotational indeterminacy: Recall that there is an infinite number of factor patterns which fit the data equally well when EFA models have more than one factor. Rotation is used to find the most interpretable factor pattern for a given model, but other, less interpretable rotations yield statistically equivalent factor patterns.

 **Section recap**

### Identification of path analysis models

**Identification** is a property of a given structural equation model which determines whether it is possible to obtain unique estimates of the parameters from the observed data. If a model is too complex, then it may not be identified, and thus, there may be more than one set of parameter estimates which explain the observed data equally well.

Often (but not always), computer software will warn users that a model may not be iden-tified. It is important to understand why such warning messages occur.

## The *t*-rule for identification

Formal identification rules have been established for path analysis models (for further details, see Bollen, 1989) as well as for other types of structural equation models. The first of these, the **t-rule**, provides a necessary but not sufficient criterion for determining whether a model is identified.

The t-rule states that t, the number of unknown parameter values to be estimated (i.e., the number of free parameters), must be less than or equal to the number of nonredundant elements in the covariance matrix of observed variables:

$$t \leq \frac{(P+Q)(P+Q+1)}{2},$$

where P is the number of endogenous variables and Q is the number of exogenous variables. Recall that a covariance matrix, **S**, is a symmetric matrix, meaning that the values below the diagonal are repeated above the diagonal. Given that sum (P + Q) is the total number of observed variables, the right-hand term of this expression is a generic formula for arriving at a count of the total number of variance terms (i.e., the number of diagonal elements in **S**) plus the number of covariance terms (i.e., the number of elements in **S** that are below the diagonal) without counting the same covariance terms twice (i.e., without also counting the number of elements in **S** that are above the diagonal).

Next, the quantity

$$\left[\frac{(P+Q)(P+Q+1)}{2}\right] - t = df \qquad (9.9)$$

gives the **degrees of freedom** (df) for a given path analysis model. Therefore, the t-rule states that a model is not identified if the degrees of freedom is negative: If a model's degrees of freedom is negative, then the model is said to be **underidentified**. Identified models with positive degrees of freedom are referred to as **overidentified**, whereas identified models with zero degrees of freedom (e.g., the model in Figure 9.4) are called **just-identified** or **saturated** models. Although it may be possible to obtain unique parameter estimates for a path model with df = 0 (pending other identification requirements), such models are often considered exploratory because they lack parsimony, and consequently, many standard model fit statistics (see later) will suggest that model fit is perfect.

Returning to our example path analysis model for social support and depression (Figure 9.7), there are P = 2 endogenous variables and Q = 3 exogenous variables, for a total of five observed variables. Thus, the number of nonredundant elements in the observed covariance matrix is (5 × 6) / 2 = 15. The free parameters to be estimated from the data consist of

- 3 exogenous variable variances (diagonal elements of Φ)
- 3 covariance terms among the exogenous variables (off-diagonal elements of Φ)
- 4 regression coefficients (one free element in **B**, three free elements in Γ)
- 2 error variance terms (diagonal elements of Ψ; the model does not specify any residual covariances)

Thus, the model has a total of 12 parameters to estimate, and so the model df is 15 − 12 = 3. Therefore, the example model passes the t-rule for identification. Remember, though, that although a model must pass the t-rule, doing so is not sufficient for establishing that it is identified.

 Section recap

### The t-rule for identification

The **t-rule** is a necessary but not sufficient criterion for model identification: For a model to be identified, $t$, the number of unknown parameter values to be estimated, must be less than or equal to the number of nonredundant elements in the covariance matrix of observed variables:

$$t \le \frac{(P+Q)(P+Q+1)}{2},$$

where $P$ is the number of endogenous variables and $Q$ is the number of exogenous variables. The quantity

$$\left[ \frac{(P+Q)(P+Q+1)}{2} \right] - t$$

gives the **degrees of freedom** ($df$) for a given path analysis model.

If a model's $df$ is negative, then the model is **underidentified**; identified models with $df > 0$ are **overidentified**; and identified models with $df = 0$ are called **just-identified** or **saturated** models.

## The recursive rule

The **recursive rule** is sufficient but not necessary for identification of a path analysis model. The recursive rule states that a path analysis model is identified if it is a **recursive model**. Generally speaking, a model is recursive if it has no reciprocal relations or feedback loops. More formally, a path analysis model is recursive if both of the following conditions hold:

- The endogenous variables can be ordered so that the only free elements of **B** are either all in its lower triangle or all in its upper triangle (e.g., if there are two endogenous variables, then it is arbitrary as to which is $Y_1$ and which is $Y_2$, but this ordering will affect whether a path from one to the other appears in the lower triangle or upper triangle of β).
- The only free elements of **Ψ** are on its diagonal.

The social support and depression example model (Figure 9.7) is recursive because its **B** is lower triangle and **Ψ** is diagonal:

$$\mathbf{B} = \begin{bmatrix} 0 & 0 \\ \beta_{21} & 0 \end{bmatrix}, \ \mathbf{\Psi} = \begin{bmatrix} \sigma^2_{\zeta_1} & 0 \\ 0 & \sigma^2_{\zeta_2} \end{bmatrix}.$$

Thus, the model passes the recursive rule.

But the model depicted in Figure 9.9 model is **nonrecursive** because its **B** has free elements both above and below the diagonal. Specifically, for this model

$$\mathbf{B} = \begin{bmatrix} 0 & \beta_{12} \\ \beta_{21} & 0 \end{bmatrix},$$

although its $\Psi$ is diagonal:

$$\Psi = \begin{bmatrix} \text{VAR}(\zeta_1) & \\ 0 & \text{VAR}(\zeta_2) \end{bmatrix}.$$

Next, the model in Figure 9.4 described earlier is also nonrecursive. Although that model has no free parameters in **B**, its $\Psi$ is not diagonal; that is, it includes a free error covariance parameter:

$$\Psi = \begin{bmatrix} \text{VAR}(\zeta_1) & \\ \text{COV}(\zeta_1,\zeta_2) & \text{VAR}(\zeta_2) \end{bmatrix}.$$

Many nonrecursive models are nonetheless identified; keep in mind that the recursive rule is sufficient but not necessary. There are methods which provide both necessary and sufficient criteria for establishing model identification, but these are a little too complex for the scope of this text (see Bollen, 1989, for further details).

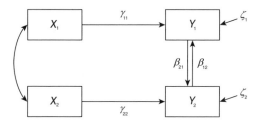

**Figure 9.9** Example of a nonrecursive model

 Section recap

### The recursive rule

The **recursive rule** is sufficient but not necessary for identification of a path analysis model. The recursive rule states that a path analysis model is identified if it is a **recursive model**.

A path analysis model is recursive if the endogenous variables can be ordered so that the only free elements of $\beta$ are all in its lower triangle and if $\Psi$ is a diagonal matrix. Otherwise, the model is **nonrecursive**.

## PATH ANALYSIS: MODEL ESTIMATION

### The covariance structure hypothesis

Once a model is specified and data are collected, the sample data are used to estimate the model's free parameters. Recall from Chapters 1 and 2 that the most common estimation method in simple and multiple regression analysis is OLS. In OLS regression, parameter values are chosen that minimize the sum of squared residuals, which represent the difference between the observed $Y$ values and the predicted (or model-implied) $\hat{Y}$ values. Thus, in standard OLS regression, the focus is on finding parameter estimates (i.e., regression slope coefficients) that fit the model to individual observations. Yet, for EFA, as explained in Chapter 8, the goal was to find parameter estimates that optimally fit the model to observed correlations rather than to individual observations. But in SEM, the focus is on finding the parameter estimates that optimally fit the model to observed covariances (and sometimes means) rather than to individual observations.

The rationale for this focus on covariances comes from the **covariance structure hypothesis**, which forms the basis for model estimation in SEM. Define $\Sigma$ as the population covariance matrix for all observed variables to be included in a given model. Next, let $\theta$ represent a vector of free model parameters. In a path analysis model, this $\theta$ is a hypothetical string of regression slopes, error variances (and possibly error covariances), and the variances and covariances among the exogenous variables. Now, let $\Sigma_{\theta}$ represent the population covariance matrix expressed as a function of $\theta$, the free parameters. This matrix, $\Sigma_{\theta}$, is the **model-implied covariance matrix**, or *predicted covariance matrix*. The covariance structure hypothesis states that if the model is correctly specified, then

$$\Sigma = \Sigma_{\theta}.$$

In other words, if the hypothesized model is the true, population data-generating model for the research phenomena of interest, then the population covariance matrix is exactly reproduced by the model parameters. Consequently, each observed population covariance can be expressed as a function of model parameters.

In the process of model estimation, parameter estimates are chosen to make the estimated model-implied covariance matrix, $\Sigma_{\theta}$, match the sample covariance matrix, **S**, as closely as possible according to some criterion. If the model is correct, $\Sigma_{\theta} = \Sigma$ by the covariance structure hypothesis, and as the sample size grows infinitely, **S** will equal $\Sigma$; therefore, $\Sigma_{\theta}$ will equal $\Sigma$ (see Bollen, 1989, for a more complete explanation). In sum, following the covariance structure hypothesis, it makes sense to fit the model to the sample covariance matrix. It is important to keep in mind, though, that covariances represent linear relations, and so SEM generally implies a strong assumption that all variables are linearly associated (although there are methods for modeling nonlinear associations within SEM).

Consequently, most types of structural equation models can be estimated directly from a sample covariance matrix. (Important exceptions are models that also incorporate a mean structure, such as growth curve models and multiple-group models of measurement invariance.) That is, the sample covariances (and variances) provide sufficient information to estimate models; one does not need a complete $N \times P$ dataset to estimate many structural equation models. An artefact of this result is that if a published research article reports the covariances among the observed variables used in the article (or, alternatively, if the correlations are reported along with the standard deviations of the variables, the covariances can be recreated[2]), readers can attempt to replicate any SEM analyses reported in the paper using one of the fitting functions described later, and they can even estimate alternative models that may not have been reported.

---

[2]But misleading results can be obtained if just correlations are analyzed (without being converted into covariances using standard deviation information); see Cudeck, 1989.

To demonstrate the covariance structure hypothesis, consider the simple, linear regression model presented earlier as Equation 9.1 and depicted in Figure 9.1:

$$Y_i = \gamma X_i + \zeta_i.$$

If this linear regression model is correct for a particular population, then we can take the variance of both sides of the equation:

$$\text{VAR}(Y) = \text{VAR}(\gamma X + \zeta)$$

and then separate the right-hand side into two variance terms:

$$\text{VAR}(Y) = \text{VAR}(\gamma X) + \text{VAR}(\zeta). \tag{9.10}$$

Next, because of the variance of a random variable (e.g., $X$) multiplied by a constant (e.g., $\gamma$) equals the constant squared times the variance of the variable, Equation 9.10 is equivalent to

$$\text{VAR}(Y) = \gamma^2 \text{VAR}(X) + \text{VAR}(\zeta_i). \tag{9.11}$$

Now, if the best-fitting linear regression slope is calculated as

$$\gamma = \text{COV}(Y,X) \,/\, \text{VAR}(X),$$

then

$$\text{COV}(Y,X) = \gamma \text{VAR}(X). \tag{9.12}$$

The population covariance matrix $\Sigma$ for the variables in this model consists of only the variance of $Y$, the variance of $X$, and the covariance between them. Therefore, given Equations 9.11 and 9.12, the covariance structure hypothesis expression $\Sigma = \Sigma_\theta$ for this simple regression model expands to

$$\begin{pmatrix} \text{VAR}(Y) & \\ \text{COV}(Y,X) & \text{VAR}(X) \end{pmatrix} = \begin{pmatrix} \gamma^2\text{VAR}(X) + \text{VAR}(\zeta) & \\ \gamma\text{VAR}(X) & \text{VAR}(X) \end{pmatrix} = \begin{pmatrix} \gamma^2\phi + \psi & \\ \gamma\phi & \phi \end{pmatrix}.$$

This equation shows the expression of the population covariance matrix as a function of the model's free parameters, which are the regression slope ($\gamma$), the variance of the exogenous variable ($\phi = \text{VAR}(X)$), and the error variance ($\psi = \text{VAR}(\zeta)$).

Returning to the general matrix form of the path analysis model (i.e., Equation 9.8), the model-implied covariance matrix $\Sigma_\theta$ can be broken down into (a) the implied covariances among the endogenous variables, $\Sigma_{\mathbf{YY}|\theta}$; (b) the implied covariances among the exogenous variables, $\Sigma_{\mathbf{XX}|\theta}$; and (c) the implied covariance of $\mathbf{Y}$ with $\mathbf{X}$, $\Sigma_{\mathbf{YX}|\theta}$. Specifically, these model-implied covariance matrices are:

$$\Sigma_{\mathbf{YY}|\theta} = (\mathbf{I} - \mathbf{B})^{-1}(\Gamma\Phi\Gamma' + \Psi)[(\mathbf{I} - \mathbf{B})^{-1}]' \,,$$

$$\Sigma_{\mathbf{XX}|\theta} = \Phi,$$

and

$$\Sigma_{YX|\theta} = \Phi\Gamma'[(I - B)^{-1}]' \,.$$

The complete model-implied covariance matrix is then

$$\Sigma_\theta = \begin{bmatrix} \Sigma_{YY|\theta} & \\ \Sigma_{XY|\theta} & \Sigma_{XX|\theta} \end{bmatrix}.$$

Once again, the goal of estimation is to find numerical values for the free parameters so as to match these model-implied covariances to the observed sample covariances as closely as possible.

## Section recap

### The covariance structure hypothesis

As with other modeling procedures, model **estimation** in SEM is the process of obtaining estimates of a given model's parameters from the observed sample data.

The **covariance structure hypothesis** provides the theoretical basis for estimating models from the sample covariance matrix.

The covariance structure hypothesis states that if a hypothesized model is perfectly correct, then the **model-implied covariance matrix** ($\Sigma_\theta$) equals the population covariance matrix ($\Sigma$). The model-implied covariance matrix expresses the variances and covariances of the observed variables as a function of a model's parameters.

In the context of path analysis, the complete model-implied covariance matrix can be partitioned into the implied covariance matrix among endogenous variables, $\Sigma_{YY|\theta}$; the implied covariance matrix among the exogenous variables, $\Sigma_{XX|\theta}$; and the implied covariance of **Y** with **X**, $\Sigma_{YX|\theta}$.

## Maximum likelihood estimation

There are several common approaches to optimizing the match between the estimated model-implied covariance matrix, $\widehat{\Sigma}_\theta$, and the sample covariance matrix, **S**. Each of these approaches works through a **fitting function**, also known as a *discrepancy function*, with which parameter estimates are found to optimize the match between $\widehat{\Sigma}_\theta$ and **S** according to some criterion.[3] This implementation of fitting functions parallels that presented in Chapter 8 for EFA.

---

[3] It is also possible to adapt these fitting functions to fit structural equation models to the observed correlation matrix, **R**. Nevertheless, for certain types of models, including path analysis models, doing so may alter the model being studied, produce incorrect values for model fit statistics, or produce incorrect standard errors of the parameter estimates (Cudeck, 1989).

By far the most common estimation method for SEM is maximum likelihood (ML). The ML fitting function expressed in terms of covariance structure[4] is

$$F_{ML} = \log|\widehat{\Sigma}_\theta| + \text{tr}(\mathbf{S}\,\widehat{\Sigma}_\theta^{-1}) - \log|\mathbf{S}| - (P + Q), \tag{9.13}$$

where again $Q$ is the number of exogenous variables and $P$ is the number of endogenous variables in the model. The goal is to find the parameter estimates that lead to the $\widehat{\Sigma}_\theta$ that makes the value of $F_{ML}$ as small as possible. Minimizing $F_{ML}$ serves to maximize the likelihood of obtaining $\widehat{\Sigma}_\theta$ from observed data randomly sampled from a multivariate normal distribution with covariances determined by the model specification.

As was the case in Chapter 6 for ML estimation of multilevel models and in Chapter 8 for estimation of EFA models, finding the parameter estimates for a structural equation model that minimize $F_{ML}$ again requires a computerized iterative algorithm; unlike OLS regression, there are no closed-form formulas for calculating the estimates. In essence, SEM software first calculates a set of initial parameter estimates called *start values* to obtain an initial version of $\widehat{\Sigma}_\theta$ which is plugged into the ML fitting function along with the observed $\mathbf{S}$ to get an initial value for $F_{ML}$. Next, the program adjusts the parameter estimates to improve (i.e., decrease) $F_{ML}$, and it keeps adjusting the parameter estimates until the improvement in $F_{ML}$ becomes trivial (where 'trivial' is defined by some arbitrary stopping value), which is known as *convergence*. These steps of parameter estimate adjustments are known as *iterations*. With SEM software, the user can typically control the start values, the maximum number of potential iterations, and the stopping rule for the algorithm, although the default choices for these options are usually adequate. With a saturated model (i.e., a model with $df = 0$), the program will eventually find the parameter estimates that make $F_{ML} = 0$, whereas for an overidentified model (i.e., a model with $df > 0$), the final, minimized value of $F_{ML}$ will be greater than zero. For an expanded description of this procedure, see Ferron and Hess (2007).

It is important to recognize, though, that for a given model, the estimation algorithm may reach its maximum number of iterations before $F_{ML}$ has been adequately minimized; this result is known as *nonconvergence*. This situation is usually indicative of model underidentification or other model misspecification; although the user might increase the maximum number of iterations allowed for the estimation algorithm or change start values to facilitate convergence, more often than not, no final solution can be obtained without changing the model specification itself. A similar problem occurs when the estimation algorithm successfully converges to a final solution, but that particular set of parameter estimates is statistically invalid, which is known as an *improper solution*. Improper solutions are often characterized by negative error variance estimates, but the problems can be more subtle, such as a nonpositive definite predicted covariance matrix. SEM software will alert the user when nonconvergence or improper solutions occur, and at that point, it is incumbent on the user to revise the model; parameter estimates and other results obtained with a nonconverged or improper solution are not trustworthy and should not be reported. For further information about the causes and consequences of nonconvergence and improper solutions, see Chen, Bollen, Paxton, Curran, and Kirby (2001).

---

[4]In Chapter 8, the ML fitting function was expressed in terms of correlation structure.

## Section recap

### Maximum likelihood estimation

**Maximum likelihood** (ML) estimation of structural equation models uses an iterative algorithm to find the set of parameter estimates that produces the population model-implied covariance matrix ($\widehat{\Sigma}_\theta$) that matches the sample covariance matrix (**S**) as closely as possible according to the ML fitting function (or discrepancy function):

$$F_{ML} = \log|\widehat{\Sigma}_\theta| + \text{tr}(\mathbf{S}\widehat{\Sigma}_\theta^{-1}) - \log|\mathbf{S}| - (P + Q),$$

where $P$ is the number of endogenous variables in the model and $Q$ is the number of exogenous variables.

Each iteration of the estimation algorithm consists of using a different set of parameter estimates represented with $\Sigma_\theta$ to find a value of $F_{ML}$. When the algorithm has found the $\Sigma_\theta$ that leads to the smallest value of $F_{ML}$ it can find, the algorithm has reached convergence.

Occasionally, the estimation algorithm converges to a set of parameter estimates which is characterized as an improper solution. Improper solutions consist of invalid parameter estimates, such as negative residual variances or model-implied correlations which are greater than +1 or less than –1.

## Properties of ML

The popularity of ML as an estimation method for SEM is a result of its large-sample statistical properties. These properties hold as long as the model being estimated is the properly specified, true population model (including the strong assumption of linearity) and as long as the errors (e.g., the $\zeta$ vector in path analysis models) have a multivariate normal distribution. Specifically, when these assumptions are met, ML produces parameter estimates which are *asymptotically unbiased, consistent*, and *efficient* (Bollen, 1989; Browne, 1984). In other words, as the sample size grows to infinity, ML parameter estimates become equal to their true population values (i.e., consistent and unbiased) and no other estimation method will give smaller parameter estimate standard errors (efficiency).

Additionally, as the sample size approaches infinity, ML parameter estimates are normally distributed which, like OLS multiple regression, allows the construction of normal-theory confidence intervals and $t$ or $Z$ tests for parameter estimate significance testing. Furthermore, the asymptotic distribution of the quantity $(N - 1)F_{ML}$ is a $\chi^2$ distribution with degrees of freedom equal to that of the model specification (i.e., Equation 9.9),[5] which leads to the development of model fit statistics which are described later in this chapter.

Finally, ML estimation does have a degree of robustness to assumption violation. Browne (1984) showed that the ML parameter estimates remain consistent even under violation of

---

[5]Technically, $(N - 1)F_{ML}$ has a *central* $\chi^2$ distribution only if the model being estimated is correct in the population. Otherwise, it has a *noncentral* $\chi^2$ distribution.

normality and that the other properties described earlier hold when the *multivariate kurtosis* is not excessive. This issue of distributional assumptions for SEM is discussed further later in this chapter.

 Section recap

### Properties of maximum likelihood

As long as the model being estimated is the properly specified population model and the observed variable errors (i.e., $\zeta$ in path analysis models) follow a multivariate normal distribution, then parameter estimates obtained with ML

- Are unbiased and converge to their true values (i.e., they are *consistent*) as the sample size increases
- Have standard errors which are smaller (i.e., they are *efficient*) than can be obtained with any other estimator
- Are normally distributed which allows construction of normal-theory confidence intervals and $t$ or $Z$ tests for significance (similar to multiple regression)

Additionally, once the minimum value of $F_{ML}$ is obtained, the quantity $(N-1)F_{ML}$ can be used to calculate certain model fit statistics.

Finally, ML estimates are robust to violation of the multivariate normality assumption, especially if the multivariate kurtosis of the observed variable errors is not excessive.

## Least-squares estimation

In addition to ML, other prominent estimation methods in SEM include **unweighted least squares** (ULS), **generalized least squares** (GLS), and **weighted least squares** (WLS). A general form of the fitting function for these estimators is

$$F_{LS} = (\tfrac{1}{2})\mathrm{tr}(\{[\mathbf{S} - \widehat{\Sigma}_{\theta}]\mathbf{W}^{-1}\}^2). \tag{9.14}$$

Thus, whereas ML optimizes the match between $\widehat{\Sigma}_{\theta}$ and $\mathbf{S}$ according to the theoretical likelihood criterion, the $F_{LS}$ function optimizes the match according to the minimization of the squared residual covariance matrix, $\mathbf{S} - \Sigma_{\theta}$, via weight matrix $\mathbf{W}$. Like ML and analogous to least-squares estimation of EFA models as presented in Chapter 8, an iterative algorithm is used to find the set of parameter estimates producing the model-implied covariance matrix that leads to the smallest obtainable value of $F_{LS}$. More specifically, when $\mathbf{W} = \mathbf{I}$, Equation 9.14 gives the ULS fitting function, whereas setting $\mathbf{W} = \mathbf{S}$ is commonly referred to as GLS.[6] Under general conditions, this GLS estimator has many of the same desirable statistical properties as

---

[6] Any consistent estimator of the population covariance matrix $\Sigma$ can be used as the weight matrix in GLS, but $\mathbf{S}$ is the most common (Bollen, 1989).

ML (see Bollen, 1989, for details), whereas a potential advantage of ULS is that convergence can be obtained more easily when ML and GLS encounter difficulties.

Finally, the $F_{LS}$ fitting function in Equation 9.14 is a special case of a more general WLS fitting function developed in Browne (1984; also see Bollen, 1989). When the weight matrix for this WLS function is the estimated *asymptotic covariance matrix* of **S**, then the *arbitrary distribution function*, or ADF, is obtained. The ADF estimator has the theoretical advantage of making no a priori assumption about the distribution of the observed variables (aside from having finite kurtosis), but unfortunately, in practice, ADF estimation generally does not work well because the asymptotic covariance matrix is difficult to calculate with realistic sample sizes.

Yet another important form of least-squares estimation is known as *two-stage least squares* (2SLS), which is commonly used to estimate nonrecursive models. 2SLS estimates are also commonly used as start values for ML and other estimators requiring iterative algorithms. Description of this procedure is beyond the scope of this text, but see Murnane and Willett (2011) for an accessible treatment.

 Section recap

### Least-squares estimation

As an alternative to ML estimation of structural equation models, least-squares estimation optimizes the match between the model-implied covariance matrix and the sample covariance matrix by minimizing the (weighted) squared residual covariance matrix.

In particular, an iterative algorithm is used to find the parameter estimates that minimize the least-squares fitting function

$$F_{LS} = (\tfrac{1}{2})\mathrm{tr}(\{[\mathbf{S} - \Sigma_\theta]\mathbf{W}^{-1}\}^2),$$

where **W** is a weight matrix. If **W** is an identity matrix, then this is the **unweighted least-squares** (ULS) fitting function; if **W** = **S**, then this is a **generalized least-squares** (GLS) fitting function; finally, if **W** is the asymptotic covariance matrix of **S**, then this is the asymptotically distribution free (ADF) fitting function.

GLS maintains many of the same desirable statistical properties as ML, whereas ULS estimation of certain models may lead to convergence when ML and GLS do not.

Another form of least squares estimation, 2SLS, is often used to estimate nonrecursive models.

## Standard error estimation and inference

Recall from Chapters 1 and 2 that with classic OLS regression, we can construct a confidence interval for a slope parameter and test the significance of the parameter estimate $\hat{\beta}$ using the standard error of the slope estimate, $s_{\hat{\beta}}$ (e.g., Equation 1.13). The coefficients in a path analysis model, that is, the free parameters in the $\Gamma$ and **B** matrices are also (partial) regression slopes, and as mentioned, when the model is estimated using ML (or GLS), these coefficients have a normal sampling distribution (as long as the sample size is large). Thus, if we have estimates of their standard errors, then we can apply the same approach from regular

OLS regression to construct confidence intervals and perform significance tests for these path coefficients. But rather than using the closed-form OLS standard error formula given in Chapter 2 (i.e., Equation 2.10), when models are estimated using ML or GLS, standard error estimates are obtained as the square root of the diagonal elements from the **asymptotic covariance matrix** of the parameter estimates. This asymptotic covariance matrix gives information about the multivariate sampling distribution of the path coefficients (as well as of the other model parameters) and is the inverse of the so-called *information matrix* (which is calculated from the second-order partial derivatives of the log-likelihood of the population parameters; see Ferron and Hess, 2007, for a pedagogical description).

Because structural equation models are often estimated using large samples, the significance test of a parameter estimate is commonly treated as a basic $Z$ test (which is equivalent to a so-called Wald test). In general, any parameter estimate obtained via ML or GLS estimation divided by its standard error estimate produces a statistic with a standard normal distribution (i.e., a $Z$ statistic) when $N$ is large (i.e., $N > 250$; otherwise the test statistic should be referred to as a $t$ distribution). For example, one can test whether a given $\hat{\gamma}$ parameter estimate significantly differs from zero with

$$Z = \frac{\hat{\gamma}}{\hat{\sigma}_{\hat{\gamma}}},$$

where $\hat{\sigma}_{\hat{\gamma}}$ is the estimated standard error of $\hat{\gamma}$. This $Z$ is considered significant with $\alpha = .05$ (two-tailed) if it exceeds the critical value 1.96 (or is less than –1.96), although SEM software will print an exact $p$ value. Additionally, and again with large $N$, a 95% confidence interval for the population parameter estimate $\gamma$ is obtained with

$$\hat{\gamma} \pm (1.96\,\hat{\sigma}_{\hat{\gamma}}),$$

which is an application of the formula for a 95% confidence interval around any normally distributed parameter estimate.

## Multiple $R^2$: Proportion of variance explained

In a path analysis model, the $\hat{\gamma}$ and $\hat{\beta}$ parameter estimates are themselves unstandardized effect-size statistics, just as $\hat{\beta}$ slope estimates obtained using OLS regression are effect-size statistics, as explained in Chapters 1 and 2. Another concept from multiple regression which can be applied to path analysis models (and all structural equation models) is the use of proportion-of-variance-explained statistics (i.e., so-called coefficients of determination), which are a type of standardized effect-size measure representing the total effect of a set of predictors on a given outcome variable (in contrast to a single slope coefficient which represents the partial effect of a single predictor).

Specifically, recall that in multiple regression, the $R^2$ statistic represents the proportion of outcome variable variance that is explained by the linear combination of the predictor variables. In a path analysis model, this statistic can also be obtained for each endogenous variable, with

$$R^2_{Y_p} = 1 - \frac{\hat{\psi}_{pp}}{\hat{\sigma}^2_{Y_p}},$$

where $\hat{\psi}_{pp}$ is the error variance estimate for the $p$th endogenous variable and $\hat{\sigma}^2_{Y_p}$ is the model-implied total variance of the $p$th endogenous variable from $\Sigma_\theta$.[7] Hence, $R^2_{Y_p}$ estimates the proportion of variance in $Y_p$ explained by its direct predictors in the path model.

 **Section recap**

### Standard errors, inference, and $R^2$ statistics

Standard errors of parameter estimates in SEM are obtained from the diagonal of the **asymptotic covariance matrix** of the parameter estimates, which describes the multivariate sampling distribution of the estimates.

These standard errors can be used to calculate confidence intervals and Wald test statistics (i.e., either $Z$ or $t$ tests) for parameter estimates in a path analysis model using the same normal-theory formulas that are used for OLS multiple regression.

A multiple $R^2$ statistic can be calculated for the $p$th endogenous variable $Y_p$ in a path analysis model with

$$R^2_{Y_p} = 1 - \frac{\hat{\psi}_{pp}}{\hat{\sigma}^2_{Y_p}}'$$

where $\hat{\psi}_{pp}$ is the error variance estimate for the $p$th endogenous variable and $\hat{\sigma}^2_{Y_p}$ is the model-implied total variance of the $p$th endogenous variable from $\Sigma_\theta$.

As with OLS multiple regression, this $R^2$ statistic estimates the proportion of variance in $Y_p$ explained by its direct predictors in the path model.

## Results for the social support and depression model

As with any statistical modeling procedure, before estimating the social support and depression model depicted in Figure 9.7, it is important to examine descriptive statistics and graphs of the data. Figure 9.9 gives a scatterplot matrix for each of the five observed variables in the model using the (simulated) sample of $N = 214$ cases. In this figure, we can see that none of the univariate distributions shows a radical departure from a normal distribution. Univariate normality is necessary, but not sufficient, for multivariate normality, which is an assumption for ML estimation (and discussed in further detail later). Additionally, none of the bivariate scatterplots shows any strong pattern in the data that would not be reasonably represented with a linear model. Because the path analysis model will be fitted to the product-moment covariances among these variables, we want to make sure that it is reasonable to summarize each bivariate relation with a straight line.

Descriptive statistics for the five variables are given in Table 9.1. Corroborating the visualizations in Figure 9.10, the correlations among the variables range from weak to moderate, whereas the univariate skewness and kurtosis statistics do not suggest any substantial

---

[7]An alternative formula simply uses the observed sample variance of $Y_p$ in place of $\hat{\sigma}^2_{Y_p}$.

deviation from normal distributions. Thus, it appears reasonable to fit the hypothesized model to the observed covariance matrix using the ML method described earlier to obtain estimates of the model's free parameters. But before interpreting these parameter estimates, it is important to evaluate the overall fit of the model to the data. Thus, the principles and procedures for examining model fit are addressed next.

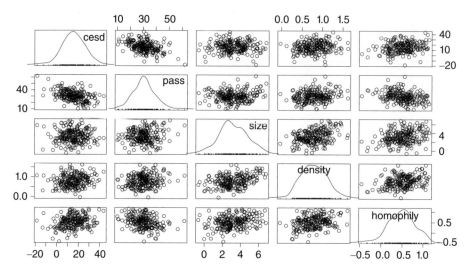

**Figure 9.10** Scatterplot matrix of five observed variables in social support and depression example

**Table 9.1** Correlations and univariate descriptive statistics of five observed variables in social support and depression example

|  | CESD | PASS | Size | Density | Homophily |
|---|---|---|---|---|---|
| CESD | 1.00 | – | – | – | – |
| PASS | −.43 | 1.00 | – | – | – |
| Size | −.01 | .12 | 1.00 | – | – |
| Density | .17 | .19 | .39 | 1.00 | – |
| Homophily | .24 | −.31 | .29 | .30 | 1.00 |
| M | 15.40 | 30.70 | 3.20 | 0.80 | 0.50 |
| SD | 10.20 | 8.30 | 1.50 | 0.30 | 0.30 |
| Skewness | −0.10 | 0.35 | 0.07 | 0.16 | −0.17 |
| Kurtosis | 0.27 | 0.68 | −0.31 | −0.29 | −0.03 |

Note. $N = 214$. $M$ = mean; $SD$ = standard deviation.

## MODEL FIT EVALUATION

An important part of most SEM analyses is the evaluation of the extent to which a hypothesized model fits the data. Good model–data fit lends general support to the overall theory or set of hypotheses that lead to the model specification. Poor model–data fit implies that the model is misspecified in some way (e.g., important parameters have been omitted) which in turn implies that estimates of the individual parameters in the model are incorrect to some extent. Thus, a model's estimates should not be interpreted if the model does not adequately fit the data. It is important to keep in mind that it is impossible for an overidentified model to fit observed data perfectly (see, e.g., MacCallum, 2003); model fit is a matter of degree rather than an all-or-nothing proposition.

Additionally, it is important to recognize that it is possible for two different models with different hypothesized effects to have an identical fit to the data, which occurs when two separate models produce the same model-implied covariance matrix, $\Sigma_\theta$. Such models are called **equivalent models**. Although some instances of equivalent models will be pointed out in this and subsequent chapters, it is advisable to consult a broader treatment of the concept (e.g., Hershberger and Marcoulides, 2013; Williams, 2012) and keep in mind that when one obtains a good fitting model, it is likely that there is an equally well-fitting equivalent model that may not have been considered.

As a quick aside, model fit can always be improved (in an absolute sense) by adding more free parameters. Taking this principle to its extreme, if a model has degrees of freedom equal to 0, that is, if it is a just-identified model, SEM fit statistics will always suggest that it has perfect fit (given the assumptions of the estimator used, such as linearity and multivariate normality for ML estimation). But such an occurrence does not imply that a model is conceptually useful; a just-identified, saturated model likely has unnecessary, trivial parameters. A general goal of many SEM applications is to describe the associations among a set of variables parsimoniously by using a model with a small number of theoretically important free parameters that still adequately fits the data.

 Section recap

### Model fit evaluation

Good model–data fit lends general support to the overall theory or set of hypotheses that lead to the model specification, whereas poor model–data fit implies that the model is misspecified in some way, which then implies that estimates of the individual parameters in the model are incorrect to some extent.

Yet, it is impossible for an overidentified model to fit data perfectly. Model fit is a matter of degree.

Two separate models which produce the same model-implied covariance matrix are called **equivalent models**. It is important to keep in mind that when one obtains a good fitting model, there is likely to be an equally well-fitting equivalent model that may not have been considered.

Model fit can always be improved (in an absolute sense) by adding more free parameters. But a general goal of path analysis modeling and SEM overall is to obtain the most parsimonious model, i.e., the simplest model with the fewest free parameters, that still adequately fits the data.

## $\chi^2$ exact-fit test

As mentioned previously, the minimized value of the fitting function used to estimate a model (e.g., $F_{ML}$) also leads to a model fit statistic; a version of this test statistic was presented in Chapter 8 as the ML minimum fit-function $\chi^2$ **exact-fit test**, which is also sometimes referred to as the $\chi^2$ *goodness-of-fit test*. In the current context, if the true population model is estimated, then the statistic

$$T = (N - 1)F_{min},$$ (9.15)

where $F_{min}$ is the minimized value of the fitting function used to estimate the model under consideration, is asymptotically (i.e., with increasingly large $N$) distributed as a central $\chi^2$ statistic (i.e., $T \sim \chi^2$) with degrees of freedom equal to

$$\left[ \frac{(P+Q)(P+Q+1)}{2} \right] - t.$$

This degrees-of-freedom calculation was described earlier as Equation 9.9 in the context of model identification. This test statistic $T$ can thus be treated as a $\chi^2$ statistic to evaluate the null hypothesis that the population covariance matrix among the observed variables equals the model-implied covariance matrix:

$$H_0: \Sigma = \Sigma_\theta.$$

More loosely speaking, the null hypothesis is that the model fits the data *exactly*. Thus, a significant $\chi^2$ suggests that the model does not fit the data perfectly, and therefore, the model is misspecified and potentially important parameters have been left out (i.e., fixed to zero). When the depression and social support example model (i.e., Figure 9.7) is estimated using ML, we obtain $\chi^2$ (3) = 19.23, which is significant with $p < .001$. Thus, the hypothesized model does not fit the data perfectly. Remember from Chapter 8, though, that perfect fit is an overly ambitious goal, and so other statistics measuring the degree of misfit for this model are presented later.

There are two general problems with the $\chi^2$ exact-fit test. The first is that it tests the hypothesis that the model fits the data perfectly; that is, the specified model is exactly correct in the population and any lack of fit in the sample arises only from sampling error. But once again, no statistical model can ever be expected to be perfect, even at the population level, and so the null hypothesis for this test is unrealistic; rejection of exact fit is not particularly informative. The second problem with the $\chi^2$ exact-fit test arises because of the first. Specifically, because no model can be perfectly specified, as $N$ increases, it becomes more likely that this $\chi^2$ test will become significant as a result of the omission of parameters representing weak, trivial effects that cannot be easily replicated. In this situation, the only way to obtain a nonsignificant $\chi^2$ may be to respecify the model by introducing parameters that are sample specific or have nonsensical interpretations. Reality is complex, but the best substantive theories (and thus the best statistical models implied by them) are as simple, or as parsimonious, as possible, while still explaining the major regularities in empirical data.

That being said, path analysis models typically have low degrees of freedom, which is associated with low power for the $\chi^2$ exact-fit test, and thus, it is common to obtain a nonsignificant result with path analysis models. When models include latent variables (as in Chapter 10), the degrees of freedom tend to be larger than for path analysis models, and consequently, $\chi^2$ fit tests are often significant, even for good models.

## Section recap

### $\chi^2$ exact-fit test

The null hypothesis that the population covariance matrix among the observed variables equals the model-implied covariance matrix ($H_0$: $\Sigma = \Sigma_\theta$) can be tested with the statistic

$$T = (N - 1)F_{min},$$

where $F_{min}$ is the minimized value of the fitting function used to estimate the model under consideration.

If the correct population model is estimated, then this test statistic $T$ is asymptotically distributed as a central $\chi^2$ statistic (i.e., $T \sim \chi^2$).

A major problem with this $\chi^2$ **exact-fit test** is that the null hypothesis being evaluated is known to be false a priori: No model can ever be expected to fit its data perfectly. Furthermore, as $N$ increases, this test is more likely to reject a given model unless trivial, potentially nonsensical or unreplicable parameters are freed.

Thus, structural equation models are usually evaluated with alternative model fit statistics.

---

## Root-mean-square error of approximation (RMSEA) fit statistic

To reiterate, the exact-fit test statistic $T = (N - 1)F_{min}$ is asymptotically distributed as a central $\chi^2$ statistic when the estimated model is correctly specified, but strictly speaking, exactly correct model specification is impossible. Consequently, the statistic $T = (N - 1)F_{min}$ asymptotically follows a *noncentral* $\chi^2$ distribution. Readers might not be familiar with the concept of noncentral distributions,[8] but the key idea for the present context is that the noncentral $\chi^2$ distribution is characterized by a *noncentrality parameter*, which reflects the degree to which a model is misspecified. Specifically, the noncentrality parameter of a structural equation model can be estimated as

$$\frac{T - df}{(N - 1)},$$

where $df$ is the model degrees of freedom. This insight led to the development of a model fit statistic now known as the **root-mean-square error of approximation** (see Steiger, 1990), or **RMSEA**, model fit statistic.

RMSEA can be expressed as

$$RMSEA = \sqrt{\frac{T - df}{df(N - 1)}},$$

---

[8]When their corresponding null hypothesis is false, a test statistic such as $F$ or $\chi^2$ has a noncentral distribution rather than the standard, central distribution it would have if the null hypothesis were true. The central distributions are used to obtain *p*-values because *p*-values represent a probability given a true null hypothesis.

where, again, $T$ is the $T = (N - 1)F_{min}$ statistic just described;[9] an alternative formula for RMSEA was given in Chapter 8 as Equation 8.9. Smaller values of RMSEA indicate better model fit, with RMSEA = 0 being set as the lowest possible value. Importantly, the model $df$ is included in the denominator of RMSEA to penalize model complexity; more specifically, RMSEA estimates the per degree of freedom amount of discrepancy between the model-implied covariance matrix $\Sigma_\theta$ and the population covariance matrix $\Sigma$ (Browne and Cudeck, 1993). Therefore, RMSEA penalizes researchers for fitting overly complex models which is in direct contrast to the $\chi^2$ exact-fit test which can reward unnecessary model complexity. For this reason and more generally, with the soundness of the statistical theory behind it, RMSEA has become one of the most popular model fit statistics in SEM and it is almost always reported in modern applications.

Following Browne and Cudeck (1993) and MacCallum, Browne, and Sugawara (1996), the applied research literature mainly adheres to the rough guidelines that an RMSEA less than .05 represents *close fit*, values between .05 and .08 indicate acceptable fit, values between .08 and .10 indicate mediocre fit, and an RMSEA above .10 suggests that an estimated model fits the data poorly. It is important to keep in mind, though, that these are only rough guidelines that do not hold in all situations; we return to this point later. In contrast to the test of exact fit, the results of simulation studies also have shown that RMSEA is not overly sensitive to sample size as long as $N$ is greater than 200 or so (e.g., Curran et al., 2003).

Another important quality of RMSEA is that its relation to the noncentral $\chi^2$ distribution allows the construction of confidence intervals, and as an alternative to using the standard $\chi^2$ exact-fit test, RMSEA can be used to test hypotheses of close fit (see MacCallum et al., 1996). That is, the null hypothesis for the $\chi^2$ exact-fit test implies RMSEA = 0, or perfect fit. Alternatively, a potential null hypothesis for the test of close fit is

$$H_0:\text{RMSEA} < .05.$$

Here, the idea of close fit reflects the idea that although a given model is unlikely to be exactly correct in the population, the model may still come close to reproducing the population covariance matrix in the sense of having a population RMSEA less than .05 (i.e., the RMSEA that would be obtained if one were to have access to the population covariance matrices, $\Sigma$ and $\Sigma_\theta$, rather than to the sample-based estimates of them, $S$ and $\Sigma_\theta$, respectively). Failure to reject the close-fit null hypothesis means that population-level close fit cannot be ruled out based on the current data. Most SEM software produces this close-fit test as a default output using the null value of RMSEA < .05 (alternative null values such as .06 or .04 could be used instead). Additionally, by convention, most SEM software automatically produces a 90% confidence interval estimate of population RMSEA; it has become common practice to report this confidence interval in published applications of SEM.

For the initial social support and depression model (i.e., Figure 9.7) estimated with ML, the point estimate of RMSEA is .159, with a 90% confidence interval of (.096, .230). Thus, although the lower limit of the confidence interval dips below .10, the RMSEA suggests that the model fits the data poorly. Not surprisingly, the test of close fit is also significant ($p = .003$), rejecting the null hypothesis that population RMSEA is less than .05.

---

[9]If the quantity $T - df$ is negative, the value of RMSEA is set equal to 0.

━━ Section recap ━━━━━━━━━━━━━━━━━━━━━━━━━━━

### Root-mean-square error of approximation (RMSEA) fit statistic

The **root-mean-square error of approximation**, or **RMSEA**, fit statistic can be expressed as

$$RMSEA = \sqrt{\frac{T - df}{df(N - 1)}},$$

where $T$ is the $T = (N - 1)F_{min}$ statistic described earlier and $df$ is the model degrees of freedom. Smaller values of RMSEA indicate better model fit.

An important feature of RMSEA is that it includes an adjustment for model parsimony, such that simpler models (i.e., models with greater $df$) have lower values of RMSEA than more complex models, all else being equal.

As an alternative to the $\chi^2$ exact-fit test, which implies RMSEA = 0, it is possible to test the null hypothesis of *close fit* using RMSEA, for example, to test the null hypothesis

$$H_0:RMSEA < .05.$$

Furthermore, it is common practice to report a 90% confidence interval for RMSEA.

___

## Baseline fit indices

A class of descriptive model fit statistics, known as **baseline fit indices**, assesses the improvement in fit of the hypothesized model relative to a **baseline model**, which is typically specified as the **independence** or **null** model. In the null model, the free parameters include the variances among the observed variables, but all covariances among observed variables are fixed to zero and there are no directional regression effects (i.e., the only free parameters are the diagonal elements of a $\Phi$ matrix, whereas all elements $\Gamma$ and $\mathbf{B}$ are fixed to 0).[10] To illustrate, a path diagram of the null model for the social support and depression example is in Figure 9.11.

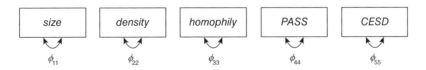

**Figure 9.11** Null model for social support and depression example

The two most commonly reported baseline fit indices are the **Tucker-Lewis index** (**TLI**; Tucker and Lewis, 1973), which is equivalent to the **non-normed fit index** (**NNFI**; Bentler

___

[10]The default null model for some SEM software includes free parameters for the covariances among the exogenous variables of the hypothesized model (while the relations between exogenous and endogenous variables continue to be fixed to zero, as are any relations among endogenous variables).

and Bonett, 1980), and the **comparative fit index** (**CFI**; Bentler, 1990). Both of these fit indices begin with a calculation of the exact-fit $\chi^2$ test statistic for the null model (i.e., the test statistic $T$ defined in Equation 9.15 obtained when the null model is estimated) which is then compared with the exact-fit $\chi^2$ test statistic for the hypothesized model. Specifically, the formula for the TLI is

$$\text{TLI} = 1 - \frac{(\chi_H^2 - df_H)/(\chi_0^2 - df_0)}{df_H / df_0},$$

where $\chi_H^2$ and $\chi_0^2$ are the exact-fit test statistics for the hypothesized and null models, respectively, and $df_H$ and $df_0$ are the model degrees of freedom for the hypothesized and null models, respectively. The formula for the CFI is

$$\text{CFI} = 1 - \frac{\chi_H^2 - df_H}{\chi_0^2 - df_0}.$$

These fit indices tend to range from 0 to 1 (although TLI values above 1 occur when $\chi_H^2 / df_H$ < 1), with larger values (e.g., > .90 or .95) indicative of better model–data fit. Additionally, because both TLI and CFI account for the degrees of freedom of the hypothesized model, like the RMSEA, these fit statistics favour more parsimonious models, all else being equal. Finally, unlike the $\chi^2$ exact-fit test and (to some extent) RMSEA, the TLI and CFI are not overly sensitive to sample size.

For the social support and depression example, the null model in Figure 9.11 has $df_0 = 10$, and ML estimation produces $\chi_0^2 = 173.99$. As reported earlier, the hypothesized social support and depression model has $df = 3$ and ML estimation produces an exact-fit test statistic of $\chi^2 = 19.23$. These values lead to TLI = 0.67 and CFI = 0.90 (guidelines for interpreting model fit statistics are discussed later).[11]

## Standardized root-mean-square residual

The *root-mean-square residual* (RMR) statistic was presented in Chapter 8 in the context of EFA. In the SEM context, this statistic is more commonly called the **standardized root-mean-square residual** (**SRMR**). Recall that the EFA model is most commonly fitted to the sample correlation matrix, **R**, by finding the model-implied correlation matrix, $\hat{\mathbf{P}}$, that most closely matches **R**. The RMR statistic was defined as the square root of the mean of the squared elements in the residual correlation matrix, $\mathbf{R} - \hat{\mathbf{P}}$. Although it is possible to fit a given SEM to a sample correlation matrix, it is much more common to fit a structural equation model to a sample covariance matrix, which then produces a **residual covariance matrix**, $(\mathbf{S} - \Sigma_\theta)$, instead of a residual correlation matrix.

If a model fits the data well, the elements of the residual covariance matrix will all be near zero. But each element of $(\mathbf{S} - \Sigma_\theta)$ depends on the scales of the two variables involved, and so an index representing the average of the residual covariances is difficult to interpret. Consequently, SRMR is calculated by standardizing the elements of the residual covariance matrix and then taking the square root of the mean of the squared elements of these

---

[11]When the null model includes freed covariances among the exogenous variables, $df_0 = 7$, $\chi_0^2 = 110.87$, and so TLI = .64 and CFI = .84 for the social support and depression model.

standardized covariances. SRMR therefore can be interpreted as similar to an average residual correlation, and it is equivalent to the RMR statistic in EFA.

Values of SRMR below .08 are commonly considered indicative of reasonable model–data fit. The hypothesized social support and depression model obtains SRMR = .07, which suggests that the model may fit the data adequately in contrast to the previous model fit evidence from the RMSEA, TLI, and CFI fit statistics.

To conclude the treatment of model fit statistics so far, because different statistics are influenced by different aspects of model fit, it has become standard practice to report several fit statistics for each estimated model. In their widely cited paper, Hu and Bentler (1999) recommended that SRMR be reported in addition to other descriptive fit statistics (e.g., RMSEA, CFI, and TLI). Specifically, Hu and Bentler showed that, for certain types of models estimated using ML, adequate fit is evident when SRMR is close to .08 or less, RMSEA is close to .06 or less, and CFI or TLI is close to .95 or greater. It is critical to keep in mind, though, that although they have been adopted in a variety of published studies using SEM, these suggested values for model fit statistics are only rough guidelines that do not generalize across all types of models (see Marsh, Hau, and Wen, 2004). In general, the best practices for evaluating model fit involve considering more than one type of fit index, not adhering to the Hu and Bentler guidelines too strictly and, ideally, comparing model fit across two or more competing models which have been hypothesized a priori. Additional fit statistics for comparing alternative, competing models are addressed later in this chapter.

 Section recap

### Descriptive model fit statistics

A class of descriptive model fit statistics, known as **baseline fit indices**, assesses the improvement in fit of the hypothesized model relative to a **baseline model**, which is usually specified to be a **null model**.

In the typical null model, the only free parameters are the variances among the observed variables (i.e., the only free parameters are the diagonal elements of a $\Phi$ matrix, whereas $\Gamma$ and $B$ are fixed to $0$).

Two of the most popular baseline fit statistics in modern applications of SEM include the **comparative fit index (CFI)** and the **Tucker-Lewis index (TLI**, which is equivalent to the **non-normed fit index**, or **NNFI**). These statistics range from 0 to (approximately) 1, with larger values indicative of better model fit.

The **standardized root-mean-square residual (SRMR)** model fit statistic is a function of the average (squared) value of the residual covariance matrix ($S - \Sigma_\theta$) produced by a fitted SEM. Because the residual covariance matrix depends on the scale of the observed variables, SRMR represents the average standardized value of the residual covariance matrix, with values closer to 0 indicative of better model fit.

In practice, researchers should report values of several model fit statistics to help evaluate whether a hypothesized SEM adequately represents the major regularities in the data. It is important to recognize that the highly cited guidelines of Hu and Bentler (1999) do not apply to all models. Ideally, then, researchers will compare fit of two or more models which have been hypothesized a priori.

## Model evaluation and revision: Residual covariances

When a model fits the data poorly, its individual parameter estimates are not trustworthy and should not be interpreted. Of course, a model might fit poorly as a result of problems with the data, such as outliers, non-normality, nonlinear relations, multicollinearity, and so on, just as these issues are problematic for OLS multiple regression, as presented in Chapter 2. The preliminary descriptive analyses (Table 9.1 and Figure 9.10) of the social support and depression data did not reveal any of these concerns, however. Otherwise, poor model fit is indicative of misspecification in that important parameters have been left out of the hypothesized model. That is, one or more directional regression effects or nondirectional covariance parameters have been fixed to 0 erroneously but should be freed.

In the social support and depression example, the combination of the RMSEA (including its 90% confidence interval), TLI, and CFI suggested that the initial hypothesized model in Figure 9.7 does not fit the data adequately. The SRMR = .07, though, indicates that the model fit may not be especially bad in terms of residual covariances. But it is important to keep in mind that although the average residual covariance or correlation might be small (representing good 'global' fit of the model), it is still possible for one or two individual elements of the residual covariance matrix to be large (indicating localized misfit). Hence, it is useful to examine the complete residual covariance matrix itself, which in turn may provide hints as to why the other fit statistics indicated inadequate overall model fit.

Once again, though, because residual covariances depend on the scales of the observed variables, their absolute size is difficult to interpret. Instead, each residual covariance can be divided by its estimated standard error, leading to what are commonly referred to as **standardized residual covariances**. The standardized residual covariances are in an approximate $Z$ score metric, and so they can be considered large when they approach 2 or are greater. Alternatively, residual covariances can be converted into residual correlations, which are interpretable in the same manner as residual correlations in EFA, as covered in Chapter 8. In short, large elements (in absolute value) of the residual covariance or correlation matrix indicate bivariate relations that have not been well explained by the fitted model.

Table 9.2 displays both the standardized residual covariances (above the diagonal) and the residual correlations (below the diagonal) for the fitted social support and depression model in Figure 9.7. Notice that wherever the model included a direct path from one variable to another (i.e., a freed $\gamma$ or $\beta$ parameter, such as the $\gamma_{11}$ path from size to PASS), the corresponding residual covariance or correlation equals 0. Conversely, the elements of the $\Gamma$ and $B$ matrices that were fixed to 0 in the hypothesized model have corresponding nonzero values in the residual covariance and correlation matrices. In Table 9.2, there is a particularly large residual covariance ($Z = 4.10$) between the CESD and density variables, corresponding to a residual correlation of $r_{residual} = .25$. The initial model in Figure 9.7 implies that the relation between CESD and density is completely explained by the indirect effect through PASS, but the large residual covariance indicates that overall model fit will likely improve substantially if we add a direct effect from density to CESD. Similarly, there is a nonzero residual relation between CESD and homophily (residual covariance $Z = 1.77$, residual correlation $r_{residual} = .11$) that was not captured by the initial model, implying that the relation between CESD and homophily also is not completely explained by an indirect effect through PASS. But this latter residual covariance is not particularly strong; perhaps we can obtain adequate overall model fit by adding only a direct effect from density to CESD without also adding a direct effect from homophily to CESD; the results from doing so are presented later. Just adding the direct effect from density to CESD moves us away from a strictly confirmatory mode into a slightly more exploratory mode of data analysis and, thus, increases the likelihood that we capitalize on chance sampling error; revising the model further to free a direct path from homophily to CESD would further decrease model parsimony and increase the likelihood of capitalizing on chance.

**Table 9.2** Standardized residual covariances (above the diagonal) and residual correlations (below the diagonal) in social support and depression example

|  | CESD | PASS | Size | Density | Homophily |
|---|---|---|---|---|---|
| CESD | – | -0.01 | 0.68 | 4.10 | 1.77 |
| PASS | .00 | – | 0.00 | 0.00 | 0.00 |
| Size | .04 | .00 | – | 0.00 | 0.00 |
| Density | .25 | .00 | .00 | – | 0.00 |
| Homophily | .11 | .00 | .00 | .00 | – |

 Section recap

### Residual covariances

Poor or inadequate model fit can be caused by a host of issues, such as influential outliers, nonlinear relations among variables, and violations of distributional assumptions. Otherwise, inadequate model fit is indicative of model misspecification in that important parameters have been fixed erroneously instead of freely estimated.

Fixed parameters contributing to inadequate model fit may be uncovered by inspecting the **standardized residual covariances** among the observed variables (which are in an approximate Z score metric) or, alternatively, the residual correlations.

## Model evaluation and revision: Modification indices

Another method for identifying potential sources of model misfit is to conduct a so-called 'specification search' by inspecting **modification indices**, which SEM software typically computes as univariate *Lagrange-multiplier* statistics (see Bollen, 1989: 298–99). A modification index (MI) from an estimated model may be calculated for any parameter that has been constrained to equal a particular value (including a parameter that has been completely omitted because it is implicitly fixed to 0). The MI gives the amount that the model's exact-fit $\chi^2$ value would decrease (i.e., improve) if the corresponding parameter were to be freely estimated. Because each MI corresponds to a $\chi^2$ change based on freeing a single parameter, it can be considered a 1 degree-of-freedom $\chi^2$ value. With $df = 1$, the critical value for $\alpha = .05$ is $\chi^2 = 3.84$. Thus, a MI can be considered 'significant' if it exceeds 3.84. Note that this is a univariate, one-at-a-time significance testing rationale; one should never revise a model by freeing all parameters with large MIs. A much better strategy is to respecify a poorly fitting model by freeing the single parameter with the largest MI that is also substantively defensible and then determine whether this revised model fits; if not, one might proceed to consider freeing other parameters with large MIs, continuing to do so one parameter at a time.

Although MIs can be valuable for diagnosing model misfit, these statistics have certainly been abused in many applied studies using SEM. Researchers may be sorely tempted to rely on MIs with the sole goal of obtaining a well-fitting model, but doing so is dangerous. Large MIs often reflect aspects of data that are sample specific, as a result of chance, and are not likely to replicate. As soon as one revises a hypothesized model based on MIs, one has moved into an exploratory mode of data analysis, in the same way that revising a model based on inspecting residual covariances moves one into a more exploratory mode. Ideally, then, the revised model should be cross-validated with a new, independent sample. Additionally, blindly relying on MIs for the sole purpose of obtaining a well-fitting model can introduce parameters that do not make sense with respect to the research application or are statistically illegal (e.g., the covariance between an exogenous variable and an error term) and can make a model underidentified. In short, MIs should be used carefully, if at all, and any published model that has been developed using MIs should be regarded with an extra dose of skepticism.

Returning to the social support and depression example, the largest MIs for the initial hypothesized model in Figure 9.7 all correspond to the relation between density and CESD, which is consistent with what we observed earlier from the residual covariance matrix. Specifically, MI = 17.25 is the amount that the initial model's $\chi^2$ fit statistic is expected to decrease if we free a direct effect from density to CESD (i.e., free the $\gamma_{22}$ parameter). Next, MI = 16.04 corresponds to a nondirectional covariance between density and the CESD error term, $\zeta_2$; this, however, is a nonsensical, illegal parameter. Finally, MI = 15.11 corresponds to a direct effect from CESD to density. Including a freed parameter for this relation would make density an endogenous variable (this freed parameter would correspond to an element of a new $3 \times 3$ **B** matrix), the model would become nonrecursive, and, most importantly, the model would contradict the theoretical stance that low social support is a precursor of higher depression, instead implying that higher depression somehow predicts a changed social support network density. In sum, in this example, the only one of the three largest MIs that suggests a model revision that makes any sense corresponds to the regression of CESD on density (i.e., a freed $\gamma_{22}$ parameter).

 Section recap

### Modification indices

An alternative way to find the sources of inadequate model-data fit is to conduct a specification search using **modification indices**. A modification index (MI) from an estimated model may be calculated for any parameter that has been fixed to equal a particular value.

An MI gives the amount that the model's exact-fit $\chi^2$ would improve if the corresponding parameter were to be freely estimated.

Carelessly relying on MIs to improve model fit is problematic for a few reasons:

- Large MIs may be sample specific, leading to freed parameters which capitalize on chance and, thus, may not be replicable.
- Large MIs may correspond to parameters which are nonsensical conceptually or statistically.
- Freeing certain parameters based on large MIs may cause a model to become underidentified.

If one undertakes a model revision exercise using MIs, then parameters should be freed one at a time until adequate model fit is obtained, rather than freeing all parameters with large MIs.

Regardless, a model revised using MIs (or residual covariances) should be considered exploratory and eventually should be cross-validated using a separate, independent sample.

## Revised social support and depression model

As shown, both the residual covariance (or correlation) matrix and the MIs suggested that the initial social support and depression model in Figure 9.7 did not adequately account for the relation between density and CESD; the model hypothesized that the relation between these two variables could be completely explained by an indirect effect of density on CESD through PASS. A sensible revision to the model retains this indirect effect but also specifies a nonzero direct effect of density on CESD. That is, the revised model will be identical to the original model except the direct effect from density to CESD will be included by freeing the $\gamma_{22}$ parameter. Keeping size as $X_1$, density as $X_2$, and homophily as $X_3$, the parameter matrices for this revised model are identical to those for the original model, except $\gamma_{22}$ is now free. So now the model's scalar equations are

$$Y_1 = \gamma_{11}X_1 + \gamma_{12}X_2 + \gamma_{13}X_3 + \zeta_1$$

and

$$Y_2 = \beta_{21}Y_1 + \gamma_{22}X_2 + \zeta_2.$$

Thus, the revised matrix equation is

$$\begin{bmatrix} Y_1 \\ Y_2 \end{bmatrix} = \begin{bmatrix} 0 & 0 \\ \beta_{21} & 0 \end{bmatrix}\begin{bmatrix} Y_1 \\ Y_2 \end{bmatrix} + \begin{bmatrix} \gamma_{11} & \gamma_{12} & \gamma_{13} \\ 0 & \gamma_{22} & 0 \end{bmatrix}\begin{bmatrix} X_1 \\ X_2 \\ X_3 \end{bmatrix} + \begin{bmatrix} \zeta_1 \\ \zeta_2 \end{bmatrix}, \tag{9.16}$$

with $\Phi$ continuing to be the completely free covariance matrix for the exogenous variables and $\Psi$ continuing to be a diagonal matrix containing the variances in $\zeta$. This revised model is depicted in Figure 9.12.

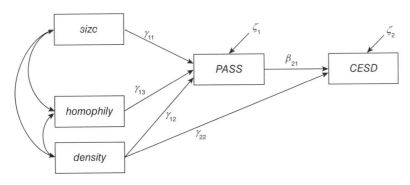

**Figure 9.12** Revised social support and depression model

When this revised model is estimated using ML, the model fit is much improved compared with the initial model. Specifically, the exact fit test is nonsignificant, $x^2$ (2) = 1.25, $p$ = .54. Consistent with this result, RMSEA = 0 (with 90% CI of .00 to .12), CFI = 1.00, TLI = 1.03, and SRMR = .01. Additionally, a quick check of the residual correlations indicates all are near zero. Therefore, the revised model in Figure 9.12 fits the data well.

## Model comparison statistics

Because the originally hypothesized model in Figure 9.7 is formally **nested** within the revised model in Figure 9.12, one can test whether the fit of the two models significantly differs using a **likelihood-ratio test**, which is more informally known as a $x^2$ **difference test** (likelihood-ratio tests were also described in Chapter 6 for comparing nested multilevel models). In general, Model B is nested within Model A when it is possible to write Model B as a special case of Model A by constraining one or more parameters of Model A to obtain Model B. Here, the original model in Figure 9.7 can be considered a special case of the revised model in Figure 9.12 because if $\gamma_{22}$ in the revised model is fixed to equal 0, then the matrix equation for the revised model (Equation 9.16) becomes identical to that for the original model (Equation 9.7). Consequently, the difference between the exact-fit $x^2$ values of the two models is itself treated as a $x^2$ statistic:

$$\chi^2_{difference} = \chi^2_B - \chi^2_A ,$$

where $\chi^2_B$ is the exact-fit $x^2$ value of the more restricted model (Model B) and $\chi^2_A$ is the exact-fit $x^2$ value of the less restricted model (Model A). The degrees of freedom of this $\chi^2_{difference}$ statistic is then equal to the difference between the $df$ values of Model B and Model A.

Therefore, with the current example, we have

$$\chi^2_{difference} = 19.23 - 1.25 = 17.98,$$

where 19.23 is the $x^2$ test statistic from the original model (the more restricted model in Figure 9.7) and 1.25 is the $x^2$ value from the revised model (the revised, less restricted model in Figure 9.12). The original model has $df$ = 3, whereas the revised model has $df$ = 2, and so this $\chi^2_{difference}$ is evaluated against the central $x^2$ distribution with $df$ = 1. Therefore, this $\chi^2_{difference}$ is clearly significant, $x^2$ (1) = 17.98, $p < .001$, confirming that the fit of the original model is significantly worse than the fit of the revised model.

Although the $x^2$ difference or likelihood-ratio test for the current example is based on $df$ = 1, the procedure can be used to compare nested models which differ by more than one parameter restriction. For example, likelihood-ratio tests can be used in a manner analogous to the hierarchical regression procedure outlined in Chapter 2 to test the joint significance of a set of direct effects. Specifically, a model with several free parameters in $\Gamma$ or $\mathbf{B}$ can be compared with a more restricted version of the same model in which a subset of the previously free parameters in $\Gamma$ or $\mathbf{B}$ is fixed to zero. The likelihood-ratio test comparing these two models provides a test of the joint significance of the set of parameter estimates in the former model that was fixed to form the latter model. Likelihood-ratio tests can also be used to test the joint significance of one or more error covariance parameter estimates in $\Psi$.

The fits of different models for the same observed variable set are also commonly compared using so-called information criterion statistics, particularly Akaike's information criterion (*AIC*) and the Bayesian information criterion (*BIC*), which were introduced in Chapter 6 in the context of multi-level modeling. Two advantages of both of these statistics are that the models being compared do not need to be nested and that there is a penalty for model complexity. The particular value of *AIC* or *BIC* for a single model is not itself interpretable, but for two models being compared, the model with the lower value of *AIC* is said to fit the data better, and likewise for *BIC*. In the current example, ML estimation of the original model produces *AIC* = 3,930.62 and *BIC* = 3,950.81, whereas ML estimation of the revised model produces *AIC* = 3,914.64 and *BIC* = 3,938.20. Therefore, both *AIC* and *BIC* indicate that the revised model fits the data better than the original model.

 Section recap

### Model comparison statistics

Model B is formally **nested** within Model A if Model B can be written as a special case of Model A by constraining one or more of its parameters to obtain Model B.

A **likelihood-ratio test** (also known as a $\chi^2$ **difference test**) can be used to determine whether overall model fit significantly differs across nested models. Specifically, the test statistic is

$$\chi^2_{difference} = \chi^2_B - \chi^2_A ,$$

where $\chi^2_B$ is the exact-fit $\chi^2$ value of Model B and $\chi^2_A$ is the exact-fit $\chi^2$ value of Model A.

If this $\chi^2_{difference}$ is significant, then the fit of the more restricted model (Model B) is significantly worse than the fit of the less restricted model (Model A).

The fit of competing model sets is also commonly compared using so-called information criterion statistics, particularly Akaike's information criterion (*AIC*) and the Bayesian information criterion (*BIC*). The particular value of *AIC* or *BIC* for a single model is not itself interpretable, but for two models being compared, the model with the lower value of *AIC* is said to fit the data better, and likewise for *BIC*.

## Estimated model interpretation

Because the revised model in Figure 9.12 fits the data well, it is suitable to interpret its individual parameter estimates. Simply obtaining adequate model fit is usually not sufficient to support the a priori hypotheses (or answer exploratory research questions) that guided the model specification: It is also important to assess whether the estimates of the key parameters are in the expected direction and whether their strength supports the more specific aspects of the research questions. As explained previously, the estimates of the free $\gamma$ and $\beta$ parameters are multiple regression coefficient estimates, and so they are interpreted in the same manner, and these interpretations may be complemented with confidence intervals and significance tests. Furthermore, just as regression coefficients in OLS regression may be standardized, so too can parameter estimates in path analysis, but the same caveats regarding standardized estimates described in Chapter 2 apply for path analysis models.

**Table 9.3**  Parameter estimates from revised social support and depression model

| Path | Parameter | Estimate | SE | 95% CI | Z | p |
|------|-----------|----------|-----|--------|---|---|
| PASS → CESD | $\beta_{21}$ | −0.59 | 0.07 | (−0.74, −0.44) | 7.96 | <.001 |
| density → CESD | $\gamma_{22}$ | 8.88 | 2.05 | (4.86, 12.89) | 4.33 | <.001 |
| size → PASS | $\gamma_{11}$ | 0.79 | 0.38 | (0.05, 1.52) | 2.10 | .036 |
| density → PASS | $\gamma_{12}$ | 7.30 | 1.88 | (3.61, 10.98) | 3.88 | <.001 |
| homophily › PASS | $\gamma_{13}$ | −11.90 | 1.81 | (−15.45, −8.36) | 6.58 | <.001 |

Referring to the results for the revised social support and depression model in Table 9.3, the estimated slope for the linear regression of CESD on PASS is $\hat{\beta}_{21} = -0.53$, which is significant with $Z = 6.97$, $p < .001$. This slope estimate is the unstandardized effect size for the relation between PASS and CESD: Each one-point increase in PASS is associated with a 0.53 decrease in CESD. The 95% confidence interval around this effect indicates that the sample data are consistent with a population effect in the range of −0.74 to −0.44. Furthermore, we also see in Table 9.3 that each exogenous characteristic of social support networks (size, density, and homophily) significantly predicts the PASS endogenous variable, with the estimates of the corresponding $\gamma$ parameters once again indicating the size of these linear relations. As a further expression of effect size for the specific paths in this model, the $R^2$ statistic for CESD is .25, indicating that 25% of variance in this endogenous variable is explained by its direct predictors (PASS and density), whereas $R^2$ for PASS is .20, indicating that 20% of variance in this endogenous variable is explained by its direct predictors, which are the support network exogenous variables (size, density, and homophily).

Next, corresponding to the main conceptual research hypotheses, the model was specified such that PASS was a hypothesized mediator of the relations between the social support network characteristics and the CESD outcome variable. Thus, there are three indirect effects of interest: (1) the indirect effect of size on CESD through PASS, (2) the indirect effect of density on CESD through PASS, and (3) the indirect effect of homophily on CESD through PASS. The methods for testing indirect effects outlined in Chapter 5 can be applied here. First, using the joint test, we can see in Table 9.3 that each constituent direct effect parameter that comprises these three indirect effects is statistically significant, thereby indicating that the indirect effects themselves are also significant. But moving beyond a basic interest in statistical significance, we can also obtain point estimates of these indirect effects as the product of the estimated coefficients making up a particular indirect effect and use bootstrapping to obtain confidence intervals for the indirect effects. For example, the estimated indirect effect of size on CESD through PASS is the product $\hat{\gamma}_{11}\hat{\beta}_{21} = (0.79) \times (-0.59) = -0.46$, and a percentile bootstrap 95% confidence interval estimate of the indirect effect is (−0.98, −0.01). Table 9.4 summarizes these indirect-effect estimates for the social support and depression example, and it further indicates that each of these indirect effects may be considered statistically significant because none of the percentile bootstrap confidence intervals overlaps zero. For further discussion of path models including multiple indirect effects, see Preacher and Hayes (2008).

In sum, although the original hypothesized model was revised slightly to add an extra parameter (i.e., $\gamma_{22}$, the direct path from density to CESD), the collection of parameter estimates, in terms of their direction, strength, and statistical significance, combines to confirm the major hypotheses that guided the model specification, namely, that aspects of social support networks (represented by the size, density, and homophily variables) combine to predict perceived social support (represented by PASS), which in turn predicts depression (measured with CESD) among low-income older adults.

**Table 9.4**   Estimated indirect effects for revised social support and depression example

| Indirect effect | Parameter | Estimate | 95% bootstrap percentile CI |
|---|---|---|---|
| size → PASS → CESD | $\gamma_{11}\beta_{21}$ | −0.46 | (−0.98, −0.01) |
| density → PASS → CESD | $\gamma_{12}\beta_{21}$ | −4.30 | (−6.65, −2.43) |
| homophily → PASS → CESD | $\gamma_{13}\beta_{21}$ | 7.02 | (4.46, 9.87) |

 **Section recap**

### Estimated model interpretation

Obtaining adequate model fit is usually not enough to answer the research questions or hypotheses that guided the model specification: It is also important to interpret the key parameter estimates in terms of their direction and strength.

The estimates of the free $\gamma$ and $\beta$ parameters in a path analysis model are interpreted in the same manner as in other multiple regression coefficient estimates and may be supplemented with confidence intervals and significance tests.

Furthermore, indirect-effect estimates from path analysis models can be obtained as the product of the relevant path coefficient estimates, which in turn can be evaluated with the joint test and bootstrap confidence intervals.

## ASSUMPTIONS AND DIAGNOSTICS FOR PATH ANALYSIS MODELS

Because the path analysis models addressed in this chapter all specify linear associations among the variables, it should be no surprise that many of the same principles of assumption checking and diagnostics covered in earlier chapters are applicable in the current context. Yet again, the foremost concern is the appropriateness of the linear functional form the regression equations. For the social support and depression example in this chapter, recall that the data were artificial and simulated to be consistent with a known population covariance matrix, which produces variables with linear bivariate associations; these were illustrated in Figure 9.10. With real data, though, because structural equation models are fitted directly to an observed covariance matrix (which serves as a summary of the associations among the variables), it is important that a linear relation be an adequate representation of each bivariate association, just as was the case in Chapter 8 for EFA. And so once again, observed variables which are discrete (i.e., dichotomous or ordinally scaled) or 'limited' in other ways (e.g., censored so as to produce floor or ceiling effects) can be especially problematic for this fundamental linearity assumption. In the context of path analysis models, though, when an observed exogenous variable is dichotomous, it is guaranteed to be linearly associated with each continuous endogenous latent variable. For this reason, dichotomous exogenous variables can be included in path analysis without concern. Furthermore, nominally or ordinally scaled exogenous variables can also be included using a dummy or contrast coding variable scheme as described in Chapter 3 in the context of OLS multiple regression.

Recall from earlier that the ML fitting function derives from an assumption that the data are multivariate normally distributed. More precisely, though, this assumption applies to the multivariate distribution of the errors $\zeta$ from the individual regression equations comprising a given path analysis model, analogous to how the normal distribution assumption for OLS regression pertains to the error term $\varepsilon_i$ and not the observed predictor or outcome variables themselves. Equivalently, we can say that the endogenous variables $\mathbf{Y}$ are assumed to follow a multivariate normal distribution *conditional on* the exogenous variables $\mathbf{X}$. An important implication, then, is that there is no need for the exogenous variables to be normally distributed. Despite its basis in ML estimation, this normality assumption for $\zeta$ generalizes to the GLS fitting function for the purposes of evaluating model fit and using estimated standard errors for hypothesis tests and constructing confidence intervals. See Bollen (1989: 126–28) for further details and explanation of this issue.

In practice, researchers typically evaluate the normal distribution assumption by examining the univariate distribution of each endogenous variable as well as by evaluating the multivariate kurtosis of the set of endogenous variables $\mathbf{Y}$ using, for instance, Mardia's (1970) multivariate kurtosis measure. Recall from earlier that parameter estimates obtained with ML (or GLS; Bollen, 1989) remain consistent even under violation of the multivariate normal distribution assumption; therefore, as long as $N$ is large, the parameter estimates are reasonably trustworthy. But non-normality does affect the accuracy of model fit statistics and parameter estimate standard errors. Regardless of whether non-normality is discovered, researchers often apply procedures to obtain robust fit statistics and standard errors because they are easy to implement with modern SEM software; these methods are presented in Chapter 10. For the social support and depression example of the current chapter, artificial data were simulated directly from a multivariate normal population distribution, and so there is no need to assess the normal distribution assumption or implement robust methodology for these example analyses.

 Section recap

### Assumptions and diagnostics for path analysis models

Because structural equation models are fitted directly to an observed covariance matrix, it is important that a linear relation be an adequate representation of each bivariate association among the variables in a path analysis model.

For ML and GLS estimation of path analysis models, the endogenous variables $\mathbf{Y}$ are assumed to follow a multivariate normal distribution conditional on the exogenous variables **X**. An important implication of this statement is that there is no need for the exogenous variables to be normally distributed.

The normal distribution assumption of ML and GLS estimation of path analysis models may be checked by examining the univariate distribution of each endogenous variable as well as by evaluating the multivariate kurtosis of the set of endogenous variables **Y** using, for instance, Mardia's (1970) multivariate kurtosis measure.

---

# CHAPTER SUMMARY

**Structural equation modeling** (**SEM**) is a general framework encompassing a wide variety of statistical models as special cases. Structural equation models can incorporate any number of independent or predictor variables and any number of dependent or outcome variables, as well as both observed variables and latent variables. To introduce the major principles of SEM, the current chapter focused on **path analysis** models, which include only observed variables and no latent variables:

- A key advantage of path analysis models is that a variable can appear as a predictor in one equation and as an outcome in another equation, which allows any number of mediation or indirect effects to be included in a single model.
- The **specification** of a given SEM provides a formal statement of the parametric associations among variables using either a set of one or more equations or, equivalently, a **path diagram**.
- **Identification** is a property of a given SEM which determines whether it is possible to obtain unique estimates of the parameters from the observed data.
- The **covariance structure hypothesis** states that if a hypothesized model is perfectly correct, then the **model-implied covariance matrix** ($\Sigma_{\theta}$) equals the population covariance matrix ($\Sigma$). The model-implied covariance matrix expresses the variances and covariances of the observed variables as a function of a model's parameters.
- Because structural equation models are fitted directly to an observed covariance matrix, it is important that a linear relation be an adequate representation of each bivariate association among the variables in a path analysis model.

# RECOMMENDED READING

Ferron, J.M., & Hess, M.R. (2007). Estimation in SEM: A concrete example. *Journal of Educational and Behavioral Statistics, 32,* 110–20.

- The authors offer a clear, pedagogical description of ML estimation using a simple example model. Knowledge of basic calculus (i.e., partial derivatives) is needed, however.

MacCallum, R.C. (2003). Working with imperfect models. *Multivariate Behavioral Research, 38,* 113–39.

- This paper offers a philosophical but comprehensible discussion of the notion that no statistical model can ever be an exactly correct representation of empirical phenomena. The practical implications of this fact are addressed using the common factor model and SEM more generally as a modeling context.

Preacher, K.J., & Hayes, A.F. (2008). Asymptotic and resampling strategies for assessing and comparing indirect effects in multiple mediator models. *Behavior Research Methods, 40,* 879–91.

- This paper presents a variety of prototypical path models which all include more than one indirect effect and discusses procedures for testing these indirect effects. Practical guidance regarding computer implementation is also presented.

# STRUCTURAL EQUATION MODELING II: LATENT VARIABLE MODELS

## CHAPTER OVERVIEW

Whereas Chapter 9 presented structural equation models consisting of only observed variables, that is, path analysis models, the current chapter and Chapter 11 focus on models which
also incorporate latent variables. Nonetheless, many of the basic principles from Chapter 9
(and prior chapters, for that matter) readily extend to latent variable models, and as such,
these principles provide a solid foundation for the current chapter. The current chapter also
draws on ideas from exploratory factor analysis presented in Chapter 9. The main topics of
this chapter include:

- Confirmatory factor analysis (CFA)

  o  Model specification, identification, and estimation
  o  Model fit evaluation

- Assumption violation and remedies
- CFA with polychoric correlations for item-level variables
- Structural regression models

  o  Model specification, identification, and estimation

**Table 10.0**   Greek letter notation used in this chapter

| Greek letter | English name | Represents |
|---|---|---|
| $\lambda$ | Lowercase 'lambda' | Factor loading parameter |
| $\eta$ | Lowercase 'eta' | Latent variable (endogenous) |
| $\varepsilon$ | Lowercase 'epsilon' | Regression error term (unique factor) |
| $\Lambda$ | Uppercase 'lambda' | Factor loading matrix |
| $\Psi$ | Uppercase 'psy' | Covariance matrix for $\eta$ (in CFA) or $\zeta$ (in structural regression models) |
| $\psi$ | Lowercase 'psy' | Element in $\Psi$ |
| $\Theta$ | Uppercase 'theta' | Error covariance matrix |
| $\Sigma$ | Uppercase 'sigma' | Population covariance matrix among observed variables |
| $\theta$ | Lowercase 'theta' | Vector of all model parameters |
| $\chi$ | Lowercase 'chi' | $\chi^2$ distribution |
| $\sigma$ | Lowercase 'sigma' | Covariance parameter ($\sigma^2$ is variance) |
| $\rho$ . | Lowercase 'rho' | $\rho$ (in bold) is a vector of model-implied population correlations; $\rho$ (in italics, not bold) is population reliability |
| $\xi$ | Lowercase 'ksi' or 'xi' | Latent variable (exogenous) |
| $\delta$ | Lowercase 'delta' | Regression error term (unique factor) |
| $\gamma$ | Lowercase 'gamma' | Slope parameter in regression of $\eta$ on $\xi$ |
| $\zeta$ | Lowercase 'zeta' | Regression error term |
| $\beta$ | Lowercase 'beta' | Slope parameter in regression of $\eta$ on a different $\eta$ |
| $\Gamma$ | Uppercase 'gamma' | Matrix of $\gamma$ parameters |
| $B$ | Uppercase 'beta' | Matrix of $\beta$ parameters |
| $\Phi$ | Uppercase 'phi' | Covariance matrix of $\xi$ |
| $\phi$ | Lowercase 'phi' | Element in $\Phi$ |

*Note.* Some of these Greek letters may have been used for different purposes in previous chapters.

# WHAT ARE LATENT VARIABLE MODELS?

In the behavioural and social sciences, all manner of research studies involve important but abstract concepts or constructs. Examples of constructs include 'academic ability', 'political conservatism', 'prejudice', 'depression', 'short-term memory', 'life satisfaction', and the list goes on forever. Given their abstract quality, researchers can never observe such constructs directly and instead must devise operational instruments which attempt to measure them (often, but not always, the instruments are questionnaires). This attempt is never perfectly successful, and so the instruments always have some degree of measurement error. It is not stated often, but typically the variables in ordinary least-squares (OLS) regression and path analysis structural equation models are assumed to be measured without error. Measurement error, or a lack of reliability for the operational variables, produces biased regression coefficient estimates.

Using **confirmatory factor analysis** (or **CFA**), a specific type of structural equation modeling (SEM), one can model the relations between observed, operational variables and the constructs they are purported to represent. Next, by incorporating these statistical associations between observed variables and hypothetical constructs, directional regression relations among the constructs themselves can be modeled using a comprehensive type of SEM known as a *structural regression model*. These structural regression models feature the major strength of SEM, which is the ability to obtain regression coefficients (i.e., *structural coefficients*) for the associations among hypothetical constructs which are not biased by the measurement error of the observed variables in the model. Unlike the path analysis models presented in Chapter 9, both CFA and structural regression models are models which use latent variables to represent hypothetical constructs.[1] Thus, the current chapter focuses on models with latent variables. Yet, the major concepts of SEM covered in Chapter 9 – model specification, identification, and estimation – carry over to the latent variable models of this chapter.

# CONFIRMATORY FACTOR ANALYSIS

A CFA model is essentially a *measurement model* representing the casual relations between one or more unobserved, or latent, variables and a set of observed variables. Usually, these latent variables represent meaningful constructs which are soundly based in conceptual theory, and so the purpose of the model is to indicate how well a set of operational, observed variables relates to the constructs. This measurement model can then be expanded to form part of a fuller structural regression model, as shown later in this chapter. The standard CFA model is an instantiation of Thurstone's (1947) common factor model, which, as explained in Chapter 8, forms the basis of both exploratory factor analysis (EFA) and CFA. The distinction between the EFA and CFA models is explained later in this chapter.

## Research example for CFA

Toplak et al. (2009) used CFA to examine a set of hypothesized measurement models for the symptoms of Attention-Deficit Hyperactivity Disorder (ADHD) as represented by 18 parental-report items of the Strengths and Weaknesses of ADHD symptoms and Normal Behaviour Scale (SWAN; see Swanson et al., 2012) collected from a sample of $N = 164$ adolescents with attention difficulties. The parents' responses to each of the 18 items provide the set of observed variables for the hypothesized measurement models which varied according to the number and type of latent variables serving as causal influences on the observed variables; these models are described in greater detail throughout this chapter.

This dataset is available on the text's webpage (https://study.sagepub.com/flora) along with annotated input and output from popular statistical software packages showing how to reproduce the analyses presented in this chapter.

Each of the item-response variables used for these CFA models has a seven-point ordinal response scale ranging from –3 (*far below average*) to +3 (*far above average*). Recall from Chapter 8

---

[1]Not all latent variables are meant to represent meaningful constructs. Some latent variables serve different purposes in statistical models. See Bollen (2002).

that item-level variables such as these are potentially problematic as outcome variables for linear models such as EFA and here for CFA. Yet, when the items have more than five categories, the results of methodological research suggest that it is usually safe to treat them as linearly associated continuous variables by fitting models to the observed product-moment covariance matrix (rather than, for instance, to a polychoric correlation matrix), at least for the purposes of CFA and SEM more generally (Rhemtulla, Brosseau-Liard, and Savalei, 2012). For the current example, Figure 10.1 gives a scatterplot matrix for a subset of five items from the complete dataset of 18 ADHD symptom items from the SWAN. The discrete nature of these variables is apparent, but the scatterplots are still somewhat similar in appearance to what would be obtained with truly continuous variables and it seems reasonable to summarize each bivariate relation with a straight-line model; as such, the product-moment correlations corresponding to the variable pairs in the scatterplot matrix are in Table 10.1. Nonetheless, even when items have more than five categories and they are to be treated as continuous variables in subsequent CFA modeling, as in the current example, it is still important to consider other aspects of their distributions, as explained later in this chapter.

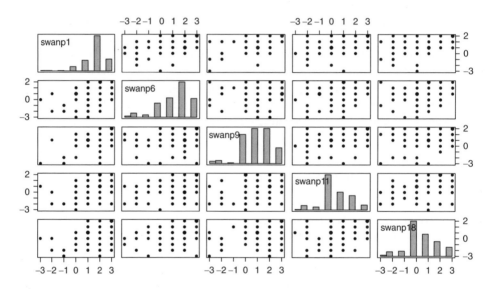

**Figure 10.1** Scatterplot matrix of a subset of five items from the 18 ADHD symptom items

**Table 10.1** Product-moment correlations among a subset of five items from the 18 ADHD symptom items

|  | SWAN1 | SWAN6 | SWAN9 | SWAN11 | SWAN18 |
|---|---|---|---|---|---|
| SWAN1 | 1 | – | – | – | – |
| SWAN6 | .45 | 1 | – | – | – |
| SWAN9 | .52 | .29 | 1 | – | – |
| SWAN11 | .26 | .23 | .24 | 1 | – |
| SWAN18 | .32 | .33 | .19 | .36 | 1 |

*Note. N = 164.*

## CFA: Model specification

In that CFA is an application of the common factor model, which was introduced in Chapter 8, the model specifies that a given observed variable (or **indicator**) $Y$ is linearly regressed on $K$ latent variables (or factors):

$$Y_{pi} = \left( \sum_{k=1}^{K} \lambda_{pk} \eta_{ki} \right) + \varepsilon_{pi}, \tag{10.1}$$

where $Y_{pi}$ is the value of the $p$th observed variable for individual case $i$; $\eta_{ki}$ is that person's unobservable score on the $k$th latent variable; $\lambda_{pk}$ is the partial regression slope, or **factor loading**, relating $\eta_{ki}$ to $Y_{pi}$; and $\varepsilon_{pi}$ is the error or disturbance term for the case $i$; the total number of observed variables is $P$, and the total number of latent variables is $K$. Equation 10.1 is equivalent to Equation 8.1; the only difference is that the notation has changed slightly to be more consistent with the 'LInear Structural RELations' (LISREL; as introduced in Chapter 9) approach to specifying structural equation models as opposed to common notation for EFA used in Equation 8.1.

Furthermore, because Equation 10.1 is a scalar equation for just one of $P$ observed variables, the model contains a whole set of $P$ scalar regression equations. Once again, as was the case for EFA, these separate scalar equations can be compactly represented using a single matrix equation:

$$\mathbf{Y} = \mathbf{\Lambda}\mathbf{\eta} + \mathbf{\varepsilon}, \tag{10.2}$$

where $\mathbf{Y}$ is the $P \times 1$ vector of observed variables, $\mathbf{\Lambda}$ is the $P \times K$ factor loading matrix, $\mathbf{\eta}$ is the $K \times 1$ vector of latent variables, and $\mathbf{\varepsilon}$ is the $P \times 1$ vector of error or disturbance terms. Equation 10.2 is equivalent to Equation 8.2 given for the EFA model, but once again, the notation is slightly changed to reflect LISREL notation for SEM.

The critical difference between the EFA and CFA implementations of the common factor model is that with CFA, certain factor loadings are fixed or constrained to zero a priori to represent hypotheses about which factors directly affect a given observed variable, whereas in EFA, all factor loading parameters are freely estimated. This distinction is exemplified later using the ADHD symptom variables described earlier. Consequently, in CFA, there are many elements of $\mathbf{\Lambda}$ fixed to zero to reflect an a priori hypothesis about the overall factor pattern, effectively removing the rotational indeterminacy problem of EFA, whereas in EFA, all elements of $\mathbf{\Lambda}$ are freely estimated and then $\mathbf{\Lambda}$ is rotated to aid interpretation. More often than not, in fact, a CFA model is specified so that a given observed variable has a nonzero factor loading for one and only one latent variable; such a factor pattern is known as an **independent clusters solution** (McDonald, 1999). Additionally, researchers typically use CFA when there is a strong hypothesis about the value of $K$, the total number of latent variables for the model, whereas a major aspect of EFA often includes a somewhat atheoretical examination of the optimal number of latent variables or factors. But, as demonstrated later, CFA can also be used to compare competing models with differing numbers of factors.

As with EFA, the factor loadings are the major parameters that are the focus in CFA. The other parameters of the model are incorporated in the $K \times K$ latent variable covariance matrix $\mathbf{\Psi}$. This covariance matrix is often converted into a correlation matrix for interpretation, and as such, it is analogous to the interfactor correlation matrix obtained from an oblique rotation in EFA. Lastly, $\mathbf{\Theta}_{\varepsilon}$ is the $P \times P$ covariance matrix for the error terms. In EFA, this matrix is necessarily constrained to be diagonal, but in CFA, off-diagonal elements of $\Theta_\varepsilon$ can be freely estimated to represent nonzero covariation between the error terms for a given pair of observed variables, as demonstrated later in this chapter. Most often, though, $\Theta_\varepsilon$ is diagonal in CFA as it is in EFA.

 Section recap

### CFA model specification

Like exploratory factor analysis (EFA), **confirmatory factor analysis** (CFA) involves developing and evaluating measurement models which represent the associations between observed variables and unobserved, or latent, variables, which often are intended to represent hypothetical constructs.

CFA is an application of the common factor model which, using LISREL notation for SEM, specifies that a given observed variable (or **indicator**) $Y$ is linearly regressed on $K$ latent variables (or factors):

$$Y_{pi} = \left( \sum_{k=1}^{K} \lambda_{pk} \eta_{ki} \right) + \varepsilon_{pi} \text{,}$$

where

$Y_{pi}$ is the value of the $p$th observed variable for individual case $i$

$\eta_{ki}$ is that person's unobservable score on the $k$th latent variable

$\lambda_{pk}$ is the partial regression slope, or **factor loading**, relating $\eta_{ki}$ to $Y_{pi}$

$\varepsilon_{pi}$ is the error or disturbance term for case $i$

Because a CFA involves a set of $P$ observed variables, these separate scalar equations for each of them can be combined into a single matrix equation:

$$\mathbf{Y} = \boldsymbol{\Lambda}\boldsymbol{\eta} + \boldsymbol{\varepsilon},$$

where

$\mathbf{Y}$ is the $P \times 1$ vector of observed variables

$\boldsymbol{\Lambda}$ is the $P \times K$ factor loading matrix

$\boldsymbol{\eta}$ is the $K \times 1$ vector of latent variables

$\boldsymbol{\varepsilon}$ is the $P \times 1$ vector of error or disturbance terms

The CFA model parameters also include the $K \times K$ latent variable covariance matrix and $\Theta_\varepsilon$, which is the $P \times P$ covariance matrix for the error terms. Although $\Theta_\varepsilon$ is usually restricted to be diagonal, its off-diagonal elements can be freely estimated to represent nonzero covariation between the error terms for a given pair of observed variables.

The critical difference between the EFA and CFA implementations of the common factor model is that with CFA, certain factor loadings are fixed to 0 based on a priori hypotheses about which factors directly affect a given observed variable, whereas in EFA, all factor loadings in $\boldsymbol{\Lambda}$ are freely estimated.

Often a CFA model is specified so that a given observed variable has a nonzero factor loading for one and only one latent variable; such a factor pattern is known as an **independent clusters solution**.

## A two-factor model specification for the ADHD symptoms

To illustrate model specification in CFA, we return to the ADHD example described earlier. Among other potential models, Toplak et al. (2009) hypothesized that a two-factor model might be appropriate for the 18 observed ADHD symptom variables because two major constructs are associated with ADHD, inattention and hyperactivity, and the SWAN questionnaire items were explicitly written to capture these constructs. More specifically, the researchers hypothesized that:

1. The first nine items are indicators of a latent variable, or factor, representing the inattention construct.
2. The second nine items are indicators of another latent variable representing the hyperactivity construct.
3. Because many children with inattention problems also have problems with hyperactivity, the two latent variables should be correlated.

With that in mind, consider the first observed variable, $Y_1$, an item purported to represent a symptom of the inattention construct or latent variable. Applying the traditional CFA model to the two-factor model hypothesis described in the previous paragraph implies that Equation 10.1 can be adapted for observed variable $Y_1$ with

$$Y_{1i} = \lambda_{11}\eta_{1i} + \lambda_{12}\eta_{2i} + \varepsilon_{1i}, \tag{10.3}$$

where $Y_{1i}$ is the parental rating of the inattention symptom described in item 1 for child $i$, $\eta_{1i}$ is that child's unobserved score on the inattention latent variable, $\lambda_{11}$ is the linear partial regression slope (the factor loading) relating $\eta_1$ to $Y_1$, $\eta_{2i}$ is the unobserved score on the hyperactivity latent variable for child $i$, $\lambda_{12}$ is the factor loading relating $\eta_2$ to $Y_1$, and $\varepsilon_{1i}$ is the regression error for child $i$ from $Y_1$ (i.e., the difference between the predicted value of $Y_{1i}$ given $\eta_{1i}$ and $\eta_{2i}$ and the actual observed value of $Y_{1i}$). Thus, Equation 10.3 is a simplified version of Equation 10.1 in which there are only two latent variables (or factors).

But because $Y_1$ is purported to represent inattention and not hyperactivity, the factor loading for the hyperactivity latent variable can be fixed to zero (i.e., $\lambda_{12} = 0$), and so Equation 10.3 reduces to

$$Y_{1i} = \lambda_{11}\eta_{1i} + 0\eta_{2i} + \varepsilon_{1i}$$

or simply

$$Y_{1i} = \lambda_{11}\eta_{1i} + \varepsilon_{1i}.$$

Observed variables $Y_2$ through $Y_9$ are also hypothetical inattention items, and so their equations are

$$Y_{2i} = \lambda_{21}\eta_{1i} + \varepsilon_{2i},$$
$$Y_{3i} = \lambda_{31}\eta_{1i} + \varepsilon_{3i},$$
$$\dots$$
$$Y_{9i} = \lambda_{91}\eta_{1i} + \varepsilon_{9i}.$$

Next, observed variable $Y_{10}$ is hypothesized to measure hyperactivity ($\eta_2$) and not inattention ($\eta_1$); thus, its equation is

$$Y_{10i} = 0\eta_{1i} + \lambda_{10,2}\eta_{2i} + \varepsilon_{10i}$$

or simply

$$Y_{10i} = \lambda_{10,2}\eta_{2i} + \varepsilon_{10i}.$$

Similarly, the remaining items are also hypothesized indicators of hyperactivity, leading to

$$Y_{11i} = \lambda_{11,2}\eta_{2i} + \varepsilon_{11i},$$

$$Y_{12i} = \lambda_{12,2}\eta_{2i} + \varepsilon_{12i},$$

$$\ldots$$

$$Y_{18i} = \lambda_{18,2}\eta_{2i} + \varepsilon_{18i}.$$

Therefore, there is a separate linear regression equation for each of the 18 observed variables. These individual regression equations can be collected into a single matrix equation:

$$
\begin{bmatrix} Y_1 \\ Y_2 \\ \vdots \\ Y_9 \\ Y_{10} \\ Y_{11} \\ \vdots \\ Y_{18} \end{bmatrix}
=
\begin{bmatrix} \lambda_{1,1} & 0 \\ \lambda_{2,1} & 0 \\ \vdots & \vdots \\ \lambda_{9,1} & 0 \\ 0 & \lambda_{10,2} \\ 0 & \lambda_{11,2} \\ \vdots & \vdots \\ 0 & \lambda_{18,2} \end{bmatrix}
\begin{bmatrix} \eta_1 \\ \eta_2 \end{bmatrix}
+
\begin{bmatrix} \varepsilon_1 \\ \varepsilon_2 \\ \vdots \\ \varepsilon_9 \\ \varepsilon_{10} \\ \varepsilon_{11} \\ \vdots \\ \varepsilon_{18} \end{bmatrix}.
$$

This matrix expression is an instantiation of the general form given as Equation 10.2 in which there are $P = 18$ observed variables in $\mathbf{Y}$ simultaneously regressed on $K = 2$ latent variables in $\eta$. The factor loading matrix in this equation is an example of an independent clusters factor pattern because each of the 18 observed variables has a nonzero factor loading on only one of the two latent variables (i.e., each row of $\Lambda$ has only one nonzero element).

Finally, as mentioned, there is an explicit expectation that the inattention and hyperactivity factors are correlated with each other. This association between these two latent variables is captured by the covariance parameter in the $2 \times 2$ covariance matrix of the latent variables, $\Psi$:

$$
\Psi = \begin{bmatrix} \psi_{11} = \mathrm{VAR}(\eta_1) & \\ \psi_{21} = \mathrm{COV}(\eta_1,\eta_2) & \psi_{22} = \mathrm{VAR}(\eta_2) \end{bmatrix},
$$

where $\psi_{11}$ is the variance of $\eta_1$ (inattention), $\psi_{22}$ is the variance of $\eta_2$ (hyperactivity), and $\psi_{21}$ is the covariance between the inattention and hyperactivity latent variables. The remaining parameters of this two-factor CFA model are in the $P \times P$ covariance matrix of the error terms, $\Theta_\varepsilon$. In the two-factor model example for the 18 ADHD items, $\Theta_\varepsilon$ is an $18 \times 18$ covariance matrix. Furthermore, if we hypothesize that the inattention and hyperactivity latent variables (and the correlation between them) completely account for the covariances among the observed item response variables, then $\Theta_\varepsilon$ is restricted to be a diagonal matrix; the error covariances among the observed variables are all fixed to zero, and each diagonal element of $\Theta_\varepsilon$ is the variance of an error term, $VAR(\varepsilon_p)$, associated with a given observed variable $Y_p$.

Figure 10.2 gives a path diagram depicting the two-factor model for the 18 ADHD items according to the LISREL representation introduced in Chapter 9. As with path analysis models, rectangles represent observed variables, but the CFA model also contains latent variables, which are represented by ovals. Also consistent with diagrams for path analysis models, straight, single-headed arrows connecting two variables represent directional partial regression slope parameters. In the CFA context, the factor loadings ($\lambda$ parameters) are slope coefficients for the regression of the observed variables on the latent variables. Furthermore, curved, double-headed arrows again represent nondirectional, free covariance parameters. Here, the $\psi_{21}$ coefficient represents the freely estimated covariance between the two latent variables (or correlation, if the latent variables are standardized). Finally, each $\varepsilon$ term, representing the error from the regression of an observed variable on one or more latent variables, also connects to its respective observed variable with a single-headed arrow.

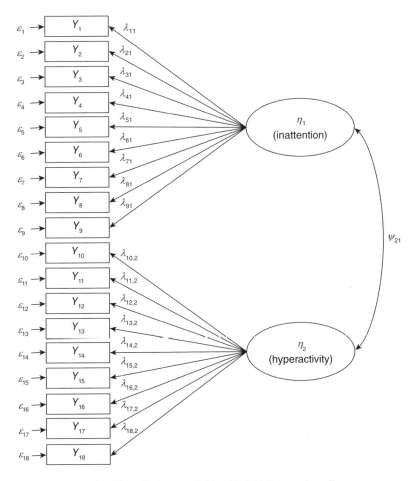

**Figure 10.2** Hypothesized two-factor model for 18 ADHD symptom items

From this path diagram, we can easily obtain the linear regression equation for a given observed variable by tracing the arrows pointing at it back to the origin of the arrows. For example, in Figure 10.2, two things are pointing directly at observed variable $Y_{10}$: latent variable $\eta_2$ and error term $\varepsilon_{10}$. Thus, the regression equation for $Y_{10}$ is

$$Y_{10} = \lambda_{10,2}\eta_2 + \varepsilon_{10}.$$

An alternative depiction of the same model adhering to the more elaborate path diagramming conventions presented by Ho et al. (2012) is in Figure 10.3. With this approach, error terms $\varepsilon$ are enclosed in small ovals to represent the idea that they too are a type of latent variable and their implied regression coefficient linking them to the observed variables is fixed equal to 1. Next, there are also small, curved bidirectional arrows – one for each latent variable and one for each latent error term – representing the free variance parameters in the model, which are, respectively, the diagonal elements of $\Psi$ (the covariance matrix of latent variables) and the diagonal elements of $\Theta_\varepsilon$ (the covariance matrix of the errors).

In addition to this two-factor model, Toplak et al. (2009) also specified a set of competing CFA models for the 18 ADHD items; the specification of these alternative models is

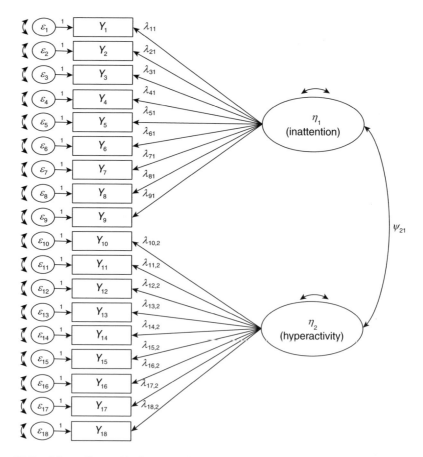

**Figure 10.3** Alternative path diagram of hypothesized two-factor model for 18 ADHD symptom items

presented later. Next, we continue to focus on the two-factor model for the purpose of describing model identification in CFA.

## CFA: Model identification

The concept of model identification was described in Chapter 9 in the context of path analysis; the basic principles addressed there extend to CFA models. To reiterate, model identification refers to the idea that the known information from the data (e.g., the variances and covariances among the observed variables) must be adequate to arrive at unique, proper estimates of the model's free parameters.

An added complication regarding identification of CFA models arises as a result of the presence of latent variables. Because a latent variable is unobserved, its scale is unknown and arbitrary. Thus, for a CFA model to be identified, constraints must be imposed on the model to establish a scale for each latent variable. Interpretation of the remaining free parameters then follows from the constraints used to set the latent variable scales. There is an infinite number of ways to set the latent variable scales, but the two most common methods are to

1. Constrain one factor loading parameter equal to one for each latent variable (i.e., for each column of $\Lambda$, fix one element equal to 1)
2. Constrain the variance of each latent variable equal to one (i.e., fix each diagonal element of $\Psi$ equal to 1)[2]

Next, we demonstrate these two approaches using the two-factor model for the ADHD symptoms.

## Constraining factor loadings to scale latent variables

This first approach is sometimes called the **marker indicator** (or reference variable) method for latent variable scaling. This method dictates that each column of the factor loading matrix $\Lambda$ must have one element constrained to 1. Applying this approach to our example two-factor model for ADHD symptoms, we might choose $Y_1$, the first listed observed variable purported to relate to the inattention factor, as the marker indicator for that latent variable. Specifically, we set the scale of the inattention factor ($\eta_1$) by fixing the factor loading relating $Y_1$ to $\eta_1$ equal to 1, so $\lambda_{11} = 1$. Next, $Y_{10}$ is the first listed observed variable purported to relate to the hyperactivity factor, so $Y_{10}$ is chosen as the marker indicator for hyperactivity. Then the scale of the hyperactivity factor ($\eta_2$) is established by fixing the factor loading relating $Y_{10}$ to $\eta_2$ equal to 1, so $\lambda_{10,2} = 1$. As a result of these factor loading constraints, the factor loading matrix is

---

[2]Incidentally, in standard applications of EFA, an inherent consequence of modeling correlation structure rather than covariances is that the factor variances are fixed to 1 which thus establishes the factors' scales.

$$\Lambda = \begin{bmatrix} 1 & 0 \\ \lambda_{2,1} & 0 \\ \vdots & \vdots \\ \lambda_{9,1} & 0 \\ 0 & 1 \\ 0 & \lambda_{11,2} \\ \vdots & \vdots \\ 0 & \lambda_{18,2} \end{bmatrix},$$

where elements not fixed to 0 or 1 are free factor loading parameters.

The choice of which observed variable is chosen as the marker indicator for a given latent variable is arbitrary. Most often, the marker indicator is simply taken as the first listed observed variable with a nonzero loading for a given factor, as is done in this example and as is the default specification in SEM software. But, if the marker indicator has a weak relation to the corresponding latent variable, then model estimation difficulties (e.g., nonconvergence or improper solutions) may arise (this phenomenon may be termed an instance of *empirical underidentification*).

Using the marker indicator method, the variances of the latent variables (i.e., diagonal elements of $\Psi$) remain free parameters, but the variance of a given latent variable will equal the variance of the corresponding marker indicator minus the error variance for that observed variable (as a function of the model-implied covariance structure, defined later in this chapter). For example, if $Y_1$ is the marker indicator of $\eta_1$, then

$$\psi_{11} = \text{VAR}(\eta_1) = [\text{VAR}(Y_1) - \text{VAR}(\varepsilon_1)].$$

Consequently, the free factor loadings (i.e., $\lambda$ parameters) for a given latent variable are interpreted relative to the strength of the relation between the marker indicator and that latent variable. For example, if $\lambda_{11}$ is fixed to 1, then $\lambda_{21}$ gives the linear regression relation between $\eta_1$ (inattention in the ADHD example) and the second observed indicator ($Y_2$) relative to the linear relation between inattention and $Y_1$. Thus, if $\lambda_{21} > 1$, then the relation between inattention and $Y_2$ is stronger than the relation between inattention and $Y_1$. Often, though, these original, unstandardized values of the $\lambda$ coefficients are not directly interpreted; because the latent variables have an unknown and therefore arbitrary scale, researchers typically interpret standardized factor loadings instead, which are defined later.

## Constraining factor variances to scale latent variables

The other common approach to establishing scales for the latent variables is to fix their variances equal to 1. Specifically, all diagonal elements of $\Psi$ are constrained to equal 1. Applying this approach to the two-factor ADHD model, $\Psi$ becomes

$$\Psi = \begin{bmatrix} 1 & \\ \psi_{21} & 1 \end{bmatrix},$$

meaning that the variances of both the inattention latent variable ($\eta_1$) and the hyperactivity latent variable ($\eta_2$) are fited to 1. As a result, off-diagonal elements of $\Psi$ are now correlations;

here, $\psi_{21}$ represents the correlation between the inattention and hyperactivity factors. Following from this approach, all nonzero factor loadings can be freely estimated, and so for the two-factor ADHD model

$$\Lambda = \begin{bmatrix} \lambda_{1,1} & 0 \\ \lambda_{2,1} & 0 \\ \vdots & \vdots \\ \lambda_{9,1} & 0 \\ 0 & \lambda_{10,2} \\ 0 & \lambda_{11,2} \\ \vdots & \vdots \\ 0 & \lambda_{18,2} \end{bmatrix}.$$

Thus, whereas $\lambda_{1,1}$ and $\lambda_{10,1}$ were both fixed to 1 in the marker indicator approach, they are now free parameters.

Interpretation of unstandardized factor loadings is different when latent variable variances are constrained to 1 than when the marker indicator approach is used. Specifically, the free factor loadings for a given latent variable are interpreted relative to the variance of the latent variable. Keeping in mind that a factor loading is a type of linear regression slope coefficient (see Equation 10.1), a particular $\lambda$ represents the predicted change in the corresponding observed variable for a one-unit increase in the latent variable; because the latent variable variance is 1, then a one-unit increase corresponds to an increase equal to 1 standard deviation on the latent variable scale. For example, $\lambda_{21}$ gives the expected difference in $Y_2$ associated with a 1 standard-deviation increase on $\eta_1$ (inattention); this interpretation of $\lambda_{21}$ is somewhat simpler than that given earlier under the marker indicator method.

Overall, with the latent variables scaled to have variances equal to 1, the factor loadings can be considered partially standardized regression coefficients. More often, though, researchers interpret so-called **completely standardized** factor loadings, which reflect a hypothetical situation in which both the latent variables (i.e., the predictors in regression Equation 10.1) and the observed variables (the outcome variables in Equation 10.1) have variances equal to 1. Recall from Chapter 2 that a regression coefficient can be standardized as a function of the ratio of the variance of the predictor variable to the outcome variable. Analogously, then, in this CFA context, a completely standardized factor loading $\lambda^*$ for the relation between latent variable $\eta_k$ and observed variable $Y_p$ is obtained with

$$\lambda^*_{p,k} = \lambda_{p,k} \frac{\text{VAR}(\eta_k)}{\text{VAR}(Y_p)},$$

where $\lambda_{p,k}$ is either the unstandardized factor loading obtained from the marker indicator approach or the partially standardized factor loading obtained by fixing $\text{var}(\eta_k) = 1$. Thus, regardless of which method one uses to scale the latent variables, SEM software can automatically convert the factor loading estimates into completely standardized factor loadings.

More generally, these different methods for establishing the scale of the latent variables lead to **equivalent models** in that model fit is identical across the two model specifications and the same standardized parameter estimates are obtained (and predicted values for the observed variables are also identical under both methods). In other words, the two approaches for scaling the latent variables simply lead to different representations of what is the same model.

(The concept of equivalent models was also presented in Chapter 9 for path analysis models.) Nonetheless, there are situations in which the estimation algorithm (e.g., maximum likelihood estimation) fails to converge to a final set of parameter estimates when one approach is used to scale the latent variables, but using another approach to scale the latent variables does lead to successful convergence.

 Section recap

### CFA model identification

The basic principles of model identification presented for path analysis models extend to CFA models. In general, there must be a sufficient amount of known information to arrive at proper, unique estimates of the unknown parameter values.

Additionally, for a CFA model to be identified, constraints must be imposed on the model to establish a scale for each latent variable. The two most common ways to scale the latent variables are:

1. Constrain one factor loading parameter equal to one for each latent variable (i.e., for each column of $\Lambda$, fix one element equal to 1), which is known as the **marker indicator** method. The choice of which observed variable is chosen as the marker indicator for a given latent variable is arbitrary.
2. Constrain the variance of each latent variable equal to one (i.e., fix each diagonal element of $\Psi$ equal to 1).

Different methods of scaling the latent variables produce equivalent models. Therefore:

- Unstandardized factor loading estimates differ depending on which approach is used to scale the latent variables, but **completely standardized** factor loadings are identical.
- Model fit is not affected by the method used to scale the latent variables.

## The *t*-rule for identification

Introduced in Chapter 9 for path analysis models, the *t*-rule also provides a necessary but not sufficient criterion for identification of CFA models. Specifically, the *t*-rule states that the number of nonredundant elements in the observed covariance matrix must equal or exceed the number of parameters to be estimated.

Returning to the two-factor CFA model for the 18 ADHD items, there are $(18 \times 19) / 2 = 171$ unique elements in the observed covariance matrix. No matter how we scale the latent variables, there will be 37 free parameters to estimate. In particular, if we use the marker indicator approach, there will be 16 free factor loadings ($\lambda_{21}, \lambda_{31},..., \lambda_{91}$ and $\lambda_{11,2}, \lambda_{12,2},..., \lambda_{18,2}$), 3 free elements in the latent variable covariance matrix ($\psi_{11}, \psi_{21},$ and $\psi_{22}$), and the 18 error variances (variances of $\varepsilon_1$ through $\varepsilon_{18}$, i.e., the diagonal elements of $\Theta_\varepsilon$); this sums to 37 free parameters. If instead we scale the latent variables by constraining their variances, there will be 18 free factor loadings ($\lambda_{11}, \lambda_{21},..., \lambda_{91}$ and $\lambda_{10,2}, \lambda_{11,2},..., \lambda_{18,2}$), the latent variable correlation ($\psi_{21}$), and again the variances of $\varepsilon_1$ through $\varepsilon_{18}$; this also sums to 37 free parameters. Thus, regardless of how the latent variable scales are established, the degrees of freedom for this two-factor model is $171 - 37 = 134$, and so the two-factor model specification passes the $t$-rule.

## Two sufficient identification rules for CFA

### Three-indicator rule

Researchers often informally state that in CFA there should be at least three indicators per latent variable, meaning that there should be at least three observed variables with freely estimated, nonzero factor loadings for each latent variable in a model. Although this rule-of-thumb has some validity with respect to accuracy and precision of parameter estimation and model fit, it also helps ensure model identification. More formally, a sufficient, but not necessary, identification rule for CFA is known as the **three-indicator rule**. Three criteria must be met for a given CFA model specification to pass the three-indicator rule, namely:

1.  There must be at least three observed variables with nonzero factor loadings for each latent variable; in other words, each column of $\Lambda$ must have at least three nonzero elements (although some of the nonzero elements may be fixed to 1 to scale latent variables).
2.  The model must have an independent clusters factor pattern. That is, each observed variable must have a nonzero loading on only one latent variable; that is, each row of $\Lambda$ must have one and only one nonzero element (again, some nonzero elements may be fixed to 1 to scale latent variables).
3.  The $\varepsilon$ error terms must be mutually uncorrelated; in other words, $\Theta_\varepsilon$ must be diagonal so that all error covariances are fixed to 0.

Referring to the parameter matrices presented earlier for the specification of the two-factor model for the ADHD items, it is clear that this model passes the three-indicator rule and therefore is identified.

### Two-indicator rule

The three-indicator rule, however, is somewhat stricter than is needed to guarantee model identification, at least with respect to the number of indicators per latent variable. Another sufficient, but not necessary, identification rule for CFA is the **two-indicator rule**, which has five criteria that must be met:

1.  The model must have more than one latent variable; that is, the length of $\eta$ must be greater than one.
2.  There must be at least two observed variables with nonzero factor loadings for each latent variable; in other words, each column of $\Lambda$ must have at least two nonzero elements (again, some nonzero elements may be fixed to 1 to scale the latent variables).
3.  Like the three-indicator rule, there must be an independent clusters factor pattern such that each row of $\Lambda$ has one and only one nonzero element (again, some of these may be fixed to 1).
4.  Also like the three-indicator rule, $\Theta_\varepsilon$ must be diagonal.
5.  Each latent variable must freely covary with at least one other latent variable; that is, each row of $\Psi$ must have at least one nonzero off-diagonal element.

Because we know that the two-factor model for the ADHD items passes the three-indicator rule and is therefore identified, there is no need to check whether it passes the two-indicator rule. But to be thorough, one can review the parameter matrices for this two-factor model and confirm that it does also pass the two-indicator rule.

 Section recap

### Identification rules for CFA

As with path analysis models, the $t$-rule provides a necessary but not sufficient criterion for identification of CFA models. Specifically, the number of nonredundant elements in the observed covariance matrix must equal or exceed the number of parameters to be estimated.

Two rules which are sufficient but not necessary for identification of CFA models are the **three-indicator rule** and the **two-indicator rule**.

For a given CFA model specification to pass the three-indicator rule:

- There must be at least three observed variables with nonzero factor loadings for each latent variable; i.e., each column of $\Lambda$ must have at least three nonzero elements.
- The model must have an independent clusters factor pattern such that each observed variable has a nonzero loading on only one latent variable; i.e., each row of $\Lambda$ must have one and only one nonzero element.
- The $\varepsilon$ error terms must be mutually uncorrelated; i.e., $\Theta_\varepsilon$ must be diagonal so that all error covariances are fixed to 0.

For a given CFA model specification to pass the two-indicator rule:

- The model must have more than one latent variable; i.e., the length of $\eta$ must be greater than one.
- The model must have at least two observed variables with nonzero factor loadings for each latent variable; i.e., each column of $\Lambda$ must have at least two nonzero elements.
- There must be an independent clusters factor pattern.
- $\Theta_\varepsilon$ must be diagonal.
- Each row of $\Psi$ must have at least one nonzero off-diagonal element.

## CFA: Model estimation

As explained in Chapter 9 in the context of path analysis, following from the covariance structure hypothesis, most structural equation models are fitted directly to the covariance matrix among observed variables rather than being fitted to individual case-by-case observations; this principle extends to CFA. As with path analysis, the goal of estimation is to find the set of parameter estimate values that optimizes the match between the fitted **model-implied covariance matrix**, $\widehat{\Sigma}_0$, and the sample covariance matrix, **S**, according to some criterion (e.g., a maximum likelihood or least-squares criterion).

In CFA, the population model-implied covariance matrix is

$$\Sigma_\theta = \Lambda\Psi\Lambda' + \Theta_\varepsilon,$$

where $\Lambda$, $\Psi$, and $\Theta_\varepsilon$ are the parameter matrices defined earlier in this chapter. Considering the two-factor model for the 18 ADHD items, if that model is correct, we should observe a particular pattern of covariation among those observed variables. Specifically:

1.   The first nine items should strongly covary with each other because they are all caused by the same construct, inattention.
2.   The second nine items should strongly covary with each other because they are all caused by the hyperactivity construct.
3.   The inattention items should also covary with the hyperactivity items to some extent because the inattention and hyperactivity constructs are correlated.

The goal of estimation, then, is to find the specific parameter estimates (i.e., estimates of the free elements in $\Lambda$, $\Psi$, and $\Theta_\varepsilon$) which produce the best match between this hypothesized pattern of covariation and the (18 × 18) sample covariance matrix among the ADHD items.

Like path analysis models, CFA models are also commonly estimated using maximum likelihood (ML). Specifically, the ML discrepancy function presented in Chapter 9 (Equation 9.13) is also used here for CFA:

$$F_{ML} = \log|\widehat{\Sigma_\theta}| + \text{tr}(S\,\widehat{\Sigma_\theta}^{-1}) - \log|S| - P,$$

where $\widehat{\Sigma_\theta}$ is the fitted model-implied covariance matrix (based on estimates of $\Lambda$, $\Psi$, and $\Theta_\varepsilon$) and $P$ is the total number of observed variables ($P = 18$ in our ADHD example). The desirable statistical properties of ML detailed in Chapter 9 hold in this CFA context as well (including obtaining parameter standard errors using the asymptotic covariance matrix of the estimates). Furthermore, as alternatives to ML, the least-squares fitting functions described in Chapter 9, such as generalized least squares (GLS) and unweighted least squares (ULS), can also be used to estimate CFA models. Keep in mind that the desirable properties of ML and GLS depend on the assumption that the observed variables follow a multivariate normal distribution.

Like EFA, CFA is commonly used when the observed variables are Likert-type or dichotomous items from a test or questionnaire, but recall that such items produce ordered categorical variables that cannot be linearly associated or normally distributed. Thus, the product-moment covariance matrix $S$ may provide an inaccurate summary of the associations among the items and the multivariate normal distribution assumption of the ML estimator is necessarily violated (see Flora et al., 2012). Thus, the estimation procedures just described may not be appropriate if one is modeling ordered categorical observed variables, such as the 18 ADHD items. But as described earlier, if the item-level variables have more than five ordered categories, it is usually safe to treat them as continuous variables and fit CFA models directly to their covariance matrix using ML. The assumption of multivariate normality, however, remains a concern which we address later.

 Section recap

### Model estimation for CFA

As with path analysis, the goal of estimation is to find the set of parameter estimate values that optimizes the match between the fitted model-implied covariance matrix, $\widehat{\Sigma}_\theta$, and the sample covariance matrix, **S**, according to some criterion (e.g., maximum likelihood or least squares).

In CFA, the population model-implied covariance matrix is

$$\Sigma_\theta = \Lambda\Psi\Lambda' + \Theta_\varepsilon,$$

where $\Lambda$, $\Psi$, and $\Theta_\varepsilon$ are the parameter matrices defined earlier.

CFA models are commonly applied to item-level variables, which are typically categorical and, therefore, not linearly related or normally distributed. Thus, it is often inappropriate to fit models to the product-moment covariance matrix **S** using ML estimation, which assumes multivariate normally distributed data.

## CFA: Model fit evaluation

The same general principles and specific statistical approaches used to evaluate the fit of path analysis models can also be used to evaluate the fit of CFA models. In fact, because CFA models typically are characterized by many more degrees of freedom than path analysis models, model fit assessment tends to be a much riskier enterprise for CFA.

When the hypothesized two-factor model is fitted to the sample covariance matrix of the 18 ADHD items using ML, model fit is not acceptable. Specifically, for the $\chi^2$ exact-fit test, we obtain $\chi^2$ (134) = 343.15, $p < .0001$, rejecting the null hypothesis that the fitted covariance matrix perfectly matches the population covariance matrix. Recall, however, that we do not take this $\chi^2$ exact-fit test seriously because the perfect fit null hypothesis is too stringent (especially when a model has such large degrees of freedom). Yet, other popular model fit statistics (i.e., those defined in Chapter 9) also indicate that the two-factor model fits the ADHD data poorly. In particular, the root-mean-square error of approximation (or RMSEA) = .104, the comparative fit index (CFI) = .82, the Tucker-Lewis index (TLI) = .80, and the standardized root-mean-square residual (SRMR) = .10. The popular guidelines summarized in Chapter 9 regarding values of these fit statistics that are indicative of good or poor fit may be generalized to CFA; in fact, most of these guidelines were developed with latent variable models such as CFA in mind rather than with path analysis models.

Additionally, as with path analysis, residual covariances and modification indices can help identify sources of misfit for CFA models. But in the particular context of CFA, residual covariances and modification indices do not directly inform researchers about whether a model has the ideal number of latent variables. Furthermore, as discussed in Chapter 9, using these statistics to guide the creation of a new model can be a dangerous practice. Instead, it is good scientific and statistical practice to conceive of several models a priori whose fit to data can be compared; here, we are doing a confirmatory analysis after all. Fortunately, Toplak et al. (2009) proposed a series of alternative models a priori which we can compare with this initial two-factor model that did not fit the data adequately. Therefore, some alternative models for the 18 ADHD items are presented in the following sections.

## Section recap

### Model fit evaluation with CFA

The same principles and model fit statistics applied to evaluate model fit assessment for path analysis models also apply to CFA models.

Residual covariances and modification indices do not directly inform researchers about whether a model has the ideal number of latent variables.

## Correlated error terms in CFA

Most often, and so far in our two-factor ADHD example, the regression errors $\varepsilon$ in a CFA model are not allowed to correlate (i.e., covariances among $\varepsilon$ are fixed to zero), which implies that the error covariance matrix $\Theta_\varepsilon$ is a diagonal matrix. But sometimes there may be a theoretically appropriate reason to specify one or more free covariances among the error terms; in such cases, $\Theta_\varepsilon$ is no longer a diagonal matrix. The two-factor model for the 18 ADHD items derives from a hypothesis that inattention and hyperactivity constructs are the two major causes of the pattern of covariation among the observed variables. But the literature also suggests that the last three items (i.e., $Y_{16}$, $Y_{17}$, and $Y_{18}$), in addition to being related to hyperactivity, are also related to a separate psychological construct, impulsivity. Thus, these three items may be more strongly related to each other than can be explained by their relation with the more general hyperactivity factor. We can model this possibility by allowing the covariances among the $\varepsilon_{16}$, $\varepsilon_{17}$, and $\varepsilon_{18}$ error terms to be nonzero, free parameters. Consequently, $\Theta_\varepsilon$ becomes:

$$
\Theta_\varepsilon =
\begin{bmatrix}
\sigma^2_{\varepsilon_1} \\
0 & \sigma^2_{\varepsilon_2} \\
0 & 0 & \sigma^2_{\varepsilon_3} \\
0 & 0 & 0 & \sigma^2_{\varepsilon_4} \\
0 & 0 & 0 & 0 & \sigma^2_{\varepsilon_5} \\
0 & 0 & 0 & 0 & 0 & \sigma^2_{\varepsilon_6} \\
0 & 0 & 0 & 0 & 0 & 0 & \sigma^2_{\varepsilon_7} \\
0 & 0 & 0 & 0 & 0 & 0 & 0 & \sigma^2_{\varepsilon_8} \\
0 & 0 & 0 & 0 & 0 & 0 & 0 & 0 & \sigma^2_{\varepsilon_9} \\
0 & 0 & 0 & 0 & 0 & 0 & 0 & 0 & 0 & \sigma^2_{\varepsilon_{10}} \\
0 & 0 & 0 & 0 & 0 & 0 & 0 & 0 & 0 & 0 & \sigma^2_{\varepsilon_{11}} \\
0 & 0 & 0 & 0 & 0 & 0 & 0 & 0 & 0 & 0 & 0 & \sigma^2_{\varepsilon_{12}} \\
0 & 0 & 0 & 0 & 0 & 0 & 0 & 0 & 0 & 0 & 0 & 0 & \sigma^2_{\varepsilon_{13}} \\
0 & 0 & 0 & 0 & 0 & 0 & 0 & 0 & 0 & 0 & 0 & 0 & 0 & \sigma^2_{\varepsilon_{14}} \\
0 & 0 & 0 & 0 & 0 & 0 & 0 & 0 & 0 & 0 & 0 & 0 & 0 & 0 & \sigma^2_{\varepsilon_{15}} \\
0 & 0 & 0 & 0 & 0 & 0 & 0 & 0 & 0 & 0 & 0 & 0 & 0 & 0 & 0 & \sigma^2_{\varepsilon_{16}} \\
0 & 0 & 0 & 0 & 0 & 0 & 0 & 0 & 0 & 0 & 0 & 0 & 0 & 0 & 0 & \sigma_{\varepsilon_{16},\varepsilon_{17}} & \sigma^2_{\varepsilon_{17}} \\
0 & 0 & 0 & 0 & 0 & 0 & 0 & 0 & 0 & 0 & 0 & 0 & 0 & 0 & 0 & \sigma_{\varepsilon_{16},\varepsilon_{18}} & \sigma_{\varepsilon_{17},\varepsilon_{18}} & \sigma^2_{\varepsilon_{18}}
\end{bmatrix}
,
$$

where $\sigma^2_{\varepsilon_p}$ is the variance of $\varepsilon_p$ (i.e., the variance of the regression error for the $p$th observed variable) and $\sigma_{\varepsilon_p, \varepsilon_{p+1}}$ is the covariance between the error term of the $p$th observed variable and the error term of the next observed variable. For example, $\sigma_{\varepsilon_{16}, \varepsilon_{17}}$ is the covariance between the error terms of $Y_{16}$ and $Y_{17}$. The path diagram for the two-factor ADHD model, revised to include these error covariances, is in Figure 10.4. This path diagram is almost the same as the one in Figure 10.2, except now there are curved, double-headed arrows representing covariances among the error terms of the three impulsivity items, $Y_{16}$, $Y_{17}$, and $Y_{18}$.

The original two-factor model depicted in Figure 10.2 is formally nested within the current model (the concept of nested models was described in Chapters 6 and 9). Specifically, if the three error covariance parameters of the current model are all fixed to zero, then we end up with the original model which had a diagonal $\Theta_\varepsilon$. Therefore, we can use a likelihood-ratio test to determine whether adding the three freed error covariances significantly improves model fit. For the current model with three free error covariances, we obtain $\chi^2 (131) = 313.93$, and so the difference between the $\chi^2$ statistics for the two models is $\Delta\chi^2 = 343.15 - 313.93 = 29.32$. Thus, the likelihood-ratio test statistic is $\chi^2 (3) = 29.22$, which is significant with $p < .0001$. Therefore, adding the freed error covariance terms did significantly improve model fit. Yet, the overall fit of this revised two-factor model is still inadequate with RMSEA $= .097$, CFI $= .85$,

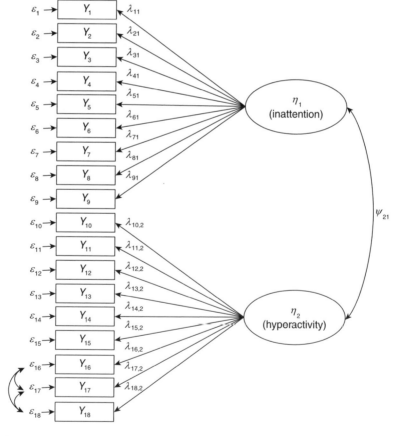

**Figure 10.4** Two-factor model for 18 ADHD symptom items with error covariances among impulsivity items

TLI = .82, and SRMR = .11. At this point, we could inspect the residual covariance matrix or modification indices to help determine the reasons for the poor fit of these two-factor models, but because Toplak et al. (2009) hypothesized alternative models with differing numbers of latent variables, it is preferable to proceed by estimating these alternative models.

 **Section recap**

### Correlated error terms in CFA

In certain situations, there is a theoretically appropriate reason to specify one or more free covariances among the errors $\varepsilon$ in a CFA model. In such cases, the error covariance matrix $\Theta_\varepsilon$ is no longer a diagonal matrix.

A likelihood-ratio test may be used to test whether model fit significantly improves when one or more error covariances is freely estimated compared with a model with diagonal $\Theta_\varepsilon$.

## One-factor model for the ADHD symptoms

Among the models Toplak et al. (2009) considered for the 18 ADHD items was a simple one-factor model, which is justifiable based on the idea that ADHD is a single psychological disorder. The regression matrix equation for this one-factor model is

$$\begin{bmatrix} Y_1 \\ \vdots \\ Y_{18} \end{bmatrix} = \begin{bmatrix} \lambda_{1,1} \\ \vdots \\ \lambda_{18,1} \end{bmatrix} \eta_1 + \begin{bmatrix} \varepsilon_1 \\ \vdots \\ \varepsilon_{18} \end{bmatrix}.$$

Additionally, because this model consists of only a single latent variable, the covariance matrix of latent variables $\Psi$ is simply a $1 \times 1$ matrix containing the variance of the single factor:

$$\Psi = [\psi_{11}] = [\text{VAR}(\eta_1)].$$

Furthermore, we return to specifying a diagonal $\Theta_\varepsilon$; that is, all error covariances are fixed to 0. A path diagram of this one-factor model is in Figure 10.5. But when this model is estimated using ML, it fits the data even more poorly than either of the two-factor models considered earlier, with RMSEA = .150, CFI = .63, TLI = .58, and SRMR = .13.

## Three-factor model for the ADHD symptoms

Yet another candidate model for the 18 ADHD items considered by Toplak et al. (2009) was a three-factor model, which was characterized by an inattention factor for the first nine items along with separate latent variables for the hyperactivity and impulsivity items. The regression matrix equation for this model is

$$
\begin{bmatrix} Y_1 \\ \vdots \\ Y_9 \\ Y_{10} \\ \vdots \\ Y_{15} \\ Y_{16} \\ Y_{17} \\ Y_{18} \end{bmatrix} = \begin{bmatrix} \lambda_{11} & 0 & 0 \\ \vdots & 0 & 0 \\ \lambda_{91} & 0 & 0 \\ 0 & \lambda_{10,2} & 0 \\ 0 & \vdots & 0 \\ 0 & \lambda_{15,2} & 0 \\ 0 & 0 & \lambda_{16,3} \\ 0 & 0 & \lambda_{17,3} \\ 0 & 0 & \lambda_{18,3} \end{bmatrix} \cdot \begin{bmatrix} \eta_1 \\ \eta_2 \\ \eta_3 \end{bmatrix} + \begin{bmatrix} \varepsilon_1 \\ \vdots \\ \varepsilon_{18} \end{bmatrix}.
$$

Now because there are three latent variables in $\eta$, their covariance matrix $\Psi$ has the dimension $3 \times 3$. The path diagram for this model is in Figure 10.6. Yet, following ML estimation, even this model fits the data inadequately, with RMSEA = .098, CFI = .84, TLI = .82, and SRMR = .10.

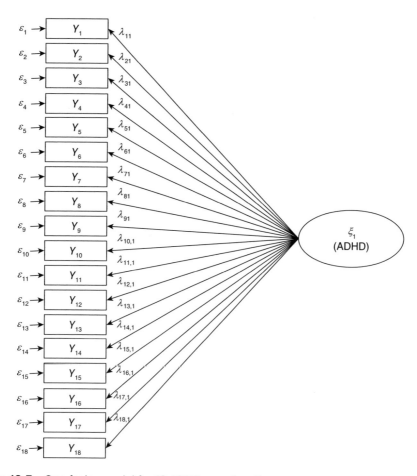

**Figure 10.5**   One-factor model for 18 ADHD symptom items

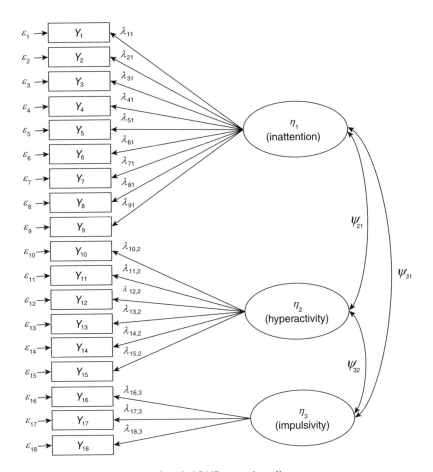

**Figure 10.6** Three-factor model for 18 ADHD symptom items

## A bifactor model for the ADHD symptoms

Finally, Toplak et al. (2009) also hypothesized that a **bifactor model** may be appropriate for the 18 ADHD items. This hypothesis reflects the notion that all 18 ADHD symptoms assessed with the SWAN questionnaire are caused by a single, underlying psychological disorder, but some symptoms tend to co-occur with each other more strongly than with other symptoms; that is, inattention symptoms tend to co-occur with each other, as do hyperactivity symptoms, but all symptoms arise from a single ADHD disorder. A bifactor model may be considered an extension of a one-factor model in that there is a single, dominant factor which directly influences all observed variables; this factor is commonly known as a **general factor**. Yet, the general factor may not be sufficient to explain all of the covariances among certain groups of observed variables. Thus, **specific factors** (also called *group factors*) are specified to explain the covariances among observed variables which are not accounted for by the general factor. The name *bifactor* makes sense when one realizes that a given observed variable is directly influenced by two latent variables – the general factor and one of the specific factors – despite that the complete model has more than two latent variables. Although bifactor models were originally developed decades ago, they are becoming more popular in modern applications of both CFA and EFA (Reise, 2012).

To demonstrate a bifactor model for the 18 ADHD items, the first item, $Y_1$, is hypothesized to be influenced by both the general factor and a specific factor capturing extra covariation among the inattention items. Thus, the scalar regression equation for the $Y_1$ observed variable is

$$Y_{1i} = \lambda_{11}\eta_{1i} + \lambda_{12}\eta_{2i} + \varepsilon_{1i},$$

where $\eta_1$ is the general factor and $\eta_2$ is a specific factor representing the covariance among hyperactivity items not explained by the general factor. In comparison, $Y_{10}$ is hypothesized to be influenced by the general factor and a specific factor capturing extra covariation among the hyperactivity items. Thus, the scalar regression equation for $Y_{10}$ is

$$Y_{10i} = \lambda_{10,1}\eta_{1i} + \lambda_{10,3}\eta_{3i} + \varepsilon_{1i},$$

where $\eta_1$ is again the general factor but now $\eta_3$ is a specific factor representing the covariance among hyperactivity items not explained by the general factor. The complete regression matrix equation for the 18 ADHD items is

$$
\begin{bmatrix} Y_1 \\ \vdots \\ Y_9 \\ Y_{10} \\ \vdots \\ Y_{18} \end{bmatrix}
=
\begin{bmatrix}
\lambda_{1,1} & \lambda_{1,2} & 0 \\
\vdots & \vdots & \vdots \\
\lambda_{9,1} & \lambda_{9,2} & 0 \\
\lambda_{10,1} & 0 & \lambda_{10,3} \\
\vdots & \vdots & \vdots \\
\lambda_{18,1} & 0 & \lambda_{18,3}
\end{bmatrix}
\begin{bmatrix} \eta_1 \\ \eta_2 \\ \eta_3 \end{bmatrix}
+
\begin{bmatrix} \varepsilon_1 \\ \vdots \\ \varepsilon_{18} \end{bmatrix},
$$

where items $Y_1$ to $Y_9$ are inattention items and items $Y_{10}$ to $Y_{18}$ are hyperactivity items. Thus, $\eta_2$ is a specific factor capturing the shared covariance among inattention symptoms that is not explained by the general factor and $\eta_3$ is a specific factor capturing the shared covariance among hyperactivity symptoms that is not explained by the general factor.

Importantly, the covariances between the general factor and the specific factors must be fixed to zero for model identification; additionally, although it is not necessary for the covariance between the specific factors to be set to zero, the traditional bifactor model does so. Therefore, $\Psi$ is fixed to be a diagonal matrix:

$$
\Psi =
\begin{bmatrix}
\psi_{11} = \text{VAR}(\eta_1) & & \\
0 & \psi_{22} = \text{VAR}(\eta_2) & \\
0 & 0 & \psi_{33} = \text{VAR}(\eta_3)
\end{bmatrix}.
$$

Furthermore, the error covariance matrix $\Theta_\varepsilon$ is once again constrained to be diagonal. The path diagram for this bifactor model is in Figure 10.7. For further details on identification and interpretation of bifactor models, see Yung, Thissen, and McLeod (1999) and Chen, West, and Sousa (2006); these articles also compare bifactor models to *higher order* factor models which also involve a type of general factor (i.e., the higher order, or second-order, factor).

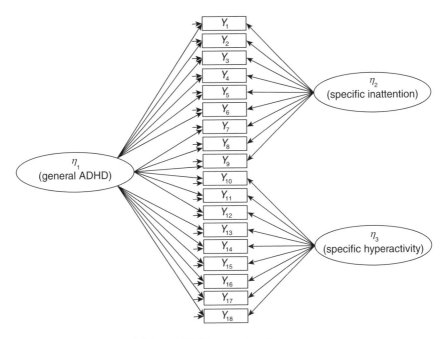

**Figure 10.7** A bifactor model for 18 ADHD symptom items

Using ML estimation, the bifactor model fits the data for the 18 ADHD items well, with RMSEA = .050, CFI = .96, TLI = .95, and SRMR = .05. Given that the model fits well, we next turn to examining the individual parameter estimates, particularly the factor loading estimates; keep in mind that these results are based on having scaled the latent variables by fixing their variances to 1. Because the model was estimated using ML, parameter estimate standard errors are obtained from the asymptotic covariance matrix of the parameter estimates (as described in Chapter 9); these standard error estimates are then used to construct significance tests (i.e., $Z$ tests) of the null hypothesis that a given parameter is zero. Finally, the standard error values printed by most SEM software correspond to the unstandardized parameter estimates; researchers often do not recognize that the standard errors of the completely standardized estimates are different, which implies that conclusions about the statistical significance of unstandardized factor loading estimates may be erroneously generalized to the completely standardized estimates.[3]

The factor loading estimates (along with the corresponding standard errors and $p$ values) from the estimated bifactor model for the 18 ADHD items are in Table 10.2. All 18 items have significant, positive loadings on the general ADHD factor, with completely standardized factor loading estimates ranging from 0.193 to 0.817. This result, coupled with the good fit of the bifactor model overall, suggests that there is a single, general underlying cause of all 18 ADHD symptoms as measured by the parental report SWAN. Yet, we do see that some items are more strongly related to their respective specific factor than to the general factor, indicating that

---

[3]Some software, such as Mplus®, explicitly outputs distinct standard error values for both unstandardized and standardized estimates.

there is something beyond general ADHD psychopathology accounting for the variability of these items. Because the specific factors represent influences on the items over and above the influence of the general ADHD factor, it is tricky to interpret the specific inattention and hyperactivity latent variables. For instance, the specific inattention factor captures aspects of inattention that are not shared with the general ADHD psychopathology, which arguably is not the same thing as a basic inattention construct. It may be safest to consider a specific factor an artefact which is in the model to account for the multidimensionality of the data despite primary interest in a single, broad general factor.

Finally, $R^2$ statistics can be calculated for each observed variable in a CFA model with

$$R_p^2 = 1 - \frac{s_{\varepsilon_p}^2}{s_p^2}$$

(10.4)

for the $p$th observed variable, where $s_{\varepsilon_p}^2$ is the estimated variance of $\varepsilon_p$ (i.e., an estimated diagonal element of $\Theta_\varepsilon$) and $s_p^2$ is the estimated variance of $Y_p$. After the bifactor model was fitted to the 18 ADHD items, their corresponding $R^2$ statistics ranged from .19 (for item 8 on the SWAN) to .73 (for item 14).

**Table 10.2**  Factor loading estimates for 18 ADHD symptom items

| Observed Y | General factor ($\eta_1$) $\hat{\lambda}$ ($\hat{\lambda}^*$) | $SE_{\hat{\lambda}}$ | p | Specific inattention ($\eta_2$) $\hat{\lambda}$ ($\hat{\lambda}^*$) | $SE_{\hat{\lambda}}$ | p | Specific hyperactivity ($\eta_2$) $\hat{\lambda}$ ($\hat{\lambda}^*$) | $SE_{\hat{\lambda}}$ | p |
|---|---|---|---|---|---|---|---|---|---|
| SWAN1 | 0.38 (0.37) | 0.10 | <.001 | 0.57 (0.54) | 0.13 | <.001 | 0 | – | – |
| SWAN2 | 0.51 (0.44) | 0.11 | <.001 | 0.48 (0.42) | 0.09 | <.001 | 0 | – | – |
| SWAN3 | 0.74 (0.64) | 0.10 | <.001 | 0.26 (0.22) | 0.10 | .008 | 0 | – | – |
| SWAN4 | 0.34 (0.39) | 0.08 | <.001 | 0.44 (0.51) | 0.07 | <.001 | 0 | – | – |
| SWAN5 | 0.25 (0.21) | 0.11 | .022 | 0.91 (0.77) | 0.13 | <.001 | 0 | – | – |
| SWAN6 | 0.56 (0.42) | 0.12 | <.001 | 0.45 (0.34) | 0.12 | <.001 | 0 | – | – |
| SWAN7 | 0.22 (0.19) | 0.10 | .034 | 0.90 (0.80) | 0.11 | <.001 | 0 | – | – |
| SWAN8 | 0.53 (0.44) | 0.11 | <.001 | −0.04 (−0.03) | 0.24 | .878 | 0 | – | – |
| SWAN9 | 0.29 (0.23) | 0.12 | .017 | 1.00 (0.80) | 0.10 | <.001 | 0 | – | – |
| SWAN10 | 0.56 (0.49) | 0.11 | <.001 | 0 | – | – | 0.42 (0.37) | 0.11 | <.001 |
| SWAN11 | 0.59 (0.49) | 0.13 | <.001 | 0 | – | – | 0.64 (0.53) | 0.12 | <.001 |
| SWAN12 | 0.49 (0.40) | 0.17 | .004 | 0 | – | – | 0.58 (0.47) | 0.15 | <.001 |
| SWAN13 | 0.56 (0.45) | 0.17 | .001 | 0 | – | – | 0.87 (0.70) | 0.13 | <.001 |
| SWAN14 | 0.44 (0.36) | 0.19 | .020 | 0 | – | – | 0.94 (0.78) | 0.15 | <.001 |
| SWAN15 | 1.05 (0.76) | 0.13 | <.001 | 0 | – | – | 0.32 (0.23) | 0.26 | .208 |
| SWAN16 | 0.97 (0.76) | 0.12 | <.001 | 0 | – | – | 0.21 (0.17) | 0.28 | .448 |
| SWAN17 | 0.90 (0.70) | 0.12 | <.001 | 0 | – | – | 0.43 (0.34) | 0.18 | .019 |
| SWAN18 | 1.07 (0.82) | 0.11 | <.001 | 0 | – | – | −0.02 (−0.01) | 0.16 | .918 |

Note. $\hat{\lambda}$ = unstandardized factor loading estimate; $\hat{\lambda}^*$ = completely standardized factor loading estimate; $SE_{\hat{\lambda}}$ = standard error of factor loading estimate; $p$ values are for Z tests based on $Z = \hat{\lambda} / SE_{\hat{\lambda}}$.

 **Section recap**

### Bifactor models

A **bifactor model** may be considered an extension of a one-factor model in that there is a single, dominant factor, or **general factor**, which directly influences all observed variables. Additionally, **specific factors** are specified to explain the covariation among subsets of observed variables which is not accounted for by the general factor.

The covariances between the general factor and the specific factors must be fixed to 0 for model identification; additionally, although it is not necessary for the covariance(s) between specific factors to be set to 0, the traditional bifactor model does so. Therefore, $\Psi$ is fixed to be diagonal.

## Assumption violation and remedies for CFA

The major concepts for assumption checking and model diagnostics covered in Chapter 8 (for EFA) and Chapter 9 (for path analysis) extend to CFA. The primary issue in the current context is that it is common for CFA models to be fitted to variables which are responses to individual items within a test or questionnaire, and such item-level variables usually have a binary or ordered-categorical scale of measurement. Strictly speaking, then, the linear factor model is not appropriate for such observed variables. But as mentioned earlier in this chapter, when item-level observed variables have more than five response options, they can be safely treated as continuous variables (as long as their univariate distributions are approximately symmetric) and modeled according to the linear regression matrix equation of Equation 10.2 using ML estimation (Rhemtulla et al., 2012).

Nonetheless, recall from Chapter 9 that use of ML estimation still carries an assumption that the endogenous variables follow a multivariate normal distribution, conditional on any exogenous covariates. In CFA models, all observed variables are endogenous (i.e., each observed variable is an outcome regressed on one or more latent variables; cf. Equation 10.2), and there are no exogenous observed variables. In the current example, the 18 ADHD items, if treated as continuous observed variables, are characterized by substantial multivariate kurtosis, with Mardia's (1970) statistic = 23.08 (West, Finch, and Curran, 1995, suggest that values of Mardia's statistic greater than 3 are indicative of problematic kurtosis). As described in Chapter 9, as long as $N$ is large, parameter estimates are reasonably trustworthy for models fitted to kurtotic data, but model fit statistics and standard error estimates are affected by multivariate kurtosis. Consequently, the previous results for the ADHD example were based on robust corrections to the model fit statistics and parameter standard errors; these robust corrections are described next.

## Robust maximum likelihood: The Satorra-Bentler method

The most commonly used estimation methods in SEM (i.e., ML and GLS) assume that the observed variables follow a multivariate normal distribution (conditional on any exogenous covariates). Any multivariate normal distribution can be completely characterized by its mean vector and covariance matrix because all normal distributions have the same skewness (i.e., skewness = 0) and kurtosis (typically scaled to equal 0). As a result, the observed covariance matrix **S** provides a sufficient summary of the data for fitting many models, if the multivariate normality assumption is tenable. Browne (1984; also see Bollen, 1989) showed that ML (and by extension, GLS) retains its desirable properties (i.e., asymptotic unbiasedness, consistency, and efficiency) as long as there is no excess multivariate kurtosis in the data. Furthermore, parameter estimates remain consistent (i.e., they equal their true values as $N$ approaches infinity) even under the condition of excess kurtosis,[4] although model fit statistics and standard errors of parameter estimates are adversely affected. Specifically, multivariate kurtosis tends to produce exact-fit $\chi^2$ statistics which are too large (which in turn affects other fit statistics) and standard errors which are too low.

Therefore, a prominent approach to handling non-normal data in SEM is to retain parameter estimates obtained with ML but to adjust the ML-based model fit statistics and standard errors according to the degree of observed multivariate kurtosis. In particular, the exact-fit test statistic $T = (N - 1)F_{min}$ (Equation 9.15) does not follow a $\chi^2$ distribution when the data used to fit the model are characterized by excess kurtosis, and so the **Satorra-Bentler scaled** $\chi^2$ test statistic (SB $\chi^2$; Satorra and Bentler, 1988, 1994) is an adjustment of $T$ that depends on the extent of kurtosis in the data. Specifically, SB $\chi^2$ equals $T / k$, where $k$ is known as a *scaling correction factor*. This scaling correction is a complex function of the degree of multivariate kurtosis in the data. Similar logic is used to obtain **robust standard errors** (specifically known as *sandwich standard errors*) which are also based on adjustments which account for excess kurtosis. Unfortunately, the formulas behind these robust corrections to the model test statistic and standard errors are too complex to present here; for a pedagogic explanation of the underlying statistical logic, see Savalei (2014).

Recall from Chapter 9 that prominent model fit statistics such as RMSEA, CFI, and TLI are calculated as a function of the exact-fit test statistic $T$. Robust versions of these model fit statistics may be obtained by using the SB $\chi^2$ in their formulas rather than the original, unadjusted test statistic $T$, and most SEM software which implements the Satorra-Bentler method also automatically calculates corresponding fit statistics in this manner. But Brosseau-Liard and Savalei (2014; also Brosseau-Liard, Savalei, and Li, 2012) have shown that simply substituting the SB $\chi^2$ for the unadjusted test statistic $T$ in the formulas for RMSEA, CFI, and TLI produces statistics which are not adequate estimates of their population analogs.[5] Instead, proper robust versions of these fit statistics can be calculated according to the following formulas (Brosseau-Liard and Savalei, 2014; Brosseau-Liard et al., 2012):

$$\text{RMSEA}_{robust} = \sqrt{\frac{T - k \cdot df}{(N - 1)df}} ,$$

$$\text{CFI}_{robust} = 1 - \frac{T - k \cdot df}{T_0 - k_0 \cdot df_0} ,$$

---

[4]But multivariate kurtosis must still be finite for parameter estimates to be consistent. Technically, kurtosis is not defined for categorical variables and so the promise of consistent parameter estimates may not hold when categorical variables (such as Likert-type items) are treated as continuous.

[5]There is no need to adjust SRMR for non-normality because residual covariances are only a function of the parameter estimates themselves which remain consistent under non-normality.

and

$$\text{TLI}_{robust} = 1 - \left( \frac{T - k \cdot df}{T_0 - k_0 \cdot df_0} \cdot \frac{df_0}{df} \right),$$

where as before, $T$ is the uncorrected model exact-fit test statistic $T = (N - 1)F_{min}$ from Equation 9.15, $k$ is the Satorra-Bentler scaling correction factor, $df$ is the model degrees of freedom, and $T_0$, $k_0$, and $df_0$ are, respectively, the uncorrected model test statistic, scaling correction factor, and degrees of freedom of the corresponding null model. Unfortunately, standard SEM software does not currently report these robust fit statistics, but they are easy to calculate as long as the SEM software can report $k$ and $k_0$.[6] The RMSEA, CFI, and TLI fit statistics reported earlier for the ADHD example were in fact calculated from Brosseau-Liard and Savalei's formulas.

Another important consideration emerges when SB $\chi^2$ statistics are used for nested model comparisons, that is, for likelihood-ratio tests. Specifically, the difference between two SB $\chi^2$ statistics is not itself distributed as $\chi^2$; consequently, this difference must also be adjusted according to the scaling correction factors of each SB $\chi^2$ to obtain a correct likelihood-ratio test. In particular, if SB $\chi_1^2$ is the SB $\chi^2$ of a given Model 1 and SB $\chi_2^2$ is the SB $\chi^2$ of a more con-strained Model 2 nested within Model 1, then the **Satorra-Bentler scaled $\chi^2$ difference** test statistic (Satorra and Bentler, 2001) is

$$\text{SB } \chi_{difference}^2 = (\text{SB } \chi_2^2 \times k_2 - \text{SB } \chi_1^2 \times k_1) / k_d,$$

where $k_1$ is the scaling correction factor for Model 1 and $k_2$ is the scaling correction factor for Model 2. In this SB $\chi_{difference}^2$ formula, $k_d$ is the difference test scaling correction such that

$$k_d = \frac{(df_2 \times k_2 - df_1 \times k_1)}{df_2 - df_1}.$$

Earlier in this chapter, a likelihood-ratio test was used to compare the two-factor model with diagonal $\Theta_\varepsilon$ for the ADHD items to a two-factor model with free error covariances among impulsivity items. This earlier result was not a correct $\chi^2$ difference test, however, because the $\chi^2$ values used were in fact SB $\chi^2$ statistics. The corrected likelihood-ratio test comparing these two models is SB $\chi_{difference}^2$ (3) = 20.38, based on scaling correction factors = 1.14 and 1.12 for the two models, respectively.

Although implementations of the Satorra-Bentler robust model fit statistics and stand-ard errors may be the most common approach to handling non-normal data in SEM, other potential remedies include the use of transformations (i.e., to bring observed data closer to data approximating a sample from a multivariate normal distribution) and bootstrapping (to obtain model fit tests and standard errors which do not depend on any formal distribution assumption for the observed data). Bootstrapping in particular has earned a fair deal of atten-tion as an alternative to the Satorra-Bentler robust procedure; see Hancock and Liu, 2012, for an overview of bootstrapping in the context of SEM.

---

[6]Software may not report $k_0$, but if it reports the SB $\chi^2$ of the null model, $k_0$ can be calculated as $k_0 = T_0 / \text{SB } \chi_0^2$.

 Section recap

**Assumption violation and remedies for CFA models**

The major concepts for assumption checking and model diagnostics for EFA and path analysis extend to CFA.

ML (and, by extension, GLS) estimation retains its desirable properties as long as there is no excess multivariate kurtosis in the data. Furthermore, parameter estimates remain consistent even under the condition of excess kurtosis, although model fit statistics and standard errors of parameter estimates are adversely affected.

A common method for handling non-normal data in SEM is to retain parameter estimates obtained with ML but to adjust model fit statistics and standard errors according to the degree of observed multivariate kurtosis using the **Satorra-Bentler scaled** $\chi^2$ test statistic and **robust standard errors**.

Robust versions of descriptive model fit statistics such as RMSEA, CFI, and TLI are also a function of the **scaling correction factor** used to calculate the SB $\chi^2$ test statistic.

The **Satorra-Bentler scaled** $\chi^2$ **difference** test statistic should be used to obtain likelihood-ratio tests for model comparisons which are robust to non-normality.

As an alternative to the Satorra-Bentler procedure, robust model fit statistics and standard errors can instead be obtained using bootstrapping.

## CFA with polychoric correlations for item-level variables

It is important to keep in mind that the methods for handling non-normal data just described are still primarily meant for models fitted to continuous endogenous variables and do not necessarily work well when endogenous variables are categorical, ordinally scaled variables such as Likert-type item responses. The main problem with treating such categorical variables as if they are continuous is not so much that the variables are non-normal but that their interrelations are nonlinear. This issue is exactly as described in Chapter 8 in the context of EFA. Indeed, much of the methodological research on factor analysis of categorical variables has been focused more on the CFA context than on the EFA context. Therefore, when the observed variables for a CFA model are ordered categorical variables with five or fewer categories, it is generally preferable to fit the model to a matrix of polychoric correlations rather than to the observed product-moment covariance matrix.

Polychoric correlations were defined and described in Chapter 8, and paralleling their application to EFA, use of polychoric correlations implies that the matrix regression equation for the CFA model is

$$\mathbf{Y^*} = \Lambda\eta + \varepsilon,$$

which is a slight modification of Equation 10.2 to indicate that the latent variables in $\eta$ are linear predictors of a set of latent response variables in the vector $\mathbf{Y^*}$ rather than the observed categorical variables $\mathbf{Y}$. As explained in Chapter 8, these latent response variables are connected to the observed variables according to a set of threshold parameters (via Equation 8.11).

These threshold parameters are included in the count of free parameters to determine the model's identification status and degrees of freedom.

Because the model pertains to the linear regression of $\mathbf{Y}^*$ on $\eta$, the model-implied covariance matrix is expressed as the covariance among $\mathbf{Y}^*$:

$$\Sigma_\Theta^* = \Lambda\Psi\Lambda' + \Theta_\varepsilon,$$

where $\Sigma_\Theta^*$ is the model-implied covariance matrix among the set of latent response variables in $\mathbf{Y}^*$. Now, because the individual latent response variables have an unknown scale, they are usually fixed as standard normal variables, which sets their variance equal to 1. Consequently, the error covariance matrix can be expressed as

$$\Theta_\varepsilon = \mathbf{I} - diag(\Lambda\Psi\Lambda'),$$

and the model-implied covariance matrix is in fact a population correlation matrix. Furthermore, because this equation shows that the error variances in $\Theta_\varepsilon$ are completely determined by the parameters in $\Lambda$ and $\Psi$, the error variances are not included in the count of free parameters to determine the model's identification status and overall degrees of freedom.

Therefore, the goal of estimation is to find the parameter estimate values that produce the estimated model-implied covariance matrix $\hat{\Sigma}_\Theta^*$ that matches the sample polychoric correlation matrix, $\mathbf{R}_{polychoric}$, as closely as possible. Asymptotically, this match is optimized according to a weighted least-squares (WLS) criterion:

$$F_{WLS} = (\mathbf{r} - \rho)'\mathbf{W}^{-1}(\mathbf{r} - \rho),$$

where $\mathbf{r}$ consists of the unique elements of the sample polychoric correlations arranged into a vector, $\rho$ consists of the corresponding elements of the model-implied correlation matrix, and $\mathbf{W}$ is a weight matrix. The theoretically correct weight matrix is the asymptotic covariance matrix of the polychoric correlations (Muthén, 1984), but in practice, this weight matrix is difficult to estimate, requiring extremely large $N$ for accurate results. Consequently, simplified forms of WLS are much more commonly used. Specifically, diagonally weighted least squares (DWLS),

$$F_{DWLS} = (\mathbf{r} - \rho)'\mathbf{V}^{-1}(\mathbf{r} - \rho),$$

where $\mathbf{V}$ consists of only the diagonal elements of the optimal weight matrix $\mathbf{W}$, and unweighted least squares (ULS),

$$F_{ULS} = (\mathbf{r} - \rho)'\mathbf{I}^{-1}(\mathbf{r} - \rho),$$

both lead to unbiased parameter estimates, with slightly better performance from ULS (Forero, Maydeu-Olivares, and Gallardo-Pujol, 2009).

Yet, the parameter estimates from DWLS or ULS estimation are statistically inefficient because they do not include the information from the full weight matrix. Consequently, the model fit statistics and standard error estimates that result are inaccurate unless they are corrected for this inefficiency. Robust fit statistics and standard errors may be obtained in a manner analogous to the Satorra-Bentler method described earlier; see Savalei and Rhemtulla (2013) for details. It is important to note, though, that even with these robust methods, the issue of sparseness, in which the cross-tabulation of two categorical variables has cells with zero frequency, is problematic for CFA as with EFA (Savalei, 2011). This general procedure of CFA with polychoric correlations – obtaining estimates via DWLS or ULS along with robust fit statistics and standard errors – has become a popular approach for CFA with ordered categorical, item-level observed variables, and it is easily implemented using most modern SEM software packages.[7]

Returning to the ADHD example, Toplak et al. (2009) also fitted a series of CFA models to the 18 ADHD symptom reports from the Schedule for Affective Disorders and Schizophrenia for School-Age Children (KSADS; Kaufman et al., 1997). Whereas the SWAN questionnaire produced item responses with seven-point scales, the KSADS items were scored using a three-point rating scale (1 = *symptom not present*, 2 = *subthreshold symptom*, and 3 = *symptom present*). Therefore, it was especially important to treat the KSADS item response variables as categorical variables explicitly because there were fewer than five observed categories for a given item. Toplak et al. found that the bifactor model depicted in Figure 10.7 fit the KSADS data well according to robust fit statistics when the model was fitted to the observed polychoric correlations using DWLS estimation.

> The KSADS data are also available on the text's webpage (https://study.sagepub.com/flora) along with annotated input and output from popular statistical software packages showing how to fit CFA models to polychoric correlations.

 **Section recap**

### CFA with polychoric correlations for item-level variables

When the observed variables for a CFA model are ordered categorical variables (such as item responses) with five or fewer categories, it is generally preferable to fit the model to a matrix of polychoric correlations rather than to the observed product-moment covariance matrix.

Use of polychoric correlations implies that the CFA model is

$$\mathbf{Y^*} = \Lambda\eta + \varepsilon,$$

indicating that the latent factors in $\eta$ are linear predictors of a set of latent response variables in the vector $\mathbf{Y^*}$. These latent response variables are connected to the observed categorical variables $\mathbf{Y}$ via threshold parameters.

For model estimation, the match between the estimated model-implied covariance matrix $\hat{\Sigma}^*_\Theta$ and the sample polychoric correlation matrix is optimized according to a weighted least-squares (WLS) criterion:

---

[7]This method is implemented as 'ULSMV' or 'WLSMV' in the Mplus program. Indeed, because of the relative popularity of Mplus, the term *WLSMV* is sometimes used as a shorthand name for fitting CFA models to polychoric correlations using DWLS with robust fit statistics. But the more general use of the term *WLSMV* is regrettable because similar (but not identical) procedures are also available in the LISREL and EQS programs, as well as in the lavaan package (Rosseel, 2012) for R.

$$F_{WLS} = (\mathbf{r} - \rho)'\mathbf{W}^{-1}(\mathbf{r} - \rho),$$

where $\mathbf{r}$ consists of the unique elements of the sample polychoric correlations arranged into a vector, $\rho$ consists of the corresponding elements of the model-implied correlation matrix, and $\mathbf{W}$ is a complex weight matrix.

In practice, CFA models are most commonly fitted to polychoric correlations using diagonally weighted least squares (DWLS), which uses only the diagonal elements of the optimal weight matrix, or unweighted least squares (ULS), which uses an identity matrix as the weight matrix.

Robust fit statistics and standard errors accompanying DWLS or ULS estimation are obtained in a manner analogous to the Satorra-Bentler method described earlier.

# STRUCTURAL REGRESSION MODELS

As explained at the beginning of this chapter, the major strength of SEM is the ability to model measurement error explicitly, that is, the ability to model the associations between fallible observed, operational variables and the underlying constructs, or latent variables, which the observed variables are purported to represent. In particular, the generic CFA model represents the measurement model for a set of $P$ observed variables denoted as the vector $\mathbf{Y}$ with

$$\mathbf{Y} = \Lambda_{\mathbf{Y}}\eta + \varepsilon, \tag{10.5}$$

where $\mathbf{Y}$ is the $(P \times 1)$ vector of observed indicators, $\Lambda_{\mathbf{Y}}$ is a $(P \times K)$ factor loading matrix, $\eta$ is a $(K \times 1)$ vector of latent variables, and $\varepsilon$ is a $(P \times 1)$ vector of measurement error terms. This equation is simply a repeat of Equation 10.2, except now the factor loading matrix has a subscript to indicate that it pertains to the measurement model for a set of $\mathbf{Y}$ observed variables. If a different set of $Q$ observed variables is collected in a vector $\mathbf{X}$, its measurement model may also be expressed as a CFA model with

$$\mathbf{X} = \Lambda_{\mathbf{X}}\xi + \delta, \tag{10.6}$$

where $\mathbf{X}$ is the $(Q \times 1)$ vector of observed indicators, $\Lambda_{\mathbf{X}}$ is a $(Q \times M)$ matrix of factor loadings, $\xi$ is a $(M \times 1)$ vector of latent variables, and $\delta$ is a $(Q \times 1)$ vector of error terms. The overall purpose of structural regression models is to obtain the linear regression associations, or **structural regression coefficients**, among the latent variables themselves, that is, to regress $\eta$ on $\xi$, while accounting for measurement model relations between the observed variables in $\mathbf{X}$ and $\mathbf{Y}$ and the corresponding latent variables in $\xi$ and $\eta$. As a result, these structural regression coefficients represent the true linear regression associations among the hypothetical constructs and are not affected by the degree of measurement error in the observed variables in $\mathbf{X}$ and $\mathbf{Y}$.

To delineate this important concept, let's return to a simple path analysis model in which an observed outcome variable $Y$ is regressed on a single observed predictor variable $X$. This model is depicted in Figure 10.8, and the corresponding regression equation is

$$Y_i = \gamma^*(X_i) + \zeta_i^*. \tag{10.7}$$

This model is identical to the path analysis model presented in Chapter 9 in Equation 9.1, except here the regression coefficient is expressed as $\gamma^*$ to denote that it is affected by measurement error in $X$ and $Y$ (consequently, the regression disturbance term is analogously denoted as $\zeta^*$). Given that this simple path model has no explicit measurement model for $X$ or $Y$, it's as if each observed variable is a perfect operationalization of its own underlying construct, with $X = \xi$ and $Y = \eta$. Therefore, the alternative path diagram in Figure 10.9 is an equivalent representation of the same model but expanded to include these trivial measurement relations between $X$ and $\xi$ and between $Y$ and $\eta$. Because the two path diagrams in Figures 10.8 and 10.9 represent the same model, their structural regression parameter $\gamma^*$ is the same. In other words, the simple regression of $Y$ on $X$ is identical to the regression of $\eta$ on $\xi$ but only under the strong assumptions that $Y$ is a perfect operationalization of $\eta$ and $X$ is a perfect operationalization of $\xi$.

In general, standard path analysis models such as those presented in Chapter 9 imply that the observed variables are perfect indicators of their underlying constructs, with no measurement error, which is an unrealistic scenario for much research in the behavioural and social sciences. As soon as we allow for the fact that there is in fact likely to be measurement error in the observed variables, a path analysis model evolves into a latent variable model with explicit measurement errors for the observed variables. Returning to the simple path analysis model, Figure 10.9 shows that the measurement model equation for $X$ is

$$X = 1\xi \tag{10.8}$$

and the measurement model for $Y$ is

$$Y = 1\eta, \tag{10.9}$$

with no error terms in either equation, although they are specific (but trivial) instantiations of the more general form in Equations 10.6 and 10.5, respectively. If we expand Equations 10.8 and 10.9 to include nonzero measurement errors, they become

$$X_i = 1\xi_i + \delta_i \tag{10.10}$$

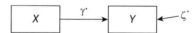

**Figure 10.8** Path diagram for simple regression model

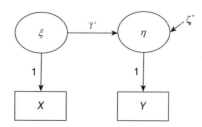

**Figure 10.9** Alternative path diagram for simple regression model explicitly showing that observed variables are assumed to be perfect indicators of latent variables

and

$$Y_i = 1\eta_i + \varepsilon_i. \tag{10.11}$$

This expansion leads to a slightly different structural regression equation than was obtained when $X$ and $Y$ were assumed to be free of measurement error. Specifically, we now have

$$\eta_i = \gamma(\xi_i) + \zeta_i. \tag{10.12}$$

If these expanded measurement model equations (Equations 10.10 and 10.11) are estimated simultaneously with the structural model Equation 10.12, then the structural coefficient $\gamma$ is corrected for the measurement error in $X$ and $Y$, in contrast to the coefficient $\gamma^*$ from Equation 10.7 which is biased as a result of ignoring measurement error in $X$ and $Y$. The full structural equation model represented by Equations 10.10 to 10.12 is depicted in Figure 10.10; notice how it is only slightly different from the path diagram in Figure 10.9, the difference being the presence of the $\delta$ and $\varepsilon$ measurement error terms, which then leads to the structural regression parameter $\gamma$ being different from $\gamma^*$.

The difference between the structural parameter $\gamma$ and parameter $\gamma^*$ from the simple path analysis model is the extent to which $\gamma^*$ is biased as a result of measurement error; measurement error also has ramifications for model fit assessment. Additionally, the consequences of ignoring measurement error by using path analysis models of the type detailed in Chapter 9 become more serious as such models become more complex. For a complete discussion of this issue, see Cole and Preacher (2014).

The model depicted in Figure 10.10 is a simple example of a complete or full SEM, a **structural regression model**, consisting of both a **measurement model** portion and a **structural model** portion. The structural model specifies the regression relations among the latent variables (e.g., Equation 10.12), which are the hypothetical constructs of interest, whereas the measurement model specifies the relations between the latent variables and the observed variables that are used to measure them (e.g., Equations 10.5 and 10.6). A more complete description of full structural regression models is presented later.

One problem with the full SEM in Figure 10.10 is that it is not identified unless the measurement error variances (i.e., VAR($\delta$) and VAR($\varepsilon$)) are each fixed to equal a specific value (identification of full structural equation models is addressed in further detail later).

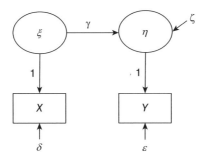

**Figure 10.10** Path diagram of structural regression model showing that regression of $\eta$ on $\xi$ is adjusted for measurement error in $Y$ and $X$

The correct values for the measurement error variances can be obtained, though, from the **reliability** of each observed variable. Drawing from classical test theory (e.g., Algina and Penfield, 2009), the total variance of an observed variable is the sum of its *true score* variance and error variance.[8] Given this relation, the reliability of an observed variable is formally defined as the ratio of true score variance to error variance.[9] In other words, if we consider latent variable $\xi$ an unobserved true score variable being measured by observed variable $X$, then

$$\rho_{XX} = \text{VAR}(\xi) \,/\, \text{VAR}(X),$$

where $\rho_{XX}$ is the reliability of $X$. Given this definition, it can be shown algebraically from the measurement model for $X$ in Equation 10.10 that

$$\text{VAR}(\delta) = (1 - \rho_{XX})\text{VAR}(X). \tag{10.13}$$

Likewise, if we consider latent variable $\eta$ an unobserved true score variable being measured by observed variable $Y$, then

$$\text{VAR}(\varepsilon) = (1 - \rho_{YY})\text{VAR}(Y), \tag{10.14}$$

where $\rho_{YY}$ is the reliability of $Y$. Consequently, if the values of $\rho_{XX}$ and $\rho_{YY}$ are available, then these Equations 10.13 and 10.14 can be used to determine fixed values for $\text{VAR}(\delta)$ and $\text{VAR}(\varepsilon)$ in the specification of the structural regression model in Figure 10.10, which in turn makes the model identified. This method can be generalized to larger models with more than one observed $X$ or $Y$. That is, Equations 10.13 and 10.14 can be applied to expand any path analysis model into a full structural regression model that accounts for measurement error in **X** and **Y**. A major challenge, though, is obtaining accurate reliability estimates for each observed variable.

The method described in the previous paragraph is applicable when a study provides only one observed variable, or indicator, for a given latent variable. Yet, it has been demonstrated that more accurate structural regression coefficients are obtained when each latent variable is measured by multiple indicators (Coffman and MacCallum, 2005; Cole and Preacher, 2014). This concept invokes a type of SEM that is essentially a synthesis of a CFA model – that is, a measurement model for the relations between observed and latent variables – and a path model – that is, a structural model for hypothesized directional, regression relations, but among latent rather than observed variables. We focus further on this type of full SEM, or structural regression model, next.

---

[8] A definition of the true score concept is beyond our scope here, but for further details, see Nunnally and Bernstein (1994; especially pp. 216–27) or Algina and Penfield (2009; especially pp. 93–96).

[9] Popular reliability measures such as coefficient alpha (i.e., 'Cronbach's alpha'), test-retest reliability, and interrater reliability can be considered different sample-based methods for estimating this more formal and more general true score reliability (see Nunnally and Bernstein, 1994).

## Section recap

### Structural regression models

The main purpose of structural regression models is to obtain the linear regression associations, or **structural regression coefficients**, among latent variables themselves, that is, to regress a set of latent outcomes in $\eta$ on a set of latent predictors in $\xi$, while accounting for the fact that the observed variables in **Y** and **X** are imperfect measures of the constructs represented by $\eta$ and $\xi$, respectively.

Consequently, structural regression coefficients represent the true linear regression associations among hypothetical constructs and are not affected by the degree of measurement error in the observed variables in **X** and **Y**.

A full SEM, or **structural regression model**, consists of both a **measurement model** portion and a **structural model** portion. The structural model specifies the regression relations among the latent variables, whereas the measurement model specifies the relations between the latent variables and the observed variables that are used to measure them.

One approach to incorporating a measurement model into a structural regression model is to constrain error variances of observed variables based on their **reliability**, which is formally defined as the ratio of true score variance (i.e., latent variable variance) to total observed score variance (i.e., observed variable variance). This approach is most applicable when a study contains only one observed indicator of a given latent variable.

More accurate structural regression coefficients are obtained when each latent variable is measured by multiple observed indicators.

## Research example for structural regression models: Healthcare utilization

Ullman (2007) developed a model to address a series of research questions from a larger study of female adults: Do age, stress, and poor sense of self directly predict perceived ill health and healthcare utilization? Does perceived ill health directly predict healthcare utilization? Does perceived ill health serve as an intervening variable between the age, life stress and poor sense of self predictors and the healthcare utilization outcome?

In this study, age and stress were both measured with single indicators. Thus, although the concept of stress is probably best conceived of as a hypothetical construct, the study provides only an operationalization which is likely distorted by measurement error (the age indicator, on the other hand, can be presumed to be mostly error free). In contrast, the poor sense of self construct was represented by three reverse-scored indicators: A self-esteem test, a martial satisfaction test, and a locus of control test.[10] Perceived ill health was represented

---

[10]Of course, the self-esteem, marital satisfaction, and locus of control tests themselves are also imperfect measures of hypothetical constructs, but here they are simply being used as indicators of the more general sense of self construct.

by two indicators reported by each participant: the number of mental health problems and the number of physical health problems. Finally, healthcare utilization was represented by two indicators: the frequency of prescription drug use and the number of visits to health professionals. See Ullman (2007) for details. In sum, the hypothesized model consists of nine observed variables – scores on measures of age, stress, self-esteem, marital satisfaction, locus of control, mental health problems, physical health problems, prescription drug use, and visits to health professionals – along with three latent variables with multiple indicators – sense of self, perceived ill health, and healthcare utilization.

This dataset is also available on the text's webpage (https://study.sagepub.com/flora) along with annotated input and output from popular statistical software packages showing how to reproduce the SEM analyses presented later.

A scatterplot matrix for the nine observed variables from a sample of $N = 445$ is in Figure 10.11, whereas descriptive statistics for this sample are in Table 10.3. This figure shows that most of the observed variables are characterized by positive skewness. Thus, it may be important to account for non-normality when calculating model fit statistics and parameter standard errors for the ensuing estimated models. Additionally, fitted LOWESS curves suggest that a few of the bivariate associations (e.g., between stress and marital satisfaction) could be more precisely represented with nonlinear functions rather than with the linear associations assumed by fitting the model to the covariance matrix among these observed variables. Nonetheless, in the following analyses, this potential nonlinearity is ignored only for the sake of demonstrating a basic SEM analysis; a more complete

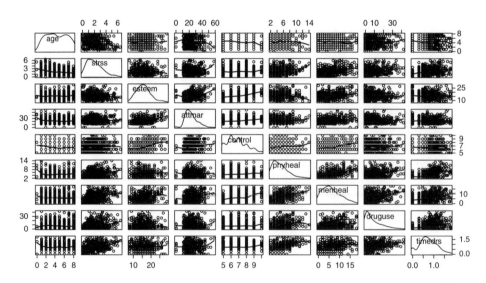

**Figure 10.11** Scatterplot matrix for nine observed variables in healthcare utilization example: age = *age*; strss = *stress*; esteem = *self-esteem*; attmar = *marital satisfaction*; control = *locus of control*; phyheal = *physical health problems*; menheal = *mental health problems*; druguse = *prescription drug use*; timedrs = *visits to health professionals*

**Table 10.3** Correlations, means, and standard deviations among observed variables for healthcare utilization example

| | 1. | 2. | 3. | 4. | 5. | 6. | 7. | 8. | 9. |
|---|---|---|---|---|---|---|---|---|---|
| 1. Age | 1 | – | – | – | – | – | – | – | – |
| 2. Stress | −.29 | 1 | – | – | – | – | – | – | – |
| 3. Self-esteem | .02 | −.10 | 1 | – | – | – | – | – | – |
| 4. Marital satisfaction | −.10 | .11 | .30 | 1 | – | – | – | – | – |
| 5. Locus of control | −.14 | .06 | .34 | .20 | 1 | – | – | – | – |
| 6. Physical health problems | .02 | .30 | .08 | .08 | .11 | 1 | – | – | – |
| 7. Mental health problems | −.09 | .39 | .22 | .24 | .29 | .50 | 1 | – | – |
| 8. Prescription drug use | −.04 | .31 | −.05 | .08 | .07 | .41 | .37 | 1 | – |
| 9. Visits to health professionals | −.02 | .34 | −.02 | .04 | .04 | .58 | .35 | .40 | 1 |
| M | | 4.39 | 2.01 | 15.79 | 22.83 | 6.74 | 4.94 | 6.15 | 8.66 | 0.73 |
| SD | | 2.23 | 1.31 | 3.97 | 8.92 | 1.27 | 2.35 | 4.21 | 9.14 | 0.41 |

Note. N = 445. M = mean; SD = standard deviation.

modeling of these data should include attempts to account these nonlinear associations (e.g., by including polynomial functions).

## Structural regression models: Specification

A full structural regression model can be broken into three components which are ultimately estimated simultaneously. These components are (1) the structural model, which is a model for the pattern of regression relations among the latent variables; (2) the measurement model for $\xi$, which relates exogenous latent variables to their observed indicators; and (3) the measurement model for $\eta$, which relates endogenous latent variables to their observed indicators. (Many texts and treatments of SEM do not explicitly distinguish between measurement models for $\xi$ and $\eta$ and instead describe a single measurement model for the entire system, but I find it is informative to keep them separate in keeping with LISREL notation.)

## Structural model

The matrix regression equation for the general structural model is

$$\eta = B\eta + \Gamma\xi + \zeta, \tag{10.15}$$

where, as before, $\eta$ is a $(K \times 1)$ vector of latent variables and $\xi$ is a $(M \times 1)$ vector of latent variables. Thus, $B$ is a $(K \times K)$ matrix of coefficients for the regression of $\eta$ on $\eta$, $\Gamma$ is a $(K \times M)$ matrix of coefficients for the regression of $\eta$ on $\xi$, and $\zeta$ is a $(K \times 1)$ vector of error or disturbance terms. In other words, in Equation 10.15, each endogenous latent variable (i.e., a $\eta$ variable) is regressed on the other endogenous latent variables as well as on the exogenous latent variables (i.e., $\xi$ variables) according to the pattern of fixed and free coefficients in $B$ and $\Gamma$.

It is helpful to realize that Equation 10.15 is essentially the same as the path analysis model of Equation 9.8 but with $\eta$ substituted for $\mathbf{Y}$ and $\xi$ substituted for $\mathbf{X}$; that is, Equation 10.15 just specifies a path analysis model among latent variables rather than among observed variables. Consequently, the regression coefficients in $\mathbf{B}$ and $\Gamma$ are now structural regression coefficients representing the linear associations among the hypothetical constructs of interest and are not biased by measurement error; estimates of these regression parameters are ultimately the primary results of interest. But to be able to estimate this structural model, we need to relate the latent variables to observed variables, which is where the measurement models come in.

Further drawing on the analogy to path analysis models from Chapter 9, the structural model also involves two covariance matrices. Specifically, $\Phi$ is the $(M \times M)$ covariance matrix among the exogenous latent variables, $\xi$. All nonredundant elements of $\Phi$ are almost always freely estimated, which is consistent with the path analysis specification that allows all exogenous variables in $\mathbf{X}$ to covary freely. Next, $\Psi$ is the $(K \times K)$ covariance matrix of regression errors in $\zeta$. Again, consistent with path analysis, $\Psi$ is often fixed to be a diagonal matrix, but it is possible to free off-diagonal elements to represent covariances among error terms from different regression equations.

## Measurement model

The measurement model for $\xi$ was already presented earlier as Equation 10.6:

$$\mathbf{X} = \Lambda_x\xi + \delta,$$

where, once again, $\mathbf{X}$ is a $(Q \times 1)$ vector of observed indicators, $\Lambda_x$ is a $(Q \times M)$ matrix of factor loadings, $\xi$ is a $(M \times 1)$ vector of latent variables, and $\delta$ is a $(Q \times 1)$ vector of error terms. Additionally, $\Theta_\delta$ is the $(Q \times Q)$ covariance matrix among the error terms in $\delta$; as with CFA, this covariance matrix is often constrained to be diagonal, but off-diagonal elements can be freed to represent measurement error covariances.

Likewise, the measurement model for $\eta$ was presented earlier as Equation 10.5:

$$\mathbf{Y} = \Lambda_y\eta + \varepsilon,$$

where $\mathbf{Y}$ is the $(P \times 1)$ vector of observed indicators, $\Lambda_y$ is a $(P \times K)$ factor loading matrix, $\eta$ is a $(K \times 1)$ vector of latent variables, and $\varepsilon$ is a $(P \times 1)$ vector of measurement error terms. Here, $\Theta_\varepsilon$ is the $(P \times P)$ covariance matrix among the error terms in $\varepsilon$; this matrix also is often constrained to be diagonal, but again it is possible to free off-diagonal elements to represent error covariances.

Putting the structural and measurement models together, a full structural regression model includes eight parameter matrices whose elements must be specified as free or fixed parameters before the model is estimated (SEM software makes doing so easy). These eight matrices are $\mathbf{B}$, $\Gamma$, $\Phi$, $\Psi$, $\Lambda_x$, $\Theta_\delta$, $\Lambda_y$, and $\Theta_\varepsilon$. Next, we see how these parameter matrices are specified for the healthcare utilization example.

## Specification of healthcare utilization model

A path diagram of Ullman's (2007) hypothesized model is in Figure 10.12. From this figure, we see that perceived ill health and healthcare utilization are endogenous latent variables, whereas sense of self is an exogenous latent variable. Additionally, age and stress are exogenous covariates which are not explicit indicators of any latent variable. Because there are two endogenous latent variables, the hypothesized structural model can be characterized by two scalar regression equations. The first of these is the regression of perceived ill health ($\eta_1$) on age ($X_1$), stress ($X_2$), and sense of self ($\xi_3$):

$$\eta_1 = \gamma_{11}X_1 + \gamma_{12}X_2 + \gamma_{13}\xi_3 + \zeta_1.$$

The second scalar regression equation for the structural model is the regression of healthcare utilization ($\eta_2$) on age, stress, and perceived ill health:

$$\eta_2 = \gamma_{21}X_1 + \gamma_{22}X_2 + \beta_{21}\eta_1 + \zeta_2.$$

To combine these two scalar equations into a single matrix equation consistent with Equation 10.15, it is helpful to set $X_1 = \xi_1$ and $X_2 = \xi_2$ (to link age and stress to their own exogenous latent variables). Then, the matrix structural regression equation is

$$\begin{bmatrix} \eta_1 \\ \eta_2 \end{bmatrix} = \begin{bmatrix} 0 & 0 \\ \beta_{21} & 0 \end{bmatrix}\begin{bmatrix} \eta_1 \\ \eta_2 \end{bmatrix} + \begin{bmatrix} \gamma_{11} & \gamma_{12} & \gamma_{13} \\ \gamma_{21} & \gamma_{22} & 0 \end{bmatrix}\begin{bmatrix} \xi_1 \\ \xi_2 \\ \xi_3 \end{bmatrix} + \begin{bmatrix} \zeta_1 \\ \zeta_2 \\ \zeta_3 \end{bmatrix}.$$

Next, $\Phi$ is a ($3 \times 3$) covariance matrix among the exogenous latent variables (given $X_1 = \xi_1$ and $X_2 = \xi_2$), whereas $\Psi$, the ($2 \times 2$) covariance matrix among error terms, is restricted to be diagonal because the model does not specify a free covariance between $\zeta_1$ and $\zeta_2$.

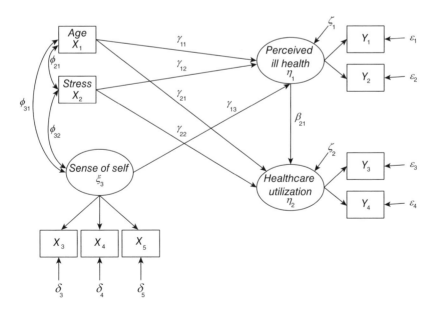

**Figure 10.12** Hypothesized healthcare utilization model: self-esteem = $X_3$; marital satisfaction = $X_2$; locus of control = $X_5$; mental health problems = $Y_1$; physical health problems = $Y_2$; prescription drug use = $Y_3$; visits to health professionals = $Y_4$

Regarding the measurement model for $\xi$, the five observed variables in $\mathbf{X}$ are regressed on three latent variables. In particular, the previous paragraph has already stated measurement equations for $X_1$ and $X_2$, which are

$$X_1 = \xi_1$$

and

$$X_2 = \xi_2,$$

indicating that age and stress are treated as error-free indicators of latent variables $\xi_1$ and $\xi_2$. Next, the three indicators of sense of self are self-esteem ($X_3$), marital satisfaction ($X_4$), and locus of control ($X_5$), so the measurement equations for these observed variables are

$$X_3 = \lambda_{33}\xi_3 + \delta_3,$$
$$X_4 = \lambda_{43}\xi_3 + \delta_4,$$

and

$$X_5 = \lambda_{53}\xi_3 + \delta_5.$$

Applying Equation 10.6, these scalar measurement equations can be collected into the matrix equation

$$
\begin{bmatrix} X_1 \\ X_2 \\ X_3 \\ X_4 \\ X_5 \end{bmatrix} =
\begin{bmatrix} 1 & 0 & 0 \\ 0 & 1 & 0 \\ 0 & 0 & \lambda_{33} \\ 0 & 0 & \lambda_{43} \\ 0 & 0 & \lambda_{53} \end{bmatrix}
\begin{bmatrix} \xi_1 \\ \xi_2 \\ \xi_3 \end{bmatrix} +
\begin{bmatrix} 0 \\ 0 \\ \delta_3 \\ \delta_4 \\ \delta_5 \end{bmatrix}.
$$

The ($5 \times 5$) error covariance matrix among $\delta$ is then

$$
\Theta_\delta =
\begin{bmatrix}
0 & & & & \\
0 & 0 & & & \\
0 & 0 & \text{VAR}(\delta_3) & & \\
0 & 0 & 0 & \text{VAR}(\delta_4) & \\
0 & 0 & 0 & 0 & \text{VAR}(\delta_5)
\end{bmatrix}.
$$

This matrix contains only three free elements: Because there are no error terms in the measurement equations for age ($X_1$) or stress ($X_2$), the two diagonal elements referring to VAR($\delta_1$) and VAR($\delta_2$) are fixed to 0, and all off-diagonal elements are also fixed to 0 because the model does not hypothesize any covariances among the measurement errors of the individual variables in $\mathbf{X}$.

Finally, the scalar measurement equations regarding the measurement model for $\eta$ are

$$Y_1 = \lambda_{11}\eta_1 + \varepsilon_1,$$
$$Y_2 = \lambda_{21}\eta_1 + \varepsilon_2,$$
$$Y_3 = \lambda_{32}\eta_2 + \varepsilon_3,$$

and

$$Y_4 = \lambda_{42}\eta_2 + \varepsilon_4,$$

where $Y_1$ is mental health problems, $Y_2$ is physical health problems, $Y_3$ is prescription drug use, and $Y_4$ is visits to health professionals. Equation 10.5 is applied to collect these scalar equations into a matrix equation with

$$\begin{bmatrix} Y_1 \\ Y_2 \\ Y_3 \\ Y_4 \end{bmatrix} = \begin{bmatrix} \lambda_{11} & 0 \\ \lambda_{21} & 0 \\ 0 & \lambda_{32} \\ 0 & \lambda_{42} \end{bmatrix} \begin{bmatrix} \eta_1 \\ \eta_2 \end{bmatrix} + \begin{bmatrix} \varepsilon_1 \\ \varepsilon_2 \\ \varepsilon_3 \\ \varepsilon_4 \end{bmatrix}.$$

Additionally, the error covariance matrix $\Theta_\varepsilon$ is then a diagonal (4 × 4) matrix because the model does not hypothesize any covariances among the measurement errors of the individual variables in **Y**.

 **Section recap**

### Specification of structural regression models

A full structural regression model can be broken into three components which are ultimately estimated simultaneously:

**(1)** The structural model is essentially a path model among latent variables rather than among observed variables:

$$\eta = B\eta + \Gamma\xi + \zeta,$$

where
$\eta$ is a ($K \times 1$) vector of latent variables and $\xi$ is a ($M \times 1$) vector of latent variables
B is a ($K \times K$) matrix of coefficients for the regression of $\eta$ on $\eta$
$\Gamma$ is a ($K \times M$) matrix of coefficients for the regression of $\eta$ on $\xi$
$\zeta$ is a ($K \times 1$) vector of error or disturbance terms
Furthermore, $\Phi$ is the ($M \times M$) covariance matrix for $\xi$; usually all elements of this matrix are freely estimated.
Additionally, $\Psi$ is the ($K \times K$) covariance matrix among the regression errors in $\zeta$; usually this matrix is fixed to be diagonal, but it is possible to estimate free error covariance parameters.

**(2)** The measurement model for $\xi$ is essentially a CFA model:

$$X = \Lambda_x\xi + \delta,$$

where
**X** is a ($Q \times 1$) vector of observed indicators
$\Lambda_x$ is a ($Q \times M$) matrix of factor loadings

*(Continued)*

(Continued)

$\xi$ is a $(M \times 1)$ vector of latent variables

$\delta$ is a $(Q \times 1)$ vector of error terms

**(3)** The measurement model for $\eta$ is also similar to a CFA model:

$$Y = \Lambda_Y \eta + \varepsilon,$$

where

**Y** is a $(P \times 1)$ vector of observed indicators

$\Lambda_Y$ is a $(P \times K)$ factor loading matrix

$\eta$ is a $(K \times 1)$ vector of latent variables

$\varepsilon$ is a $(P \times 1)$ vector of measurement error terms

Additionally, $\Theta_\varepsilon$ is the $(P \times P)$ covariance matrix among the error terms in $\varepsilon$ and $\Theta_\delta$ is the $(Q \times Q)$ covariance matrix among the error terms in $\delta$. These matrices are often constrained to be diagonal, but again it is possible to free off-diagonal elements to represent error covariances.

---

## Structural regression models: Identification

First, it is important to note that the measurement model specification just given for the health-care utilization model does not yet establish the scales of the latent variables $\xi_3$, $\eta_1$, and $\eta_2$. Just as latent variables must be given a scale as a part of model identification in CFA, so too must latent variables be given a scale to identify full structural regression models. In the healthcare utilization example, let's presume the latent variable scales are set using the marker indicator approach described earlier in the context of CFA, that is, by constraining a factor loading equal to 1 for one indicator of each latent variable. This constraint was already imposed earlier to set the scales for $\xi_1$ and $\xi_2$ because 1 is the implicit regression coefficient in the equations $X_1 = \xi_1$ and $X_2 = \xi_2$. Next, the scale of $\xi_3$ can be set by fixing $\lambda_{33} = 1$ in the $\Lambda_X$ matrix, and the scales of $\eta_1$ and $\eta_2$ can be set fixing $\lambda_{11} = 1$ and $\lambda_{32} = 1$ in the $\Lambda_Y$ matrix. The latent variables could instead be scaled by constraining their variance parameters, but in practice, the marker indicator approach tends to lead to more stable estimation of full structural regression models.

## The *t*-rule for identification

As with any SEM, the number of parameters to be estimated in a structural regression model must be less than the number of nonredundant elements of the observed covariance matrix, which is the *t*-rule of identification initially described in Chapter 9. In the healthcare utilization example, there are nine observed variables and so their covariance matrix has 45 nonredundant elements (observed variances and covariances). The model has a total of 25 free parameters to be estimated: two free parameters in $\Lambda_X$, three in $\Theta_\delta$, six in $\Phi$, two in $\Lambda_Y$, four in $\Theta_\varepsilon$, two in $\Psi$, five in $\Gamma$, and one in **B**. Therefore, the model has $(45 - 25) = 20$ degrees of freedom and passes the *t*-rule for identification. Remember, however, that the *t*-rule is necessary but not sufficient for overall model identification.

## Two-step rule

The **two-step rule** is sufficient, but not necessary, for establishing the identification status of a structural regression model with both exogenous and endogenous latent variables. If both of its 'steps' are passed, then the overall model is identified.

### Step 1

The first step essentially involves establishing identification of the measurement model portion of the full model. Specifically, one recasts the complete model as a CFA model: All latent variables in both $\xi$ and $\eta$ are considered freely correlated with each other, but there are no

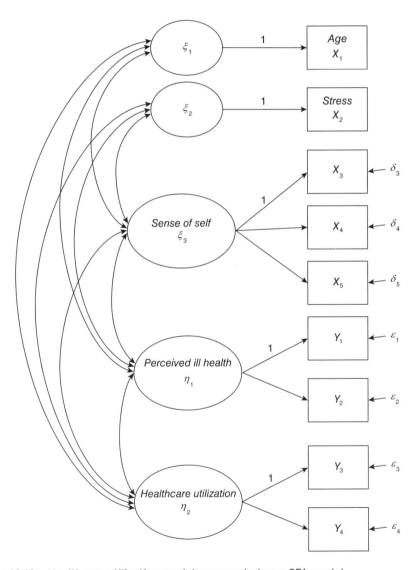

**Figure 10.13** Healthcare utilization model represented as a CFA model

directional relations among them (i.e., ignore the $\Upsilon$ and **B** matrices, and instead expand $\Phi$ to include covariances among both $\xi$ and $\eta$). Then, determine whether this CFA model would be identified (there is no actual need to estimate it, though).

Figure 10.13 presents the healthcare utilization model reformulated as a CFA model in which each latent variable is scaled according to the marker indicator approach. Because $\xi_1$ and $\xi_2$ each have only a single indicator, this CFA model does not pass either the three-indicator rule or the two-indicator rule for CFA model identification explained earlier in this chapter. But those rules are not necessary for identification. It turns out this CFA model is identified, though, because the equations $X_1 = \xi_1$ and $X_2 = \xi_2$ do not have error terms and the remaining latent variables do adhere to the two-indicator rule.

## Step 2

The second step of the two-step rule is to imagine the structural model portion of the full model as if the latent variables were observed variables without any measurement error and to ignore the measurement model for the actual observed variables. In other words, this step involves treating the structural model among latent variables as though it were a path analysis model among observed variables. Then, determine whether this hypothetical path analysis model is identified.

Figure 10.14 shows the structural model portion of the healthcare utilization example recast as a path analysis model. This imagined path analysis model is recursive (because **B** is lower-triangular and $\Psi$ is diagonal); therefore, it is identified according to the recursive rule of identification discussed in Chapter 9.

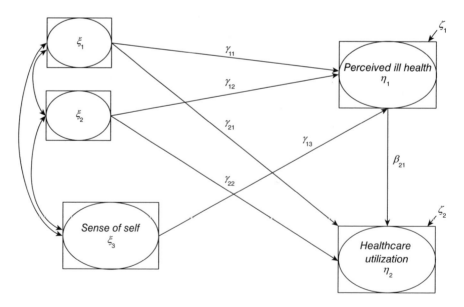

**Figure 10.14** Structural model of healthcare utilization example represented as a path analysis model (oval latent variables are enclosed in rectangles to represent the idea that they are being imagined as observed variables)

In sum, passing both steps of the two-step rule is sufficient for establishing identification of the full structural regression model. In the healthcare example, both steps of the two-step rule are passed, indicating that the overall model is identified.

## Section recap

### Identification of structural regression models

Just as latent variables must be given a scale as a part of model identification in CFA, so too must latent variables be given a scale to identify full structural regression models.

As with any SEM, it is necessary for the number of parameters to be estimated in a structural regression model to be less than the number of nonredundant elements of the observed covariance matrix, which is the $t$-rule of identification.

The **two-step rule** is sufficient but not necessary to establish identification of structural regression models:

**Step 1**: Recast the full model as a CFA model in which all latent variables freely covary but there are no directional regression relations among them. Is this CFA model identified?

**Step 2**: Ignore the measurement model and imagine the structural model portion of the full model as a path analysis model. Is this path analysis model identified?

If the answer to both Step 1 and Step 2 is yes, then the full structural regression model is identified.

## Structural regression models: Estimation

The same estimation methods used with path analysis and CFA can be used to fit full structural regression models, and consequently, the same model fit statistics are available. Once again, the goal of estimation is to find the set of parameter estimate values that optimizes the match between the fitted model-implied covariance matrix, $\widehat{\Sigma}_\theta$, and the sample covariance matrix, $\mathbf{S}$, according to some criterion (e.g., a maximum likelihood or least-squares criterion). Similar to path analysis, the population model-implied covariance matrix $\Sigma_\theta$ for the full structural regression model can be broken into (1) $\Sigma_{YY\theta}$, which is the implied covariances among $\mathbf{Y}$, the observed indicators of the endogenous latent variables; (2) $\Sigma_{XX\theta}$, which is the implied covariances among $\mathbf{X}$, the observed indicators of the exogenous latent variables; and (3) $\Sigma_{YX\theta}$, which is the implied covariance of $\mathbf{Y}$ with $\mathbf{X}$. Specifically, these model-implied covariance matrices are

$$\Sigma_{YY\theta} = \Lambda_Y(\mathbf{I} - \mathbf{B})^{-1}(\Gamma\Phi\Gamma' + \Psi)[(\mathbf{I} - \mathbf{B})^{-1}]'\Lambda'_Y + \Theta_\varepsilon,$$

$$\Sigma_{XX\theta} = \Lambda_X\Phi\Lambda'_X + \Theta_\delta,$$

and

$$\Sigma_{YX\theta} = \Lambda_Y(\mathbf{I} - \mathbf{B})^{-1}\Gamma\Phi\Lambda'_X.$$

These three submatrices are then collected into the complete model-implied covariance matrix

$$\Sigma_\theta = \begin{bmatrix} \Sigma_{YY\theta} & \\ \Sigma_{XY\theta} & \Sigma_{XX\theta} \end{bmatrix}.$$

The same ML fitting function (or an alternative least-squares fitting function) presented earlier for CFA, as well as in Chapter 9 for path analysis, is minimized by finding estimates of the free parameters in this overall model-implied covariance matrix that match the sample covariance matrix as closely as possible.

In practice, it is often advisable to follow a two-step procedure when estimating a full structural regression model (Anderson and Gerbing, 1988; also see Mulaik and Millsap, 2000). With this method, one first estimates the measurement model as a CFA model (e.g., the model in Figure 10.13 for the healthcare utilization example) before estimating the full structural regression model itself. Because structural regression models are often large and complex, it can be difficult to pinpoint reasons behind poor model–data fit, nonconvergence, or improper solutions. This two-step method can help reveal the source of such problems; one may discover a need to revise the measurement model which ultimately becomes reflected in a respecification of the full model itself. Furthermore, when a measurement model is especially large, it may be advantageous to break it into smaller models, each using only a subset of the observed variables (for example, one CFA model relating the variables in **X** to their latent variables and another relating **Y** to their latent variables) and to estimate these one at a time and potentially revise them before attempting to estimate the complete measurement model or the structural regression model itself.

 **Section recap**

### Estimation of structural regression models

The same general procedure of model estimation presented earlier for path analysis and CFA is also applied to estimation of structural regression models. Consequently, the same model fit statistics are available.

The model-implied covariance matrix $\Sigma_\theta$ for the full structural regression model can be broken into

(1) $\Sigma_{YY\theta}$, which is the implied covariances among **Y**, the observed indicators of the endogenous latent variables
(2) $\Sigma_{XX\theta}$, which is the implied covariances among **X**, the observed indicators of the exogenous latent variables
(3) $\Sigma_{YX\theta}$, which is the implied covariance of **Y** with **X**

In practice, it is often advisable to follow a two-step procedure when estimating a full structural regression model:

In the first step, estimate the measurement model relating all latent variables to observed variables as a CFA model, and then in the second step, estimate the full structural regression model.

## Results for healthcare utilization example

Recall that popular estimation methods (i.e., ML and least-squares estimators) carry an assumption that the errors in the equations for all endogenous observed variables (i.e., the terms in the $\delta$ and $\varepsilon$ vectors) must follow a multivariate normal distribution to obtain correct model fit statistics and parameter standard errors. In Figure 10.11, it is clear that the univariate distributions of the observed variables of the healthcare utilization example substantially deviate from normality; consequently, it would not be surprising for any linear model fitted to these data to produce non-normal residuals. Therefore, although the health-care utilization model can be validly estimated using ML, it is important to obtain model fit statistics and standard errors which are robust to non-normality using a procedure such as the Satorra-Bentler method described earlier in this chapter.

Before estimating the complete healthcare utilization structural regression model, the corresponding measurement model (i.e., the model in Figure 10.13) was first estimated using ML according to the two-step procedure mentioned earlier. This initial measurement model leads to an improper solution, though; specifically, the estimated latent variable covariance matrix is nonpositive definite. Because the estimated measurement model is improper, its individual parameter estimates are invalid for interpretational purposes, but they can still be inspected for hints about the cause of the improper solution. Here, the estimated correlation (i.e., the standardized covariance) between the perceived ill health ($\eta_1$) and healthcare utilization ($\eta_2$) latent variables is excessively large, $r = .97$. Thinking carefully about the indicators of these latent variables, one would expect a strong correlation between physical health problems ($Y_2$) and visits to health professionals ($Y_4$) regardless of the psy-chological mechanism meant to be captured by the regression of a healthcare utilization latent variable on a perceived ill health latent variable. Of course people with more health problems will go to the doctor more often. Thus, it seems reasonable to free the covariance between the errors of $Y_2$ and $Y_4$.

When the measurement model is respecified to include this error covariance and estimated with ML, a proper solution is obtained. Furthermore, the measurement model fits the data adequately: Although the exact fit null hypothesis is rejected, SB $\chi^2$ (18) = 54.14, $p < .001$, the descriptive fit statistics are indicative of adequate model–data fit, with $RMSEA_{robust} = .070$, $CFI_{robust} = .95$, $TLI_{robust} = .90$, and SRMR = .045.

Subsequently, the full structural regression model originally depicted in Figure 10.12 was also respecified to include a free covariance between the errors for $Y_2$ and $Y_4$. With this slight model respecification, $\Theta_\varepsilon$ is no longer diagonal; instead

$$\Theta_\varepsilon = \begin{bmatrix} VAR(\varepsilon_1) & & & \\ 0 & VAR(\varepsilon_2) & & \\ 0 & 0 & VAR(\varepsilon_3) & \\ 0 & COV(\varepsilon_4\varepsilon_2) & 0 & VAR(\varepsilon_4) \end{bmatrix}.$$

Figure 10.15 presents a path diagram for this final model.

When this final model is estimated using ML, the overall fit is adequate with SB $\chi^2$ (19) = 62.93, $p < .001$, $RMSEA_{robust} = .075$, $CFI_{robust} = .94$, $TLI_{robust} = .88$, and SRMR = .051. At this point, we are ready to take a look at the parameter estimates, with the $\hat{\gamma}$ and $\hat{\beta}$ estimates being of

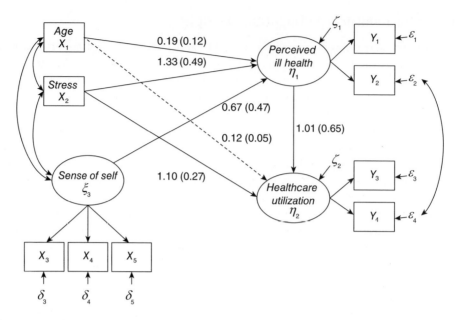

**Figure 10.15** Revised healthcare utilization model (values represent unstandardized structural regression estimates [with completely standardized estimates in parentheses]; dashed line indicates a nonsignificant estimate)

primary interest because they are estimates of the structural regression parameters representing the hypothesized directional associations among the latent variables, or psychological constructs, of interest. Figure 10.15 presents this final model along with the estimated structural regression coefficients, whereas Table 10.4 gives more complete results for the estimated model.

Overall, older age, greater stress, and a poorer sense of self significantly predict higher levels of the perceived ill health latent variable. Next, greater stress and higher perceived ill health significantly predict increased levels of the healthcare utilization latent variable. Because these structural regression effects represent the associations among latent variables, which have an arbitrary scale, it is reasonable to interpret the corresponding completely standardized estimated coefficients perhaps more so than the unstandardized estimates. For instance, each 1 standard-deviation increase in the poor sense of self latent variable predicts about 0.5 of a standard-deviation decrease in the perceived ill health latent variable (i.e., $\hat{\gamma}_{13}^* = 0.47$). Because the latent variables were scaled using the marker indicator approach, their variance is a function of both the variance of the marker indicator and the measurement error variance for that indicator (as explained earlier in this chapter), which makes interpretation of the unstandardized structural regression estimates considerably awkward.

Whereas these structural regression coefficient estimates represent the significant direct effects in the structural model, it is also clear that there are substantial indirect effects in the model. In particular, the healthcare utilization latent variable is indirectly predicted by age, stress, and the sense of self latent variable through the perceived ill health latent variable. Here, the inferential methods for indirect effects described in Chapter 5 potentially come into play.

**Table 10.4**  Parameter estimates of revised healthcare utilization model

| Endogenous latent variable  Predictor | Estimate | robust SE | z | p | B* |
|---|---|---|---|---|---|
| Structural model results | | | | | |
| Perceived ill health | | | | | |
| Age | 0.186 | 0.080 | 2.32 | .020 | 0.118 |
| Stress | 1.325 | 0.143 | 9.30 | <.001 | 0.494 |
| Sense of self | 0.671 | 0.124 | 5.43 | <.001 | 0.466 |
| Healthcare utilization | | | | | |
| Age | 0.124 | 0.130 | 0.96 | .338 | 0.051 |
| Stress | 1.102 | 0.269 | 4.11 | <.001 | 0.266 |
| Perceived ill health | 1.005 | 0.163 | 6.17 | <.001 | 0.651 |
| Measurement model results | | | | | |
| Sense of self | | | | | |
| Self-esteem | 1.000 | – | – | – | 0.612 |
| Marital satisfaction | 1.607 | 0.271 | 5.94 | <.001 | 0.438 |
| Locus of control | 0.291 | 0.054 | 5.40 | <.001 | 0.558 |
| Perceived ill health | | | | | |
| Mental health problems | 1.000 | – | – | – | 0.832 |
| Physical health problems | 0.416 | 0.043 | 9.68 | <.001 | 0.619 |
| Healthcare utilization | | | | | |
| Prescription drug use | 1.000 | – | – | – | 0.591 |
| Visits to health professionals | 0.044 | 0.006 | 7.79 | <.001 | 0.580 |

*Note.* N = 445. B* = completely standardized parameter estimate.

For example, adhering to the test of joint significance for an indirect effect, we can say that poor sense of self has a significant indirect effect on healthcare utilization through perceived ill health because both $\hat{\gamma}_{13} = 0.67$ and $\hat{\beta}_{21} = 1.01$ are statistically significant.[11] Alternatively, most SEM software packages are capable of generating percentile bootstrap confidence intervals around indirect effects, which also can be used to establish their statistical significance as well as give a range of plausible population values for the indirect effect.

Finally, just as $R^2$ statistics can be obtained for path analysis models and CFA models, they can also be calculated for structural regression models. In particular, although Equation 10.4

[11]Here, the significance of the unstandardized estimates is reported because the standard errors in Table 10.4 pertain to these estimates rather than to the standardized estimates. Not all SEM software is capable of reporting proper standard errors for standardized parameter estimates.

can be used to obtain an $R^2$ statistic for each observed variable, $R^2$ statistics for the endogenous latent variables (i.e., variables in $\eta$) are probably of greater interest in most applications. For a given latent variable $\eta_k$, $R^2$ can be calculated as

$$R^2_{\eta_k} = 1 - \frac{\hat{\psi}_{kk}}{\hat{\sigma}^2_{\eta_k}},$$

where $\hat{\psi}_{kk}$ is the estimated diagonal element of $\Psi$ corresponding to the residual variance of $\eta_k$ and $\hat{\sigma}^2_{\eta_k}$ is the estimated model-implied total variance of $\eta_k$. It is important to recognize that most SEM software reports the residual variance of endogenous latent variables under a column in the output which is simply labeled 'Variances'; this value is of course smaller than the total variance of a given endogenous latent variable, which itself is usually not reported.[12] Fortunately, though, SEM software does unambiguously report $R^2$ statistics for endogenous latent variables as well as for observed variables. For the healthcare utilization example, $R^2 = .43$ for perceived ill heath, indicating that 43% of this latent variable's variance is accounted for by the set of its direct predictors which were age, stress, and the sense of self exogenous latent variable. Next, $R^2 = .65$ for the healthcare utilization latent variable, indicating that 65% of its variance is explained by its direct predictors which were age, stress, and the perceived ill health latent variable.

## CHAPTER SUMMARY

The current chapter drew on principles from exploratory factor analysis (EFA) and path analysis to develop structural equation models which incorporate latent variables, specifically **confirmatory factor analysis** (CFA) models and full, **structural regression models**:

- Like EFA, CFA involves developing and evaluating models which represent the associations between observed variables and latent variables that often are intended to represent hypothetical constructs.
- The critical difference between EFA and CFA is that with CFA, certain factor loadings are fixed to 0 based on a priori hypotheses about which factors directly affect a given observed variable, whereas in EFA, all factor loadings in $\Lambda$ are freely estimated.
- The main purpose of structural regression models is to obtain the linear regression associations, or **structural regression coefficients**, among latent variables themselves while accounting for the fact that the observed variables are imperfect measures of the constructs represented by the latent variables.
- Consequently, structural regression coefficients represent true linear regression associations among hypothetical constructs and are not affected by the degree of measurement error in the observed variables.
- The **structural model** portion of a full structural regression model specifies the regression relations among the latent variables, whereas the **measurement model** portion specifies the relations between the latent variables and the observed variables.

---

[12]Estimates of the total variances of the endogenous latent variables are the diagonal elements of a matrix calculated as $(\mathbf{I} - \hat{\mathbf{B}})^{-1}(\hat{\Gamma}\hat{\Phi}\hat{\Gamma}' + \hat{\Psi})[(\mathbf{I} - \hat{\mathbf{B}})^{-1}]'$.

- The basic principles of model identification presented for path analysis models extend to models with latent variables.
- Additionally, for a CFA or structural regression model to be identified, constraints must be imposed on the model to establish a scale for each latent variable.
- The same principles and model fit statistics applied to evaluate model fit assessment for path analysis models also apply to latent variable models.
- The major concepts for assumption checking and model diagnostics for EFA and path analysis extend to CFA and structural regression models.
- A common method for handling non-normal data in SEM is to adjust model fit statistics and standard errors according to the degree of observed multivariate kurtosis using the **Satorra-Bentler scaled** $\chi^2$ test statistic and **robust standard errors**.
- Robust versions of descriptive model fit statistics such as RMSEA, CFI, and TLI are also a function of the **scaling correction factor** used to calculate the SB $\chi^2$ test statistic.
- When the observed variables for a latent variable model are ordered categorical variables (such as item responses) with five or fewer categories, it is generally preferable to fit the model to a matrix of polychoric correlations rather than to the observed product-moment covariance matrix.

## RECOMMENDED READING

Bollen, K.A. (2002). Latent variables in psychology and the social sciences. *Annual Review of Psychology, 53*, 605–34.

- This is an interesting, nontechnical paper discussing various definitions of latent variables and their roles in statistical models.

Cole, D.A., & Preacher, K.J. (2014). Manifest variable path analysis: Potentially serious and misleading consequences due to uncorrected measurement error. *Psychological Methods, 19*, 300–15.

- This paper convincingly describes and demonstrates the advantages of full structural regression models over path analysis models (and ordinary multiple regression models, for that matter) which do not account for measurement error in observed variables.

DeCarlo, L.T. (1997). On the meaning and use of kurtosis. *Psychological Methods, 2*, 292–307.

- Introductory statistics courses and texts often give a deficient presentation of kurtosis. Consequently, students and researchers alike have difficulty distinguishing symmetric distributions with nonzero kurtosis from normal distributions with differing variances. This tutorial paper defines kurtosis clearly and carefully and uses a series of idealized graphs to illustrate the concepts.

Jackson, D.L., Gillaspy, J.A., & Purc-Stephenson, R. (2009). Reporting practices in confirmatory factor analysis: A review and some recommendations. *Psychological Methods, 14*, 6–23.

- This article presents a literature review assessing the extent to which applications of CFA follow methodological recommendations. In so doing, the article succinctly explains these best methodological practices for CFA (which generalize to other latent variable models).

Savalei, V. (2014). Understanding robust corrections in structural equation modeling. *Structural Equation Modeling, 21,* 149–60.

- Textbooks presenting SEM (including this one!) usually state that the mathematical underpinnings of the Satorra-Bentler robust corrections for non-normality are 'too complex to present here' or something along those lines. This *Teacher's Corner* paper effectively demystifies how the corrections work by drawing an analogy with a sandwich.

# GROWTH CURVE MODELING

## CHAPTER OVERVIEW

There are many methods available for analysing longitudinal and repeated measures data, but growth curve modeling (GCM) has rapidly become one of the most popular because its generality and flexibility allows GCM to handle data from many different types of longitudinal studies and to address many different research questions. Additionally, as this chapter shows, growth curve models can be specified and estimated using either a structural equation modeling (SEM) or a multilevel modeling (MLM) approach. The main topics of this chapter include:

- Advantages of GCM over repeated-measures analysis of variance (ANOVA) and multivariate analysis of variance (MANOVA)
- Unconditional linear growth curve models

    o   Model specification, identification, and estimation using SEM
    o   Model specification, identification, and estimation using MLM

- Coding *time* to change the trajectory intercept
- Specification of conditional linear growth curve models
- Growth curve models for nonlinear change

    o   Unconditional and conditional quadratic growth curve models
    o   Unconditional and conditional piecewise linear growth curve models

**Table 11.0**   Greek letter notation used in this chapter

| Greek letter | English name | Represents |
|---|---|---|
| $\lambda$ | Lowercase 'lambda' | Factor loading parameter |
| $\eta$ | Lowercase 'eta' | Latent variable (growth factor) |
| $\varepsilon$ | Lowercase 'epsilon' | Regression error term |

*(Continued)*

**Table 11.0** (Continued)

| Greek letter | English name | Represents |
|---|---|---|
| Λ | Uppercase 'lambda' | Factor loading matrix |
| Θ | Uppercase 'theta' | Error covariance matrix |
| $\sigma$ | Lowercase 'sigma' | $\sigma^2$ is for variance parameters |
| $\mu$ | Lowercase 'mu' | Population mean; $\mu$ (in bold) is a vector of mean or intercept parameters |
| $\zeta$ | Lowercase 'zeta' | Regression error term |
| Ψ | Uppercase 'psy' | Covariance matrix for $\eta$ (in unconditional GCMs) or $\zeta$ (in conditional GCMs) |
| $\psi$ | Lowercase 'psy' | Element in Ψ |
| Σ | Uppercase 'sigma' | Population covariance matrix among observed variables |
| $\theta$ | Lowercase 'theta' | Vector of all model parameters |
| $\chi$ | Lowercase 'chi' | $\chi^2$ distribution |
| $\beta$ | Lowercase 'beta' | Level 1 regression parameter in MLM (intercept or slope, depending on subscript) |
| $\gamma$ | Lowercase 'gamma' | Level 2 regression parameter in MLM (intercept or slope, depending on subscript); Regression parameter in SEM conditional model |
| Γ | Uppercase 'gamma' | Matrix of $\gamma$ parameters |
| $\delta$ | Lowercase 'delta' | Regression error term |
| $\tau$ | Lowercase 'tau' | $\tau^2$ is Level 2 error variance; $\tau$ is covariance between different Level 2 error terms |
| Φ | Uppercase 'phi' | Covariance matrix of exogenous variables |

*Note.* Some of these Greek letters may have been used for different purposes in previous chapters.

## WHAT IS GROWTH CURVE MODELING?

**Growth curve modeling** (GCM) has rapidly become the standard approach to analysing longitudinal data in the behavioural and social sciences, especially when a study includes measures of the same variable on more than two occasions, as with so-called panel studies and other types of longitudinal research studies. In particular, growth curve models are used to represent how scores on a given variable change over time or across repeated observation. Even when a study involves only two measurement occasions (i.e., participants are observed only twice), GCM procedures are applicable, although with some limitations (see Willett, 1989). Furthermore, GCM is also useful for repeated-measures experimental data (e.g., Mirman, 2014), even if the interest lies in changes across different experimental conditions (which may be arbitrarily ordered) rather than in change over time per se. Traditionally, such data have been analysed using repeated-measures analysis of variance (ANOVA) or multivariate ANOVA (i.e., MANOVA), but we now know that the GCM approaches outlined in this chapter offer important advantages over these traditional methods (e.g., Quené and van den Bergh, 2004), which themselves can be expressed as highly restricted, special cases of a more general growth curve model.

Growth curve modeling can be carried out either as a type of SEM or as a type of MLM. In the SEM framework, GCM is often referred to as *latent trajectory modeling* or as *latent growth modeling* because individual differences in change over time are represented using latent variables. In MLM, individual differences in change over time are instead captured as random effects. Yet, under many conditions, growth curve models fitted using SEM and MLM produce identical results; with longitudinal data, SEM and MLM simply give us two ways to fit what is essentially the same model (see Bauer, 2003; Curran, 2003; MacCallum, Kim, Malarkey, and Kiecolt-Glaser, 1997). In some situations, there are advantages to using SEM rather than MLM, particularly when one wishes to expand the growth curve model to a larger model in which the growth factors become predictors of other endogenous outcomes. In other situations, the MLM approach may be advantageous, such as when the *time* variable takes on different values for different research participants (i.e., the time points at which each participant is observed vary from participant to participant). This chapter presents both the SEM and MLM frameworks for GCM, although there is more emphasis on the SEM perspective.

 Section recap

### Growth Curve Modeling

**Growth curve modeling** (GCM) can be implemented using either SEM or MLM.
 GCM is applicable to any type of longitudinal or repeated-measures data.
 The general purpose of GCM is to model change over time or across repeated measurements.

## Research example for GCM

An example dataset used in Chapters 4 and 5 involved a measure of heavy alcohol-use behaviour observed among adolescents, some of whom were classified as children of alcoholics (COAs), whereas the rest were control participants who did not have an alcoholic parent. Although the examples in these previous chapters used the alcohol-use variable observed at a single time point for each participant, it turns out that the larger study includes longitudinal alcohol-use data. Specifically, the current dataset of $N = 355$ adolescents includes repeated measures of the alcohol-use variable observed approximately annually from 11 to 15 years of age (see Flora et al., 2007, and references therein for further details). Thus, the *time* variable in this example is age measured in units of years.

This longitudinal dataset is available on the text's webpage (https://study.sagepub.com/flora) along with annotated input and output from popular statistical software packages showing how to reproduce the analyses presented in this chapter.

Table 11.1 presents descriptive statistics for the alcohol-use variable as a function of age and parental alcoholism. Several important features of the data are apparent in the table. First, the number of participants observed at each age is not consistent. Longitudinal studies often bear this feature whereby not all study participants are observed at every measurement occasion. A common reason for obtaining such incomplete data is participant **attrition**, meaning that participants drop out of a study before it is completed. In addition to attrition, though, the study for the current example is characterized by a *cohort-sequential design*, also known as an *accelerated longitudinal design*: Specifically, the study design itself has only three measurement occasions, or *waves*, which occurred approximately annually. But because participants had varying ages at each wave of data collection, longitudinal data are available across five different ages. For example, one cohort of participants was observed at ages 11, 12, and 13, whereas another cohort was observed at ages 12, 13, and 14. In studies of human development, it is particularly important for the *time* variable to reflect participant age as closely as possible, and depending on the design of a longitudinal study, measurement wave may not have a one-to-one correspondence with age, as is the case for the current example. Hence, in these situations, it is important to re-code the data so that the *time* variable represents age rather than wave (see Mehta and West, 2000). As we will see, having different participants observed at different time points creates missing data which must be appropriately handled when fitting growth curve models using SEM. But because longitudinal data are organized differently for MLM, this issue is not explicitly manifest as missing data when growth curve models are fitted using MLM.

**Table 11.1** Means and standard deviations of heavy alcohol use by age and parental alcoholism

| Age | Full sample | | | Control participants | | | COA participants | | |
|---|---|---|---|---|---|---|---|---|---|
| | *n* | *M* | *SD* | *n* | *M* | *SD* | *n* | *M* | *SD* |
| 11 | 70 | 0.04 | 0.15 | 32 | 0.07 | 0.20 | 38 | 0.02 | 0.09 |
| 12 | 150 | 0.11 | 0.35 | 69 | 0.08 | 0.23 | 81 | 0.13 | 0.43 |
| 13 | 246 | 0.19 | 0.44 | 112 | 0.09 | 0.24 | 134 | 0.27 | 0.54 |
| 14 | 271 | 0.44 | 0.85 | 125 | 0.17 | 0.34 | 146 | 0.67 | 1.06 |
| 15 | 185 | 0.82 | 1.18 | 83 | 0.36 | 0.58 | 102 | 1.19 | 1.40 |

*Note.* Total $N = 355$. COA = child of alcoholic, $M$ = mean; $SD$ = standard deviation.

Next, Table 11.1 shows that the mean level of alcohol use increases with age for both control and COA participants, although within each age these means are higher for COAs than for controls (except age 11). But although these means indicate that the average level or amount of alcohol use increases over time, they tell us nothing about how the amount of alcohol use of any given individual participant changes over time. We can see from the standard deviations that there is substantial variability in the alcohol-use scores within any one age, and that this variability is greater at older ages, but we still do not know about individual variability in how alcohol use changes over time. That is, some adolescents likely have greater increases in their alcohol use than do others, and it is also possible that some adolescents decrease their alcohol use over time or simply maintain the same level of alcohol use (in particular, maintaining zero alcohol use).

To simplify the presentation of models for linear change over time, the next several sections of this chapter make use of the data only from ages 13, 14, and 15. Later, models for nonlinear change over time are fitted to the full data from ages 11 to 15.

## Individual trajectories

Given the observations made in the previous paragraph, we would like to specify and estimate a statistical model which includes parameters for representing both the average **trajectory** and individual differences, or variability, in trajectories. The term *trajectory* is often used in longitudinal data analysis simply to refer to the pattern of change in outcome variable scores across time.

If one could overcome the challenge of having unbalanced, incomplete longitudinal data mentioned earlier, repeated-measures ANOVA or MANOVA could be used to test mean comparisons and thereby to determine whether a mean trajectory involves any change, but such an analysis would be deficient. First, because they merely involve significance testing, these approaches would not directly provide parameter estimates which characterize the average trajectory.[1] Second, and perhaps more importantly, because repeated-measures ANOVA and MANOVA focus on mean comparisons, their underlying models do not explicitly recognize that there may be substantial, theoretically important individual differences (i.e., intraindividual heterogeneity) in trajectories over time. In fact, these methods involve strict assumptions regarding individual variability; Table 11.1 shows that the standard deviations of the alcohol-use scores vary substantially across age and parental alcoholism, suggesting that any strong assumptions about homogeneity of variance would likely be problematic for these data. In contrast, growth curve models feature parameters which quantify the extent of individual differences in trajectories in addition to parameters which describe the average trajectory. Furthermore, it is straightforward to expand growth curve models to include variables which explain or predict individual differences in change over time. For example, later in this chapter, parental alcoholism will be used both to predict the level of heavy alcohol use at a given age and to predict changes in alcohol use across age.

Figure 11.1 gives separate scatterplots for the longitudinal data of each of $n = 6$ adolescents drawn from the larger sample of the alcohol-use example; each scatterplot has the main outcome variable, heavy alcohol use, on the $y$-axis, whereas the *time* variable, age, is on the $x$-axis. To aid visualization of the individual trajectory for each adolescent, the scatterplots have been enhanced with a linear regression line estimated using ordinary least squares (OLS);[2] each line was estimated separately using the data from the six adolescents as six separate datasets. In the figure, each participant has an increasing level of alcohol use from age 13 to 15, except the first participant (in the top left panel) who shows a slight decrease in alcohol use. But even among those with increasing alcohol use, the extent of the increase varies substantially from one adolescent to the next, as indicated by the varying magnitude of the slopes of the individual regression lines. Furthermore, there is also some variability in the starting point, or intercept, of the individual linear trajectories; that is, the level of alcohol use observed at age 13 varies among these six adolescents.

---

[1]So-called 'trend analysis' is often used as a follow-up to repeated-measures ANOVA to test whether a mean trajectory is linear, quadratic, or follows some other polynomial form. But this analysis also does not explicitly produce parameter estimates which represent the mean trajectory.

[2]The functional form of these individual trajectories must be linear because there are only three data points for a given participant; an individually estimated trajectory with a more complex form (e.g., quadratic) would be underidentified.

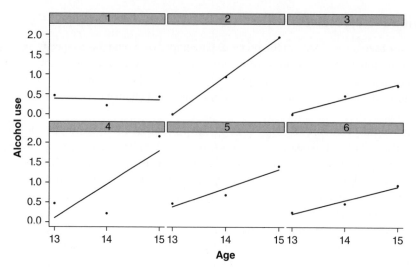

**Figure 11.1**   Separate scatterplots of alcohol use by age for each of n = 6 participants with individual linear trajectories fitted with OLS

Once we specify a growth curve model using SEM or MLM, we will not estimate a separate trajectory for each of the $N = 355$ adolescents in the entire sample, as was done to create Figure 11.1 with just $n = 6$ participants. Instead, the models will contain parameters which summarize the distribution of the individual trajectories. Specifically, models with a linear functional form of change over time will include parameters representing the mean trajectory as well as the variance of the individual intercepts and variance of the individual slopes.

 Section recap

### Individual trajectories

Traditional ANOVA and MANOVA approaches to analysis of repeated-measures or longitudinal data focus on testing mean differences, implicitly assuming that each individual in the population follows the same trajectory over time.

Instead, modern GCM approaches explicitly recognize that there is likely to be substantial variability across individual trajectories, including parameters to represent the mean trajectory as well as individual differences in trajectories.

## GCM: Data organization

Although SEM and MLM provide two approaches for representing growth curve models in general, the way that repeated-measures or longitudinal data are organized differs across these approaches. These different data organizations lead to *time* being treated as a categorical variable in the context of SEM but as a continuous variable with MLM. Fortunately, several prominent statistical software packages have built-in functions for reorganizing longitudinal data, so there is no need for users to program their own function or, worse yet, to re-enter the data manually.

In particular, for the SEM implementation of GCM, the data need to be organized in a so-called **wide format**, which is also referred to as a *person-level format* (Singer and Willett, 2003), in which each person (or other unit of observation) has a single row of data and the multiple observations of the outcome variable over time are represented as separate, multiple outcome variables. This format is presented in Table 11.2 for a subset of five cases from the adolescent alcohol-use example dataset. As discussed earlier, these data are taken from a study with a cohort-sequential design, which creates missing values that are *missing by design*. For instance, in Table 11.2, we see that the first participant's alcohol use was observed at ages 11, 12, and 13 but not at age 14 or 15, whereas the second participant was observed at ages 12, 13, and 14 but not at age 11 or 15.

**Table 11.2**  Wide-format longitudinal alcohol use data of $n = 5$ adolescents

| Participant ID | alc11 | alc12 | alc13 | alc14 | alc15 | COA | gender |
|---|---|---|---|---|---|---|---|
| 1 | 0.00 | 0.00 | 0.47 | – | – | 1 | 0 |
| 2 | – | 0.00 | 0.97 | 2.38 | – | 1 | 1 |
| 3 | – | – | 1.16 | 0.47 | 1.63 | 1 | 1 |
| 4 | – | 0.25 | 0.22 | 1.69 | – | 0 | 0 |
| 5 | – | – | 0.00 | 0.00 | 0.97 | 0 | 1 |

Note. alc11 = age 11 alcohol use; alc12 = age 12 alcohol use; alc13 = age 13 alcohol use; alc14 = age 14 alcohol use; alc15 = age 15 alcohol use; COA = child of alcoholic; COA = 1 for participants with an alcoholic parent, COA = 0 for control participants; gender = 1 for male, gender = 0 for female.

For the MLM implementation of GCM, the data instead need to be organized in a **long format**, which is also known as a *person-period format* (Singer and Willett, 2003). In this format, each person has multiple rows of data, one for each measurement occasion, and the multiple observations of the outcome variable are represented as a single variable along with a separate *time* variable to distinguish among them. Table 11.3 presents the same data as Table 11.2 but organized in long format. Now, we see that there is a single alcohol-use variable, but the age variable represents *time* to distinguish the alcohol-use observations taken from the same adolescent. Furthermore, whereas the cohort-sequential design led to missing data for the wide-format dataset, the long-format dataset does not explicitly represent this feature as missing data. Instead, if a given participant is not observed at a particular age, then the long format simply does not include a row of data for that age. For example, the first participant (ID = 1) was observed at ages 11, 12, and 13, and so there is a row of data for each of those measurement occasions, but this participant was not observed at age 14 or 15, and so there is no need to include rows for those potential but unobserved measurement occasions. Linking the current use of MLM with the logic of MLM presented in Chapter 6, the repeated measures of the longitudinally observed alcohol-use variable are nested within different participants, so the different measurement occasions are the Level 1 units of observation, whereas the separate adolescent research participants are the Level 2 units of observation.

Finally, notice how the COA and gender variables are represented in the long-format data-set. Although these variables are not longitudinally observed (i.e., the COA and gender status of each participant only need to be observed once because these values do not change over time), it is still necessary to repeat the values of these variables in each row corresponding to the same participant. For example, the fact that the first participant (ID = 1) is female is reflected in all three rows of data corresponding to ID = 1. In the current context, COA and gender are examples of **time-invariant covariates**, meaning that they are covariates or predictors which maintain the same value over time for each participant. Many analyses of longitudinal data also incorporate **time-varying covariates**, which do take on different values at different measurement occasions. As with the primary outcome variable, time-varying covariates also need to be organized according to either a long or a wide format, depending on whether MLM or SEM is being used to model the data.

**Table 11.3**  Long-format longitudinal alcohol use data of $n = 5$ adolescents

| Participant ID | alc | age | COA | gender |
|---|---|---|---|---|
| 1 | 0.00 | 11 | 1 | 0 |
| 1 | 0.00 | 12 | 1 | 0 |
| 1 | 0.47 | 13 | 1 | 0 |
| 2 | 0.00 | 12 | 1 | 1 |
| 2 | 0.97 | 13 | 1 | 1 |
| 2 | 2.38 | 14 | 1 | 1 |
| 3 | 1.16 | 13 | 1 | 1 |
| 3 | 0.47 | 14 | 1 | 1 |
| 3 | 1.63 | 15 | 1 | 1 |
| 4 | 0.25 | 12 | 0 | 0 |
| 4 | 0.22 | 13 | 0 | 0 |
| 4 | 1.69 | 14 | 0 | 0 |
| 5 | 0.00 | 13 | 0 | 1 |
| 5 | 0.00 | 14 | 0 | 1 |
| 5 | 0.97 | 15 | 0 | 1 |

Note. alc = alcohol use; COA = child of alcoholic; COA = 1 for participants with an alcoholic parent, COA = 0 for control participants; gender = 0 for female, gender = 1 for male.

 Section recap

### Data organization for growth curve models

Although SEM and MLM can both be used for growth curve modeling, the data organization differs across these frameworks.

For GCM using SEM, the data need to be in a **wide format** in which each individual has only one row of data, with multiple variables used to represent the distinct longitudinal or repeated measurements observed for that individual.

For GCM using MLM, the data need to be in a **long format** in which each individual has multiple rows of data, with one row for each longitudinal or repeated measurement. Additionally, there must be an identification (ID) variable to distinguish individuals (i.e., the units of observation) as well as a *time* variable.

## GROWTH CURVE MODELS FOR LINEAR CHANGE

### Unconditional linear growth model: SEM specification

We begin by examining unconditional growth curve models for linear change over time, meaning that the model is specified to represent individual trajectories with a linear functional form, but the trajectories are not conditioned upon any predictor variables or covariates; that is, the model does not include any variables to predict or explain individual differences in the pattern of change over time for the longitudinally observed outcome variable.

As described earlier, a major feature of a growth curve model, whether implemented with SEM or MLM, is that the model explicitly represents individual trajectories in addition to mean values. Thus, an equation with SEM notation to represent a within-person, individual linear growth trajectory is

$$Y_{ti} = \eta_{0i} + \lambda_t \eta_{1i} + \varepsilon_{ti}, \tag{11.1}$$

where $Y_{ti}$ represents the value of the observed outcome variable for individual $i$ at *time* $= t$, $\eta_{0i}$ is the value of the **latent intercept factor** for individual $i$, $\eta_{1i}$ is the value of the **latent slope factor** for individual $i$, $\lambda_t$ is a factor loading specific to *time* $= t$, and $\varepsilon_{ti}$ is the prediction error at *time* $= t$ for individual $i$. Equation 11.1 resembles a simple linear regression equation in that the intercept factor $\eta_0$ gives the predicted value of $Y$ when $\lambda_t$ equals 0 and the slope factor $\eta_1$ gives the predicted difference in $Y$ when $\lambda_t$ increases by 1. A crucial difference, though, between Equation 11.1 and a simple linear regression equation (cf. Equation 1.5) is that here, both the intercept factor and the slope factor are indexed by the subscript $i$, indicating that there is a different value of $\eta_0$ and $\eta_1$ for each individual in the population. In this way, the model allows each individual to follow her own linear growth trajectory.

Additionally, Equation 11.1 indicates that there is a separate regression equation for each time point or measurement occasion $t$. These separate equations can be collected into a single matrix equation

$$\mathbf{Y}_i = \mathbf{\Lambda}\mathbf{\eta}_i + \mathbf{\varepsilon}_i, \tag{11.2}$$

where $\mathbf{Y}_i$ is a $T \times 1$ vector of scores for individual $i$ on the repeated outcome variable $Y$, $\mathbf{\Lambda}$ is a $T \times 2$ factor loading matrix, $\mathbf{\eta}_i$ is the $2 \times 1$ vector of scores on the latent growth factors (i.e., the intercept and slope factors) for individual $i$, and $\mathbf{\varepsilon}_i$ is a $T \times 1$ vector of error or disturbance terms capturing the deviations of observed $Y$ scores from model-implied $Y$ scores for individual $i$.

A crucial feature of this model is that in each element the factor loading matrix $\mathbf{\Lambda}$ is fixed, or constrained, to specify linear change over time across the $T$ repeated measures of $Y$. First, in Equation 11.1, there is an implicit coefficient of 1 for the intercept factor, such that Equation 11.1 can be equivalently written as

$$Y_{ti} = 1\eta_{0i} + \lambda_t \eta_{1i} + \varepsilon_{ti}.$$

Therefore, each element of the first column of $\Lambda$ is fixed to equal 1 so that $\eta_0$ does in fact represent the individual trajectory intercept. Next, the elements of the second column of $\Lambda$ correspond to the coefficients of $\eta_1$ (i.e., the $\lambda_t$ term in Equation 11.1) and are fixed to equal $t - 1$ for all $T$ rows (corresponding to the different measurement occasions of $Y$) so that $\eta_1$ represents the individual trajectory linear slope (assuming that the repeated measures of $Y$ are observed at equally spaced time points; that is, consecutive measurement occasions are consistently separated by the same amount of time, e.g., annual measurement occasions).[3] In other words, when the time points are equally spaced, the factor loadings for the slope latent variable are constrained to be equally spaced values (typically integer values).

To demonstrate with the adolescent alcohol-use example, a growth curve model for linear change across ages 13, 14, and 15 can be specified with

$$
\begin{bmatrix} Y_1 \\ Y_2 \\ Y_3 \end{bmatrix} = \begin{bmatrix} 1 & 0 \\ 1 & 1 \\ 1 & 2 \end{bmatrix} \begin{bmatrix} \eta_0 \\ \eta_1 \end{bmatrix} + \begin{bmatrix} \varepsilon_0 \\ \varepsilon_1 \\ \varepsilon_2 \end{bmatrix}, \tag{11.3}
$$

where $Y_1$ is the age 13 alcohol-use variable, $Y_2$ is the age 14 alcohol-use variable, and $Y_3$ is the age 15 alcohol-use variable. As stated earlier, the intercept factor $\eta_0$ represents the predicted value of $Y$ when $\lambda_t$ equals 0. Thus, with the current application, the intercept factor represents the predicted amount of alcohol use at age 13 (i.e., the initial measurement occasion for this example), which is made evident if we write out the scalar equation for $Y_1$:

$$
Y_{1i} = 1\eta_{0i} + 0\eta_{1i} + \varepsilon_{0i},
$$

which of course reduces to

$$
Y_{1i} = \eta_{0i} + \varepsilon_{0i},
$$

and so the predicted value of alcohol use at age 13 for individual $i$ is $\hat{Y}_{1i} = \eta_{0i}$. Next, the scalar equation for $Y_2$, the age 14 alcohol-use variable, is

$$
Y_{2i} = 1\eta_{0i} + 1\eta_{1i} + \varepsilon_{1i},
$$

and the scalar equation for $Y_3$, the age 15 alcohol-use variable, is

$$
Y_{3i} = 1\eta_{0i} + 2\eta_{1i} + \varepsilon_{2i}.
$$

From these scalar equations, one can adapt the usual interpretation of a regression slope parameter to see that $\eta_1$ represents the predicted linear change in alcohol use per one-year increase in age.

Finally, each $\varepsilon_{ti}$ in Equation 11.1 is a time-specific and individual-specific error term capturing the deviation of an observed value on the outcome $Y_t$ from the predicted value falling on the model-implied trajectory. Referring back to Figure 11.1, these error terms are analogous to the residuals from each person's linear trajectory. In the figure, the second individual (in the top middle panel) would have small values of $\varepsilon$ at all three time points

---

[3]If the time points are unequally spaced, the fixed elements of $\Lambda$ can be adjusted accordingly.

(ages 13, 14, and 15); in contrast, the fourth individual (in the bottom-left panel) would have larger values of $\varepsilon$, especially at age 14. The covariance matrix for $\varepsilon_i$ has dimension $T \times T$ and is typically specified to be a diagonal matrix, implying that these individual-level error terms are assumed uncorrelated across time, but it is possible to free the off-diagonal covariance parameters. Such error covariance parameters are often nonzero in implementations of GCM (reflecting the idea that the *autocorrelation* among repeated measures is not completely explained by the growth factors), but nonzero error covariances (i.e., residual covariances) often imply that the functional form of change over time is misspecified (e.g., a model for linear growth is incorrectly implemented to represent nonlinear change over time). In the current three time-point example, we might therefore specify $\Theta_\varepsilon$ as

$$\Theta_\varepsilon = \begin{bmatrix} \mathrm{VAR}(\varepsilon_1) = \sigma_1^2 & & \\ 0 & \mathrm{VAR}(\varepsilon_2) = \sigma_2^2 & \\ 0 & 0 & \mathrm{VAR}(\varepsilon_3) = \sigma_3^2 \end{bmatrix}.$$

With MLM, it is also common to specify equality constraints for the diagonal elements of $\Theta_\varepsilon$ (e.g., $\sigma_1^2 = \sigma_2^2 = \sigma_3^2$), a type of homogeneity of variance assumption, but in the SEM implementation of GCM, these parameters are more typically allowed to differ freely.

As mentioned earlier, the goal of GCM is not to estimate a separate trajectory for each and every individual in a sample but to summarize the distribution of individual trajectories using parameters representing their central tendency and variability. In particular, a matrix equation for $\eta_0$ and $\eta_1$ is

$$\eta_i = \mu_\eta + \zeta_i, \tag{11.4}$$

which, for the current model for linear change, corresponds to

$$\begin{bmatrix} \eta_0 \\ \eta_1 \end{bmatrix} = \begin{bmatrix} \mu_0 \\ \mu_1 \end{bmatrix} + \begin{bmatrix} \zeta_0 \\ \zeta_1 \end{bmatrix},$$

where $\mu_0$ is the population mean of $\eta_{0i}$, that is, the mean of the individual trajectory intercepts, and $\mu_1$ is the population mean of $\eta_{1i}$, that is, the mean of the individual linear slopes. Therefore, $\zeta_{0i}$ is an error term representing the deviation of an individual's latent intercept value from the mean intercept and $\zeta_{1i}$ is an error term representing the deviation of an individual's latent slope from the mean slope. Next, the covariance matrix for $\zeta_i$ is

$$\Psi = \begin{bmatrix} \mathrm{VAR}(\zeta_0) = \psi_{11} & \\ \mathrm{COV}(\zeta_0, \zeta_1) = \psi_{21} & \mathrm{VAR}(\zeta_1) = \psi_{22} \end{bmatrix},$$

and so $\psi_{11}$, the variance of $\zeta_{0i}$, captures the overall extent of individual deviations from the mean intercept, whereas $\psi_{22}$, the variance of $\zeta_{1i}$, captures the extent of individual deviations from the mean slope. In other words, because the model does not (yet) include any predictors of the latent growth factors, $\psi_{11}$ and $\psi_{22}$ describe the population variance of the latent intercept factor $(\eta_{0i})$ and the population variance of the latent slope factor $(\eta_{1i})$, respectively. Finally, $\psi_{21}$ is the population covariance between $\zeta_{0i}$ and $\zeta_{1i}$; if $\psi_{21}$ is positive, then individuals with higher intercepts tend to have higher slopes and if $\psi_{21}$ is negative, then individuals with higher intercepts tend to have lower slopes.

Figure 11.2 presents a path diagram for a linear growth curve model across three repeated measures of an outcome variable $Y_t$. Astute readers have likely already noticed that this model bears a striking resemblance to the general CFA model described in Chapter 10 in that both models involve regressing a set of observed variables ($\mathbf{Y}$) on a set of latent variables ($\eta$). But there are two critical differences between the typical CFA model and the current growth curve model: First, the growth curve model explicitly includes a **mean structure**, which is represented using the triangle in Figure 11.2. In path diagramming conventions, the triangle with a value of 1 inside it is used to represent a constant (rather than an observed or latent variable) equal to 1; the latent variable means $\mathbf{\mu}_\eta$ in Equation 11.4 are the coefficients of this constant term. That is, Equation 11.4 can be expressed as

$$\eta_i = 1 \times \mathbf{\mu}_\eta + \zeta_i.$$

CFA models, on the other hand, are typically specified without explicitly incorporating the means of the latent variables (they are implicitly constrained to equal 0). Second, the factor loadings in $\Lambda$ are highly constrained in GCM to establish the functional form of

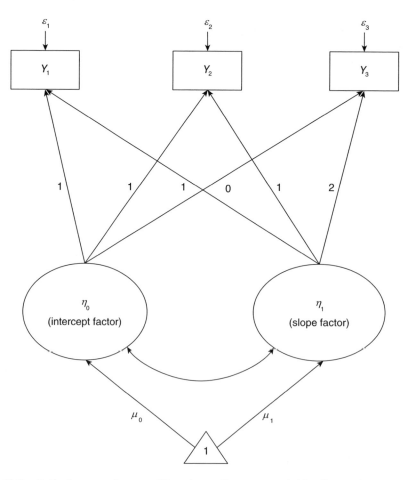

**Figure 11.2** Path diagram of unconditional growth curve model for linear change

change (i.e., simple linear change at this point of the chapter) across the repeated outcome variables in **Y** (see Equation 11.3; also the fixed factor loadings are given in Figure 11.2), whereas in CFA, the factor loading matrix contains a combination of freely estimated elements and elements fixed to 0 (as explained in Chapter 10).

## Section recap

### SEM specification of the unconditional linear growth curve model

The within-person, individual linear growth trajectory can be written as

$$Y_{ti} = \eta_{0i} + \lambda_t \eta_{1i} + \varepsilon_{ti},$$

where

$Y_{ti}$ represents the value of the observed outcome variable for individual $i$ at $time = t$
$\eta_{0i}$ is the value of the **latent intercept factor** for individual $i$
$\eta_{1i}$ is the value of the **latent slope factor** for individual $i$
$\lambda_t$ is a factor loading specific to $time = t$
$\varepsilon_{ti}$ is the prediction error at $time = t$ for individual $i$
A matrix equation for the individual linear growth trajectory is

$$\mathbf{Y}_i = \mathbf{\Lambda}\mathbf{\eta}_i + \mathbf{\varepsilon}_i,$$

where

$\mathbf{Y}_i$ is a $T \times 1$ vector of scores for individual $i$ on the repeated outcome variable $Y$
$\mathbf{\Lambda}$ is a $T \times 2$ factor loading matrix
$\mathbf{\eta}_i$ is the $2 \times 1$ vector of scores on the latent intercept and slope factors for individual $i$
$\mathbf{\varepsilon}_i$ is a $T \times 1$ vector of error or disturbance terms
The elements of the factor loading matrix $\mathbf{\Lambda}$ are constrained to establish $\eta_0$ and $\eta_1$ as the linear trajectory intercept and slope, respectively, such that all factor loadings for $\eta_0$ equal 1 and the factor loadings for $\eta_1$ equal $t - 1$ for all $T$ rows.

The unconditional linear growth curve model consists of parameters to summarize the population distribution of individual trajectories:

$\mathbf{\mu}_\eta$ is the vector of latent variable means consisting of $\mu_0$, the population mean of the individual intercepts, and $\mu_1$, the population mean of the individual slopes.

$\mathbf{\Psi}$ is the covariance matrix for the individual deviations from the latent variable means, such that $\psi_{11}$ and $\psi_{22}$ are the variance of the individual intercepts and the individual slopes, respectively, whereas $\psi_{21}$ is the covariance between individual intercepts and slopes.

## Unconditional linear growth model: Model identification

The basic concepts of model identification detailed in Chapters 9 and 10 also apply to the current use of SEM for implementing GCM. In particular, the $t$-rule of identification that the model degrees of freedom must be greater than or equal to 0 is still pertinent. In the current context, though, because growth curve models involve mean structure in addition to covariance structure, the *t*-rule is slightly more complex.

Specifically, although all factor loadings of the linear growth curve model are fixed parameters, the latent variable means, $\mu_0$ and $\mu_1$, are now free parameters to be estimated. Therefore, for the example growth curve model with three observed variables in **Y**, there are eight free parameters to estimate: the two latent variables means ($\mu_0$ and $\mu_1$), the latent variable variances and covariance (i.e., the three elements of **Ψ**), and the variances of the within-time error terms (i.e., the three diagonal elements of $\mathbf{\Theta}_\varepsilon$). Because there are three observed variables in **Y**, the observed covariance matrix has $(3 \times 4) / 2 = 6$ unique elements, but because the model also contains a mean structure, the means of the observed variables are also used to estimate the model. Therefore, the model degrees of freedom is calculated as (number of observed variances and nonredundant covariances + number of observed variable means) – (number of free parameters to estimate), which for the current linear model is $(6 + 3) – (8) = 1$ degree of freedom.

It is straightforward to see that if **Y** contains only two repeated-measure variables, then the model for linear change becomes underidentified unless other parameter constraints are applied (e.g., fixing the variance of the latent slope factor to zero, $\psi_{22} = 0$). In contrast, if the number of time points increases such that the number of observed variables in **Y** increases, then the model degrees of freedom increases. Furthermore, models for nonlinear change over time involve additional free parameters, which in turn requires additional observed variables in **Y** for model identification.

 **Section recap**

### Identification of the unconditional linear growth curve model

The same principles of model identification that were described for other types of structural equation models apply to growth curve models.

But because growth curve models involve mean structure in addition to covariance structure, the model degrees of freedom is also a function of the number of observed variable means and the number of growth factor means.

## Unconditional linear growth model: SEM estimation

As with the structural equation models described in Chapters 9 and 10, growth curve models are most often estimated using maximum likelihood (ML) according to the ML fitting function, which again is minimized so that the match between parameter estimates and sample data is optimized. But because the model now incorporates mean structure, the ML fitting function for GCM is slightly more complex than that given in Chapter 9 (cf. Equation 9.13):

$$F_{ML} = \ln|\widehat{\boldsymbol{\Sigma}}_\theta| + \text{tr}(\mathbf{S}\ \widehat{\boldsymbol{\Sigma}}_\theta{}^{-1}) - \ln|\mathbf{S}| - T - (\bar{\mathbf{Y}} - \hat{\boldsymbol{\mu}}_\theta)'\ \widehat{\boldsymbol{\Sigma}}_\theta{}^{-1}(\bar{\mathbf{Y}} - \hat{\boldsymbol{\mu}}_\theta), \tag{11.5}$$

where $\widehat{\Sigma}_\theta$ is the fitted model-implied covariance matrix, $S$ is the sample covariance matrix among the observed variables in $Y$, $T$ is the total number of observed variables (e.g., $T = 3$ repeated measures of $Y$ in our current linear growth curve model example), $\overline{Y}$ is the vector of means for the observed variables in $Y$, and $\hat{\mu}_\theta$ is the fitted model-implied vector of population means for the observed variables (not to be confused with the vector of latent variable means in Equation 11.4).

As in Chapter 10 for CFA, the model-implied covariance structure is

$$\Sigma_\theta = \Lambda\Psi\Lambda' + \Theta_\varepsilon,$$

only now with $\Lambda$, $\Psi$, and $\Theta_\varepsilon$ specified according to a growth curve model rather than according to CFA. The model-implied mean structure is

$$\mu_\theta = \Lambda\mu_\eta,$$

where $\mu_\eta$ is the vector of latent variable means given earlier in Equation 11.4.

The ML fitting function in Equation 11.5 is applicable only to cases with complete data; that is, the sample covariance matrix $S$ and mean vector $\overline{Y}$ are calculated using data only from individual cases with nonmissing observations for all $T$ measurement occasions of the longitudinal outcome $Y_t$. As mentioned earlier, missing data are extremely common in longitudinal research, and missingness is a prominent feature of the adolescent alcohol-use example data presented earlier. Given the presence of incomplete data, that is, cases with missing values, a viable ML estimation procedure is known as **direct ML** or *full-information ML*. This approach shares the desirable asymptotic properties (i.e., unbiasedness, consistency, and efficiency) of the complete-data ML method presented in earlier chapters.

Direct ML works on the principle that a model likelihood function is calculated for each case using only those variables that are observed (i.e., nonmissing) for that case. Specifically, with direct ML, a distinct *log-likelihood* value (ln L) is calculated for each case $i$ in the sample:

$$\ln L_{\theta i} = K_i - 1/2 \ln|\widehat{\Sigma}_\theta| - 1/2 (Y_i - \hat{\mu}_{\theta i})' \hat{\Sigma}_{\theta i}^{-1} (Y_i - \hat{\mu}_{\theta i}),$$

where $K_i$ is a constant unrelated to the parameters $\theta$, $Y_i$ is the vector of observed variable values for case $i$, and $\hat{\Sigma}_{\theta i}$ and $\hat{\mu}_{\theta i}$ are the subset of model-implied covariances and means corresponding to the nonmissing variables observed for case $i$. Next, these individual, case-specific log-likelihoods are summed to compute the total log-likelihood value for all cases:

$$\ln L_\theta = \sum_{i=1}^{N} \ln L_{\theta i}.$$

In practice, a computerized algorithm is used to choose the parameter estimates that optimize the match between the observed data with the individual-level model-implied means and covariances, which in turn maximizes the latter log-likelihood function for the full sample. It turns out that when all cases have complete data, this direct ML log-likelihood function is equivalent to the ML discrepancy function of Equation 11.5. Furthermore, the direct ML approach also may be used to estimate any structural equation model from a dataset with missing values, not just growth curve models.

The Satorra and Bentler (1988, 1994) scaled $\chi^2$ statistic described in Chapter 10 does not perform as well for calculating model fit statistics which are robust to non-normality when structural equation models are estimated using direct ML to account for missing data. Instead, a similar test statistic developed by Yuan and Bentler (2000), specifically their T2* statistic, is generally recommended for this scenario (but see Savalei, 2010, and Savalei and Falk, 2014, for further details and potentially superior approaches for testing model fit when data are characterized by both non-normality and missingness).

 Section recap

### Estimation of the unconditional linear growth curve model with SEM

Like other types of structural equation models, growth curve models are most commonly estimated using maximum likelihood (ML).

But because mean structure is a critical aspect of GCM, the ML fitting function simultaneously optimizes the match both between the observed covariance matrix and the model-implied covariance matrix and between the observed means and the model-implied means.

In the context of incomplete cases (i.e., missing data), **direct ML**, also known as *full-information ML*, can be used to estimate the model using all data from all cases, regardless of the pattern of missingness.

## Unconditional linear growth curve model: SEM results for alcohol-use example

The unconditional model for linear growth, estimated using direct ML to incorporate incomplete cases, fits the alcohol-use data from ages 13 to 15 adequately according to robust model fit statistics calculated based on the Yuan-Bentler T2* statistic,[4] with $\chi^2(1) = 3.28$, $p < .001$, robust root-mean-square error of approximation (RMSEA$_{robust}$) = .078, robust comparative fit index (CFI$_{robust}$) = .98, robust Tucker-Lewis index (TLI$_{robust}$) = .95, and standardized root-mean-square residual (SRMR) = .025.

The parameter estimates for this model are in Table 11.4. First, the estimated mean of the latent intercept factor is $\hat{\mu}_0 = 0.20$, which represents the mean level of alcohol use at the initial measurement occasion, which is age 13. Next, the estimated mean of the latent slope factor $\hat{\mu}_1 = 0.27$ represents the average amount that the alcohol-use variable is predicted to increase per year. Importantly, though, there is nonzero variance in the individual slopes with $\hat{\psi}_{22} = 0.18$; it is informative to translate this variance estimate to a standard deviation statistic, $\sqrt{\hat{\psi}_{22}} = 0.42$, which seems substantial given that the mean of the individual

---

[4]The Yuan-Bentler T2* statistic is available in several SEM software packages, particularly EQS, Mplus, and the lavaan package in R.

trajectory slopes is 0.27.[5] The covariance between the individual intercepts and slopes, $\hat{\psi}_{21} = 0.02$, is nonsignificant ($p = .81$) and corresponds to a weak correlation, $r = .12$, which indicates that there is little association between the participants' level of alcohol use at age 13 and their subsequent linear increase in alcohol use.[6]

Finally, Table 11.4 also indicates that the separate time-specific residual variances are strongly discrepant across the three measurement occasions (i.e., $\sigma_1^2 = 0.01$, $\sigma_2^2 = 0.30$, $\sigma_3^2 = 0.44$). In particular, the unexplained variance of age 13 alcohol use is much smaller than the residual variances of the age 14 and age 15 alcohol-use variables. Thus, for the current example, it seems that it would be incorrect (i.e., a source of model misspecification) to restrict these diagonal elements of $\Theta_\varepsilon$ to be equal over time, as is often done in applications of GCM (particularly using the MLM approach).

**Table 11.4**   Results for unconditional linear growth curve model of alcohol use from ages 13 to 15

| Parameter | Estimate | Robust SE | Z | p |
|---|---|---|---|---|
| $\mu_0$ (latent intercept mean) | 0.202 | 0.030 | 6.65 | <.001 |
| $\mu_1$ (latent slope mean) | 0.271 | 0.039 | 7.02 | <.001 |
| $\psi_{11}$ (latent intercept variance) | 0.205 | 0.140 | 1.46 | .143 |
| $\psi_{22}$ (latent slope variance) | 0.175 | 0.100 | 1.75 | .080 |
| $\psi_{21}$ (intercept, slope covariance) | 0.022 | 0.092 | 0.24 | .813 |
| $\sigma_1^2$ (age 13 error variance) | 0.007 | 0.133 | 0.05 | .958 |
| $\sigma_2^2$ (age 14 error variance) | 0.297 | 0.096 | 3.09 | .002 |
| $\sigma_3^2$ (age 15 error variance) | 0.435 | 0.267 | 1.63 | .103 |

Note. $N = 352$. See Footnote 5 for comments regarding $p$ values for the variance estimates.

## Unconditional linear growth model: MLM specification

Looking at the long-format data structure in Table 11.3 can facilitate understanding of the MLM approach to representing longitudinal or repeated-measures data. In particular, this data format shows that certain observations of the longitudinal outcome variable are non-independent in the sense that there are repeated observations nested or clustered within

[5]This conclusion is reached despite that the Wald test of this variance estimate is nonsignificant, $Z = 1.75$, $p = .08$. Wald tests of variance estimates are problematic because the null hypothesis that a population variance equals zero lies on the boundary of the parameter space, which in this case means that the parameter cannot be less than the null hypothesis value (variances cannot be negative). Some authors (e.g., Snijders and Bosker, 2012) have suggested that the $p$ value from a Wald test of a variance estimate should be divided in half, implying a one-tailed test, because the alternative hypothesis should be that the variance parameter is greater than zero. In the current example, doing so does in fact produce a significant test of the latent slope variance, $p = .04$.

[6]This correlation is easily obtained from SEM software output as the completely standardized estimate of the covariance between intercepts and slopes (i.e., the standardized covariance between $\eta_0$ and $\eta_1$).

the same individual person. For instance, in Table 11.3, the first three rows of data all come from the same research participant (ID = 1), the next three rows come from the second participant (ID = 2), and so on. In Chapter 6, MLMs were presented for cross-sectional data in which the data for different people (e.g., individual students) were nonindependent because the participants were clustered within larger groups (e.g., university classes). Here, with longitudinal data, MLMs are applicable because the data for different observations taken at different measurement occasions are clustered within individual people. In other words, in the cross-sectional applications emphasized in Chapter 6, individual people are the Level 1 units of observation and different groups of people formed the Level 2 units. But in the current longitudinal data context, the separate repeated measurements are the Level 1 units of observation and the individual people themselves are the Level 2 units.[7]

As just presented, in the SEM approach to specifying a growth curve model for unconditional linear growth, or change over time, intercept and slope latent variables are used to capture individual variability in linear trajectories. These latent variables represent the idea that each individual may have her or his own starting point (i.e., a value for the intercept latent variable, $\eta_0$) and linear change over time (i.e., a value for the slope latent variable, $\eta_1$). The analogous (indeed, equivalent) model from the MLM perspective is a random-slopes model. Adapting the notation used in Chapter 6, the Level 1 equation of an unconditional model for linear growth is

$$Y_{ti} = \beta_{0i} + \beta_{1i}X_t + \varepsilon_{ti} \text{ (Level 1)}, \tag{11.6}$$

where $Y_{ti}$ is the value of the outcome variable observed at measurement occasion $t$ for individual $i$ and $X_t$ is the value of the *time* variable at measurement occasion $t$. Furthermore, $\beta_{0i}$ is the random intercept representing the predicted level of the outcome variable for individual $i$ when the *time* variable $X_t$ equals 0; in other words, $\beta_{0i}$ is the intercept of the individual trajectory for person $i$. Next, $\beta_{1i}$ is the random slope giving the predicted change of the outcome variable for a one-unit increase in the *time* variable $X_t$; that is, $\beta_{1i}$ is the slope of the individual trajectory for person $i$. Finally, $\varepsilon_{ti}$ is the error term giving the deviation of the model-implied value of $Y$ at time $t$ for person $i$ from that person's observed value at time $t$. Notice also that this Level 1 equation is the same as Equation 11.1 for the specification of the model using SEM, only with different notation.

At this point, we assume that the *time* variable $X_t$ is defined such that $X_t = 0$ at the first (or initial) measurement occasion. Consequently, the intercept $\beta_{0i}$ represents the **initial status** of individual $i$, that is, the predicted level of the outcome variable for individual $i$ at the first measurement occasion. In the current example in which we wish to specify a growth curve model for adolescent alcohol use from ages 13 to 15, this specification implies that $X_t$ is set equal to 0 for observations made at age 13. Next, for the slope $\beta_{1i}$ to represent the predicted change in alcohol use per one-year increase in age, $X_t = 1$ for age 14

---

[7]Of course, in longitudinal studies, it is also possible for individuals to be clustered within larger units, which then leads to three (or more) levels of the data hierarchy. For example, some waves of the larger study from which the current adolescent alcohol use data are drawn also include data from the original adolescent participants' siblings. This larger longitudinal data structure therefore includes repeated observations nested within participants who are then nested within families.

observations and $X_t = 2$ for age 15 observations. More generally, then, the *time* variable is defined as $X_t =$ (years of age) – 13. In other words, *time* is centered at age 13.

The Level 2 equation for the random intercepts of the unconditional linear model is

$$\beta_{0i} = \gamma_{00} + \delta_{0i} \text{ (Level 2a)}, \tag{11.7}$$

where $\gamma_{00}$ is the mean of the intercepts of the individual trajectories and $\delta_{0i}$ is the difference between the individual intercept for person $i$ and the mean intercept. Next, the Level 2 equation for the individual slopes is

$$\beta_{1i} = \gamma_{10} + \delta_{1i} \text{ (Level 2b)}, \tag{11.8}$$

where $\gamma_{10}$ is the mean of the slopes of the individual trajectories and $\delta_{1i}$ is the difference between the individual slope for person $i$ and the mean slope. Equations 11.7 and 11.8, taken together, are essentially the same as Equation 11.4 from the SEM framework; these equations express the intercept and slope of the linear trajectory of individual $i$ as a function of a mean plus that individual's deviation from the mean.

In addition to the fixed-effect parameters, $\gamma_{00}$ and $\gamma_{10}$, which describe the mean linear trajectory, the model also includes the random-effect variance parameters, $\text{VAR}(\delta_{0i}) = \tau_{00}^2$ and $\text{VAR}(\delta_{1i}) = \tau_{11}^2$, which describe the extent of the individual variability around the mean intercept and slope, respectively. Furthermore, the parameter $\tau_{01}$ represents the covariance between the individual intercepts and slopes. Finally, the Level 1 variance parameter $\text{VAR}(\varepsilon_{ti}) = \sigma^2$ again represents the variance across individuals within a given time-point or measurement occasion. As stated earlier, it is conventional in MLM to assume that this parameter $\sigma^2$ remains constant across all time points, but it is possible to relax this assumption and estimate a model such that $\text{VAR}(\varepsilon_{ti}) = \sigma_t^2$ varies across time points. Finally, it is also possible to estimate covariances among the $\varepsilon_{ti}$ terms using MLM, as is the case with SEM.

At this point, it should be clear that the parameters of the SEM unconditional linear growth curve model directly map onto the MLM parameters. This correspondence between the SEM and MLM specifications is summarized in Table 11.5.

**Table 11.5** Correspondence between SEM and MLM specifications of unconditional linear growth curve model

|  | SEM notation | MLM notation |
|---|---|---|
| Individual-level intercept | $\eta_{0i}$ | $\beta_{0i}$ |
| Individual-level slope | $\eta_{1i}$ | $\beta_{1i}$ |
| Mean of individual intercepts | $\mu_0$ | $\gamma_{00}$ |
| Mean of individual slopes | $\mu_1$ | $\gamma_{10}$ |
| Intercept variance | $\text{VAR}(\eta_{0i}) = \psi_{11}$ | $\text{VAR}(\delta_{0i}) = \tau_{00}^2$ |
| Slope variance | $\text{VAR}(\eta_{1i}) = \psi_{22}$ | $\text{VAR}(\delta_{1i}) = \tau_{11}^2$ |
| Intercept, slope covariance | $\text{COV}(\eta_{0i}, \eta_{1i}) = \psi_{21}$ | $\text{COV}(\delta_{0i}, \delta_{1i}) = \tau_{10}$ |

 Section recap

### MLM specification of the unconditional linear growth curve model

In the MLM framework, repeated (i.e., longitudinal) observations of the same variable are Level 1 units of analysis, whereas individual persons are Level 2 units of analysis. That is, repeated observations are nested within individuals.

Given this perspective, the Level 1 equation of the unconditional linear model is

$$Y_{ti} = \beta_{0i} + \beta_{1i}X_t + \varepsilon_{ti},$$

indicating that the longitudinally observed outcome variable is regressed on a variable $X_t$ representing *time*. This Level 1 equation represents the linear trajectory for a given individual $i$.

The intercept $\beta_{0i}$ and slope $\beta_{1i}$ from the Level 1 equation vary randomly across individuals, leading to the Level 2 equations:

$$\beta_{0i} = \gamma_{00} + \delta_{0i}$$

and

$$\beta_{1i} = \gamma_{10} + \delta_{1i},$$

where $\gamma_{00}$ and $\gamma_{10}$ are the mean of the individual intercepts and individual slopes, respectively.

The variability of the individual trajectories is captured by the Level 2 random-effects variance parameters, with $\mathrm{VAR}(\delta_{0i}) = \tau_{00}^2$ and $\mathrm{VAR}(\delta_{1i}) = \tau_{11}^2$ representing the variance of the individual intercepts and the variance of the individual slopes, respectively.

The parameters of the MLM specification of the unconditional linear growth curve model map directly onto the parameters from the SEM specification.

## Unconditional linear growth model: MLM identification, estimation, and fit evaluation

The concept of model identification is typically not directly addressed in treatments of MLM, but the same principles from using SEM for GCM apply. In particular, as a general rule of thumb, it is important for there to be at least three longitudinal observations of the outcome variable $Y$ for at least a large subset of individuals (although some may have only one or two observations). If not, it may be necessary to restrict certain random effects variance parameters to 0 to avoid nonconvergence or an improper solution. If a nonlinear functional form of growth is specified (as discussed later in this chapter), then more than three observations of $Y$ are required for the purposes of model identification.

Next, the full-information ML (FIML) estimation method introduced in Chapter 6 for MLM is equivalent to the direct ML procedure outlined earlier for SEM. Yet, the host of overall model fit statistics produced with SEM software is generally not available from MLM applications. Instead, in the context of MLM, model fit is typically addressed by comparing a hypothesized, candidate model with one or more hierarchically nested alternative models. When a study consists of more than three time points, in the context of MLM, it is customary to use likelihood-ratio tests to compare models with different polynomial functions of *time*, for example, to compare a model with a linear functional form of growth with a model specifying a quadratic functional form (as discussed later).

To demonstrate another type of model fit comparison, as mentioned previously, MLM applications of growth curve models often assume a constant variance $\sigma^2$ for the Level 1 error terms, $\varepsilon_{ti}$, although it is possible to estimate separate variance parameters for each time point, $\sigma_t^2$. In fact, the model with constant Level 1 error variance can be viewed as a model specified with the constraint that $\sigma_1^2 = \sigma_2^2 = \sigma_3^2$ (for a model fitted to data with only three time points), and therefore, the constant-Level 1 variance model is nested within (i.e., it is a restricted version of) a model with freely varying Level 1 error variances. As described in Chapter 6, a likelihood-ratio test can be used to compare such nested models as can Bayesian Information Criterion (*BIC*) statistics. For the adolescent alcohol-use example, the model with constant Level 1 variance (*BIC* = 1,523) fits the data worse than the less restricted model with separate Level 1 variances (*BIC* = 1,485), $\chi^2$ (2) = 50.64, $p < .001$.

## Section recap

### Identification, estimation, and model fit of growth curve models with MLM

The principles of model identification from SEM also apply to MLM. Furthermore, the FIML estimation procedure for MLM is equivalent to FIML estimation of structural equation models.

But many of the popular model fit statistics from SEM are not generally available with MLM. Instead, in the MLM context, the concept of model fit is typically investigated by comparing nested models.

## Unconditional linear growth model: MLM results for alcohol-use example

When the unconditional linear growth curve model (with separate Level 1 variances) is fitted to the adolescent alcohol-use example as a multilevel model using FIML, the parameter estimates obtained do indeed match (within rounding error) those reported earlier when the same model is estimated as a structural equation model (see Table 11.4). In particular, the fixed-effect intercept estimate $\hat{\gamma}_{00}$ = 0.202 is the mean of the individual trajectory intercepts, representing the predicted level of alcohol use at the initial time point (i.e., age 13), whereas the intercept variance estimate $\hat{\tau}_{00}^2$ = 0.204 describes the extent of the individual differences around the mean intercept. Next, the fixed-effect slope estimate $\hat{\gamma}_{10}$ = 0.271 is the mean of the individual trajectory slopes, representing the predicted per-year increase in alcohol use, whereas the slope variance estimate $\hat{\tau}_{11}^2$ = 0.174 describes the extent of the individual differences around the mean slope. One challenge, however, is that robust standard errors can be more difficult to obtain for MLMs as a result of software limitations, whereas robust standard errors are easily obtained in most SEM software packages. The adolescent alcohol-use variable is strongly non-normal, which in turn produces non-normal errors; therefore, robust standard errors are preferable for this example. These values are provided in Table 11.4 using the SEM implementation.

## Coding *time* to change the trajectory intercept

In the example analysis, the MLM fixed intercept estimate and the SEM intercept factor mean represented the predicted level of alcohol use at age 13, which was the first time point of the data used to fit the unconditional linear model. It is easy, however, to change the meaning of the trajectory intercept by simply changing the way that the *time* variable is centered. As described earlier, in the MLM specification, the *time* variable was defined as $X_t = \text{age} - 13$, or centered at age 13. If instead we would like to know the predicted level of alcohol use at age 15, we could simply re-center *time* as $X_t = \text{age} - 15$, and re-estimate the model using this new *time* variable.

An equivalent procedure in SEM involves changing the fixed elements of the factor loading matrix from

$$\Lambda = \begin{bmatrix} 1 & 0 \\ 1 & 1 \\ 1 & 2 \end{bmatrix}$$

to

$$\Lambda = \begin{bmatrix} 1 & -2 \\ 1 & -1 \\ 1 & 0 \end{bmatrix}.$$

Notice that the latter factor loading matrix is formed by subtracting 2 from each element of the second column of the original factor loading matrix, which corresponds to the factor loadings of the slope latent variable, $\eta_1$. At first, it may seem strange that changing the factor loadings of the slope latent variable effectively changes the interpretation of the intercept, but why this is so becomes clear when one considers Equation 11.1, the scalar equation for an individual trajectory:

$$Y_{ti} = \eta_{0i} + \lambda_t \eta_{1i} + \varepsilon_{ti}.$$

As described earlier, this equation shows that the intercept factor $\eta_0$ gives the predicted value of $Y$ when $\lambda_t$ equals 0. These $\lambda_t$ coefficients for $\eta_1$ correspond to the second column of the factor loading matrix $\Lambda$, whereas 1 is the implicit coefficient for the intercept latent variable, $\eta_0$, which explains why the elements of the first column of $\Lambda$ are all fixed to 1. Therefore, if the coefficient $\lambda_t$ for the slope latent variable is fixed to 0 for time point $t = 15$ years of age (i.e., the third time point in the current example), then the latent intercept variable represents the predicted level of $Y$ (i.e., alcohol use) at age 15. The factor loadings for the previous two time points are fixed to -2 and -1 because the corresponding measurement occasions (i.e., age 13 and 14, respectively) occurred at 2 and 1 units of *time* (i.e., years of age) before age 15, the time point with $\lambda_t$ fixed to 0; doing so maintains the linear functional form of the growth trajectory. For a more formal, detailed description of the logic behind specifying the fixed factor loadings in $\Lambda$, see Biesanz, Deeb-Sossa, Papadakis, Bollen, and Curran (2004: 33–36).

With the factor loading matrix modified as explained in the previous paragraph and the alcohol-use linear growth curve model re-estimated, the resulting parameter estimates are in Table 11.6. In particular, the estimated mean of the intercept factor is $\hat{\mu}_0 = 0.74$, which now represents the predicted level of alcohol use at age 15 rather than at age 13. Furthermore, the estimated variance of the intercept factor has changed to $\hat{\psi}_{11} = 0.99$; this variance of the individual intercepts now indicates the extent of individual differences in age 15 alcohol use. Additionally, the estimated covariance between the individual trajectory intercepts and slopes, $\hat{\psi}_{21} = 0.37$, now corresponds to a correlation of $r = .89$, indicating that there is a strong positive association between the extent to which alcohol use increases over time (i.e., individual trajectory slopes) and the age 15 level of alcohol use (i.e., individual trajectory intercepts). Comparing Table 11.6 with the results in Table 11.4 (i.e., results obtained when the intercept factor represented age 13 alcohol use), the remaining parameter estimates (and corresponding standard errors) have not changed: Whereas adjusting the slope factor loadings as described earlier changes the parameters involving the individual intercepts, it does not affect parameters involving the individual slopes nor does it affect the age-specific error variance parameters. Furthermore, overall model fit also does not change when the $\lambda_t$ coefficients are adjusted to alter the meaning of the intercepts (i.e., two models with time centered in different ways are statistically equivalent). Finally, the same pattern of results and conclusions is also obtained with MLM when the *time* variable is re-centered to adjust the meaning of the fixed and random-intercept parameters.

**Table 11.6** Results for unconditional linear growth curve model of alcohol use from ages 13 to 15 with time centered at age 15

| Parameter | Estimate | Robust SE | z | p |
|---|---|---|---|---|
| $\mu_{\eta_0}$ (latent intercept mean) | 0.744 | 0.079 | 9.48 | <.001 |
| $\mu_{\eta_1}$ (latent slope mean) | 0.271 | 0.039 | 7.02 | <.001 |
| $\psi_{11}$ (latent intercept variance) | 0.992 | 0.301 | 3.30 | <.001 |
| $\psi_{22}$ (latent slope variance) | 0.175 | 0.100 | 1.75 | .080 |
| $\psi_{21}$ (intercept, slope covariance) | 0.372 | 0.151 | 2.46 | .014 |
| $\sigma_1^2$ (age 13 error variance) | 0.007 | 0.133 | 0.05 | .958 |
| $\sigma_2^2$ (age 14 error variance) | 0.297 | 0.096 | 3.09 | .002 |
| $\sigma_3^2$ (age 15 error variance) | 0.435 | 0.267 | 1.63 | .103 |

*Note.* N = 352.

 **Section recap**

### Coding *time* to change the trajectory intercept

The trajectory intercept does not necessarily need to represent the level of the outcome variable Y at the first or initial measurement occasion.

*(Continued)*

(Continued)

Using MLM, the intercept represents the predicted level of Y when the *time* variable $X_t$ equals 0. Thus, $X_t$ can be centered so that the intercept represents the predicted level of Y at any time point.

Using SEM, adjusting the fixed $\lambda_t$ factor loadings for the slope latent variable serves to center time; the intercept latent variable represents the predicted level of Y for the time point at which $\lambda_t = 0$.

Centering time to change the interpretation of the intercept does not change the mean or variance of the individual trajectory slopes, nor does it change overall model fit.

## Conditional linear growth model: Specification with SEM and MLM

The growth curve models presented so far are all *unconditional* models in the sense that although they include parameters to represent individual differences in growth trajectories, they do not include any variables to explain or predict these individual differences. In other words, the trajectories are not conditioned upon any predictor variables, nor are the trajectories themselves used as predictors of any outcome variables. Often, however, researchers hypothesize that interindividual variability in growth trajectories can be explained or predicted by other variables. For instance, in the adolescent alcohol-use example, we can incorporate gender and parental alcoholism as predictors of both the individual trajectory intercepts and the individual slopes.

Before estimating conditional growth curve models, it is good practice to estimate unconditional growth curve models first to determine the optimal functional form of change over time for a longitudinal outcome variable (e.g., to determine whether a growth curve model for linear change is adequate or whether a more complex model for nonlinear change is more appropriate) and to describe the average trajectory and the extent of individual heterogeneity around the average trajectory. In the previous analyses, we did find that a model for linear change is adequate for the alcohol-use variables observed from ages 13 to 15 and that there are substantial individual differences in the linear trajectory intercepts and slopes. Next, we would like to expand this model to include gender and parental alcoholism as predictors of these intercepts and slopes. As mentioned earlier, these predictor variables are time-invariant because they are assumed to remain constant over time (at least during the course of the longitudinal study). Incorporating time-invariant predictors is straightforward with both the SEM and MLM frameworks.

Specifically, in the SEM implementation of GCM, the regression of the repeated outcome variable $Y_{ti}$ on the latent intercept and slope factors, $\eta_{0i}$ and $\eta_{1i}$, using Equation 11.1 does not change when time-invariant predictors are introduced. But Equation 11.4 for $\eta_{0i}$ and $\eta_{1i}$ themselves does change. In the unconditional growth curve model, Equation 11.4 represented an individual's values on these latent growth factors simply as a function of the factor means plus individual deviation from the means. In the conditional growth curve model, this expression is expanded to include a vector of predictors of the growth factors:

$$\eta_i = \mu_\eta + \Gamma X_i + \zeta_i, \tag{11.9}$$

where $\eta_i$ again represents the $K \times 1$ vector of scores on the latent growth factors for individual $i$ (for linear growth, $K = 2$ for the intercept and slope factors), $\mathbf{X}_i$ is a $Q \times 1$ vector of scores on $Q$ predictor variables for the same individual $i$, and $\boldsymbol{\Gamma}$ is a $K \times Q$ matrix of regression coefficients for the linear regression of $\eta_i$ on $\mathbf{X}_i$. It is important to recognize that $\boldsymbol{\mu}_\eta$ is now a $K \times 1$ vector of regression intercept parameters whose elements represent the predicted values of the latent growth factors for an individual whose values in $\mathbf{X}_i$ all equal zero; $\eta$ is no longer simply the vector of growth factor means. Furthermore, instead of just representing deviations from the growth factor means, $\zeta_i$ is now a $K \times 1$ vector of regression error terms. Consequently, the diagonal elements of $\boldsymbol{\Psi}$, which is the covariance matrix for $\zeta_i$, are now error variances representing the variability in the growth factors that remains beyond the variance explained by $\mathbf{X}$. Finally, the model's parameter set also includes $\boldsymbol{\Phi}$, the $Q \times Q$ matrix of covariances among the exogenous predictors $\mathbf{X}$.

Equation 11.9 provides a type of structural regression model for predicting latent variables which can be shown to represent a special case of the general structural regression model presented in Chapter 10 (i.e., Equation 10.15). With that in mind, working within the SEM framework allows Equation 11.9 to be revised so that the predictors are latent variables (i.e., $\mathbf{X}$ can be replaced with a vector of latent variables $\xi$), which allows the regression coefficients in $\boldsymbol{\Gamma}$ to be corrected for measurement error in $\mathbf{X}$. This capability is one advantage of modeling longitudinal data using SEM rather than MLM.

Applying the adolescent alcohol-use example, we would like to model individual linear trajectories in alcohol use from age 13 to age 15 as a function of gender and parental alcoholism (i.e., whether an individual is a COA or not; see Chapter 4). For this application, Equation 11.9 reduces to

$$\begin{bmatrix} \eta_0 \\ \eta_1 \end{bmatrix} = \begin{bmatrix} \mu_0 \\ \mu_1 \end{bmatrix} + \begin{bmatrix} \gamma_{01} & \gamma_{02} \\ \gamma_{11} & \gamma_{12} \end{bmatrix} \begin{bmatrix} X_1 \\ X_2 \end{bmatrix} + \begin{bmatrix} \zeta_0 \\ \zeta_1 \end{bmatrix},$$

which corresponds to the separate scalar equations

$$\eta_{0i} = \mu_0 + \gamma_{01}X_{1i} + \gamma_{02}X_{2i} + \zeta_{0i}$$

giving the regression of the latent intercept factor on $X_1$ and $X_2$, and

$$\eta_{1i} = \mu_1 + \gamma_{11}X_{1i} + \gamma_{12}X_{2i} + \zeta_{1i}$$

giving the regression of the latent slope factor on $X_1$ and $X_2$, where $X_1$ is the gender variable and $X_2$ is the binary parental alcoholism variable. A path diagram of this conditional linear growth curve model is in Figure 11.3.

Just as the intercept and slope latent variables can be regressed on one or more predictors using SEM, the random intercepts and slopes in MLM can also be regressed on one or more predictors. Specifically, the Level 2 equations from the unconditional model (Equations 11.7 and 11.8) are expanded to

$$\beta_{0i} = \gamma_{00} + \sum_{p=1}^{P} \gamma_{0p}X_{pi} + \delta_{0i} \quad \text{(Level 2a)} \tag{11.10}$$

and

$$\beta_{1i} = \gamma_{10} + \sum_{p=1}^{P} \gamma_{1p}X_{pi} + \delta_{1i} \quad \text{(Level 2b)}, \tag{11.11}$$

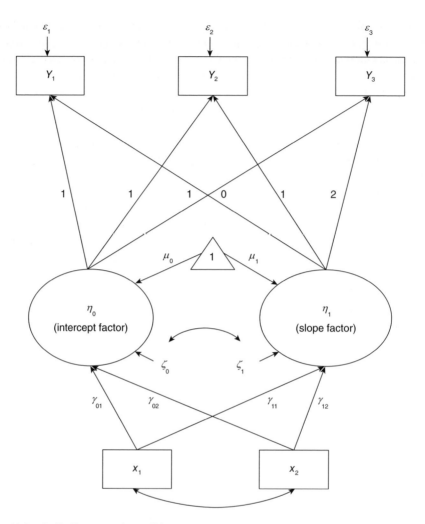

**Figure 11.3** Path diagram of conditional growth curve model for linear change

where $X_{pi}$ is the value on the $p$th of $P$ predictors for individual $i$.[8] It is important not to confuse these $X_p$ predictors with the *time* variable $X_t$ in the Level 1 equation of the growth curve model. Paralleling interpretation of the SEM parameters, the $\gamma_{00}$ and $\gamma_{10}$ fixed-effect parameters no longer represent the mean intercept and slope, respectively, and instead are interpretable as regression intercept parameters such that $\gamma_{00}$ gives the predicted trajectory intercept (i.e., $\hat{\beta}_0$) for a hypothetical individual with a value of 0 on each of the $P$ predictors and $\gamma_{10}$ gives the predicted trajectory slope (i.e., $\hat{\beta}_1$) for a hypothetical individual with a value of 0 on each of the $P$

---

[8]In Chapter 6, a Level 2 predictor was represented as $W_j$, with the subscript $j$ indexing different groups or clusters, which are the Level 2 units in multilevel models with hierarchically nested cross-sectional data. Here, each Level 2 predictor is instead represented as $X_j$, with the subscript $i$ indexing different individuals, which are the Level 2 units in multilevel models for longitudinal or repeated-measures data nested within individuals.

predictors. Furthermore, $\text{VAR}(\delta_{0i}) = \tau_{00}^2$ and $\text{VAR}(\delta_{1i}) = \tau_{11}^2$ are now error variance parameters which describe the extent of individual differences in trajectories that remains over and above the variance explained by the $P$ predictors. For a reason explained shortly, any predictor of the random slopes included in Equation 11.11 ordinarily should also be included as a predictor of the random intercepts in Equation 11.10, but it is reasonable to include predictors of the intercepts which are not also predictors of the slopes.

Returning to the adolescent alcohol-use example, as shown earlier for the SEM approach, we would like to model the individual linear trajectories from ages 13 to 15 as a function of two predictors, gender $(X_1)$ and parental alcoholism $(X_2)$. For this application, Equations 11.10 and 11.11 reduce to

$$\beta_{0i} = \gamma_{00} + \gamma_{01}X_{1i} + \gamma_{02}X_{2i} + \delta_{0i}$$

and

$$\beta_{1i} = \gamma_{10} + \gamma_{11}X_{1i} + \gamma_{12}X_{2i} + \delta_{1i}.$$

When these Level 2 equations for the random intercepts and slopes are combined with the Level 1 equation for the linear model (i.e., Equation 11.6) to obtain the reduced-form equation, the result is

$$Y_{ti} = \gamma_{00} + \gamma_{01}X_{1i} + \gamma_{02}X_{2i} + \gamma_{10}X_t + \gamma_{11}X_{1i}X_t + \gamma_{12}X_{2i}X_t + \delta_{1i}X_t + \delta_{0i} + \varepsilon_{ti}. \qquad (11.12)$$

This combined equation shows that including one or more predictors of the random slopes in a conditional growth curve model effectively introduces cross-level interaction(s) in the overall model analogously to the situation described in Chapter 6 for multilevel models with cross-sectional data (cf. Equation 6.16). Specifically, here we see that because both gender $(X_1)$ and parental alcoholism $(X_2)$ were included as predictors of the random slopes, the combined model includes two cross-level interaction terms, specifically, the product of gender and *time* $(X_1X_t)$ and the product of parental alcoholism and *time* $(X_2X_t)$. Consequently, these interactions can be probed using simple-slope analyses described in Chapter 4; for instance, we could compare the predicted trajectory (i.e., the simple slope of *time*) for boys with nonalcoholic parents with the predicted trajectory for boys who are COAs. Incidentally, although the SEM specification of conditional growth curve models does not explicitly represent the prediction of the latent slope variable from one or more predictors using interaction terms, such effects nonetheless still represent the moderation of the trajectory slope by these predictors; see Curran, Bauer, and Willoughby (2004) for further explanation of this issue. Finally, Equation 11.12 also reveals the reason that it is important that any variable included as a predictor of the random slopes in Equation 11.11 also be included as a predictor of the random intercepts in Equation 11.10: Because a predictor of the slopes ends up being involved in cross-level interactions with the *time* variable in the reduced-form equation (e.g., $X_1X_t$), its lower order constituent (e.g., $X_1$) is also included in the reduced-form equation if it was included as a predictor for the random intercepts; consequently, the model adheres to the 'principle of marginality' for interactions (see Footnote 3 in Chapter 4).

 Section recap

### Specification of conditional linear growth curve models

In conditional growth curve models, time-invariant covariates or predictors are incorporated in the SEM framework by including them as predictors of the latent intercept and slope factors:

$$\eta_i = \mu_\eta + \Gamma X_i + \zeta_i.$$

Consequently, the variables in **X** can explain individual differences in both the level (i.e., the latent intercepts) and the slope of the individual trajectories.

Equivalently, time-invariant predictors are incorporated in the MLM representation of a conditional growth curve model by including them as Level 2 predictors of the random intercepts and slopes:

$$\beta_{0i} = \gamma_{00} + \sum_{p=1}^{P} \gamma_{0p} X_{pi} + \delta_{0i},$$

$$\beta_{1i} = \gamma_{10} + \sum_{p=1}^{P} \gamma_{1p} X_{pi} + \delta_{1i}.$$

When these conditional Level 2 equations are combined with the Level 1 equation, the resulting reduced-form equation reveals that the Level 2 regression of the random slopes on a given predictor $X_p$ produces a cross-level interaction between $X_p$ and the *time* variable $X_t$.

This cross-level interaction can be probed using a simple-slope analysis to determine the predicted trajectory slope for a hypothetical individual with a given value on the predictor $X_p$.

## Conditional linear growth model: Results for alcohol-use example

Table 11.7 displays the results obtained when FIML is used to estimate the conditional linear growth curve model in which individual trajectories of heavy alcohol use from ages 13 to 15 are regressed on gender and parental alcoholism. The model was specified such that *time* was centered at age 13; thus, the intercept factor represents the level of alcohol use at age 13. First, although gender was not a significant predictor of either the intercept or slope factors, parental alcoholism was significantly associated with both latent growth factors. Specifically, because parental alcoholism was coded such that COA = 0 for control participants and COA = 1 for participants with an alcoholic parent, the estimated coefficients for this COA variable represent the predicted mean differences between these two groups (holding constant the weak gender effects). Thus, $\hat{\gamma}_{02} = 0.206$, the partial regression coefficient for the relation between parental alcoholism and the intercept factor, indicates that the mean level of age 13 alcohol use is 0.206 higher among COAs than among controls, whereas $\hat{\gamma}_{12} = 0.299$, the partial regression coefficient for the relation between parental alcoholism and the slope factor, indicates that the mean per-year increase in alcohol use is 0.299 higher among COAs than among control participants.

**Table 11.7** Results for linear growth curve model of alcohol use from ages 13 to 15 conditioned on gender and parental alcoholism (COA)

| Parameter | Estimate | Robust SE | Z | p |
|---|---|---|---|---|
| $\gamma_{01}$ (coefficient for gender effect on intercept factor) | −0.083 | 0.053 | 1.57 | .118 |
| $\gamma_{02}$ (coefficient for COA effect on intercept factor) | 0.206 | 0.054 | 3.84 | <.001 |
| $\gamma_{11}$ (coefficient for effect of gender on slope factor) | 0.036 | 0.067 | 0.54 | .591 |
| $\gamma_{12}$ (coefficient for effect of COA on slope factor) | 0.299 | 0.068 | 4.38 | <.001 |
| $\mu_0$ (intercept of intercept factor) | 0.217 | 0.087 | 2.50 | .012 |
| $\mu_1$ (intercept of slope factor) | 0.057 | 0.106 | 0.54 | .592 |
| $\psi_{11}$ (intercept factor error variance) | 0.198 | 0.136 | 1.46 | .145 |
| $\psi_{22}$ (slope factor error variance) | 0.163 | 0.092 | 1.77 | .076 |
| $\psi_{21}$ (intercept, slope error covariance) | −0.002 | 0.090 | 0.02 | .984 |
| $\sigma_1^2$ (age 13 error variance) | 0.000 | 0.131 | 0.00 | .994 |
| $\sigma_2^2$ (age 14 error variance) | 0.300 | 0.091 | 3.30 | <.001 |
| $\sigma_3^2$ (age 15 error variance) | 0.408 | 0.244 | 1.67 | .094 |

*Note.* $N = 352$. For these results, *time* was centered at age 13. gender = 1 for male, gender = 0 for female; COA = child of alcoholic; COA = 1 for participants with an alcoholic parent, COA = 0 for control participants.

It is straightforward to go one step further and calculate the mean trajectory for each of four groups of adolescents: female controls, male controls, female COAs, and male COAs.

To do so, it is helpful to revisit the equations for the latent growth factors:

$$\eta_{0i} = \mu_0 + \gamma_{01}X_{1i} + \gamma_{02}X_{2i} + \zeta_{0i}$$

and

$$\eta_{1i} = \mu_1 + \gamma_{11}X_{1i} + \gamma_{12}X_{2i} + \zeta_{1i},$$

where $X_1$ is the gender variable (coded female = 0 and male = 1) and $X_2$ is the COA variable. From these equations, it is clear that the estimates $\hat{\mu}_0$ and $\hat{\mu}_1$ describe the estimated mean linear trajectory for female control participants because they are the individuals who have a value of 0 for both $X_1$ and $X_2$.[9] Thus, $\hat{\mu}_0 = 0.217$ represents the mean level of alcohol use at age 13 among female controls and $\hat{\mu}_1 = 0.057$ represents the predicted per-year increase in alcohol use for female controls. For male controls ($X_1 = 1$, $X_2 = 0$), the predicted mean trajectory intercept is

$$(\hat{\mu}_0 + \hat{\gamma}_{01}) = (0.217 - 0.083) = 0.134$$

---

[9]Although gender was not a significant predictor of the intercept and slope growth factors, the results obtained nonetheless are still conditional on gender, and so it would be somewhat misleading to use the intercept estimates $\hat{\mu}_0$ and $\hat{\mu}_1$ to represent mean trajectories for both genders.

and the predicted mean trajectory slope is

$$(\hat{\mu}_1 + \hat{\gamma}_{11}) = (0.057 + 0.036) = 0.093.$$

Next, female COA participants ($X_1 = 0$, $X_2 = 1$) have a predicted mean intercept of

$$(\hat{\mu}_0 + \hat{\gamma}_{02}) = (0.217 - 0.206) = 0.423$$

and a predicted mean slope of

$$(\hat{\mu}_1 + \hat{\gamma}_{12}) = (0.057 + 0.299) = 0.356,$$

and finally the predicted mean intercept for male COAs ($X_1 = 1$, $X_2 = 1$) is

$$(\hat{\mu}_0 + \hat{\gamma}_{01} + \hat{\gamma}_{02}) = (0.217 - 0.083 + 0.206) = 0.340$$

and the male COA predicted mean slope is

$$(\hat{\mu}_1 + \hat{\gamma}_{11} + \hat{\gamma}_{12}) = (0.057 + 0.299 + 0.206) = 0.562.$$

Figure 11.4 presents a simple graph of these predicted, or model-implied, mean trajectories. The figure makes it clear that adolescents with an alcoholic parent have much higher predicted levels of alcohol use at any given age than do control participants and that the increase in alcohol use is much stronger for COAs than for controls, whereas gender differences are much weaker than the parental alcoholism effect.

Calculation of such model-implied trajectories becomes somewhat more labour-intensive if a given time-invariant predictor $X_p$ is continuous, but the current example shows that doing so is simply a matter of plugging different values of $X_p$ into the equations for the growth factors. Alternatively, different model-implied trajectories at particular values of a predictor

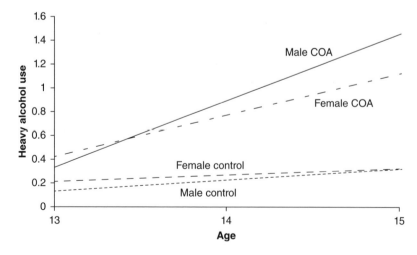

**Figure 11.4** Mean model-implied trajectories by gender and parental alcoholism

$X_p$ can be obtained by recoding $X_p$ (i.e., centering) and then re-estimating the model (analogous to probing interactions with a simple-slope analysis), which has the added benefit of obtaining significance tests or confidence intervals for each model-implied trajectory slope (see Curran et al., 2004).

## Incorporating a time-varying predictor

In the adolescent alcohol-use example, gender and parental alcoholism are time-invariant covariates; these are variables whose values are presumed not to change over time for a given participant. In the same study from which those example data were drawn, there were several potential time-varying predictors of the longitudinal, repeated measures of adolescent alcohol use. For example, adolescent externalizing behaviour is a potential time-varying predictor of alcohol use; a given participant's level of externalizing behaviour is likely to change over time, just as the outcome variable itself, alcohol use, also changes. There are several approaches to incorporating time-varying predictors in growth curve models, and properly choosing among them can be difficult. One concern is that the nature of causality dictates that a cause must precede its effect; therefore, it is often sensible to use an observation of a time-varying variable from a previous time point to predict an outcome variable at a current time point. But the timing of the observations in a given study might not adequately represent the actual timing of how the causal process unfolds, leading to biased estimates of an effect (Cole and Maxwell, 2003). Another concern is that the time-varying predictor itself follows a particular trajectory over time, and not accounting for this trajectory in the model for the longitudinally observed outcome variable of interest can also lead to biased effects in that within-person variability becomes confounded with between-persons variability (Curran and Bauer, 2011). Finally, it can also be critical to account for the interaction between the time-varying predictor and the *time* variable itself in the prediction of a longitudinally observed outcome variable.

A complete description of one or more reasonable approaches to incorporating time-varying covariates is beyond the scope of this text. Curran and Bauer (2011) reviewed approaches to incorporating time-varying predictors using the MLM framework; their general principles also extend to the SEM framework. An alternative approach for incorporating time-varying covariates in growth curve models using SEM involves so-called *parallel-process* growth curve models (also termed *bivariate* or *multivariate* growth curve models; Bollen and Curran, 2006) in which the latent growth factors of a longitudinally observed outcome variable may be regressed on or simply correlated with the latent growth factors of a time-varying predictor. MacCallum et al. (1997) presented both the SEM approach to parallel-process growth curve models and an implementation of an equivalent model using the MLM framework.

## GROWTH CURVE MODELS FOR NONLINEAR CHANGE

Because change over time is complex for many phenomena, when longitudinal or repeated-measures data are extended to include more than three time points, it often turns out that trajectories display considerably nonlinear patterns such that models specifying a simple linear functional form of change are inadequate. In the adolescent alcohol-use example, the models for linear change over time were fitted to data only from ages 13, 14, and 15 (i.e., three discrete time points). But, as presented at the beginning of this chapter, the alcohol-use variable was also observed at ages 11 and 12. A simple line plot of the means of this alcohol-use variable across all five ages (see Table 11.1 for descriptive statistics), conditional on parental alcoholism, is in Figure 11.5. In this figure, it is clear that on average, the trajectory of alcohol use from ages 11 to 15 is nonlinear for both COAs and control participants. Specifically, for both groups, the alcohol-use means increase slightly from ages 11 to 13 but then increase more steadily from ages 13 to 15. The fact that the trajectory of the means is nonlinear implies that individual trajectories are also nonlinear for many participants.[10] Consequently, it is desirable to specify and estimate a growth curve model with a nonlinear functional form of change for these data spanning age 11 to age 15 (indeed, a simple unconditional linear growth curve model fits the complete data from age 11 to 15 poorly, $RMSEA_{robust} = .178$, SRMR = .133).

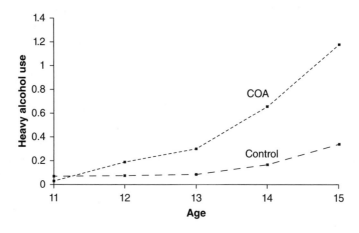

**Figure 11.5** Trajectory of observed means of heavy alcohol use by parental alcoholism

There are many potential approaches to specifying nonlinear trajectories using growth curve models. Perhaps the most popular approach is to specify a quadratic function of time, which is a certain type of polynomial function and essentially a generalization of the polynomial regression procedure touched on in Chapter 2. Quadratic growth curve models are straightforward to specify and estimate, but interpretation of the parameter estimates can be challenging, particularly when the quadratic trajectories are conditioned on predictors. Another common approach is to represent nonlinear trajectories with a set of connected linear trajectories, which is known as a *piecewise* linear functional form (also known as linear *splines*). Piecewise linear growth curve models are also straightforward to specify but are considerably easier to interpret than quadratic or other polynomial growth curve models. Yet, for certain types of data, it may be that neither a polynomial growth curve model nor a piecewise growth curve model provides a reasonable representation of the data-generating process; for an overview of alternative approaches for nonlinear growth curve models using SEM, see Grimm, Ram, and Hamagami (2011).

---

[10]The converse is not necessarily true: It is possible for individual trajectories to follow nonlinear patterns while the means of the longitudinal variable display an approximately linear trend over time.

## Section recap

### Growth curve models for nonlinear change

As the number of time points or repeated measurements of an outcome variable increases, it becomes more likely that trajectories should be modeled with a nonlinear functional form of change.

There are many approaches to specifying growth curve models for nonlinear change. Probably the most popular approach is to specify a quadratic growth curve model, but such models can be difficult to interpret. Piecewise linear growth curve models are typically easier to interpret compared with other growth curve models for nonlinear change.

---

# Unconditional quadratic growth curve model: Specification with SEM and MLM

An equation to represent a within-person, individual quadratic growth trajectory using SEM notation is

$$Y_{ti} = \eta_{0i} + \lambda_t \eta_{1i} + \lambda_t^2 \eta_{2i} + \varepsilon_{ti}, \tag{11.13}$$

where, like for the linear growth curve model (Equation 11.1), $Y_{ti}$ represents the value of the observed outcome variable for individual $i$ at $time = t$, $\eta_{0i}$ is again the value of the latent intercept factor for individual $i$, $\eta_{1i}$ is the value of the latent linear factor for individual $i$, $\lambda_t$ is a factor loading specific to time $t$, and $\varepsilon_{ti}$ is the prediction error at $time = t$ for individual $i$. But, expanding from the linear model, Equation 11.13 for the quadratic growth curve model includes a third latent variable, $\eta_{2i}$, which is the value of the **latent quadratic factor** for individual $i$; this factor captures the extent of the curvature of the individual trajectory. With MLM notation, the Level 1 equation of a quadratic growth curve model can be expressed as

$$Y_{ti} = \beta_{0i} + \beta_{1i}X_t + \beta_{2i}X_t^2 + \varepsilon_{ti},$$

which is equivalent to Equation 11.13 of the SEM framework. Here, $\beta_{0i}$ is the random-intercept value for individual $i$, $\beta_{1i}$ is the random linear slope value for individual $i$, $\beta_{2i}$ is the value of the random quadratic term for individual $i$, and $X_t$ is again the *time* variable which is necessary for the implementation of GCM using MLM.

Equation 11.13 implies a separate equation for each time point $t$; collecting these separate scalar equations into a matrix equation leads to the same form presented earlier as Equation 11.2:

$$\mathbf{Y}_i = \mathbf{\Lambda}\boldsymbol{\eta}_i + \boldsymbol{\varepsilon}_i,$$

where $\mathbf{Y}_i$ is again a $T \times 1$ vector of scores for individual $i$ on the repeated outcome variable $Y$, but now $\mathbf{\Lambda}$ is a $T \times 3$ factor loading matrix and $\boldsymbol{\eta}_i$ is the $3 \times 1$ vector of scores on the three latent growth factors (i.e., the intercept, linear, and quadratic factors) for individual $i$. Finally, $\varepsilon_i$ is again the $T \times 1$ vector of error or disturbance terms capturing the within-time deviations of observed $Y$ scores from model-implied $Y$ scores for individual $i$.

Next, as with linear growth curve models, Equation 11.4 can be applied to the unconditional quadratic model to represent the individual values of the growth factors as a function of the means of the growth factors and individual deviations from the mean:

$$\eta_i = \mathbf{\mu}_\eta + \zeta_i$$

which, for the quadratic model, corresponds to

$$\begin{bmatrix} \eta_0 \\ \eta_1 \\ \eta_2 \end{bmatrix} = \begin{bmatrix} \mu_0 \\ \mu_1 \\ \mu_2 \end{bmatrix} + \begin{bmatrix} \zeta_0 \\ \zeta_1 \\ \zeta_2 \end{bmatrix},$$

where $\mu_0$ is the population mean of the individual trajectory intercepts, $\mu_1$ is the population mean of the individual *instantaneous* linear slopes (explained shortly), and $\mu_1$ is the population mean of the individual-level curvature of the quadratic trajectory. Therefore, $\zeta_{0i}, \zeta_{1i}$, and $\zeta_{1i}$ represent the deviations of an individual's values on the three respective growth factors from the means of these factors. Next, the covariance matrix for the individual deviations in $\zeta_i$ is

$$\Psi = \begin{bmatrix} \text{VAR}(\zeta_0) = \psi_{11} & & \\ \text{COV}(\zeta_0, \zeta_1) = \psi_{21} & \text{VAR}(\zeta_1) = \psi_{22} & \\ \text{COV}(\zeta_0, \zeta_2) = \psi_{31} & \text{COV}(\zeta_1, \zeta_2) = \psi_{32} & \text{VAR}(\zeta_2) = \psi_{33} \end{bmatrix},$$

and so $\psi_{11}$, $\psi_{22}$, and $\psi_{33}$ describe the population variances of the latent intercept factor ($\eta_{0i}$), latent linear factor ($\eta_{1i}$), and latent quadratic factor ($\eta_{2i}$). The off-diagonal elements of $\Psi$ are the covariances among these latent growth factors.

The matrix equation in the previous paragraph is equivalent to the Level 2 equations for the MLM implementation of an unconditional quadratic growth curve model. Specifically, the Level 2 equations for the random intercepts ($\beta_{0i}$) and instantaneous linear slopes ($\beta_{1i}$) are identical to Equations 11.7 and 11.8 given earlier in this chapter for the unconditional linear growth curve model. Additionally, the Level 2 equation for the random quadratic effect is

$$\beta_{2i} = \gamma_{20} + \delta_{2i} \quad \text{(Level 2c)},$$

where $\gamma_{20}$ is the mean of the quadratic curvature components of the individual trajectories and $\delta_{2i}$ is the difference between the curvature of the trajectory for person $i$ and the mean $\gamma_{20}$. Now the fixed-effect parameters $\gamma_{00}, \gamma_{10}$, and $\gamma_{20}$ describe the mean trajectory, whereas the random-effect variance parameters – $\text{VAR}(\delta_{0i}) = \tau_{00}^2$, $\text{VAR}(\delta_{1i}) = \tau_{11}^2$, and $\text{VAR}(\delta_{2i}) = \tau_{22}^2$ – describe the extent of the individual variability around the mean intercept, instantaneous linear slope, and quadratic curvature, respectively.

To demonstrate with the adolescent alcohol-use example, a growth curve model for quadratic change in heavy alcohol use across ages 11 to 15 can be specified as a structural equation model by applying Equation 11.2 with

$$\begin{bmatrix} Y_0 \\ Y_1 \\ Y_2 \\ Y_3 \\ Y_4 \end{bmatrix} = \begin{bmatrix} 1 & 0 & 0 \\ 1 & 1 & 1 \\ 1 & 2 & 4 \\ 1 & 3 & 9 \\ 1 & 4 & 16 \end{bmatrix} \begin{bmatrix} \eta_0 \\ \eta_1 \\ \eta_2 \end{bmatrix} + \begin{bmatrix} \varepsilon_0 \\ \varepsilon_1 \\ \varepsilon_2 \\ \varepsilon_3 \\ \varepsilon_4 \end{bmatrix},$$

where $Y_0$ is the age 11 alcohol-use variable, $Y_1$ is age 12 alcohol use, $Y_2$ is age 13 alcohol use, $Y_3$ is age 14 alcohol use, and $Y_4$ is age 15 alcohol use. The first two columns of the factor loading matrix $\Lambda$ are fixed in the same way that the factor loadings would be fixed for a linear growth curve model, but the third column of $\Lambda$, which contains the factor loadings for the quadratic factor $\eta_2$, is fixed so that each element equals the square of the corresponding factor loading for the linear factor $\eta_1$. With this model specification, the intercept factor $\eta_0$ represents the predicted amount of alcohol use at age 11 (i.e., the predicted value of $Y$ when $\lambda_t$ equals 0). Next, the linear factor $\eta_1$ represents the instantaneous linear change in alcohol use which is occurring at age 11 (i.e., the predicted linear slope obtained when $\lambda_t$ equals 0); more technically, $\eta_1$ is the slope of the line that is tangent to the curve of the model-implied nonlinear trajectory. Finally, $\eta_2$ captures the extent of the curvature of the individual trajectory and is proportional to the amount that $\eta_1$ differs as *time* passes. Figure 11.6 presents a path diagram of this model.

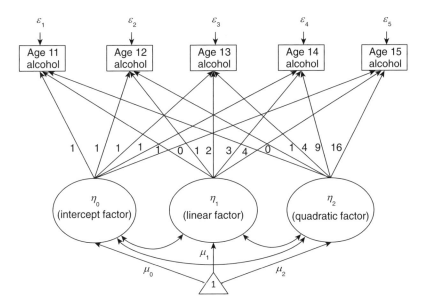

**Figure 11.6** Path diagram of unconditional growth curve model for quadratic change in adolescent alcohol use

As explained earlier, centering *time* changes the meaning of the intercept factor of a linear growth curve model. With a quadratic growth curve model, centering time changes the interpretation of both the intercept and the linear growth factors. For instance, in the previous paragraph, *time* was centered at age 11, but if *time* is centered at age 13 instead, the matrix equation for the quadratic growth curve model is

$$
\begin{bmatrix} Y_0 \\ Y_1 \\ Y_2 \\ Y_3 \\ Y_4 \end{bmatrix} = \begin{bmatrix} 1 & -2 & 4 \\ 1 & -1 & 1 \\ 1 & 0 & 0 \\ 1 & 1 & 1 \\ 1 & 2 & 4 \end{bmatrix} \begin{bmatrix} \eta_0 \\ \eta_1 \\ \eta_2 \end{bmatrix} + \begin{bmatrix} \varepsilon_0 \\ \varepsilon_1 \\ \varepsilon_2 \\ \varepsilon_3 \\ \varepsilon_4 \end{bmatrix}.
$$

Now, the intercept factor $\eta_0$ represents the predicted amount of alcohol use at age 13 and $\eta_1$ represents the instantaneous linear change in alcohol use which is occurring at age 13. The meaning of the quadratic factor $\eta_2$ remains unchanged. Furthermore, eventual model fit is not affected by such a respecification of $\Lambda$ to center *time*. For further explanation of alternative specifications of quadratic growth curve models, see Biesanz et al. (2004).

 Section recap

### Specification of unconditional quadratic growth curve models

A within-person, individual quadratic growth trajectory can be expressed using SEM notation with

$$
Y_{ti} = \eta_{0i} + \lambda_t \eta_{1i} + \lambda_t^2 \eta_{2i} + \varepsilon_{ti}.
$$

This is an expansion of the equation for a linear trajectory with the addition of a third latent variable, $\eta_{2i}$, which is the value of the **latent quadratic factor** for individual *i*; this factor captures the extent of the curvature of the individual trajectory.

With MLM notation, the Level 1 equation of a quadratic growth curve model can be expressed as

$$
Y_{ti} = \beta_{0i} + \beta_{1i} X_t + \beta_{2i} X_t^2 + \varepsilon_{ti},
$$

which is an expansion of the Level 1 equation for a linear growth curve model with the addition of a random quadratic term, $\beta_{2i}$.

Using both SEM and MLM, the distributions of the individual intercepts, linear slopes, and quadratic curvature components are summarized with parameters representing their means and variances, as well as with covariances among these components.

In a quadratic growth curve model, the linear component of the trajectory represents the *instantaneous* linear change occurring at the time point for which $\lambda_t$ equals 0 (using SEM) or the *time* variable $X_t = 0$. Changing the centering of *time* therefore changes both the trajectory intercept and the linear term.

## Unconditional quadratic growth curve model: Results for alcohol-use example

Before moving to model estimation, it is important to point out that as a general rule of thumb, it is necessary to have at least four time points (measurement occasions) at which Y is observed for a quadratic growth curve model to be overidentified (see Bollen and Curran, 2006: 121–23, for additional details). Here, the alcohol-use outcome is observed at five discrete ages, resulting in an overidentified unconditional quadratic model. In general, the more complex a nonlinear functional form of growth is, the more repeated observations are needed for model identification.

Using FIML estimation, the unconditional quadratic model has a close fit to the adolescent alcohol-use data,[11] YB $\chi^2$ (5) = 4.98, $p$ = .42, RMSEA$_{robust}$ = .000, CFI$_{robust}$ = 1.00, TLI$_{robust}$ = 1.00, and SRMR = .101. Keep in mind that identical fit statistics are obtained regardless of how *time* is centered to specify the model.

Parameter estimates of the unconditional quadratic model, obtained with *time* centered at age 11, are given in Table 11.8. First, note that the quadratic factor mean estimate, $\hat{\mu}_2$ = 0.047, is significant ($p$ < .001); interpreting this parameter estimate directly is difficult, but overall it suggests that there is substantial curvature in the average trajectory of alcohol use, which is no surprise given Figure 11.5. Furthermore, the estimated variance of the quadratic factor ($\hat{\psi}_{33}$ = 0.012, one-tailed $p$ = .03) indicates that the individual trajectories vary substantially with respect to their amount of curvature. Interpretation of the other parameter estimates is less vague: The estimated mean of the intercept growth factor, $\hat{\mu}_0$ = 0.049, indicates the predicted level of age 11 alcohol use. The estimated mean of the linear growth factor, $\hat{\mu}_1$ = –0.011, indicates that the instantaneous linear change in alcohol use which is occurring at age 11 is slightly below zero, on average. At first glance, this estimate may be confusing because it suggests that the overall level of alcohol use is decreasing at age 11, which is not consistent with the trajectory of means in Figure 11.5. Yet, this estimate is not significantly different from zero ($p$ = .73), and there is substantial interindividual heterogeneity in the linear growth factor ($\hat{\psi}_{22}$ = 0.097, $p$ = .05).

This negative value of $\hat{\mu}_1$ also reflects a mathematical feature (often, a limitation) of the quadratic growth curve model which is that the underlying quadratic function (i.e., Equation 11.13) is the equation for a parabola, and as such, the model-implied trajectory necessarily features a 'turning point' (which is either a minimum or a maximum) around which the trajectory shifts from increasing values of $Y$ to decreasing values of $Y$ (or vice versa). In the current example, it seems from Figure 11.5 that this turning point is likely to be near age 11, which is the age at which alcohol use is near its minimum (on average), with alcohol use increasing as age increases. But the nature of the quadratic function is such that if alcohol use increases from this minimum onward, then the function also implies decreasing levels of alcohol use during time points prior to the minimum. In the current example, this implied decrease is mainly outside of the range of the data (i.e., alcohol use is not observed before age 11) and, thus, ultimately has little substantive impact on the interpretation of the estimated mean trajectory.

It is informative to contrast parameter estimates obtained with *time* centered at age 11 with estimates of the unconditional quadratic model instead obtained with *time* centered at age 13; these estimates are also given in Table 11.8. Recall that changing the centering of *time* does not affect model fit. Furthermore, both the quadratic factor mean estimate ($\hat{\mu}_2$ = 0.047) and the estimated variance of the quadratic factor ($\hat{\psi}_{33}$ = 0.012) remain unchanged. But now,

---

[11]Referring back to Table 11.1, the alcohol use variable observed at age 11 has a much lower standard deviation than that observed at later ages. For this reason, the residual variance of the age 11 alcohol-use variable was fixed to 0 to avoid obtaining an improper solution for the quadratic GCM.

the estimated mean of the intercept growth factor is $\hat{\mu}_0 = 0.214$, representing the mean level of alcohol use at age 13 rather than at age 11. Furthermore, the variance of intercept factor is now $\hat{\psi}_{11} = 0.156$, indicating that there is greater individual variability in alcohol use at age 13 than at age 11 (where $\hat{\psi}_{11}$ was just 0.022). Next, whereas the mean of the linear growth factor was $\hat{\mu}_1 = -0.011$ with *time* centered at age 11, we now have $\hat{\mu}_1 = 0.176$ with *time* centered at age 13. This difference helps illuminate the nonlinear nature of the model-implied mean trajectory: Whereas the instantaneous linear change at age 11 was negative but nonsignificant, the instantaneous linear change at age 13 is positive and significantly greater than 0 ($p < .001$). This interpretation is consistent with the nonlinear pattern of means shown in Figure 11.5, where it is clear that at early ages (e.g., from ages 11 to 12), there is a much smaller change

**Table 11.8** Results for unconditional quadratic growth curve model of alcohol use from ages 11 to 15

*Time centered at age 11*

| Parameter | Estimate | Robust SE | z | p |
|---|---|---|---|---|
| $\mu_0$ (intercept factor mean) | 0.049 | 0.020 | 2.34 | .017 |
| $\mu_1$ (linear factor mean) | −0.011 | 0.032 | 0.35 | .729 |
| $\mu_2$ (quadratic factor mean) | 0.047 | 0.010 | 4.90 | <.001 |
| $\psi_{11}$ (intercept factor variance) | 0.022 | 0.012 | 1.75 | .080 |
| $\psi_{22}$ (linear factor variance) | 0.097 | 0.049 | 1.99 | .047 |
| $\psi_{33}$ (quadratic factor variance) | 0.012 | 0.006 | 1.87 | .062 |
| $\psi_{21}$ (intercept, linear covariance) | −0.003 | 0.026 | 0.11 | .916 |
| $\psi_{31}$ (intercept, quadratic covariance) | −0.002 | 0.009 | 0.22 | .825 |
| $\psi_{32}$ (linear, quadratic covariance) | −0.026 | 0.017 | 1.53 | .126 |

*Time centered at age 13*

| Parameter | Estimate | Robust SE | z | p |
|---|---|---|---|---|
| $\mu_0$ (intercept factor mean) | 0.214 | 0.027 | 7.78 | <.001 |
| $\mu_1$ (linear factor mean) | 0.176 | 0.019 | 9.38 | <.001 |
| $\mu_2$ (quadratic factor mean) | 0.047 | 0.010 | 4.90 | <.001 |
| $\psi_{11}$ (intercept factor variance) | 0.156 | 0.041 | 3.82 | <.001 |
| $\psi_{22}$ (linear factor variance) | 0.079 | 0.022 | 3.56 | <.001 |
| $\psi_{33}$ (quadratic factor variance) | 0.012 | 0.006 | 1.87 | .062 |
| $\psi_{21}$ (intercept, linear covariance) | 0.061 | 0.019 | 3.23 | .001 |
| $\psi_{31}$ (intercept, quadratic covariance) | −0.006 | 0.011 | 0.59 | .559 |
| $\psi_{32}$ (linear, quadratic covariance) | 0.022 | 0.011 | 2.06 | .040 |
| $\sigma_1^2$ (age 11 error variance) | 0.000 | – | – | – |
| $\sigma_2^2$ (age 12 error variance) | 0.068 | 0.040 | 1.71 | .088 |
| $\sigma_3^2$ (age 13 error variance) | 0.049 | 0.038 | 1.28 | .201 |
| $\sigma_4^2$ (age 14 error variance) | 0.311 | 0.090 | 3.47 | .001 |
| $\sigma_5^2$ (age 15 error variance) | 0.278 | 0.292 | 0.95 | .340 |

*Note.* $N = 355$. $\sigma_t^2$ estimates with *time* centered at 11 are identical to those with *time* centered at 13.

in alcohol use, but as age reaches 13 and older, alcohol use increases more steadily. It is also important to keep in mind, though, that there are still substantial individual differences in the linear growth factor ($\hat{\psi}_{22} = 0.079$ with *time* centered at age 13).

## Conditional quadratic growth curve models

It is straightforward to expand the quadratic growth curve model to include predictors of the intercept, linear, and quadratic growth factors. Analogous to the conditional linear growth curve model presented earlier, with the factor loadings fixed so that *time* is centered at age 13, we could test the association between parental alcoholism and the intercept factor to estimate the association between parental alcoholism and age 13 alcohol use, or we could test the association between parental alcoholism and the linear factor to estimate the association between parental alcoholism and the amount of linear change in alcohol use which is occurring at age 13. Furthermore, the quadratic factor itself can be regressed on parental alcoholism. But, interpreting the association between a predictor variable and a quadratic growth factor is particularly challenging, although an adaptation of the simple-slope approach for probing interactions can be helpful (see Biesanz at al., 2004, for an illustration).

## Unconditional piecewise growth curve model: Specification with SEM and MLM

In statistics generally (not just with longitudinal models), it is common to represent a non-linear data pattern using a series of joined line segments (so-called linear *splines*) rather than trying to specify and estimate a complex nonlinear function. In the context of GCM, the **piecewise** linear growth curve model provides one approach to representing nonlinear trajectories using a set of two or more linear segments (another, more exploratory, method using linear splines is the *freed-loading* model; e.g., Bollen and Curran, 2006: 98–103). The chief advantage of piecewise linear growth curve models is that their parameters are much easier to interpret conceptually than those for more complex models for nonlinear change over time. Furthermore, piecewise linear growth curve models can be tailored to test hypotheses about changes which occur during specific segments of time; for example, a piecewise linear growth curve model can be used to determine whether the slope changes significantly after a particular point in time (e.g., after the onset of a treatment or intervention) or to determine whether a particular covariate has a different effect on the trajectory during one segment of time compared with a different time period (Flora, 2008).

Returning to the adolescent alcohol-use example, in Figure 11.5, it appears that the change in the mean level of alcohol use from age 11 up to age 13 is approximately linear, and then from age 13 to age 15, the change also appears linear but with a steeper slope than from ages 11 to 13. To represent this pattern, an unconditional piecewise linear growth curve model can be specified using SEM to have three latent growth factors: an intercept factor, $\eta_0$, representing the predicted level of Y (i.e., alcohol use) at the measurement occasion for which *time* equals zero; one linear slope factor, $\eta_1$, representing the linear change in Y during the first set of measurement occasions (i.e., ages 11 to 13); and a second linear slope factor, $\eta_2$, representing the linear change in Y during the second set of measurement occasions (i.e., ages 13 to 15).

More specifically, the longitudinally observed outcome variable $Y_{ti}$ is regressed on these latent growth factors such that

$$Y_{ti} = \eta_{0i} + \lambda_{1t}\eta_{1i} + \lambda_{2t}\eta_{2i} + \varepsilon_{ti}, \qquad (11.14)$$

where $\lambda_{1t}$ is the factor loading specific to *time* = $t$ and constrained so that $\eta_1$ represents the slope of $Y$ during the first segment of *time* and $\lambda_{2t}$ is the factor loading fixed so that $\eta_2$ represents the slope of $Y$ during the second segment of *time*. With the MLM framework, the Level 1 equation of a piecewise linear growth curve model can be expressed as

$$Y_{ti} = \beta_{0i} + \beta_{1i}X_{1t} + \beta_{2i}X_{2t} + \varepsilon_{ti},$$

where $X_{1t}$ and $X_{2t}$ are separate *time* variables coded to represent the passage of time during the first and second time segments of the model (see Raudenbush and Bryk, 2002: 178–79). As with the linear and quadratic growth curve models, the $T$ scalar equations implied by Equation 11.14 can be combined into a matrix equation of the form given earlier as Equation 11.2:

$$\mathbf{Y}_i = \boldsymbol{\Lambda}\boldsymbol{\eta}_i + \boldsymbol{\varepsilon}_i,$$

where $\Lambda$ is now a $T \times 3$ factor loading matrix and $\boldsymbol{\eta}_i$ is the $3 \times 1$ vector of scores on the three latent growth factors (i.e., the intercept and two linear factors) for individual $i$.

Next, Equation 11.4 can be applied to the unconditional piecewise linear model to represent the individual values for the growth factors as a function of their means and individual deviations from the mean:

$$\boldsymbol{\eta}_i = \boldsymbol{\mu}_{\boldsymbol{\eta}} + \boldsymbol{\zeta}_i,$$

which, for the piecewise linear growth curve model, corresponds to

$$\begin{bmatrix} \eta_0 \\ \eta_1 \\ \eta_2 \end{bmatrix} = \begin{bmatrix} \mu_0 \\ \mu_1 \\ \mu_2 \end{bmatrix} + \begin{bmatrix} \zeta_0 \\ \zeta_1 \\ \zeta_2 \end{bmatrix}.$$

Because there are three latent growth factors, the covariance matrix $\Psi$ for $\zeta_i$ has dimension $3 \times 3$; elements $\psi_{11}$, $\psi_{22}$, and $\psi_{33}$ describe the population variances of the latent intercept factor, the linear slope factor for the first time segment, and the linear slope factor for the third time segment, respectively, with off-diagonal elements of $\Psi$ giving the covariances among these latent growth factors.

The matrix equation in the previous paragraph is equivalent to the Level 2 equations for the MLM implementation of an unconditional piecewise linear growth curve model. Specifically, the Level 2 equation for the random intercepts ($\beta_{0i}$) is identical to Equation 11.7, and now there are Level 2 equations for each of the two random linear slopes:

$$\beta_{1i} = \gamma_{10} + \delta_{1i} \quad \text{(Level 2b)}$$

and

$$\beta_{2i} = \gamma_{20} + \delta_{2i} \quad \text{(Level 2c)},$$

where $\gamma_{10}$ is the mean of the individual trajectory slopes during the first time segment, $\delta_{1i}$ is the deviation from $\gamma_{10}$ of the individual slope for person $i$ during that same time segment, $\gamma_{20}$ is the mean slope during the second time segment, and $\delta_{2i}$ is the individual deviation from $\gamma_{20}$ for person $i$. Now the random-effect variance parameters – $VAR(\delta_{0i}) = \tau_{00}^2$, $VAR(\delta_{1i}) = \tau_{11}^2$, and $VAR(\delta_{2i}) = \tau_{22}^2$ – describe the extent of the individual variability around the mean intercept, variability around mean slope for the first time period, and slope variability for the second time period, respectively.

To demonstrate with the adolescent alcohol-use example, a piecewise linear growth curve model for heavy alcohol use across ages 11 to 15 can be specified as a structural equation model by applying Equation 11.2 with

$$
\begin{bmatrix} Y_0 \\ Y_1 \\ Y_2 \\ Y_3 \\ Y_4 \end{bmatrix} = \begin{bmatrix} 1 & -2 & 0 \\ 1 & -1 & 0 \\ 1 & 0 & 0 \\ 1 & 0 & 1 \\ 1 & 0 & 2 \end{bmatrix} \begin{bmatrix} \eta_0 \\ \eta_1 \\ \eta_2 \end{bmatrix} + \begin{bmatrix} \varepsilon_0 \\ \varepsilon_1 \\ \varepsilon_2 \\ \varepsilon_3 \\ \varepsilon_4 \end{bmatrix},
$$

where again $Y_0$ is the age 11 alcohol-use variable, $Y_1$ is age 12 alcohol use, $Y_2$ is age 13 alcohol use, $Y_3$ is age 14 alcohol use, and $Y_4$ is age 15 alcohol use. In this matrix equation, the second column of $\Lambda$ corresponds to the $\lambda_{1t}$ coefficients in Equation 11.14, showing that $\eta_1$ captures linear change from age 11 to age 13 because the $\lambda_{1t}$ coefficients increase by one unit per year from age 11 (where $\lambda_1 = -2$) to age 13 (where $\lambda_1 = 0$) but remain constant thereafter (i.e., $\lambda_1 = 0$ for ages 13, 14, and 15). Next, the third column of $\Lambda$ corresponds to the $\lambda_{2t}$ coefficients in Equation 11.14 so that $\eta_2$ represents linear change from ages 13 to 15 because the $\lambda_{2t}$ coefficients are constant up until age 13 (i.e., $\lambda_2 = 0$ for ages 11, 12, and 13) but then increase by one unit per year from age 13 (where $\lambda_2 = 0$) to age 15 (where $\lambda_2 = 2$). Notice also that these fixed values in $\Lambda$ serve to center time at age 13 because both $\lambda_1$ and $\lambda_2$ are fixed to 0 in the row of $\Lambda$ corresponding to age 13; thus, the intercept factor $\eta_0$ represents the amount of alcohol use at age 13. A path diagram of this model is in Figure 11.7.

In the model specification in the previous paragraph, time is centered at age 13, but as with the other models outlined earlier, the fixed elements of $\Lambda$ can be transformed to center time at any age. For instance, the matrix equation for a piecewise linear model with time instead centered at age 11 is

$$
\begin{bmatrix} Y_0 \\ Y_1 \\ Y_2 \\ Y_3 \\ Y_4 \end{bmatrix} = \begin{bmatrix} 1 & 0 & 0 \\ 1 & 1 & 0 \\ 1 & 2 & 0 \\ 1 & 2 & 1 \\ 1 & 2 & 2 \end{bmatrix} \begin{bmatrix} \eta_0 \\ \eta_1 \\ \eta_2 \end{bmatrix} + \begin{bmatrix} \varepsilon_0 \\ \varepsilon_1 \\ \varepsilon_2 \\ \varepsilon_3 \\ \varepsilon_4 \end{bmatrix}.
$$

Now, the intercept factor $\eta_0$ represents the predicted amount of alcohol use at age 11, but $\eta_1$ still represents the linear change in alcohol use from age 11 to 13 and $\eta_2$ still represents the linear change in alcohol use from age 13 to 15. Furthermore, eventual model fit is not affected by this respecification of $\Lambda$. For additional explanation, see Flora (2008).

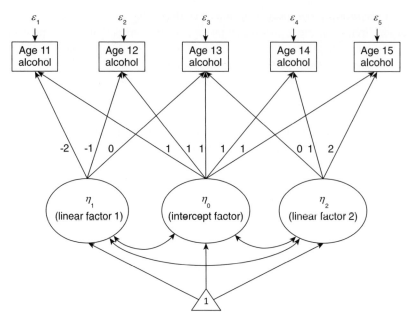

**Figure 11.7** Path diagram of unconditional growth curve model for piecewise linear change in adolescent alcohol use

 Section recap

### Specification of unconditional piecewise linear growth curve models

The piecewise linear growth curve model is an approach to representing nonlinear trajectories using a set of two or more linear segments. The parameters of piecewise linear growth curve models are much easier to interpret than those for more complex models for nonlinear change over time.

An individual piecewise linear growth trajectory can be expressed using SEM notation with

$$Y_{ti} = \eta_{0i} + \lambda_{1t}\eta_{1i} + \lambda_{2t}\eta_{2i} + \varepsilon_{ti},$$

where $\lambda_{1t}$ is the factor loading specific to $time = t$ and constrained so that $\eta_1$ represents the linear slope of $Y$ during the first segment of $time$, and $\lambda_{2t}$ is the factor loading fixed so that $\eta_2$ represents the linear slope of $Y$ during the second segment of $time$.

The Level 1 equation of a piecewise linear growth curve model can be expressed using MLM notation with

$$Y_{ti} = \beta_{0i} + \beta_{1i}X_{1t} + \beta_{2i}X_{2t} + \varepsilon_{ti},$$

where $X_{1t}$ and $X_{2t}$ are separate $time$ variables coded to represent the passage of time during the first and second time segments.

Using both SEM and MLM, the distributions of the individual intercepts and both linear slopes are summarized with parameters representing their means and variances, as well as with covariances among these components.

## Unconditional piecewise growth curve model: Results for alcohol-use example

Before moving to model estimation, it is also important to consider identification issues for the piecewise linear growth curve model. In short, it is generally necessary for there to be at least three time points (measurement occasions) at which Y is observed for each segment of time, or linear 'piece' of the trajectory; thus, at least five measurement occasions are needed for a model with two linear pieces because one time point is shared by the two time segments (see Bollen and Curran, 2006: 124–25, for additional details). For the current alcohol-use example, three time points are used for the first linear piece (ages 11, 12, and 13) and three time points are used for the second linear piece (ages 13, 14, and 15), resulting in an overidentified unconditional piecewise linear growth curve model.

Using FIML estimation, the unconditional piecewise linear model has a close fit to the adolescent alcohol-use data,[12] YB $\chi^2(6) = 5.71$, $p = .46$, RMSEA$_{robust} = .000$, CFI$_{robust} = 1.00$, TLI$_{robust} = 1.00$, SRMR $= .088$. Parameter estimates of the unconditional piecewise linear model, obtained with *time* centered at age 13, are given in Table 11.9.

The major result from these parameter estimates is that the mean of the first linear slope factor, $\hat{\mu}_1 = 0.076$, is much smaller than the mean of the second slope factor, $\hat{\mu}_2 = 0.278$, which indicates that the average increase in alcohol use from ages 11 to 13 is slight, whereas the average increase in alcohol use from ages 13 to 15 is much steeper. This slope difference is consistent with Figure 11.5 which clearly shows that there is a greater average increase in alcohol use at the later ages. Furthermore, the parameter estimates $\hat{\mu}_1 = 0.076$ and $\hat{\mu}_2 = 0.278$ of the current piecewise linear model map more directly onto this data pattern than do the growth factor mean estimates obtained earlier with the unconditional quadratic model.

Moving beyond the estimated mean trajectory, it is also noteworthy that there is substantial variability in the individual slopes for both the first time segment ($\hat{\psi}_{22} = 0.051$, $p = .004$) and the second time segment ($\hat{\psi}_{33} = 0.195$, $p = .003$), although the variance estimate is notably greater for the second time period. Thus, both from ages 11 to 13 and from ages 13 to 15, the individual trajectories have slopes which vary substantially around the mean slopes given by $\hat{\mu}_1$ and $\hat{\mu}_2$.

## Conditional piecewise growth curve models

The unconditional piecewise linear growth curve model is easily expanded to a conditional model with the latent growth factors conditioned on one or more predictor variables or covariates in a manner that parallels expanding the basic linear unconditional growth curve model to a linear conditional model. In particular, whereas interpretation of regression coefficients relating a predictor variable to a quadratic growth factor is somewhat awkward, in contrast, interpretation of coefficients relating a predictor variable to a linear slope factor is straightforward.

For instance, continuing with the adolescent alcohol-use example, we can expand the unconditional piecewise linear model presented earlier to include gender and parental

---

[12]As also occurred for the unconditional quadratic growth curve model, the residual variance of the age 11 alcohol-use variable was fixed to 0 to avoid obtaining an improper solution for the piecewise growth curve model. The covariance between the two linear growth factors, $\eta_1$ and $\eta_2$, was also fixed to 0 to facilitate convergence.

**Table 11.9** Results for unconditional piecewise linear growth curve model of alcohol use from ages 11 to 15

| Parameter | Estimate | Robust SE | z | p |
|---|---|---|---|---|
| $\mu_0$ (intercept factor mean) | 0.197 | 0.028 | 6.95 | <.001 |
| $\mu_1$ (mean of linear factor 1) | 0.076 | 0.016 | 4.78 | <.001 |
| $\mu_2$ (mean of linear factor 2) | 0.278 | 0.040 | 6.94 | <.001 |
| $\psi_{11}$ (intercept factor variance) | 0.196 | 0.068 | 2.88 | .004 |
| $\psi_{22}$ (variance of linear factor 1) | 0.051 | 0.017 | 2.98 | .003 |
| $\psi_{33}$ (variance of linear factor 2) | 0.195 | 0.070 | 2.77 | .006 |
| $\psi_{21}$ (intercept, $\eta_1$ covariance) | 0.095 | 0.033 | 2.86 | .004 |
| $\psi_{31}$ (intercept, $\eta_2$ covariance) | 0.002 | 0.036 | 0.05 | .960 |
| $\psi_{32}$ ($\eta_1$, $\eta_2$ covariance) | 0.00ª | – | – | – |
| $\sigma_1^2$ (age 11 error variance) | 0.00ª | – | – | – |
| $\sigma_2^2$ (age 12 error variance) | 0.090 | 0.043 | 2.11 | .035 |
| $\sigma_3^2$ (age 13 error variance) | 0.008 | 0.055 | 0.15 | .880 |
| $\sigma_4^2$ (age 14 error variance) | 0.310 | 0.092 | 3.38 | .001 |
| $\sigma_5^2$ (age 15 error variance) | 0.400 | 0.254 | 1.57 | .116 |

Note. $N = 355$. ªThese parameters were fixed to 0 to allow the model to converge to a proper solution.

alcoholism as predictors of both the linear slope factor from ages 11 to 13 and the linear slope factor from ages 13 to 15 (as well as regressing the intercept factor on these predictors). Doing so demonstrates an advantage of piecewise linear growth curve models over quadratic growth curve models: Unlike the quadratic growth curve model, the piecewise model allows a direct, natural method for testing and interpreting the effect of a predictor during one timeframe (e.g., ages 11 to 13) compared with the effect during another timeframe (e.g., ages 13 to 15). With the current example, the separate time segments were selected based on the observed data primarily to allow the model to capture the nonlinear longitudinal trajectory pattern. In other research contexts, the different time segments of a piecewise growth curve model can be specified a priori to represent theoretically important timeframes, such as longitudinal change occurring before and after the implementation of a treatment or intervention; consequently, one can easily model how the treatment affects the trajectory after it is implemented or model the differential effects of a predictor during these separate timeframes.

Returning to the alcohol-use example, Equation 11.9 can be adapted to incorporate gender ($X_1$) and the dichotomous parental alcoholism variable ($X_2$) as exogenous predictors of the intercept factor ($\eta_0$) and the two linear slope factors ($\eta_1$ and $\eta_2$):

$$\begin{bmatrix} \eta_0 \\ \eta_1 \\ \eta_2 \end{bmatrix} = \begin{bmatrix} \mu_0 \\ \mu_1 \\ \mu_2 \end{bmatrix} + \begin{bmatrix} \gamma_{01} & \gamma_{02} \\ \gamma_{11} & \gamma_{12} \\ \gamma_{21} & \gamma_{22} \end{bmatrix} \begin{bmatrix} X_1 \\ X_2 \end{bmatrix} + \begin{bmatrix} \zeta_0 \\ \zeta_1 \\ \zeta_2 \end{bmatrix},$$

where the $\gamma$ parameters are the coefficients in the linear regression of the latent growth factors on $X_1$ and $X_2$. Because this is now a conditional model, $\Psi$ is a 3 × 3 covariance matrix for the regression error terms in $\zeta$, with diagonal elements of $\Psi$ representing the growth factor variance that remains beyond the variance explained by **X**. Finally, the model's parameter set also includes $\Phi$, the $Q \times Q$ covariance matrix for exogenous predictors **X**. A path diagram of the model is in Figure 11.8.

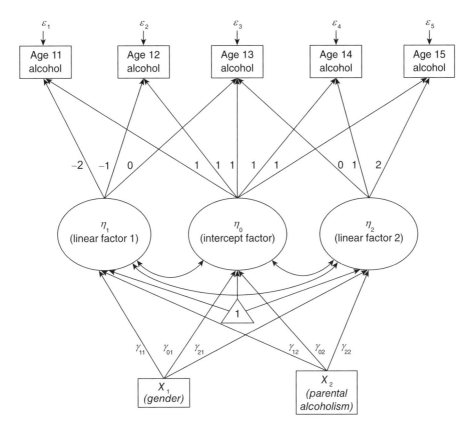

**Figure 11.8** Path diagram of piecewise linear growth curve model in adolescent alcohol use conditioned on gender and parental alcoholism

When this conditional piecewise linear model is fitted to the alcohol-use data using FIML, gender does not significantly predict any of the growth factors (using robust standard errors). But parental alcoholism is significantly related to both linear slope factors ($\hat{\gamma}_{12} = 0.12$, $Z = 4.01$, $p < .001$ and $\hat{\gamma}_{22} = 0.31$, $Z = 4.52$, $p < .001$) as well as the intercept factor ($\hat{\gamma}_{02} = 0.20$, $Z = 3.88$, $p < .001$). Interpretation of these effects proceeds in a manner which is essentially the same as that for the simple conditional linear model presented earlier. Specifically, because parental alcoholism was coded such that $0 = $ control and $1 = $ COA, the estimate $\hat{\gamma}_{12} = 0.12$ indicates that the mean linear slope from age 11 to age 13 of adolescents with an alcoholic parent (COAs) is 0.12 greater than the age 11 to age 13 slope of adolescents without an alcoholic parent (control participants). Next, $\hat{\gamma}_{22} = 0.31$ indicates that the mean linear slope from age 13 to age 15 of COAs is 0.31 greater than the age 13 to age 15 slope of control participants. Finally, because the model was specified so that the intercept factor represents the level of alcohol use at age 13, $\hat{\gamma}_{02} = 0.20$ indicates that the predicted level (or mean) of age 13 alcohol use is 0.20 greater for COAs than for controls. Therefore, it is evident that parental alcoholism is a stronger predictor of the increase in adolescent alcohol use from ages 13 to 15 than of the increase in alcohol use from ages 11 to 13; this conclusion would have been considerably more difficult to reach using a conditional quadratic growth curve model.

 — Section recap ▬▬▬▬▬▬▬▬▬▬▬▬▬▬▬▬▬▬▬▬▬▬▬▬

### Conditional piecewise growth curve models

The unconditional piecewise linear growth curve model is easily expanded to a conditional model with the latent growth factors (or individual growth random effects) conditioned on one or more predictor variables just as the basic linear unconditional growth curve model can be expanded to a linear conditional growth curve model.

Interpretation of regression coefficients relating a predictor variable to a linear slope factor from a piecewise growth curve model is straightforward, whereas interpretation of regression coefficients relating a predictor variable to a quadratic growth factor is somewhat awkward.

## CHAPTER SUMMARY

Growth curve modeling (GCM) has become one of the most popular methods for analysing longitudinal and repeated-measures data because its generality and flexibility allows GCM to handle data from many different types of studies and address many different research questions. This chapter showed how growth curve models can be specified and estimated using either a structural equation modeling (SEM) or a multilevel modeling (MLM) approach:

- Traditional ANOVA and MANOVA approaches focus on testing mean differences, implicitly assuming that each individual in the population follows the same trajectory over time, whereas GCM explicitly recognizes that there is likely to be substantial variability across individual trajectories.
- The unconditional linear growth curve model consists of parameters to summarize the distribution of individual trajectories.
- In the SEM framework, repeated (i.e., longitudinal) observations of the same variable are used as indicators of latent intercept and latent slope factors. In the MLM framework, repeated (i.e., longitudinal) observations are Level 1 units of analysis, whereas individual persons are Level 2 units of analysis. That is, repeated observations are nested within individuals.
- The parameters of the MLM specification of the unconditional linear growth curve model map directly onto the parameters from the SEM specification.
- The same principles of model identification that were described for other types of structural equation models apply to growth curve models, but because growth curve models involve mean structure in addition to covariance structure, the model degrees of freedom is also a function of the number of observed variable means and the number of growth factor means.

- In conditional growth curve models, time-invariant covariates or predictors are incorporated in the SEM framework by including them as predictors of the latent intercept and slope factors. Using MLM, time-invariant predictors $X_p$ are incorporated by including them as Level 2 predictors of the random intercepts and slopes.
- As the number of time points or repeated measurements of an outcome variable increases, it becomes more likely that the trajectory should be modeled with a nonlinear functional form of change.
- There are many approaches to specifying growth curve models for nonlinear change. Probably the most popular approach is to specify a quadratic growth curve model, but such models can be difficult to interpret.
- Piecewise linear growth curve models are typically easier to interpret compared with other growth curve models for nonlinear change.

## RECOMMENDED READING

Biesanz, J.C., Deeb-Sossa, N., Aubrecht, A.M., Bollen, K.A., & Curran, P.J. (2004). The role of coding time in estimating and interpreting growth curve models. *Psychological Methods, 9,* 30–52.

- Adapting a didactic style with example analyses, this paper gives a formal, detailed presentation of how different effects of *time* can be specified using the SEM factor loading matrix of a growth curve model and the implications for interpreting results.

Curran, P.J., Bauer, D.J., & Willoughby, M.T. (2004). Testing and probing main effects and interactions in latent curve analysis. *Psychological Methods, 9,* 220–37.

- Using examples, this paper describes and demonstrates how simple slope analyses for probing interactions in a regression model can be used to examine the associations between predictor variables and the latent slope factor in a growth curve model.

Flora, D.B. (2008). Specifying piecewise latent trajectory models for longitudinal data. *Structural Equation Modeling, 15,* 513–33.

- This *Teacher's Corner* paper provides a detailed description of the specification of piecewise growth curve models through the use of several examples (including an expanded description of the alcohol-use example used in this chapter). The paper moves on to present the specification of three-piece growth curve models and hybrid linear-quadratic piecewise growth curve models.

Grimm, K.J., Ram, N., & Hamagami, F. (2011). Nonlinear growth curves in developmental research. *Child Development, 82,* 1357–71.

- Using a nontechnical, applied context, this paper describes and demonstrates several approaches to modeling nonlinear trajectories, moving beyond the usual polynomial (e.g., quadratic) trajectory models.

MacCallum, R.C., Kim, C., Malarkey, W.B., & Kiecolt-Glaser, J.K. (1997). Studying multivariate change using multilevel models and latent curve models. *Multivariate Behavioral Research, 32,* 215–53.

- This paper was among the first to show that the SEM and MLM approaches to modeling longitudinal data are essentially the same. Furthermore, this paper describes how so-called parallel process models, in which the growth trajectories of two separate variables are modeled simultaneously, may be specified and interpreted in the SEM and MLM frameworks.

Quené, H., & van den Bergh, H. (2004). On multi-level modeling of data from repeated measures designs: A tutorial. *Speech Communication, 43,* 103–21.

- This paper clearly and comprehensively contrasts the MLM approach to growth curve modeling with repeated-measures ANOVA, detailing the important advantages of MLM. As the title indicates, the presentation is given with the context of repeated-measures experimental data in mind.

# REFERENCES

Achenbach, T., & Edelbrock, C. (1981). The classification of child psychopathology: A review and analysis of empirical efforts. *Psychological Bulletin, 85,* 1275–1301.

Agresti, A. (2002). *Categorical data analysis* (2nd edn.). Hoboken, NJ: Wiley.

Algina, J., & Penfield, R.D. (2009). Classical test theory. In R.E. Millsap & A. Maydeu-Olivares (Eds), *The SAGE handbook of quantitative methods in psychology* (pp. 93–122). Los Angeles, CA: SAGE.

American Psychological Association [APA]. (2010). *Publication manual of the American Psychological Association* (6th edn.). Washington, DC: Author.

Anderson, J.C., & Gerbing, D.W. (1988). Structural equation modeling in practice: A review and recommended two-step approach. *Psychological Bulletin, 103,* 411–23.

Anscombe, F.J. (1973). Graphs in statistical analysis. *The American Statistician, 27,* 17–21.

Baguley, T. (2009). Standardized or simple effect size: What should be reported? *British Journal of Psychology, 100,* 603–17.

Barendse, M.T., Oort, F.J., & Timmerman, M.E. (2015). Using exploratory factor analysis to determine the dimensionality of discrete responses. *Structural Equation Modeling, 22,* 87–101.

Baron, R.M., & Kenny, D.A. (1986). The moderator-mediator variable distinction in social psychological research: Conceptual, strategic and statistical considerations. *Journal of Personality and Social Psychology, 51,* 1173–82.

Barratt, S. (1994). Impulsivity: Integrating cognitive, behavioral, biological, and environmental data. In W.B. McCown, J.L. Johnson, & M.B. Shure (Eds), *The impulsive client: Theory, research, and treatment* (pp. 39–56). Washington, DC: American Psychological Association.

Bartholomew, D.J. (2007). Three faces of factor analysis. In R. Cudeck & R.C. MacCallum (Eds), *Factor analysis at 100: Historical developments and future directions* (pp. 9–21). Mahwah, NJ: Lawrence Erlbaum.

Bauer, D.J. (2003). Estimating multilevel linear models as structural equation models. *Journal of Educational and Behavioral Statistics, 28,* 135–67.

Bauer, D.J., & Curran, P.J. (2005). Probing interactions in fixed and multilevel regression: Inferential and graphical techniques. *Multivariate Behavioral Research, 40,* 373–400.

Baumann, J.F., Seifert-Kessell, N., & Jones, L.A. (1992). Effect of think-aloud instruction on elementary students' comprehension monitoring abilities. *Journal of Reading Behavior, 24,* 143–72.

Bentler, P.M. (1990). Comparative fit indexes in structural models. *Psychological Bulletin, 107,* 238–46.

Bentler, P.M., & Bonett, D.G. (1980). Significance tests and goodness of fit in the analysis of covariance structures. *Psychological Bulletin, 88,* 588–606.

Bentler, P.M., & Weeks, D.G. (1980). Linear structural equations with latent variables. *Psychometrika, 45,* 289–308.

Berk, R.A. (2004). *Regression analysis: A constructive critique.* Thousand Oaks, CA: SAGE.

Biesanz, J.C., Deeb-Sossa, N., Papadakis, A.A., Bollen, K.A., & Curran, P.J. (2004). The role of coding time in estimating and interpreting growth curve models. *Psychological Methods, 9,* 30–52.

Biesanz, J.C., Falk, C.F., & Savalei, V. (2010). Assessing mediational models: Testing and interval estimation for indirect effects. *Multivariate Behavioral Research, 45,* 661–701.

Bollen, K.A. (1989). Causality and causal models. In K.A. Bollen, *Structural equations with latent variables* (pp. 40–79). New York: Wiley.

Bollen, K.A. (2002). Latent variables in psychology and the social sciences. *Annual Review of Psychology, 53,* 605–34.

Bollen, K.A., & Curran, P.J. (2006). *Latent curve models: A structural equation perspective.* Hoboken, NJ: Wiley.

Box, G.E.P. (1979). Robustness in the strategy of scientific model building. In R.L. Launer & G.N. Wilkonson (Eds), *Robustness in Statistics: Proceedings of a Workshop.* New York: Academic Press.

Box, G.E.P., & Cox, D.R. (1964). An analysis of transformations. *Journal of the Royal Statistical Society, 26*(Series B), 211–43.

Briggs, N.E., & MacCallum, R.C. (2003). Recovery of weak common factors by maximum likelihood and ordinary least squares estimation. *Multivariate Behavioral Research, 38,* 25–56.

Brosseau-Liard, P.E., & Savalei, V. (2014). Adjusting incremental fit indices for nonnormality. *Multivariate Behavioral Research, 49,* 460–70.

Brosseau-Liard, P.E., Savalei, V., & Li, L. (2012). An investigation of the sample performance of two nonnormality corrections for RMSEA. *Multivariate Behavioral Research, 47,* 904–30.

Browne, M.W. (1984). Asymptotically distribution-free methods for the analysis of covariance structures. *British Journal of Mathematical and Statistical Psychology, 37,* 62–83.

Browne, M.W. (2001). An overview of analytic rotation in exploratory factor analysis. *Multivariate Behavioral Research, 36,* 111–50.

Browne, M.W., & Cudeck, R. (1992). Alternative ways of assessing model fit. *Sociological Methods and Research, 21,* 230–58.

Browne, M.W., & Cudeck, R. (1993). Alternative ways of assessing model fit. In K.A. Bollen & J.S. Long (Eds), *Testing structural equation models* (pp. 136–62). Newbury Park, CA: SAGE.

Buss, A.H., & Perry, M.P. (1992). The aggression questionnaire. *Journal of Personality and Social Psychology, 63,* 452–59.

Byrne, B.M. (1998). *Structural equation modeling with LISREL, PRELIS, and SIMPLIS: Basic concepts, applications, and programming.* Mahwah, NJ: Lawrence Erlbaum.

Carroll, J.D., Green, P.E., & Chaturvedi, A. (1997). *Mathematical tools for applied multivariate analysis: Revised edition.* San Diego, CA: Academic Press.

Cattell, R.B. (1966). The scree test for the number of factors. *Multivariate Behavioral Research, 1,* 245–76.

Chao, Y.-C.E., Zhao, Y., Kupper, L.L., & Nylander-French, L.A. (2008). Quantifying the relative importance of predictors in multiple linear regression analyses for public health studies. *Journal of Occupational and Environmental Hygiene, 8,* 519–29.

Chassin, L., Flora, D.B., & King, K.M. (2004). Trajectories of alcohol and drug use and dependence from adolescence to adulthood: The effects of familial alcoholism and personality. *Journal of Abnormal Psychology, 113,* 483–98.

Chen, F.F., Bollen, K., Paxton, P., Curran, P.J., & Kirby, J. (2001). Improper solutions in structural equation models: Causes, consequences, and strategies. *Sociological Methods and Research, 29,* 468–508.

Chen, F.F., West, S.G., & Sousa, K.H. (2006). A comparison of bifactor and second-order models of quality of life. *Multivariate Behavioral Research, 41,* 189–225.

Coffman, D.L., & MacCallum, R.C. (2005). Using parcels to convert path analysis models into latent variable models. *Multivariate Behavioral Research, 40,* 235–59.

Coffman, D.L., & Zhong, W. (2012). Assessing mediation using marginal structural models in the context of confounding and moderation. *Psychological Methods, 17,* 642–64.

Cohen, J. (1968). Multiple regression as a general data-analytic system. *Psychological Bulletin, 70,* 426–43.

Cohen, J. (1994). The earth is round ($p < .05$). *American Psychologist, 49,* 997–1003.

Cohen, J., Cohen, P., West, S.G., & Aiken, L.S. (2003). *Applied multiple regression/correlation analysis for the behavioral sciences* (3rd edn.). Mahwah, NJ: Lawrence Erlbaum.

Cole, D.A., & Maxwell, S.E. (2003). Testing mediational models with longitudinal data: Questions and tips in the use of structural equation modeling. *Journal of Abnormal Psychology, 112,* 558–77.

Cole, D.A., & Preacher, K.J. (2014). Manifest variable path analysis: Potentially serious and misleading consequences due to uncorrected measurement error. *Psychological Methods, 19,* 300–15.

Compas, B.E., Davis, G.E., Forsythe, C.J., & Wagner, B.M. (1987). Assessment of major and daily life events during adolescence: The Adolescent Perceived Events Scale. *Journal of Consulting and Clinical Psychology, 55,* 534–41.

Compas, B.E., Wagner, B.M., Slavin, L.A., & Vannatta, K. (1986). A prospective study of life events, social support, and psychological symptomatology during the transition from high school to college. *American Journal of Community Psychology, 14,* 241–57.

Crawford, C.B., & Ferguson, G.A. (1970). A general rotation criterion and its use in orthogonal rotation. *Psychometrika, 35,* 321–32.

Cudeck, R. (1989). The analysis of correlation matrices using covariance structure models. *Psychological Bulletin, 105,* 317–27.

Curran, P.J. (2003). Have multilevel models been structural equation models all along? *Multivariate Behavioral Research, 38,* 529–69.

Curran, P.J., & Bauer, D.J. (2011). The disaggregation of within-person and between-person effects in longitudinal models of change. *Annual Review of Psychology, 62,* 583–619.

Curran, P.J., Bauer, D.J., & Willoughby, M.T. (2004). Testing and probing main effects and interactions in latent curve analysis. *Psychological Methods, 9,* 220–37.

Curran, P.J., Bollen, K.A., Chen, F., Paxton, P., & Kirby, J. (2003). The finite sampling properties of the RMSEA: Point estimates and confidence intervals. *Sociological Methods and Research, 32,* 208–52.

Derogatis, L.R., Lipman, R.S., Rickels, K., Uhlenhuth, E.H., & Covi, L. (1974). The Hopkins Symptom Checklist. *Pharmacopsychiatry, 7,* 79–110.

Diez Roux, A.V. (2002). A glossary for multilevel analysis. *Journal of Epidemiology & Community Health, 56,* 588–94.

Dunn, E.W., Biesanz, J.C., Human, L.J., & Finn, S. (2007). Misunderstanding the affective consequences of everyday social interactions: The hidden benefits of putting one's best face forward. *Journal of Personality and Social Psychology, 92,* 990–1005.

Edwards, J.R. (2009). Seven deadly myths of testing moderation in organizational research. In C.E. Lance & R.J. Vandenberg (Eds), *Statistical and methodological myths and urban legends: Doctrine, verity and fable in the organizational and social sciences* (pp. 143–60). New York: Routledge.

Efron, B., & Tibshirani, R. (1993). *An introduction to the bootstrap.* New York: Chapman & Hall/CRC.

Enders, C.K., & Tofighi, D. (2007). Centering predictor variables in cross-sectional multilevel models: A new look at an old issue. *Psychological Methods, 12,* 121–38.

Fabrigar, L.R., Wegener, D.T., MacCallum, R.C., & Strahan, E.J. (1999). Evaluating the use of exploratory factor analysis in psychological research. *Psychological Methods, 4,* 272–99.

Ferron, J.M., & Hess, M.R. (2007). Estimation in SEM: A concrete example. *Journal of Educational and Behavioral Statistics, 32,* 110–20.

Fisher, R.A. (1922). On the mathematical foundations of theoretical statistics. *Philosophical Transactions of the Royal Society of London, Series A, 222,* 309–68.

Flora, D.B. (2008). Specifying piecewise latent trajectory models for longitudinal data. *Structural Equation Modeling, 15,* 513–33.

Flora, D.B., & Curran, P.J. (2004). An empirical evaluation of alternative methods of estimation for confirmatory factor analysis with ordinal data. *Psychological Methods, 9,* 466–91.

Flora, D.B., Khoo, S.-T., & Chassin, L. (2007). Moderating effects of a risk factor: Modeling longitudinal moderated mediation in the development of adolescent heavy drinking. In T.D. Little, J.A. Bovaird, & N.A. Card (Eds), *Modeling contextual effects in longitudinal studies* (pp. 231–54). Mahwah, NJ: Lawrence Erlbaum.

Flora, D.B., LaBrish, C., & Chalmers, R.P. (2012). Old and new ideas for data screening and assumption testing for exploratory and confirmatory factor analysis. *Frontiers in Psychology (Quantitative Psychology and Measurement), 3* (55). doi:10.3389/fpsyg.2012.00055

Forero, C.G., & Maydeu-Olivares, A. (2009). Estimation of IRT graded response models: Limited versus full information methods. *Psychological Methods, 3,* 275–99.

Forero, C.G., Maydeu-Olivares, A., & Gallardo-Pujol, D. (2009). Factor analysis with ordinal indicators: A Monte Carlo study comparing DWLS and ULS estimation. *Structural Equation Modeling, 16,* 625–41.

Fox, J. (2003). Effect displays in R for generalised linear models. *Journal of Statistical Software, 8,* 1–27.

Fox, J. (2008). *Applied regression analysis and generalized linear models.* Thousand Oaks, CA: SAGE.

Fox, J. (2009). *A mathematical primer for social statistics.* Thousand Oaks, CA: SAGE.

Fox, J., & Weisberg, S. (2011). *An R companion to applied regression* (2nd edn.). Thousand Oaks, CA: SAGE.

Frick, R.W. (1999). Defending the statistical status quo. *Theory and Psychology, 9,* 183–89.

Friedman, L., & Wall, M. (2005). Graphical views of suppression and multicollinearity in multiple linear regression. *The American Statistician, 59,* 127–36.

Garrido, L.E., Abad, F.J., & Ponsoda, V. (2013). A new look at Horn's parallel analysis with ordinal variables. *Psychological Methods, 18,* 454–74.

Garrido, L.E., Abad, F.J., & Ponsoda, V. (2016). Are fit indices really fit to estimate the number of factors with categorical variables? Some cautionary findings via Monte Carlo simulation. *Psychological Methods, 21,* 93–111.

Gelman, A., & Hill, J. (2007). *Data analysis using regression and multilevel/hierarchical models.* New York: Cambridge University Press.

Graham, J.M. (2008). The general linear model as structural equation modeling. *Journal of Educational and Behavioral Statistics, 33,* 485–506.

Green, S.B., & Thompson, M.S. (2006). Structural equation modeling for conducting tests of differences in multiple means. *Psychosomatic Medicine, 68,* 706–17.

Green, S.B., & Thompson, M.S. (2012). A flexible structural equation modeling approach for analyzing means. In R.H. Hoyle (Ed.), *Handbook of structural equation modeling* (pp. 393–416). New York: Guilford Press.

Grimm, K.J., Ram, N., & Hamagami, F. (2011). Nonlinear growth curves in developmental research. *Child Development, 82,* 1357–71.

Hamermesh, D.S., & Parker, A.M. (2005). Beauty in the classroom: Instructors' pulchritude and putative pedagogical productivity. *Economics of Education Review, 24,* 369–76.

Hancock, G.R., & Liu, M. (2012). Bootstrapping standard errors and data-model fit statistics in structural equation modeling. In R. Hoyle (Ed.), *Handbook of structural equation modeling* (pp. 296–306). New York: Guilford Press.

Hart, T.A., Flora, D.B., Palyo, S.A., Fresco, D.M., Holle, C., & Heimberg, R.G. (2008). Development and examination of the Social Appearance Anxiety Scale. *Assessment, 15,* 48–59.

Hershberger, S.L., & Marcoulides, G.A. (2013). The problem of equivalent structural models. In G.R. Hancock & R.O. Mueller (Eds), *Structural equation modeling: A second course* (pp. 3–39). Charlotte, NC: Information Age.

Ho, R.M., Stark, S., & Chernyshenko, O. (2012). Graphical representation of structural equation models using path diagrams. In R.H. Hoyle (Ed.), *Handbook of structural equation modeling* (pp. 43–55). New York: Guilford Press.

Horn, J.L. (1965). A rationale and test for the number of factors in factor analysis. *Psychometrika, 30,* 179–85.

Howell, D.C. (2007). *Statistical methods for psychology* (6th ed.). Belmont, CA: Thomson Wadsworth.

Hu, L.T., & Bentler, P.M. (1999). Cutoff criteria for fit indexes in covariance structure analysis: Conventional criteria versus new alternatives. *Structural Equation Modeling, 6,* 1–55.

Imai, K., Keele, L., & Tingley, D. (2010). A general approach to causal mediation analysis. *Psychological Methods, 15,* 309–34.

Jennrich, R.I. (2007). Rotation methods, algorithms, and standard errors. In R. Cudeck & R.C. MacCallum (Eds), *Factor analysis at 100: Historical developments and future directions* (pp. 315–35). Mahwah, NJ: Lawrence Erlbaum.

Jennrich, R.I., & Bentler, P.M. (2012). Exploratory bi-factor analysis: The oblique case. *Psychometrika, 77,* 442–54.

Jones, L.V. (1952). Tests of hypotheses: One-sided vs. two-sided alternatives. *Psychological Bulletin, 49,* 43–46.

Jöreskog, K.G. (1969). A general approach to confirmatory maximum likelihood factor analysis. *Psychometrika, 34,* 183–202.

Jöreskog, K.G. (1970). A general method for analysis of covariance structures. *Biometrika, 57,* 239–51.

Jöreskog, K.G. (1973). A general method for estimating a linear structural equation system. In A. Goldberger & O.D. Duncan (Eds), *Structural equation models in the social sciences* (pp. 85–112). New York: Academic Press.

Jöreskog, K.G., & Sörbom, D. (1974). LISREL III [Computer software]. Chicago, IL: Scientific Software International.

Jöreskog, K.G., & Sörbom, D. (2015). LISREL 9.20 [Computer software]. Skokie, IL: Scientific Software International.

Kaufman, J., Birmaher, B., Brent, D., Rao, U., Flynn, C., Moreci, P., Williamson, D., & Ryan, N. (1997). Schedule for affective disorders and schizophrenia for school-age children – present and lifetime version (K-SADS-PL): Initial reliability and validity data. *Journal of the American Academy of Child and Adolescent Psychiatry, 36,* 980–88.

Kelley, K., & Preacher, K.J. (2012). On effect size. *Psychological Methods, 17,* 137–52.

King, G. (1986). How not to lie with statistics: Avoiding common mistakes in quantitative political science. *American Journal of Political Science, 30,* 666–87.

Kromrey, J.D., & Foster-Johnson, L. (1998). Mean centering in moderated multiple regression: Much ado about nothing. *Educational and Psychological Measurement, 58,* 42–67.

Lane, D.M., & Sandor, A. (2009). Designing better graphs by including distributional information and integrating words, numbers, and images. *Psychological Methods, 14,* 239–57.

Lee, C.-T., Zhang, G., & Edwards, M.C. (2012). Ordinary least squares estimation of parameters in exploratory factor analysis with ordinal data. *Multivariate Behavioral Research, 47,* 314–39.

MacCallum, R.C. (2003). Working with imperfect models. *Multivariate Behavioral Research, 38,* 113–39.

MacCallum, R.C. (2009). Factor analysis. In R.E. Millsap & A. Maydeu-Olivares (Eds), *The SAGE handbook of quantitative methods in psychology* (pp. 123–47). Thousand Oaks, CA: SAGE.

MacCallum, R.C., Browne, M.W., & Sugawara, H.M. (1996). Power analysis and determination of sample size for covariance structure modeling. *Psychological Methods, 1,* 130–49.

MacCallum, R.C., Kim, C., Malarkey, W.B., & Kiecolt-Glaser, J.K. (1997). Studying multivariate change using multilevel models and latent curve models. *Multivariate Behavioral Research, 32,* 215–53.

MacCallum, R.C., Zhang, S., Preacher, K.J., & Rucker, D.D. (2002). On the practice of dichotomization of quantitative variables. *Psychological Methods, 7,* 19–40.

MacKinnon, D.P., Krull, J.L., & Lockwood, C.M. (2000). Equivalence of the mediation, confounding and suppression effect. *Prevention Science, 4,* 173–81.

MacKinnon, D.P., Lockwood, C.M., Hoffman, J.M., West, S.G., & Sheets, V. (2002). A comparison of methods to test the significance of the mediated effect. *Psychological Methods, 7,* 83–104.

MacKinnon, D.P., Lockwood, C.M., & Williams, J. (2004). Confidence limits for the indirect effect: Distribution of the product and resampling methods. *Multivariate Behavioral Research, 39,* 99–128.

Mardia, K.V. (1970). Measures of multivariate skewness and kurtosis with applications. *Biometrika, 57,* 519–30.

Marsh, H.W., Hau, K.T., & Wen, Z. (2004). In search of golden rules: Comment on hypothesis-testing approaches to setting cutoff values for fit indexes and dangers in overgeneralizing Hu and Bentler's (1999) findings. *Structural Equation modeling, 11,* 320–41.

Matsueda, R.L. (2012). Key advances in the history of structural equation modeling. In R.H. Hoyle (Ed.), *Handbook of structural equation modeling* (pp. 17–42). New York: Guilford Press.

Maxwell, S.E., & Delaney, H.D. (1990). *Designing experiments and analyzing data: A model comparison perspective.* Belmont, CA: Wadsworth.

Maxwell, S.E., & Delaney, H.D. (2004). *Designing experiments and analyzing data: A model comparison perspective* (2nd edn.). Mahwah, NJ: Lawrence Erlbaum.

McArdle, J.J., & McDonald, R.P. (1984). Some algebraic properties of the Reticular Action Model for moment structures. *British Journal of Mathematical and Statistical Psychology, 37,* 234–51.

McCrae, R.R., & Costa, P.T. (2004). A contemplated revision of the NEO Five-Factor Inventory. *Personality and Individual Differences, 36,* 587–96.

McDonald, R.P. (1999). *Test theory: A unified treatment.* New York: Routledge.

Mehta, P.D., & West, S.G. (2000). Putting the individual back into individual growth curves. *Psychological Methods, 5,* 23–43.

Meyer, T.J., Miller, M.L., Metzger, R.L., & Borkovec, T.D. (1990). Development and validation of the Penn State Worry Questionnaire. *Behaviour Research and Therapy, 28,* 487–95.

Mirman, D. (2014). *Growth curve analysis and visualization using R.* Boca Raton, FL: CRC Press.

Monette, G. (1990). Geometry of multiple regression and interactive 3-D graphics. In J. Fox & J.S. Long (Eds), *Modern methods of data analysis* (pp. 209–56). Newbury Park, CA: SAGE.

Mulaik, S.A., & Millsap, R.E. (2000). Doing the four-step right. *Structural Equation Modeling, 7,* 36–73.

Murnane, R.J., & Willett, J.B. (2011). *Methods matter: Improving causal inference in educational and social science research.* New York: Oxford University Press.

Muthén, B. (1984). A general structural equation model with dichotomous, ordered categorical, and continuous latent variable indicators. *Psychometrika, 49,* 115–32.

Myung, I.J. (2003). Tutorial on maximum likelihood estimation. *Journal of Mathematical Psychology, 47,* 90–100.

Nissim, R., Flora, D.B., Cribbie, R.A., Zimmermann, C., Gagliese, L., & Rodin, G. (2010). Factor structure of the Beck Hopelessness Scale in individuals with advanced cancer. *Psycho-Oncology, 19,* 255–63.

Nunnally, J.C., & Bernstein, I.H. (1994). *Psychometric theory* (3rd edn.). New York: McGraw-Hill.

Olsson, U. (1979). Maximum likelihood estimation of the polychoric correlation coefficient. *Psychometrika, 44,* 443–60.

Pearl, J. (2000). *Causality: Models, reasoning, and inference.* Cambridge, England: Cambridge University Press.

Pedhazur, E.J. (1997). *Multiple regression in behavioral research: Explanation and prediction* (3rd edn.). Toronto, ON, Canada: Wadsworth.

Pek, J., & Flora, D.B. (In press). Reporting effect sizes in original psychological research: A discussion and tutorial. *Psychological Methods.* doi:dx.doi.org/10.1037/met0000126

Pek, J., & Hoyle, R.H. (2016). On the (in)validity of tests of simple mediation: Threats and solutions. *Social and Personality Psychology Compass, 10,* 150–63.

Preacher, K.J., & Hayes, A.F. (2008). Asymptotic and resampling strategies for assessing and comparing indirect effects in multiple mediator models. *Behavior Research Methods, 40,* 879–91.

Preacher, K.J., & MacCallum, R.C. (2003). Repairing Tom Swift's electric factor analysis machine. *Understanding Statistics, 2,* 13–43.

Preacher, K.J., & Merkle, E.C. (2012). The problem of model selection uncertainty in structural equation modeling. *Psychological Methods, 17,* 1–14.

Preacher, K.J., Rucker, D.D., & Hayes, A.F. (2007). Addressing moderated mediation hypotheses: Theory, methods, and prescriptions. *Multivariate Behavioral Research, 42,* 185–227.

Preacher, K.J., Zhang, G., Kim, C., & Mels, G. (2013). Choosing the optimal number of factors in exploratory factor analysis: A model selection perspective. *Multivariate Behavioral Research, 48,* 28–56.

Quené, H., & van den Bergh, H. (2004). On multi-level modeling of data from repeated measures designs: A tutorial. *Speech Communication, 43,* 103–21.

Raudenbush, S.W., & Bryk, A.S. (2002). *Hierarchical linear models: Applications and data analysis methods* (2nd edn.). London, England: SAGE.

Reichardt, C.S. (2009). Quasi-experimental design. In R.E. Millsap & A. Maydeu-Olivares (Eds), *The SAGE handbook of quantitative methods in psychology* (pp. 46–71). Los Angeles, CA: SAGE.

Reise, S.P. (2012). The rediscovery of bifactor measurement models. *Multivariate Behavioral Research, 47,* 667–96.

Rhemtulla, M., Brosseau-Liard, P.E., & Savalei, V. (2012). When can categorical variables be treated as continuous? A comparison of robust continuous and categorical SEM estimation methods in non-ideal conditions. *Psychological Methods, 17,* 354–73.

Richards, J.M. (1982). Standardized versus unstandardized regression weights. *Applied Psychological Measurement, 6,* 201–12.

Rodgers, J.L. (2010). The epistemology of mathematical and statistical modeling: A quiet methodological revolution. *American Psychologist, 65,* 1–12.

Rosseel, Y. (2012). *lavaan*: An R package for structural equation modeling. *Journal of Statistical Software, 48,* 1–36.

Rozeboom, W.W. (1960). The fallacy of the null-hypothesis significance test. *Psychological Bulletin, 57,* 416–28.

Rubin, D.B. (1974). Estimating causal effects of treatments in randomized and nonrandomized studies. *Journal of Educational Psychology, 66,* 688–701.

Sarason, I.G., Levine H.M., Basham, R.B., & Sarason, B.R. (1983). Assessing social support: The Social Support Questionnaire. *Journal of Personality and Social Psychology, 44,* 127–39.

Satorra, A., & Bentler, P.M. (1988). Scaling corrections for chi-square statistics in covariance structure analysis. *ASA 1988 Proceedings of the Business and Economic Statistics Section* (pp. 308–13). Alexandria, VA: American Statistical Association.

Satorra, A., & Bentler, P.M. (1994). Corrections to test statistics and standard errors in covariance structure analysis. In A. von Eye & C.C. Clogg (Eds), *Latent variables analysis: Applications for developmental research* (pp. 399–419). Thousand Oaks, CA: SAGE.

Satorra, A., & Bentler, P.M. (2001). A scaled difference chi-square test statistic for moment structure analysis. *Psychometrika, 66,* 507–14.

Savalei, V. (2010). Small sample statistics for incomplete nonnormal data: Extensions of complete data formulae and a Monte Carlo comparison. *Structural Equation Modeling, 17,* 245–68.

Savalei, V. (2011). What to do about zero frequency cells when estimating polychoric correlations. *Structural Equation Modeling, 18,* 253–73.

Savalei, V. (2014). Understanding robust corrections in structural equation modeling. *Structural Equation Modeling, 21,* 149–60.

Savalei, V., & Falk, C.F. (2014). Robust two-stage approach outperforms robust full information maximum likelihood with incomplete nonnormal data. *Structural Equation Modeling, 21,* 280–302.

Savalei, V., and Rhemtulla, M. (2013). The performance of robust test statistics with categorical data. *British Journal of Mathematical and Statistical Psychology, 66,* 201–23.

Scott-Lennox, J.A., & Lennox, R.D. (1995). Sex-race differences in social support and depression in lower-income older adults. In R.H. Hoyle (Ed.), *Structural equation modeling: Concepts, issues, and applications* (pp. 199–216). Thousand Oaks, CA: SAGE.

Singer, J.D., & Willett, J.B. (2003). *Applied longitudinal data analysis.* Oxford, England: Oxford University Press.

Snijders, T.A.B., & Bosker, R.J. (2012). *Multilevel analysis: An introduction to basic and advanced multilevel modeling.* London, England: SAGE.

Sobel, M.E. (1982). Asymptotic confidence intervals for indirect effects in structural equation models. In S. Leinhardt (Ed.), *Sociological Methodology 1982* (pp. 290–312). San Francisco, CA: Jossey-Bass.

Steiger, J.H. (1990). Structural model evaluation and modification: An interval estimation approach. *Multivariate Behavioral Research, 25,* 173–80.

Steiger, J.H., & Lind, J. (1980, May). *Statistically based tests for the number of common factors.* Paper presented at the annual meeting of the Psychometric Society, Iowa City, IA.

Steinberg, L., & Thissen, D. (2006). Using effect sizes for research reporting: Examples using item response theory to analyze differential item functioning. *Psychological Methods, 11,* 402–15.

Sterba, S.K. (2009). Alternative model-based and design-based frameworks for inference from samples to populations: From polarization to integration. *Multivariate Behavioral Research, 44,* 711–40.

Strobl, C., Malley, J., & Tutz, G. (2009). An introduction to recursive partitioning: Rationale, application and characteristics of classification and regression trees, bagging, and random forests. *Psychological Methods, 14,* 323–48.

Swanson, J.M., Schuck, S., Porter, M.M., Carlson, C., Hartman, C.A., Sergeant, J.A., Clevenger, W., Wasdell, M., McCleary, R., Lakes, K., & Wigal, T. (2012). Categorical and dimensional definitions and evaluations of symptoms of ADHD: History of the SNAP and the SWAN rating scales. *The International Journal of Educational and Psychological Assessment, 10,* 51–70.

Thomas, R.D., Hughes, E., & Zumbo, B.D. (1998). On variable importance in linear regression. *Social Indicators Research, 45*, 253–75.

Thurstone, L.L. (1947). *Multiple factor analysis*. Chicago, IL: University of Chicago Press.

Toplak, M.E., Pitch, A., Flora, D.B., Iwenofu, L., Ghelani, K., Jain, U., & Tannock, R. (2009). The unity and diversity of inattention and hyperactivity/impulsivity in ADHD: Evidence for a general factor with separable dimensions. *Journal of Abnormal Child Psychology, 37*, 1137–50.

Tucker, L.R., & Lewis, C. (1973). A reliability coefficient for maximum likelihood factor analysis. *Psychometrika, 38*, 1–10.

Ullman, J.B. (2007). Structural equation modeling. In B.G. Tabachnick and L.S. Fidell (Eds), *Using multivariate statistics* (5th edn.), (pp. 676–780). New York: Allyn and Bacon.

Wagner, B.M., Compas, B.E., & Howell, D.C. (1988). Daily and major life events: A test of an integrative model of psychosocial stress. *American Journal of Community Psychology, 16*, 189–205.

Wand, M.P., & Jones, M.C. (1995). *Kernel smoothing*. London, England: Chapman & Hall.

West, S.G., Finch, J.F., & Curran, P.J. (1995). Structural equation models with non-normal variables: Problems and remedies. In R.H. Hoyle (Ed.), *Structural equation modeling: Concepts, issues and applications* (pp. 56–75). Newbury Park, CA: SAGE.

Widaman, K.F. (2007). Common factors versus components: Principals and principles, errors and misconceptions. In R. Cudeck & R.C. MacCallum (Eds), *Factor analysis at 100: Historical developments and future directions* (pp. 177–203). Mahwah, NJ: Lawrence Erlbaum.

Wilkinson, L., & The Task Force on Statistical Inference (1999). Statistical methods in psychology journals: Guidelines and explanations. *American Psychologist, 54*, 594–604.

Willett, J.B. (1989). Some results on reliability for the longitudinal measurement of change: Implications for the design of studies of individual growth. *Educational and Psychological Measurement, 49*, 587–602.

Williams, L.J. (2012). Equivalent models: Concepts, problems, alternatives. In R.H. Hoyle (Ed.), *Handbook of structural equation modeling* (pp. 247–60). New York: Guilford Press.

Wirth, R.J., & Edwards, M.C. (2007). Item factor analysis: Current approaches and future directions. *Psychological Methods, 12*, 58–79.

Yuan, K.H., & Bentler, P.M. (2000). Three likelihood-based methods for mean and covariance structure analysis with nonnormal missing data. *Sociological Methodology, 30*, 165–200.

Yung, Y.F., Thissen, D., & McLeod, L.D. (1999). On the relationship between the higher-order factor model and the hierarchical factor model. *Psychometrika, 64*, 113–28.

# INDEX

Page numbers followed by f = figure; n = notes; t = table

addition and subtraction: matrices 218–20
adjusted means 106–7
Akaike's Information Criterion (AIC) 200–1, 329
algebra. see matrix algebra
analysis of covariance. see ANCOVA
analysis of regression variance. see ANOVA
ANCOVA 88, 104–8, 110
ANOVA. see also MANOVA
   formal expression as a multiple regression
      model 96
   general linear model 88–9
   and growth curve modeling 390, 393
   random-effects ANOVA model 172–3. see
      also unconditional multilevel model
   regression ANOVA
     multiple regression 54–8, 56t, 93–7, 94t
     multiple regression (contrast codes)
       99–101, 103
assumptions 361
   confirmatory factor analysis 351, 361–4
   exploratory factor analysis 256–7, 280–3,
     281f, 282f
   growth curve modeling 393, 407
   multilevel modeling 164–5, 205–8, 206f,
     207f, 208f
   multiple regression: categorical predictors
     108, 110–11
   multiple regression: continuous predictors
     72–3, 77–8, 81, 86
   path analysis 311–12, 331–3
   simple linear regression 18–20, 21, 26, 29–31
asymptotic covariance matrix 121, 121n, 177,
   313–15, 351, 365

Baron, R.M. 152, 153n
baseline fit indices 321–2, 321f
Bauer, D.J. 121, 123, 141, 204, 391, 419
Baumann, J.F. 90, 91, 98, 105, 107
Bayesian Information Criterion (BIC) 200–1,
   329, 409
Beck Hopelessness Scale 278–9, 278t, 279t

Bentler, P.M. 269n, 287, 321, 363, 404
Bernstein, I.H. 267, 370n
between-cluster effects. see within-cluster
   effect and between-clusters effect
Biesanz, J.C. 150, 152, 153n, 410, 424, 427
bifactor model 357–61, 359f, 360t, 366
Bollen, K.A. 145, 286, 288, 301, 303, 306,
   307, 311, 313, 325, 337n, 362, 419,
   425, 427, 431
bootstrapping 153–6, 155f, 297, 330–1, 331t,
   363, 385
Bosker, R.J. 166n, 176, 182, 205, 405n
Box, G.E.P. 4, 80
Browne, M.W. 263, 264, 268, 311, 313, 320, 362
Bryk, A.S. 176, 177, 195, 205, 206, 207, 428

Carroll, J.D. 214, 225
categorical moderators 114–31
   probing an interaction: multicategory
     moderator 128–31, 129t, 130t
   probing an interaction: simple-slope analysis
     118–25, 121f, 122t, 124f
   research example 114–15, 115f, 115t
   specification and interpretation:
     dichotomous moderator 116–18, 117t
   specification and interpretation:
     multicategory moderator 125–8,
     125t, 127t
categorical observed variables with EFA 275
   polychoric correlations 276–7, 277f
   research example 278–80, 278t, 279t
categorical predictors. see multiple regression:
   categorical predictors
causality 145–7, 146n, 152, 153n, 157–60,
   286, 419
centering continuous predictors 135, 139,
   140–2
Chen, F.F. 310, 358
cluster mean centering 191–2, 197–9, 199t
clustering 166–7, 190–9, 190f. see also
   multilevel modeling

coding *time* to change the trajectory intercept 410–12, 411t
coefficient of determination. *see* R²
Coffman, D.L. 146n, 370
Cohen, J. 6, 7, 8, 79, 80, 89, 100, 102, 140
Cole, D.A. 369, 370, 419
common factor model
  estimation of 247–50
    maximum likelihood estimation 256–7
    model-implied and residual correlation matrices 253–5, 254t, 255t
    principal axis estimation 250–2
    unweighted least-squares estimation 253, 255
  specification of 241–5, 242t, 244t
common factors, optimal number of 257–8
  Kaiser criterion 258
  model fit statistics 262–4
  parallel analysis 259–61, 259f, 261f, 261t
  scree plots 258–9
communality and uniqueness (EFA) 245–7
complex comparisons 97, 99, 101–2
conditional linear growth model
  incorporating a time-varying predictor 419
  research example 416–19, 417t, 418f
  specification with SEM and MLM 412–19, 414f, 417t, 418f
conditional multilevel models 179–90
  including level 1 and level 2 predictors 187–90, 189t
  incorporating a level 2 predictor 186–7, 187t
  random-intercepts model 179–83, 180f, 182t
  random-slopes model 183–5, 184f
conditional piecewise growth curve models 431–4, 432t, 433f
conditional quadratic growth curve models 427
confidence intervals 7
  exploratory factor analysis 264–5
  multiple regression 58, 77, 80, 81, 123
  path analysis 297, 311–12, 330–1
  simple linear regression model 22–3, 26, 29
confirmatory factor analysis
  assumption violation and remedies 361
    robust maximum likelihood: The Satorra-Bentler method 361–4
  correlated error terms
    two-factor model example 353–5, 354f
  polychoric correlations for item-level variables 364–7
  research example
    bifactor model 357–61, 359f, 360t
    one-factor model 355
    three-factor model 355–7, 356f, 357f
    two-factor model 341–5, 343f, 344f, 353–5, 354f
constant variance. *see also* homogeneity of variance
  growth curve modeling 409
  multiple regression 73, 74–7, 74f, 75f, 76f

simple linear regression 21
continuous moderators 131–42
  centering continuous predictors 140–2
  model specification and interpretation 132–3, 133t
  probing an interaction 133–40, 136t, 137t, 138f, 138t
  research example 131–2, 131t, 132f
continuous observed variables with EFA 240–1
  research example 241–7, 273–5, 274t
    communality and uniqueness 245–7
    specification of the common factor model 241–5
continuous outcome variables 24–6
continuous predictors. *see* multiple regression: continuous predictors
contrast-code variables 97–103
  improved contrasts 100–3, 101t, 102t
  model specification 97–9, 99t
  regression ANOVA and interpretation of results 99–100
contrast matrix 98–9, 99t, 100–3, 101t
Cook's distance 33–9, 36–7t, 39f, 84–5, 84f
correlated error terms
  confirmatory factor analysis
    research example 353–5, 354f
  two-factor model example 353–5, 354f
correlation 16–17. *see also* product-moment correlation
  multilevel modeling 169–70
  multiple correlation 52–4
  multiple regression 47–9
  polychoric correlations 275, 276–8, 277f, 364–7
correlation coefficient 16–17
correlation matrices 216–17, 216t, 217t, 231–2, 235, 248–63, 269–71, 322, 324, 365
  residual correlation matrices 253–7, 254t, 255t
covariance. *see also* ANCOVA; asymptotic covariance matrix
  intercept-slope covariance 199–201
  multiple regression 292–5
  residual covariances 322–5, 325t
  simple linear regression model 15–16, 18
  variance and covariance 228–30
covariance matrices 217, 224, 228–33, 235–6
  growth curve modeling 399–404
  latent variable models 339–40, 342–5, 350–61, 365–6, 374–7, 381–2
  path analysis 302–5, 309–14, 331–2
covariance structure hypothesis 306–9
covariance structure modeling 286
covariate 62n. *see also* predictor variable
criterion. *see* outcome variable
cross-level interactions 202–5, 204t
Cudeck, R. 263, 264, 307n, 309n, 320
Curran, P.J. 121, 123, 141, 204, 264, 282, 320, 391, 415, 419, 425, 427, 431

data organization: growth curve modeling
  394–7, 395t, 396t
dependent variable. *see* outcome variable
descriptive model fit statistics. *see* baseline fit
  indices
deviance test 199–201
DFFITS 34
diagnostic methods. *see* regression diagnostics
dichotomous moderator 116–18, 117t
dichotomous outcomes 26–7
dichotomous predictors 24–7, 24f
dichotomous variables 90, 92–3, 93t, 114–15
discrepancy
  linear regression 33, 34–9, 36–7t, 36f,
    38f, 39f
  multiple regression 83–5, 84f
distribution of residuals 29–30, 29f, 30f, 79, 109
division: matrices 224–7
dummy-code variables
  multiple regression: categorical predictors
    92–7
    ANOVA model as a multiple regression
      model 96
    model specification 92–3, 93t
    regression ANOVA and interpretation of
      results 93–5, 94t
  multiple regression: interactions 125–8,
    128–31
  simple linear regression 24f

effect size 8–10, 21, 40
  and significance testing 6–9
eigenvalue-one rule. *see* Kaiser criterion
eigenvalues and eigenvectors 235–6, 258–61,
  259f, 261f, 261t
Enders, C.K. 191n, 192, 203
equivalent models 317, 348
error sum of squares 19, 19n
errors 2–4, 10. *see also* regression diagnostics
  confirmatory factor analysis 353–5, 361–4,
    365–7
  growth curve modeling 409–10
  multilevel modeling 165, 167, 176, 206–8
  multiple regression 61, 72–3, 78, 86
  path analysis 299–301, 311–15, 322
  simple linear regression model 21, 29–30
estimated model interpretation 329–31,
  330t, 331t
estimation. *see also* model estimation
  multiple regression 46–9, 48t
  simple linear regression 19–20
exogenous variables 297–301, 304–5, 307–9,
  310–11, 330, 332–3
explanatory variable. *see* predictor variable
exploratory factor analysis 238
  assumptions and diagnostics 280–3,
    281f, 282f
  with categorical observed variables 275
    polychoric correlations 276–7, 277f
    research example 278–80, 278t, 279t

with continuous observed variables 240–1
  research example 241–7, 273–5, 274t
definition 239–40
determining the optimal number of
    common factors 257–8
  Kaiser criterion 258
  parallel analysis 259–61, 259f, 261f, 261t
  scree plots 258–9
estimation of the common factor model
    247–50
  maximum likelihood estimation 256–7
  model-implied and residual correlation
      matrices 253–5, 254t, 255t
  principal axis estimation 250–2
  unweighted least-squares estimation
      253, 255
factor rotation 265–8, 266f, 266t, 267t, 268f
  factor pattern versus factor structure
      271–3
  orthogonal and oblique rotations
      269–71, 270t
research example
  communality and uniqueness 245–7
  specification of the common factor model
      241–5, 242t, 244t
using model fit statistics to determine
    optimal number of factors
  minimum fit-function $X^2$ exact-fit test 263
  root-mean-square error of approximation
      263–4
  root-mean-square residual 262

factors. *see also* latent variables
  factor analysis. *see* confirmatory factor
      analysis; exploratory factor analysis
  factor loading. *see* confirmatory factor
      analysis; exploratory factor analysis;
      factor rotation
  factor pattern versus factor structure 271–3
  factor rotation 265–8, 266f, 266t, 267t, 268f
    factor pattern versus factor structure
        271–3
    orthogonal and oblique rotations
        269–71, 270t
  factor structure versus factor pattern 271–3
Ferron, J.M. 310, 314
Fisher, R.A. 7, 8, 88
fitted value. *see* predicted values
Flora, D.B. 8, 114, 275, 280, 282, 351, 391,
  427, 429
Forero, C.G. 275, 365
formal model comparisons: multilevel
    modeling 199–202
Fox, J. 26, 47, 64, 74, 77, 82, 141, 214

Garrido, L.E. 278, 280
general linear model 88–90. *see also* ANCOVA;
    ANOVA; multiple regression
general model specification form 299–301, 299f
growth curve modeling 389

data organization 394–7, 395t, 396t
definition 390–1
individual trajectories 393–4, 394f
linear change
  coding *time* to change the trajectory
    intercept 410–12, 411t
  conditional linear growth model
    incorporating a time-varying
      predictor 419
    research example 416–19, 417t, 418f
    specification with SEM and MLM
      412–19, 414f, 417t, 418f
  unconditional linear growth model
    MLM identification, estimation & fit
      evaluation 408–10
    MLM specification 405–8, 407t
    model identification 401–2
    research example 404–5, 405t, 409–10
    SEM estimation 402–5, 405t
    SEM specification 397–401, 400f
nonlinear change 419–21, 420f
  conditional piecewise growth curve
    models 431–4, 432t, 433f
  conditional quadratic growth curve
    models 427
  unconditional piecewise growth curve
    model
    research example 431
    specification with SEM and MLM
      427–30, 430f
  unconditional quadratic growth curve
    model
    research example 424–7, 426t
    specification with SEM and MLM 421–7,
      423f, 426t
  research example 391–2, 392t

Hamermesh, D.S. 167, 169
hat values 32, 34–9, 36–7t, 38f, 83, 83f
Hayes, A.F. 297, 330
heteroscedastic residuals 30–2, 31f. *see also*
  transformations; weighted least squares
hierarchical data 166–7. *see also* multilevel
  modeling
hierarchical linear modeling. *see* multilevel
  modeling
hierarchical regression 68–70, 70t, 82, 85,
  105–6, 125–8, 143
Ho, R.M. 302, 344
homogeneity of regression 110–12
homogeneity of variance 21, 26, 30–2, 75, 80,
  206–7
homoscedasticity 21
  homoscedastic versus heteroscedastic
    residuals 30–2

improper solutions 176, 257, 310–11, 346, 382
improved contrasts 100–3, 101t, 102t
independence
  multilevel modeling 164–7
  multiple regression 73

independent clusters solution 267, 339–40
independent variable. *see* predictor variable
indirect effects 145–7, 145f
  estimation and inference 151–60, 152t, 155f,
    157f, 158t, 159f
  moderated indirect effect 158–60, 159f
  multiple regression
    estimation and inference for the indirect
      effect 151–60, 152t, 155f, 157f,
      158t, 159f
  path analysis
    model specification 296–8, 296f, 298f
    research example 149–51, 150f, 151f, 156–8,
      157f, 158t
  simple indirect-effect model 147–9
individual trajectories 393–4, 394f, 397,
  407–8
inference. *see* statistical inference
influence
  linear regression 33–4, 34–9, 36–7t, 36f,
    38f, 39f
  multiple regression 83–5, 84f
interactions. *see* multiple regression:
  interactions
intercept estimate 20, 22, 25, 94, 100–1
intercept-only model 12–14, 21, 23, 55. *see*
  *also* unconditional multilevel model
intercept-slope covariance 199–201
item-level variables. *see* categorical observed
  variables with EFA

Jennrich, R.I. 268, 269n
joint significance of $\hat{\alpha}$ and $\hat{\beta}$ 152–3

Kaiser criterion 258
Kenny, D.A. 152, 153n

latent growth modeling. *see* growth curve
  modeling
latent trajectory modeling. *see* growth curve
  modeling
latent variable models 239–40, 335
  confirmatory factor analysis 337
    assumption violation and remedies 361
      robust maximum likelihood: The
        Satorra-Bentler method 361–4
    correlated error terms
      research example 353–5, 354f
      two-factor model 353–5, 354f
    identification rules
      the *t*-rule 348–9
      three-indicator rule 349
      two indicator rule 349–50
    model estimation 350–2
    model fit evaluation 352–3
    model identification 345
      constraining factor loadings to scale
        latent variables 345–6
      constraining factor variances to scale
        latent variables 346–8
      rules: the *t*-rule 348–9

rules: three-indicator rule 349
rules: two-indicator rule 349–50
model specification 339–40
two-factor model example 341–5, 343f, 344f
polychoric correlations for item-level variables 364–7
research example 337–8, 338f, 338t
bifactor model 357–61, 359f, 360t
one-factor model 355
three-factor model 355–7, 356f, 357f
two-factor model 341–5, 343f, 344f, 353–5, 354f
correlated error terms: research example 353–5, 354f
definition 336
identification rules
the *t*-rule 348–9
three-indicator rule 349
two indicator rule 349–50
model estimation 350–2
model fit evaluation 352–3
model identification 345
constraining factor loadings to scale latent variables 345–6
constraining factor variances to scale latent variables 346–8
rules: the *t*-rule 348–9
rules: three-indicator rule 349
rules: two-indicator rule 349–50
model specification 339–40
two-factor model example 341–5, 343f, 344f
structural regression models 367–71, 368f, 369f
model estimation 381–2
research example 383–6, 384f, 385t
model identification 378
The *t*-rule 378
two-step rule 379–81, 379f, 380f
model specification
measurement model 374
research example 374–8, 375f
structural model 373–4
research example 371–3, 372f, 373t
least-squares estimation 253, 255, 312–13
Lennox, R.D. 289, 299
Level 1 equations (unconditional model) 172–3, 183–4
Level 1 predictors (conditional multilevel models) 179, 187–9
centering 191–2, 192t
cross-level interactions 202–5, 204t
reincorporating 192–5, 193f, 194t
Level 2 equations (unconditional multilevel model) 173–4, 183–4, 192–5.193f, 194t
Level 2 predictors (conditional multilevel models) 186–9
cross-level interactions 202–5, 204t
leverage
linear regression 32, 34–9, 36–7t, 36f, 38f, 39f
multiple regression 83–5, 83f, 84f
likelihood-ratio test 199–201, 328–9

linear factor analysis model. *see* common factor model; continuous observed variables
linear regression. *see* simple linear regression model
linearity. *see also* multicollinearity
multiple regression 72–3, 74–6, 74f, 75f, 76f
simple linear regression 27–9, 28f
LISREL modeling. *see* structural equation modeling
longitudinal data. *see* growth curve modeling

MacCallum, R.C. 88, 243n, 248, 249, 256, 258, 317, 320, 370, 391, 419
MacKinnon, D.P. 148, 152, 154
MANOVA 287, 390, 393–4
Mardia, K.V. 333, 361
marginal effect. *see* partial effect and marginal effect
marker indicator method 345–6
matrix algebra 213–14
elementary matrix algebra
addition and subtraction 218–20
division 224–7
multiplication 220–4
matrices and simple matrix operations 214–18, 216t, 217t
for statistical applications
correlations 231–2
eigenvalues and eigenvectors 235–6
linear regression 233–5
means 227–8
standard deviation 231
variance and covariance 228–30
maximum likelihood
exploratory factor analysis 256–7
latent variable models 361–4
multilevel modeling 176–7
path analysis 309–12
unconditional linear growth model 402–4
Maxwell, S.E. 7, 106, 107, 419
McDonald, R.P. 267, 268, 287, 338
mean 227–8
means-as-outcomes model 186–7
measurement model 369–71, 374
mediation. *see* multiple regression: model mediation and other indirect effects
minimum fit-function $X^2$ exact-fit test 263
mixed modeling. *see* multilevel modeling
model comparison statistics 328–9
model estimation
confirmatory factor analysis 350–2
multiple regression 151–60, 152t
joint significance of $\hat{\alpha}$ and $\hat{\beta}$ 152–3
a moderated indirect effect 158–60, 159f
P=2 or more predictors 64
percentile bootstrap confidence intervals 153–6, 155f
research example for modeling a nonexperimental indirect effect 156–8, 157f, 158t
two predictors 46–9, 48t

path analysis
  covariance structure hypothesis 306–9
  least-squares estimation 312–13
  maximum likelihood estimation 309–11
  multiple $R^2$: proportion of variance
    explained 314–15
  properties of maximum likelihood
    311–12
  research example 315–16, 316f, 316t
  standard error estimation and inference
    313–14
  simple linear regression 19–20
  structural regression models 381–2
    research example 383–6, 384f, 385t
  unconditional linear growth model 402–5,
    405t, 408–10
  unconditional multilevel model 175–8
model fit evaluation
  confirmatory factor analysis 352–3
  path analysis 316–17, 330t
    baseline fit indices 321–2, 321f
    estimated model interpretation
      329–31
    model comparison statistics 328–9
    model evaluation and revision:
      modification indices 325–7
    model evaluation and revision: residual
      covariances 324–5, 325t
    research example 327–8, 327f
    root-mean-square error of approximation
      fit statistic 319–21
    standardized root-mean-square residual
      322–3
    $X^2$ exact-fit test 317–19
  unconditional linear growth model 408–10
model fit statistics
  minimum fit-function $X^2$ exact-fit test 263
  root-mean-square error of approximation
    263–4
  root-mean-square residual 262
model identification
  confirmatory factor analysis 345
    constraining factor loadings to scale latent
      variables 345–6
    constraining factor variances to scale
      latent variables 346–8
    rules: the $t$-rule 348–9
    rules: three-indicator rule 349
    rules: two-indicator rule 349–50
  path analysis
    the recursive rule 305–6, 306f
    research example 302–3
    the $t$-rule 303–5
  structural regression models 378
    rules: the $t$-rule 378
    rules: two-step rule 379–81, 379f, 380f
  unconditional linear growth model 401–2,
    408–10
model-implied correlation matrices 248–9,
  253–5, 254t, 255t

model-implied covariance matrix 307–9
model-implied value. see predicted values
model mediation and other indirect
    effects 144
  estimation and inference for the indirect
    effect 151–60, 152t, 155f, 157f,
    158t, 159f
  mediation and indirect effects 145–7, 145f
  research example 149–51, 150f, 151f
  specification of the simple indirect-effect
    model 147–9
model specification
  common factor model 241–5, 242t, 244t
  conditional linear growth model 412–19,
    414f, 417t, 418f
  confirmatory factor analysis 339–40
    two-factor model example 341–5,
      343f, 344f
  multiple regression
    continuous moderators 132–3, 133t
    contrast-code variables 97–9, 99t
    dichotomous moderator 116–18, 117t
    dummy-code variables 92–3, 93t
    multicategory moderators 125–8, 125t, 127t
    P = 2 or more predictors 63–4
    simple indirect-effect model 147–9
    two predictors 44–6, 46f
  path analysis 289–90
    general model specification form
      299–301, 299f
    mediation and other indirect effects
      models 296–8, 296f, 298f
    multiple regression model 291–3, 292f
    multivariate multiple regression model
      293–5, 293f, 295f
    research example 301–2, 301f
    simple regression model 290–1
  simple linear regression 18–19
  structural regression models
    measurement model 374
    research example 374–8, 375f
    structural model 373–4
  unconditional linear growth model 397–401,
    400f, 405–8, 407t
  unconditional piecewise growth curve
    model 427–30, 430f
  unconditional quadratic growth curve
    model 421–7, 423f, 426t
modeling revolution 6–7
moderated indirect effect 158–60, 159f
moderation 114. see also multiple regression:
    interactions
modification indices 325–7
multicategory moderators
  probing an interaction 128–31, 129t, 130t
  specification and interpretation 125–8,
    125t, 127t
multicategory predictors 90. see also
    contrast-code variables; dummy-code
    variables

multicollinearity 81–3
multilevel modeling 163. *see also* growth curve modeling; hierarchical linear modeling
  assumption checking 205–8, 206f, 207f, 208f
  conditional multilevel models 179–90
    including level 1 and level 2 predictors 187–90, 189t
    incorporating a level 2 predictor 186–7, 187t
    random-intercepts model 179–83, 180f, 182t
    random-slopes model 183–5, 184f
  cross-level interactions 202–5, 204t
  definition 164
  distinguishing within-cluster effect from between-clusters effect 190–9, 190f
    alternative approach 195–7, 196t
    centering a level 1 predictor 191–2, 192t
    reincorporating the level 1 means 192–5, 193f, 194t
    revisiting the random-slopes model 197–9, 199t
  formal model comparisons 199–202
  nonindependent observations 164–71
    research example 168–71, 168t, 170f, 171f
    sources of nonindependence 165–7
  three-level models 205
  unconditional multilevel model 171–8
    estimation and inference 175–8
    model specification 171–5
multiple correlation 52–4
multiple linear regression model. *see* multiple regression
multiple $R^2$: proportion of variance explained 314–15
multiple regression: categorical predictors 87
  ANCOVA model and beyond 104–8
    interpretation of results 106–7
    model specification 104–6
  contrast-code variables 97–103
    improved contrasts 100–3, 101t, 102t
    model specification 97–9, 99t
    regression ANOVA and interpretation of results 99–100
  dummy-code variables 92–7
    ANOVA model as a multiple regression model 96
    model specification 92–3, 93t
    regression ANOVA and interpretation of results 93–5, 94t
  general linear model 88–90
  regression diagnostics 108–11, 109f, 110f
  research example 90–1, 91f, 91t
multiple regression: continuous predictors 42
  definition 43
  P=2 or more predictors 62–3
    hierarchical regression 68–70, 70t
    inference and model comparisons 64–6
    model estimation 64
    model specification 63–4

simultaneous regression 66–7, 67t
stepwise regression 71–2
regression diagnostics 72–3
  assumption violation and remedies 77–8
  linearity and constant variance 74–6, 74f, 75f, 76f
  multicollinearity 81–3
  normality 76–7, 76f
  outliers and influential observations 83–5, 84f
  polynomial regression 78–9
  transformations 79–80
  weighted least squares 80–1
research example 43–4, 44f
two predictors
  inference 54–8, 56t
  model estimation 46–9, 48t
  model specification 44–6, 46f
  multiple correlation 52–4
  partial effect and marginal effect 49–52, 50f, 51f
  standardized regression coefficients 59–62
multiple regression: interactions 113
  categorical moderators 114–31
    probing an interaction: multicategory moderator 128–31, 129t, 130t
    probing an interaction: simple-slope analysis 118–25, 121f, 122t, 124f
    research example 114–15, 115f, 115t
    specification and interpretation: dichotomous moderator 116–18, 117t
    specification and interpretation: multicategory moderator 125–8, 125t, 127t
  continuous moderators 131–42
    centering continuous predictors 140–2
    model specification and interpretation 132–3, 133t
    probing an interaction 133–40, 136t, 137t, 138f, 138t
    research example 131–2, 131t, 132f
  statistical moderation 114
multiple regression model 291–3, 292f
multiple regression: model mediation and other indirect effects 144
  estimation and inference for the indirect effect 151–60, 152t
  joint significance of $\hat{\alpha}$ and $\hat{\beta}$ 152–3
  a moderated indirect effect 158–60, 159f
  percentile bootstrap confidence intervals 153–6, 155f
  research example for modeling a nonexperimental indirect effect 156–8, 157f, 158t
  mediation and indirect effects 145–7, 145f
  research example 149–51, 150f, 151f
  specification of the simple indirect-effect model 147–9
multiplication: matrices 220–4
multivariate models 214. *see also* matrix algebra

multivariate multiple regression model 293–5, 293f, 295f
Murnane, R.J. 145, 286
mutually orthogonal 98, 102–3
Myung, I.J. 5, 176

nested models
    growth curve modeling 409
    latent variable models 354, 363
    multilevel modeling 199–200, 201–2, 211
    path analysis 327f, 328–9
nesting 166–7. *see also* multilevel modeling
Nissim, R. 278, 279
nominal variables 24–6
nonconvergence 176, 256–7, 310
nonindependent observations 73, 164–71, 168t, 170f, 171f. *see also* multilevel modeling
normality 29, 73, 76–7, 76f
notational practice 10
null hypotheses 6–9, 21–3, 29, 101–3, 111, 152–3
Nunnally, J.C. 267, 370n

oblique rotations 269–71, 270t
OLS estimation
    multiple regression 47–9, 64, 77–8, 151
    simple linear regression model 19–20, 21
one-factor model 273–4, 355–6, 356f
orthogonal and oblique rotations 269–71, 270t
outliers 32–4, 83–5, 84f

P=2 or more predictors 62–3
    hierarchical regression 68–70, 70t
    inference and model comparisons 64–6
    model estimation 64
    model specification 63–4
    simultaneous regression 66–7, 67t
    stepwise regression 71–2
parallel analysis 259–61, 259f, 261f, 261t
parallelism 110–12
partial effect and marginal effect 49–52, 50f, 51f
partial regression coefficient 45–6, 46f
partial regression slope 45–6, 46f, 64–6
path analysis 285, 288–9
    assumptions and diagnostics 331–3
    model estimation
        covariance structure hypothesis 306–9
        least-squares estimation 312–13
        maximum likelihood estimation 309–11
        multiple $R^2$: proportion of variance explained 314–15
        properties of maximum likelihood 311–12
        research example 315–16, 316f, 316t
        standard error estimation and inference 313–14
    model fit evaluation 316–17
        baseline fit indices 321–2, 321f
        estimated model interpretation 329–31, 330t, 331t
        model comparison statistics 328–9

model evaluation and revision: modification indices 325–7
model evaluation and revision: residual covariances 324–5, 325t
    research example 327–8, 327f
    root-mean-square error of approximation fit statistic 319–21
    standardized root-mean-square residual 322–3
    $X^2$ exact-fit test 317–19
model identification
    the recursive rule 305–6, 306f
    research example 302–3
    the *t*-rule 303–5
model specification 289–90
    general model specification form 299–301, 299f
    mediation and other indirect effects models 296–8, 296f, 298f
    multiple regression model 291–3, 292f
    multivariate multiple regression model 293–5, 293f, 295f
    research example 301–2, 301f
    simple regression model 290–1
    research example 289
Pearson's correlation. *see* product-moment correlation
Pedhazur, E.J. 6, 60, 71, 286
Pek, J. 8, 146
percentile bootstrap confidence intervals 153–6, 155f, 159
piecewise growth curve model
    conditional 431–4, 432t, 433f
    unconditional 427–30, 430f, 431
point-biserial correlation 26n
polychoric correlations 275, 276–8, 277f, 364–7
polynomial regression 78–9, 281, 420
Preacher, K.J. 8, 249, 258, 264, 297, 330, 369, 370
predicted values 2–4, 4f, 6, 17, 18
predictor selection methods 71–2
principal axis estimation 250–2
principal components analysis 249–50
probing an interaction
    continuous moderators 133–40, 136t, 137t, 138f, 138t
    multicategory moderator 128–31, 129t, 130t
    simple-slope analysis 118–25, 121f, 122t, 124f
product-moment correlation 16–18, 26n, 67, 231–2, 239–41, 275, 282–3
product-moment covariance 15, 18, 230–1, 351–2

quadratic growth curve model 421–7, 423f, 426t

$R^2$
    confirmatory factor analysis 360
    hierarchical regression 68–70
    multilevel modeling 165
    multiple regression 50n, 52–4, 64–6, 126–8

path analysis 314–15
regression ANOVA 93–5
simple regression 23, 24, 35
stepwise regression 71–2
structural regression models 385–6
random effects 174–5, 200, 205
random-effects ANOVA model 172–3. *see also*
 unconditional multilevel model
random-intercepts model 179–83, 180f, 182t
random-slopes model 183–5, 184f, 197–9, 199t
rank-order correlation. *see* Spearman's
 correlation
Raudenbush, S.W. 176, 177, 195, 205, 206,
 207, 428
the recursive rule 305–6, 306f
regression ANOVA 54–8, 56t, 93–5, 94t,
 99–100
regression diagnostics
 multiple regression: categorical predictors
 108–11, 109f, 110f
 multiple regression: continuous predictors
 72–3
 assumption violation and remedies 77–8
 linearity and constant variance 74–6, 74f,
 75f, 76f
 multicollinearity 81–3
 normality 76–7, 76f
 outliers and influential observations
 83–5, 84f
 polynomial regression 78–9
 transformations 79–80
 weighted least squares 80–1
 simple linear regression 27–39
 distribution of residuals 29–30
 examining outliers and unusual cases
 32–4
 homoscedastic versus heteroscedastic
 residuals 30–2
 leverage, discrepancy, and influence 34–9
 linearity 27–9, 28f
regressor. *see* predictor variable
residual correlation matrices 253–7, 254t, 255t
residual covariances 322–5, 325t, 352–3
residuals. *see also* transformations; weighted
 least squares
 distribution of 29–30, 29f, 30f
 homoscedastic versus heteroscedastic
 residuals 30–2, 31f
 multiple regression 74–7, 74f, 75f, 76f
 simple linear regression 13, 14, 17, 18, 19n,
 29–30, 29f, 30f
 studentized residuals 33, 34–9, 36–7t, 39f,
 84, 84f, 124f
response variable. *see* outcome variable
Rhemtulla, M. 338, 361, 364, 366
Richards, J.M. 60
robust maximum likelihood 361–4
Rodgers, J.L. 5, 6, 7
root-mean-square error of approximation
 263–4

root-mean-square error of approximation fit
 statistic 319–21
root-mean-square residual 262

Satorra, A. 362, 363, 404
The Satorra-Bentler method 361–4
Savalei, V. 362, 366, 404
Scott-Lennox, J.A. 289, 299
sequential regression. *see* hierarchical
 regression
significance testing
 and effect sizes 6–9
 simple linear regression 21–3
simple indirect-effect model 145f, 147–9,
 151–2, 152t, 156–60, 158t, 296
simple linear regression model 9. *see also*
 simple regression models
 dichotomous predictors 24–7, 24f
 estimation 19–20
 intercept-only model 12–14, 21, 23
 matrices 233–5
 single predictor model 15–18, 15f, 17f, 21, 23
 specification 18–19
 statistical inference 21–4
simple regression models 9–27
 dichotomous outcome? 26–7
 model estimation 19–20
 model specification 18–19
 path analysis/structural equation modeling
 model specification 290–1
 research example 11–18, 11f, 12f, 12t, 15f, 17f
 intercept-only model 12–14, 21, 23
 single predictor model 15–18, 15f, 17f,
 21, 23
 simple regression with a dichotomous
 predictor 24–6, 24f
 statistical inference 21–4
simple-slope analysis
 probing an interaction 118–25, 121f,
 122t, 124f
 continuous moderators 131–9
 multicategory moderators 128–31,
 129t, 130t
simultaneous regression 66–7, 67t, 69
Snijders, T.A.B. 166n, 176, 182, 205, 405n
Spearman's correlation 17
specification. *see* model specification
standardized regression coefficients 59–62
standardized root-mean-square residual 322–3
statistical inference 6
 model-based approach 7–8
 multiple regression
 P=2 or more predictors 64–6
 two predictors 54–8, 56t
 simple linear regression model 21–4
statistical mediation. *see* multiple regression:
 model mediation and other indirect effects
statistical models: demonstrated with simple
 regression
 basic regression diagnostic concepts 27–39

data-based illustration of leverage, discrepancy, and influence 34–9, 36–7f, 36–7t, 38f, 39f
distribution of residuals 29–30, 29f, 30f
examining outliers and unusual cases 32–4
homoscedastic versus heteroscedastic residuals 30–2, 31f
linearity 27–9, 28f
definition 2–6, 4f
significance testing and effect sizes 6–9
simple regression models 9–27
dichotomous outcome? 26–7
model estimation 19–20
model specification 18–19
research example 11–18, 11f, 12f, 12t, 15f, 17f
simple regression with a dichotomous predictor 24–6, 24f
statistical inference 21–4
statistical moderation 114. *see also* multiple regression: interactions
Steiger, J.H. 263, 319
stepwise regression 71–2
structural equation modeling 286–8. *see also* growth curve modeling; latent variable models; path analysis
structural model 369–71, 373–4
structural regression models 367–71, 368f, 369f
model estimation 381–2
research example 383–6, 384f, 385t
model identification 378
The *t*-rule 378
two-step rule 379–81, 379f, 380f
model specification
measurement model 374
research example 374–8, 375f
structural model 373–4
research example 371–3, 372f, 373t
studentized residuals 33, 34–9, 36–7t, 39f, 84, 84f, 124f
suppression 50n

the *t*-rule 303–5, 348–9, 378
three-factor model 355–7, 356f, 357f
three-indicator rule 349
three-level models 205
Thurstone, L.L. 239, 241, 267, 337
time
coding *time* to change the trajectory intercept 410–12, 411t
incorporating a time-varying predictor 419
Topiak, M.E. 337, 341, 344, 352, 355, 357, 366
trajectories
coding *time* to change the trajectory intercept 410–12, 411t
individual trajectories 393–4, 394f, 397, 407–8

transformations 79–80
two-factor model 353–5, 354f
two indicator rule 349–50
two predictor multiple linear progression
inference 54–8, 56t
model estimation 46–9, 48t
model specification 44–6, 46f
multiple correlation 52–4
partial effect and marginal effect 49–52, 50f, 51f
standardized regression coefficients 59–62
two-step rule 379–81, 379f, 380f

Ullman, J.B. 371, 372, 374
unconditional linear growth model
MLM identification, estimation & fit evaluation 408–10
MLM specification 405–8, 407t
model identification 401–2
research example 404–5, 405t, 409–10
SEM estimation 402–5, 405t
SEM specification 397–401, 400f
unconditional multilevel model 171–8
estimation and inference 175–8
model specification 171–5
unconditional piecewise growth curve model
research example 431
specification with SEM and MLM 427–30, 430f
unconditional quadratic growth curve model
research example 424–7, 426t
specification with SEM and MLM 421–7, 423f, 426t
uniqueness (EFA) 245–7
unweighted least-squares estimation 253, 255

variance and covariance 228–30
variance-components model. *see* unconditional multilevel model
variance inflation factor 81–3
violation. *see* assumption violation

Wald test 177–8, 314, 315
weighted least squares (WLS) 80–1, 313
West, S.G. 361, 392
Wilkinson, L. 6, 7, 8
Willett, J.B. 145, 286, 390, 395
within-cluster effect and between-clusters effect 190–9, 190f
alternative approach 195–7, 196t
centering a level 1 predictor 191–2, 192t
reincorporating the level 1 means 192–5, 193f, 194t
revisiting the random-slopes model 197–9, 199t

$X^2$ exact-fit test 317–19